MODERN MATHEMATICS AND ECONOMIC ANALYSIS

MODERN MATHEMATICS AND ECONOMIC ANALYSIS

by Blaine Roberts
and David L. Schulze UNIVERSITY OF FLORIDA

W · W · NORTON & COMPANY · INC · NEW YORK

First Edition

Library of Congress Cataloging in Publication Data

Roberts, Blaine, 1944–
 Modern mathematics and economic analysis.

 Includes bibliographies.
  1. Economics, Mathematical. I. Schulze, David L., joint author. II. Title.
HB74.M3R56   510   72-7283
ISBN 0-393-09392-1

PRINTED IN THE UNITED STATES OF AMERICA

1 2 3 4 5 6 7 8 9 0

Contents

Preface

The genesis of this book was the fact that the widely varied mathematical techniques currently being applied in economics (and other social sciences) have been scattered through a large number of different sources, often with different notations and presumptions of knowledge. Our aim has been to draw these techniques together in a single volume that is consistent in presentation and thorough in coverage. Thus the scope of the text is broader than most books on mathematical economics or mathematics for economists. This permits the book to be used flexibly by undergraduates, graduate students, and professional economists.

We have written this book for both beginning and advanced courses in mathematics for economic analysis. It is also adaptable to graduate mathematics courses in other social sciences and business or to applied mathematics courses at the undergraduate level.

A one-term beginning (for undergraduates), or remedial (for graduates), course could cover the first five sections of Chapter 2 (set theory), Chapter 4 (functions and matrix algebra), Chapter 5 (differential calculus), and Section 6.1 (Riemann integration). The second-quarter beginning course might include Chapter 7 (differential equations), Chapter 8 (difference equations), Sections 11.1 and 11.4 (linear programming), Section 12.1 (the simplex method), and Sections 13.1 and 13.2 (simple game theory).

Courses in mathematical economics, *per se*, would cover the remainder of Chapter 2 (morphisms, convex sets, and separating hyperplanes), Chapter 3 (basic measurement theory), Section 6.2 (Stieltjes integrals), Chapter 9 (fixed-point theorems, existence, uniqueness, and stability), Chapter 10 (calculus of variations), Chapters 11 and 12 (theory and algorithms of mathematical programming), Chapter 13 (game theory), and Chapter 14 (control theory).

In addition to its function as a textbook, this volume should serve as a useful reference work for professional economists, not only because it covers most of the current mathematical techniques but also because it is self-contained. We include the basic concepts and theorems upon which the advanced techniques are based, and have proved the most important results in each chapter. Problems are provided at the end of each section to emphasize the important aspects covered.

A workbook for the text is also available which summarizes the chapter, gives a detailed step-by-step solution to the problems in the text, and contains additional problems and their answers.

A bibliography is given at the end of each chapter which contains the references cited in the chapter and selected additional sources.

The organization of the book follows a logical format: beginning with the concept of mathematics; then developing the basic tenets of set theory; measure theory; functions; matrix theory; derivative and integral calculus; difference calculus; existence, uniqueness, and stability of simultaneous equations; calculus of variations; mathematical programming; game theory; and concluding with control theory.

Several aspects of this organization should be mentioned. Chapters 7 and 8 present the techniques for solving single differential and difference equations as well as systems of equations. Chapter 9 treats much the same topic, but on more sophisticated, theoretical levels. It seems more expedient to provide the student with the tools for solving such equations and equation systems before discussing the more difficult theoretical questions of the existence, uniqueness, and stability of such solutions. This organization makes the previous suggestions about the use of the book in beginning and advanced courses more practical.

In addition, Chapter 10 (calculus of variations), Section 12.3 (dynamic programming), and Chapter 14 (control theory) are highly interrelated. This organization was adopted for several reasons: first, the calculus of variations depends heavily on the theory of differential equations and follows those chapters; second, dynamic programming is one of many special cases of mathematical programming and so is placed in that chapter; finally, control theory, to be fully understood, requires a knowledge of both of the preceding and therefore follows them in the text. These topics may, of course, be taken up in the order originally given.

We would like to express our appreciation to Karl A. Fox, Chairman of the Department of Economics, Iowa State University, for providing both intellectual and administrative support for our efforts. Without his help and stimulation this project would have never become a reality. In addition, the College of Business Administration, University of Florida, provided administrative support. We owe a special debt of gratitude to Stanley Fisher, of the University of Chicago, and to Michael Manove, of the University of Michigan, who read preliminary drafts and made many valuable suggestions, and to Edmund S. Phelps, of Columbia University, for his role of advisory editor to W. W. Norton & Company, Inc. Gerard Gaudet, of the University of Pennsylvania, closely read final versions of the manuscript and helped eliminate many errors. Frank Casey, David Hatcher, and Somchai Richupan, our former graduate assistants, suffered through various stages of the manuscript and made valuable comments. We also owe thanks to our students both at Iowa State and the University of Florida who have used various portions of the book while still in manuscript form. Books would not exist in a form other than pages of manuscript in a state of disarray were it not for an editor. Donald S. Lamm, of W. W. Norton, performed this service exceedingly well.

Finally, each author has agreed to blame the other for any errors in the text.

MODERN
MATHEMATICS
AND
ECONOMIC
ANALYSIS

Chapter 1

Introduction

1.1 MATHEMATICS DEFINED

The primary characteristic of mathematics is abstraction from real-world data. It is an abstraction from empirical concepts in order to derive generalizations about these environmental phenomena. This does not greatly distinguish it from any other particular science, including logic, the study of the principles of reason. Basically, logic boils down to deciding and clarifying what one means, or what information statements convey. If we were to classify logic as the first order of abstraction—since it represents the "rules" for abstraction—then mathematics would be the second order of abstraction.

Mathematics is usually associated with numbers or, more specifically, quantities. However, this does not encompass the whole realm of mathematics. It is an application of the rules of logic to obtain relations and *general* conclusions about the environment. The fact that the quantitative characteristics of real-world phenomena are usually amenable to abstraction and generalization provides this usual association between "numbers" and "mathematics."

Our modern number system is the foundation of all mathematics. Without this system of numbers we all take for granted, most techniques in this book could not exist even in the mind of the world's most brilliant man. In such an event we should more accurately refer to him as the world's most intelligent savage. As Karl Menninger has pointed out in his fascinating book,[1] the development of number systems paralleled the rise of civilization. The degree of sophistication of a culture's number system is a reliable index of its level of development.

The first step in developing a number system is to disassociate numbers from objects. It may have been conceivable within a particular culture to add one apple and two apples and get three apples—or to add one deer and one deer to get a pair of deer—but not to add 1 and 2 or 1 and 1. The abstraction of quantity (a particular characteristic) of deer or apples from the deer or apples themselves, a necessary step for a number system to exist, was never attained. This fact is apparent in many ancient languages where the terms for two apples, two deer, two horses, two people, and so on, have absolutely

[1] Menninger (1969).

3

nothing in common. There were no separate words meaning simply "one" or "two."

Many primitive cultures had a number system composed of only three numbers: one, two, and many.[2] They had no way of distinguishing between, for example, 100 horses and 150 horses. Why? Because in their primitive culture there was no need to make such a distinction. The number "many" was good enough. As civilization developed, men began to raise horses. As it became obvious that there was an important difference between having many or few horses, the number system was extended to systems like 1, 2, . . . , 1000; many. As commerce developed it also became necessary to perform the basic mathematical operations of addition, subtraction, multiplication, and division.

The point here is that both the number system and the operations that can be performed on the system grew as man's needs for them developed.

For many centuries the number system 1, 2, . . . , n; many, coupled with the simplest arithmetic operations, served man's needs adequately. As civilization developed and the problems that men were interested in solving became more and more complex, inexorable pressure was created to expand the number system and the techniques available for manipulating it. Before man could build the Tower of Babel (a formidable project, we are told) he had to have some rudimentary knowledge of geometry. Today, before man could reach the moon, he had to have a knowledge of the calculus of variations and optimal control theory. Thus the entire history of mathematical analysis can be viewed as an unceasing attempt to develop techniques either to answer more difficult questions or to give more precise answers to existing questions. The growth of mathematics parallels the growth of man's knowledge of himself and the universe.

The close nexus between mathematics, logic, and, in turn, philosophy means that mathematics is a *way* of characterizing the aspects of the real world. More specifically, it is a way of characterizing or looking at the similar, general, and abstract aspects of the real world. Consequently, mathematics defines properties or concepts in ways that are efficient or useful. Consider the common assumption of continuity. Whether anything is really continuous, for example, time, is a moot question in both philosophy and physics. Yet whether it is or not, to assume so is useful in many cases since the techniques of calculus can then be applied. The results are often "good enough" approximations to reality to aid in understanding the environment.

Mathematics is simply a language, a special language with rigid rules for

---

[2] The number system the typical two- or three-year old uses is very similar to these primitive systems. Any number of pieces of candy over two or three is, most likely, "lotsa" candy. In the two-year-old world, "lotsa" is a perfectly reasonable number. As he grows up it becomes more relevant to distinguish between 10 and 12 pieces of candy, and his number system expands.

structuring statements. Communication by mathematics is consequently very precise and concise. It can be thought of as symbolic logical shorthand. As such there need be no difference between saying something in "mathematics" and saying something in English, just as one may describe some facet of the environment in English or in French. However, due to their inexactness, to say the same thing in literary languages as in mathematics one must often spend paragraphs clarifying and restating to eliminate the ambiguities not present in the mathematical version. This, of course, is the enormous advantage of mathematics: to be able to deal simply and accurately with complex phenomena.

Unfortunately, this advantage carries with it a disadvantage. The disadvantage is that of interpreting or "translating" a real-world problem into mathematics and back again. Although this is not a formal problem but simply a matter of correct translation, it is often a significant practical problem. The exact mathematics that are relevant to some empirical problem may be both difficult and debatable. But this is not the "fault" of mathematics, it is the fault of the mathematician—the user of the language. It is as much an error as translating a German idiom literally into English or vice versa. The criticism of mathematical models as being irrelevant, if valid, is a criticism of the model builder, not of the tools. If invalid, it is frequently a failure to communicate—a failure of the critic to understand the language of mathematics—equivalent to saying that things written in Greek are hard to understand and therefore irrelevant.

Another criticism of the mathematical approach is its tendency to avoid relevant problems and only analyze problems that are easily translated and interpreted in their mathematical dress. Again, this amounts to a criticism of what is or is not relevant. If one does not like a mathematical model—a particular interpretation of reality—one should correct the situation and analyze the problem including the omitted parameters, variables, or whatever. If a mathematical representation of a question is inadequate, it may be because a more relevant description is not possible at the present; the problems created by including such omissions have not been solved. In this case the solution is to alleviate the inadequacies. If something is missing, complaining of its absence does not result in its inclusion.

1.2   THEORY DEFINED

Simply stated, theory is the selection of apparently unrelated statements and the demonstration of a relation between them. In an empirical science the statements are often complexly intertwined, with literally billions of agents interacting with each other. So complex is this environment relative to the capacities of human mentality that the only possible way of comprehending it is through abstraction. The only way for the individual to understand his complicated milieu is to reduce the scope, eliminate "minor" influences, and concentrate on "major" or important aspects. Thus theory is a simplification of the environment. This obvious relation between theory as a simplification process—or a selection of specific elements to be analyzed—and the nature of mathematics is what makes theory so amenable to mathematical analysis.

Theory is, at best, nothing more than a clear and precise form of communication. Further, the more precise, the better—everything else being equal.[3] In its ultimate form, theory reduces itself to a tautology—a tautology that relates one concept to another. The value of theory depends upon the obviousness and importance of the concepts and their relations. Clearly and precisely relating apparently diverse concepts can greatly improve the knowledge of man and his ability to cope with his world. To show the minimal assumptions that imply a particular conclusion, and that a result follows from the existence of particular hypotheses, should be the ultimate goal of theory.

1.3   THE PLACE OF MATHEMATICS IN ECONOMIC THEORY

The place of mathematics in economics depends upon what is useful and efficient in given contexts. A priori, mathematics is not limited to a particular area of economic analysis nor specifically required in any area. However, the history of economic thought indicates that the properties of rigor and conciseness are extremely useful in solving economic problems. In this context mathematics is mind-expanding. Reducing a problem to mathematical language expands one's ability to handle many more concepts than would be possible with a literary approach.

References

1. ALEKSANDROV, A. D., A. N. KALMOGOROV, and M. A. LAVRENT'EV (1963), *Mathematics: Its Content, Methods, and Meaning* (tr. by K. Hirsch), Cambridge, Mass.: M.I.T. Press.
2. MENNINGER, KARL (1969), *Number Words and Number Symbols, a Cultural History of Numbers*, Cambridge, Mass.: M.I.T. Press.

[3] Of course, usually everything else at a given point in time is not equal. This is the reason for having a theory at all. Increased precision requires increased complexity.

Chapter 2

Set Theory

2.1 SETS

Intuitively, a set is any collection of physical or abstract entities. Thus the collection of all students at Iowa State University or of all integer powers of e both qualify as sets. A set may be described in two ways: by giving the rule by which membership in the set is determined as we did above, or by listing all the members, or elements, of the set. We shall use capital letters to represent sets and lower case letters to represent arbitrary elements of the set. If x is a member of set X we write "$x \in X$" (read alternatively as "x is in X" or "x belongs to X"). If x is not a member of X we write "$x \notin X$" ("x is not in X" or "x does not belong to X").

Suppose X is the set of all positive integers greater than 5 and less than 10. The following two statements are then equivalent descriptions of X:

(1) $$X = \{6, 7, 8, 9\}$$

(2) $$X = \{x \mid x \in I, 5 < x < 10\}$$

In (1) we have simply listed the elements of X, enclosing them in braces to indicate that they form a set. The order in which these elements are listed is completely immaterial. A set is completely defined by its elements independently of the order in which they are listed.

In (2) we have given, in set notation, the rule for determining the elements of set X. Equation (2) should be read "X is the set of all elements x such that x is an integer (I is the standard abbreviation for the set of integers) and x is greater than 5 and less than 10." Note that the vertical bar in (2) stands for "such that"; the x preceding it is an arbitrary element of X, while the specific relation each member of X must satisfy follows the vertical bar. In defining sets this way, the description following the vertical bar must be satisfied by each element of the set. Furthermore, it cannot be satisfied by elements that are not members of the set.

Another example may make the notation of (2) clearer.

$$Y = \{y \mid y \in R, y \leq 0\}$$

should be read "Y is the set of all elements y such that y is a real number

7

(R is a standard notation for the set of all real numbers) and y is less than or equal to zero." Thus the set Y is simply the set of all nonpositive real numbers.

Problems

2.1–1   Describe the following sets in the notation of Equation (2).

      (a) $y = \sqrt{x}$, $x \geq 0$ (d) $y = 5$

      (b) $y = \sqrt{x}$, $-\infty < x$, $< \infty$ (e) $y \geq 2x + 1$

      (c) $y = 5x^3 - 3x^2 + x^{-2}$ (f) $y = 5xz^2 + 2x^2z$

2.2   SUBSETS

A fundamental axiom of set theory is the **axiom of extent**.

AXIOM 2.2–1   Two sets A and B are equal ($A = B$) if and only if every member of A is a member of B and every member of B is a member of A.

This axiom is the basis for our earlier statement that a set is independent of the order in which its elements are listed.

Another important concept is that of a subset.

DEFINITION 2.2–1   Set A is a **subset** of set B if and only if every element of A is also an element of B.

The statement that A is a subset of B can be written as either

$$A \subseteq B \quad \text{or} \quad B \supseteq A$$

These two equivalent statements are read "A is contained in, or is equal to, B" and "B contains, or is equal to, A."

DEFINITION 2.2–2 A is a **proper subset** of B if and only if A is a subset of B and B is not a subset of A.

If A is a proper subset of B we write

$$A \subset B \quad \text{or} \quad B \supset A$$

read "A is contained in B" and "B contains A."

DEFINITION 2.2–3   The **null** (empty or void) **set**, $\varnothing$, is the set containing no elements.

DEFINITION 2.2–4 A is an **improper subset** of B if and only if $A = B$ or A is the null set ($A = \varnothing$).

AXIOM 2.2–2   The null set is a subset of every set.

The preceding axiom and two definitions lead to the conclusion that every set has two improper subsets: the set itself and the null set.

Example 1.   List all the subsets of $A = \{a, b, c, d\}$. The two improper subsets are $\emptyset$ and A. There are four proper subsets of one element, $\{a\}$, $\{b\}$, $\{c\}$, and $\{d\}$; six of two elements, $\{a, b\}$, $\{a, c\}$, $\{a, d\}$, $\{b, c\}$, $\{b, d\}$, and $\{c, d\}$; and four of three elements, $\{a, b, c\}$, $\{a, b, d\}$, $\{a, c, d\}$, and $\{b, c, d\}$. This set of four elements thus has a total of 16 subsets: two improper and 14 proper subsets.

The concept of a subset is vital to the following theorem.

Theorem 2.2–1   Two sets, A and B, are equal if and only if A is a subset of B and B is a subset of A.

PROOF   In proving all "if and only if" statements, a two-stage proof is required. We must prove that the "if" portion is true and also prove the "only if" portion of the statement. In effect we must demonstrate the statements: (1) If $A \subseteq B$ and $B \subseteq A$, then $A = B$; and (2) if $A = B$, then $A \subseteq B$ and $B \subseteq A$.

To prove statement (1), assume $A \subseteq B$ and $B \subseteq A$. It then follows that every $x \in A$ is in B and that every $x \in B$ is also in A. By the axiom of extent (Axiom 2.2–1), we know that A must equal B. To prove statement (2), assume $A = B$. Then by the axiom of extent, every element of A is an element of B. Thus $A \subseteq B$. Also, by the same axiom, every element of B is an element of A. Thus $B \subseteq A$.   QED[1]

Problems

2.2–1   List all the subsets of
(a) $A = \{1, -2, 3, -10, 5\}$ (c) $C = \emptyset$
(b) $B = \{b_1, b_2, b_3, b_4, b_5, b_6\}$ (d) $D = 0$

2.2–2   Which of the subsets in Problem 2.2–1 are improper subsets? Proper subsets?

2.2–3   If $A \subset B \subset C \subset A$, prove that $A = B = C$.

2.2–4   Explain how the axiom of extent implies that sets are independent of the order of their elements.

2.2–5   How do the requirements for proving an "if and only if" theorem differ from those for proving an "if" theorem?

---

[1] QED is the abbreviation for the Latin phrase *quod erat demonstrandum*, meaning "which was to be demonstrated." It is used to mark the end of a proof.

2.3   COMBINATIONS OF SETS

There are three important and frequently encountered operations for obtaining a new set from existing sets. For two sets S and T, these operations are as given in Definition 2.3–1.

DEFINITION 2.3–1[2]

(1) **Union:** $S \cup T = \{x \mid x \in S \text{ or } x \in T\}$.
(2) **Intersection:** $S \cap T = \{x \mid x \in S \text{ and } x \in T\}$.
(3) **Difference:** $S - T = \{x \mid x \in S \text{ and } x \notin T\}$.

Verbally, these new sets may be described as follows: $S \cup T$ ("S union T") is the set composed of all elements that are either members of S, members of T, or members of both S and T; $S \cap T$ ("S intersect T") is the set composed of all elements that are members of both S and T; and $S - T$ ("S difference T") is the set composed of all elements of S that are not also members of T.

At this point it is convenient to introduce the use of Venn diagrams for illustrating sets and the operations on sets. Even though Venn diagrams are extremely useful for illustrative purposes, it should be noted at the outset that they cannot be used to establish the formal validity of any statement or theorem in set theory. Venn diagrams are simply representations of sets by geometric figures (see Figures 2.3–1 to 2.3–4).

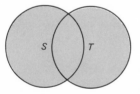

Figure 2.3–1 $S \cup T$.

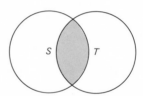

Figure 2.3–2 $S \cap T$.

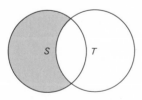

Figure 2.3–3 $S - T$.

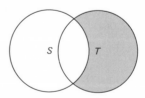

Figure 2.3–4 $T - S$.

[2] A fourth operation of complementarity is sometimes used. The complement of S in T, written $\tilde{S}^T$, is identical to $T - S$, while the complement of T in S, written $\tilde{T}^S$ is identical to $S - T$. A more general set $\tilde{S}$ (S complement) is defined as all elements in the universal set, U, that are not in S. This is identical to $U - S$.

Example 1.   Let

$$S = \{a, b, c, d, e\}$$

$$T = \{b, c, d, f, g\}$$

Then $S \cup T = \{a, b, c, d, e, f, g\}$, $S \cap T = \{b, c, d\}$, $S - T = \{a, e\}$, and $T - S = \{f, g\}$.

These set operations conform to certain basic laws, which we present as theorems.

Theorem 2.3–1   *Commutative Law of Union and Intersection*

$$A \cup B = B \cup A \quad \text{and} \quad A \cap B = B \cap A$$

where A and B are any arbitrary sets.

Theorem 2.3–2   *Associative Law of Union and Intersection*

$$A \cap (B \cap C) = (A \cap B) \cap C \quad \text{and} \quad A \cup (B \cup C) = (A \cup B) \cup C$$

where A, B, and C are any arbitrary sets.

Theorem 2.3–3   *Distributive Law of Union and Intersection*

(a) $A \cup (B \cap C) = (A \cup B) \cap (A \cup C)$

(b) $A \cap (B \cup C) = (A \cap B) \cup (A \cap C)$

where A, B, and C are any arbitrary sets.

Theorem 2.3–4   *De Morgan's Formulas*

(a) $(A - B) \cap (A - C) = A - (B \cup C)$

(b) $(A - B) \cup (A - C) = A - (B \cap C)$

where A, B, and C are any arbitrary sets.

Theorem 2.3–5   If A and B are sets, $A - B$ and $B - A$ are not in general equal. (Set difference is not commutative.)

Theorem 2.3–6 $A - (B - C)$ is not in general equal to $(A - B) - C$, where A, B, and C are any arbitrary sets. (Set difference is not associative.)

We shall present the proofs of Theorems 2.3–3(a) and 2.3–6 to illustrate general techniques. The reader should work through the proofs of the other theorems.

PROOF OF THEOREM 2.3–3(a)

$$A \cup (B \cap C) = (A \cup B) \cap (A \cup C)$$

To prove the equality of these two sets we must show that (1) $A \cup (B \cap C) \subseteq (A \cup B) \cap (A \cup C)$ and (2) $(A \cup B) \cap (A \cup C) \subseteq A \cup (B \cap C)$.

Part 1. $A \cup (B \cap C) \subseteq (A \cup B) \cap (A \cup C)$. Let $x \in A \cup (B \cap C)$. This implies that $x \in A$ or $x \in (B \cap C)$. $x \in (B \cap C)$ implies that $x \in B$ and $x \in C$. Thus $x \in A \cup (B \cap C)$ implies that $x \in A$ or $x \in B$ and $x \in C$. $x \in A$ implies that $x \in (A \cup B)$ and $x \in (A \cup C)$. $x \in B$ and $x \in C$ implies that $x \in (A \cup B)$ and $x \in (A \cup C)$. Thus $A \cup (B \cap C) \subseteq (A \cup B) \cap (A \cup C)$, since every element of the set on the left is also an element of the set on the right.

Part 2. $(A \cup B) \cap (A \cup C) \subseteq A \cup (B \cap C)$. Let $x \in (A \cup B) \cap (A \cup C)$. This implies that $x \in (A \cup B)$ and $x \in (A \cup C)$. $x \in (A \cup B)$ implies that $x \in A$ or $x \in B$. $x \in (A \cup C)$ implies that $x \in A$ or $x \in C$. The last three statements imply that $x \in A$ or $x \in B$ and $x \in C$. Thus $(A \cup B) \cap (A \cup C) \subseteq A \cup (B \cap C)$.   QED

Parts 1 and 2 constitute the proof of the theorem. The reader may care to draw a Venn diagram to illustrate this theorem.

PROOF OF THEOREM 2.3–6 $A - (B - C)$ is not in general equal to $(A - B) - C$. To prove this theorem we need only demonstrate one case in which these two sets are unequal. Suppose B is the empty set. Then $B - C$ is the set of all elements not in C, and $A - (B - C)$ is the set of all elements in both A and C. Thus $A - B = A$ and $A - C$ is the set of all elements in A not in C.   QED

We shall present another method of proof for this theorem for illustrative purposes.

Let $x \in A - (B - C)$. This implies that $x \in A$ and $x \notin (B - C)$. $x \notin (B - C)$ implies either that $x \notin B$ and $x \notin C$ or that $x \notin B$ but $x \in C$. Let $x \in (A - B) - C$. This implies that $x \in (A - B)$ and $x \notin C$. We thus have a contradiction since in the second case we find $x \notin C$ and in the first case x may be an element of C.   QED

The Venn diagram in Figure 2.3–5 illustrates the theorem. The black area is included in $A - (B - C)$ while it is not in the set $(A - B) - C$. What about the crosshatched area?

We conclude this section with the following definition.

DEFINITION 2.3–2   Two sets, A and B, are **disjoint** if $A \cap B = \varnothing$.
Disjoint sets are simply sets with no elements in common.

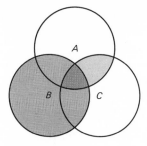

Figure 2.3–5   *Theorem 2.3–6.*

Problems

2.3–1   Prove Theorems 2.3–1, 2.3–2, and 2.3–3(b).

2.3–2   Illustrate the theorems in Problem 2.3–1 with Venn diagrams.

2.3–3   Given the following sets:

$A = \{a, b, c\}$
$B = \{b, e, f, g\}$
$C = \{a, b, g, e, c\}$
$D = \{f, b, a, g, h, j, c\}$

Calculate

(a) $A \cap D$

(b) $A \cup C$

(c) $B \cup (C \cap D)$

(d) $(B - A) \cap (D \cup C)$

(e) $(A - B) \cap (B - A)$

(f) $(A \cap D) \cap (C \cap D)$

(g) $(B \cup C) \cup (A \cup D)$

(h) $D - [A - (B \cap A)]$

2.3–4   Translate the following statements into set-theory notation, where

A is the set of all Angolans
B is the set of all bakers
C is the set of all candlestick makers
F is the set of all females
M is the set of all males
O is the set of all orange-juice drinkers
W is the set of all whiskey drinkers

(a) (Example) Some Angolan bakers are female whiskey drinkers. (Ans. $A \cap B \cap F \cap W \neq \varnothing$.)

(b) Angolan bakers always drink whiskey.

(c) All females who do not drink whiskey are either Angolans or bakers.

(d) There are no female candlestick makers in Angola.

(e) Angolans who are neither bakers nor candlestick makers are whiskey-drinking females.

(f) No male Angolan orange-juice drinker is a baker.

2.3–5   Prove: $(A \cup B) \cap \tilde{B} = A$ if and only if $A \cap B = \varnothing$. (Remember that $\tilde{B} = U - B$ for U, an arbitrary universal set that contains both A and B.)

2.3–6 If $n(A)$ is the number of elements in set A and if $n(U) = 300$, $n(A) = 55$, $n(B) = 75$, $n(C) = 70$, $n(A \cap B) = 30$, $n(A \cap C) = 15$, $n(B \cap C) = 25$, and $n(A \cap \tilde{B} \cap \tilde{C}) = 20$, find

(a) $n(A \cup B)$ (d) $n(\tilde{A} \cap \tilde{B} \cap \tilde{C})$

(b) $n(A \cap B \cap C)$ (e) $n(\tilde{A} \cap B \cap \tilde{C})$

(c) $n[(A \cap B) \cup (A \cap C) \cup (B \cap C)]$

2.4 ORDERED PAIRS, CARTESIAN PRODUCTS, RELATIONS, AND ORDERED SETS

As we have seen, sets are independent of the order in which their elements are listed. Ordered pairs (triples, or n-tuples) are sets of two elements (three elements, or n elements), where the order of the elements is of crucial importance. The **axiom of pair equality** embodies this concept.

AXIOM 2.4–1   Axiom of Pair Equality   The ordered pair (a, b) is equal to the ordered pair (c, d) if and only if $a = c$ and $b = d$.

Ordered triples can be defined with reference to ordered pairs.

DEFINITION 2.4–1   The **ordered triple** (a, b, c) is the ordered pair $(a, (b, c))$.

The axiom of pair equality extends in a natural way to ordered triples. Thus the ordered triple (a, b, c) equals the ordered triple (e, f, g) if and only if $a = e$, $b = f$, and $c = g$.

Another frequently encountered operation is the sum of two (or more) sets.

DEFINITION 2.4–2   Given two sets A and B, the **sum** of A and B, $A + B$, is the set $C = \{c_{ij}\}$, where $c_{ij} = (a_i + b_j)$ for all $a_i \in A$ and $b_j \in B$.

This definition applies to sets whose elements may or may not be ordered n-tuples. The most useful applications of set addition occur when the elements of A and B are ordered n-tuples. In such a case the representative elements of A and B are

$$a_i = (\alpha_i^1, \alpha_i^2, \ldots, \alpha_i^n)$$

and

$$b_j = (\beta_j^1, \beta_j^2, \ldots, \beta_j^n)$$

Then $c_{ij} = (\alpha_i^1 + \beta_j^1, \alpha_i^2 + \beta_j^2, \ldots, \alpha_i^n + \beta_j^n)$. Figure 2.4–1 illustrates this operation graphically.

Finding the general shape of the set $A + B$ is illustrated in Figure 2.4–2. $A + B$ will be enclosed in the four lines $X_{A(\max)} + X_{B(\max)}$, $X_{A(\min)} + X_{B(\min)}$, $Y_{A(\max)} + Y_{B(\max)}$, and $Y_{A(\min)} + Y_{B(\min)}$. Its general shape, of course, depends on the shapes of A and B.

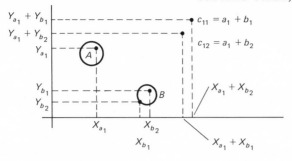

Figure 2.4–1 $A + B.$

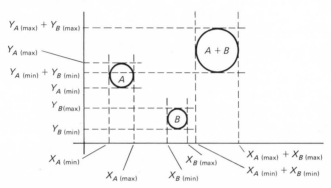

Figure 2.4–2 *General shape of* $A + B.$

Example 1. Suppose there are 10 firms in a given economy, each producing five different outputs. Let A_i be the set of all possible output combinations for producer i. Each element in A_i is thus an ordered 5-tuple, each component representing an output level of a particular commodity. The reader should be able to verify that the set $A_1 + A_2 + A_3 + \cdots + A_{10}$ represents all possible output combinations for the economy as a whole if the range of outputs of producer i is not influenced by the production of producer j.

The concept of an ordered pair is essential in understanding the concept of a Cartesian product of two sets.

DEFINITION 2.4–3 The **Cartesian product of two sets**, A and B, is the set $A \times B$ ("A cross B"), where

$$A \times B = \{(a, b) \mid a \in A \quad \text{and} \quad b \in B\}$$

The Cartesian product of two sets is a set whose elements are ordered pairs, the first element of each pair being a member of the first set and the second element of each pair being an element of the second set.

The idea of the Cartesian product can be readily extended as follows.

DEFINITION 2.4–4   The **Cartesian product of** n **sets** (where n is a positive integer) is the set $A_1 \times A_2 \times A_3 \times \cdots \times A_n$, where $A_1 \times \cdots \times A_n = \{(a_1, a_2, \ldots, a_n) \mid a_1 \in A_1, a_2 \in A_2, \ldots, a_n \in A_n\}$. If $A_i = A_j$ for all i and j, then we have the Cartesian product of A with itself n times, $A \times A \times \cdots \times A$. Or more simply, A^n.

In this case the Cartesian product is a set whose elements are ordered n-tuples.

Given an arbitrary set A it is, of course, possible to form the Cartesian product $A \times A$. Following Definition 2.4–3, $A \times A = \{(a, b) \mid a \in A$ and $b \in A\}$. $A \times A$ contains all the possible pairings of the elements of A. The Cartesian product of a set with itself leads directly to the notion of a binary relation.

DEFINITION 2.4–5   A **binary relation** on A is a subset R of the Cartesian product of A with itself ($A \times A$). If an ordered pair (a, b) is an element of R we write $a \, R \, b$ ("a is related to b by R" or "a is in the relation R to b").

DEFINITION 2.4–6   A binary relation R is an **equivalence relation** on A if and only if R has the following properties:

(1) R is *reflexive:* $a \, R \, a$ for all $a \in A$.
(2) R is *symmetric:* If $a \, R \, b$, then $b \, R \, a$ for a and $b \in A$.
(3) R is *transitive:* If $a \, R \, b$ and $b \, R \, c$, then $a \, R \, c$ for $a, b,$ and $c \in A$.

Some examples should help make these concepts clearer.

Example 2.   Let A be the set of all possible commodity bundles a particular consumer can choose among. Let P be the preference relation. Thus $a \, P \, b$ means bundle a is preferred to bundle b. Is P a relation in the sense of Definition 2.4–5? Clearly it is, because there must be some elements of A that the individual can rank by this relation. Thus there must be a set of bundles (a, b), where a is preferred to b. Thus P is a binary relation on A.

Is P an equivalence relation? If it is, it must satisfy conditions (1)–(3) of Definition 2.4–6. P is clearly not reflexive, as it makes no sense to say that one particular bundle is preferred to itself. Neither is P symmetric, since if a is preferred to b, b certainly is not preferred to a. For a rational consumer we would hope that P is transitive. If a is preferred to b and b is preferred to c, then a should be preferred to c. Even the transitivity of P is open to question on an empirical basis.

Example 3.   Let A be defined as in Example 2, and let I be the indifference relation. Thus $a \, I \, b$ means the consumer is indifferent between bundles a and *b.* The reader should be able to verify that *I* is in fact a relation in the sense of Definition 2.4–5. But is it an equivalence relation? Clearly *I* is reflexive: *a I a* for all $a \in I$. *I* is also symmetric, since if the consumer is indifferent between *a* and *b* he is also indifferent between *b* and *a*. In most simple models of consumer behavior *I* is also transitive, since if *a I b* and *b I c*, the consumer will be indifferent between *a* and *c*. Thus, in standard utility analysis *I* is an equivalence relation.[3]

Example 4.   Let *A* be the set of positive integers, and let *R* be the relation "is a multiple of 2 of." Thus 6 *R* 3. Describe the subset *R* of $A \times A$. Is *R* an equivalence relation? If not, which properties does it fail to satisfy and why?

The concept of an equivalence relation leads directly to two important concepts: a partition of a set and an equivalence class.

DEFINITION 2.4–7   A **partition** *P* of a set *A* is a set whose elements are nonempty subsets of *A* that have the following properties:

(1) all distinct elements of *P* are disjoint; and
(2) every element of *A* is a member of some element of *P*.

A partition of a set *A* is thus a set of subsets of *A*, where each element of *A* is in one and only one of the subsets. Figure 2.4–3 illustrates one of the many possible partitions of an arbitrary set *A*. Here the set *A* has been partitioned into 16 distinct, disjoint subsets $A_1, A_2, \ldots, A_{16}$. Every element $a \in A$ is a member of one and only one of these subsets. The partition in this case is

$$P = \{A_1, A_2, \ldots, A_{16}\}$$

where, as noted above, every element of *P* is itself a set.

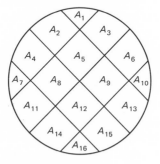

Figure 2.4–3   *A partition of A.*

[3] The same empirical objection has been made to the transitivity of *I*, as was noted earlier when discussing the transitivity of *P*.

Of all the possible partitions of a given set, one of the most useful and frequently encountered is a partition into equivalence classes.

DEFINITION 2.4–8 Let E be an equivalence relation on a set A. Then for each element $x \in A$ define a set A_x, where

$$A_x = \{y \mid y \in A \quad \text{and} \quad (x, y) \in E\}$$

The set A_x is called the **equivalence class** of element x.

For a given element of set A, its equivalence class under the equivalence relation E is simply the set of all elements of A for which $a \, E \, b$ holds. Note that different equivalence relations will in general define different sets of equivalence classes.

The relation between partitions and equivalence classes is contained in the following theorem.

Theorem 2.4–1 Let $\bar{E}$ be the set of all equivalence classes of a set A under an equivalence relation E. Then $\bar{E}$ is a partition of A.

PROOF We must show that the two properties of a partition in Definition 2.4–7 are satisfied. To prove that the first property holds, let A_x and A_y be two members of $\bar{E}$, and assume they have an element w in common. This means that $x \, E \, w$ and $y \, E \, w$. By the properties of the equivalence relation E, $x \, E \, w$ and $y \, E \, w$ imply:

(1) $\qquad\qquad x \, E \, w$ and $w \, E \, y \qquad$ (by symmetry of E)

(2) $\qquad\qquad x \, E \, y \qquad$ (by transitivity of E)

(2) implies that $A_x \supseteq A_y$.

(3) $\qquad\qquad w \, E \, x$ and $y \, E \, w \qquad$ (by symmetry)

(4) $\qquad\qquad y \, E \, x \qquad$ (by transitivity)

(4) implies that $A_x \subseteq A_y$. Thus, if two equivalence classes have an element in common, they are equal. Consequently, distinct equivalence classes must be disjoint. Thus the first property of partitions is satisfied.

To prove the second property of partitions, let x be an arbitrary element of A. Then $\bar{E}$ has A_x as an element by definition. Then, by the reflexive property of E, $x \, E \, x$, and we have shown that every element of A belongs to an element of the partition.   QED

The converse of Theorem 2.4–1 is also true: Every partition of a set A is induced by an equivalence relation. The proof of this statement is omitted.[4]

---

[4] See Deskins (1964), p. 12.

We conclude this section by defining the concepts of linearly ordered, partially ordered, and well-ordered sets and by discussing the relation between the various concepts of ordering and relations.

DEFINITION 2.4–9   Let R be a binary relation on a set A. R is a **linear order** (or a **total order**) on A if and only if:

(1) either $a\ R\ b$ or $b\ R\ a$ for a and b, any two distinct elements of A;
(2) there is no element $a \in A$ for which $a\ R\ a$; and
(3) if $a\ R\ b$ and $b\ R\ c$, then $a\ R\ c$ for a, b, and $c \in A$.

DEFINITION 2.4–10   Let R be a binary relation on a set A. R is a **partial order** on A if and only if:

(1) $a\ R\ a$ for every $a \in A$;
(2) both $a\ R\ b$ and $b\ R\ a$ cannot be true if a and b are distinct elements of A;[5] and
(3) $a\ R\ b$ and $b\ R\ c$ implies $a\ R\ c$ for a, b, and $c \in A$.

Simply stated, the basic difference between a linear order and a partial order on a set A is that under a linear order any two elements of A are directly comparable, while under a partial order any two arbitrary elements of A are not necessarily directly comparable.

Lattice diagrams (sometimes called modal diagrams) are often used to illustrate the ordering in sets with a finite number of elements. In diagrams of this sort, comparable elements of the set under the relation R (elements a and b for which $a\ R\ b$ holds) lie on the same line or are connected by a series of line segments. Arrows are used to indicate the direction in which the relation runs. Figures 2.4–4 and 2.4–5 illustrate a linear and a partial order for sets of four elements. In Figure 2.4–4 all four elements are directly comparable— that is, $a\ R\ b$, $a\ R\ c$, $a\ R\ d$, $b\ R\ c$, $b\ R\ d$, and $c\ R\ d$—while in Figure 2.4–5 elements d and c are not comparable—c is not in the relation with d and vice versa. This is clear from the figure, since elements c and d are not connected by a line segment or a series of line segments.

Before defining the notion of a well-ordered set, we introduce the following concepts.

Theorem 2.4–2   Let A be a set partially ordered by a relation R. Then every subset of A is also partially ordered under R, while some subsets of A may be totally ordered under A. (R may be a linear order on some subsets of A).

---

[5] A relation with this property is said to be antisymmetric; that is, $a\ R\ b$ and $b\ R\ a$ if and only if $a = b$.

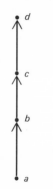

Figure 2.4–4   *Linear order.*

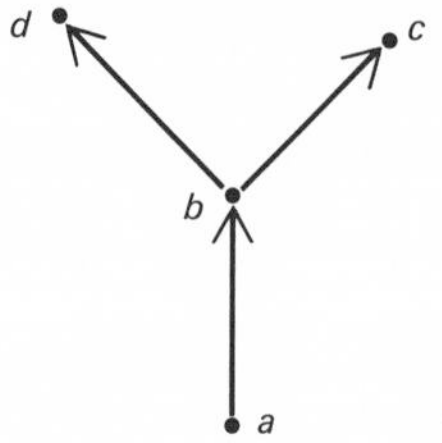

Figure 2.4–5   *Partial order.*

DEFINITION 2.4–11   Let A be a set partially ordered under a relation R. Then:

(1) an element $a \in A$ is a **first element** of A if $a R x$ for all $x \in A$;
(2) an element $z \in A$ is a **last element** of A if $x R z$ for all $x \in A$;
(3) an element $b \in A$ is a **minimal element** of A if $x R b$ implies $x = b$ for all $x \in A$; and
(4) an element $y \in A$ is a **maximal element** of A if $y R x$ implies $y = x$ for all $x \in A$.

Theorem 2.4–3   If a set A has a first element a (last element z), under a partial order R, then the first element (last element) is unique.

The proof of this theorem should be worked through by the reader.

In Figure 2.4–4 element a is both a first and a minimal element, while element d is both a last and a maximal element. In Figure 2.4–5, a is a first and a minimal element. There is no last element, although both d and c are maximal elements. In Figure 2.4–6, what are the first, last, maximal, and minimal elements, if any?

We can now define a well-ordered set.

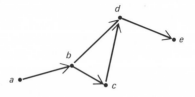

Figure 2.4–6   *An ordered set.*

DEFINITION 2.4–12 An ordered set A is **well ordered** if and only if each of its nonempty subsets has a first element.

Theorem 2.4–4 Every well-ordered set is totally ordered.

PROOF Let A be well ordered by relation R. Then for any two elements x and $y \in A$, the subset $\{x, y\}$ has a first element by the definition of a well ordered set. This fact implies that either $x \ R \ y$ or $y \ R \ x$ (depending on which element is the first element of the subset $\{x, y\}$). Consequently, A is totally ordered by R since any two arbitrary elements are comparable. QED

The converse of Theorem 2.4–4 is not true; every totally ordered set is not well ordered. To show this we need only give an example of a totally ordered set that is not well ordered. Let A be the set of all rational numbers, and let R be the relation "less than or equal to." Clearly, A is totally ordered by this relation. Consider an arbitrary subset A' of A. $A' = \{x \mid x \in A, x > 5\}$. A' has no first element (why?). Thus A is not well ordered by the relation $\leq$.

Problems

2.4–1 If $A = \{1, 2, 3, 4\}$ and $B = \{-1, 0, 1\}$ calculate $A + B$.

2.4–2 Discuss the relationship between the axiom of extent and the axiom of pair equality.

2.4–3 If $A = \{a, b, c\}$ and $B = \{e, f, b\}$, what are
(a) $A \times A$ (c) $B \times A$
(b) $A \times B$ (d) $A \times B \times A$

2.4–4 If $A = \{$red marshmallow, blue marshmallow, chalk, steel$\} = \{r, b, c, s\}$ and R is the binary relation "is softer than" (thus $a \ R \ b$ is read "a is softer than b"), what subset of $A \times A$ does R define?

2.4–5 Which of the following relations on the real numbers are (a) reflexive, (b) symmetric, and (c) transitive? Which are equivalence relations?
(a) $>$ (c) $<$
(b) $\geq$ (d) $=$

2.4–6 Show that the indifference relation, I, is an equivalence relation on the set of all commodity bundles. Prove that I effects a partition of the set and describe the equivalence classes.

2.4–7 Let A be the set of all people living on a particular block in Gainesville, Florida. Describe at least three different equivalence relations on this set and describe the partition each induces.

2.4–8 Let A be the set of positive integers from 1 to 10. Show that a relation of the form $a_i/a_j = a_k$ for a_i, a_j, and $a_k \in A$ is an equivalence relation. What partition of A does it induce?

2.4–9   Let A be the same set as in Problem 2.4–4, with the following relations:
R_1 "is harder than," R_2 "is just as hard, but no harder than," and R_3 "is as
heavy per handful as."
(a) Is R_1 a linear or partial order on A?
(b) What kind of relation is R_2? What are its elements?
(c) What kind of order does R_3 define on A? Is $(r, b) \in R_3$? (r, c)? (s, b)?
(c, s)?
(d) What are the first, last, maximal, and minimal elements, if any, under
each of the three relations?

2.4–10   Prove Theorem 2.4–3.

2.5   FUNCTIONS AND MAPPINGS

Functions are one of the most basic concepts in mathematics. In this section we shall develop the concept of a mapping or map and show how this
concept is related to the familiar concept of a function.

Consider two sets A and B, where A is the set of all students in a particular
class and B is the set of all chairs in the classroom. There is a natural association between these two sets—namely, the particular chair in which a particular
student sits. Let $A = \{a_1, a_2, \ldots, a_{43}\}$ and $B = \{b_1, b_2, \ldots, b_{50}\}$. If
student i sits in chair j then we associate element a_i from set A with element b_j
from set B. This correspondence between the elements of sets A and B is
called a **mapping of** A **into** B. The unique element of set B associated with an
element of set A is called the **image** of the element of A under the mapping.
Thus $b_j \in B$ is the image of $a_i \in A$.

There are two basic types of maps to be considered: "into" and "onto"
maps. In the example above, the mapping was A into B since not every element
of B was an image of an element of A. There are more chairs than students.
If, however, there were the same number of chairs as students, the mapping
would be an "onto" mapping since each chair would be occupied, that is,
every element of B would be an image of an element of A.

Suppose either our students are very friendly or the chairs are very large,
so that more than one student sits in a particular chair. Thus one element in
B would be the image of one, two, or more distinct elements in A. Such a
relationship between sets A and B is still a mapping. If, however, one student
were to occupy two chairs simultaneously, this would not be a mapping from
A to B since one element of A would have two distinct elements in B as images.

Mappings can be described in several different ways. Let the mapping in our
example be ρ. Then one description of ρ would be to list the ordered pairs of
each student and his chair. ρ then is simply the set of these ordered pairs,

$$\rho = \{(a_1, b_5), (a_2, b_{31}), \ldots, (a_{43}, b_{27})\}$$

where the ordered pair (a_i, b_j) simply means student i sits in chair j. This way of describing a mapping leads to the following definition of a map.

DEFINITION 2.5–1   A mapping of a set A into[6] a set B is a subset of the Cartesian product of A and B ($A \times B$) in which each element of A appears *once* and *only once* as the first element of an ordered pair. A is the **domain** of the mapping, while B is called the **codomain** of the mapping. If the mapping is onto, B is called the **range** of the mapping.

Sometimes a mapping is described by using an arrow to connect elements of A with their image in B. For our example we could write:

$$\rho : a_1 \mapsto b_5$$
$$a_2 \mapsto b_{31}$$
$$\vdots$$
$$a_{43} \mapsto b_{27}$$

Venn diagrams can also be used to describe a mapping pictorially when the number of elements in each set is small. See, for example, Figure 2.5–1, where each element in A is connected to its image in B by an arrow. Note that the map in Figure 2.5–1 is into, but not onto, since element b_4 is not an image of any element in A.

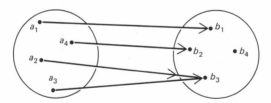

Figure 2.5–1   *Map ρ: A into B.*

Having defined the term map, it should be clear that a function is simply a special mapping.

DEFINITION 2.5–2   A **function** is a mapping of a set A into a set B, where the elements of A and B are numbers.

The type of function with which the reader is probably most familiar is a real-valued function. If R is the set of real numbers, a real-valued function is simply a subset of $R \times R$; or in other words, a set whose elements are ordered pairs, where each element in the ordered pairs is a real number.

[6] When the term "A into B" is used, this does not rule out the possibility of the mapping being an onto map, unless it is specified that the map is "into, but not onto."

Example 1. $y = f(x) = 2x^2 + 3$. This says that y is a function of x and the rule for determining the value of y for any value of x is given. The function f is not $2x^2 + 3$ but is

$$f = \{(x, y) \mid y = 2x^2 + 3, x \in R\}$$

that is, the set of ordered pairs satisfying the "rule" $y = 2x^2 + 3$. Note that the description of f could also be written as

$$f = \{(x, 2x^2 + 3) \mid x \in R\}$$

In typical functional notation the value of y when $x = x_1$ is indicated by $y_1 = f(x_1)$. An alternative notation used in abstract algebra to denote the image of an element $a \in A$ under the mapping (function) f is $af \in B$. This notation is particularly useful when considering composite mappings. Suppose f is a map from A into B and g is a map from B into C. Then f transforms $a \in A$ to $af \in B$. The effect of the mapping g is to map $af \in B$ to $(af)g \in C$. The effect of applying f and then g is to form a new mapping denoted by $g \circ f$ (read "f composed with g") which is a map from A into C. Alternatively, the composite mapping $g \circ f$ can be defined as

$$g \circ f = \{(a, a(g \circ f)) \mid a \in A\}$$

where $a(g \circ f) = (af)g$ for $af \in B$ and $a(g \circ f) \in C$.

Figure 2.5–2 illustrates a composite mapping, where $a_1 f = b_1$, $b_1 g = c_1 = a_1(g \circ f)$, and so on. In functional notation, $a_1(g \circ f) = g[f(a_1)]$.

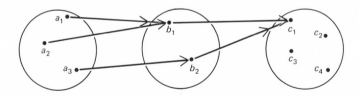

Figure 2.5–2 $g \circ f$.

The question of when such a composite mapping is defined is answered in the following theorem.

Theorem 2.5–1   Given a mapping f from A into B and a mapping g from B into C, the composite mapping $g \circ f$ of A into C is defined if the range of f is equal to the domain of g.

Since the domain of g is the whole set B, the theorem implies that f must be a mapping of A onto B for $g \circ f$ to be defined.

No formal proof of this theorem will be presented.[7] Note, however, that since g is a mapping from B to C, every element of B has an image in C under

[7] See MacLane and Berkhoff (1967).

g. Thus, if every element in *B* is not the image of at least one element of *A* under *f*, then *g* ∘ *f* is not the function *f* followed by the function *g* as defined, since *g* maps every element of *B* into an element of *C*. We could, however, define a new set $B' = B - \{b \in B \mid b$ is not an image of an element of *A* under *f*\} and a new map *g'* from *B'* to *C* such that $b'g' = bg$ for all $b' \in B'$. Then the composite map *g'* ∘ *f* would be a map from *A* to *C*. See Figure 2.5–3.

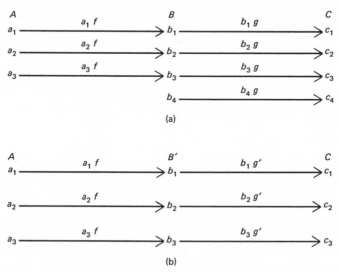

(a)

(b)

Figure 2.5–3   (*a*) *g* ∘ *f* not defined. (*b*) *g'* ∘ *f* defined.

Composite mappings involving more than two maps may be defined provided the domains and ranges of "adjacent" maps are equal.

We turn now to a discussion of one-to-one mappings.

DEFINITION 2.5–3   A mapping *α* of a set *A* into a set *B* is a **one-to-one mapping of *A* into *B*** if each element of *A* has a distinct image in *B*; that is, $a_1\alpha = a_2\alpha$ if and only if $a_1 = a_2$ for all $a \in A$. (If a_1 and a_2 have the same image in *B* under *α*, then a_1 is equal to a_2.)

DEFINITION 2.5–4   A mapping *β* of a set *A* onto a set *B* is a **one-to-one mapping of *A* onto *B*** if (1) each element of *A* has a distinct image in *B* and (2) each element in *B* is the image of an element in *A*.

Figures 2.5–4 and 2.5–5 illustrate these mappings. (Note that neither *f* nor *g* in Figure 2.5–2 is one-to-one.) From Figure 2.5–4 it is clear that when a one-to-one mapping of *A* onto *B*, *β*, exists, we can also define a one-to-one map of *B* onto *A* denoted by *β'*. These two maps, *β* and *β'*, together are called a

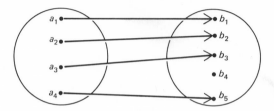

Figure 2.5–4   *One-to-one into.*

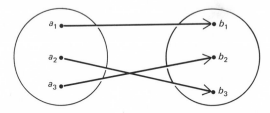

Figure 2.5–5   *One-to-one onto.*

one-to-one correspondence between A and B. Some terms based on the ideas of one-to-one mappings are defined below.

DEFINITION 2.5–5   Two sets have the **same number of elements** if a one-to-one correspondence exists between them.

DEFINITION 2.5–6   A set A **has n elements** if there is a one-to-one mapping from A onto the subset $\{1, 2, \ldots, n\}$ of the positive integers.

DEFINITION 2.5–7   If a set has n elements the set is a **finite set**.

DEFINITION 2.5–8   An **infinite set** is a set for which there is a one-to-one correspondence between it and one of its proper subsets.

DEFINITION 2.5–9   An infinite set is **countable** or **denumerable** if there is a one-to-one correspondence between it and the set of all positive integers.

As an example of Definition 2.5–8, consider the set of all positive integers. Show that the mapping $\gamma : i\gamma = 2i$ for $i \in I^+$ is a one-to-one mapping of I^+ onto E, the set of all positive even integers. Once this has been shown, we conclude that I^+ is an infinite set in the sense of Definition 2.5–8. Furthermore, I^+ is a denumerable set, since it is obviously possible to construct a one-to-one correspondence between a set and itself.

Before discussing the concept of an inverse mapping we define an identity mapping, I.

DEFINITION 2.5–10   An **identity mapping**, I, is a one-to-one map of a set A onto itself such that $xI = x$ for all $x \in A$.

We have already used, without mentioning explicitly, the fact that any mapping f from A to B can be written as the composite of two maps, $f = g \circ h$, where h is an onto map (but not necessarily one-to-one) and g is a one-to-one into map.

DEFINITION 2.5–11   Consider two mappings: j from T to S and k from S to T such that the composite mapping $k \circ j$ is defined. $k \circ j$ is a map from T to itself. If $k \circ j$ is the identity map on T, I_T, then k is a **left inverse** of j and j is a **right inverse** of k. If furthermore, $j \circ k$ (a map from S to itself) is the identity map on S, I_S, then j is also a **left inverse** of k and k is a **right inverse** of j. In such a case k is called the **inverse** of j and j the **inverse** of k.

Intuitively, j undoes what k does and vice versa. Notationally, $j = k^{-1}$ and $k = j^{-1}$. We can then write that $(xj)k = x$ for all $x \in T$ and $(yk)j = y$ for all $y \in S$.

Theorem 2.5–2   If α is a one-to-one mapping of A onto B, then α has a unique inverse. The converse is also true.

PROOF   *Part 1: uniqueness of* α^{-1}. Let α be a one-to-one mapping of A onto B. Then for every $a \in A$, $a\alpha = b \in B$. Since each $b \in B$ is the image of only one element $a \in A$, it follows that the mapping β from B to A, where $b\beta = a$, is one-to-one from B onto A. Then $a(\alpha \circ \beta) = b\beta = a$ and $\beta \circ \alpha = I_B$. Thus $\alpha = \beta^{-1}$ and $\beta = \alpha^{-1}$. Suppose that these inverses are not unique, that is, γ is also an inverse of α and ρ is also an inverse of β. Then $\alpha \circ \beta = \beta \circ \alpha = I, \alpha \circ \gamma = \gamma \circ \gamma = I$ (only this case will be considered), and $\rho \circ \beta = \beta \circ \gamma = I$. Then

$$\beta \circ \alpha \circ \gamma = \beta \circ (\alpha \circ \gamma) = \beta \circ I = \beta$$

and

$$\beta \circ \alpha \circ \gamma = (\beta \circ \alpha) \circ \gamma = I \circ \gamma = \gamma$$

so that $\beta = \gamma$ and the inverse of α is unique.

Part 2: α^{-1} unique implies α is one-to-one A onto B. Suppose α is unique. Suppose for any two distinct elements a_1 and $a_2 \in A$, $a_1\alpha = a_2\alpha$. Then $(a_1\alpha)\alpha^{-1} = (a_2\alpha)\alpha^{-1}$ so that $a_1 = a_2$, a contradiction of our assumption that a_1 and a_2 are distinct elements of A. Therefore α is a one-to-one mapping. To show that α is onto, note that for any element $b \in B$ we have $(b\alpha^{-1})\alpha = b(\alpha^{-1} \circ \alpha) = b$. Consequently, b is the image of $a = b\alpha^{-1} \in A$ and the mapping is onto.   QED

Often mappings that have the properties of continuity or monotonicity are useful. We conclude this section with the following definitions.

DEFINITION 2.5–12   Given that f is a mapping from a denumerable set A to another denumerable set B. Let $a_1, a_2, \ldots, a_n$ be any arbitrary sequence of elements of A. Then f is a **continuous mapping** if

$$f(\lim_{n \to \infty} a_n) = \lim_{n \to \infty} f(a_n)$$

In other words, for f to be continuous the image of the limit of the sequence must be the same element in B as is the limit of the image of a_n as n is made arbitrarily large. The existence of these limits implies that the rule for determining the sequence $a_1, a_2, \ldots$ must be known.

DEFINITION 2.5–13   Given that f is a mapping from A to B and that A and B are ordered by R_a and R_b. Then f is a **monotonically increasing** mapping if for any two elements a_1 and $a_2 \in A$, $a_1 R_a a_2$ implies $f(a_1) R_b f(a_2)$. f is **monotonically decreasing** if for the same two elements in A, $f(a_2) R_b f(a_1)$.

The concepts of continuous and monotonic maps are generalizations of the better-known concepts of continuous and monotonic functions.[8]

Problems

2.5–1   Let $S = \{a, b, c, d\}$ and let $T = \{1, 2, 3, 4, 5\}$.
    (a) Construct a mapping from S to T that is into but not one-to-one.
    (b) Is it possible to construct a one-to-one mapping from S onto T? S into T? T onto S? T into S? Explain.

2.5–2   Let $f = \{(x, 2x - 1) \mid x \in R\}$ and $g = \{(x, 3x) \mid x \in R\}$. Describe the composite mappings $f \circ g$ and $g \circ f$. What are the domains and ranges of f, g, $g \circ f$, and $f \circ g$? Does $f \circ g = g \circ f$? Why or why not?

2.5–3   Show that the set of all positive integers is an infinite set.

2.5–4   For $A = \{a_1, a_2, a_3, a_4\}$ and $B = \{b_1, b_2, b_3, b_4\}$.
    (a) Show that $f: a_i \mapsto b_i$ is a one-to-one, onto map.
    (b) Find the inverse of f and show that it is unique.
    (c) What is $f \circ f^{-1}$?

2.5–5   Let $A = \{1, 2, 3, 4\}$ and let $B = \{8, 9, 10, 11\}$. If A is ordered by R_a, "greater than," and B is ordered by R_b, "less than," construct, if possible, a monotonically increasing and a monotonically decreasing mapping from A to B.

2.5–6   Prove: If α is a one-to-one mapping of A onto B, and β is a one-to-one mapping of B onto C, then $(\beta \circ \alpha)^{-1} = \alpha^{-1} \circ \beta^{-1}$.

2.5–7   Given the following one-to-one mappings of $A = \{a_1, a_2, a_3, a_4\}$ onto itself:
I: $a_1 I = a_1$, $a_2 I = a_2$, $a_3 I = a_3$, $a_4 I = a_4$
α: $a_1 \alpha = a_2$, $a_2 \alpha = a_3$, $a_3 \alpha = a_4$, $a_4 \alpha = a_1$
β: $a_1 \beta = a_4$, $a_2 \beta = a_1$, $a_3 \beta = a_2$, $a_4 \beta = a_3$

---

[8] The relation between a continuous and/or monotonic mapping for arbitrary sets and a continuous and/or monotonic mapping for sets of numbers is the subject matter of measure theory and is discussed in detail in Chapter 3.

$\gamma: a_1\gamma = a_3, \quad a_2\gamma = a_4, \quad a_3\gamma = a_1, \quad a_4\gamma = a_2$

Verify that

(a) $\beta = \alpha^{-1}$

(b) $\alpha \circ \gamma = \gamma \circ a$

(c) $\gamma^{-1} = \gamma$

(d) $\alpha^{-1} = \alpha^3$

(where $\alpha^3 = \alpha \circ \alpha \circ \alpha$).

2.6 BINARY OPERATIONS AND MORPHISMS

In Section 2.4 we discussed the concept of a binary relation on a set A, which was a subset of $A \times A$, a set of ordered pairs. Relations, as we saw, resulted in the comparability of certain (and perhaps all) elements of A. Binary relations can be viewed as a mapping from A, or some subset of A, to a subset of $A \times A$. Binary operations, on the other hand, combine two elements of A to produce a third element of A. Some of the most familiar binary operations are those of addition, subtraction, and multiplication. Formally, we have the following definition.

DEFINITION 2.6–1 A **binary operation**, denoted by $\square$, on a set A is a mapping from $A \times A$ into A. In other words, for each ordered pair (a_1, a_2) in $A \times A$ the operation $\square$ determines a unique element of A, $a_1 \square a_2$. If the element $a_1 \square a_2$ is not a member of A, then $\square$ is not a binary operation on A.

Example 1. Let A be the set of all real numbers. Then addition, denoted by $+$, is a binary operation on A. Any pair of real numbers can be added and their sum is always another real number. The statement that the set of all real numbers is "closed under addition" is equivalent to saying that $+$ is a binary operation on the set of real numbers.

Example 2. The set of integers, I, is not closed with respect to the operation division, $\div$, since $I_1 \div I_2$, where I_1 and $I_2 \in I$ may be a rational number, not an integer. Thus $\div$ is not a binary operation on I. It is, however, a binary operation on the set of rational numbers, as the reader can verify.

Example 3. Construct a set whose elements are real numbers on which neither addition nor multiplication are binary operations.

DEFINITION 2.6–2 A binary operation, $\square$, on a set A is **commutative** if $a_1 \square a_2 = a_2 \square a_1$ for all a_1 and $a_2 \in A$.

DEFINITION 2.6–3 A binary operation, $\square$, on a set A is **associative** if $(a_1 \square a_2) \square a_3 = a_1 \square (a_2 \square a_3)$ for all a_1, a_2, and $a_3 \in A$.

Example 4. Addition on the set of all real numbers, R, is both commutative and associative, since $x_1 + x_2 = x_2 + x_1$ for x_1 and $x_2 \in R$ and since $x_1 + (x_2 + x_3) = (x_1 + x_2) + x_3$ for all x_1, x_2, and $x_3 \in R$.

DEFINITION 2.6–4   Given two binary operations, $\square$ and Δ, defined on a set A. $\square$ is **left distributive** with Δ if $a_1 \square (a_2 \Delta a_3) = (a_1 \square a_2) \Delta (a_1 \square a_3)$. $\square$ is **right distributive** with Δ if $(a_1 \Delta a_2) \square a_3 = (a_1 \square a_3) \Delta (a_2 \square a_3)$. If $\square$ is both right and left distributive with Δ, then $\square$ is said to be **distributive** with Δ.

Example 5.   Addition and multiplication are both left and right distributive with respect to each other and thus are distributive with each other on R. Are the operations of set union and intersection distributive? Are the operations of union and difference distributive?

DEFINITION 2.6–5   A set A has a **unit element** (identity element or unit), 1_A, under the binary operation $\square$ if $1_A \square a = a = a \square 1_A$ for all elements $a \in A$.

DEFINITION 2.6–6   A set A has a **zero element** (null element or zero), O_A, under the binary operation $\square$ if $O_A \square a = O_A = a \square O_A$ for all elements $a \in A$.

The notations for the unit element and zero element are chosen to underline the fact that they behave like one and zero in the real numbers.

DEFINITION 2.6–7   The **inverse** of $a \in A$ under the binary operation $\square$ is an element $b \in A$ such that $a \square b = b \square a = 1_A$.

Example 6.   Consider the real numbers, R, under addition, $+$. The identity element in R under $+$ is 0, since $0 + r = r + 0 = r$ for all $r \in R$. The set R has no zero element under addition, since there is no element $O_R \in R$ such that $O_R + r = r + O_R = O_R$ for all $r \in R$. Consider R under multiplication, $(\cdot)$. The unit element of R under $(\cdot)$ is 1 while the zero element of R under $(\cdot)$ is 0.

Just as it was possible to define ternary and higher-order relations, higher-order operations can also be defined. A third-order, or ternary, operation is a mapping from ordered triples of a set to another element of the same set. An *n*-ary operation is a mapping from ordered *n*-tuples of a set to single elements of the set.

For a particular set A, more than one binary or higher-order operation may be defined. The notation $\langle A, \square, O, \Delta \rangle$ indicates that the operations $\square$, O, and Δ (assumed to be binary unless otherwise indicated) are defined on the set A.

DEFINITION 2.6–8   An **algebraic system** is a set upon which one or more binary or higher-order operations are defined.

Modern or abstract algebra is largely concerned with describing the characteristics of algebraic systems and the relationships that exist between different algebraic systems. One of the most important concepts in abstract algebra is that of a morphism.[9]

DEFINITION 2.6–9   A **morphism** is a mapping, μ, from a set A on which a binary operation $\square$ is defined to a set B on which a binary operation O is defined such that $\mu(a_1 \square a_2) = \mu a_1 \; O \; \mu a_2$.

To qualify as a morphism, not only must μ be a mapping from A to B, but also μ must preserve operations. That is, if $a_1 \square a_2 = a_3$ for a_1, a_2, and $a_3 \in A$, then μa_3, (the image of a_3 in B under μ) must be equal to $\mu a_1 \; O \; \mu a_2$, which is the element of B obtained by combining images of a_1 and a_2 under the operation O.

Some specific types of morphisms are given in the following definitions.

DEFINITION 2.6–10   Given μ is a morphism between $\langle A, \square \rangle$ and $\langle B, O \rangle$: (1) μ is an **isomorphism** if it is a one-to-one mapping of A onto B; (2) μ is an **epimorphism** if it is a mapping of A onto B; and (3) μ is a **monomorphism** if it is a one-to-one mapping of A into B.

DEFINITION 2.6–11   Given μ, a morphism from $\langle A, \square \rangle$ to $\langle A, \square \rangle$. (1) μ is an **endomorphism** and (2) if, in addition, μ is a one-to-one mapping of A onto A, then it is an **automorphism**.

Isomorphisms are the most important type of morphisms. The reasons for this are as follows: (1) Given one algebraic system whose properties are known, any algebraic systems that are isomorphic to it have the same properties (two algebraic systems are isomorphic if there is an isomorphism from one system to the other); and (2) in analyzing algebraic systems, it is often convenient to replace one system with another system isomorphic to it, since they have the same properties. Note also that a monomorphism, m, from $\langle A, \square \rangle$ to $\langle B, O \rangle$ defines an isomorphism m' from $\langle A, \square \rangle$ to $\langle B', O \rangle$, where $B' = \{b \mid b \in B$ and $b = ma$ for all $a \in A\}$.

Example 7.   Let $A = \{a_1, a_2, a_3, a_4\}$ and $B = \{b_1, b_2, b_3, b_4\}$. The operations $\square$ on A and O on B are defined in the following operation tables:

$\square$	a_1	a_2	a_3	a_4
a_1	a_1	a_2	a_3	a_4
a_2	a_2	a_4	a_1	a_3
a_3	a_3	a_1	a_4	a_2
a_4	a_4	a_3	a_2	a_1

O	b_1	b_2	b_3	b_4
b_1	b_3	b_4	b_1	b_2
b_2	b_4	b_1	b_2	b_3
b_3	b_1	b_2	b_3	b_4
b_4	b_2	b_3	b_4	b_1

Such tables are read as follows: To find $a_4 \square a_1$, find the element in the a_4 row and the a_1 column. Thus $a_4 \square a_1 = a_4$. $(a_1 \square a_4 = a_4)$.

---

[9] Morphisms are also sometimes called homomorphisms.

Verify that the mapping $\alpha : a_1 \rightarrow b_3$, $a_2 \rightarrow b_4$, $a_3 \rightarrow b_2$, and $a_4 \rightarrow b_1$ is an isomorphism between $\langle A, \square \rangle$ and $\langle B, O \rangle$. First we must check that α is a one-to-one mapping of A onto B. Every element of B is an image of an element in A, so α is onto. Also, every element of B is the image of only one element in A, so α is also one-to-one. Next, we must check to see if α preserves the operations, that is, does $\alpha(a_i \square a_j) = \alpha a_i \, O \, \alpha a_j$ for all a_i and $a_j \in A$?

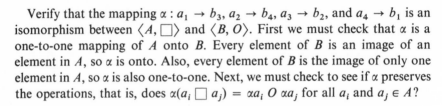

Check $a_2 \square a_3$.

(1) $\qquad\qquad\qquad\qquad\qquad a_2 \square a_3 = a_1$

(2) $\qquad\qquad\qquad\qquad\qquad\qquad \alpha a_2 = b_4$

(3) $\qquad\qquad\qquad\qquad\qquad\qquad \alpha a_3 = b_2$

(4) $\qquad\qquad\qquad\qquad\qquad\; b_4 \, O \, b_2 = b_3$

(5) $\qquad\qquad\qquad\qquad\qquad\qquad \alpha a_1 = b_3$

So the operations are preserved for this case. Verification of the other cases is left as an exercise. All possible combinations must be verified to ensure that $\langle A, \square \rangle$ is indeed isomorphic to $\langle B, O \rangle$.

We conclude this section with the following theorems.

Theorem 2.6–1   The inverse of an isomorphism is an isomorphism.

PROOF   If f is an isomorphism from $\langle A, \square \rangle$ to $\langle B, O \rangle$, we must show that f^{-1}, a mapping from B to A, satisfies $f^{-1}(b_1 \, O \, b_2) = f^{-1}b_1 \square f^{-1}b_2$, for all elements b_1 and $b_2 \in B$. Apply f to both sides of this equation. Then $f[f^{-1}(b_1 \, O \, b_2)] = b_1 \, O \, b_2 = f[f^{-1}b_1 \square f^{-1}b_2]$. Since f is an isomorphism, $f[f^{-1}b_1 \square f^{-1}b_2] = (ff^{-1}b_1) \, O \, (ff^{-1}b_2) = b_1 \, O \, b_2$.   QED

Theorem 2.6–2   The relation $\simeq$ ("is isomorphic to") is an equivalence relation. That is, $\simeq$ is:

(a) reflexive, $\langle A, \square \rangle \simeq \langle A, \square \rangle$;
(b) symmetric, $\langle A, \square \rangle \simeq \langle B, O \rangle$ implies $\langle B, O \rangle \simeq \langle A, \square \rangle$; and
(c) transitive, if $\langle A, \square \rangle \simeq \langle B, O \rangle$ and $\langle B, O \rangle \simeq \langle C, \Delta \rangle$, then $\langle A, \square \rangle \simeq \langle C, \Delta \rangle$.

PROOF   (a) The mapping I_A (the identity map) establishes the isomorphism (specifically an automorphism) between $\langle A, \square \rangle$ and itself.

(b) The symmetry of $\simeq$ is proved in Theorem 2.6–1.

(c) If α is the isomorphism from $\langle A, \square \rangle$ to $\langle B, O \rangle$ and β the isomorphism from $\langle B, O \rangle$ to $\langle C, \Delta \rangle$, then $\beta \circ \alpha$ is the isomorphism from $\langle A, \square \rangle$ to $\langle C, \Delta \rangle$.   QED

The implications of Theorem 2.6–2 are quite important. Since $\simeq$ is an equivalence relation, the set of all algebraic systems is partitioned into equivalence classes by $\simeq$. The members of a particular class are algebraic systems that are isomorphic to each other. All members of an equivalence class will have exactly the same algebraic properties. The theorem also provides a method of building up new isomorphisms, $f \circ g$, from known isomorphisms f and g.

In all the preceding we have spoken of morphisms that preserve operations. Another entire class of morphisms are those that preserve relations. The definitions of morphisms of this type are completely analogous to those given above if one simply changes the term "operation" to "relation."

Problems

2.6–1 What is the difference between a binary relation and a binary operation?

2.6–2 Which arithmetic operations are commutative, distributive, and associative on the set of real numbers? Which are not?

2.6–3 Complete the verification $\alpha(a_1 \ \square \ a_j)$ in Example 7.

2.6–4 Construct morphisms between the following algebraic systems:
   (a) $\langle R^-, + \rangle$ and $\langle R^+, + \rangle$
   (b) $\langle$even integers, $+ \rangle$ and $\langle$odd integers, $+ \rangle$
   (c) $\langle R, - \rangle$ and $\langle R, - \rangle$

2.6–5 For the sets $A = \{a_1, a_2\}$ and $B = \{b_1, b_2\}$.
   (a) Define two operations on each set Δ_A, O_A, Δ_B, and O_B that are commutative and associative.
   (b) Define an isomorphism between A and B. (You may have to redefine the operations.)
   (c) Find the inverse of your isomorphism in (b), thus verifying that $\simeq$ is symmetric.

2.6–6 Construct an abstract algebraic system that is isomorphic to the positive integers under addition. Can you relate such a system to utility theory?

2.6–7 Give examples of binary relations that are
   (a) symmetric and transitive but not reflexive
   (b) reflexive and symmetric but not transitive
   (c) reflexive and transitive but not symmetric

2.6–8 (a) Show that $\langle I^+, + \rangle$ and $\langle A, + \rangle$, where $A = \{2x, x \in I^+\}$ are isomorphic.
   (b) Is $\langle I^+, + \rangle$ isomorphic to $\langle B, + \rangle$, where $B = \{3x - 1, x \in I^+\}$.
   (c) Is $\langle A, + \rangle$ isomorphic to $\langle B, + \rangle$?

2.7 TYPES OF ALGEBRAIC SYSTEMS

In the previous section we defined the general notion of an algebraic system and discussed the concept of a morphism—a relation between algebraic systems. In this section we describe the most common types of algebraic systems.

DEFINITION 2.7–1   A set G on which a binary operation O is defined forms a **group** with respect to this operation if for arbitrary elements in G:

(1) $(g_1 \ O \ g_2) \ O \ g_3 = g_1 \ O \ (g_2 \ O \ g_3)$ (O is associative);
(2) there is an element $g_u \in G$ such that $g_u \ O \ g_i = g_i \ O \ g_u = g_i$ for all $g_i \in G$ (G has an identity element); and
(3) for every element $g \in G$ there is an element g^{-1} such that $g \ O \ g^{-1} = g^{-1} \ O \ g = g_u$ (the existence of inverses).

If, in addition, the operation O is commutative, that is, $g_1 \ O \ g_2 = g_2 \ O \ g_1$ for every g_1 and $g_2 \in G$, then the group is an **abelian group**.

Example 1.   The set of all integers, I, forms a group with respect to addition. 0 is the identity element and the inverse of any integer is its negative. I is not a group under the operation of multiplication, since every integer does not have an inverse that is also an integer.

DEFINITION 2.7–2   A set R forms a **ring** with respect to the binary operations of addition and multiplication if for every r_1, r_2, and $r_3 \in R$:

(1) addition is associative, $(r_1 + r_2) + r_3 = r_1 + (r_2 + r_3)$;
(2) addition is commutative, $r_1 + r_2 = r_2 + r_1$;
(3) there is an additive identity element (zero), $r + 0 = r$;
(4) there are additive inverses, $r + (-r) = 0$;
(5) multiplication is associative $(r_1 \cdot r_2) \cdot r_3 = r_1 \cdot (r_2 \cdot r_3)$; and
(6) multiplication and addition are distributive, $(r_1 + r_2) \cdot r_3 = r_1 \cdot r_3 + r_2 \cdot r_3$.

If, in addition to the properties listed above, multiplication is commutative $(a \cdot b = b \cdot a)$, then the ring is a **commutative ring**. If a ring has a multiplicative identity $(a \cdot 1 = 1 \cdot a = a)$, it is a **ring with unity**.

Example 2.   The reader should be able to verify that the sets of integers, rational numbers, real numbers, and complex numbers each form rings with respect to the operations of ordinary addition and multiplication.

DEFINITION 2.7–3   An **integral domain**, D, is a commutative ring with unity having no divisors of zero. A ring has divisors of zero if the product of two (or more) nonzero elements of the ring is zero.

Example 3.   The rings in Example 2 are all integral domains.

DEFINITION 2.7–4   A **division ring** is a ring whose nonzero elements form a group under multiplication.

Example 4.   The real, rational, and complex numbers are division rings. Is the set of integers a division ring?

DEFINITION 2.7–5   A **field** is a ring whose nonzero elements form a commutative (abelian) group under multiplication.

Example 5.   The real, rational, and complex numbers are fields. Do the integers form a field?

A more familiar algebraic system is defined below.

DEFINITION 2.7–6   Given a field F and an additive abelian group V, and scalar multiplication of V by F that associates with each element $f \in F$ and $v \in V$ the element $fv \in V$. Then V is a **vector space** over F provided (where u is the unit element of F):

(1) $f(v_1 + v_2) = fv_1 + fv_2$;
(2) $(f + f_1)v_1 = fv_1 + f_1v_1$;
(3) $f(f_1 v_1) = (ff_1)v_1$; and
(4) $uv_1 = v_1$

hold for all f and $f_1 \in F$ and v_1 and $v_2 \in V$.

Elements of V are vectors. Multiplication of a vector $v_1 = (a, b)$ by a scalar (an element of the field F) is defined in the normal way: $fv_1 = f(a, b) = (fa, fb)$. The sum of two vectors $v_1 = (a, b)$ and $v_2 = (c, d)$ is given by $v_1 + v_2 = (a + c, b + d)$.

DEFINITION 2.7–7   A set K, having the binary operations addition and multiplication, together with scalar multiplication by elements of a field F, is a **linear algebra** over F provided:

(1) K is a vector space under addition and scalar multiplication over F;
(2) multiplication is associative;
(3) addition and multiplication are distributive;
(4) K has a multiplicative unit element; and
(5) $(fk_1)k_2 = k_1(fk_2) = f(k_1k_2)$ for all $f \in F$ and k_1 and $k_2 \in K$.

Example 6.   The field of complex numbers is a linear algebra over the field of real numbers.

DEFINITION 2.7–8   A set B on which binary operations $\cup$ and $\cap$ are defined is a **Boolean algebra** if:

(1) $\cup$ and $\cap$ are commutative;
(2) B has an identity element 0 with respect to $\cup$ and an identity element 1 with respect to $\cap$;
(3) each operation distributes with the other;
(4) for each element $b \in B$ there is an element $\bar{b} \in B$ such that $b \cup \bar{b} = 1$ and $b \cap \bar{b} = 0$.

Problems

2.7–1   Verify the statements made in the examples of Section 7.

2.7–2   What sort of algebraic system does the set of all commodity bundles with the preference and indifference relations form? Do any restrictions or additions need to be made to create an algebraic system? Which ones, if any?

2.7–3   Verify that $(R \times R)$ and R form a vector space with appropriately defined multiplication and addition.

2.8   CONVEX SETS AND SEPARATING HYPERPLANES

In this section we develop the concepts of concave and convex sets and prove an important theorem, Minkowski's separating hyperplane theorem. Some preliminary concepts are first defined.

DEFINITION 2.8–1   An **interior point** of a set A is an element $a \in A$ such that every point in an arbitrarily small ε neighborhood of a is also an element of A. In two dimensions ε (epsilon) is the length of the radius of a circle centered at a. The collection of all interior points of A is called the interior of A, denoted Å.

DEFINITION 2.8–2   A **boundary point** of a set A is an element b such that some points in an arbitrarily small ε neighborhood of it are elements of A, while some points in the neighborhood are not elements of A. The collection of boundary points of A is called the **boundary of** A, denoted by δA.

DEFINITION 2.8–3   An **exterior point** of A is an element e such that every point in an arbitrarily small ε neighborhood of e is not an element of A.

Figure 2.8–1 illustrates these three concepts. In the figure the dotted circles around a, b, and e are greatly enlarged ε neighborhoods of these three points.

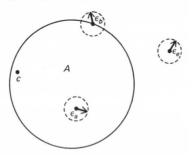

Figure 2.8–1   *Interior, boundary, and exterior points.*

It is important to note that these ε neighborhoods should be considered to be circles with infinitely small radii. Otherwise, a point like c might incorrectly be classified as a boundary point when it is clearly an interior point. Why?

A set may or may not have its boundary points as elements of the set; also, a set may or may not have one or more exterior points as elements.

DEFINITION 2.8–4   A set that contains its boundary points is a **closed** set. A set that does not contain its boundary points is an **open** set.

DEFINITION 2.8–5   If A is an open set, the set $A \cup \delta A$ is the **closure** of A.

Other common types of sets are bounded and unbounded sets. To define these types, sets are given a certain orientation (or location) in space by introducing a coordinate system (x and y axes in a two-dimensional space; x, y, and z axes in three-dimensional space; etc.).

DEFINITION 2.8–6   A set is **bounded** if it can be completely enclosed in a circle (sphere or hypersphere) of finite radius centered at the origin of the coordinate system. A set is unbounded if it cannot be so enclosed.

Figure 2.8–2 illustrates a bounded set in two-dimensional space. Here A is completely contained in the circle with radius r and is thus a bounded set.

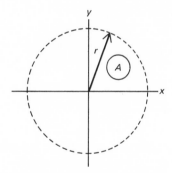

Figure 2.8–2   *A is a bounded set.*

Example 1.   The set of real numbers $\{x \mid 5 < x < 10\}$ is a bounded set, while the set of real numbers $\{x \mid x \leq 2\}$ is an unbounded set. The set of numbers (x, y) such that $x + y \geq 5$ is an unbounded set.

Note that a bounded or unbounded set may be either open or closed. The first set in Example 1 is open, while the second set is closed. Is the third set open or closed? What points would have to be included to make the first set a closed set?

DEFINITION 2.8–7   A **compact set** is a set that is both bounded and closed.

The concepts of boundary and interior points are crucial to developing the concepts of convex and concave sets.

DEFINITION 2.8–8   A set A is a **strictly convex** set if and only if for every two elements a_1 and a_2 either in A or in δA, if A is an open set, each point on the *straight* line segment between a_1 and a_2 is an interior point of A. A is a **convex** (weakly convex or quasiconvex) set if some of the points on the line segment between a_1 and a_2 are boundary points of A while the rest are interior points of A.

DEFINITION 2.8–9   A set A is a **strictly concave set** if and only if, for every two elements a_1 and a_2 in δA,[10] each point on the line segment between a_1 and a_2 is an exterior point of A. A is **concave** (weakly concave or quasiconcave) if some of the points on the line segment from a_1 to a_2 are boundary points while the rest are exterior points of A.

DEFINITION 2.8–10   A set A is **neither concave nor convex** if for some pairs of elements a_1 and a_2 in δA the line segment $a_1 a_2$ contains interior points of A, while for other pairs b_1 and b_2 in δA the line segment $b_1 b_2$ contains exterior points of A.[11]

Figure 2.8–3 illustrates these types of sets.

Example 2.   Production functions that have increasing marginal product(s) for the variable factor(s) are sets that are neither concave nor convex when the production set is defined as all possible outputs for a particular combination of inputs, not just the maximum output. The set of all combinations of commodities preferred or indifferent to a given bundle of commodities is a closed, unbounded, strictly convex set in standard utility theory. Input sets—the set of all combinations of inputs that produce at least a given amount of output or a greater amount—are closed, unbounded, strictly convex sets if an infinite number of production processes are available. If only a finite number of processes are available, these sets are closed, unbounded, and quasiconvex. Many other economic examples of concave and convex sets could be cited.

We now prove a theorem of wide-spread economic application.

[10] What can be said about any two elements in A?

[11] Definitions 2.8–8 through 2.8–10 have used the fact that any point c on the line segment between a and b must satisfy the relation $c = \lambda a + (1 - \lambda)b$, where λ is a positive number, $0 \leq \lambda \leq 1$. Simply stated, any point on a line segment can be expressed as a weighted sum of the two end points.

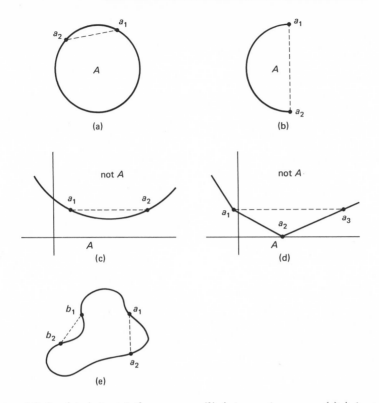

Figure 2.8–3   (*a*) A *is strictly convex.*   (*b*) A *is quasiconvex.*   (*c*) A *is strictly concave.*   (*d*) A *is quasiconcave.*   (*e*) A *is neither convex nor concave.*

Theorem 2.8–1   *Minkowski's Separating Hyperplane Theorem*   Given that two sets S and T are convex and have no interior points in common. Then there exists a vector a and a scalar b such that $\omega \in S$ implies $a\omega \le b$ and $\omega \in T$ implies $a\omega \ge b$.[12]

Before proceeding to a formal proof, note that if the sets S and T can be graphed in two dimensions; every element of these sets is in fact an ordered pair. $s_i = (x_{1i}, x_{2i})$ for all $s \in S$ and $t_j = (x_{1j}, x_{2j})$ for all $t \in T$, where the coordinate system is the $x_1 x_2$ plane. The vector a in this case is a vector of two elements $a = (\alpha_1, \alpha_2)$. The graph of a is thus a straight line. If S and T are representable in n dimensions, then elements of S and T are ordered n-tuples and a is a vector of n components. The graph of a in such a case is an n-dimensional plane or hyperplane.

Figure 2.8–4 illustrates the theorem for the two-dimensional case. In two dimensions, the theorem says that given two convex sets with no interior

---

[12] What sort of algebraic system must be defined on these sets?

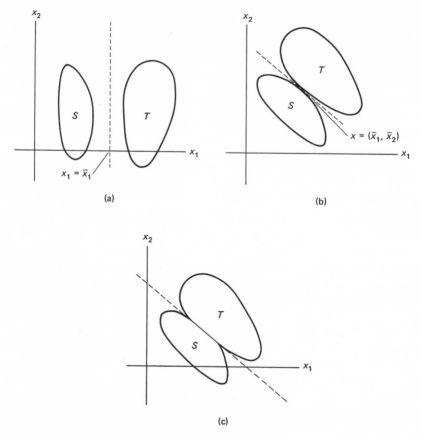

Figure 2.8–4 (*a*) *S and T are disjoint, strictly convex sets.* (*b*)$S \cap T = \omega$.
(*c*) *S and T are quasiconvex.*

points in common, it is possible to find a line (the dotted lines in Figure 2.8–4 are examples) such that all interior points of S lie on one side of the line while all interior points of T lie on the other side of the line, that is, the line "separates" S and T. In Figure 2.8–4a there are clearly an infinite number of lines that separate S and T. Consider the one drawn. The equation of this line is $x_1 = \bar{x}_1$. The vector, a, and scalar, b, are obtained from the equation of the separating hyperplane (in this case, simply a line). Writing the equation of the line as $1x_1 + 0x_2 = \bar{x}_1$, we compare this to the general equation of the separating hyperplane for the two-dimensional case: $a_1x_1 + a_2x_2 = b$, where a_1 and a_2 are the components of the vector a. Thus, in this example $a_1 = 1$ and $a_2 = 0$ so that $a = (1, 0)$ while $b = \bar{x}_1$. Now, for any element $\omega \in S$, where $\omega = (x_1, x_2)$, we have $a\omega = (1, 0)(x_1, x_2) = (1)x_1 + 0x_2 = x_1 < b = \bar{x}_1$, since clearly every x_1 component of S is less than $\bar{x}_1$. Likewise, for all elements ω in T, $a\omega > b$ since all x_1 components of elements of T are greater than $\bar{x}_1$.

In Figure 2.8–4 the equation of the line through point $x = (\bar{x}_1, \bar{x}_2)$ is, in point-slope form,

$$x_2 = -\frac{x_2^0 - \bar{x}_2}{\bar{x}_1}(x_1 + x_2^0)$$

or

(1)
$$(x_2^0 - \bar{x}_2)x_1 + \bar{x}_1 x_2 = \bar{x}_1 x_2^0$$

In this case $a = (x_2^0 - \bar{x}_2, \bar{x}_1)$ and $b = \bar{x}_1 x_2^0$. For point x, which is an element of both S and T, we have $ax = (x_2^0 - \bar{x}_2, \bar{x}_1)(\bar{x}_1, \bar{x}_2) = (\bar{x}_1)(x_2^0 - \bar{x}_2) + \bar{x}_1\bar{x}_2 = \bar{x}_1 x_2^0 = b$.

Let l be the set of points lying on the line and thus satisfying (1). For each point in l, x_l, define the set "northeast of x_l" ($\mathrm{NE}x_l$) as the set of all ordered pairs (x_1, x_2) such that either or both of the components are greater than or equal to the corresponding component of x_l. Figure 2.8–5 shows an example of this set. On the boundary of $\mathrm{NE}x_l$, the relations indicated in the figure hold, while in the interior of $\mathrm{NE}x_l$, $x_1 > x_{l_1}$ and $x_2 > x_{l_2}$ must hold. Therefore, since $ax_l = b$, $ay \geq b$ for all $y \in \mathrm{NE}x_l$. Thus, for $\omega \in T \cap \mathrm{NE}x_l$, a subset of $\mathrm{NE}x_l$, $a\omega \geq b$. Now consider the set NE_l defined as the union of all sets $\mathrm{NE}x_l$ for all $x \in l$. Clearly, the set T is a subset of NE_l and thus all $\omega \in T$ must satisfy $a\omega \geq b$. $x = (\bar{x}_1, \bar{x}_2)$ is the only element of T for which $ax = b_1$. For all other elements of T we have $a\omega > b$.

In a similar manner we could define sets "southwest of x_l" ($\mathrm{SW}x_l$) and "southwest of l" (SW_l) and show that for all points $\omega \in S$, except $x = (\bar{x}_1, \bar{x}_2)$, $a\omega < b$. The reader is urged to work this out.

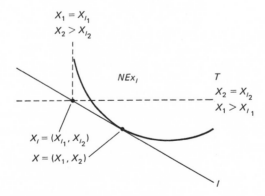

Figure 2.8–5 *The set NEx_l.*

Figure 2.8–4c is drawn to illustrate that S and T may have an infinite number of boundary points in common and still be separable. With this background, we shall now prove the theorem for the general case of n dimensions.

PROOF OF THEOREM 2.8–1   The general equation of the separating hyperplane in n dimensions is $a_1 x_1 + a_2 x_2 + \cdots + a_n x_n = b$. Thus $a = (a_1, a_2, \ldots, a_n)$ and elements of S and T are ordered n-tuples, $(x_1, x_2, \ldots, x_n)$.

There are many alternative proofs of this theorem. The following is a two-part proof by contradiction.

Given: (1) S and T convex, and (2) $S \cap T = \{i \mid i \in \delta S, i \in \delta T\}$ (S and T have no interior points in common). Since S is convex, there exists a vector a and a scalar b such that $as \leq b$ for all $s \in S$ and $as' = b$ for some $s' \in \delta S$. Such a hyperplane is called a **supporting plane** for S.[13] Also $at' = b$ for some $t' \in \delta T$. Assume that $a\bar{t} < b$ for some $\bar{t} \in T$. Then $a\bar{t} = c < b$. There exists a subset $\bar{S} \subset S$ such that $a\bar{s} = c$ for all $\bar{s} \in \bar{S}$. Then $a\bar{s} = c = a\bar{t}$ implies that $\bar{t} = \bar{s}'$ for $\bar{s}' \in \bar{S}$ by the convexity of S and T. Furthermore, $\bar{S}$ must be composed of elements in $\mathring{S}$ (the interior of S) since $a\bar{s} < b$ for all $\bar{s} \in \bar{S}$. Thus $S \cap T$ contains elements in $\mathring{S}$, a contradiction of assumption (2). Consequently, $a\bar{t}$ is not less than b for any $\bar{t} \in T$, which implies that $at \geq b$ for all $t \in T$. QED

The applications of this theorem are numerous. A few will be presented below. The reader can undoubtedly think of many more.

Example 3. Consider a world of two commodities, x and y. Let B be the set of all combinations of x and y a consumer can buy given P_x, the price of x, P_y, the price of y, and z, his income. $B = \{(x, y) \mid P_x x + P_y y \leq z, x, y \geq 0\}$. B is customarily called the budget space and is a quasiconvex set. For a given bundle of commodities $X_1 = (x_1, y_1)$, define the set "no worse than X_1", $\mathring{X}_1$, as the set of all bundles that are preferred or indifferent to bundle X_1. $\mathring{X}_1$ is thus a closed, unbounded, strictly convex set. Figure 2.8–6

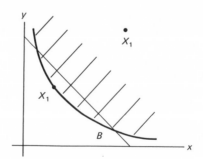

Figure 2.8–6   *B and X_1.*

---

[13] The reader should work Problems 2.8–1 and 2.8–2 at this point.

illustrates these sets. For some bundle X_i, $\mathring{X}_i \cap B = \{X_i\}$, where $X_i \in \delta B$ and $X_i \in \delta \mathring{X}_i$. Thus the separating hyperplane theorem says there exists a hyperplane (in this two-dimensional case, a line) separating these two convex sets. The equation $P_x x + P_y y = z$ is the equation of the required line. Thus, in terms of the theorem, $a = (P_x, P_y)$ and $b = z$. Clearly, all bundles on or below the line satisfy $P_x x + P_y y \leq z$, while all bundles above the line satisfy $P_x x + P_y y \geq z$. Figure 2.8–7 shows these two sets and the separating line, l. This is nothing more than the introductory diagram for constrained utility maximization. This simple example underlines one important aspect of the theorem: Often in economic examples the elements of the vector a are prices, while the scalar b represents a fixed level of income, outlay, cost, or so forth.

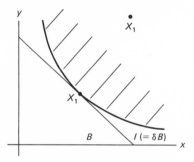

Figure 2.8–7   *Constrained utility maximization.*

Another basic concept in set theory, considered here because of its close relation to the concept of a separating hyperplane, is the notion of maximizing (or minimizing) a linear function on a set. Consider the family of linear functions $a_1 x + a_2 y = \beta$. a_1 and a_2 are constants, while β varies over all real numbers. Different values of β yield a family of individual parallel lines, as shown in Figure 2.8–8. If a_1 and a_2 are positive, β increases as one moves away from the origin along the arrow in Figure 2.8–8.

Theorem 2.8–2   For any closed set A with no exterior points and a linear function f, such that $A \cap f \neq \varnothing$,[14] maximum and minimum values of f on the set A occur at boundary points of A.

No formal proof of this theorem will be given.[15] Figure 2.8–9 illustrates the theorem for a set A that is neither concave nor convex and a linear function $f(a_1 x + a_2 y = \beta)$. f attains a maximum on A at point 1 simply means that

[14] $A \cap f$ is defined since both are subsets of $R \times R$. See Definition 2.5–2 and the discussion following Theorem 2.8–1.

[15] MacLane and Birkhoff (1967).

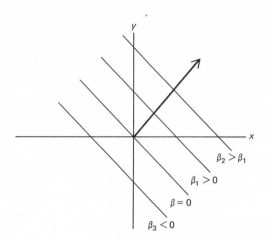

Figure 2.8–8

$a_1x_1 + a_2y_1 \geq a_1\bar{x} + a_2\bar{y}$ for all $(\bar{x}, \bar{y}) \in A$. Likewise, at point 2, $a_1x_2 + a_2y_2 \leq a_1\bar{x} + a_2\bar{y}$ for all $(\bar{x}, \bar{y}) \in A$. In this example these last two statements could be replaced by strict inequalities. How would you define this operation if A were an open set? An unbounded set?

The following theorem relates the concepts of maximizing a function on a set and of summing two or more sets.

Theorem 2.8–3   Given two sets A and B and a linear function $f(a_1x + a_2y = \beta)$. If f reaches its maximum (minimum) at $b \in B$ and $a \in A$, then f

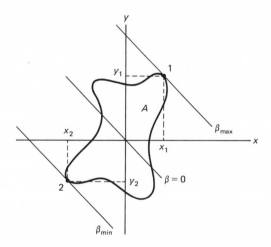

Figure 2.8–9 β_{max} *and* β_{min} *on* A, *where* a_1 *and* $a_2 > 0$.

reaches its maximum (minimum) on $A + B$ at c, where $c = a + b$. The converse is also true.

Figure 2.8–10 illustrates this theorem.

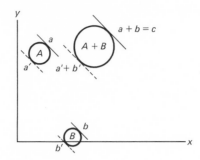

Figure 2.8–10   *Illustration of Theorem 2.8–3.*

PROOF   Let a' be any point in A and b' any point in B. Then $a' + b' = c'$, some point in $A + B$. So $f(a') + f(b') = f(c')$, where $f(a') = a_1 x'_a + a_2 y'_a$, $f(b') = a_1 x'_b + a_2 y'_b$, and $f(c') = a_1 x'_c + a_2 y'_c$. (These definitions imply that we have set $\beta = 0$, transforming f to a homogeneous function.) Then $f(a) + f(b) = f(c)$. Furthermore, $f(a') \le f(a)$ for all $a' \in A$ and $f(b') \le f(b)$ for all $b' \in B$. Thus $f(c') \le f(c)$ for all c' in $A + B$.

PROOF OF THE CONVERSE   Given f reaches its maximum on $A + B = C$ at $c = a + b$. Assume that for some $a' \in A, f(a') > f(a)$. Then $c' = a' + b$ is in C and $f(c') = f(a') + f(b) > f(c)$. This contradiction shows that f reaches its maximum on A at a. Assume that for some $b' \in B, f(b') > f(b)$. Then $c'' = a + b'$ and $f(c'') = f(a) + f(b') > f(c)$. This contradiction shows that f reaches its maximum on B at b.   QED

Example 4.   Consider the producers and their production sets described in Example 1 in Section 2.4. If f is a profit function, $P_{x_1} X_1 + P_{x_2} X_2 + P_{x_3} X_3 + P_{x_4} X_4 + P_{x_5} X_5$, where the constants in f are the prices of the five goods and the variables are the quantities of each good, each producer will maximize his profits by producing a bundle of outputs lying on the boundary of his production set. For f defined as a profit function, we must assume that one or more of the X's are inputs used by the producer that enter the function as negative numbers measuring the amount of the particular input used. Then the point of $A_1 + A_2 + \cdots + A_{10}$ at which f is at a maximum is simply the sum of the maximum profit points for each producer. Thus each producer maximizing his profits leads to a point of profit maximization for the economy as a whole. This point lies in the boundary of $A_1 + A_2 + \cdots + A_{10}$ and is thus an efficient production point in the sense that no more of one output can be produced without reducing the output of one or more of the other goods.

Example 5.   Consider the production set, P, obtained by adding the production sets of all producers in an economy and a consumption set, C, defined to be the set of all bundles of outputs greater than or equal to the minimum amounts necessary to sustain a subsistence standard of living (however defined). The set $P \cap C$ is the set of all producible bundles of commodities whose consumption ensure a standard of living greater than or equal to the minimum level. This is sometimes called the attainable set. See Figure 2.8–11 for a case of one input and one output.

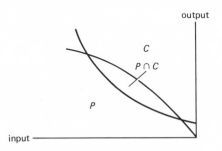

Figure 2.8–11 $P \cap C$.

For a given point $x_0 \in P \cap C$, denote the set "no worse than x_0" by $\mathring{X}_0$, the collection of all bundles preferred or indifferent to x_0. For a Robinson Crusoe economy the sets $\mathring{X}_i$ are defined by Crusoe's preference function. For a multiperson economy, it is by no means clear how the $\mathring{X}_i$ are defined since they depend on, in this case, the successful definition of community indifference curves. (Why not define $\mathring{X}_0$ as the set sum of all individuals no worse than x_0 sets?)

Under assumptions of strict convexity of $P \cap C$, C, and the preference ordering that defines the sets $\mathring{X}_i$, Koopmans shows that if x_1 is a best point in $P \cap C$ then there is a system of prices such that x_1 is a point that maximizes revenue in P and also that x_1 yields more utility than any other point in C costing the same or less.[16] Figure 2.8–12 illustrates this proposition for the two-dimensional case. l is a line separating the attainable set and the no worse than x_1 set, $\mathring{X}_1$. Thus there is a vector a and a scalar b such that $ax_1 = b$ or $a_1 y_1 + a_2 y_2 = b$. Here a_1 is the price of input y_1, a_2 is the price of y_2, and b is the producer's total revenue from selling bundle x_1. Also, b is the consumer's cost of buying x_1. Thus x_1 maximizes utility given a fixed level of income b and also maximizes the producer's profit. Thus x_1 is the bundle that

[16] Koopmans (1957) p. 32.

will be selected independently by the producers and the consumers given the existence of the price system (a_1, a_2). This independent selection of x_1 by producers and consumers means that decentralized decision making (each producer maximizing his profits and each consumer maximizing his utility) leads to the same equilibrium point (x_1) as the actions of a planning agency could ensure, but without the costs involved in organizing and operating such an agency. In a real sense, it is an Adam Smith's "invisible hand," using the concepts of set sums, separating hyperplanes, and maximizing a linear function on a set.

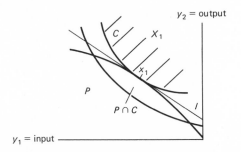

Figure 2.8–12

Example 6. Professor Koopmans has shown under what conditions the existence of a perfectly competitive equilibrium implies that such a state is also Pareto optimal.[17] He also describes what conditions must hold for a Pareto optimal state to imply the existence of a perfectly competitive equilibrium. Because of the economic importance of these issues and the use their proofs make of the tools described above, we shall summarize his arguments.

I. *Competitive equilibrium implies Pareto optimality.* Koopmans[1] basic postulates are as follows.

P1. There are a given number of decision makers—producers, consumers, and resource owners—and a fixed (finite) number of commodities, some of which are inputs (types of labor) and the rest outputs. Each decision maker makes one choice, which is representable as a point in commodity space.

P2. Each consumer has a complete preference ordering over his consumption set, x, each element of which is an ordered n-tuple of all commodities, including labor and other inputs. Each consumer's preference ordering and consumption set is independent from every other decision maker's choice.

P3. Each producer is constrained to a production set, Y, that is independent of the choices of all other decision makers.

[17] Koopmans (1957).

P4. Each resource holder owns a nonnegative amount of each nonlabor input and cannot supply more of any input than he owns.

P5. If a point in a consumer's consumption set is not a point of complete saturation, there is another point in an arbitrarily small neighborhood of the point preferred to it.

These definitions are needed:

D1. A bundle of choices (commodities) is a **balancing bundle** if for every commodity the net amounts chosen by producers and resource holders are equal to the amounts chosen by all consumers.

D2. A **competitive equilibrium** is a balancing bundle for which P1–P4 hold, together with a system of prices, P_i, one for each commodity, such that, given that values are calculated at those prices ($\sum P_i x_i$):

(a) each consumer's choice yields a maximum of utility in the sense that any other choice with higher utility costs more than the original choice;

(b) each producer's choice yields maximum profits; and

(c) the value of inputs sold by each resource holder is the maximum value he can obtain.

D3. A **Pareto optimum** is a balancing bundle of choices satisfying P1–P4 such that there is no other balancing bundle satisfying the same postulates in which at least one consumer would be better off while no other consumer would be worse off.

A competitive equilibrium maximizes the profit function on each producer's production set. By Theorem 2.8–3 the profit function is at a maximum on the aggregate production set at the point $\bar{p}$, which is the sum of all the individual producer's maximum points. Given an individual consumer's choice x_i, it follows that the value function is at a minimum at this point on the no worse than x_i set, $\mathring{X}_i$. The aggregate set of no worse than x_i sets, $\sum \mathring{X}$, is obtained from the individual sets $\mathring{X}_i$ and depends on all consumer's choices and not just i's choice x_i. By Theorem 2.8–3 the value function reaches its minimum value on $\sum \mathring{X}_i$ at a point $\bar{x}$ that is the sum of the points of individual consumer's minima.

We suppose the original state is a competitive equilibrium. Thus $\bar{p} = \bar{x}$. See Figure 2.8–13. Suppose this point is not a Pareto optimum. Then there must be some bundle x' that is both a balancing bundle and is preferred by consumer i to his original choice, while every other consumer's choice is no worse than his original choice. It must be true, however, that the value of the alternative choice for consumer i is greater than the value of his original choice, while the value of every other consumer's alternative choice cannot be lower than his original choice [D2(a)]. Thus the value of x' is higher than the value of the original choice $\bar{x}$. But $\bar{p}$ was already a maximum value on the production set and therefore the value of the producer's choices cannot be increased. Thus the alternative bundle x' cannot be a balancing bundle. This

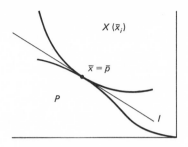

Figure 2.8–13   *A competitive equilibrium.*

is a contradiction to the definition of competitive equilibrium and shows that the original state must, in fact, have been a Pareto optimal state as well.

To show that Pareto optimality implies the existence of a competitive equilibrium, it is necessary to assume that P and $\sum \mathring{X}_i$ are convex (but not strictly convex). If not, it is possible to have the situation shown in Figure 2.8–14. Here x is a Pareto optimum point (Why?) but not a competitive equilibrium. (Why?) To show that Pareto optimality implies a competitive equilibrium, assume that $\bar{x}$ is a Pareto optimal point. Then, by D3, $\bar{x}$ is a balancing bundle and consumers have maximized utility. This implies that there exists a hyperplane separating the set $\sum \mathring{X}_i$ from the production set. Therefore $\bar{x}$ is also a point of competitive equilibrium. P4 implies that, given positive prices, resources are used to the extent of their availability. Thus requirements (a), (b), and (c) of a competitive equilibrium are satisfied by a Pareto optimal point.

These propositions do not depend on the existence of a competitive market structure. Indeed, a planning agency could set prices at their required level and reach point $\bar{x}$ just as a market economy could.

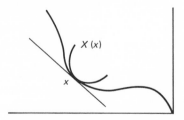

Figure 2.8–14   *A Pareto optimum point that is not a competitive equilibrium.*

Problems

2.8–1   Prove that at least one supporting hyperplane exists for every bounded, convex set S. (Hint: all points in $\mathring{S}$ must lie completely on one side of the supporting hyperplane for S.)

2.8–2   Show that every separating hyperplane is a supporting hyperplane for both sets, but that hyperplanes supporting either S or T need not separate S and T.

2.8–3   Verify the following statements.
(a) The union of two convex sets is not, in general, a convex set. (Under what conditions would the union be a convex set?)
(b) The intersection of two convex sets is a convex set.

2.8–4   What can be said about the union and intersection of two concave sets? Of a convex and a concave set?

2.8–5   Analyze the theory of cost minimization from the point of view of convex sets and separating hyperplanes. Specify all the sets and the equation of the separating hyperplane.

References

1. BIRKHOFF, G., and S. MACLANE (1965), *A Survey of Modern Algebra*, 3rd ed., New York: Macmillan.
2. DESKINS, W. E. (1964), *Abstract Algebra*, New York: Macmillan.
3. KOOPMANS, T. (1957), *Three Essays on the State of Economic Science*, New York: McGraw-Hill.
4. MACDUFFEE, C. (1940), *An Introduction to Abstract Algebra*, New York: Wiley.
5. MACLANE, S., and G. BIRKHOFF (1967), *Algebra*, New York: Macmillan.
6. MOORE, J. (1962), *Elements of Abstract Algebra*, New York: Macmillan.

Chapter 3

Basic Measurement Theory

3.1 THE REPRESENTATION PROBLEM

In Chapter 2 we presented the logical rules for conceptualizing different aspects of our environment. We discussed the classification of objects into sets and the ways these sets can be altered (set operations) or related to other sets (maps). The basic concern in this chapter is the rationale for assigning numbers to elements of these sets and the degree to which these assignments are meaningful and unique. The reason for this is the economy afforded by relating sets to a set of numbers. In this way, we do not have to develop an arithmetic for one set, the set of all economists or the set of all birds in North America, but we can develop an abstract set of relations that apply to characteristics of a variety of sets.

The first problem is to show how arithmetic operations can be applied to a set of arbitrary elements. This is accomplished by proving that an arbitrary set is homomorphic to a set of numbers. A set A is homomorphic to set B if there exists a morphism (Definition 2.6–9) from A to B. Two sets are isomorphic if the mapping is one-to-one onto. Thus, if our conceptualization of some empirical phenomena can be shown to have the same structure as a set of numbers, then arithmetic operations can be applied to these numbers alone to derive conclusions about the phenomena. The problem, then, amounts to defining a mapping from a set A to a set of numbers B.

In Chapter 2 we defined a binary relation on a set A as being a subset R of the Cartesian product of $A \times A$.[1] Thus an n-ary relation on a set A is a subset, R, of ordered n-tuples such that if $(a_1, \ldots, a_n)$ is in R, the n-tuples $(a_1, \ldots, a_n)$ satisfy the requirement or rule of the relation R.

DEFINITION 3.1–1   A **relational system**, denoted $\langle A, R_1, \ldots, R_m \rangle$, is a set A, together with m specified relations, $R_1, \ldots, R_m$.

---

[1] Definition 2.4–5.

Example 1. Suppose A is the set of all economic goods produced in the United States in 1970. If R_1 is the unary (1-ary) relation, "goods that are exported," then R_1 defines the subset (also denoted by the symbol R_1) of goods produced in the United States in 1970 that were exported.

Example 2. If R_2 were the quarternary (4-ary) relation, "the difference in dollar value between a_1 and a_2 is equal to the difference in dollar value between a_3 and a_4," then R_2 would be the set of all 4-tuples such that a_1 differed from a_2 by the same dollar amount that a_3 differed from a_4.

Example 3. If R_3 were the equivalence relation (a binary or 2-ary relation), "all commodities of the same weight," then R_3 would be the set of all ordered pairs (a_1, a_2) such that a_1 was equal in weight to a_2. Thus a relational system is any specified set A and any specified number of relations of any type (any n-ary size).

This leads immediately to the notion of special types of relational systems, some of which are now defined.

DEFINITION 3.1–2   An equivalence relation[2] E on the set $A = \{a_{hj}\}$, is a **congruence relation** for the relational system $\langle A, R_1, \ldots, R_m \rangle$ if and only if for *each* relation R_i on A, $a_{hj}Ea_{gj}$ for all $j = 1, \ldots, k$ implies that $R_i(a_{h_1}, \ldots, a_{hk}) = R_i(a_{g_1}, \ldots, a_{gk})$.

Definition 3.1–2 states that a congruence relation possesses a substitution property. If, for example, A is the set of all economic goods produced in the United States in 1970, and R_1 is the quarternary relation, "the difference in weight between a_1 and a_2 is equal to the difference in weight between a_3 and a_4," then the equivalence relation E, "a_1 is equal in weight to a_j," would be a congruence relation for R_1. Any economic good that was equal in weight to a_1 could be *substituted* for a_1 and the relation R_1 would still hold. Consequently, a congruence relation for the relational system $\langle A, R_1, \ldots, R_m \rangle$ would be one where this substitution property held for *each* of the specified relations on the set A.

DEFINITION 3.1–3   A **relational system** $\langle A, R_1, \ldots, R_m \rangle$ is **irreducible** if and only if the equivalence relation E is the only congruence relation for the system $\langle A, R_1, \ldots, R_m \rangle$.

For example, suppose $\langle A, E, P, I \rangle$ is a relational system, where $A = \{goods\}$, $E =$ "is equal in weight to," $P =$ "is preferred to," and $I =$ "is indifferent to." E and I are both equivalence relations. That is, they are transitive, reflexive, and symmetric binary relations defined on A. I is also a con-

---

[2] See Definition 2.4–6.

gruence relation for $\langle A, P \rangle$, that is, if $a\ P\ b$, $a\ I\ c$, then $c\ P\ b$. However, two goods of equal weight would not necessarily be preferred to a third (i.e., $a\ E\ c$, $a\ P\ b$ does not imply $c\ P\ b$). Thus the system is not an irreducible relational system. E has nothing, in general, to do with either I or P. $\langle A, P, I \rangle$ would be an irreducible relational system.

DEFINITION 3.1–4   A **numerical relational system** $\langle A, R_1, \ldots, R_m \rangle$ is one where A is the set of real numbers.

DEFINITION 3.1–5   An **empirical relational system** $\langle A, R_1, \ldots, R_m \rangle$ is one where A is *any* identifiable set of entities, such as commodities, weights, attitude statements, and so forth.[3]

We are now in a position to define the concept of a scale.

DEFINITION 3.1–6   An ***n*-dimensional scale** is a morphism, α, of an irreducible empirical relational system $\langle A, T_1, \ldots, T_m \rangle$ into an n-dimensional numerical relational system $\langle R^n, S_1, \ldots, S_m \rangle$, where R^n is equal to the nth Cartesian product of the set of real numbers. T_i and S_i, for $i = 1, \ldots, m$, are sets of specified relations on A and R^n. Furthermore, T_i is the same type of relation as S_i (e.g., both are binary, n-ary, etc.).

Thus a one-dimensional scale is a mapping from an empirical set to the set of real numbers R. Scales are not in general unique. That is, often there are several different morphisms that will serve as a scale. In fact the classification of types of scales is based upon the relative uniqueness of the set of permissible mappings.

Problems

3.1–1   Find k for the following k-ary relations in the relational system $\langle A, R_1, R_2, R_3 \rangle$ where $A = \{$all students at the University of Florida$\}$.
  (a) $R_1 = $ "a_1 is married to a_2"
  (b) $R_2 = $ "a_1 is a senior, a_2 is a junior, a_3 is a sophomore, and a_4 is a freshman"
  (c) $R_3 = $ "a_1 is homecoming queen, a_2 is first runner up, and a_3 is second runner up"

3.1–2   Which of the following are congruence relations for the set A and the relations R_1, R_2, and R_3 in Problem 3.1–1?
  (a) $E = $ "a_i lives in the same house as a_j" for $\langle A, R_1 \rangle$
  (b) $E = $ "a_i is in the same class as a_j" for $\langle A, R_2 \rangle$
  (c) $E = $ "a_i is in the same sorority as a_j" for $\langle A, R_3 \rangle$

3.1–3   An irreducible relational system is one where there is only one acceptable

---

[3] That is, something other than a numerical relational system.

congruence relation for the relational system. Explain why or why not the relational system in Problem 3.1–1 is irreducible.

3.1–4   Define the congruence relation for the following relational systems:
  (a) $\langle A, R_1 \rangle$, $A = \{\text{all commodities}\}$
    $R_1 = \text{“}a_1$ is worth twice as much as $a_2\text{”}$
  (b) $\langle A, R_1, R_2 \rangle$, $A = \{\text{factors of production}\}$
    $R_1 = \text{“}a_1$ is more productive than $a_2\text{”}$
    $R_2 = \text{“the difference in total output of }a_1$ and a_2 is equal to the difference in output of a_3 and $a_4\text{”}$

3.2   CLASSIFICATION AND FORMATION OF SCALES[4]

Coupling the definition of a scale with the set of admissible transformations for that scale, it is easy to define different types of scales.

Let α be a one-dimensional scale of the irreducible relational system $\langle A, T_1, \ldots, T_m \rangle$ into $\langle R, S_1, \ldots, S_m \rangle$ and let Γ_R be the set of admissible transformations of α.[5]

DEFINITION 3.2–1   (1) α is a **nominal** scale if Γ_R is the set of all one-to-one mappings from R to R.

(2) α is an **ordinal** scale if Γ_R is the set of all monotonically increasing, continuous mappings from R to R.

(3) α is an **interval** scale if Γ_R is the set of all positive linear transformations of α. (That is, if $\alpha : a_1 \to x \in R$ and $\beta \in \Gamma_R$, then $\beta : x \to \delta x + \gamma$ for $\gamma \in R$ and $\delta \in R^+$ is the set of positive real numbers.)

(4) A **difference** scale is one where Γ_R is the set of mappings differing from α by a constant. (That is, if $\alpha : a_1 \to x \in R$ and $\beta \in \Gamma_R$, then $\beta : x \to x + \gamma$ for $\gamma \in R$).

(5) A **ratio** scale is one where Γ_R is the set of mappings differing from α by a positive multiple. (That is, if $\alpha : a_1 \to x \in R$ and $\beta \in \Gamma_R$, then $\beta : x \to \delta x$ for $\delta \in R^+$.)

(6) α is an **absolute** scale if $\alpha : A \to R$ is the only permissible mapping. That is, the only permissible transformation of α is the identity transformation.

Nominal scales are those that merely classify the elements of an empirical set. For example, the numbers assigned to the players of a basketball team have no significance aside from the classification. And because they do classify,

---

[4] In this section we deal with one-dimensional scales. Each definition is easily extended to an n-dimensional scale by replacing R with R^n.

[5] Alternatively, Γ_R is also the set of all endomorphisms on $\langle R, S_1, \ldots, S_m \rangle$. An endomorphism (Definition 2.6–11) is a morphism from $\langle R, S_1, \ldots, S_m \rangle$ to $\langle R, S_1, \ldots, S_m \rangle$.

the mapping must be one-to-one—two members of the same team cannot have the same number. On the other hand, consider a football squad of 44 men with four individuals for each position. If the relations specified for this set are R_1: "the individual's name is Dawson," R_2: "the individual's name is Livingston," R_3: "the individual's name is Lee," and R_4: "the individual's name is Podalak," then if B is the set of positive integers and $\{S_i\} = I^+$,[6] it is easy to construct a mapping for $\langle A, R_1, R_2, R_3, R_4 \rangle$ into $\langle B, \{S_i\} \rangle$.[7] Furthermore, the class of endomorphisms that are admissible is infinite. That is, B could have been the set of all negative numbers and S_i: -1.037409, for some i, and the scale have been valid. This example illustrates the simplicity and usefulness of choosing one particular mapping over another. Also, if the relational system includes T: "any four integers between 0 and 19," with B being the set of positive integers and R_5: "those four who play quarterback," then seeing an individual with the number 16 conveys the information that he is a quarterback but says nothing about his name, weight, or so forth unless other relations are known.

An ordinal scale preserves a ranking relation on an empirical set. The binary relations of preference and indifference, P and I, discussed in Chapter 2 are examples of ranking relations.[8] Given that A is the consumption set for an individual, P: "is preferred to," and I: "is indifferent to," it is possible to find a mapping α from this empirical relational system to the set of real numbers, where Γ_R is the set of positive monotonic transformations of α, that is, α is an ordinal scale. This is proved formally in the following theorem.[9]

Theorem 3.2–1   Let $\langle A, I, P \rangle$ be an empirical relational system, where I: "is indifferent to" and P: "is preferred to" such that for any a_1 and $a_2 \in A$, either $a_1 \, I \, a_2$, $a_1 \, P \, a_2$, or $a_2 \, P \, a_1$; and for any a_1, a_2, and $a_3 \in A$ if $a_1 \, P \, a_2$ and $a_2 \, P \, a_3$, then $a_1 \, P \, a_3$. Then $\langle A, I, P \rangle$ can be represented by an ordinal one-dimensional scale if and only if it has a countable (or denumerable) base.[10] Such a system is called a completely ordered and connected system—or a complete order.

Before proving Theorem 3.2–1, we need the following definition:

DEFINITION 3.2–2   A **base**, B_0, for the set A is a subset of the set of all

---

[6] That is, $\{S_i\}$ is the set of "naming" relations for the positive integers, e.g., $S_{18} = 18$.

[7] Note that the numerical relational system has an infinite number of relations defined on it, while the empirical system only has five.

[8] Cf. Examples 2 and 3 in Section 2.4.

[9] This was first proved by Debreu (1954).

[10] A countable set is one having a one-to-one correspondence between it and all positive real numbers. See Definition 2.5–9.

open subsets of A such that each open subset of A is equal to the union of some members of B_0. A set may have any number of different bases.[11,12]

For an example of a base of a set, consider the real line R. For any two real numbers r_1 and r_2, where $r_1 < r_2$, the set

$$(r_1, r_2) = \{x \in R \mid r_1 < x < r_2\}$$

is called an **open interval** of R. The collection B_0 of all open intervals of R forms a base for R, since R can be expressed as the union of such open intervals.

PROOF OF THEOREM   To prove the if portion, assume that the set has a countable base. Then all open subsets of $A = \{\alpha_i\}$ can be represented by its base, $B_0 = \{\beta_1, \beta_2, \ldots\}$; that is, $\alpha_j = \bigcup \beta_i \in B_0$.[13] This means that each and every element in A is contained in the union of some members of its base; for example, if $a_i \in A$, then $a_i \in \bigcup \beta_j$. Then a mapping, m, can be constructed from A to R in the following way: Let $m(\beta_j) = j \in I^+$. Suppose $a_i \in \beta_j \cup \beta_{j+1}$ and $a_{i+1} \in \beta_j \bigcup \beta_{j-1}$; then if a_{i+1} is preferred to a_i, let $m(\beta_{j-1}) = j - 1 \in I^+$. Since the base is countable there exists between the positive integers $j - 1$ and j some rational number that can be assigned to every a_i. Clearly, the mapping is monotonic and continuous since, regardless of the number of elements that are between a_{i+1} and a_i according to the preference ordering on A, there exists a rational number for each.

On the other hand, suppose that $m : A \to R$ is a continuous, monotonic mapping and A does not have a countable base. This means that there is no one-to-one correspondence between the real numbers, R, and the family of open subsets in A. This in turn implies either that (1) there is an element of A, $a_i \notin \bigcup \beta_j$ or (2) $m(\beta_j) = m(\beta_k)$ for $j \neq k$, or (3) there exists some $j \in I^+$ such that $m(\beta_k) \neq j$, for all k and for some h, and g, where $m(\beta_h) = j - 1$ and $m(\beta_g) = j + 1$. (1), (2), and (3) are easily seen to contradict the assumption that $m : A \to R$ is continuous and monotonic. (1) implies that m is *not* continuous, since there is no open set in the neighborhood of a_i and the mapping from A to R must have a discontinuity between a_i and some other $a_j \in A$. (2) implies that for $a_i \, P \, a_j$, $m(a_i) = m(a_j)$, which contradicts the assumption of monotonicity. (3) is an obvious violation of the continuity assumption.   QED

From the proof of Theorem 3.2–1, the arbitrary method of constructing the mapping from the consumption set to the real line implies that Γ_R is the

[11] The set of all open subsets of $A = \{\alpha_i\}$ is the topology of A, while the pair $(A, \{\alpha_i\})$ is the topological space of A.

[12] The base of a set is analogous to the concept of a basis of a vector space. This will be discussed in Section 4.3.

[13] $\bigcup \beta_i$ is shorthand notation for the union of all β_i, i.e., $\bigcup \beta_i = \beta_1 \cup \beta_2 \cup \beta_3 \ldots$.

set of all monotonic transformations of m. That is, if $g \in \Gamma_R$ is a monotonic transformation of m and $m: a \to x$ and $m: b \to y$ such that $x > y$, then $g(x) > g(y)$. If $x = y$, then $g(x) = g(y)$. This observation is proved in the following theorem.

Theorem 3.2–2   Let $\langle A, I, P \rangle$ be an empirical relational system with I: "indifference" and P: "preference." If m and n both map $\langle A, I, P \rangle$ into the real number system, then n is a monotonic transformation of m.

PROOF   The domain of both m and n is the same, $viz.$, $\langle A, I, P \rangle$. Since each mapping $\langle A, I, P \rangle$ is isomorphic to some subset of R (say R_1 for n and R_2 for m) the range of the inverses of m and n, defined on their respective subsets, is the same, $viz.$, the set $\langle A, I, P \rangle$. This means that the range of m (n) is equal to the domain of m^{-1} (n^{-1}), which is R_1 (R_2). Consequently, the composition of m and n^{-1}, $m \circ n^{-1}$, has domain R_1 and range R_2. This means that n is a monotonic transformation of m, since both m and n are both continuous, monotonic mappings to the real numbers.   QED

What sorts of preference orderings does Theorem 3.2–1 preclude? Perhaps the most common example is a lexicographic ordering. Basically, a lexicographic ordering has subsets that cannot be related to a common denominator in terms of preferences. For example, suppose A contains two goods: rice and meat. If more rice is preferred to less, *ceteris paribus*, and more meat to less meat, but more meat is always preferred to less meat regardless of the amount of rice associated with each quantity of meat, then the ordering is lexicographic. In effect, this means that no quantity of rice, no matter how large, could be substituted for any amount of meat, no matter how small. There is no trade-off between rice and meat. In terms of a two-dimensional diagram, this would be represented as in Figure 3.2–1, where U_0, U_1, $U_2 \ldots$ are indifference curves for meat and there is another ordering along each curve for rice. This consumption set and its associated orderings does not have a

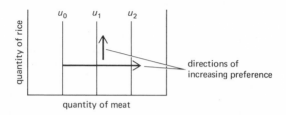

Figure 3.2–1   *A graphical representation of a lexicographic ordering for rice and meat.*

countable base, since there is a one-to-one correspondence between both meat and rice and the real number system.

An obvious extension of this example is stated in Theorem 3.2–3.

Theorem 3.2–3   Let $\langle A, I, P \rangle$ be an empirical relational system as in Theorem 3.2–1. Then $\langle A, I, P \rangle$ can be represented by an n-dimensional ordinal scale if it is composed of n distinct subsets each of which has a countable base.

The proof of Theorem 3.2–3 is quite similar to Theorem 3.2–1 and is omitted. The utility functions of Theorem 3.2–3 are termed multidimensional (or vector) utility functions.

Another aspect of the completely ordered empirical relational system $\langle A, I, P \rangle$ is that it requires an arbitrarily fine degree of discrimination. For example, suppose for two commodity baskets, a_0 and a_n, $a_n P a_0$. But for a series of commodity baskets between a_0 and a_n, the individual is unable to discern a difference between any two; that is, $a_0 I a_1, a_1 I a_2, \ldots, a_{n-1} I a_n$; but $a_n P a_0$ (Cf. Figure 3.2–3). In other words, there is a definite difference between a_0 and a_n, but just where this difference occurs between the two is not clear. Luce (1956) introduced a generalization of Theorem 3.2–1 with the notion of a semiordered relational system.

DEFINITION 3.2–3   A **semiordered relational system** (or simply, a semi-order) is an empirical relational system $\langle A, I, P \rangle$, such that the following axioms hold for all $a_1, a_2, a_3,$ and $a_4 \in A$:

(1) for any a_1 and a_2 either $a_1 I a_2$, $a_1 P a_2$, or $a_2 P a_1$;
(2) if $a_1 P a_2$ and $a_3 P a_4$, then either $a_1 P a_4$ or $a_3 P a_2$;
(3) if $a_1 P a_2$ and $a_2 P a_3$, then $a_1 P a_3$.

In a semiorder, the transitivity of the binary "preference" relation P defined on A holds for sufficiently large differences. In psychology this is known as a *just noticeable difference* (jnd). For example, suppose an individual is able to semiorder the commodity space A, composed of beer and wine. Being usually under the influence of one or the other, he can distinguish between the number of bottles (10-oz) but not the number of ounces. That is, he is indifferent between a basket of 3.1 bottles of beer and 4.5 bottles of wine and a basket containing three bottles of beer and four bottles of wine. However, the axioms of Definition 3.2–3 assert that he would be able to differentiate between commodity baskets where either commodity differed by 10 oz or more. For the following baskets:

a_1: (1.3 b, 6.7 w) = (1.3 bottles of beer and 6.7 bottles of wine), etc.
a_2: (2.5 b, 6.7 w)
a_1^*: (5.4 b, 6.5 w)
a_2^*: (3 b, 6 w)

a_3: (4 b, 7 w)
a_4: (5 b, 6 w)
a_5: (2 b, 7 w)
a_6: (3.7 b, 8 w)

axiom (1) of Definition 3.2–3 asserts that

$$a_2 \ P \ a_1, \text{ since more is preferred to less;}$$

axiom (2) asserts that

$$\text{if } a_1^* \ P \ a_2^* \text{ and } a_3 \ P \ a_4, \text{ then either } a_1^* \ P \ a_4, \text{ or } a_3 \ P \ a_2^*;$$

axiom (3) asserts that

if $a_4 \ P \ a_2^* \ P \ a_5$, then for any a_6 such that $a_6 \ P \ a_4$ it must be that $a_6 \ P \ a_5$.

As an illustration, the lines in Figure 3.2–2 represent preference orderings of commodity baskets. If line 1 fulfills axiom (2), what must be true for the distance between a_1 and a_2 in terms of *just noticeable differences*? What can be asserted about the jnd between a_1, a_2, a_3, a_4, and a_5 if a_1, a_2, and a_3 satisfy axiom (3)?

line 1 a_1, a_2, a_3, a_4 satisfy axion (2) of Definition 3.2–3;
          i.e., $a_1 P a_2$ and $a_3 P a_4$

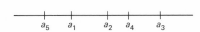

line 2 a_1, a_2, a_3 satisfy axion (3) of Definition 3.2–3;
          i.e., $a_1 P a_2$ and $a_2 P a_3$

Figure 3.2–2   *Graphical representation of Definition 3.2–3.*

Although a semiordered relational system cannot be mapped into an ordinary numerical relational system, the indifference classes are both thick and arbitrarily defined (see Figure 3.2–3). However, it can be represented by a numerical semiorder.[14]

DEFINITION 3.2–4   A numerical relational system $\langle R_1, \gg_\delta \rangle$ is termed a **numerical semiorder** if and only if:

(1) $R_1 \subset R$, the set of real numbers; and

[14] First proved by Scott and Suppes (1958).

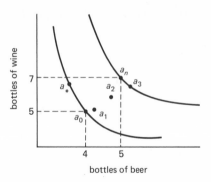

Figure 3.2–3 *Graphical representation of a semiorder for beer and wine.*

(2) $\gg_\delta$ is a binary relation on R_1 such that for all x and $y \in R_1$, $x \gg_\delta y$ if and only if $x > y + \delta$.

In the foregoing definition, δ can be interpreted as the measure of a just noticeable difference and the following representation theorem can be proven.

Theorem 3.2–4 A semiordered relational system $\langle A, I, P \rangle$ is homomorphic to some (can be represented by a) numerical semiorder.

PROOF   We have to show how such a mapping could be constructed and that it is a homomorphism. First of all, it is possible to form an equivalence relation, E, on A from the relations I and P that is stronger than I. Specifically, $a_0 \, E \, a_*$ if and only if $a_0 \, I \, a_i$ implies $a_* \, I \, a_i$ for all such a_i.[15]

Let the equivalence classes so constructed be represented by $a_0, a_1, \ldots,$ $a_i, \ldots$ such that either $a_i \, P \, a_{i-k}$ or $a_i \, I \, a_{i-k}$.[16] Further, if $a_i \, I \, a_{i-k}$, then $a_{i-j} \, I \, a_{i-k}$ for all $0 < j < k < i$.[17] Define the function $m: A \to R$ as follows: let $m(a_0) = 0$, $\delta = 1$, then for $i \in I^+$:

(1) If $a_j \, I \, a_0$, let

$$m(a_j) = \frac{j}{j + \delta} = \frac{j}{j + 1}$$

(2) If $a_i \, P \, a_0$ and $a_{i-1} \, I \, a_0$, then let

$$m(a_i) = \delta = 1$$

[15] An E class for a_0 corresponds to the curve running through a_0 in Figure 3.2–3.

[16] a_{i-k} is the equivalence class that is k units in back of i. For example, let $i = 5, k = 2$; then for $a_0, a_1, a_2, a_3, a_4, a_5, \ldots$ either $a_5 \, P \, a_3$ or $a_5 \, I \, a_3$. Further, if $a_5 \, I \, a_3$ then $a_5 \, I \, a_4$.

[17] For such equivalence classes, what can be said about the indifference classes?

(3) If $a_{i+j} \ I \ a_i$, $a_{i+j} \ P \ a_j$, and $a_{i+j-1} \ I \ a_j$, then let

$$m(a_{i+j}) = \frac{j}{j+1} + 1$$

(4) If $a_k \ P \ a_i$, and $a_{k-1} \ I \ a_i$, then let

$$m(a_k) = 2$$

(5) If $a_{k+j} \ I \ a_k$, $a_{k+j} \ P \ a_{i+j}$, and $a_{k+j-1} \ I \ a_{i+j}$, then let

$$m(a_{k+j}) = \frac{j}{j+1} + 2$$

and so on for all a_i.[18]

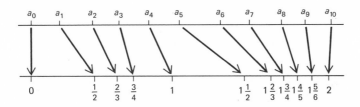

The set $\{a_0, a_1, \ldots, a_i, \ldots\}$ can be shown to be isomorphic to some numerical system (hence $\langle A, 1, P \rangle$ is homomorphic to some numerical system) if $m(a_{j+1}) > m(a_j)$ for all i.

[18] For example: for $a_0, a_1, a_2, a_3, a_4, a_5$,

$$m(a_0) = 0$$

(1) Let $j = 3$. If $a_3 \ I \ a_0$, then

$$m(a_3) = \frac{3}{3+1} = \frac{3}{4}$$
$$m(a_2) = \tfrac{2}{3}$$
$$m(a_1) = \tfrac{1}{2}$$

(2) Suppose that for $i = 4$, $a_4 \ P \ a_0$. Since $a_{4-1} = a_3$ and $a_3 \ I \ a_0$, then

$$m(a_4) = 1$$

(3) Next suppose that for $j = 2$, $a_6 \ I \ a_4$, $a_6 \ P \ a_2$, and $a_5 \ I \ a_2$, then

$$m(a_6) = \frac{2}{2+1} + 1 = 1\tfrac{2}{3}$$

(4) Let $k = 10$ if $a_{10} \ P \ a_4$. But $a_9 \ I \ a_4$, then

$$m(a_{10}) = 2$$

This constructed mapping is illustrated below. Verify that $m(a_5) + 1\tfrac{1}{2}$, $m(a_7) = 1\tfrac{3}{4}$, $m(a_8) = 1\tfrac{4}{5}$, and $m(a_9) = 1\tfrac{5}{6}$.

Clearly, $m(a_0) = 0 < m(a_i) = 1 < m(a_k) = 2 < \cdots$; and also, since for any $a_j \, I \, a_i$, we have

$$n - 1 < \frac{j}{j + 1} + n - 1 < n$$

This precludes $m(a_j)$ overlapping with the integers assigned to the equivalence classes $a_0, a_i, a_k, \ldots$. If $m(a_{j+1}) > m(a_j)$, for $a_{j+1} \, I \, a_j$, then it must be true that

$$\frac{j + 1}{j + 1 + n} > \frac{j}{j + n} \qquad \text{for any } n \in I^+$$

Therefore $m(a_{j+1}) > m(a_j)$ for all $a_j \in \{a_0, a_1, \ldots, a_i, \ldots\}$, and the set of equivalence classes is isomorphic to some numerical order system. To show that the numerical system is a semiorder, we have to show that $a_j \, P \, a_{j-r}$, for some $0 < r < j$ if and only if $m(a_j) \geq m(a_{j-r}) + 1$. First, if $m(a_{i+j}) = m(a_j) + 1$, then by construction $a_{i+j} \, P \, a_j$. Therefore, if $m(a_j) \geq m(a_{j-r}) + 1$, then $a_j \, P \, a_{j-r}$. Second, to show that $a_j \, P \, a_{j-r}$ implies that $m(a_j) \geq m(a_{j-r}) + 1$, note that $a_{i+j} \, P \, a_j$ and $a_{i+j-1} \, I \, a_j$ implies that $m(a_{i+j}) = m(a_j) + 1$; therefore, it cannot be true that $a_{i+j-r} \, P \, a_j$ for $r > 0$ by the construction of $\{a_0, a_1, \ldots, a_i, \ldots\}$. Consequently, since $m(a_{j+1}) > m(a_j)$, if $a_j \, P \, a_{j-r}$ it must be true that $m(a_j) \geq m(a_{j-r}) + 1$.   QED

There are several interesting aspects of the numerical semiorder so constructed. First, R_1 is not a continuous subset of R, since there are "gaps" between the numbers assigned to the last a_{i-1}, which was indifferent to a_0, and to the a_i receiving an integral value. Since $m(a_i) = 1$, and $m(a_{i-1}) = (i - 1)/i$, there will be a gap unless there are an infinite number of equivalence classes between a_i and a_0. Furthermore, these "gaps" will be equivalent only if the number of equivalence classes between any two a's assigned an integer is equal.[19] Finally, the theorem does not assert that just noticeable differences of an individual's ordering are equal in a physical sense, but the mapping measures it as if the just noticeable differences were equal between a_0, a_i, $a_k, \ldots$ [where $m(a_0) = 0$, $m(a_i) = 1$, $m(a_k) = 2$, etc.]. On the other hand, the mapping does not necessarily measure a jnd as equal between any other a_h and a_j, although in terms of some physical construct they may very well be.

Clearly, there is nothing unique about such a mapping. First of all, δ may be selected at any real value ≥ 1 and the above definition followed by replacing 1 with δ, 2 with 2δ, and so on. The rule of when to create a "gap," that is, when $a_i \, P \, a_0$ but $a_{i-1} \, I \, a_0$, is also completely arbitrary. Thus the set of "admissible" endomorphisms, Γ_R, is unknown at present, and it appears

---

[19] Cf. the example in footnote 18, page 61. The number of classes between a_0 and a_4 is 3, and between a_4 and a_{10} is 5. The "gap" between a_3 and a_4 is $\frac{1}{4}$, but between a_9 and a_{10} it is only $\frac{1}{6}$.

unlikely that an admissible transformation of m exists that has the properties of traditional algebra. This illustrates its lack of usefulness *vis-à-vis* the ordinal mapping discussed in Theorem 3.2–1.[20]

Interval scales give more information about their associated empirical relational system than do ordinal scales. Interval scales preserve a *metrical operation* defined on the empirical system rather than only a ranking, a binary relation. We shall prove in Theorem 3.2–6 that they also preserve quarternary relations.

DEFINITION 3.2–5   A **metrical operation** defined on a set A is commutative, associative (hence, distributive), and continuous.[21]

The following theorem relates interval scales to an irreducible empirical relational system that includes a metrical operation. First we need to define a limit relation.

DEFINITION 3.2–6   The **limit relation,** L, holds for the elements $(a_0, a_1, a_2, \dots)$ of A [denoted as $L: (a_0, a_1, a_2, \dots)$] if and only if

$$a_0 = \lim_{i \to \infty} a_i$$

Theorem 3.2–5   Let $\langle A, I, P, L, \square \rangle$ be a completely ordered and connected, irreducible relational system,[22] where L: "limit relation holds" and $\square$ is an operation defined on A. There exists a monotonic and continuous mapping m such that $m(a_1 \square a_2) = \alpha\, m(a_1) + \beta\, m(a_2) + \gamma$ for α, β, and $\gamma \in R$, where α and $\beta \neq 0$ if and only if $\square$ is a metrical operation. Consequently, m is an interval scale and unique up to a positive linear transformation.

PROOF   For the if portion, assume that $\square$ is a metrical operation on A. Then there exists a homomorphism, g, by Theorem 3.2–1, from A to R that

---

[20] This is an interesting example of the mix of realism and usefulness, or applicability, in theoretical models. Most would agree that individuals are only able to semiorder the commodity space. Yet a comparison of the results of such a semiordering and resulting consumer demand shows that there is very little difference between the usual approach and the semiorder and the consequences for demand curves. In other words, the assumption of the ability of individuals to calculate infinitesimal differences selects the essential characteristics of the assumption of a semiorder, yet it is significantly easier to utilize. The criterion of Occam's razor does not apply, and so which is better depends upon the question to be analyzed. Experiments with individuals might require the increased realism of the semiorder —but market demand is just as realistically analyzed, and much more efficiently, by an ordinal utility function. Cf. Section 3.4.

[21] See Definitions 2.6–1–2.6–4. The following approach to interval scales largely follows Pfanzagl (1968).

[22] Cf. Theorem 3.2–1.

is monotonic and continuous. On the image of A, $g(A) \subset R$, we can define the function $\phi(r_1, r_2)$ as follows:

$$\phi(r_1, r_2) = g[g^{-1}(r_1) \,\square\, g^{-1}(r_2)]$$

It can be shown[23] that there exists an increasing monotonic and continuous function $f: R \to R$, such that

$$\phi(r_1, r_2) = f^{-1}[\alpha f(r_1) + \beta f(r_2) + \gamma]$$

for α, β, and $\gamma \in R$, where α and $\beta \neq 0$. Therefore

$$g[g^{-1}(r_1) \,\square\, g^{-1}(r_2)] = f^{-1}[\alpha f(r_1) + \beta f(r_2) + \gamma]$$

Letting $g^{-1}(r_1) = a_1$, $g^{-1}(r_2) = a_2$, and $f[g(a)] = m(a)$, it immediately follows that

$$m(a_1 \,\square\, a_2) = \alpha m(a_1) + \beta m(a_2) + \gamma$$

The only if portion is easily proved by noting that if m is a homomorphism such that $m(a_1 \,\square\, a_2) = \alpha m(a_1) + \beta m(a_2) + \gamma$, a metrical operation on R, then $\square$ must also be a metrical operation on A.

To show uniqueness, assume that m_1 and m_2 both exist. Then

$$m_1(a_1 \,\square\, a_2) = \alpha_1 m_1(a_1) + \beta_1 m_1(a_2) + \gamma_1$$

$$m_2(a_1 \,\square\, a_2) = \alpha_2 m_2(a_1) + \beta_2 m_2(a_2) + \gamma_2$$

Letting $m_1(a_1) = r_1$, $m_1(a_2) = r_2$, and $f(r_1) = m_2[m^{-1}(r_1)]$, then $f(\alpha_1 r_1 + \beta_1 r_2 + \gamma_1) = \alpha_2 f(r_1) + \beta_2 f(r_2) + \gamma_2$. Aczél (1966) shows that this necessarily implies that $\alpha_1 = \alpha_2$ and $\beta_1 = \beta_2$. Therefore $f(r_1) = m_2[m^{-1}(r_1)] = \alpha_3 r_1 + \gamma_3$, which is to say, the mapping is unique up to a positive linear transformation if $\alpha_3 > 0$. It must be, since it is an increasing monotonic function. QED

Interval scales also preserve a quarternary relation, a special type of metrical operation, defined on an empirical system. Since a quarternary relation relates four elements of the set, the usual interpretation of such a relation is that of distance.

DEFINITION 3.2–7   An **ordered distance system**[24] is a relational system $\langle A, I, P, D \rangle$ and a map $m: A \to A \times A$, where D is both a quarternary relation on A and a binary relation on $A \times A$ written as $ab\,D\,cd$ such that for all a, b, c, d, e, and $f \in A$:

(1) $a\,P\,b$ if and only if not $ab\,D\,aa$;
(2) $a\,I\,b$ if and only if $ab\,D\,ba$ and $ba\,D\,ab$;

[23] Aczél (1966).

[24] Suppes and Winet (1955), Suppes and Zinnes (1963), Pfanzagl (1968).

(3) if *ab D cd* and *cd D ef*, then *ab D ef*;

(4) either *ab D cd* or *cd D ab*;

(5) if *ab D cd*, then *ac D bd*;

(6) for each $a \in A$, $A \times \{a\}$ is connected in $A \times A$; and

(7) the mapping $m : a \rightarrow (a, b)$ for $(a, b) \in A \times A$ is monotonic, continuous, and one-to-one.

Example 1. For a numerical ordered distance system, *ab D cd* would be interpreted as "the difference between *a* and *b* is greater than or equal to the difference between *c* and *d*." Thus (1) says that "*a* is greater than *b*" if $a - b \geq a - a$, while (2) says that "*a* is equal to *b*" (*a I b*) if $a - b \geq b - a$ and $b - a \geq a - b$. (3) and (4) hold since the numerical system is transitive and complete.

Example 2. If the consumer's consumption space and his ordering over that space form an ordered distance system, then by (3) and (4) the ordering is transitive and complete with respect to preference, *P*, and indifference, *I*. It is also transitive and complete with respect to differences in utility between two pairs. For example, if the difference in utility between two apples and three bananas is greater than the difference in utility between a cantaloupe and two dogberry sundaes, which in turn is greater than the difference in utility between two eggs and a flatfish sandwich, then the utility difference between the apples and bananas is greater than the difference between the eggs and the sandwich. Or, given the prices of the commodities, if the difference between the utility of $5[25] and $10 is greater than the utility difference of $6 and $11, then by (5) the difference in utility between $5 and $6 is greater than the difference between $10 and $11. (6) says that the individual has a complete and transitive preference ordering over all pairs (a_i, a_j), where a_i is given and a_j is any element of *A*, such that the ordering has a denumerable (countable) base. (7) states that each element in *A* is associated with an ordered pair in $A \times A$ and that this association, as given by *m*, is continuous, monotonic, and one-to-one. Thus, if a_i provides more satisfaction than a_j, then the pair (a_i, b) must provide more satisfaction than (a_j, b).

For such an ordered distance system, $\langle A, I, P, D \rangle$ the following theorem can be proved.

Theorem 3.2–6 For any ordered distance system, there exists a homomorphism, *m*, which is an interval scale; that is,

$$ab \ D \ cd \quad \text{if and only if} \quad m(a) - m(b) \leq m(c) - m(d)$$

where *m* is monotonically increasing, continuous, and unique up to a linear transformation.

---

[25] The utility of $5 is defined as the maximum utility attainable from $5 expenditure on commodities.

The proof of this is similar to Theorem 3.2–5 and is omitted.[26] Also, it should be noted that Theorems 3.2–5 and 3.2–6 can be extended to multidimensional interval scales in much the same manner as a one-dimensional ordinal scale can be extended to an n-dimensional ordinal scale.

Another example of interval scales is the von Neumann–Morgenstern[27] system of utility. In their book *The Theory of Games and Economic Behavior*, von Neumann and Morgenstern have presented eight axioms that give rise to an interval scale for such an empirical relational system.[28] What we want to do here is to present the axioms and show how they imply the existence of an ordered distance system.

DEFINITION 3.2–8 $\langle A, I, P, h \rangle$ is a **von Neumann–Morgenstern system of utility,** where I and P are binary operations on A and h is a ternary operation on A, if and only if the following axioms are satisfied for every a_1, a_2, and $a_3 \in A$; and every α and β, where $0 < \alpha, \beta < 1$; and where $h(a_1, \alpha, a_2)$ is denoted as $a_1 \alpha a_2$:

   (1*) I and P create a complete and transitive ordering of indifference classes on A;
   (2*) $a_1 \alpha a_2 \in A$;
   (3*) $a_1 \alpha a_2 = a_2(1 - \alpha)a_1$;
   (4*) $(a_1 \alpha a_2)\beta a_2 = a_1 \alpha \beta a_2$;
   (5*)   if $a_1 \ I \ a_2$, then $(a_1 \alpha a_3) \ I \ (a_2 \alpha a_3)$;
   (6*)   if $a_1 \ P \ a_2$, then $a_1 \ P \ (a_1 \alpha a_2)$ and $(a_1 \alpha a_2) \ P \ a_2$;
   (7*)   if $a_1 \ P \ a_2$, $a_2 \ P \ a_3$, then there exists a γ, $0 < \gamma < 1$, such that $a_2 \ P \ (a_1 \gamma a_3)$; and
   (8*)   if $a_1 \ P \ a_2$ and $a_2 \ P \ a_3$, then there exists a $\gamma \in (0, 1)$ such that $(a_1 \gamma a_3) \ P \ a_2$.

Axiom (1*) together with the assumption of connectedness is sufficient to create an ordinal scale, as was demonstrated in Theorem 3.2–1. The remaining axioms are much more restrictive. To put it simply, the remaining axioms create an ordered distance system where the "measure" of distance is that of utility differences. The ternary operation that satisfies the above axioms, along with I and P, imply the existence of quarternary relation, D, that satisfies the axioms of an ordered distance system[29]. Thus the eight von Neumann–Morgenstern axioms regarding an individual's ordering of a

---

[26] See Suppes and Winet (1955) and Pfanzagl (1968).

[27] von Neumann and Morgenstern (1947).

[28] See also Luce and Suppes (1965) for a discussion of various axiom systems and the utility measures that can be derived from these systems.

[29] The reader is encouraged to work through the proof. Hint: *ab D cd* implies that either *aαb P cαd* or *aαb I cαd*.

consumption space are sufficient to generate an ordered distance system. In a von Neumann–Morgenstern system of utility, the ternary operation is interpreted as a numerical probability. Hence, for example, (8*) says that if prospect a_1 (commodity bundle, amount of money, etc.) is preferred to prospect a_2, which in turn is preferred to prospect a_3, then there exists a lottery ticket $(a_1 \gamma a_3)$ which has the outcome of a_1 with some probability γ between 0 and 1 and the outcome of a_3 with a probability $1 - \gamma$ that is preferred to outcome a_2. The question raised with such a system of axioms is whether they impose a realistic or a restrictive set of conditions of their real-world counterpart which is being approximated by such a model.

Difference scales are those that have a unique unit of measure, in the ordinary sense of the word, but have an arbitrary origin. In other words, any transformation of a difference scale must take place by either the addition or subtraction of some constant to preserve the relations of the empirical system, that is, to be a permissible transformation. Difference scales are little used. However, there are some applications in psychology.[30]

An example of such a well-structured empirical system that possesses only a difference scale would be the set of all animals and the relation on this empirical set would be the "difference in number of feet." One could map a one-footed protozoa into any real number as long as the map for human beings differed from that of the single-footed protozoa by one. Although such a mapping would be a difference scale, unique up to any arbitrary origin, it does not appear to be a very useful method of analyzing an empirical set. In most cases where a difference scale exists, it is possible to specify additional relations on the set so that a more useful scale can be derived.

In contrast to difference scales, ratio scales have a unique origin, although the unit of measure assigned to the empirical set is arbitrary. Scales of weight or mass are ratio scales. The choice of measure (e.g., pounds or ounces) is arbitrary, but a zero weight or mass is meaningful under any choice of measure and is the unique origin. The following theorem from Suppes and Zinnes (1963) relates an extensive relational system to a ratio scale.

DEFINITION 3.2–9 An **extensive relational system** $\langle A, R, \square \rangle$ is a relational system where R is a binary relation and $\square$ is a binary operation that satisfy the following seven axioms for a_1, a_2, and $a_3 \in A$:

   (1) if $a_1 \ R \ a_2$ and $a_2 \ R \ a_3$, then $a_1 \ R \ a_3$;
   (2) $a_1 \ R \ a_1$;
   (3) $a_1 \ \square \ (a_2 \ \square \ a_3) = (a_1 \ \square \ a_2) \ \square \ a_3$;
   (4) if $a_1 \ R \ a_2$, then $a_1 \ \square \ a_3 \ R \ a_2 \ \square \ a_3$;

---

[30] See Pfanzagl (1968) and Suppes and Zinnes (1963) for further discussion and additional references.

(5) if not $a_1 \, R \, a_2$, then there exists $a_3 \in A$ such that $a_1 \, R \, a_2 \, \square \, a_3$ and $a_2 \, \square \, a_3 \, R \, a_1$;

(6) $a_1 \, \square \, a_2 \, R \, a_1$ cannot occur; and

(7) If $a_1 \, R \, a_2$, then $a_2 \, R \, a_1 \, \square \cdots \square \, a_1$.

With respect to weights, for example, the binary relation in Definition 3.2–9 would be interpreted as "less heavy or equal to," while $\square$ would be "combination of weights." Axiom (1) establishes transitivity, while axioms (2) and (3) establish reflexiveness and the associativity of the operation $\square$, respectively. Axiom (4) says that if a_1 is not heavier than a_2, then a combination of a_1 and any a_3 is not heavier than a_2 and a_3. Axiom (6) states that weight is always positive. Axiom (7) is sometimes termed the Archimedean axiom and states that if a_1 is not heavier than a_2, then some multiple of a_1 is heavier than a_2.

Theorem 3.2–7   If $\langle A, R, \square \rangle$ is an empirical extensive relational system, and $(N, \leq, +)$ is an extensive numerical system, then there is a homomorphic mapping $m: A \to N$. Further, any two numerical relational systems that are homomorphic to $\langle A, R, \square \rangle$ are related by a positive transformation. Hence m is a ratio scale.

We omit the proof of Theorem 3.2–7.[31]

Absolute scales, being unique up to the identity transformation,[32] are the most limited kind of scale. This in turn implies that the empirical relational system for which such a mapping is defined must be relatively more structured than those associated with other scales.

Suppose that $\langle A, R_1, \ldots, R_i, \ldots \rangle$ is an empirical relational system, where A is the set of all conceivable commodity baskets and R_i is the 1-ary relation; "the number of different commodities in basket a is i." The map $m(a) = i \in I$ is then an absolute scale for $\langle A, R_1, \ldots, R_i, \ldots \rangle$ since the only admissible transformation is the identity map: $\phi: m(a) \to m(a)$.

Problems

3.2–1   Classify the following scales according to Definition 3.2–1:
    (a) centigrade temperature
    (b) social security numbers
    (c) teacher evaluation scores, where best is 4 and worst is 1
    (d) Troy weights
    (e) mileage between two cities

3.2–2   What kind of scale is appropriate for the following relational systems?
    (a) $\langle A, R_1 \rangle$, $A = \{\text{commodities}\}$ and the relation is an individual's evaluation of the quality of one commodity compared to that of another

---

[31] See Suppes (1957), Suppes and Zinnes (1963).

[32] $m: a \to a$ for all $a \in A$ is an identity transformation.

(b) $\langle A, R_1 \rangle$, $A = \{$durable goods$\}$, where the relation R is "the life of a_1 is longer than a_2" where if a_1 and a_2 expire within a month of each other there is no significant difference in the length of their lives

(c) $\langle A, R_1 \rangle$, $A = \{$entrants in a yodeling contest$\}$, $R_1 = $ "a_1 is not the same yodeler as a_2"

3.2–3 Suppose $A = \{$beer, bread, cheese, wine, chips, champagne$\}$ and that Mr. Casey has the following preferences: He is indifferent to chips and cheese, indifferent to beer and bread, prefers champagne to wine, prefers wine to chips, and prefers cheese over bread. If Mr. Casey is rational in the sense that his preferences are transitive, then:

(a) Construct a suitable utility scale for Mr. Casey's preferences from the set of numbers $\{1, 2, 3, 4, 5, 6, 7, 8, 9, 10\}$.

(b) If $U(\text{bread}) = 5$, find $U(\text{beer})$.

(c) If $U(\text{champagne}) = 4$, what is $U(\text{chips})$?

(d) If $U(\text{wine}) = 8$, what are permissible values for $U(\text{champagne})$?

3.2–4 If an individual is unable to distinguish between two sounds differing in loudness by less than a decibel, construct a just noticeable difference scales for the sounds $\{a, b, c, d, e\}$, where the decibels are 2.7, 3.2, 3.6, 4.3, and 5.0, respectively. Use the method outlined in Theorem 3.2–4.

3.2–5 Suppose an individual who maximizes expected utility is indifferent between having \$100 with certainty and owning a lottery ticket paying \$1000 with a probability of 0.5 and \$50 with probability of 0.5. If we let the utility of \$50 $= 0$ and the utility of \$1000 $= 1$, what is the utility of \$100? Is marginal utility increasing, decreasing, or constant between \$50 and \$100?

3.2–6 Suppose an individual who maximizes expected utility receives 10 units of utility from \$500, 2 units from \$100, and 3 units of utility from \$200. What would have to be the probability, p, of a lottery ticket with p payoff of \$500 and $(1 - p)$ payoff of \$100 in order for the individual to be indifferent between the lottery ticket and \$200 with certainty?

3.2–7 Construct another suitable utility scale for the values \$100, \$200, and \$500 in Problem 3.1–6.

3.3   MEANINGFULNESS

In Sections 3.1 and 3.2 we have discussed the extent to which various types of empirical relational systems are related to numerical relational systems. Now the question becomes, given that we have a mapping of an empirical set to the set of real numbers, what statements are meaningful in terms of a numerical system? Consider the following statements:

(1) If Herbert Klotzmeyer's money income is increased by \$100, this will increase his utility by 10%.

(2) The quantity of labor used in the production of kazoos plus the

quantity of labor used in the production of mouth-harps is a constant.
(3) Social welfare is a weighted average of individual utilities.
(4) The difference in the utility of three apples and three oranges is greater than the difference in the utility of a shotgun and a rifle.
(5) The quantity of land times the quantity of capital is greater than the value of land times the value of capital.

Clearly, the meaningfulness of any one of the above depends upon the uniqueness of the scale being used to make a statement about the empirical system. In (1), if utility is defined as unique up to an ordinal scale, then the assertion of a 10% increase in the numerical value assigned to Herb's preference ordering makes no sense. Given another arbitrary mapping from the commodity set to the real numbers, the $100 increase in income might cause a 1%, 300%, or any percentage change.

More precisely, we define meaningfulness in the following way:

DEFINITION 3.3–1   A statement of an n-ary numerical relation, S_i, from a specified (irreducible) numerical relational system $\langle N_1, S_1, \ldots, S_i, \ldots, S_m \rangle$ meant to correspond to a specified (irreducible) empirical relational system $\langle A, R_1, \ldots, R_i, \ldots, R_m \rangle$ *is* **meaningful** if for any two admissible mappings, $m_1: A \to N_1, m_2: A \to N_1$, the relation S_i holds.

In (1)

$$S_i: \text{"} \frac{U(a_1 + \$100) - U(a_1)}{U(a_1)} = 10\% \text{"}$$

does not hold for $U^*(a) = [U(a)]^2$ (or, in general, any monotonic transformation of $U: A \to N_1$), and thus the numerical statement S_i is not meaningful by Definition 3.2–1.

Consider statement (2). The empirical set is apparently labor used in different activities. The truth or validity of (2) depends entirely upon the specified relations on the empirical set. Since for (2) to be a meaningful statement, the empirical relational system must be specified such that the mapping is an absolute scale with the metrical operations implied by (2) holding. For example, the empirical relational system would have to specify unambiguously the origin and unit of measure—man-days, units of kazoos produced, and so on.

Mathematically, (3) says:

(3a)
$$W = \sum_{i=1}^{n} \alpha_i U_i$$

First of all, this says that a relational system exists on the set that includes not only all individual utilities but also social welfare, something to which few are willing to agree. Further, suppose W' and U_i' are positive linear, admissible transformations of W and U_i that are unique up to an interval scale; therefore, it follows that

$$W' = \sum_{i=1}^{n} \alpha_i U_i'$$

or if $W' = \beta W + \gamma$, and $U_i' = \beta U_i + \gamma$, then

$$\beta W + \gamma = \sum_{i=1}^{n} \alpha_i(\beta U_i + \gamma) = \beta \sum_{i=1}^{n} \alpha_i U_i + \gamma \sum_{i=1}^{n} \alpha_i$$

which does not reduce to (3a). If the scale were unique up to a similarity transformation, that is,

$$W' = \beta W \quad \text{and} \quad U_i' = \beta U_i$$

then (3a) holds. This example illustrates that for many numerical statements to be meaningful the associated empirical systems must be structured to such a degree that the system is neither useful nor realistic. This is further discussed in the following section.

Statement (4) implies that the utility measure of commodities is cardinal. That is, for any two admissible mappings, U and U', one must be at least a linear transformation of the other. Thus, if

$$U(a) - U(o) > U(s) - U(r)$$

where $U: A \to R_1$, for a, o, s, and $r \in A = \{\text{commodities}\}$,

$$R_1 \subset R$$

then for

$$U'(a) - U'(o) > U'(s) - U'(r)$$

where $U': A \to R_2$ and $R_2 \subset R$, it must be true that

$$U' = \beta U + \gamma$$

for $\beta \in R^+$ and $\gamma \in R$.

What relations are implied by statement (5)?

In many respects, Definition 3.3–1 is quite a restrictive interpretation of "meaningfulness." A generalization of the definition would permit the numerical statement to depend upon the parameters of the admissible transformations of a mapping m but not on the specific elements of A. For example, suppose that m_1 and m_2 are admissible mappings forming a scale, then a numerical statement such as:

(6) $m_1(a) = \alpha m_2(a)$ for $a \in A$ and $\alpha \in R$, where $\alpha \neq 0$

would not, in general, be meaningful by Definition 3.2–1 unless the mappings m_1 and m_2 were unique. A generalization would be that (6) is meaningful if, for transformations m_3 of m_1 and m_4 of m_2.

(7) $m_3(a) = \beta m_4(a)$ for $a \in A$, where β is a constant

Suppose that

$$s\, m_1(a) = m_3(a) \quad \text{and} \quad t\, m_2(a) = m_4(a)$$

where s and t are real numbers. Then (7) says that

$$s\, m_1(a) = \beta\, t\, m_2(a)$$

Consequently, if β is equal to $(s/t)\alpha$, (6) is equal to (7) for all nonzero values of s and t and the empirical system is *meaningfully parameterized* according to the following definition.

DEFINITION 3.3–2 Let $S_{\phi(m)}$ be an m-ary relation on an irreducible numerical relational system under the mapping m. The family of such relations, $S = \{S_{\phi(m)}\}$ is **meaningfully parameterized** by ϕ if and only for any $m_0: A \to N_1$, where $N_1 \subset R$ and for $\gamma \in \Gamma_R$ [the set of admissible transformations of m_0, that is, $m_1 = \gamma(m_0)$], it is true that

$$S_{\phi(m_0)} = \gamma S_{\phi[\gamma(m_0)]}$$

Example 1. Ragnar Frisch[33] proposed that the empirical relation between utility, U, and money income, M, was

$$(1) \qquad\qquad U = \frac{\alpha}{\ln M - \ln \beta} \quad {}^{34}$$

Frisch's law is meaningfully parameterized if the mappings U and M are unique up to positive multiples, that is, if for all other admissible mappings

$$U^* = \delta_1 U \quad \text{and} \quad M^* = \delta_2 M$$

the law is meaningfully parameterized if

$$U^* = \frac{\alpha^*}{\ln M^* - \ln \beta}$$

where α^* and β^* depend upon δ_1 and δ_2. Letting $\alpha^* = \delta_1 \alpha$ and $\beta^* = \delta_2 \beta$, then

$$\frac{\alpha}{\ln M - \ln \beta} = U = \frac{1}{\delta_1} U^* = \frac{1}{\delta_1} \frac{\delta_1 \alpha}{\ln \delta_2 M - \ln \delta_2 \beta} = \frac{\alpha}{\ln M - \ln \beta}$$

which is to say, Frisch's law *is* meaningfully parameterized.

---

[33] Frisch (1936).

[34] $\ln x$ is the natural logarithm of x. If $\ln x = y$, then $e^y = x$, where e is the natural number $2.71828\ldots$. $\log_a x$ is the logarithm of x to the base a, i.e., $\log_a x = y$ means $a^y = x$, where a is any positive constant.

Waugh (1935), however, proposed that

$$U = \frac{\alpha}{\ln \ln M - \ln \ln \beta}$$

which is not a meaningful parametric relationship. If it were, then

$$\frac{\alpha}{\ln \ln M - \ln \ln \beta} = \frac{1}{\delta_1} \frac{f_1(\delta_1, \delta_2)}{\ln \ln \delta_2 M - \ln \ln f_2(\delta_1, \delta_2)}$$

which implies that

$$\ln \ln M = \frac{K_1}{\alpha} \ln \ln \delta_2 M - K_2$$

where

$$K_1 = \frac{f_1(\delta_1, \delta_2)}{\delta_1} \quad \text{and} \quad K_2 = K_1 \ln \ln \beta + \alpha \ln \ln f_2(\delta_1, \delta_2)$$

This holds only if $\delta_2 = 1$.

Example 2.[35]   Suppose that

(2) $m_1(a) = \alpha \log m_2(a)$

is a numerical statement. In spite of the fact that m_1 is related to the logarithm of m_2, if m_1 is unique up to a positive multiple and m_2 is unique up to a power transformation, then for $m_1(a)$ admissibly transformed into $\delta_1 m_1(a)$ and $m_2(a)$ transformed into $[m_2(a)]^{\delta_2}$, then the numerical statement (2) becomes

$$\delta_1 m_1(a) = \alpha^* \log [m_2(a)^{\delta_2}]$$

which is equivalent to (2) if $\alpha^* = (\delta_1/\delta_2)\alpha$. In other words, $\delta_1 m_1(a) = (\delta_1/\delta_2)\alpha \log [m_2(a)^{\delta_2}] = \delta_1\alpha \log m_2(a)$. Equation (2) is meaningfully parameterized only when m_1 is a ratio scale and m_2 is unique up to a power transformation.

Problems

3.3–1   If the following statements are meaningful according to Definition 3.3–1, then what kind of scale is implied to exist?

(a) Student b is twice as good as student a.

(b) The temperature change on Tuesday was greater than the change on Wednesday.

(c) The price of commodity a is one-half the price of commodity b.

(d) The correct measure of social welfare is Gross National Product.

---

[35] Due to Suppes and Zinnes (1963).

3.3–2   Which of the following statements are meaningful for an ordinal scale? An interval scale? A ratio scale?
(a) The value of x over y is 10% greater than the value of w over z.
(b) x is better than y.
(c) x is only 0.8 of y.
(d) x is equivalent to y.

3.3–3   Suppose we have the following law, which relates money income (M) to utility U:

$$U = a + bM$$

and further that U is unique up to a positive multiple (i.e., $U^* = \delta_1 U$) and M is unique up to a positive multiple (i.e., $M^* = \delta_2 M$). Is the above law meaningfully parameterized by a and b? (Hint: For any other admissible measures U^* and M^* you must be able to find an a^* and b^* such that $U^* = a^* + b^* M$ and a^* and b^* depend only upon δ_1 and δ_2.)

3.3–4   Suppose that aggregate consumption, C, is related to aggregate income by the following law:

$$C = a + b \ln Y$$

Since both consumption and income measured in dollars are unique up to a positive multiple, do a and b meaningfully parameterize the relation between C and Y?

3.4   USEFULNESS VERSUS REALISM

As has probably been apparent throughout this chapter, the type of scale (and its uniqueness, monotonicity, etc.) associated with any empirical relational system depends upon the nature of the set and the number and type of relations that are specified for that set. For any empirical set, the actual number of relations that could be specified is usually quite large. However, the very nature and purpose of any scientific analysis is to simplify and generalize in order to explain, predict, and, perhaps, control. Clearly, then, the number and kind of relations that are specified for a particular empirical set depend upon the relevant questions to be answered by the measurement. In most cases one will find a trade-off between realism (i.e., a greater degree of detailed relational specification) and usefulness (simplicity, lack of extraneous detail, etc.).

Given that one has alternative ways of specifying a particular empirical set and its associated relations (as is more common in economics and the social sciences than in the physical sciences), can one compare two different scales and evaluate one as better or worse than another? In most cases, which is the better will depend upon the question at hand. Scales of entire social systems tend to become a morass of incomprehensible symbols: post-, super-, pre-subscripts, and so on, unless the specified relations are limited to the relevant (useful and/or important) aspects of such an encompassing empirical set. On the other hand, when gleaning information for an analysis of Good Greasy Foods Inc.'s sales for next year, it may be necessary and desirable to specify detailed relations and derive exacting scales of measurement for these sets.[36]

Value judgments as to relevance aside, are there unambiguous cases where one scale is better than another? Clearly, if two scales are equal with respect to simplicity but one is more useful than another, then the latter is better.[37] An example of such a scale comparison is the question of ordinal or cardinal utility.

As discussed in Section 3.2, cardinal utility is a more detailed description of the empirical system commodities. The set of admissible transformations is limited to positive linear transformations. However, since an ordinal scale provides the identical amount of information for demand theory in economics and concomitantly requires a less rigid specification of the relations that hold on the empirical set of commodities, it is preferred. Comparing the postulates of Theorem 3.2–1 and Theorem 3.2–5, one can easily see that in order for an interval scale to exist, the relations must be specified more exactly. If this is not a realistic specification of its real-world counterpart, that is, an individual consumer's ability to discern and calculate, then the analysis is misleading and unnecessary. This principle is known as Occam's razor and says to shave off the extraneous relations that are irrelevant to the question at hand as long as equivalent information can be obtained.

Comparing Theorems 3.2–1 and 3.2–4, one can see that 3.2–4 is more general in the sense that the relations specified for the empirical set are less presumptious than those in 3.2–1. In Theorem 3.2–4 the ability of the consumer need not be nearly so exacting and precise as that required in Theorem 3.2–1. However, notice what happens to the usefulness of the resulting scales. When the question is one of aggregate demand, Theorem 3.2–1 is a sufficient approximation to reality so that it may be used as a theoretical basis of analysis. However, if the question were to explain and/or predict the buying habits of Mrs. Roberts on a given Saturday in Ames, Iowa, even the greater realism of Theorem 3.2–4 would probably not be sufficient.

Problems

3.4–1 Which of the following of the given pairs is (*i*) a more realistic scale, (ii) a more useful scale, (iii) a preferred scale? Why?

---

[36] This question in and of itself is a question of measurement. That is, the discussion is whether or not we can construct a measurement of various types of scales. In most cases the relations that hold over the set of possible scales is unknown, a priori.

[37] That is, without knowing the relations that hold over the set of all scales, a lexicographic ordering is possible.

(a) cardinal utility or ordinal utility scale for measuring individual preference
(b) absolute scale or nominal scale in numbering all hockey players
(c) nominal scale or ordinal scale for measuring the hardness of rocks
(d) an ordinal scale or an interval scale for measuring the brightness of colors

References

1. ACZÉL, J. (1966), *Lectures on Functional Equations and Their Applications*, New York: Academic.
2. DEBREU, G. (1954), "Representation of a Preference Ordering by a Numerical Function," in R. M. Thrall, C. H. Coombs, and R. L. Davis (eds.), *Decision Processes*, New York: Wiley.
3. FRISCH, RAGNAR (1936), "The Problem of Index Numbers" *Econometrica*, 4:1–38.
4. LUCE, R. D. (1956), "Semiorders and a Theory of Utility Discrimination," *Econometrica*, 24:178–191.
5. ———— and P. SUPPES (1965), "Preference, Utility, and Subjective Probability" in R. D. Luce, R. R. Bush, and E. Galanter (eds.), *Handbook of Mathematical Psychology*, vol. III, New York: Wiley.
6. PFANZAGL, J. (1968), *Theory of Measurement*, New York: Wiley.
7. SCOTT, D., and P. SUPPES (1958), "Foundational Aspects of Theories of Measurement," *Journal of Symbolic Logic*, 23:113–128.
8. SUPPES, P. (1957), *Introduction to Logic*, New York: Van Nostrand Reinhold.
9. ———— and M. WINET (1955), "An Axiomatization of Utility Based on the Notion of Utility Differences," *Management Science*, 1:259–270.
10. ————and J. L. ZINNES (1963), "Basic Measurement Theory" in R. D. Luce, R. R. Bush, and E. Galanter (eds.), *Handbook of Mathematical Psychology*, vol. I, New York: Wiley.
11. VON NEUMANN, J., and O. MORGENSTERN (1947), *The Theory of Games and Economic Behavior*, 2nd ed., Princeton, N.J.: Princeton University Press.
12. WAUGH, F. W. (1935), "The Marginal Utility of Money in the United States from 1917–1921 and from 1922–1932," *Econometrica*, 3:376–399.

Chapter 4

Functions and Matrix Algebra

4.1 FUNCTIONS

In the next four chapters we review the concepts and applications of matrix algebra and the ordinary calculus. Much, if not all, of the material in later chapters requires a sound understanding of these techniques.

Functions have already been defined in Chapter 2. We shall be dealing with functions of both one variable, $y = f(x)$, and more than one variable, $y = f(x_1, x_2, \ldots, x_m)$. In this familiar notation, y is dependent variable, or value of the function, while the x's are the independent variables. If the value of the dependent variable is uniquely determined by the value(s) assigned to the independent variable(s), the function is single-valued. If there is more than one value for the dependent variable given the value(s) of the independent variable(s), the function is multivalued. Multivalued functions may be decomposed into single-valued functions. Note that in the terminology developed in Chapter 2, multivalued functions should, strictly speaking, be called relations and not functions. Why?

Example 1. Express the multivalued function $y^2 + 3x^2 = 5$ as two single-valued functions. $y = +\sqrt{5 - 3x^2}$ and $y = -\sqrt{5 - 3x^2}$ are the required functions. Verify that they are single-valued.

We shall follow the customary procedure and refer to both single- and multi-valued functions as functions. Note that a single-valued function may have different sets of values of the independent variables yielding the same value of the dependent variable and not violate the definition of a function given in Chapter 2. See Figure 4.1–1.

Functions can be classified either by their structure or by their particular properties. We conclude this section with descriptions of some of the various types.

Functions may be written implicitly or explicitly. One way of writing a function explicitly is to indicate what independent variables determine the

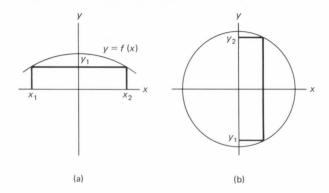

Figure 4.1–1   (*a*) *Single-valued function.*   (*b*)*Multivalued function.*

value of the dependent variable. $y = f(x_1, x_2, \ldots, x_n)$ is an example. In such a case we may or may not know the exact form of the function f. Another implicit form of a function is given by [1]

$$(1) \qquad\qquad \ln y + 3x - 5 = 0$$

The explicit form of Equation (1) is simply

$$(2) \qquad\qquad y = e^{5-3x}$$

Equation (2) is in explicit form, since we have "explicitly" solved Equation (1) for y. Note that some implicit functions, such as $y + 2\ln y + 3x = 5$, cannot be solved explicitly for the dependent variable y (written in explicit form). Such functions can be solved for y through various approximation techniques.

DEFINITION 4.1–1   An **algebraic function** is a function that can be expressed in terms of finite polynomials and/or roots of finite polynomials.

The most common types of algebraic functions are constant functions, polynomial functions, and rational functions.

DEFINITION 4.1–2   A **constant function** is a function whose range consists of only one element.[2]

Example 2. $y = 5$ is a constant function.

---

[1] ln y is the natural logarithm of y, defined by the relation $e^{\ln y} = y$ (see Definition 4.1–6 and footnote 34 in Chapter 3).

[2] See Chapter 2 for the definitions of the domain and range of a function.

DEFINITION 4.1–3   A **polynomial function** of one variable is a function that can be written as

$$y = a_0x^0 + a_1x^1 + a_2x^2 + \cdots + a_nx^n$$

where $(a_0, a_1, \ldots, a_n)$ is a vector of constant coefficients and $(x^0, x^1, x^2, \ldots, x^n)$ a vector of integral powers of x.

DEFINITION 4.1–4   A **rational function** is a function that can be written as a ratio of polynomial functions.

Example 3.

$$y = \frac{5x^2 + 3}{x^3 - 2}$$

is a rational function.

Note that constant functions are a special type of polynomial function with $n = 0$. What are polynomial functions called when $n = 1, n = 2$, and $n = 3$? The function $y = \sqrt{x^4 - x + 3}$ is not a rational function, but it is algebraic. Why?

Nonalgebraic functions are called **transcendental functions.** The following definitions give the major types of transcendental functions.

DEFINITION 4.1–5   An **exponential function** is a function where the independent variable appears as an exponent.

Example 4. $y = 2e^x$ and $y = 10^{(x^2-3)}$ are exponential functions.

DEFINITION 4.1–6   A **logarithmic function (log function)** is one in which either the dependent, independent, or both variables appear as logarithms.

Example 5.   The functions $\ln y = x$ and $y = 5 \log_b x^2$ are both log functions.

An obvious and close relation exists between exponential and log functions based on the definitions of natural and base b logarithms. The following pairs of functions are equivalent:

(1) $y = e^x$ and $\ln y = x$

(2) $y = b^{2x}$ and $\log_b y = 2x$

(3) $y = 10^{2x}$ and $\log_{10} y = 2x$

DEFINITION 4.1–7   A **trigonometric (circular or sinusoidal) function** is a function in which either the dependent, independent, or both variables appear as sines, cosines, or other trigonometric relations.[3]

Example 6. $y = 3 \sin x$ and $\cos y - 4 \tan x + 3 \sec x = 5$ are trigonometric (trig) functions.

DEFINITION 4.1–8   An **inverse trigonometric function** is one involving the inverse sine ($\sin^{-1}$), inverse cosine ($\cos^{-1}$), and so on.

Example 7. $y = \sin^{-1} x$ and $\tan^{-1} x + 3 \csc^{-1} y = 4$ are inverse trig functions.

Functions may also be classified by their domains and ranges. A function whose domain and range is restricted to the real numbers is called a real-valued function. Complex-valued functions are defined in an analogous way.

Other important types of functions (continuous, differentiable, homogeneous, monotone, etc.) will be defined later.

Problems

4.1–1   Why are multivalued functions relations and not functions?

4.1–2   Which of the following functions $y = f(x)$, are single-valued? Multivalued? Decompose the multivalued functions into several single-valued functions.
  (a) $y = 7 \ln x + 3$ (d) $y^2 + 3x - 4 = 0$
  (b) $y = x^3 - 3x^2 + 2$ (e) $y^2 + 3x^2 - 2x + 1 = 0$
  (c) $y^2 x^2 = 5$

4.1–3   Find the explicit form of the following functions, $y = f(x)$ (if possible).
  (a) $\ln y^2 - 4x^2 - 2x + 1 = 0$ (d) $e^y = 5 \ln x$
  (b) $\sin y + \cos x = 3$ (e) $y + 2e^y = x^2 + 1$
  (c) $\ln (xy) = 1$ (f) $\log_{10} y^2 = 2x + 3$

4.1–4   Write the corresponding log and exponential functions for the functions given in Examples 4 and 5.

4.1–5   Generalize the definition of a polynomial function (Definition 4.1–3) to functions with two or more independent variables.

4.2   LINEAR SYSTEMS AND MATRICES

Before developing the tenets of calculus, it is efficient to develop a shorthand notation for systems of functions or sets of simultaneous equations. Sets of equations and rules for the simultaneous manipulation of these equations, that is, the *algebra* of simultaneous equations, is the subject matter of matrix

---

[3] See Thomas (1968), Chapters 4 and 6, for a discussion of trigonometric and inverse trigonometric functions.

algebra. In this section we shall review the characteristics of matrix algebra and note several theorems and methods of dealing with equations.

If the system of equations for which a simultaneous solution is to be found is of the form

$$a_{11}x_1 + a_{12}x_2 + \cdots + a_{1n}x_n = b_1$$
$$a_{21}x_1 + a_{22}x_2 + \cdots + a_{2n}x_n = b_2$$
$$\vdots$$
$$a_{m1}x_1 + a_{m2}x_2 + \cdots + a_{mn}x_n = b_m$$

where the a_{ij}'s and b_i's are constants, then the matrix notation for such a system is $Ax = b$, where

$$A = \begin{bmatrix} a_{11} & \cdots & a_{1n} \\ \vdots & & \vdots \\ a_{m1} & \cdots & a_{mn} \end{bmatrix}$$

is an $n \times m$ ordered array of elements,

$$x = \begin{bmatrix} x_1 \\ x_2 \\ \vdots \\ x_n \end{bmatrix}$$

is an n-dimensional vector, and

$$b = \begin{bmatrix} b_1 \\ b_2 \\ \vdots \\ b_m \end{bmatrix}$$

is an m-dimensional vector.

The obvious advantage of matrix algebra is compactness and economy of notation. The following definitions and theorems hold for matrices.

DEFINITION 4.2–1   A **matrix** of dimension $m \times n$ is an ordered collection of mn elements[4]; an ordered set of m n-dimensional vectors (or, equivalently, n m-dimensional vectors), defined on a linear algebra (Definition 2.7–7), where m and n are positive integers.

DEFINITION 4.2–2   The **transpose** of the $m \times n$ matrix A is the matrix A', where a typical element of A' is $a'_{ij} = a_{ji}$.

In other words, the transpose of a matrix A has the columns of A for rows and the rows of A for columns.

___

[4] A matrix of dimension $m \times n$ (an "m by n" matrix) is a matrix with m rows and n columns.

Since the vectors that comprise a matrix are contained in a linear algebra, the following operations hold for matrices:

DEFINITION 4.2–3

(1) The **sum of two matrices,** $A + B$, is defined if and only if A and B are of the same dimension. If $A + B = C$, then a typical element of C, c_{ij}, is equal to $a_{ij} + b_{ij}$.

(2) **Scalar multiplication** of A by a scalar s, $s(A)$, is defined as $s(a_{ij})$ for all ij. A **scalar** is any single element from a vector or any single element a_{ij} from a matrix composed of vectors. (Cf. Definition 2.7–6.)

(3) **The product of two matrices,** AB, is defined when A is $m \times n$ and B is $n \times s$. Further, if $AB = C$, then $c_{ij} = \sum_{k=1}^{n} a_{ik}b_{kj}$. (What is the dimension of the product C?)[5] If the product C exists, then A and B are said to be conformable for multiplication.

Example 1. Let

$$A = \begin{bmatrix} 2 & 3 \\ 4 & 5 \end{bmatrix} \quad B = \begin{bmatrix} -1 & 0 \\ 6 & 2 \end{bmatrix} \quad C = \begin{bmatrix} 1 & 4 \\ 0 & 6 \\ 2 & 3 \end{bmatrix}$$

Then $A + B$ is found by adding a_{ij} to b_{ij} for all the elements of A and B. Thus

$$A + B = \begin{bmatrix} 1 & 3 \\ 10 & 7 \end{bmatrix}$$

$A + C$ is not defined, since A is 2×2 and C is 3×2. The product AB is as if each row of A were run down each column of B. For example, letting $AB = D$ with a typical element of d_{ij}, then

$$d_{11} = a_{11}b_{11} + a_{12}b_{21} = -2 + 18 = 16$$

Thus

$$AB = \begin{bmatrix} 16 & 6 \\ 26 & 10 \end{bmatrix}$$

The product CA is defined and is the 3×2 matrix

$$\begin{bmatrix} 18 & 23 \\ 24 & 30 \\ 16 & 21 \end{bmatrix}$$

AC is not defined.

[5] Note that division as ordinarily thought of, A/B, is not defined for matrices.

The following theorems hold for matrices and will not be proved here.[6] However, the reader should satisfy himself that the shorthand matrix notation holds when the theorems are written out as equations.

Theorem 4.2–1   (a) The transpose of AB is the product of the transposes in reverse order:

$$(AB)' = B'A'$$

(b) Matrix multiplication is associative:

$$(AB)C = A(BC)$$

(c) Matrix multiplication is distributive with addition:

$$A(B + C) = AB + AC$$

(d) In general, matrix multiplication is not commutative:

$$AB \neq BA$$

Example 2.   Consider

$$A = \begin{bmatrix} 0 & 1 \\ 2 & 7 \end{bmatrix} \quad B = \begin{bmatrix} 1 & 6 \\ -2 & 0 \end{bmatrix} \quad C = \begin{bmatrix} 2 & 2 \\ 1 & 1 \end{bmatrix}$$

For part (a) of Theorem 4.2–1 we first have

$$AB = \begin{bmatrix} -2 & 0 \\ -12 & 12 \end{bmatrix}$$

thus

$$(AB)' = \begin{bmatrix} -2 & -12 \\ 0 & 12 \end{bmatrix}$$

Since

$$A' = \begin{bmatrix} 0 & 2 \\ 1 & 7 \end{bmatrix}$$

and

$$B' = \begin{bmatrix} 1 & -2 \\ 6 & 0 \end{bmatrix}$$

and, thus

$$B'A' = \begin{bmatrix} -2 & -12 \\ 0 & 12 \end{bmatrix}$$

which is equal to $(AB)'$.

[6] See Perlis (1958).

For part (b),

$$AB = \begin{bmatrix} -2 & 0 \\ -12 & 12 \end{bmatrix}$$

and therefore

$$(AB)C = \begin{bmatrix} -2 & 0 \\ -12 & 12 \end{bmatrix}\begin{bmatrix} 2 & 2 \\ 1 & 1 \end{bmatrix} = \begin{bmatrix} -4 & -4 \\ -12 & -12 \end{bmatrix}$$

which is equal to

$$A(BC) = \begin{bmatrix} 0 & 1 \\ 2 & 7 \end{bmatrix}\begin{bmatrix} 8 & 8 \\ -4 & -4 \end{bmatrix}$$

The reader can easily verify parts (c) and (d) in a similar manner.

DEFINITION 4.2–4   (a) m vectors $(v_1, \ldots, v_m)$ from a vector space V are **linearly dependent** if there are scalars $c_1, \ldots, c_m$ such that:
  (1) not all $c_i = 0$;
  (2) $c_1 v_1 + c_2 v_2 + \cdots + c_m v_m = 0$.
  (b) m vectors, $v \in V$, are **linearly independent** if there are no scalars $c_1, \ldots, c_m$ such that:
  (1) not all $c_i = 0$;
  (2) $c_1 v_1 + c_2 v_2 + \cdots + c_m v_m = 0$.

For example, the vectors $v_1 = (1, 2, 1)$, $v_2 = (4, 5, 4)$, $v_3 = (0, -3, 0)$ are linearly dependent, since if we let $c_1 = 4$, $c_2 = -1$, and $c_3 = 1$ we have $4(1, 2, 1) - (4, 5, 4) + (0, -3, 0) = (4, 8, 4) - (4, 5, 4) + (0, -3, 0) = (0, 0, 0) = 0$.

If $m \leq n$ one can easily find a set of m linearly independent vectors for an n-dimensional vector space from the **unit** vectors or scalar multiples of them; that is,

$$u_1 = (1, 0, \ldots, 0)$$
$$u_2 = (0, 1, \ldots, 0)$$
$$\vdots$$
$$u_m = (0, 0, \ldots, 1)$$

are the unit vectors over V and are linearly independent.

As is easily seen from Definition 4.2–4, if m vectors are *linearly dependent*, then any one is a linear combination of the others; that is, if

$$c_1 v_1 + \cdots + c_m v_m = 0$$

then

$$v_1 = \frac{c_2}{c_1} v_2 - \cdots - \frac{c_m}{c_1} v_m$$

DEFINITION 4.2–5 A **basis** for an n-dimensional vector space is a set of n n-dimensional vectors $(v_1, \ldots, v_n)$ that are linearly independent. If $(v_1, \ldots, v_n)$ is a basis for V, then every vector in V can be expressed as a linear combination of the basis vectors.

Clearly the unit vectors $u_1, \ldots, u_n$ form a basis for an n-dimensional vector space.

DEFINITION 4.2–6 An **identity matrix** is a square $(n \times n)$ matrix, where

(1) $$a_{ii} = 1, i = 1, 2, \ldots, n \text{ and}$$

(2) $$a_{ij} = 0, i \neq j$$

DEFINITION 4.2–7 A matrix A is **nonsingular** if there exists a matrix A^{-1} (A **inverse**) such that

$$AA^{-1} = A^{-1}A = I = \begin{bmatrix} 1 & 0 & \cdots & 0 \\ 0 & 1 & & \\ \vdots & & \ddots & \vdots \\ 0 & & \cdots & 1 \end{bmatrix}$$

an **identity** matrix.

Theorem 4.2–2 If A is nonsingular (i.e., if it has an inverse) then it is square and its inverse, A^{-1}, is unique.

PROOF $A^{-1}A = I$ and I is $n \times n$. If A is $m \times n$, then A^{-1} must be $n \times m$ to be conformable for multiplication with A. But $AA^{-1} = I$, so I must also be $m \times m$. Hence $m = n$; that is, A is square.

Suppose A^{-1} and A^* are inverses of A. Then

$$A^*(AA^{-1}) = A^*I = A^*$$

and $(A^*A)A^{-1} = IA^{-1} = A^{-1}$, or $A^* = A^{-1}$. QED

DEFINITION 4.2–8 The **row (column) rank** of an $m \times n$ matrix A is the number of linearly independent rows (columns) of A.

Theorem 4.2–3 The number of linearly independent rows or columns in an $n \times m$ matrix A is less than or equal to the smaller of m and n. Furthermore, the number of independent rows is equal to the number of independent columns.

PROOF Suppose $n < m$. Then A can be viewed as a collection of m vectors from an n-dimensional vector space. Each vector is a linear combination of the basis vectors $u_1, \ldots, u_n$ for the space. Since the $(n + 1)$st distinct vector in n-dimensional space must be a linear combination of the basis, it follows that the number of independent columns must be less than or equal to n. A similar argument follows for $m < n$.

Suppose that the number of independent columns, r_c, is less than the number of independent rows, r_r, which is less than or equal to both m and n; that is, $r_c < r_r \leq m, n$. This means that we have n vectors in r_c-dimensional vector space. Consequently, any row in r_c-dimensional vector space is a linear combination of r_c unit vectors, and therefore the greatest number of independent vectors is r_c, that is, $r_c = r_r$.   QED

Theorem 4.2–3 further asserts that one can establish the rank of a matrix by performing "elementary row operations" on the rows of A until A contains only zeros or ones.

DEFINITION 4.2–9   An **elementary row operation** is either (1) multiplying a row by a scalar or (2) adding a scalar product of one row to another.

In other words, elementary row operations reduce A to a matrix with all off-diagonal elements zero and all diagonal elements either one or zero.

The following illustrates this technique. Let

$$A = \begin{bmatrix} a_{11} & a_{12} & \cdots & a_{1n} \\ a_{21} & & \cdots & \\ \vdots & & & \vdots \\ a_{m1} & & \cdots & a_{mn} \end{bmatrix}$$

Divide the first row by a_{11}. Then we have

$$A = \begin{bmatrix} 1 & \dfrac{a_{12}}{a_{11}} & \cdots & \dfrac{a_{1n}}{a_{11}} \\ a_{21} & & \cdots & \\ \vdots & & & \vdots \\ a_{m1} & & & a_{mn} \end{bmatrix}$$

Subtract a_{21} times the first row from the second row to obtain

$$A'' = \begin{bmatrix} 1 & \dfrac{a_{12}}{a_{11}} & \cdots & \dfrac{a_{1n}}{a_{11}} \\ 0 & a_{22} - \dfrac{a_{21}a_{12}}{a_{11}} & \cdots & a_{2n} - \dfrac{a_{22}a_{1n}}{a_{11}} \\ a_{m1} & & \cdots & a_{mn} \end{bmatrix}$$

Follow the same procedure on the other rows to obtain the unit vector in the first column:

$$A^* = \begin{bmatrix} 1 & a_{12}^* & \cdots & a_{1n}^* \\ 0 & a_{22}^* & & \\ \vdots & \vdots & & \vdots \\ 0 & a_{m2}^* & \cdots & a_{mn}^* \end{bmatrix}$$

The next step is to divide the second row by a_{22}^*, that is, post multiply A^* by $[0, 1/a_{22}, 0, \ldots, 0]$. Next reduce the second element in every row (except row 2) to zero as we did for column 1. Continuing this process until all elements of A are zero or one, the result will be

$$\begin{bmatrix} 1 & 0 & 0 & \cdots & 0 & 0 & \cdots & 0 \\ 0 & 1 & 0 & \cdots & 0 & & & \\ 0 & 0 & 1 & \cdots & 0 & & & \vdots \\ & & & \cdots & 1 & 0 & \cdots & 0 \\ 0 & 0 & & \cdots & 0 & 0 & \cdots & 0 \\ 0 & 0 & & \cdots & 0 & 0 & \cdots & 0 \end{bmatrix}$$

or more simply expressed as

$$\begin{bmatrix} I_r & | & 0 \\ \hline 0 & | & 0 \end{bmatrix}$$

the **partitional form** of the matrix, where I_r is an $r \times r$ identity matrix.[7]

Thus r is the rank of the matrix. Essentially, what we have done is to work backwards, going from m points in r-dimensional vector space to the basis for that space, the r unit vectors.

Example 3.   Find the elementary row operations that reduce

$$A = \begin{bmatrix} 2 & 3 \\ 4 & 1 \\ 3 & 0 \end{bmatrix}$$

to a matrix with only ones or zeros. First divide row 1 by 2 to obtain:

$$\begin{bmatrix} 1 & \frac{3}{2} \\ 4 & 1 \\ 3 & 0 \end{bmatrix}$$

[7] What are the dimensions of the three zero matrices in $\begin{bmatrix} I_r & | & 0 \\ \hline 0 & | & 0 \end{bmatrix}$?

Next, subtracting 4 times the first row from the second and 3 times the first from the third will give:

$$\begin{bmatrix} 1 & \frac{3}{2} \\ 0 & -5 \\ 0 & -\frac{9}{2} \end{bmatrix}$$

We now have the first column with zeros everywhere except the first element. The next step is to divide the second row by -5. Then add $-\frac{3}{2}$ of the second row to the first, and finally add $\frac{9}{2}$ of the second row to the third. This will give

$$\begin{bmatrix} 1 & 0 \\ 0 & 1 \\ 0 & 0 \end{bmatrix}$$

Thus the rank of A is 2, which agrees with the assertion that for three vectors in two-dimensional space, one must be a linear combination of the other two.

Each elementary row operation on A is equivalent to premultiplying A by a matrix. For example, if

$$A = \begin{bmatrix} 2 & 3 \\ 4 & 1 \\ 3 & 0 \end{bmatrix}$$

then the elementary row operation of dividing the first row by 2 is equal to premultiplying A by

$$e_1 = \begin{bmatrix} \frac{1}{2} & 0 & 0 \\ 0 & 1 & 0 \\ 0 & 0 & 1 \end{bmatrix}$$

as the reader can verify.

Example 4.   In Example 3 six elementary row operations resulted in

$$\begin{bmatrix} 1 & 0 \\ 0 & 1 \\ 0 & 0 \end{bmatrix}$$

Thus we could find equivalent matrices e_1, e_2, e_3, e_4, e_5, and e_6 such that

$$e_6 e_5 e_4 e_3 e_2 e_1 A = \begin{bmatrix} 1 & 0 \\ 0 & 1 \\ 0 & 0 \end{bmatrix}$$

Verify that

$$e_2 = \begin{bmatrix} 1 & 0 & 0 \\ -4 & 1 & 0 \\ 0 & 0 & 1 \end{bmatrix}$$

is the second elementary row operation of Example 3 and find e_3.

Elementary row operations are one method by which the inverse of a matrix can be found, providing it exists. This is proved in the following theorem and illustrated in Example 5, which follows.

Theorem 4.2–4   A nonsingular, square ($n \times n$) matrix A has a rank of n. And conversely, if A has rank n it is nonsingular.

PROOF   A complete proof would require too much space, but we shall outline it. First, suppose A has rank n. Then by a series of elementary row operations A can be reduced to the $n \times n$ identity matrix I_n as outlined above. In other words, if we let e_j be the jth elementary row operation (either dividing a row by its element on the diagonal or subtracting a multiple of one row from another), then we have $e_k \cdot e_{k-1} \cdots e_1 A = I_n$. Therefore, performing the same elementary row operations on I_n gives the inverse of A; that is, $e_k \cdot e_{k-1} \cdots e_1 I_n = A^{-1}$.

Suppose A is nonsingular. Then A^{-1} exists and $A^{-1}A = I_n$. If we think of A^{-1} as a series of elementary row operations and further, since there are no other elementary row operations that reduce I_n to having rows with all zeros, the rank of A must be n.

In practice the matrices corresponding to the elementary row operations do not have to be found. By simply performing the same operation on the identity matrix as is performed on A, one will have A^{-1} when A is reduced to I. This is illustrated in Example 5.

Example 5.   Find the inverse of

$$A = \begin{bmatrix} 2 & 3 \\ 4 & 1 \end{bmatrix}$$

by elementary row operations. The technique is to begin with A and I side by side and, as elementary row operations are performed on A, to perform the same operations on I.
Thus

$$A = \begin{bmatrix} 2 & 3 \\ 4 & 1 \end{bmatrix} \qquad \begin{bmatrix} 1 & 0 \\ 0 & 1 \end{bmatrix} = I$$

First elementary row operation:

$$\begin{bmatrix} 1 & \frac{3}{2} \\ 4 & 1 \end{bmatrix} \qquad \begin{bmatrix} \frac{1}{2} & 0 \\ 0 & 1 \end{bmatrix}$$

Second elementary row operation:

$$\begin{bmatrix} 1 & \frac{3}{2} \\ 0 & -5 \end{bmatrix} \qquad \begin{bmatrix} \frac{1}{2} & 0 \\ -2 & 1 \end{bmatrix}$$

Third elementary row operation:

$$\begin{bmatrix} 1 & \frac{3}{2} \\ 0 & 1 \end{bmatrix} \qquad \begin{bmatrix} \frac{1}{2} & 0 \\ \frac{2}{5} & -\frac{1}{5} \end{bmatrix}$$

Fourth elementary row operation:

$$I = \begin{bmatrix} 1 & 0 \\ 0 & 1 \end{bmatrix} \qquad \begin{bmatrix} -\frac{1}{10} & \frac{3}{10} \\ \frac{2}{5} & -\frac{1}{5} \end{bmatrix} = A^{-1}$$

Since A has now been transformed into I, what is on the right side should be A^{-1}. And it is, since

$$\begin{bmatrix} 2 & 3 \\ 4 & 1 \end{bmatrix} \begin{bmatrix} -\frac{1}{10} & \frac{3}{10} \\ \frac{2}{5} & -\frac{1}{5} \end{bmatrix} = \begin{bmatrix} 1 & 0 \\ 0 & 1 \end{bmatrix}$$

The equivalent elementary row operation matrices for this example are

$$e_4 e_3 e_2 e_1 = \begin{bmatrix} 1 & -\frac{3}{2} \\ 0 & 1 \end{bmatrix} \begin{bmatrix} 1 & 0 \\ 0 & -\frac{1}{5} \end{bmatrix} \begin{bmatrix} 1 & 0 \\ -4 & 1 \end{bmatrix} \begin{bmatrix} \frac{1}{2} & 0 \\ 0 & 1 \end{bmatrix} = \begin{bmatrix} -\frac{1}{10} & \frac{3}{10} \\ \frac{2}{5} & -\frac{1}{5} \end{bmatrix} = A^{-1}$$

The reader should verify that the product $e_4 e_3 e_2 e_1$ gives A^{-1}. Check to see if $A^{-1}A$ also equals I.

Often people have assumed that if the number of equations were equal to the number of unknowns there was a solution. However, only if these equations are linearly independent is this true. From Theorem 4.2–3, if $A(n \times n)$ has a rank of n in the system of linear equations $Ax = b$, then A^{-1} exists and $A^{-1}Ax = A^{-1}b$. Thus $Ix = x = A^{-1}b$ is the solution.

Suppose that A is $m \times n$, $m < n$, that is, the number of equations is less than the number of unknowns, then the system is said to be **underdetermined** and will usually possess an infinite number of possible solutions. On the other hand, if $m > n$, the system of equations is said to be **overdetermined**. In general such a system will not possess a solution. However, if n of the equations are linearly independent and the $m - n$ remaining equations are linearly dependent on the first n equations, the system will possess a solution. More formally, we have the following theorem.

Theorem 4.2–5 Given the system of equations $Ax = b$. Let $C = [A, b]$, the $m \times (n + 1)$ "augmented" matrix composed of A and b.[8] Then $Ax = b$ has a solution if and only if the rank of C equals the rank of A.

[8]
$$C = \begin{bmatrix} a_{11} & a_{12} & \cdots & a_{1n} & b_1 \\ a_{21} & a_{22} & \cdots & a_{2n} & b_2 \\ \vdots & & & & \\ a_{m1} & a_{m2} & \cdots & a_{mn} & b_m \end{bmatrix}$$

PROOF   Let r be the rank of C, and let r^* be the rank of A. Since C is composed of A and another column only, $r \geq r^*$. Suppose $r > r^*$, then for r rows of A one can find constants $k_1, \ldots, k_r$ such that $k_1 a_1 + \cdots + k_r a_r = 0$. Since $Ax = b$, it follows that $k_1 a_1 x + k_2 a_2 x + \cdots + k_r a_r x = k_1 b_1 + \cdots k_r b_r = 0$ if and only if all $b_i = 0$, since not all $k_i = 0$. However, if all $b_i = 0$, then the rank of C must be equal to the rank of A. Therefore $r = r^*$ for the system to be consistent.   QED

The foregoing theorem is useful in an overdetermined system. Clearly, if A is $n \times n$, then the rank of the augmented $n \times n + 1$ matrix will be less than or equal to n. In fact, it will be equal to the rank of A. However, if we have a system with more equations than unknowns, the system may or may not have a solution.

Example 6.   Consider the following set of equations:

$$2x_1 + 3x_2 = 4$$

$$x_1 + 2x_2 = 3$$

$$3x_1 + 5x_2 = 8$$

The rank of

$$A = \begin{bmatrix} 2 & 3 \\ 1 & 2 \\ 3 & 5 \end{bmatrix}$$

is 2. However, the rank of

$$[A, b] = \begin{bmatrix} 2 & 3 & 4 \\ 1 & 2 & 3 \\ 3 & 5 & 8 \end{bmatrix}$$

is 3, and the system is inconsistent. Alternatively, if b were

$$\begin{pmatrix} 4 \\ 3 \\ 7 \end{pmatrix}$$

so that $[A, b]$ were

$$\begin{bmatrix} 2 & 3 & 4 \\ 1 & 2 & 3 \\ 3 & 5 & 7 \end{bmatrix}$$

then the rank of $[A, b]$ would also be 2 and there would be a unique solution, *viz.*, $x_1 = -1$ and $x_2 = 2$.

Problems

4.2–1   Write the following equation system in matrix form. What are the dimensions of each of the matrices?

$$5x_1 + 3x_2 - x_4 = 7$$

$$2x_2 - 3x_3 + x_5 = 2$$

$$-3x_1 - x_4 + 2x_5 = 3$$

$$-4x_2 + x_3 + x_4 = 1$$

4.2–2   Calculate the transpose of each of the matrices in Problem 4.2–1.

4.2–3   Given the following matrices:

$$A = \begin{bmatrix} 1 & 2 & 3 \\ 4 & 5 & 0 \end{bmatrix} \quad B = \begin{bmatrix} -1 & 0 & 8 \\ 7 & 3 & 2 \end{bmatrix} \quad C = \begin{bmatrix} -2 & 1 & -1 \\ 3 & 4 & 1 \\ 5 & -2 & 0 \end{bmatrix}$$

$$D = \begin{bmatrix} 1 & 1 & 1 \\ 0 & 5 & 2 \\ 7 & -1 & 4 \end{bmatrix} \quad E = \begin{bmatrix} 2 & -1 \\ 3 & 8 \\ 4 & 5 \end{bmatrix}$$

(a) Find $A + B$ and $C + D$.

(b) Find the scalar product $-2E$.

(c) Find the product CD. Which other pairs of matrices are conformable for multiplication?

(d) Calculate $B - A$. How would you define matrix subtraction in general, using only the operations given in Definition 4.2–3?

(e) Calculate AE and use it to illustrate that matrix multiplication is associative.

(f) Calculate EA, thus illustrating that matrix multiplication in general is not commutative. Construct an example where $AB = BA$ for two arbitrary matrices A and B.

(g) Find AE by the methods of Definition 4.2–2 and part (a) of Theorem 4.2–1.

(h) Construct an example from the matrices given to illustrate that matrix multiplication and addition are associative.

4.2–4   Which of the following sets of vectors are linearly independent? Dependent? Verify your conclusions.

(a) $(1, -1, 3)$
$(5, -2, 3)$
$(-3, 3, -9)$

(b) $(1, 1, 1)$
$(-1, 2, 0)$
$(4, -1, 2)$

(c) $(2, 1, -1)$
$(5, 4, -2)$
$(-3, -3, 1)$

(d) $(2, -3, 1)$
$(1, -1, 0)$
$(2, -4, 2)$

4.2–5 Find which of the following matrices are nonsingular by calculating their row and column rank.

$$A = \begin{bmatrix} 2 & 3 & 4 \\ 5 & 6 & 7 \end{bmatrix} \qquad B = \begin{bmatrix} 2 & 2 & 2 \\ 0 & 1 & 0 \\ -1 & 0 & -1 \end{bmatrix}$$

$$C = \begin{bmatrix} 2 & -1 & 1 \\ 3 & 5 & -7 \\ 4 & 0 & 1 \end{bmatrix} \qquad D = \begin{bmatrix} 1 & 5 \\ 2 & 7 \end{bmatrix}$$

42.–6 Calculate the inverse for the nonsingular matrices in Problem 4.2–5 using elementary row operations. Verify your answers.

4.2–7 Find the solution to the following system of equations by finding the inverse of the coefficient matrix, using elementary column operations.

$$x_1 + 2x_2 + x_4 = 5$$
$$2x_1 + x_2 + 2x_3 + x_4 = 2$$
$$x_2 + 3x_3 - 2x_4 = -3$$
$$-3x_1 + 7x_3 - 2x_4 = -1$$

4.2–8 Find the solution to $Ax = b$, where

$$A = \begin{bmatrix} 1 & -2 & 0 \\ 2 & 1 & 2 \\ 3 & 0 & 5 \\ 0 & 1 & 3 \end{bmatrix} \qquad x = \begin{bmatrix} x_1 \\ x_2 \\ x_3 \end{bmatrix} \qquad b = \begin{bmatrix} 1 \\ -2 \\ 6 \\ 7 \end{bmatrix}$$

4.3 DETERMINANTS AND CRAMER'S RULE

If A is an $n \times n$ matrix and a_{ij} is an element of A, then a product formed by taking one element from each row would be $a_{1j}a_{2k}a_{3l} \cdots a_{ng}$. If none of the second subscripts are equal, we have a **permutation** of the integers $(1, \ldots, n)$. For example, $(n, n-1, n-2, \ldots, 1)$ is one such permutation. The number of **transpositions** required to change a permutation back to its original order is the number of times required to restore the permutation to its original order by interchanging two integers at a time. Although this number is not unique, it will either be *always* odd or even. That is, if a given permutation requires an even number of transpositions to restore it to its original order, it cannot be restored by an odd number.

DEFINITION 4.3–1 The **determinant** of a matrix A, denoted $|A|$, is equal to the sum of *all* possible products, $(-1)^t a_{1j}a_{2k} \cdots a_{ng}$, where the series of second subscripts is a permutation of $(1, \ldots, n)$, including the natural order $(1, \ldots, n)$, and t is the number of transpositions necessary to return the permutation to its natural order.

Example 1.   Consider the 2×2 matrix

$$A = \begin{bmatrix} 1 & 2 \\ 3 & 4 \end{bmatrix}$$

The number of products in the determinant is $n! = n(n-1)(n-2)\cdots 1$, or $2! = (2)(1) = 2$ in this case. That is, there are only two ways of arranging $(1, 2)$: either $(1, 2)$ or $(2, 1)$. For the first permutation t is even ($t = 0$ or $t = 2$, etc.) and in the second case t is odd. Therefore

$$|A| = a_{11}a_{22} - a_{21}a_{12} = 1 \cdot 4 - 3 \cdot 2 = -2$$

If $n = 3$, then the number of terms in the determinant is $3! = 3 \cdot 2 \cdot 1 = 6$. These products are shown in Figure 4.3–1 by arrows: The solid arrows connect the elements with positive signs; the dashed arrows connect the elements with negative signs.

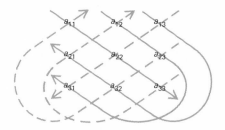

Figure 4.3–1 $|A|$ *for* $n = 3$

$$|A| = a_{11}a_{22}a_{33} + a_{12}a_{23}a_{31} + a_{13}a_{21}a_{32} - a_{13}a_{22}a_{31} - a_{11}a_{23}a_{32}$$
$$- a_{12}a_{21}a_{23}$$

Example 2.   Verify that the determinant of

$$\begin{bmatrix} 0 & 1 & 3 \\ 1 & 2 & 0 \\ 1 & 0 & 5 \end{bmatrix}$$

is equal to -11.

The following theorem points out some special properties of determinants. Often the evaluation of a determinant can be simplified by using parts of Theorem 4.3–1.

Theorem 4.3–1

(a) Interchanging one row with another (one column with another) changes the sign of the determinant of a matrix.

(b) Multiplying a row (column) by a scalar multiplies the value of the determinant by that scalar.

(c) Multiplying all rows (columns) by a scalar, k, multiplies the value of the determinant by k^n in an $n \times n$ matrix.

(d) If one row (column) is replaced by another row (column) of the matrix, then the value of the determinant is zero.

PROOF   The theorem is easily proved by referring to the definition of a determinant. In (a) we have $|A| = \sum^{n!} (-1)^t a_{1_g} a_{2j} \cdots a_{nk}$, and if we interchange any one row with another to give A^*, the number of transpositions, t, associated with each product will change by one. Hence, all terms that were positive will now be negative and vice versa. Thus $|A^*| = -|A|$.   QED

For (b), letting A^* be the matrix A with one row or column (e.g., row 1) multiplied by a scalar, k, then

$$|A^*| = \sum^{n!} (-1)^t k a_{1_g} a_{2j} \cdots a_{nk} = k \sum^{n!} (-1)^t a_{1_g} a_{2j} \cdots a_{nk} = k|A|.   \text{QED}$$

In (c), $|A^*| = \sum^{n!} (-1)^t k a_{1_g} k a_{2j} \cdots k a_{nk} = k^n \sum^{n!} (-1)^t a_{1_g} a_{2j} \cdots a_{nk} = k^n |A|$.   QED

To prove (d), simply note that the matrix now has rank less than n, since one row (column) is equal to another and hence $|A^*| = 0$.   QED

Example 3.   Let

$$A = \begin{bmatrix} 1 & 3 & 2 \\ 0 & 5 & 4 \\ 1 & 1 & 2 \end{bmatrix}$$

$$|A| = 10 + 12 + 0 - 10 - 4 - 0 = 8$$

If

$$A^* = \begin{bmatrix} 3 & 9 & 6 \\ 0 & 5 & 4 \\ 1 & 1 & 2 \end{bmatrix}$$

then, since A^* is A with row 1 multiplied by 3, $|A^*| = 24$, which the reader may easily verify.

Suppose we wish to find $|A^*|$, where

$$A^* = \begin{bmatrix} 0.01 & 0.03 & 0.02 \\ 0.00 & 0.05 & 0.04 \\ 0.01 & 0.01 & 0.02 \end{bmatrix}$$

Then

$$|A^*| = \left(\frac{1}{100}\right)^3 |A| = \frac{8}{10^6} = 0.000008$$

Verify that $|A^*| = -8$, if A^* is matrix A with the first and third columns interchanged.

By deleting rows and columns of an $m \times n$ matrix, one is left with a **submatrix** of the original matrix. For example, for

$$A = \begin{bmatrix} 3 & 2 \\ 1 & 17 \end{bmatrix}$$

any one of the elements is a submatrix of A. Similarly, A is a submatrix of B:

$$B = \begin{bmatrix} 1 & 8 & -5 \\ 4 & 3 & 2 \\ 7 & 1 & 17 \end{bmatrix}$$

Corresponding to submatrices, we also have minor determinants.

DEFINITION 4.3–2   A **minor determinant** of a matrix A is the determinant of a submatrix of A with rows and columns deleted. The minor determinant of A with the ith row and jth column deleted is denoted as

$$|A_{ij}| = \begin{vmatrix} a_{11} & \cdots & a_{1j-1} & a_{1j+1} & \cdots & a_{1n} \\ \vdots & & & & & \\ a_{i-11} & \cdots & a_{i-1j-1} & a_{i-1j+1} & \cdots & a_{i-1n} \\ a_{i+11} & \cdots & a_{i+1j-1} & a_{i+1j+1} & \cdots & a_{i+1n} \\ \vdots & & & & & \\ a_{m1} & \cdots & a_{mj-1} & a_{mj+1} & \cdots & a_{mn} \end{vmatrix}$$

A **principal minor determinant** (principal minor) of A is a determinant of a submatrix of A where the same numbered rows and columns are deleted. The **order** of the determinant is the number of remaining rows and columns.

Example 4.   The principal minor determinants of a 3×3 matrix are six in number: the three elements a_{11}, a_{22}, a_{33}, and three 2×2 determinants formed by dropping rows and columns 1, 2, and 3, respectively.

Another principal use of determinants is in finding the inverse of a matrix. This alternative method to elementary row operations is best explained with use of the definitions of a cofactor and an adjoint matrix.

DEFINITION 4.3–3   A **cofactor,** c_{ij}, of an $n \times n$ matrix A is the determinant of the matrix A, with the ith row and jth column deleted, multiplied by $(-1)^{i+j}$. That is, $c_{ij} = (-1)^{i+j}|A_{ij}|$.

DEFINITION 4.3–4   The **adjoint** of a matrix A, denoted (adj. A), is the transpose of the matrix of cofactors of A.

Since a determinant is equal to the sum of products of all possible permutations, suppose we select from each product a term a_{hi}, where h is constant and the i's form a permutation. This is equivalent to taking out a row. From the definition of a cofactor it follows that

$$|A| = a_{h1}c_{h1} + a_{h2}c_{h2} + \cdots + a_{hn}c_{hn}$$

This is called expanding a determinant by its cofactors.

Example 5.   Consider the matrix

$$A = \begin{bmatrix} 1 & 2 & 3 \\ 4 & 5 & 6 \\ 7 & 8 & 9 \end{bmatrix}$$

Then

$$|A| = 1 \cdot 5 \cdot 9 + 2 \cdot 6 \cdot 7 + 3 \cdot 8 \cdot 4 - 3 \cdot 5 \cdot 6 - 6 \cdot 8 \cdot 1 - 9 \cdot 4 \cdot 2$$

Alternatively, we may find $|A|$ by expanding it by its cofactors. To do this we may use any row or column of A. For example, if we take out the first row and multiply each element in that row by its cofactor, we shall also have the determinant of A. That is, $|A| = 1c_{11} + 2c_{22} + 3c_{33}$, where $c_{11} = 5 \cdot 9 - 6 \cdot 8$, $c_{22} = -4 \cdot 9 + 6 \cdot 7$, and $c_{33} = 4 \cdot 8 - 7 \cdot 5$. Therefore $|A| = 1(5 \cdot 9 - 6 \cdot 8) + 2(4 \cdot 9 - 6 \cdot 7) + 3(4 \cdot 8 - 7 \cdot 5)$.

Since we can expand a determinant by its cofactors, this implies that in practice we never have to find all possible products ($n!$) as stated in Definition 4.3–1. Rather we can expand an $n \times n$ matrix by its cofactors, and expand each of these in turn by their cofactors, and so on until we have a 2×2 determinant to evaluate.

We can now state the following theorem, which gives both necessary and sufficient conditions for a matrix to be nonsingular and the determinant method for finding its inverse.

Theorem 4.3–2   A square matrix A is nonsingular if and only if $|A| \neq 0$. If A is nonsingular,

$$A^{-1} = \frac{1}{|A|} \, (\text{adj. } A)$$

SKETCH OF THE PROOF[9]   The theorem is easily shown to be true by noting that since $|A| = a_{h1}c_{h1} + \cdots + a_{hn}c_{hn}$, the product of A and its adjoint, by definition, gives a diagonal matrix with the determinant in the diagonal and zeros elsewhere; that is,

$$A(\text{adj. } A) = |A|I$$

---

[9] See Perlis (1958) for a complete proof.

Rearranging, since $|A|$ is a scalar, we have

$$\frac{A(\text{adj. } A)}{|A|} = I$$

if and only if $|A|$ is not zero; hence

$$A^{-1} = \frac{1}{|A|} (\text{adj. } A) \qquad \text{QED}$$

Cramer's rule is an adaptation of Theorem 4.3–2 and is very useful in solving for specific unknowns in a system of simultaneous equations. Consider a system of n linear equations and n unknowns $(x_1, \ldots, x_n) = x$ and b an n-dimensional vector of constants. If A is a nonsingular coefficient matrix, then $x = A^{-1}b$. By Theorem 4.3–2 this can be written as

$$x = \frac{1}{|A|} (\text{adj. } A)b$$

which becomes, for any x_i,

$$x_i = \frac{b_1 c_{1i} + b_2 c_{2i} + \cdots + b_n c_{ni}}{|A|}$$

However, the numerator in the above equation is the determinant of the A matrix with the ith column deleted and replaced by the column of constants. That is, if we let

$$A = \begin{bmatrix} a_{11} & \cdots & a_{1n} \\ \vdots & & \\ a_{n1} & \cdots & a_{nn} \end{bmatrix}$$

$$A_i = \begin{bmatrix} a_{11} & \cdots & b_1 & \cdots & a_{1n} \\ & & b_2 & & \\ \vdots & & \vdots & & \vdots \\ a_{n1} & \cdots & b_n & \cdots & a_{nn} \end{bmatrix}$$

Then for the system

$$Ax = b$$

$$x_i = \frac{|A_i|}{|A|}$$

Thus, we have formally:

DEFINITION 4.3–5 **Cramer's Rule** Given a system of n linearly independent equations of n unknowns. To find the value of x_i, replace the ith column of the coefficient matrix with the column of constants to form the matrix A_i. Then

$$x_i = \frac{|A_i|}{|A|}$$

Example 6. Linear Market Model Suppose in a three-commodity world we have the following linear excess demand equations:

$$E_1 = 9 - p_1 + 2p_2 + 3p_3$$

$$E_2 = 20 - p_1 - 4p_2 + p_3$$

$$E_3 = 25 - 2p_1 + p_2 - 3p_3$$

Since the equilibrium condition is that $E_1 = E_2 = E_3 = 0$, this system can be rewritten in matrix form as

$$\begin{bmatrix} 1 & -2 & -3 \\ 1 & 4 & -1 \\ 2 & -1 & 3 \end{bmatrix} \begin{bmatrix} p_1 \\ p_2 \\ p_3 \end{bmatrix} = \begin{bmatrix} 9 \\ 20 \\ 15 \end{bmatrix}$$

or

$$Ax = b$$

To solve for p_1 by Cramer's rule, replace the first column in A with the vector b to obtain

$$A_1 = \begin{bmatrix} 9 & -2 & -3 \\ 20 & 4 & -1 \\ 25 & -1 & 3 \end{bmatrix}$$

then

$$p_1 = \frac{|A_1|}{|A|} = \frac{108 + 50 + 60 + 300 - 9 + 120}{12 + 4 + 3 + 24 - 1 + 6} = \frac{629}{48} = 13\tfrac{5}{48}$$

Similarly, solving for the remaining equilibrium prices we have

$$p_2 = \frac{|A_2|}{|A|} = \tfrac{85}{48} = 1\tfrac{37}{48} \quad \text{and} \quad p_3 = \frac{|A_3|}{|A|} = \tfrac{9}{48}$$

Problems

4.3–1 Evaluate the determinants of the following matrices.

$$A = \begin{bmatrix} 7 & -2 \\ 3 & 4 \end{bmatrix} \qquad B = \begin{bmatrix} -1 & 1 \\ 3 & -3 \end{bmatrix}$$

$$C = \begin{bmatrix} 1 & 2 & 3 \\ 7 & 6 & 5 \\ 8 & -1 & 10 \end{bmatrix} \qquad D = \begin{bmatrix} -1 & 0 & 2 \\ 4 & 1 & 3 \\ 3 & 1 & 5 \end{bmatrix}$$

4.3–2   Test the matrices in Problem 4.2–5 for nonsingularity by calculating their determinants.

4.3–3   Evaluate the determinant of the following matrix by expansion by cofactors.

$$A = \begin{bmatrix} 1 & 2 & -1 & 0 & 3 \\ 4 & 7 & 0 & 5 & -2 \\ 1 & 0 & 0 & 3 & 4 \\ 0 & 1 & 2 & -2 & 3 \\ 3 & 0 & 7 & -1 & -1 \end{bmatrix}$$

4.3–4   Calculate the inverses of the matrices in Problem 4.2–5 by the adjoint method.

4.3–5   Solve the equation system below by Cramer's rule.

$$3x_1 + 2x_2 - x_3 = 9$$
$$2x_1 - x_2 + 4x_3 = 13$$
$$7x_1 + x_2 - 5x_3 = 12$$

4.4   QUADRATIC FORMS, NEGATIVE AND POSITIVE DEFINITE MATRICES

When specific data is not available for specifying the parameters of equations, an economist often can derive qualitative information from the system. Primarily, the determination of qualitative information is used in comparative static analysis and will be covered in Section 9.5. An example would be the statement that for regular-shaped supply and demand curves, an outward shift in demand will cause price to rise and quantity sold to increase. The qualitative information is $\Delta p > 0$ and $\Delta q > 0$.

Thus it is often of interest to know the sign of a function or system of functions. When a function is quadratic, that is, $\sum_i \sum_j a_{ij} x_i x_j$, it can be written in matrix notation as

$$x'Ax$$

where A is an $n \times n$ matrix and x is an n-dimensional column vector. For example, $f(x) = 5x^2 + 3xy + 7y^2$ can be written as

$$(xy) \begin{bmatrix} 5 & \frac{3}{2} \\ \frac{3}{2} & 7 \end{bmatrix} \begin{pmatrix} x \\ y \end{pmatrix} \quad \text{or} \quad (xy) \begin{bmatrix} 5 & 3 \\ 0 & 7 \end{bmatrix} \begin{pmatrix} x \\ y \end{pmatrix}$$

DEFINITION 4.4–1 A, an $n \times n$ matrix, is
  (1) A **negative** (positive) **quasidefinite matrix** if $x'Ax < 0$ $(x'Ax > 0)$ for any real vector x, where not all $x_i = 0$ for $i = 1, \ldots, n$;

(2) A **negative** (positive) **definite matrix** if A is a symmetric matrix (i.e., $a_{ij} = a_{ji}$) and A is negative (positive) quasidefinite; and

(3) A **negative** (positive) **quasisemidefinite matrix** if $x'Ax \leq 0$ ($x'Ax \geq 0$) for any real vector $x \neq 0$.

From Definition 4.4–1 it follows that if a matrix A is quasidefinite, then $A + A'$ is a definite matrix, and $(A + A')/2$ is also a definite matrix. Consequently, if a function is quadratic it will have a positive sign regardless of the value of the variables if the matrix of coefficients is positive quasidefinite.

The following theorems establish the method for determining whether a matrix is positive (negative) definite and also whether it is a quasidefinite matrix.

Theorem 4.4–1   If an $n \times n$ matrix A is positive definite, then its principal minor determinants (principal minors) are positive.

Although we omit the proof, the following sketch is presented.[10] If A is positive definite then we must have $x'Ax > 0$ for any real x, where not all x_i are zero. Consider any principal submatrix S of A. $x'Sx$ is equivalent to $x'Ax$ if $x_i = 0$ for all the rows and columns deleted from A to get S. Thus if S is a_{ii} (i.e., all rows and columns deleted from A except i), it immediately follows that $a_{ii} > 0$ for all i. Thus all diagonal elements must be positive. Next suppose that some principal minor is negative. By similar, but much more involved, reasoning it can then be shown that one can find an x such that $x'Ax$ is negative.

Theorem 4.4–2   If an $n \times n$ matrix is negative definite, then its principal minors must alternate in sign:

$$a_{ii} < 0, \begin{vmatrix} a_{ii} & a_{ij} \\ a_{ji} & a_{jj} \end{vmatrix} > 0, \ldots$$

In the example above, where $f(x) = 5x^2 + 3xy + 7y^2$,

$$A = \begin{bmatrix} 5 & \frac{3}{2} \\ \frac{3}{2} & 7 \end{bmatrix}$$

A is positive definite, since it is symmetric and its principal minors are positive. Alternatively, $f(x)$ could have been written as

$$(xy) \begin{bmatrix} 5 & 3 \\ 0 & 7 \end{bmatrix} \begin{pmatrix} x \\ y \end{pmatrix} \quad \text{or} \quad (xy)A^* \begin{pmatrix} x \\ y \end{pmatrix}$$

---

[10] Perlis (1958).

$A*$ is a positive quasidefinite matrix. To see this, first find $(A* + A*')/2$ and check its minor determinants.[11]

Problems

4.4–1   Write the following expressions in matrix form:

(a) $x^2 + 3y^2$ (c) $x^2 - 5xy$

(b) $2x^2 - xy + y^2$

4.4–2   Indicate whether the following matrices are definite, quasidefinite, or quasi-semidefinite.

$$A = \begin{bmatrix} 2 & -\frac{1}{2} & -\frac{1}{2} \\ -\frac{1}{2} & 3 & 0 \\ -\frac{1}{2} & 0 & 5 \end{bmatrix} \quad B = \begin{bmatrix} 2 & 2 & 0 \\ 3 & 4 & -1 \\ 2 & 0 & 3 \end{bmatrix}$$

$$C = \begin{bmatrix} -2 & -2.5 & -1 \\ -2.5 & -4 & 0.5 \\ -1 & 0.5 & -3 \end{bmatrix} \quad D = \begin{bmatrix} 2 & 0 & 0 \\ 0 & 3 & 0 \\ 0 & 0 & -1 \end{bmatrix}$$

$$E = \begin{bmatrix} 1 & -\frac{1}{2} \\ \frac{1}{2} & 0 \end{bmatrix}$$

4.4-3   State the following quadratic functions in matrix form and determine if $f(x) < 0, f(x) > 0$, or $f(x) \quad 0$.

(a) $f(x) = x_1^2 - 2x_1x_2 + x_2^2$

(b) $f(x) = 5x_1^2 + 3x_2^2 + 2x_3^2 - x_1x_2 - x_1x_3$

(c) $f(x) = 6x_1^2 + 4x_2^2 + 2x_3^2 - 2x_1x_2 - 4x_1x_3 - 10x_2x_3$

(d) $f(x) = 3x_1^2 + 8x_2^2 - 4x_3^2 + x_1x_2 - x_1x_3 - 8x_2x_3$

(e) $f(x) = 15x_1x_2 + 3x_2x_3 - 3x_1x_3 - 6x_1^2 - 12x_2^2 - 9x_3^2$

4.5   CHARACTERISTIC FUNCTIONS AND CHARACTERISTIC ROOTS OF MATRICES

In this section we present some special properties of matrices.[12] In particular, characteristic roots and characteristic functions are useful concepts for analyzing the properties of square matrices.

---

[11] Negative definite matrices and quadratic forms are used in the second-order conditions for a maximum. This is discussed in detail in Section 5.4. For now, we simply state that for a continuous function, $f(x_1, \ldots, x_n)$, the first-order conditions for a maximum require the first differential to be zero, while the second-order conditions require the second differential to be negative. This is equivalent, in light of Definition 4.4–1, to requiring that the matrix of second partial derivatives, $\partial^2 f/(\partial x_i \ \partial x_j)$ be negative definite.

[12] This will be used in Chapters 9 and 14. This section can be skipped and returned to at that point.

DEFINITION 4.5–1 Associated with every $n \times n$ matrix A there is a matrix

$$[rI - A]$$

that is called the **characteristic matrix** of A. Its determinant $|rI - A| = f(r) = r^n + a_{n-1}r^{n-1} + \cdots + a_0$ is called the **characteristic function** of A and $|rI - A| = f(r) = 0$ is the **characteristic equation** of A. (The reader should satisfy himself that the determinant $|rI - A|$ will be an nth-order polynomial.)

Theorem 4.5–1 Cayley–Hamilton Theorem If A is an $n \times n$ matrix with the characteristic function $f(r) = r^n + a_{n-1}r^{n-1} + \cdots + a_0$, then A, itself, satisfies the characteristic equation; that is,

$$f(A) = A^n + a_{n-1}A^{n-1} + \cdots + a_0I + 0$$

where $A^2 = A \cdot A$, $A^3 = A \cdot A \cdot A$, and so on.

The proof of Theorem 4.5–1 is too detailed to be presented here.[13]
The characteristic equation $f(r) = 0$ can be factored linearly into

$$f(r) = (r - r_1)(r - r_2) \cdots (r - r_n)$$

DEFINITION 4.5–2 The roots $r_1, \ldots, r_n$ of the characteristic equation of an $n \times n$ matrix A are called the **characteristic roots** or **eigenvalues** of A.

Theorem 4.5–2 If there exists a nonsingular matrix T such that $T^{-1}AT = A_T$ (i.e., the matrix A is transformed into A_T by the matrix T) and A_T is a diagonal matrix,

$$A_T = \begin{bmatrix} t_1 & 0 & \cdots & 0 \\ 0 & t_2 & \cdots & 0 \\ \vdots & & & \\ 0 & & \cdots & t_n \end{bmatrix} = \text{diag.} (t_1, \ldots, t_n)$$

then the characteristic roots of A are equal to the diagonal elements of A_T, that is, $(r_1, \ldots, r_n) = (t_1, \ldots, t_n)$.

PROOF First note that the roots of A_T are $(t_1, \ldots, t_n)$. That is, $|rI - A| = (r - t_1) \cdots (r - t_n)$. Next, since $A_T = T^{-1}AT$ and $T^{-1}T = I$, we have $|rI - A_T| = |rT^{-1}T - T^{-1}AT| = |T^{-1}rT - T^{-1}AT|$ since r is a scalar. But $|T^{-1}rT - T^{-1}AT| = |T^{-1}[rI - A]T| = |T^{-1}||rI - A||T| = |rI - A|$, since the determinant of a matrix product is the product of the determinants, and $T^{-1} = 1/|T|$. Therefore $|rI - A_T| = |rI - A|$, and the roots must be equal.   QED

[13] Perlis (1958).

Example 1.   Given

$$A = \begin{bmatrix} 4 & 2 \\ 0 & -24 \end{bmatrix}$$

then

$$\begin{bmatrix} r - 4 & -2 \\ 0 & r + 24 \end{bmatrix}$$

is the characteristic matrix of A. The characteristic function is $f(r) = |rI - A| = r^2 + 20r - 96$. The characteristic equation,

$$r^2 + 20r - 96 = 0$$

can be factored linearly into

$$(r + 24)(r - 4) = 0$$

Thus the roots of the matrix A are -24 and 4. Note that A itself satisfies the characteristic equation:

$$\begin{bmatrix} 4 & 2 \\ 0 & -24 \end{bmatrix}\begin{bmatrix} 4 & 2 \\ 0 & -24 \end{bmatrix} + 20\begin{bmatrix} 4 & 2 \\ 0 & -24 \end{bmatrix} + \begin{bmatrix} -96 & 0 \\ 0 & -96 \end{bmatrix} = \begin{bmatrix} 0 & 0 \\ 0 & 0 \end{bmatrix}$$

$$\begin{bmatrix} 16 & -40 \\ 0 & 576 \end{bmatrix} + \begin{bmatrix} 80 & 40 \\ 0 & -480 \end{bmatrix} + \begin{bmatrix} -96 & 0 \\ 0 & -96 \end{bmatrix} = \begin{bmatrix} 0 & 0 \\ 0 & 0 \end{bmatrix}$$

Finally, let us find a suitable nonsingular matrix T. Since $A_T = T^{-1}AT$, then $TA_T = AT$ or

$$\begin{bmatrix} t_1 & t_2 \\ t_3 & t_4 \end{bmatrix}\begin{bmatrix} 4 & 0 \\ 0 & -24 \end{bmatrix} = \begin{bmatrix} 4 & 2 \\ 0 & -24 \end{bmatrix}\begin{bmatrix} t_1 & t_2 \\ t_3 & t_4 \end{bmatrix}$$

This means

(1) $$4t_1 = 4t_1$$

(2) $$-24t_2 = 4t_2 + 2t_4$$

(3) $$4t_3 = -24t_3$$

(4) $$-24t_4 = -24t_4$$

Equations (1) and (4) put no restrictions on t_1 and t_4, so let $t_1 = 1$ and $t_4 = 1$. Equation (3) requires that $t_3 = 0$ and from (2) we find that $t_2 = -\frac{1}{14}$. Thus

$$T = \begin{bmatrix} 1 & -\frac{1}{14} \\ 0 & 1 \end{bmatrix} \qquad T^{-1} = \begin{bmatrix} 1 & \frac{1}{14} \\ 0 & 1 \end{bmatrix} \qquad T^{-1}AT = \begin{bmatrix} 4 & 0 \\ 0 & -24 \end{bmatrix}$$

DEFINITION 4.5–3   A **characteristic vector**, x, for a square matrix A is a nonzero column vector such that $Ax = rx$, where r is a scalar.

Theorem 4.5–3   For a square matrix A and a scalar r, there exists a characteristic vector corresponding to r (i.e., there exists a vector x such that $Ax = rx$) if and only if r is a characteristic root of A.

PROOF   Let x be a nontrivial solution to the system $|A - rI|x = 0$, or equivalently, to the system $|rI - A|x = 0$. Therefore, by Theorems 4.2–4 and 4.2–5, $|rI - A| = 0$, and r must be a characteristic root of A.   QED

There are many areas of economic analysis, especially in the area of linear aggregate economic models and input–output models, where the elements of the matrix A are nonnegative (i.e., A is a *nonnegative matrix*). To round out the discussion of matrix algebra we present the following theorems for non-negative square matrices due to Debreu and Herstein (1953). Most of the proofs will be omitted since many require the use of fixed-point theorems, which are discussed in Chapter 9.

DEFINITION 4.5–4   An $n \times n$ matrix A is said to be **indecomposable** if no permutation matrix π (π is a permutation of the columns of I, an identity matrix) exists such that

$$\pi A \pi^{-1} = \begin{bmatrix} A_{11} & A_{12} \\ 0 & A_{21} \end{bmatrix}$$

where A_{11} and A_{21} are square.

Since $\pi A \pi^{-1}$ is equivalent to permuting equivalent columns and rows of A, Definition 4.5–4 says that for an indecomposable matrix A it is not possible to rearrange the columns and concomitantly rearrange the rows to get a rectangle of zeros in the bottom left-hand corner. (What would a permutation of a diagonal matrix do? Is a diagonal matrix indecomposable?)

Example 2.   The matrix

$$\begin{bmatrix} 10 & 0 & 9 & 0 \\ 6 & 2 & 5 & 2 \\ 8 & 0 & 7 & 0 \\ 4 & 2 & 3 & 2 \end{bmatrix}$$

is decomposable, because interchanging rows 1 and 4 and thus also inter-changing columns 1 and 4 results in

$$\begin{bmatrix} 2 & 2 & 3 & 4 \\ 2 & 2 & 5 & 6 \\ 0 & 0 & 7 & 8 \\ 0 & 0 & 9 & 10 \end{bmatrix}$$

Verify that π for this interchange is

$$\begin{bmatrix} 0 & 0 & 0 & 1 \\ 0 & 1 & 0 & 0 \\ 0 & 0 & 1 & 0 \\ 1 & 0 & 0 & 0 \end{bmatrix}$$

Theorem 4.5–4 If A is an indecomposable, nonnegative matrix, then:
(a) A has a characteristic root $r > 0$;
(b) r is such that its characteristic vector x_0 is positive (all elements of x_0 are greater than zero);
(c) for any other characteristic root r_i of A, $|r_i| \le r$;
(d) r increases when any element of A increases; and
(e) r is a simple root (i.e., not a complex number).

The proof is omitted except to note that (a) is proven by use of Brouwer's fixed-point theorem, which is developed in Section 9.3. Parts (b)–(e) are more or less straightforward. For details the interested reader is referred to Debreu and Herstein (1953).

Theorem 4.5–5 If A is a nonnegative square matrix, then:
(a) A has a characteristic root $r \ge 0$;
(b) r's associated characteristic vector x_0 is positive;
(c) if r_i is any characteristic root of A, $|r_i| \le r$; and
(d) r does not decrease when an element of A increases.

One should note the differences between Theorems 4.5–4 and 4.5–5. Theorem 4.5–4 applies to an $m \times n$ *indecomposable* matrix, Theorem 4.5–5 to any nonnegative *square* matrix. The similarity between the two follows from the observation that any square matrix A can be transformed by permutation matrices to

$$\pi A \pi^{-1} = \begin{bmatrix} A_1 & & & \\ & A_2 & & * \\ & 0 & \ddots & \\ & & & A_H \end{bmatrix}$$

where every A_h along the diagonal is either square and indecomposable or a single element. Therefore the properties of A are easily derived from A_h, since $|rI - A| = |rI - A_1| \cdot |rI - A_2| \cdots |rI - A_H|$.

Theorem 4.5–6 If $Ax \le sx$ for a square ($n \times n$) matrix A, a strictly positive vector x, and a scalar s, then for r, the maximum nonnegative characteristic root of A, $r \le s$. Further, if $x \ge 0$ (x is nonnegative) and if $Ax < sx$, then $r < s$. Also, the theorem holds for all inequality signs reversed.

PROOF Let $x_0 \ge 0$ be a characteristic vector of A associated with r, that is, $Ax_0 = rx_0$. Then, since $Ax \le sx$ for $x > 0$, multiplying by x_0' we have $x_0'Ax \le sx_0'x$, or $rx_0'x \le sx_0'x$. Since $x_0'x > 0$, then $r \le s$. The proofs for the remaining portions follow a similar argument.

Theorem 4.5–7 For the equation $[sI - A]x = y$, where A is a nonnegative square matrix, x and y are n-dimensional vectors, and s is a scalar,

$[sI - A]^{-1} \geq 0$ if and only if $s > r$, the maximum nonnegative character-istic root of A.

PROOF   For the if portion we shall show that $y \geq 0$ implies that $x \geq 0$, and since $x = [sI - A]^{-1}y$, then $[sI - A]^{-1} \geq 0$. Assume that $y \geq 0$ and $s > r$, and suppose that x has some negative elements. Then, by identical permutations of the rows and columns of A we can find

$$\begin{bmatrix} sI - A_1 & -A_{12} \\ -A_{21} & sI - A_2 \end{bmatrix} \begin{bmatrix} -x_1 \\ x_2 \end{bmatrix} = y$$

where $x_1 > 0$, $x_2 \geq 0$. Therefore, since $y \geq 0$, $-[sI - A_1]x_1 - A_{12}x_2 \geq 0$, and therefore $-[sI - A_1]x_1 \geq 0$, or $A_1 x_1 \geq sI$; hence, by Theorem 4.5–6, the maximum root of A_1^*, r_1, must be greater than s. But this contradicts the assumption that $r \geq r_1$ and $s > r$.

For the only if portion, since $[sI - A]^{-1} \geq 0$, there exists for $y > 0$ an $x \geq 0$. Therefore, from $sx - Ax = y$, it follows that $Ax < sx$ and, again by Theorem 4.5–6, $r < s$.   QED

If the A matrix is indecomposable, then the above theorem can be strength-ened.

Theorem 4.5–8   If A is a nonnegative, indecomposable square matrix, then for the equation $[sI - A]x = y$, $[sI - A]^{-1} > 0$ if and only if $s > r$, the maximum characteristic root of A.

The proof follows the argument of Theorem 4.5–4 by showing that $y \geq 0$ implies $x > 0$.

Example 3.   Suppose we have a simple economy with three industries, each of which have constant returns to scale. The technological relations are described in the following matrix, a Leontief input–output table[14]:

	coal	steel	trucks
coal	0.2	0.8	0
steel	0.2	0.1	0.6
trucks	0.1	0.1	0

The matrix is read as follows. For every ton of coal produced, the follow-ing inputs are needed: 0.2 ton of coal, 0.2 ton of steel, and 0.1 of a truck. 0.8 ton of coal is needed in making a ton of steel. Truck production requires

[14] Leontief (1951).

no coal. Steel production requires 10% of its own output, 0.8 ton of coal, and 0.1 of a truck. 0.6 ton of steel is used in every truck produced.

Thus, if we let A be this technological matrix, x be a vector of total output, and y be the vector of final outputs, we have the relation

(1) $$x - Ax = y$$

or

$$[I - A]x = y$$

Thus, for a given vector of final demands we can solve for the total outputs in each industry by

$$x = [I - A]^{-1}y$$

Since all outputs are nonnegative, and if we then let $x' = (1, 1, 1)$, we have

$$Ax = \begin{pmatrix} 1 \\ 0.9 \\ 0.2 \end{pmatrix}$$

Thus, solving for the scalar s in Theorem 4.5–6 we see that the maximum characteristic root of A is 1. Solving for the characteristic roots, we have

$$f(r) = |rI - A| = 0$$

or $r = 0.6$, which was guaranteed to be positive by Theorem 4.5–5. By Theorem 4.5–7, $[I - A]^{-1} \geq 0$ since $1 > r = 0.6$. A check of the matrix A shows that it is indecomposable and thus, by Theorem 4.5–8, $[I - A]^{-1} > 0$. Thus any positive vector of final demands may be produced as long as other primary factors (e.g., labor) are not used up.

Next suppose that each industry were taxed at 20% of output. Thus (1) becomes

$$0.8x - Ax = y$$

or

$$[sI - A]x = y$$

where $s = 0.8$. Since $0.8 > 0.6$, $[sI - A]^{-1} > 0$ by Theorem 4.5–8.

Another method of finding $[I - A]^{-1}$ is as follows. Suppose we multiply $[I - A]$ by $I + A + A^2 + \cdots + A^n$. This gives

$$[I - A][I + A + A^2 + \cdots + A^n] = I - A^{n+1}$$

If in the limit as n approaches infinity, A^{n+1} approaches the null matrix (matrix of all zeros), then we may approximate $[I - A]^{-1}$ by $[I + A + A^2 + \cdots + A^n]$ as closely as desired by choosing n large enough. A^{n+1} will approach the null matrix for a sufficiently large n if the column sum, $\sum_{i=1}^{n} a_{ij} < 1$ for all $j = 1, \ldots, n$.[15]

[15] See Waugh (1950).

The following three theorems are also useful in input–output type models.

Theorem 4.5–9[16]   The principal minor determinants of $[sI - A]$ of orders $1, \ldots, n$ are all positive if and only if $s > r$.

Theorem 4.5–10   If the matrix A is $n \times n$ and strictly positive ($a_{ij} > 0$, for all i and j), then for $[sI - A]$, if $s > \sum_j a_{ij}$ for all i, the cofactor of a diagonal element of $[sI - A]$ is greater than the cofactor of any off-diagonal element; that is, if c_{ij} is the cofactor of $[sI - A]$, then $c_{ii} > c_{ij}$ for all $i \neq j$.

Example 4.   Let A be the following matrix:

$$A = \begin{bmatrix} 0.2 & 0.3 & 0.3 & 0.1 \\ 0.1 & 0.1 & 0.3 & 0.1 \\ 0.3 & 0.2 & 0.1 & 0.2 \\ 0.5 & 0.2 & 0.1 & 0.1 \end{bmatrix}$$

Immediately we can say the following:
(a) the maximum characteristic root of A is 0.9 (by Theorem 4.5–6);
(b) if $s > 0.9$, then $[sI - A]^{-1} > 0$ (by Theorem 4.5–8);
(c) the principal minors of $[sI - A]$ will all be positive (by Theorem 4.5–9); and
(d) if $s > 0.9$, then the cofactor of any diagonal element is greater than that of any off-diagonal element (by Theorem 4.5–10).

Problems

4.5–1   Given $A = \begin{bmatrix} 1 & 0 \\ 3 & 1 \end{bmatrix}$

(a) Find the characteristic matrix.
(b) Find the characteristic function.
(c) Find the characteristic equation.
(d) Use your results to verify the Cayley–Hamilton theorem.
(e) Find the eigenvalues of A.
(f) Find a matrix T such that $T^{-1}AT = A_T$ as in Theorem 4.5–2, if possible.
(g) Find a characteristic vector for A.

4.5–2   In Example 3 of this section, how many tons of coal, tons of steel, and trucks would have to be produced to get one truck for final demand? How much would each industry have to produce with no taxes in order to meet the final demands of 1 ton of coal, 1 ton of steel, and 1 truck?

4.5–3   Assume the following matrix is an input–output matrix:

$$A = \begin{bmatrix} 0.2 & 0.3 & 0.3 \\ 0.1 & 0.15 & 0.4 \\ 0.2 & 0.2 & 0.45 \end{bmatrix}$$

[16] The proofs of Theorems 4.5–9 and 4.5–10 are in Debreu and Herstein (1953).

(a) Find $[sI - A]^{-1}$ for $s = 0.95$.

(b) What is the level of each industry for a final demand vector of $y = (1, 2, 0)$?

4.5-4   If the amount of labor used in the ith industry in Example 3 is a_{oi} and $a_{o1} = 0.3$ (man-years per ton of coal), $a_{o2} = 0.4$, and $a_{o3} = 0.5$, how many man-years will be required to produce a final output of $y = (1, 1, 1)$? What will be the maximum output produced in a ratio of $1:1:1$ if the amount of labor is 150 man-years.

4.5-5   Find the approximate value of $[I - A]^{-1}$ by $I + A + A^2 + \cdots + A^n$ for $n = 3$ for the matrices in (a)–(e).

(a)
$$A = \begin{bmatrix} 0.2 & 0.4 \\ 0.3 & 0.5 \end{bmatrix}$$

(d)
$$A = \begin{bmatrix} 0.1 & 0.3 & 0.5 \\ 0.4 & 0 & 0.1 \\ 0.2 & 0.4 & 0 \end{bmatrix}$$

(b)
$$A = \begin{bmatrix} 0.3 & 0.8 \\ 0.1 & 0 \end{bmatrix}$$

(e)
$$A = \begin{bmatrix} 0.1 & 0 & 0.2 \\ 0 & 0.1 & 0 \\ 0.6 & 0.4 & 0.7 \end{bmatrix}$$

(c)
$$A = \begin{bmatrix} 0.5 & 0.1 \\ 0.4 & 0.2 \end{bmatrix}$$

References

1. DEBREU, G., and I. N. HERSTEIN (1953), "Nonnegative Square Matrices," *Econometrica*, **21**:597–607.

2. HADLEY, G. (1961), *Linear Algebra*, Reading, Mass.: Addison-Wesley.

3. KEMENY, J. G., J. L. SNELL, and G. L. THOMPSON (1957), *Introduction to Finite Mathematics*, Englewood Cliffs, N.J.: Prentice-Hall.

4. LEONTIEF, WASSILY (1951), *The Structure of the American Economy*, 1919–1939, 2nd ed., New York: Oxford University Press.

5. PERLIS, SAM (1958), *Theory of Matrices*, Reading, Mass.: Addison-Wesley.

6. SCHKADE, L. L. (1967), *Vectors and Matrices*, Columbus, Ohio: Charles E. Merrill.

7. THOMAS, GEORGE (1968), *Calculus and Analytical Geometry*, 4th ed., Reading, Mass.: Addison-Wesley.

8. WAUGH, FREDERICK (1950), "Inversion of the Leontief Matrix by a Power Series," *Econometrica*, **18**:142–154.

Chapter 5

Differential Calculus

The next two chapters cover the techniques of the ordinary calculus. This chapter develops the tenets of differential calculus, primarily differentiation and the theory of extreme values.

5.1 LIMITS, CONTINUITY, AND DERIVATIVES

Given that y is a function of x, $y = f(x)$. The derivative of y with respect to x, written either as dy/dx or $f'(x)$, is defined as

(1)
$$f'(x) = \lim_{\Delta x \to 0} \frac{f(x + \Delta x) - f(x)}{\Delta x}$$

Before reviewing the definition of the ordinary (as opposed to partial) derivative, it is necessary to discuss the concept of a limit, upon which (1) is based.

DEFINITION 5.1–1 A function f defined on the domain $x_1 < a < x_2$ approaches the **limit** L as x approaches a [written $\lim_{x \to a} f(x) = L$] if, for any positive number ε, there exists a positive number δ such that the functional values $f(x)$ are within an ε distance of L whenever x is within a δ distance of a, $x \neq a$. Thus $|f(x) - L| < \varepsilon$ when $|x - a| < \delta$.

Figure 5.1–1 illustrates Definition 5.1–1. The reader should convince himself that for any positive ε it is possible to find a positive δ such that when x is within δ of a, $f(x)$ is within ε of $f(a)$. In this case $\lim_{x \to a} f(x) = f(a)$.

In Figure 5.1–2, suppose we choose L as a candidate for $\lim_{x \to a} f(x)$. First let $\varepsilon = \varepsilon_1$. Corresponding to ε_1, δ_1 fulfills the requirement for L to be the limit of $f(x)$ as $x \to a$. (Why?) But for L to be the limit, the definition must hold not just for certain values of ε, but for all positive values of ε no matter how small. As the reader can verify, for $\varepsilon = \varepsilon_2$, no δ can be found that satisfies the definition. Thus, $\lim_{x \to a} f(x)$ does not exist in this case.

In Definition 5.1–1 we allow x to approach a from either side—that is, from values greater than a and from values less than a. It is possible to define other limit concepts if we restrict the side from which x approaches a.

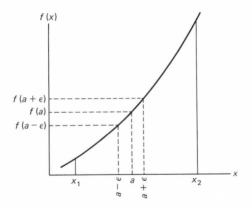

Figure 5.1–1 *Illustration of Definition 5.1–1.*

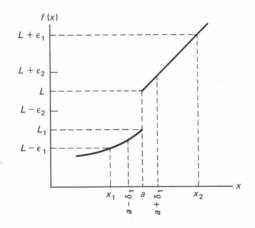

Figure 5.1–2 *Limit does not exist.*

DEFINITION 5.1–2   Given that y is a function of x defined on the domain $x_1 \leq x \leq a$. f approaches the **left side limit** L as x approaches a from the left (from values less than a), written $\lim_{x \to a^-} f(x) = L$, if for all positive numbers ε, there exists a positive number δ such that the functional values $f(x)$ are within ε of L whenever x is within δ of a. Thus

$$|L - f(x)| < \varepsilon \qquad \text{when } a - x < \delta$$

DEFINITION 5.1–3   Given that y is a function of x defined on the domain $a \leq x \leq x_2$. f approaches the **right side limit** L as x approaches a from the right (from values greater than a), written $\lim_{x \to a^+} f(x) = L$, if for all positive numbers ε, there exists a positive number δ, such that the functional values $f(x)$ are within ε of L whenever x is within δ of a. Thus

$$|f(x) - L| < \varepsilon \qquad \text{when } x - a < \delta$$

In Figure 5.1–2 $\lim_{x \to a^+} f(x) = L$ and $\lim_{x \to a^-} f(x) = L_1$.

Theorem 5.1–1 $\lim_{x \to a} f(x) = L$ if and only if $\lim_{x \to a^-} f(x) = \lim_{x \to a^+} f(x) = L$.

The proof of this theorem follows directly from Definitions 5.1–1, 5.1–2, and 5.1–3.

The following theorem describes the most fundamental properties of limits.

Theorem 5.1–2 Given that $\lim_{x \to a} f(x) = L_f$ and $\lim_{x \to a} g(x) = L_g$, then:

(a) $\displaystyle\lim_{x \to a} [f(x) + g(x)] = \lim_{x \to a} f(x) + \lim_{x \to a} g(x) = L_f + L_g$;

(b) $\displaystyle\lim_{x \to a} [f(x)g(x)] = \lim_{x \to a} f(x) \lim_{x \to a} g(x) = L_f L_g$;

(c) $\displaystyle\lim_{x \to a} \left[\frac{f(x)}{g(x)}\right] = \frac{\lim_{x \to a} f(x)}{\lim_{x \to a} g(x)} = \frac{L_f}{L_g}, \ L_g \neq 0$;

(d) $\displaystyle\lim_{x \to a} k = k$, where k is any constant; and

(e) $\displaystyle\lim_{x \to a} [kf(x)] = k \lim_{x \to a} f(x) = kL_f$.

Example 1.

(a) $\displaystyle\lim_{x \to 5} (3x^3 + 5x^2 - 2x + 3)$

$$= \lim_{x \to 5} 3x^3 + \lim_{x \to 5} 5x^2 + \lim_{x \to 5} -2x + \lim_{x \to 5} 3$$

$$= 3 \lim_{x \to 5} x^3 + 5 \lim_{x \to 5} x^2 - 2 \lim_{x \to 5} x + 3$$

$$= 3 \lim_{x \to 5} x \lim_{x \to 5} x \lim_{x \to 5} x + 5 \lim_{x \to 5} x \lim_{x \to 5} x - 2 \lim_{x \to 5} x + 3$$

$$= 3(125) + 5(25) - 2(5) + 3 = 493$$

(b) $\displaystyle\lim_{x \to 1} \left(\frac{x^2 - 1}{x - 1}\right) = \lim_{x \to 1} \left[\frac{(x - 1)(x + 1)}{x - 1}\right] = \lim_{x \to 1} (x + 1) = 2$

(c) $\displaystyle\lim_{x \to 3} \left(\frac{x^2 + 2x + 7}{x + 3}\right) = \frac{\lim_{x \to 3} (x^2 + 2x + 7)}{\lim_{x \to 3} (x + 3)} = \frac{22}{6} = \frac{11}{3}$

(d) $\displaystyle\lim_{t \to \infty} \left(\frac{t + 1}{t^2 + 1}\right)$

In such problems a convenient trick is to let $t = 1/h$ and find

$$\lim_{h \to 0} \frac{(1/h) + 1}{(1/h)^2 + 1}$$

Simplifying, we have

$$\lim_{h \to 0} \frac{(1 + h)/h}{(1 + h^2)/h^2} \quad \text{or} \quad \lim_{h \to 0} \frac{(1 + h)h}{1 + h^2} = \frac{0}{1} = 0$$

The concept of a limit leads directly to the notion of a continuous function.

DEFINITION 5.1–4 $f(x)$ **is continuous at a point** $x = a$ if and only if $\lim_{x \to a} f(x) = f(a)$.

A function for which Definition 5.1–4 holds for all values of a in its domain is called **everywhere continuous.** Piecewise-continuous functions are those that are continuous for certain ranges of x and discontinuous for a finite number of values of x. Note that under the definition functions that have "kinks" or "corners" are continuous. See Figure 5.1–3. Here $\lim_{x \to a^-} f(x) = f(a) = \lim_{x \to a^+} f(x)$. Thus $\lim_{x \to a} f(x) = f(a)$ and $f(x)$ is continuous at $x = a$. The function in Figure 5.1–2 is not continuous at $x = a$. It is, however, continuous on the right and continuous on the left at $x = a$. How are these types of continuity defined?

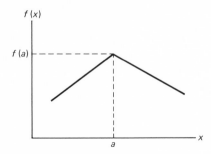

Figure 5.1–3 *A continuous function.*

We now return to the definition of the derivative given in Equation (1) on page 111. Consider Figure 5.1–4. The slope of the line joining points P and Q is

$$\frac{y_2 - y_1}{x_2 - x_1} = \frac{\Delta y}{\Delta x}$$

If we allow point Q to move along the curve closer and closer to P, the ratio $\Delta y/\Delta x$ approaches a limit. This limit is the slope of the curve at P. Changing the form in which the coordinates of P and Q are written to $P = [x_1, f(x_1)]$

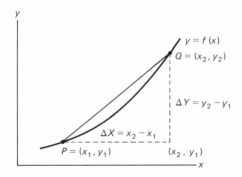

Figure 5.1–4   *The slope of* $y = f(x)$ *between* (x_1, y_1) *and* (x_2, y_2).

and $Q = [x_1 + \Delta x, f(x_1 + \Delta x)]$, we can write $\Delta y = f(x_1 + \Delta x) - f(x_1)$
so that the slope of the curve at P is given by

$$\lim_{\Delta x \to 0} \frac{\Delta y}{\Delta x} = \lim_{\Delta x \to 0} \frac{f(x_1 + \Delta x) - f(x_1)}{\Delta x}$$

This is, of course, the definition of the derivative—the measure of the instantaneous rate of change of y with respect to changes in x.

This definition of the derivative can be used actually to calculate dy/dx for specific functions. Suppose $y = 3x^3 - 2x + x^{-2}$. Then

$$\frac{dy}{dx} = \lim_{\Delta x \to 0} \left[\frac{3(x + \Delta x)^3 - 2(x + \Delta x) + (x + \Delta x)^{-2} - 3x^3 + 2x - x^{-2}}{\Delta x} \right]$$

Simplifying,

$$\frac{dy}{dx} = \lim_{\Delta x \to 0} \left[\frac{3(3x^2 \Delta x + 3x \Delta x^2 + \Delta x^3) - 2 \Delta x}{\Delta x} \right]$$

$$+ \lim_{\Delta x \to 0} \left[\frac{-2x \Delta x - \Delta x^2}{\Delta x x^2 (x^2 + 2x \Delta x + \Delta x^2)} \right]$$

$$= \lim_{\Delta x \to 0} 3(3x^2 + 3x \Delta x + \Delta x^2) - 2 + \lim_{\Delta x \to 0} \frac{-2x - \Delta x}{x^2 (x^2 + 2x \Delta x + \Delta x^2)}$$

$$= 9x^2 - 2 - 2x^{-3}$$

Note that the division by Δx was performed before Δx was allowed to approach zero.

A differentiable function is one whose derivative exists at all points on the function. This is stated more formally in Definition 5.1–5.

DEFINITION 5.1–5   A function $y = f(x)$ is **differentiable** if $\lim_{\Delta x \to 0} \Delta y / \Delta x$ exists for all values of x in the domain of the function.

The properties of differentiability and continuity are closely related, since both are based on the existence of certain limits. Given a function that is differentiable at $x = a$. Then we know that

$$f'(a) \equiv \lim_{x \to a} \frac{f(x) - f(a)}{x - a}$$

(See Figure 5.1–5.) Since $x - a \neq 0$ (why?) we can write

(2)
$$f(x) - f(a) = \frac{f(x) - f(a)}{x - a}(x - a)$$

Taking the limit as $x \to a$ on both sides of (2), we obtain

$$\lim_{x \to a} f(x) - \lim_{x \to a} f(a) = \lim_{x \to a} \frac{f(x) - f(a)}{x - a} \lim_{x \to a}(x - a)$$

or

$$\lim_{x \to a} f(x) - f(a) = f'(a)[\lim_{x \to a} x - \lim_{x \to a} a]$$

or

$$\lim_{x \to a} f(x) - f(a) = f'(a)[a - a]$$

Thus, since the right side is zero,

$$\lim_{x \to a} f(x) = f(a)$$

which is the requirement for f to be continuous at $x = a$. Thus differentiability implies continuity. The converse of this statement is not true, as the reader may verify since the continuous function in Figure 5.1–3 is not differentiable at $x = a$. (Why not?)

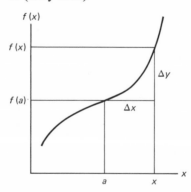

Figure 5.1–5 $y = f(x)$ *differentiable at* $x = a$.

Theorem 5.1–3 describes the most fundamental rules of differentiation for a function of one variable.

Theorem 5.1–3   Given that $y = f(x)$ is a differentiable function. Then if
(a) $f(x) = k$ (a constant), $f'(x) = 0$;
(b) $f(x) = x^n, f'(x) = nx^{n-1}$;
(c) $f(x) = kx^n, f'(x) = knx^{n-1}$;
(d) $f(x) = e^x, f'(x) = e^x$;
(e) $f(x) = e^{kx}, f'(x) = ke^{kx}$;
(f) $f(x) = k^x, f'(x) = k^x \ln k$;
(g) $f(x) = \log_a x, f'(x) = x^{-1} \log_a e$;
(h) $f(x) = \ln x, f'(x) = x^{-1}$;
(i) $f(x) = \sin x, f'(x) = \cos x$;
(j) $f(x) = \cos x, f'(x) = -\sin x$;
(k) $f(x) = \tan x, f'(x) = \sec^2 x$;
(l) $f(x) = \cot x, f'(x) = -\csc^2 x$;
(m) $f(x) = \sec x, f'(x) = \tan x \sec x$; and
(n) $f(x) = \csc x, f'(x) = -\cot x \csc x$.[1]

No attempt will be made to prove all the rules in Theorem 5.1–3. The same general technique is used in all the proofs and centers around the definition of a derivative. The proofs of parts (b) and (h) are presented as examples.
Proof of b when n is an integer:

$$\frac{dy}{dx} \equiv \lim_{\Delta x \to 0} \frac{f(x + \Delta x) - f(x)}{\Delta x} = \lim_{\Delta x \to 0} \frac{(x + \Delta x)^n - x^n}{\Delta x}$$

$$= \lim_{\Delta x \to 0} \frac{\binom{n}{0} x^n + \binom{n}{1} x^{n-1} \Delta x + \binom{n}{2} x^{n-2} \Delta x^2 + \cdots + \binom{n}{n} \Delta x^n - x^n}{\Delta x}{}^{[2]}$$

$$= \lim_{\Delta x \to 0} \left[\binom{n}{1} x^{n-1} + \binom{n}{2} x^{n-2} \Delta x + \cdots + \binom{n}{n} \Delta x^{n-1} \right]$$

$$= \binom{n}{1} x^{n-1} = nx^{n-1}$$

---

[1] Many other rules could be given. For a more complete list, see The Chemical Rubber Co., *Mathematical Tables from the Handbook of Chemistry and Physics*, Cleveland, 1964.

[2] The terms in parentheses are simply the binomial coefficients, where

$$\binom{n}{m} = \frac{n(n - 1)(n - 2) \cdots (n - m + 1)}{m(m - 1)(m - 2) \cdots (3)(2)(1)}$$

Note that $\binom{n}{0}$ is, by definition, 1. $\binom{n}{1}$ by the above definition is simply $\frac{n}{1} = n$.

Proof of h:

$$\frac{dy}{dx} = \lim_{\Delta x \to 0} \frac{f(x + \Delta x) - f(x)}{\Delta x} = \lim_{\Delta x \to 0} \frac{\ln(x + \Delta x) - \ln x}{\Delta x}$$

$$= \lim_{\Delta x \to 0} \frac{1}{\Delta x} \left[\ln \left(\frac{x + \Delta x}{x} \right) \right] = \lim_{\Delta x \to 0} \frac{1}{x} \frac{x}{\Delta x} \ln \left(1 + \frac{\Delta x}{x} \right)$$

$$= \lim_{\Delta x \to 0} \frac{1}{x} \ln \left(1 + \frac{\Delta x}{x} \right)^{x/\Delta x} = \lim_{n \to \infty} \frac{1}{x} \ln \left(1 + \frac{1}{n} \right)^{n}$$

This step follows since $n = x/\Delta x$ and $n \to \infty$ as $\Delta x \to 0$. e is by definition equal to $\lim_{n \to \infty} (1 + 1/n)^n$. Thus

$$\lim_{n \to \infty} \frac{1}{x} \ln \left(1 + \frac{1}{n} \right)^{n} = \frac{1}{x} \ln e$$

By definition $\ln e = 1$. Thus $dy/dx = 1/x$. The reader not familiar with the logarithmic operations used in the proof should consult any standard calculus book.[3]

The following theorems are often useful in evaluating limits of the quotient of two functions:

Theorem 5.1–4 *l'Hôpital's Rule 1* If $f(a) = g(a) = 0$ and if $\lim_{x \to a} f'(x)/g'(x)$ exists, then

$$\lim_{x \to a} \frac{f(x)}{g(x)} = \lim_{x \to a} \frac{f'(x)}{g'(x)}$$

Theorem 5.1–5 *l'Hôpital's Rule 2* If $f(a) = g(a) = \infty$ and if $\lim_{x \to a} f'(x)/g'(x)$ exists, then

$$\lim_{x \to a} \frac{f(x)}{g(x)} = \lim_{x \to a} \frac{f'(x)}{g'(x)}$$

For proofs of l'Hôpital's rules, see Widder (1961), pp. 260–265.

Example 2. Find $\lim_{x \to \infty} (x^2 + x)/3x^2$. This is an indeterminate form ∞/∞. By Theorem 5.1–4, $\lim_{x \to \infty} (x^2 + x)/3x^2 = \lim_{x \to \infty} (2x + 1)/6x$, which is still in the form ∞/∞. Applying l'Hôpital's rule again, we have $\lim_{x \to \infty} (2x + 1)/6x = \lim_{x \to \infty} 2/6 = 1/3$.

Example 3. Find $\lim_{x \to 1} (\ln x)/(x - 1)$. This is in the indeterminate form $0/0$. By Theorem 5.1–3, we have

$$\lim_{x \to 1} \frac{\ln x}{x - 1} = \lim_{x \to 1} \frac{1/x}{1} = 1$$

[3] Thomas (1968).

Theorem 5.1–3 applies only in cases involving one function. Theorem 5.1–6 applies when more than one function is involved.

Theorem 5.1–6   Given $f_1, f_2, \ldots, f_n$ are differentiable functions of x. Then:
(a) (Sum–difference rule)

$$\frac{d}{dx}(f_1 \pm f_2 \pm \cdots \pm f_n) = \frac{d}{dx}f_1 \pm \frac{d}{dx}f_2 \pm \cdots \pm \frac{d}{dx}f_n$$

(b) (Quotient rule)

$$\frac{d}{dx}\left(\frac{f_1}{f_2}\right) = \frac{f_2\,(d/dx)f_1 - f_1\,(d/dx)f_2}{f_2^2}$$

(c) (Product rule)

$$\frac{d}{dx}(f_1 f_2) = f_1\frac{d}{dx}f_2 + f_2\frac{d}{dx}f_1$$

PROOF   The proof of part (a) of the theorem follows directly from Theorem 5.1–2(a). For part (b) of the theorem,

$$\frac{d}{dx}\left(\frac{f_1}{f_2}\right) \equiv \lim_{\Delta x \to 0} \frac{f_1(x + \Delta x)/f_2(x + \Delta x) - f_1(x)/f_2(x)}{\Delta x}$$

$$= \lim_{\Delta x \to 0} \frac{f_1(x + \Delta x)f_2(x) - f_1(x)f_2(x + \Delta x)}{f_2(x + \Delta x)f_2(x)}\frac{1}{\Delta x}$$

Now, add and subtract $f_1(x)f_2(x)$ to the numerator:

$$= \lim_{\Delta x \to 0}\left(\frac{1}{\Delta x}\right)\frac{f_1(x + \Delta x)f_2(x) - f_1(x)f_2(x) - f_1(x)f_2(x + \Delta x) + f_1(x)f_2(x)}{f_2(x + \Delta x)f_2(x)}$$

$$= \lim_{\Delta x \to 0}\frac{1}{f_2(x + \Delta x)f_2(x)}\left\{f_2(x)\left[\frac{f_1(x + \Delta x) - f_1(x)}{\Delta x}\right]\right.$$

$$\left. - f_1(x)\left[\frac{f_2(x + \Delta x) - f_2(x)}{\Delta x}\right]\right\}$$

$$= \lim_{\Delta x \to 0}\frac{1}{f_2(x + \Delta x)f_2(x)}\left\{\lim_{\Delta x \to 0}f_2(x)\lim_{\Delta x \to 0}\left[\frac{f_1(x + \Delta x) - f_1(x)}{\Delta x}\right]\right.$$

$$\left. - \lim_{\Delta x \to 0}f_1(x)\lim_{\Delta x \to 0}\left[\frac{f_2(x + \Delta x) - f_2(x)}{\Delta x}\right]\right\}$$

$$= \frac{1}{f_2^2}\left(f_2\frac{df_1}{dx} - f_1\frac{df_2}{dx}\right)$$

The proof of part (c) of the theorem is left as an exercise. The "trick" involved is again adding and subtracting the appropriate term to the numerator of $\Delta y/\Delta x$.

Example 4.

(a) $y = x^3 - 3x^2 + 4x + 3x^{-4}$

$$\frac{dy}{dx} = 3x^2 - 6x + 4 - 12x^{-5} \qquad \text{[Theorems 5.1–3(b) and 5.1–6(a)]}$$

(b) $y = (3x^2 + 5)(\sin x)$

$$\frac{dy}{dx} = 6x \sin x + (3x^2 + 5) \cos x \qquad \text{[Theorem 5.1–6(b)]}$$

(c) $y = \dfrac{e^x}{\sin x}$

$$\frac{dy}{dx} = \frac{(\sin x)e^x - e^x \cos^x}{(\sin x)^2} \qquad \text{[Theorem 5.1–6(c)]}$$

Consider the following: $y = f(x)$ and $x = g(z)$. Both dy/dx and dx/dz can be found through the techniques described above. The two functions, f and g, also establish a functional relationship between y and z. Theorem 5.1–7 describes how to find dy/dz.

Theorem 5.1–7   Chain Rule   Given that $y = f(x)$ and $x = g(z)$ are differentiable functions of x and z, respectively, then

$$\frac{dy}{dz} \equiv \lim_{\Delta z \to 0} \frac{\Delta y}{\Delta z} \equiv \lim_{\Delta z \to 0} \frac{f[g(z + \Delta z)] - f[g(z)]}{\Delta z} = \frac{dy}{dx}\frac{dx}{dz}$$

In general, if $y = f_1(x_1)$, $x_1 = f_2(x_2), \ldots, x_{n-1} = f_n(x_n)$, then $dy/dx_i = f_1' f_2' \cdots f_i'$ for all $i \le n$.

PROOF

$$\lim_{\Delta z \to 0} \frac{\Delta y}{\Delta z} = \lim_{\Delta z \to 0} \frac{\Delta y}{\Delta x}\frac{\Delta x}{\Delta z} = \lim_{\Delta z \to 0} \frac{\Delta y}{\Delta x} \lim_{\Delta z \to 0} \frac{\Delta x}{\Delta z}$$

But $\Delta z \to 0$ implies that $\Delta x \to 0$ so

$$\lim_{\Delta z \to 0} \frac{\Delta y}{\Delta x} = \lim_{\Delta x \to 0} \frac{\Delta y}{\Delta x}$$

Then, by the definition of a derivative,

$$\lim_{\Delta x \to 0} \frac{\Delta y}{\Delta x} \lim_{\Delta z \to 0} \frac{\Delta x}{\Delta z} = \frac{dy}{dx}\frac{dx}{dy} \qquad \text{QED}$$

The chain rule appeals easily to one's intuition. The effect of a change in z on y (dy/dz) depends first on its effect on x (dx/dz) and then on the effect of that change in x on y (dy/dx).

Example 5. If $y = x^3 - 3x^2 + 4$ and $x = 2(z - 5)^{1/3}$, find dy/dz. $dy/dx = 3x^2 - 6x$ and $dx/dz = \frac{2}{3}(z - 5)^{-2/3}$, so $dy/dz = (3x^2 - 6x)\frac{2}{3}(z - 5)^{-2/3}$, or, in terms of z only, $dy/dz = [3(2[z - 5])^{2/3} - 12[z - 5]^{1/3}]\frac{3}{2}(z - 5)^{2/3}$.

Such problems can also be solved by first substituting and then performing the differentiation.

Example 6. $y = 3x^{-1} + 2x$ and $x = 3z^2$. Then $y = 3/3z^2 + 6z^2 = z^{-2} + 6z^2$. $dy/dz = -2z^{-3} + 12z$. Applying the chain rule, $dy/dx = -3x^{-2} + 2$, and $dx/dz = 6z$. Thus $dy/dz = 6z(-3x^{-2} + 2) = 6z(-3/9z^4 + 2) = -2z^{-3} + 12z$.

Often we are given an equation in implicit form to differentiate. It may be difficult or impossible to write the equation in explicit form to fit the differentiation rules given above. Theorem 5.1–8 describes the process of implicit differentiation.

Theorem 5.1–8 *Implicit Differentiation* Given $F(x, y) = 0$, an implicit function of x and y. To find dy/dx simply treat y as an unknown function of x and differentiate F with respect to x, applying the rules developed above.

Example 7. If $x^3 - 2x^2y^2 + y^4 - 5 = 0$, find dy/dx. For this relation, y cannot be solved for explicitly in terms of x, so implicit differentiation must be used.

Differentiating with respect to x:

$$\frac{d(x^3)}{dx} + \frac{d(-2x^2y^2)}{dx} + \frac{d(y^4)}{dx} + \frac{d(-5)}{dx} = 0$$

or

$$3x^2 - 2x^2\frac{d(y^2)}{dx} + \frac{y^2 d(-2x^2)}{dx} + 4y^3\frac{dy}{dx} = 0$$

or

$$3x^2 - 4x^2y\frac{dy}{dx} - 4xy^2 + 4y^3\frac{dy}{dx} = 0$$

Solving for dy/dx we obtain

$$\frac{dy}{dx} = \frac{4xy^2 - 3x^2}{4(y^3 - x^2y)} \quad \text{for} \quad 4(y^3 - x^2y) \neq 0$$

Example 8. $x^2 + y^3 - 3 = 0$. dy/dx can be found by expressing y as an explicit function of x: $y = (3 - x^2)^{1/3}$ so that

$$\frac{dy}{dx} = -\frac{2}{3}x(3 - x^2)^{-2/3}$$

Differentiating the equation implicitly, we obtain

$$2x + 3y^2 \frac{dy}{dx} = 0 \quad \text{or} \quad \frac{dy}{dx} = -\frac{2x}{3y^2}$$

But, since $y = (3 - x^2)^{1/3}$, $y^2 = (3 - x^2)^{2/3}$ and the same answer is obtained.

As the examples illustrate, the derivative of a function is itself a function derived from the original function. Hence the term derivative. This derived function can in turn be differentiated, leading to the concepts of second-, third-, and higher-order derivatives.

DEFINITION 5.1–6   (a) The **second derivative** of y with respect to x, denoted as d^2y/dx^2 or as $f''(x)$, is equal to

$$\lim_{\Delta x \to 0} \frac{f'(x + \Delta x) - f'(x)}{\Delta x}$$

provided this limit exists.

(b) The **nth derivative** of y with respect to x, d^ny/dx^n or $f^{(n)}(x)$, is equal to

$$\lim_{\Delta x \to 0} \frac{f^{(n-1)}(x + \Delta x) - f^{(n-1)}(x)}{\Delta x}$$

provided this limit exists.

Obviously, the rules for finding first-order derivatives also apply to finding second- and higher-order derivatives, since higher-order derivatives are simply derivatives of functions that have been derived in a specified manner from initial functions.

Example 9.   Find the first-, second-, and higher-order derivatives of $y = x^4 - 3x^2 + 2x$.

$$\frac{dy}{dx} = f'(x) = 4x^3 - 6x + 2$$

$$\frac{d^2y}{dx^2} = \frac{d}{dx}\left(\frac{dy}{dx}\right) = \frac{d}{dx}(4x^3 - 6x + 2) = 12x^2 - 6$$

$$\frac{d^3y}{dx^3} = f'''(x) = 24x$$

$$\frac{d^4y}{dx^4} = 24$$

$$f^{(5)} = f^{(6)} = \cdots = f^{(n)} = \cdots = 0$$

All derivatives of order 5 and higher are zero for this function. A given function may have an infinite number of nonzero derivatives. Consider, for example, $y = \sin x$ or $y = x^{-1}$.

Just as the first derivative is a measure of the rate of change of the original function, the second derivative measures the rate of change (slope) of the (first) derived function. The second derivative thus is a measure of the rate of change of the rate of change of the original function, if $y = f(x)$ is a twice-differentiable function (both f' and f'' exist). Table 5.1–1 shows various combinations of signs for $f'(x)$ and $f''(x)$ and the implication for the shape of the graph of $f(x)$. Figure 5.1–6 illustrates these four cases. Second- and higher-order derivatives also play an important part in the theories of constrained and unconstrained extrema. (See Section 5.4).

Table 5.1–1

	$f'(x)$	$f''(x)$	$f(x)$
(a)	>0	>0	Increasing at increasing rate
(b)	>0	<0	Increasing at decreasing rate
(c)	<0	<0	Decreasing at increasing rate
(d)	<0	>0	Decreasing at decreasing rate

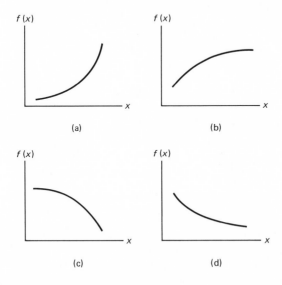

Figure 5.1–6 *Illustration of Table 5.1–1.*

A continuous function whose first derivative is positive for all values of the independent variable is called a **monotonically increasing function.** If the first derivative is negative for all values of the independent variable, the function is monotonically decreasing. Monotonicity (either increasing or decreasing) implies that the function is a one-to-one mapping. (Why?) If $y = f(x)$ is monotonic, and thus a one-to-one mapping, it follows that the **inverse function** $x = f^{-1}(y)$ is defined. (All this means is that there is only one x value associated with each y value and vice versa.) This leads to Theorem 5.1–9.

Theorem 5.1–9 If $y = f(x)$ is a monotonic function, then the inverse function $x = f^{-1}(y)$ exists and

$$\frac{dx}{dy} = \frac{1}{dy/dx} \quad \text{or} \quad f^{-1'} = \frac{1}{f'}$$

PROOF   The reader should persuade himself that $y = f(x)$ being monotonic implies that $x = f^{-1}(y)$ exists. The proof of the second part of the theorem is straightforward:

(1) $$\frac{dy}{dx} = \lim_{\Delta x \to 0} \frac{f(x + \Delta x) - f(x)}{\Delta x}$$

(2) $$\frac{dx}{dy} = \lim_{\Delta y \to 0} \frac{f^{-1}(y + \Delta y) - f^{-1}(y)}{\Delta y}$$

But, by definition $\Delta y = f(x + \Delta x) - f(x)$ and $f^{-1}(y + \Delta y) - f^{-1}(y) = \Delta x$, so (2) becomes

$$\lim_{\Delta y \to 0} \frac{\Delta x}{f(x + \Delta x) - f(x)}$$

Furthermore, $\Delta y \to 0$ implies that $\Delta x \to 0$, so

$$\lim_{\Delta x \to 0} \frac{f(x + \Delta x) - f(x)}{\Delta x} = \frac{1}{\lim_{\Delta x \to 0} \Delta x / [f(x + \Delta x) - f(x)]}$$

or

$$\frac{dy}{dx} = \frac{1}{dx/dy} \qquad \text{QED}$$

Example 10.   Let $y = x^2 - 3x$. Then $dy/dx = 2x - 3$. This function is not monotonic. But for $x < \frac{3}{2}$, $dy/dx < 0$. In this range the function is monotonically decreasing, as the reader can verify. For $x > \frac{3}{2}$, $dy/dx > 0$ and in this range the function is monotonically increasing. The inverse function rule may be applied in each monotonic segment of the function, if the domain is appropriately restricted. Thus if $x > \frac{3}{2}$, $dx/dy = 1/(2x - 3)$.

Example 11.   Let $y = 3x + 10$. Then $dy/dx = 3$. This function is clearly monotonically increasing. Solving for x explicitly,

$$x = \frac{y - 10}{3} \quad \text{and} \quad \frac{dx}{dy} = \frac{1}{3} = \frac{1}{dy/dx}$$

The reader should attempt to construct more complicated examples of monotonic functions and use them to verify the inverse function rule.

Since derivatives are themselves functions, their values will, in general, be different for different values of the independent variable. If a derivative is to be evaluated at a particular value of x, say $x = x_0$, we write $f'(x_0)$ or

$$\left. \frac{dy}{dx} \right|_{x=x_0}$$

If $f'(x) = 3x^2 - 5x + 1$,

$$\left. \frac{dy}{dx} \right|_{x=x_0} = 3(x_0)^2 - 5(x_0) + 1 = f'(x_0)$$

For $x_0 = 5$,

$$\left. \frac{dy}{dx} \right|_{x=5} = f'(5) = 51$$

Verify that $(dx/dy)|_{x=2} = 1$ in Example 10.

Problems

5.1–1   Evaluate the following limits:

(a) $\lim\limits_{x \to 2} \dfrac{x + 4}{x + 2}$

(c) $\lim\limits_{x \to 3} \dfrac{x^2 - 5x + 6}{x - 3}$

(b) $\lim\limits_{x \to -1} \dfrac{x^2 - 1}{x + 1}$

(d) $\lim\limits_{x \to \infty} \dfrac{x^2 - 2x + 3}{2x^2}$

5.1–2   Use the definition of a derivative, (1) on page 111, to find $f'(x)$ if

(a) $f(x) = \dfrac{1}{2x} - 5x^2$

(c) $f(x) = x^3 - 2x + 5$

(b) $f(x) = 2x - 1$

5.1–3   Find $f'(x)$ and $f''(x)$ if

(a) $f(x) = x^3 - 2x + 5$

(f) $f(x) = (x + 1)^4 (x - 2)^3$

(b) $f(x) = 4x^5 + 3x^2 - 2x^{-2}$

(g) $f(x) = \dfrac{x^2 - 1}{x + 5}$

(c) $f(x) = (x^2 - 5x)^2$

(h) $f(x) = (2x - 3)^2 \left(\dfrac{1}{x} - x^2 \right)^{-3}$

(d) $f(x) = (x + 5)(x^3 - 2)$ (i) $f(x) = \dfrac{3x^2}{2x - 5x^{-1} + x^{-2}}$

(e) $f(x) = x^3(x^{-2} + 5)$

5.1-4 Find dy/dx by implicit differentiation if

(a) $y = 3x^2 + 2y^{-1}$ (d) $y^3 = x^2 - x$

(b) $xy + 3x = 5$ (e) $y^2 = \dfrac{x - 1}{x^2 + y}$

(c) $\dfrac{1}{x} + \dfrac{1}{y} = 3$ (f) $y^{1/2} - x^{2/3} = 7$

5.1-5 Find dy/dz, dz/dx, and dy/dx for the following, thus verifying the chain rule:

(a) $y = z^2 + 2z;\ z = 3x^2 + 2x^{-1}$

(b) $y = \dfrac{(z + 2z^{-1})^2}{z + 2};\ z = \dfrac{x^3 - 2x}{(x + 1)^{3/2}}$

(c) $x = 2z^2 + 1;\ y = z$

(d) $x = \dfrac{z}{z^2 + 1};\ y = z^2$

5.1-6 Prove that the function $y = x^2$ is continuous for all $x \in R$.

5.1-7 For what values of x are the following functions continuous? Discontinuous?

(a) $y = x^2 - 3x + 2$ (d) $y = \dfrac{x^2 - 2}{x - 2}$

(b) $y = \dfrac{x}{x - 1}$ (e) $x^2 - y^2 = 0$

(c) $y = \dfrac{x + 2}{x^2 - 3x + 2}$

5.1-8 Are the functions in Problem 5.1-7 differentiable? If not, for what values of x are they nondifferentiable?

5.2 PARTIAL DIFFERENTIATION

In Section 5.1 we considered only cases involving one or more functions with only one independent variable. In this section we shall consider functions of more than one independent variable and their derivatives.

Given $y = f(x_1, x_2, \ldots, x_n)$, where the independent variables $x_1, x_2, \ldots, x_n$ are not themselves functionally related. If one of the independent variables, say x_i, changes in value while the others remain constant, there will be a resulting change in the dependent variable. As the change in x_i approaches zero, the ratio $\Delta y/\Delta x_i$ measures the instantaneous rate of change of y with respect to changes in x_i.

DEFINITION 5.2–1   Given $y = f(x_1, x_2, \ldots, x_n)$. The **first-order partial derivative** of y with respect to x_i, denoted by $\partial y/\partial x_i$, y_{x_i}, $f_i(x_1, x_2, \ldots, x_n)$, or f_{x_i}, measures the instantaneous rate of change of y with respect to changes in x_i, all other independent variables remaining fixed in value. Furthermore,

$$\frac{\partial y}{\partial x_i} = \lim_{\Delta x_i \to 0} \frac{\Delta y}{\Delta x_i} \equiv \lim_{\Delta x_i \to 0} \frac{f(x_1, x_2, \ldots, x_i + \Delta x_i, \ldots, x_n) - f(x_1, x_2, \ldots, x_n)}{\Delta x_i}$$

Thus, for a function of n independent variables there are n first-order partial derivatives $\partial y/\partial x_1$, $\partial y/\partial x_2$, $\ldots$, $\partial y/\partial x_n$. Figure 5.2–1 shows the graphic interpretation of first-order partial derivatives for $y = f(x_1, x_2)$. The three-dimensional figure is the graph of the function $y = f(x_1, x_2)$. Consider holding x_2 constant at $\bar{x}_2$. The solid line *FGH* shows the resulting relation between y and x_1. The slope of the line is the $\partial y/\partial x_1$, given $x_2 = \bar{x}_2$. The slope at G, shown by the tangent line drawn in, is thus

$$\left. \frac{\partial y}{\partial x_1} \right|_{\substack{x_1 = x_1^0 \\ x_2 = \bar{x}_2}} \quad \text{or} \quad f_{x_1}(x_1^0, \bar{x}_2)$$

Note that for different values of x_1, $f_{x_1}(x_1, \bar{x}_2)$ will vary. Furthermore, for different values of x_2, $f_{x_1}(x_1^0, x_2)$ will vary as is illustrated by the different tangent lines at points G, where $x_2 = \bar{x}_2$ and C, where $x_2 = \bar{\bar{x}}_2$. This simply illustrates the fact that partial derivatives are again derived functions, in general, of the same independent variables as the original function.

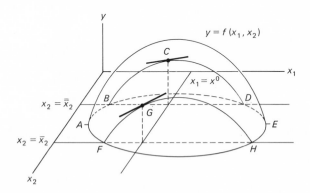

Figure 5.2–1   *Illustration of partial derivatives.*

The process of calculating partial derivatives follows the same rules as ordinary differentiation. The only thing to remember is that all independent variables other than the one being allowed to vary are treated as constants.

Example 1.

(a)
$$y = 5z^2x + 3x^{-1} + 5z$$

$$\frac{\partial y}{\partial x} = 5z^2 - 3x^{-2}$$

$$\frac{\partial y}{\partial z} = 10xz + 5$$

(b)
$$y = \frac{3x^2z^3}{\cos x \sin z}$$

$$\frac{\partial y}{\partial x} = \frac{(\cos x \sin z)6xz^3 + 3x^2z^3 (\sin x \sin z)}{(\cos x \sin z)^2}$$

$$\frac{\partial y}{\partial z} = \frac{(\cos x \sin z)9x^2z^2 - 3x^2z^3 \cos x \cos z}{(\cos x \sin z)^2}$$

Since first-order partial derivatives are themselves functions, higher-order partial derivatives can be obtained through successive differentiations in a manner analogous to that used to obtain higher-order ordinary derivatives. Consider a function of two independent variables, $y = f(x, z)$. This function has two first-order partial derivatives, f_x and f_z. Both of these functions must be differentiated with respect to both x and z to obtain all the second-order partial derivatives: $f_{xx} = \partial^2 y/\partial x^2$, $f_{xz} = \partial^2 y/(\partial x\, \partial z)$, $f_{zx} = \partial^2 y/(\partial z\, \partial x)$, and $f_{zz} = \partial^2 y/\partial z^2$. The second-order derivatives f_{xz} and f_{zx} are called cross partial or mixed partial derivatives. The following theorem is of great importance in the theory of partial differentiation.

Theorem 5.2–1   *Young's Theorem* Given that $y = f(x_1, x_2, \ldots, x_n)$ is continuous and has continuous first- and second-order partial derivatives. Then

$$f_{ij} = f_{ji} \qquad \text{for all } i \text{ and } j.[4]$$

Young's theorem assures us that the order of differentiation is immaterial in cross derivatives as long as they are continuous. Thus, in the example above $f_{zx} = f_{xz}$ and there are only three distinct second-order derivatives, given the continuity requirements hold.

[4] For a proof, see Widder (1961), page 52ff.

Example 2. Find all the first- and second-order partial derivatives of $y = (3x^2z)(z^2 - 5x)^2$.

$$\frac{\partial y}{\partial x} = 6xz(z^2 - 5x)^2 - 30x^2z(z^2 - 5x)$$

$$\frac{\partial y}{\partial z} = 3x^2(z^2 - 5x)^2 + 12x^2z^2(z^2 - 5x)$$

$$\frac{\partial^2 y}{\partial x^2} = 6z(z^2 - 5x)^2 - 120xz(z^2 - 5x) + 150x^2z$$

$$\frac{\partial^2 y}{\partial z^2} = 36x^2z(z^2 - 5x) + 24x^2z^3$$

$$\frac{\partial^2 y}{\partial x\,\partial z} = \frac{\partial^2 y}{\partial z\,\partial x} = 6x(z^2 - 5x)^2 + (24xz^2 - 30x^2)(z^2 - 5x) - 60x^2z^2$$

The reader should verify that $y_{xz} = y_{zx}$.

A function of m independent variables will have m^n partial derivatives of order n; by Young's theorem many of these will be equal. If Young's theorem applies, the number of distinct derivatives of order n is $(n + m - 1)!/n!\,(m - 1)!$. The number of distinct third-order derivatives for a function of five variables is thus $(3 + 5 - 1)!/3!\,(5 - 1)! = 35$.

The chain rule for ordinary derivatives (Theorem 5.1–5) can be generalized to composite functions of more than two variables. In partial differentiation there are many cases to consider. We shall state and prove one of the simplest cases as Theorem 5.2–2 for illustrative purposes. Other cases will be discussed as examples.

Theorem 5.2–2   Given that $z = f(x, y)$, $x = g(s, t)$, and $y = h(s, t)$ are continuous, with continuous first-order partial derivatives. Then

(1)
$$\frac{\partial z}{\partial s} = \frac{\partial f}{\partial x}\frac{\partial x}{\partial s} + \frac{\partial f}{\partial y}\frac{\partial y}{\partial s}$$

(2)
$$\frac{\partial z}{\partial t} = \frac{\partial f}{\partial x}\frac{\partial x}{\partial t} + \frac{\partial f}{\partial y}\frac{\partial y}{\partial t}$$

PROOF   By the definition of a partial derivative,

$$\left.\frac{\partial z}{\partial s}\right|_{\substack{s=s_0 \\ t=t_0}} = \lim_{\Delta s \to 0} \frac{\Delta z}{\Delta s}$$

where $\Delta z = f[g(s_0 + \Delta s, t_0), h(s_0 + \Delta s, t_0)] - f[g(s_0, t_0), h(s_0, t_0)]$. But since $g(s_0 + \Delta s, t_0) = x_0 + \Delta x$, $x_0 = g(s_0, t_0)$ and $h(s_0 + \Delta s, t_0) = y_0 +$

Δy, we have $y_0 = h(s_0, t_0)$. Since by hypothesis both h and g are continuous, $\Delta s \to 0$ implies that $\Delta x \to 0$ and $\Delta y \to 0$. Thus

$$\frac{\Delta z}{\Delta s} = f_x(x_0 + \Delta x, y_0)\frac{\Delta x}{\Delta s} + f_y(x_0 + \Delta x, y_0 + \Delta y)\frac{\Delta y}{\Delta s}$$

and

$$\lim_{\Delta s \to 0} \frac{\Delta z}{\Delta s} = f_x g_s + f_y h_s = \frac{\partial z}{\partial s} \qquad \text{QED}$$

Example 3. Let $z = 3xy^2 + 2x$; $x = -3s^2 t$; and $y = 4t^3 + s$. Thus

$$\frac{\partial f}{\partial x} = 3y^2 + 2 \qquad \frac{\partial g}{\partial s} = -6st \qquad \frac{\partial h}{\partial s} = 1 \qquad \frac{\partial f}{\partial y} = 6xy$$

and

$$\frac{\partial z}{\partial s} = \frac{\partial f}{\partial x}\frac{\partial g}{\partial s} + \frac{\partial f}{\partial y}\frac{\partial h}{\partial s} = (3y^2 + 2)(-6st) + 6xy$$

Notice the problem can also be solved by substitution and direct differentiation:

$$z = 3(-3s^2 t)(4t^3 + s)^2 - 6s^2 t$$

$$\frac{\partial z}{\partial s} = -18st(4t^3 + s)^2 - 18s^2 t(4t^3 + s) - 12st$$

The reader should convince himself that both answers are equivalent and also calculate $\partial z/\partial t$ using both methods (Theorem 5.2–2 and substitution).

The following cases represent some of the most frequently encountered applications of the chain rule.

Case 1. $y = f(x_1, x_2, x_3, \ldots, x_n)$; $x_1 = g_1(s, t)$, $x_2 = g_2(s, t), \ldots, x_n = g_n(s, t)$. Then

$$\frac{\partial y}{\partial s} = f_{x_1}g_{1_s} + f_{x_2}g_{2_s} + \cdots + f_{x_n}g_{n_s}$$

and

$$\frac{\partial y}{\partial t} = f_{x_1}g_{1_t} + f_{x_2}g_{2_t} + \cdots + f_{x_n}g_{n_t}$$

Case 2. $y = f(x)$ and $x = g(r, s, t)$. Then

$$\frac{\partial y}{\partial r} = \frac{df}{dx}\frac{\partial g}{\partial r} = \frac{df}{dx}\frac{\partial x}{\partial r}$$

$$\frac{\partial y}{\partial s} = \frac{df}{dx}\frac{\partial x}{\partial s}$$

and

$$\frac{\partial y}{\partial t} = \frac{df}{dx}\frac{\partial x}{\partial t}$$

Since y is directly a function of only one variable, x, the derivative df/dx is an ordinary and not a partial derivative. The derivatives of x with respect to r, s, and t are, of course, partial derivatives.

Case 3. $w = f(x, y, z)$, $x = g(t)$, $y = h(t)$, and $z = i(t)$. Then

$$\frac{dw}{dt} = \frac{\partial f}{\partial x}\frac{dg}{dt} + \frac{\partial f}{\partial y}\frac{dh}{dt} + \frac{\partial f}{\partial z}\frac{di}{dt}$$

Since x, y, and z are functions of t only, the ordinary derivatives dg/dt, dh/dt, and di/dt require no special comment. However, the derivative dw/dt does. A derivative of this sort is called a **total derivative** and the process of finding it is called **total differentiation.** In Case 4 we find another total derivative.

Case 4. $y = f(x, z)$ and $z = g(x)$. Then

$$\frac{dy}{dx} = \frac{\partial f}{\partial x} + \frac{\partial f}{\partial z}\frac{dz}{dx}$$

Here dy/dx is a total derivative and is composed of two parts: (1) the direct effect of a change in x on y, $(\partial f/\partial x)$, and (2) the indirect effect of x on y operating through the variable z, $(\partial f/\partial z)(dz/dx)$. dy/dx is a total derivative because it captures both the direct and indirect effect of a change in x on y. In Case 3 the total derivative dw/dt is the sum of three indirect effects of changes in t on w. We shall have more to say about total differentiation when the topics of differentials and total differentials are discussed.

There are many more cases that could be examined; they all fall into the general category of chain rules or, as they are sometimes called, composite function rules.

The calculation of higher-order derivatives for composite functions requires some care, but no new rules. As an example, suppose we have the functions in Theorem 5.2–2: $z = f(x, y)$, $x = g(s, t)$, and $y = h(s, t)$. Then

$$\frac{\partial z}{\partial s} = f_x g_s + f_y h_s \quad \text{and} \quad \frac{\partial z}{\partial t} = f_x g_t + f_y h_t$$

To find the second-order partial derivatives, one must remember (1) that the first-order derivatives f_x and f_y are themselves composite functions and (2) to apply the rule for differentiating a product of functions to the terms $f_x g_s$, and so on, with this in mind, we can write:

$$\frac{\partial^2 z}{\partial s^2} = \frac{\partial}{\partial s}(f_x g_s + f_y h_s)$$

$$= f_x\frac{\partial(g_s)}{\partial s} + g_s\frac{\partial(f_x)}{\partial s} + f_y\frac{\partial(h_s)}{\partial s} + h_s\frac{\partial(f_y)}{\partial s}$$

$$= f_x g_{ss} + f_y h_{ss} + g_s(f_{xx}g_s + f_{xy}h_s) + h_s(f_{yy}h_s + f_{yx}g_s)$$

since f_x and f_y are composite functions.

Similarly,

$$\frac{\partial^2 z}{\partial t^2} = \frac{\partial}{\partial t}(f_x g_t + f_y h_t)$$

$$= f_x g_{tt} + f_y h_{tt} + g_t(f_{xx}g_t + f_{xy}h_t) + h_t(f_{yy}h_t + f_{yx}g_t)$$

and

$$\frac{\partial^2 z}{\partial s \, \partial t} = \frac{\partial}{\partial t}(f_x g_s + f_y h_s)$$

$$= f_x \frac{\partial}{\partial t}(g_s) + g_s \frac{\partial}{\partial t}(f_x) + f_y \frac{\partial}{\partial t}(h_s) + h_s \frac{\partial}{\partial t}(f_y)$$

$$= f_x g_{st} + f_y h_{st} + g_s(f_{xx}g_t + f_{xy}h_t) + h_s(f_{yy}h_t + f_{yx}g_t)$$

The reader should write the expression for $\partial^2 z/(\partial t \, \partial s)$ and decide what must be true for the resulting expression to equal $\partial^2 z/(\partial s \, \partial t)$.

Example 4.   Find the first- and second-order partial derivatives if $z = 3x^2 + 2xy$, $x = 4t^2 s$, and $y = 7t - 3s^2$.

First-order:

$$z_x = 6x + 2y$$
$$z_y = 2x$$
$$z_s = (6x + 2y)(4t^2) + 2x(-6s)$$
$$z_t = (6x + 2y)(8ts) + 2x(7)$$

Second-order:

$$z_{xx} = 6$$
$$z_{xy} = 2$$
$$z_{yy} = 0$$
$$z_{yx} = 2$$

$$z_{ss} = 4t^2\left[\frac{\partial}{\partial s}(6x + 2y)\right] - 6s\frac{\partial(2x)}{\partial s} + 2x(-6)$$

$$= 4t^2(24t^2 - 12s) - 48t^2 s - 12x$$

$$z_{st} = 8t(6x + 2y) + 4t^2\left[\frac{\partial}{\partial t}(6x + 2y)\right] - 12s\frac{\partial x}{\partial t}$$

$$= 8t(6x + 2y) + 4t^2(48ts + 14) - 96ts^2$$

$$z_{tt} = (6x + 2y)\frac{\partial}{\partial t}(8ts) + 8ts\left[\frac{\partial}{\partial t}(6x + 2y)\right] + 14\frac{\partial x}{\partial t}$$

$$= 8s(6x + 2y) + 8ts(48ts + 14) + 112ts$$

$$z_{ts} = (6x + 2y)(8t) + 8ts\left[\frac{\partial}{\partial s}(6x + 2y)\right] + 14\frac{\partial x}{\partial s}$$

$$= 8t(6x + 2y) + 8ts(24t^2 - 12s) + 56t^2$$

As is easily verified, $z_{ts} = z_{st}$.

The methods of partial differentiation can be applied to the implicit differentiation of $f(x, y) = 0$ discussed in the last section. Since y is presumed to be a function of x we have, upon differentiation with respect to x:

$$\frac{df}{dx} + \frac{\partial f}{\partial y}\frac{dy}{dx} = 0$$

Solving for dy/dx we obtain

$$\frac{dy}{dx} = -\frac{f_x}{f_y}$$

Example 5.

$$3xy^2 + 2x^2y = 0$$
$$f_x = 3y^2 + 4xy$$
$$f_y = 6xy + 2x^2$$
$$\frac{dy}{dx} = -\frac{f_x}{f_y} = -\frac{3y^2 + 4xy}{6xy + 2x^2}$$

The reader should solve for dy/dx by the method of Section 5.1 to persuade himself that both methods provide the same answer.

Theorem 5.2–3 describes the method of finding the partial derivatives of implicit functions for the more general case.

Theorem 5.2–3 Given that $z = f(x, y)$ and the implicit function $g(x, y, z) = 0$ are continuous and have continuous first derivatives. Then

$$z_x = -\frac{g_x}{g_z}$$

and

$$z_y = -\frac{g_y}{g_z}$$

if $g_z \neq 0$.

PROOF Differentiate $g(x, y, z) = 0$ with respect to x. This yields $g_x + g_z z_x = 0$, or $z_x = -g_x/g_y$. The expression for z_y is obtained in an analogous way.

Example 6. Given that $x^2y + 3z - 2zx = 0$. Then $g_x = 2xy - 2z$, $g_z = 3 - 2x$, and $g_y = x^2$. Thus

$$z_x = -\frac{2xy - 2z}{3 - 2x} \quad \text{and} \quad z_y = -\frac{x^2}{3 - 2x}$$

Note that these derivatives do not exist for $x = \frac{3}{2}$, since at this value the denominator vanishes.

Example 7. Given $y = f(x, y)$, find dy/dx. This is a case of implicit differentiation, where the implicit function g is $f(x, y) - y = 0$. Thus

$$\frac{dy}{dx} = -\frac{g_x}{g_y} = -\frac{f_x}{f_y - 1} \quad \text{for } f_y - 1 \neq 0$$

Second-order derivatives of implicit functions may be calculated by applying the rules already at our disposal. Consider $f(x, y) = 0$, so that $dy/dx = -f_x/f_y$. Then, by the quotient rule and since y is itself a function of x:

$$\frac{d^2y}{dx^2} = \frac{f_y[\partial(-f_x)/\partial x] + f_x[\partial(f_y)/\partial x]}{(f_y)^2}$$

$$= \left\{ -f_y\left(f_{xx} + f_{xy}\frac{dy}{dx}\right) + f_x[f_{yx} + f_{yy}(dy/dx)] \right\}\left\{\frac{1}{f_y^2}\right\}$$

or, substituting for dy/dx,

$$\frac{d^2y}{dx^2} = \frac{f_y[f_{xx} + f_{xy}(-f_x/f_y)] + f_x[f_{yx} + f_{yy}(-f_y/f_x)]}{(f_y)^2}$$

In Chapter 9 we shall study simultaneous equation systems and their solutions in much detail. At this point we assume that a solution exists and examine only the method of finding the derivatives of the solution. This general method is given in Theorem 5.2–4.

Theorem 5.2–4   Given that $f(w, x, y, z)$ and $g(w, x, y, z)$ are continuous and have continuous first-order derivatives. If $w = w(y, z)$ and $x = x(y, z)$ also have the same continuity properties, the system of two equations in two unknowns,

$$f[w(y, z), x(y, z), y, z] \equiv 0$$

and

$$g[w(y, z), x(y, z), y, z] \equiv 0$$

has the following derivatives:

$$\frac{\partial w}{\partial y} = -\frac{\begin{vmatrix} \dfrac{\partial f}{\partial y} & \dfrac{\partial f}{\partial x} \\ \dfrac{\partial g}{\partial y} & \dfrac{\partial g}{\partial x} \end{vmatrix}}{\begin{vmatrix} \dfrac{\partial f}{\partial w} & \dfrac{\partial f}{\partial x} \\ \dfrac{\partial g}{\partial w} & \dfrac{\partial g}{\partial x} \end{vmatrix}} (=D) \qquad \frac{\partial w}{\partial z} = -\frac{\begin{vmatrix} \dfrac{\partial f}{\partial z} & \dfrac{\partial f}{\partial x} \\ \dfrac{\partial g}{\partial z} & \dfrac{\partial g}{\partial x} \end{vmatrix}}{D}$$

$$\frac{\partial x}{\partial y} = -\frac{\begin{vmatrix} \dfrac{\partial f}{\partial w} & \dfrac{\partial f}{\partial y} \\ \dfrac{\partial g}{\partial w} & \dfrac{\partial g}{\partial y} \end{vmatrix}}{D} \qquad \frac{\partial x}{\partial z} = -\frac{\begin{vmatrix} \dfrac{\partial f}{\partial w} & \dfrac{\partial f}{\partial z} \\ \dfrac{\partial g}{\partial w} & \dfrac{\partial g}{\partial z} \end{vmatrix}}{D}$$

if $D \neq 0$.

PROOF   Differentiate f and g with respect to y:

(1)
$$\frac{\partial f}{\partial w}\frac{\partial w}{\partial y} + \frac{\partial f}{\partial x}\frac{\partial x}{\partial y} + \frac{\partial f}{\partial y} = 0$$

(2)
$$\frac{\partial g}{\partial w}\frac{\partial w}{\partial y} + \frac{\partial g}{\partial x}\frac{\partial x}{\partial y} + \frac{\partial g}{\partial y} = 0$$

Treat $\partial w/\partial y$ and $\partial x/\partial y$ as the unknowns and solve by Cramer's rule.[5] This yields, for $\partial w/\partial y$,

$$\frac{\partial w}{\partial y} = \frac{\begin{vmatrix} -f_y & f_x \\ -g_y & g_x \end{vmatrix}}{\begin{vmatrix} f_w & f_x \\ g_w & g_x \end{vmatrix}} = -\frac{\begin{vmatrix} f_y & f_x \\ g_y & g_x \end{vmatrix}}{\begin{vmatrix} f_w & f_x \\ g_w & g_x \end{vmatrix}}$$

$\partial x/\partial y$ is solved for in the same way from (1) and (2). To solve for $\partial w/\partial z$ and $\partial x/\partial z$, first differentiate f and g with respect to z and then apply Cramer's rule. QED

Example 8.   Let

$$f = 5x^2 + 3xy - wz + xyz = 0$$
$$g = y^3 + 3x^2z - 2zw = 0$$
$$x = 5y^2z$$
$$w = z^3 - 5x^2z$$

Then

$$\frac{\partial w}{\partial z} = -\frac{\begin{vmatrix} -w + xy & 10x + 3y + yz \\ 3x^2 - 2w & 6xz \end{vmatrix}}{\begin{vmatrix} -z & 10x + 3y + yz \\ -2z & 6xz \end{vmatrix}}$$

$$= -\frac{6xz(-w + xy) - (3x^2 - 2w)(10x + 3y + yz)}{-6xz^2 + 2z(10x + 3y + yz)}$$

The reader should calculate w_y, x_z, and x_y.

The determinants in Theorem 4.3–4 are examples of *Jacobian determinants*.

DEFINITION 5.2–2   A **Jacobian** is a determinant whose elements are partial derivatives.

The denominator of the derivatives in Theorem 5.2–4 is the Jacobian of f and g with respect to w and x, written $\partial(f, g)/\partial(w, x)$. The numerator of

---

[5] See Section 4.3.

$\partial w/\partial y$ is the Jacobian of f and g with respect to y and x, written $\partial(f, g)/\partial(y, x)$. The results of the theorem, written in Jacobian notations, are

$$\frac{\partial w}{\partial y} = -\frac{\partial(f, g)}{\partial(y, w)} \bigg/ \frac{\partial(f, g)}{\partial(w, x)}$$

$$\frac{\partial w}{\partial z} = -\frac{\partial(f, g)}{\partial(z, x)} \bigg/ \frac{\partial(f, g)}{\partial(w, x)}$$

$$\frac{\partial x}{\partial y} = -\frac{\partial(f, g)}{\partial(w, y)} \bigg/ \frac{\partial(f, g)}{\partial(w, x)}$$

$$\frac{\partial x}{\partial z} = -\frac{\partial(f, g)}{\partial(w, z)} \bigg/ \frac{\partial(f, g)}{\partial(w, x)}$$

This notation has the obvious advantage of being easier and shorter. More important, it provides an easy way to remember the results. Consider the expression for $\partial x/\partial y$ and imagine that the following steps could be performed mathematically (they cannot be).

$$\frac{\partial x}{\partial y} = \frac{\partial(f, g)}{\partial(w, y)} \bigg/ \frac{\partial(f, g)}{\partial(w, x)} = \frac{\partial(f, g)}{\partial(w, y)} \frac{\partial(w, x)}{\partial(f, g)} = \frac{\partial(w, x)}{\partial(w, y)} = \frac{\partial x}{\partial y}$$

This sequence run in reverse (and with the necessary minus sign added) permits us to construct the proper expression for the derivative in question.

Suppose we had a system of three simultaneous equations: $f(w, x, y, z)$, $g(w, x, y, z)$, and $h(w, x, y, z)$, where z is the independent variable and w, x, and y are the dependent variables. Then, following the "construction" procedure outlined above, we can immediately write

$$\frac{dw}{dz} = -\frac{\partial(f, g, h)}{\partial(z, x, y)} \bigg/ \frac{\partial(f, g, h)}{\partial(w, x, y)}$$

$$\frac{dx}{dz} = -\frac{\partial(f, g, h)}{\partial(w, z, y)} \bigg/ \frac{\partial(f, g, h)}{\partial(w, x, y)}$$

$$\frac{dy}{dz} = -\frac{\partial(f, g, h)}{\partial(w, x, z)} \bigg/ \frac{\partial(f, g, h)}{\partial(w, x, y)}$$

(Why have we written dw/dz instead of $\partial w/\partial z$, etc.?) Note that the Jacobian always contains the dependent variables in the denominator, while the independent variable replaces the appropriate dependent variable in the numerator. For any of these derivatives to exist, the Jacobian in the denominator must be nonzero.

Suppose we have the following system of equations: $w = f(x, y)$ and $z = g(x, y)$. The derivatives w_x, w_y, z_x, and z_y can be calculated by the methods already at our disposal. But suppose we wanted to find x_w, x_y, and so on. They could be found if we could solve the system for x and y as functions of w and z. Technically, f and g define a transformation, and the functions expressing x and y as functions of w and z are the inverses of that transformation. Through the use of Jacobians we can find x_w, x_y, and so on without solving for them explicitly as follows. Let

$$H(w, z, x, y) = w - f(x, y) = 0$$

and

$$K(w, z, x, y) = z - g(x, y) = 0$$

Then

$$x_w = -\frac{\partial(H, K)}{\partial(w, y)} \bigg/ \frac{\partial(H, K)}{\partial(x, y)} = -\frac{\begin{vmatrix} H_w & K_w \\ H_y & K_y \\ H_x & K_x \\ H_y & K_y \end{vmatrix}}{} = -\frac{\begin{vmatrix} 1 & 0 \\ -f_y & -g_y \\ -f_x & -g_x \\ -f_y & -g_y \end{vmatrix}}{} = \frac{\begin{vmatrix} 1 & 0 \\ f_y & g_y \\ f_x & g_x \\ f_y & g_y \end{vmatrix}}{}$$

Expanding both determinants, we obtain

$$x_w = \frac{g_y}{f_x g_y - f_y g_x}$$

Similarly,

$$y_z = -\frac{\partial(H, K)}{\partial(x, z)} \bigg/ \frac{\partial(H, K)}{E\ \partial(x, y)} = -\frac{\begin{vmatrix} H_x & K_x \\ H_z & K_z \\ H_x & K_x \\ H_y & K_y \end{vmatrix}}{} = -\frac{\begin{vmatrix} -f_x & -g_x \\ 0 & 1 \\ -f_x & -g_x \\ -f_y & -g_y \end{vmatrix}}{}$$

$$= \frac{f_x}{f_x g_y - f_y g_x}$$

Example 9. If $w = 5xy + x^2$ and $z = 3x + 2y^2$, find x_z. By the method outlined above,

$$x_z = -\frac{\partial(H, K)}{\partial(z, y)} \bigg/ \frac{\partial(H, K)}{\partial(x, y)} = -\frac{\begin{vmatrix} H_z & K_z \\ H_y & K_y \end{vmatrix}}{\begin{vmatrix} H_x & K_x \\ H_y & K_y \end{vmatrix}}$$

where $H = w - 5xy + x^2 = 0$ and $K = z - 3x - 2y^2 = 0$. Then

$$x_z = -\frac{\begin{vmatrix} 0 & 1 \\ -f_y & -g_y \end{vmatrix}}{\begin{vmatrix} -f_x & -g_x \\ -f_y & -g_y \end{vmatrix}} = \frac{-f_y}{f_x g_y - g_x f_y}$$

Computing the derivatives in the formula for x_z: $f_y = 5x$, $f_x = 5y + 2x$, $g_y = 4y$, and $g_x = 3$. Thus, by the formula,

$$x_z = \frac{-5x}{4y(5y + 2x) - 15x}$$

Rather than apply this formula directly, we could differentiate both expressions with respect to z. This yields

(1)
$$0 = 5x \frac{\partial y}{\partial z} + 5y \frac{\partial x}{\partial z} + 2x \frac{\partial x}{\partial z}$$

(2)
$$1 = 3 \frac{\partial x}{\partial z} + 4y \frac{\partial y}{\partial z}$$

or

(3)
$$(5y + 2x) \frac{\partial x}{\partial z} + 5x \frac{\partial y}{\partial z} = 0$$

and

(4)
$$3 \frac{\partial x}{\partial z} + 4y \frac{\partial y}{\partial z} = 1$$

Solving (3) and (4) for x_z by Cramer's rule gives

$$x_z = \frac{\begin{vmatrix} 0 & 5x \\ 1 & 4y \end{vmatrix}}{\begin{vmatrix} 5y + 2x & 5x \\ 3 & 4y \end{vmatrix}} = \frac{-5x}{4y(5y + 2x) - 15x}$$

As one would like in a well-ordered world, the same answer is obtained through the formula and the method on which the formula is based.

Another interesting property of Jacobians has to do with transformations and their inverses.

Theorem 5.2–5   Given that $w = f(x, y)$ and $z = g(x, y)$ is a transformation with Jacobian J. Then $x = F(w, z)$ and $y = G(w, z)$ with Jacobian j is the inverse transformation if and only if $J j = 1$.

PROOF   Since

$$J = \frac{\partial(f, g)}{\partial(x, y)} = \begin{vmatrix} f_x & g_x \\ f_y & g_y \end{vmatrix}$$

we can write

$$\frac{\partial x}{\partial w} = \frac{g_y}{J} \qquad \frac{\partial y}{\partial w} = -\frac{g_x}{J} \qquad \frac{\partial x}{\partial z} = -\frac{f_y}{J} \qquad \frac{\partial y}{\partial z} = \frac{f_x}{J}$$

Thus

$$j = \frac{\partial(x, y)}{\partial(w, z)} = \begin{vmatrix} x_w & y_w \\ x_z & y_z \end{vmatrix} = \begin{vmatrix} \dfrac{g_y}{J} & \dfrac{-g_x}{J} \\ \dfrac{-f_y}{J} & \dfrac{f_x}{J} \end{vmatrix} = \begin{vmatrix} g_y & -g_x \\ -f_y & f_x \end{vmatrix} \frac{1}{J^2} = \frac{J}{J^2} = \frac{1}{J}$$

Thus

$$J j = J\left(\frac{1}{J}\right) = 1^6$$

Another useful application of Jacobians is in testing whether or not two or more functions are *functionally dependent.*

DEFINITION 5.2–3   Two functions $f(x, y)$ and $g(x, y)$ are **functionally dependent** if there exists a function of one variable, $F(z)$, such that

$$g(x, y) = F[f(x, y)]$$

Functional dependence intuitively means that one function is itself a function of the other. Simple examples of functional dependence include cases where g is a multiple of f, a power of f, and so on.

Theorem 5.2–6   Given that $f(x, y)$ and $g(x, y)$ are functionally dependent. Then their Jacobian, $\partial(f, g)/\partial(x, y)$ is equal to zero for all values of x and y.

PROOF

$$\frac{\partial(f, g)}{\partial(x, y)} = \begin{vmatrix} f_x & g_x \\ f_y & g_y \end{vmatrix}$$

But, by the definition of functional dependence, $g_x = F'f_x$ and $g_y = F'f_y$. Thus the Jacobian becomes

$$\begin{vmatrix} f_x & F'f_x \\ f_y & F'f_y \end{vmatrix} = F' \begin{vmatrix} f_x & f_x \\ f_y & f_y \end{vmatrix} = 0 \qquad \text{QED}$$

The theorem can be generalized to systems of more equations in more variables. A more interesting result is the converse of Theorem 5.2–6, which states that under certain restrictions a zero Jacobian implies functional dependence. We state the theorem without proof.[7]

Theorem 5.2–7   Given that $f(x, y)$ and $g(x, y)$ are continuous and have continuous first-order derivatives. If $\partial(f, g)/\partial(x, y) = 0$ and $f_y(\bar{x}, \bar{y}) \neq 0$, then f and g are functionally dependent in a suitably small region around $\bar{x}$ and $\bar{y}$.

[6] The reader should persuade himself that

$$\begin{vmatrix} f_x & -g_x \\ f_y & g_y \end{vmatrix} = F' \begin{vmatrix} g_y & g_x \\ -f_y & f_x \end{vmatrix}.$$

One way to do so is to expand both determinants.

[7] See Widder (1961), pages 58–59.

For most functions one can safely conclude that a Jacobian equal to zero implies their functional dependence.

Example 10.   Let $f = x + y = 0$ and $g = x^2 + 2xy + y^2 = 0$. Then

$$\frac{\partial(f, g)}{\partial(x, y)} = \begin{vmatrix} f_x & g_x \\ f_y & g_y \end{vmatrix} = \begin{vmatrix} 1 & 2x + 2y \\ 1 & 2x + 2y \end{vmatrix} = 2x + 2y - (2x + 2y) = 0$$

Since $f_y = 1$ for all x and y, f and g are functionally dependent. In terms of Definition 5.2–3, $z = f(x, y)$ and $F(z) = F[f(x, y)] = z^2 = g(x, y)$.

While the notion of a homogeneous function does not depend directly on the concepts of partial differentiation, the proof of one of the most important theorems concerning these functions (Euler's theorem) does. Both the concept of homogeneity and Euler's theorem have widespread economic uses.

DEFINITION 5.2–4   A function $f(x, y)$ is **homogeneous of degree** n if and only if for every positive number λ and ranges of x and y, $x_1 \leq x \leq x_2$ and $y_1 \leq y \leq y_2$:

$$f(\lambda x, \lambda y) = \lambda^n f(x, y) \qquad \text{for all } x_1 \leq x \leq x_2 \text{ and } y_1 \leq y \leq y_2$$

Suppose we let $\lambda = 2$. Then if f is homogeneous of degree 3, multiplying all the independent variables by 2 will multiply the value of the dependent variable by 8. Functions may be homogeneous of any degree, that is, $-\infty \leq n \leq \infty$. Nor is n restricted to integer values. The reason for and importance of specifying the region of homogeneity will be illustrated in the economic application of Euler's theorem.

Example 11. $z = x^2 y + 2y^3 + xy^2 - 10x^3$ is homogeneous of degree 3. Polynomial functions are homogeneous if the sum of the exponents of each term is equal for all terms. Thus $z = x^3 + xy - 2y^3$ is not homogeneous. The reader should verify this by applying Definition 5.2–4. The degree of homogeneity of nonpolynomial functions is not so easy to determine.

Theorem 5.2–8   (*Euler's Theorem*)   Given that $z = f(x, y)$ is continuous and has continuous first-order derivatives. Then, if $f(x, y)$ is homogeneous of degree n,

$$\frac{\partial f}{\partial x} x + \frac{\partial f}{\partial y} y = nf(x, y)$$

PROOF   Homogeneity of degree n means

(1) $$f(\lambda x, \lambda y) = \lambda^n f(x, y)$$

Differentiating the left hand side of (1) with respect to λ:

(2)
$$\frac{\partial[f(\lambda x, \lambda y)]}{\partial \lambda} = f_x \frac{\partial(\lambda x)}{\partial \lambda} + f_y \frac{\partial(\lambda y)}{\partial \lambda}$$

$$= f_x x + f_y y$$

Performing the same operation on the right hand side of (1):

(3)
$$\frac{\partial[\lambda^n f(x, y)]}{\partial \lambda} = f(x, y) \frac{\partial(\lambda^n)}{\partial \lambda} + \lambda^n \frac{\partial[f(x, y)]}{\partial \lambda}$$

$$= n\lambda^{n-1} f(x, y) + 0$$

Equating (2) and (3) and setting $\lambda = 1$, since λ can be any positive value,

$$f_x x + f_y y = nf(x, y) \qquad \text{QED}$$

Theorem 5.2–9   Converse of Euler's Theorem Given that $f(x, y)$ is continuous and has continuous first-order derivatives. If $f_x x + f_y y = nf$ for all values of x and y, then $f(x, y)$ is homogeneous to degree n.

The reader may wish to prove the converse of Euler's theorem. In the definition of homogeneity, λ was restricted to being positive. If negative λ's are allowed, Euler's theorem still holds, although the converse of Euler's theorem is no longer valid. This is the reason for the restriction on λ.

Example 12.   Euler's Theorem, Homogeneity, and Distribution Theory Euler's theorem has caused a certain confusion in economics. The converse of Euler's theorem must hold for all values of the independent variables, not just for a particular value of x and a particular value of y. Consider a production function

(1)
$$Q = Q(K, L)$$

where Q is output and K and L are factors of production. If this function has regions of both increasing and decreasing returns, then there will be one point (K^*, L^*) where the function has the properties of linear homogeneity. That is, at the point where average cost is equal to marginal cost it will be true that

$$Q^* = Q_K K^* + Q_L L^*$$

Since this only holds for one value of K and L, the function is not (linearly) homogeneous.

Suppose, on the other hand, that (1) is homogeneous. Then, by Euler's theorem we can write

$$\frac{\partial Q}{\partial K} K + \frac{\partial Q}{\partial L} L = nQ(K, L)$$

or, since $Q = Q(K, L)$,

(2)
$$\frac{\partial Q}{\partial K} K + \frac{\partial Q}{\partial L} L = nQ$$

where n is the degree of homogeneity. $\partial Q/\partial K$ and $\partial Q/\partial L$ are the marginal products of K and L (MP_K, MP_L). If $n = 1$, output is equal to the MP's times the amount of their respective input.

Suppose (2) is the production function for a firm that is a perfect competitor in both the input and output markets. To maximize profit, such a firm will hire both inputs up to the point where the value of the marginal product of each input is equal to the price of that input. For the perfectly competitive firm the value of the marginal product (VMP) is, of course, equal to the price of output times the marginal product. Thus

$$\text{VMP}_K = P_Q \text{MP}_K \quad \text{and} \quad \text{VMP}_L = P_Q \text{MP}_L$$

The profit-maximizing condition is thus

$$P_Q \text{MP}_K = P_K \quad \text{and} \quad P_Q \text{MP}_L = P_L$$

Multiplying both sides of (2) by P_Q:

(3)
$$P_Q \text{MP}_K K + P_Q \text{MP}_L L = nP_Q Q$$

If the firm maximizes profit, (3) becomes

(4)
$$P_K K + P_L L = nP_Q Q$$

If $n = 1$, (4) says that the perfectly competitive firm pays out the entire value of its output ($P_Q Q$) to the inputs. This corresponds to the statement that the competitive firm earns zero profit. If $n > 1$ the firm earns pure profits.

Suppose, following the standard assumptions of marginal productivity distribution theory, that $n = 1$ and P_Q is constant. The firm's profit function is

$$\Pi = P_Q Q - P_K K - P_L L$$

But since $Q(K, L)$ is homogeneous of degree 1, this may be written as

(5)
$$\lambda \Pi = P_Q Q(\lambda K, \lambda L) - \lambda P_K K - \lambda P_L L$$

where λ is a positive constant. The profit function is also homogeneous of degree 1 under these assumptions.

Equation (5) leads to three possibilities:

(1) Some combination of prices yields a positive profit. In this case profit can be increased without bound. There is no maximum profit, since larger values of λ (increasing the scale of operation) always increase profit.

(2) No combination of prices results in a positive or zero profit. The firm will go out of business, since any level of operation results in a loss.

(3) All combinations of prices yield negative profit, except one which results in a zero profit. This is the only situation considered by the standard marginal productivity analysis. Note that at this combination of prices the size of the firm is not determinate, since any λ (any level of operation) still results in zero profit. Thus, for the results of the marginal productivity analysis to hold an additional restraint fixing the size of firms must be introduced.

Problems

5.2–1 Calculate $\partial y/\partial x$ and $\partial y/\partial z$ using the definition of partial derivatives if $y = 3x^2z - 2xz^2 + 5z$.

5.2–2 Calculate all first- and second-order partial derivatives if:
(a) $y = xz^2w^3 - 5x^{-1}(x - w)^2$ (c) $y = (x^2 + w)^{-1/2}$
(b) $y = \dfrac{x - z^2}{w^2 + x^{-1}}$

5.2–3 Verify that Young's theorem (Theorem 5.2–1) holds for the functions in Problem 5.2–2.

5.2–4 Calculate the following derivatives:
(a) $\partial z/\partial s$ and $\partial z/\partial t$ if $z = 5x^2 - 3y$, $x = st$, and $y = t^2$
(b) $\partial z/\partial s$ and $\partial z/\partial t$ if $z = -x/y^2 - xy$, $x = s^2 + 3t$, and $y = s/3t^2$
(c) $\partial z/\partial s$ and $\partial z/\partial t$ if $z = x_1^2 + 2x_2x_3$, $x_1 = s + t$, $x_2 = s - t$, and $x_3 = st$
(d) $\partial z/\partial s$ and $\partial z/\partial t$ if $z = 3x_2^3 - x_3^2/x_1x_2$, $x_1 = s/t^2$, $x_2 = 2s$ and $x_3 = (3t^3s)^{1/2}$
(e) $\partial z/\partial s$, $\partial z/\partial t$, and $\partial z/\partial u$ if $z = 7x^2 + 3x - 5$ and $x = 2st^2/(u + 1)$
(f) dz/dt if $z = (6x - x^2)/(y^3 - 2w)$, $x = 3t^2$, $y = \sqrt{t}$, and $w = e^t + 1$
(g) dz/dt if $z = (5t^2 + 3xy)/2w^2y$, $x = t^{1/2}$, $y = w + t$, and $w = 4t^2$
(h) dz/dt if $z = 4x^t$ and $x = t + 1$
(i) dz/dt if $z = 3t^2x - 3x^2t$ and $x = 4t^{3/2}$

5.2–5 Use Theorem 5.2–3 to calculate z_x and x_y if
(a) $x^2 + 3yz = 5$ (c) $x + y + z = 1$
(b) $\dfrac{x - y}{z^2} = 1$

5.2–6 Calculate w_y, x_z, and x_y in Example 8.

5.2–7 Find all the first-order partial derivatives for the following system of simultaneous equations:

$$f = x^2y - w^2z - 3yz = 10$$
$$g = y^{-1}z + 2xw^2 - 1 = 0$$
$$x = 3yz - 2w$$
$$w = z^2 - 5xz$$

5.2–8   Given $f = x^2 + 2yx$ and $g = x^4 + 4y^2x^2 + 4x^3y$, calculate the Jacobian $\partial(f, g)/\partial(x, y)$. Are f and g functionally dependent?

5.2–9   Which of the following functions are homogeneous and of what degree?
(a) $z = x^2 - y^2 + 2xy$ (e) $z = e^x + e^y$
(b) $z = (x + y)/(x^2 + y^2)$ (f) $z = Ax^\alpha y^\beta$
(c) $z = x - 4y + y^{1/3}x^{2/3}$ (g) $z = (x^2 + y^2)^{1/2}$
(d) $z = \ln x + \ln y$

5.2–10   Show that Euler's theorem holds for those functions in Problem 5.2–9 that are homogeneous.

5.2–11   Prove the converse of Euler's theorem (Theorem 5.2–9).

5.3   DIFFERENTIALS

The ordinary derivative dy/dx may be thought of as the ratio of two differentials dy and dx. For finite changes in x and y, $\Delta y = (\Delta y/\Delta x)\,\Delta x$. Given that $y = f(x)$, then as $\Delta x \to 0$, $\Delta y/\Delta x \to dy/dx$ while $\Delta y \to dy$, the differential of y, and $\Delta x \to dx$, the differential of x. Thus dy and dx are to be interpreted as infinitesimal changes in y and x, respectively. Furthermore, as $\Delta x \to 0$ the expression $\Delta y = (\Delta y/\Delta x)\,\Delta x$ becomes $dy = f'\,dx$. Thus $f' = (dy)/(dx)$, which establishes the interpretation of the ordinary derivative as a ratio of differentials.

Example 1. Given $dy/dx = 5x^3 - 3$. Then, by definition, $dy = (5x^3 - 3)\,dx$. Figure 5.3–1 shows the graphical interpretation of dy and dx. dy is a measure of the change in y produced by a change in x equal to dx. Since dy and dx are defined only for infinitesimal changes in x, the relation $dy = f'\,dx$ serves as an approximation to the true change in y produced by a finite change in x. In Figure 5.3–1, f' is the slope of the tangent to the curve at A and is

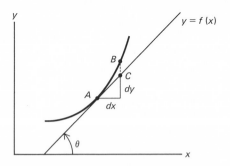

Figure 5.3–1   *Illustration of the differential $dy = f'(x)\,dx$.*

equal to tan θ, which in turn is equal to $(dy)/(dx)$. The true change in y produced by dx in Figure 5.3–1 is not dy, but is equal to $dy + CB$.

The rules for computing differentials can be found by multiplying the rules for derivatives, given in Theorem 5.1–5, by dx.

Differentials of functions of more than one independent variable can also be found. Suppose that $y = f(w, x)$ and we wish to find dy. In this case the change in y will be produced by a change in both w and x. Thus we can write $dy = (\partial f/\partial w) \, dw + (\partial f/\partial x) \, dx$. The term $(\partial f/\partial w) \, dw$ measures that portion of the total change in y resulting from a change in w, holding x constant. $\partial f/\partial w$ measures the rate of change. This, multiplied by dw, gives the actual change in y. The same interpretation of $(\partial f/\partial x) \, dx$ holds. In this case the differential dy is called a **total differential**, since it captures both sources of change in y. Suppose we hold x constant; that is, $dx = 0$. Then

$$(1) \qquad dy = \frac{\partial f}{\partial w}\bigg|_{dx=0} dw$$

In this case dy is called a **partial differential,** since only one source of change in y is measured. If we divide (1) by dw, the resulting expression,

$$\left(\frac{\partial f}{\partial w}\right) = \frac{(dy)}{(dw)}\bigg|_{dx=0}$$

clearly shows that partial derivatives can also be interpreted as a ratio of (partial) differentials.

Second-order differentials can be defined that measure the change in the first-order differential. Thus $d^2y = d(dy)$. If y is a function of only one variable, $d^2y = d(dy) = d(f' \, dx) = f''(dx)^2$. Thus the second-order derivative may also be interpreted as a ratio of two differentials d^2y and $(dx)^2$. Second-order total differentials can be obtained in the same manner. If $y = f(w, x)$, then $dy = f_w \, dw + f_x \, dx$ and $d^2y = d(dy) = d(f_w \, dw + f_x \, dx)$. By the definition of dy,

$$d^2y = \frac{\partial(f_w \, dw + f_x \, dx)}{\partial w} \, dw + \frac{\partial(f_w \, dw + f_x \, dx)}{\partial x} \, dx$$

Performing the partial differentiation,

$$d^2y = (f_{ww} \, dw + f_{xw} \, dx) \, dw + (f_{wx} \, dw + f_{xx} \, dx) \, dx$$

Collecting terms and applying Young's theorem,[8]

$$d^2y = f_{ww} \, (dw)^2 + 2f_{wx} \, dw \, dx + f_{xx} \, (dx)^2$$

---

[8] Theorem 5.2–1.

Example 2.   Given $y = 5w^2x + 3x^3w + 5$, find dy and d^2y.

$$dy = \frac{\partial f}{\partial w} dw + \frac{\partial f}{\partial x} dx = (10wx + 3x^3) dw + (5w^2 + 9x^2w) dx$$

and

$$d^2y = (10x)(dw)^2 + 2(10w + 9x^2) dw \, dx + (18xw)(dx)^2$$

Higher-order differentials may be computed in the same way as total differentials for functions of more than two independent variables.

Problems

5.3–1   Find dy and d^2y for the following functions:

(a) $y = 3x^2 - 4x$ (d) $y = 5x^2 + 3zx - 4z^2$

(b) $y^2 + 3xy - 2y = 0$ (e) $y = \dfrac{(x-1)^2}{z - 2x}$

(c) $y = 3x^2z - 4z^3w + 5xwz$

5.4   EXTREME VALUES

One of the best known and most widely applied areas of the calculus is finding extreme values (maxima and minima) of functions of one or more variables. As we shall see, differentials play a key role in these procedures. In the remainder of this chapter we shall examine the procedures for finding extreme values both with and without additional constraints.

DEFINITION 5.4–1 $y = f(x)$ attains a **strong, local, interior maximum** at $x = \bar{x}$ if and only if $dy = f'(x) \, dx < 0$ for all x arbitrarily close to $\bar{x}$, $x \neq \bar{x}$, in the domain of the function. Alternatively, it must be true that $f(\bar{x}) > f(x^0)$ for all x^0 such that $|\bar{x} - x^0| < \delta$, where δ is an arbitrarily small positive number and x^0 is in the domain of x.

DEFINITION 5.4–2 $y = f(x)$ attains a **weak, local, interior maximum** at $x = \bar{x}$ if and only if $dy = f'(x) \, dx \leq 0$ for all x such that $|\bar{x} - x| < \delta$, for δ a positive number, and $f(\bar{x}) \geq f(x')$ for all x' such that $|\bar{x} - x'| < \eta$, where η is a positive number greater than δ and x and x' are in the domain of x the function.

Figure 5.4–1 illustrates these two concepts. Clearly, $dy = 0$ for values of x close to $\bar{x}$ in Figure 5.4–1b, which is not the case in Figure 5.4–1a. Strong and weak local, interior minima may be defined in an analogous manner. For a minimum substitute $dy > 0$ and $f(\bar{x}) < f(x^0)$ in the previous definitions.

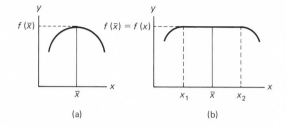

Figure 5.4–1 (a) *Strong maximum.* (b) *Weak maximum.*

The maxima defined above are called interior maxima because they do not occur at values of x on the boundary of the domain. Figure 5.4–2 shows exterior (or boundary) extreme points. The domain of x is assumed to be $x \geq 0$.

Figure 5.4–2b also illustrates why we have used the terms local maximum and local minimum. This function (at least the portion of it shown) has two local minima, $f(x_1)$ and $f(x_3)$, and two local maxima, $f(0)$ and $f(x_2)$.

DEFINITION 5.4–3 Given $y = f(x)$ attains local maxima (minima) at $f(\bar{x}_1), f(\bar{x}_2), \ldots, f(\bar{x}_n)$. Then y attains a **global maximum** (minimum) at $f(\bar{x}_1)$ if and only if $f(\bar{x}_1) \geq (\leq) f(\bar{x}_2), f(\bar{x}_3), \ldots, f(\bar{x}_n)$.

Note that global maximum or minimum points may be either weak or strong, interior or exterior.

DEFINITION 5.4–4 Local maximum and minimum points are called **extreme points. Critical values** are maxima and minima as well as inflection points.

Theorem 5.4–1 If $y = f(x)$ is continuous and has a continuous first derivative and if $x = \bar{x}$ is an extreme point, then $f'(\bar{x}) = 0$.

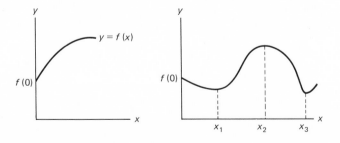

Figure 5.4–2 (a) *Exterior local minimum at* $x = 0$. (b) *Exterior local maximum at* $x = 0$.

PROOF   (for max at $x = \bar{x}$)

$$f'(\bar{x}) = \lim_{\Delta x \to 0} \frac{f(\bar{x} + \Delta x) - f(\bar{x})}{\Delta x}$$

But $f(\bar{x} + \Delta x) - f(\bar{x}) \leq 0$ by hypothesis. Thus

$$\frac{f(\bar{x} + \Delta x) - f(\bar{x})}{\Delta x} \leq 0 \qquad \text{if} \quad \Delta x > 0$$

and

$$\frac{f(\bar{x} + \Delta x) - f(\bar{x})}{\Delta x} \geq 0 \qquad \text{if} \quad \Delta x < 0$$

Also,

$$\lim_{\Delta x \to 0^+} \frac{f(\bar{x} + \Delta x) - f(\bar{x})}{\Delta x} = \lim_{\Delta x \to 0^-} \frac{f(\bar{x} + \Delta x) - f(\bar{x})}{\Delta x}$$

since $f'(\bar{x})$ is assumed to exist. But $\Delta x \to 0^-$ implies that $f'(\bar{x}) \geq 0$ and $\Delta x \to 0^+$ implies that $f'(x) \leq 0$, so $0 \geq f'(\bar{x}) \geq 0$. The only way this can be true is if

$$f'(\bar{x}) = 0 \qquad \text{QED}$$

The proof is similar if $f(\bar{x})$ is a local minimum. The theorem says only that an interior extreme point implies that the derivative is zero. It does not say that $f'(\bar{x}) = 0$ implies that $f(\bar{x})$ is an extreme point. Nor do all extreme points occur at points where the function is differentiable. Nor does it say anything about exterior extreme points where one of the two limits, $\lim_{\Delta x \to 0^-}$ and $\lim_{\Delta x \to 0^+}$, do not exist. Exterior points and points where the derivative does not exist must be examined separately.

Theorem 5.4-2   *Second Derivative Test*   Given that $f'(x)$ is continuous and $f'(\bar{x}) = 0$, then $f(\bar{x})$ is a local maximum if

$$\left. \frac{d^2 y}{dx^2} \right|_{x=\bar{x}} < 0$$

$f(\bar{x})$ is a local minimum if

$$\left. \frac{d^2 y}{dx^2} \right|_{x=\bar{x}} > \cup$$

Parts (a) and (b) of Figure 5.4–3 illustrate the theorem. Part (c) shows an inflection point at $\bar{x}$ for which $f'(\bar{x}) = 0 = f''(\bar{x})$. If $f'(x)$ had an inflection point at $\bar{x}$ in parts (a) and (b), as is possible given slight alterations in the functions shown, then $f''(\bar{x})$ would also be zero and the second-derivative test for a maximum or minimum would fail. In such a case one must apply Theorem 5.4–3.

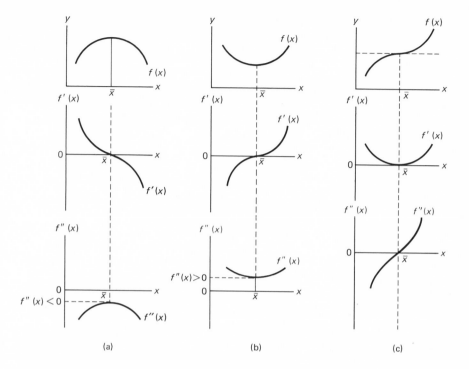

Figure 5.4–3 *(a) $f(x)$ a maximum at $\bar{x}$.   (b) $f(\bar{x})$ a minimum.   (c) An inflection point at $f(x)$.*

Theorem 5.4–3   *nth Derivative Test*   Given $f'(\bar{x}) = 0 = f''(\bar{x})$, $y = f(x)$
(a) attains a local maximum at $x = \bar{x}$ if for the first nonzero derivative, $f^{(n)}(\bar{x}) < 0$ and n is an even number;
(b) attains a local minimum if for the first nonzero derivative, $f^{(n)}(\bar{x}) > 0$ and n is an even number; and
(c) has an inflection point if the first nonzero derivative is of odd order (n an odd number).

The proofs of Theorems 5.4–2 and 5.4–3 rely on the Taylor's series expansion of a function about the point $x = \bar{x}$.

DEFINITION 5.4–5   The **Taylor's series expansion** of $y = f(x)$ about the point $x = \bar{x}$ is

(1) $f(x) = f(\bar{x}) + f'(\bar{x})(x - \bar{x}) + \dfrac{f''(\bar{x})}{2!}(x - \bar{x})^2 + \dfrac{f'''(\bar{x})}{3!}(x - \bar{x})^3$

$$+ \cdots + \frac{f^{(n)}(\bar{x})}{n!}(x - \bar{x})^n + \cdots$$

Equation (1) is an infinite series. If we disregard the terms of degree larger than n, (1) is only an approximation to $f(x)$. Usually these higher-degree terms are lumped together into a remainder term, a device that preserves the equality. Although there are several forms for the remainder term, the most useful is the Lagrange form of the remainder.

DEFINITION 5.4–6   The **Lagrange form of the remainder** in a Taylor's series expansion is

$$R_N(x, \bar{x}) = f^{(n+1)}(x_0) \frac{(x - \bar{x})^{n+1}}{(n + 1)!}$$

where x_0 is some value between x and $\bar{x}$.

With this definition we can write

$$f(x) = f(\bar{x}) + f'(\bar{x})(x - \bar{x}) + \frac{f''(\bar{x})(x - \bar{x})^2}{2!}$$

$$+ \cdots + \frac{f^{(n)}(\bar{x})(x - \bar{x})^n}{n!} + \frac{f^{(n+1)}(x_0)(x - \bar{x})^{n+1}}{(n + 1)!}$$

or

$$(2) \qquad f(x) - f(\bar{x}) = f'(\bar{x})(x - \bar{x}) + \frac{f''(\bar{x})(x - \bar{x})^2}{2!}$$

$$+ \cdots + \frac{f^n(\bar{x})(x - \bar{x})^n}{n!} + \frac{f^{(n+1)}(x_0)(x - \bar{x})^{n+1}}{(n + 1)!}$$

Going back to the definitions of maxima and minima, we can see that $f(\bar{x})$ is a maximum if the left side (and hence the right side) of (2) is negative and is a minimum if the left side is positive. Since we are free to choose any integer value for n, (2) provides the vehicle for proving the theorems.

Rather than proving all the parts of these theorems, we shall illustrate one proof and leave the rest for the reader.

SKETCH PROOF OF THEOREM   5.4–3(c)   Suppose $f'(\bar{x}) = f''(\bar{x}) = 0$ and $f'''(\bar{x}) > 0$. Then if we let $n = 2$ in (2), the equation becomes

$$f(x) - f(\bar{x}) = f'(\bar{x})(x - \bar{x}) + \frac{f''(\bar{x})(x - \bar{x})^2}{2!} + \frac{f'''(x_0)(x - \bar{x})^3}{3!}$$

By hypothesis this reduces to

$$f(x) - f(\bar{x}) = \frac{f'''(x_0)(x - \bar{x})^3}{3!}$$

One criterion for applying the Taylor's series expansion to a given function is that all the derivatives exist and are continuous.[9] Since $f'''(x)$ is continuous

---

[9] The reader not familiar with Maclaurin's and Taylor's series expansions should refer to Thomas (1968), pages 787ff.

and since x_0 is arbitrarily close to $\bar{x}$, $f'''(x_0)$ must have the same sign as $f'''(\bar{x})$. Thus $f'''(x_0) > 0$. What about the sign of $(x - \bar{x})^3$? If $\bar{x} > x$, $x - \bar{x} < 0$ and $(x - \bar{x})^3 < 0$. But if $\bar{x} < x$, $(x - \bar{x})^3 > 0$. Consequently, $f(x) - f(\bar{x})$ changes sign depending on whether $x > \bar{x}$ or $x < \bar{x}$. Thus $f(\bar{x})$ can be neither a maximum nor a minimum and must be an inflection point.

The other parts of both theorems may be proven in an analogous way.

The requirement that $f'(x) = 0$ for extreme points is often called the **first-order condition.** It is **necessary,** but not a sufficient condition, as the existence of inflection points where $f' = 0$ shows. The **sufficient, or second-order conditions** are embodied in the second derivative test or, if it fails, in the nth derivative test.

We turn now to the question of finding unconstrained critical values for functions of two or more independent variables. We shall consider specifically the case of two independent variables, $z = f(x, y)$, and then generalize the results to functions of more than two independent variables.

The first-order condition that, as before, is necessary, but not sufficient is

$$f_x = f_y = 0$$

The first-order condition fails to discriminate between extreme values and saddle points (or inflection points), as Figure 5.4–4 illustrates. In part (a), z attains a maximum at $(\bar{x}, \bar{y})$ and, as the arrows indicate, both first-order partial derivatives are zero at that point. In part (b) the point $(\bar{x}, \bar{y})$ is obviously neither a maximum nor a minimum, although $f_x = f_y = 0$. Such a point is called a **saddle point**—a name derived from the general shape of the graph of the function. Movement away from the saddle point along the line $y = \bar{y}$ decreases z, while movements away along $x = \bar{x}$ increase the value of z. In part (a) movement away from the point $(\bar{x}, \bar{y})$ in any direction reduces the value of z. In terms of the total differential, $dz = f_x\, dx + f_y\, dy$, $f_x = f_y = 0$ implies that $dz = 0$ and vice versa. $dz = 0$ is thus an alternative and equivalent statement of the first-order condition.

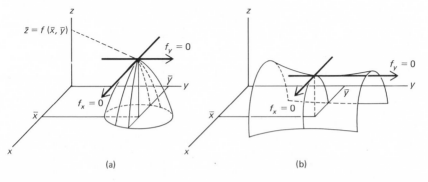

Figure 5.4–4   (a) Maximum at $(\bar{x}, \bar{y})$.   (b) Saddle point at $(\bar{x}, \bar{y})$.

Given $dz = 0$ at $(\bar{x}, \bar{y})$, the second-order condition can be stated in terms of the second-order total differential, d^2z. If $(\bar{x}, \bar{y})$ is a maximum, movements away from this point in any direction will reduce the value of z. This means that for any values of x and y arbitrarily close to $\bar{x}$ and $\bar{y}$, $x = \bar{x} \pm a$ and $y = \bar{y} \pm b$, dz evaluated at $(\bar{x} \pm a, \bar{y} \pm b)$ must be negative. This means that dz is decreasing or that $d^2z < 0$. A similar argument shows that if $(\bar{x}, \bar{y})$ is a minimum, $d^2z > 0$. For either a saddle point or an inflection point d^2z changes sign depending on the direction of movement away from $(\bar{x}, \bar{y})$. In terms of partial derivatives the second-order condition becomes

$$d^2z = f_{xx}\,(dx)^2 + 2f_{xy}\,dx\,dy + f_{yy}\,(dy)^2 \qquad \begin{array}{l} < 0 \text{ for a maximum} \\ > 0 \text{ for a minimum} \end{array}$$

This expression for d^2z is an example of a quadratic form.[10]

By Theorem 4.4–1, (a) d^2z is positive definite if $f_{xx} > 0$ and $f_{xx}f_{yy} - (f_{xy})^2 > 0$ and (b) d^2z is negative definite if and only if $f_{xx} < 0$ and $f_{xx}f_{yy} - (f_{xy})^2 > 0$. Thus d^2z being positive definite is the second-order condition for a minimum, while d^2z being negative definite is the second-order condition for a maximum.

The second-order condition is more easily generalized to functions of more variables if it is written in matrix form as

$$z = [x \; y]\begin{bmatrix} a & b \\ b & c \end{bmatrix}\begin{bmatrix} x \\ y \end{bmatrix}$$

DEFINITION 5.4–7 A determinant whose elements are second-order partial derivatives is called a **Hessian determinant,** denoted H.

In terms of the Hessian, the second-order conditions become
(a) d^2z is positive definite if the first principal minor[11] (f_{xx}) is positive and the second principal minor

$$\begin{vmatrix} f_{xx} & f_{xy} \\ f_{yx} & f_{yy} \end{vmatrix} = f_{xx}f_{yy} - (f_{xy})^2$$

is positive.
(b) d^2z is negative definite if the first principal minor is negative, while the second principal minor is positive.

Consider a quadratic form in three variables:

$$z = [x_1, \, x_2, \, x_3]\begin{bmatrix} a_{11} & a_{12} & a_{13} \\ a_{21} & a_{22} & a_{23} \\ a_{31} & a_{32} & a_{33} \end{bmatrix}\begin{bmatrix} x_1 \\ x_2 \\ x_3 \end{bmatrix}$$

[10] See Section 4.4.
[11] See Definition 4.3–2.

This corresponds to the second-order total differential of a function of three independent variables, $z = f(x_1, x_2, x_3)$,

$$d^2z = f_{11}\,(dx_1)^2 + f_{12}\,dx_1\,dx_2 + f_{13}\,dx_1\,dx_3 + f_{21}\,dx_2\,dx_1 + f_{22}\,(dx_2)^2$$
$$+ f_{23}\,dx_2\,dx_3 + f_{31}\,dx_3\,dx_1 + f_{32}\,dx_3\,dx_2 + f_{33}\,(dx_3)^2$$

where, by Young's theorem, $f_{ij} = f_{ji}$ for all $i = 1, 2, 3$ and $j = 1, 2, 3$. The matrix $A = [a_{ij}]$ is the Hessian, while x_1, x_2, and x_3 play the roles of dx_1, dx_2, and dx_3. The Hessian has three principal minors in this case:

$$D_1 = f_{11}$$

$$D_2 = \begin{vmatrix} f_{11} & f_{12} \\ f_{21} & f_{22} \end{vmatrix}$$

$$D_3 = \begin{vmatrix} f_{11} & f_{12} & f_{13} \\ f_{21} & f_{22} & f_{23} \\ f_{31} & f_{32} & f_{33} \end{vmatrix}$$

By completing the square in the expression for d^2z and applying Young's theorem, we obtain

$$d^2z = f_{11}\left(dx_1 + \frac{f_{12}}{f_{11}}\,dx_2 + \frac{f_{13}}{f_{11}}\,dx_3 \right)^2$$
$$+ \frac{f_{11}f_{22} - (f_{12})^2}{f_{11}}\left[dx_2 + \frac{f_{11}f_{33} - f_{12}f_{13}}{f_{11}f_{22} - (f_{12})^2}\,dx_3 \right]^2$$
$$+ \left[\frac{f_{11}f_{22}f_{33} - f_{11}(f_{23})^2 - f_{22}(f_{13})^2 - f_{33}(f_{12})^2 + 2f_{12}f_{13}f_{23}}{f_{11}f_{22} - (f_{12})^2} \right](dx_3)^2$$

The second-order conditions for the three variable case become d^2z positive definite if and only if:
  (a) $f_{11} > 0$;
  (b) $f_{11}f_{22} - (f_{12})^2 > 0$ (since $f_{11} > 0$); and
  (c) the numerator of the coefficient of $(dx_3)^2 > 0$ (since $f_{11}f_{22} - (f_{12})^2 > 0$).
However, $f_{11} = D_1$, $f_{11}f_{22} - (f_{12})^2 = D_2$, and D_3 is the numerator in (c). Thus, for positive definiteness, the signs of the principal minors must all be positive.

  For d^2z negative definite:
  (a) $f_{11} < 0$;
  (b) $f_{11}f_{22} - (f_{12})^2 > 0$ (since $f_{11} < 0$); and
  (c) the numerator of the coefficient of $(dx_3)^2 < 0$ (since $f_{11}f_{22} - (f_{12})^2 > 0$).
Thus, in terms of the principal minors, d^2z is negative definite if and only if the principal minors alternate in sign, beginning with $D_1 < 0$.

For functions of n independent variables the associated quadratic form (d^2z) will be positive definite if and only if all the principal minors of the Hessian are positive. For negative definiteness the principal minors must alternate in sign, beginning with $D_1 < 0$; that is, all odd-numbered principal minors are <0 while all even numbered ones are >0.

Table 5.4–1 summarizes the first- and second-order conditions for functions of one or more independent variables. It must be understood that the second-order conditions both for the constrained and unconstrained problems are incomplete. If $d^2z = 0$ for all values of the independent variables, that is, all second-order partial derivatives are identically zero, the second-order conditions fail. Nonetheless, the critical value may still be either a maximum or a minimum. In all other cases where the second-order conditions fail, the critical value will be a saddle point.

Example 1.   Find the extreme values of $f(x) = 3x^2 - 4x^3$. $f'(x) = 6x - 12x^2$. Solving for the values of x that equate $f'(x)$ to zero we obtain

$$6x(1 - 2x) = 0$$

so the extreme values are $x_1 = 0$ and $x_2 = \frac{1}{2}$. To find the nature of these extreme values we must calculate $f''(x)$ and $f'''(x)$:

$$f''(x) = 6 - 24x$$
$$f''(0) = 6 \quad \text{and} \quad f''(\tfrac{1}{4}) = 0$$
$$f'''(x) = -24 = f'''(0) = f'''(\tfrac{1}{4})$$

Thus, from Table 5.4–1, $x = 0$ is a minimum while $x = \frac{1}{2}$ is an inflection point. The function has no maximum.

Find the extreme values of $f(x, y) = x^2y - y^2x$. $f_x = 2xy - y^2$ and $f_y = x^2 - 2xy$. Then $f_x = 0$ for the following values of x and y:

(1) $(x, 0)$

and

(2) $(\tfrac{1}{2}y, y)$

while $f_y = 0$ for

(3) $(0, y)$

and

(4) $(2y, y)$

Since f_x and f_y must both be zero for the same values of y and x to satisfy the first-order conditions, solutions of the forms (3) and (4) are not critical values.

Table 5.4–1

Function	Critical Value	First Order	Second Order
$y = f(x)$	max at $x = \bar{x}$	$f'(\bar{x}) = 0$	$f''(\bar{x}) < 0$; if $f''(\bar{x}) = 0$ first nonzero derivative < 0 and of even order
	min at $x = \bar{x}$	$f'(\bar{x}) = 0$	$f''(\bar{x}) > 0$; if $f''(\bar{x}) = 0$ first nonzero derivative > 0 and of even order
	inflection pt. at $x = \bar{x}$	$f'(\bar{x}) = 0$	$f''(\bar{x}) = 0$ and first nonzero derivative is of odd order
$z = f(x, y)$	max at $(\bar{x}, \bar{y})$	$f_x = f_y = 0$	$f_{xx} < 0$ and $f_{xx}f_{yy} - (f_{xy})^2 > 0$
	min at $(\bar{x}, \bar{y})$	$f_x = f_y = 0$	$f_{xx} > 0$ and $f_{xx}f_{yy} - (f_{xy})^2 > 0$
	saddle pt. at $(\bar{x}, y)$	$f_x = f_y = 0$	d^2z neither positive nor negative definite
$z = f(x_1, x_2, \ldots, x_n)$	max at $(\bar{x}_1, \bar{x}_2, \ldots, \bar{x}_n)$	$f_{x_1} = f_{x_2} = \cdots = f_{x_n} = 0$	principal minors alternate in sign, i.e., $D_1 < 0, D_2 > 0, D_3 < 0$, etc.
	min at $(\bar{x}_1, \bar{x}_2, \ldots, \bar{x}_n)$	$f_{x_1} = f_{x_2} = \cdots = f_{x_n} = 0$	all principal minors positive, i.e., $D_1 > 0, D_2 > 0, \ldots, D_n > 0$
	saddle pt. at $(\bar{x}_1, \bar{x}_2, \ldots, \bar{x}_n)$	$f_{x_1} = f_{x_2} = \cdots = f_{x_n} = 0$	d^2z neither positive nor negative definite

Thus the only critical value for this function is $(0, 0)$, a combination of (1) and (3). To find the nature of this extreme value calculate:

(a) $$f_{xx} = 2y$$

(b) $$f_{yy} = -2x$$

and

(c) $$f_{xy} = 2x$$

Since $f_{xx}|_{(0,0)} = 0$ and $[f_{xx}f_{yy} - (f_{xy})^2]|_{(0,0)} = 4x^2|_{(0,0)} = 0$, the point $(0, 0)$ is a saddle point. No maxima nor minima exist for this function.

Functions may also be maximized or minimized subject to additional relations or constraints. The methods used to solve such problems depend on both the number of independent variables and on the nature of the constraints. Generally speaking, problems where the constraints are inequalities, and can remain inequalities in the solution, are solved through various programming techniques. Problems of this type will be discussed in Chapters 11 and 12. Problems where the constraints are equalities or where they must be equalities in the solution can be treated by more "standard" methods and are our present topic.

For functions of one independent variable, $y = f(x)$, the constraints may either be of the type $x \gtrless \alpha$, where α is a constant, or they may be functions of x and y, $G(x, y) = 0$. In problems of the first type the effect of the constraint is to limit the domain of the function. Solutions are obtained by applying the techniques for unconstrained optimization to the restricted domain, remembering to check for exterior extreme points. In the trivial case where the constraint is $x = \alpha$, the solution is simply $\bar{y} = f(\alpha)$.

Problems of the second type are simply a system of two equations, $y = f(x)$ and $G(x, y) = 0$, in two unknowns, x and y. Solving the system simultaneously and comparing y values for each solution provides the necessary information.

Example 2. Find the maximum and minimum values of $y = x^2 + \frac{1}{5}$ subject to $x + y = 0$. From the constraint, $x = -y$. Substituting, $y = y^2 + \frac{1}{5}$, or $y^2 - y + \frac{1}{5} = 0$. This quadratic equation has two solutions, one of which will be the constrained maximum value of y and the other the minimum value. By the quadratic formula,

$$y = \frac{1 \pm \sqrt{1 - (4)(1)\frac{1}{5}}}{2} = \frac{1 \pm \sqrt{\frac{1}{5}}}{2}$$

Thus $y_{max} = \frac{1}{2} + 1/2\sqrt{5}$ and $y_{min} = \frac{1}{2} - 1/2\sqrt{5}$.

Consider the following general problem: Find the extreme values of $z = f(x, y)$ subject to $G(x, y) = 0$. Problems of this type can be solved by substitution. The constraint can be rewritten as $y = g(x)$. The function to be maximized or minimized then becomes a composite function of one independent variable: $z = f[x, g(x)]$. The critical values can be found by applying the procedure for unconstrained critical values of functions of one variable.

As a practical consideration, expressing y as a function of x may either be very difficult or, in certain cases as we have already seen when discussing implicit functions, impossible. The technique of Lagrangean multipliers has been developed to overcome these difficulties.

Theorem 5.4-4   Given that $z = f(x, y)$ and $G(x, y) = 0$ are continuous and have continuous first-order partial derivatives. If $(\partial G/\partial x)^2 + (\partial G/\partial y)^2 > 0$, then the set of points (x, y) satisfying $G(x, y) = 0$, where $f(x, y)$ has maxima or minima, is included in the solutions to the following system of equations:

$$f_x + \lambda G_x = 0$$

$$f_y + \lambda G_y = 0$$

$$G(x, y) = 0$$

where λ is a Lagrangean multiplier.

If we treat x as the independent variable in $G(x, y) = 0$, we can calculate the total derivative $dz/dx = f_x - f_y(G_x/G_y) = \partial(f, G)/\partial(x, y)$. The necessary, but not sufficient, condition for z to be at a maximum or minimum is $dz/dx = 0$. To calculate dz/dx, G_y must not be zero. Thus the extreme values are included in the solutions to the equation system

$$\frac{\partial(f, G)}{\partial(x, y)} = 0 \quad \text{and} \quad G(x, y) = 0$$

If $G_y = 0$ we must treat y as the independent variable and calculate $dz/dy = f_y - f_x(G_y/G_x)$. The necessary condition is $dz/dy = 0$. Thus $dz/dy = \partial(f, G)/\partial(x, y) = 0$, and we have the same two equations to solve simultaneously. If both G_x and $G_y = 0$ the system cannot be solved. (Why?) Thus the requirement in the theorem that $(G_x)^2 + (G_y)^2 > 0$.

The use of Lagrangean multipliers leads to the same set of equations, thus proving the theorem. First, form the Lagrangean expression $L = f(x, y) + \lambda G(x, y)$. In this method we treat both x and y as independent variables. Differentiating L with respect to x and y yields

(1)
$$\frac{\partial L}{\partial x} = f_x + \lambda G_x$$

(2)
$$\frac{\partial L}{\partial y} = f_y + \lambda G_y$$

The necessary condition for functions of two variables requires that $\partial L/\partial x = \partial L/\partial y = 0$. Thus we have the system

(3) $$L_x = f_x + \lambda G_x = 0$$

(4) $$L_y = f_y + \lambda G_y = 0$$

Either of these equations may be solved for λ. From (3), $\lambda = -f_x/G_x$. Substituting into (4): $f_y - f_x(G_y/G_x) = 0 = \partial(f, G)/\partial(x, y)$. This equation together with the requirement $G(x, y) = 0$ yields the same system of simultaneous equations as before, thus proving the theorem. Strictly speaking, there are three equations to solve simultaneously for the three unknowns x, y, and λ:

(5) $$L_x = f_x + \lambda G_x = 0$$

(6) $$L_y = f_y + \lambda G_y = 0$$

(7) $$G(x, y) = 0$$

Note that Equation (7), our original constraint, is equal to $\partial L/\partial \lambda$. Thus our simultaneous system is obtained by differentiating the Lagrangean expression with respect to x, y, and λ and setting the resulting expressions equal to zero. It must be stressed that solutions to this system only satisfy the first-order condition, which is necessary but *not* sufficient. Before examining the second-order conditions we shall generalize the method by examining: (1) functions of more than two independent variables with one constraint, and (2) functions with more than two variables subject to more than one constraint.

Case 1. $z = f(x_1, x_2, \ldots, x_n)$ subject to $G(x_1, x_2, \ldots, x_n) = 0$. The Lagrangean expression is $L = f(x_1, x_2, \ldots, x_n) + \lambda G(x_1, x_2, \ldots, x_n)$. The first-order condition is satisfied by solutions to the following system of $n + 1$ simultaneous equations:

$$L_{x_1} = f_{x_1} + \lambda G_{x_1} = 0$$
$$L_{x_2} = f_{x_2} + \lambda G_{x_2} = 0$$
$$\vdots$$
$$L_{x_n} = f_{x_n} + \lambda G_{x_n} = 0$$
$$L_\lambda = G(x_1, x_2, \ldots, x_n) = 0$$

Case 2. $z = f(x_1, x_2, \ldots, x_n)$ subject to $G_1(x_1, x_2, \ldots, x_n) = G_2(x_1, x_2, \ldots, x_n) = \cdots = G_m(x_1, x_2, \ldots, x_n) = 0$ and $m \leq n$. A different Lagrangean multiplier is introduced for each constraint. Thus the Lagrangean expression is

$$L = f(x_1, x_2, \ldots, x_n) + \lambda_1 G_1(x_1, x_2, \ldots, x_n) + \lambda_2 G_2(x_1, x_2, \ldots, x_n)$$
$$+ \cdots + \lambda_m G_m(x_1, x_2, \ldots, x_n)$$

The solutions to the following system of $m + n$ simultaneous equations satisfy the first-order condition:

$$L_{x_1} = f_{x_1} + \lambda_1 G_{1_{x_1}} + \lambda_2 G_{2_{x_1}} + \cdots + \lambda_m G_{m_{x_1}} = 0$$
$$\vdots$$
$$L_{x_n} = f_{x_n} + \lambda_1 G_{1_{x_n}} + \lambda_2 G_{2_{x_n}} + \cdots + \lambda_m G_{m_{x_n}} = 0$$
$$L_{\lambda_1} = G_1(x_1, x_2, \ldots, x_n) = 0$$
$$\vdots$$
$$L_{\lambda_m} = G_m(x_1, x_2, \ldots, x_n) = 0$$

The second-order conditions, regardless of the number of constraints and/or independent variables, again involve an examination of the second-order total differential of the dependent variable, d^2z. One additional condition must be satisfied. The first-order total differential of each constraint, dG_i, $i = 1$, $2, \ldots, n$, must be zero, as should be obvious from the nature of the constraint(s). Thus the second-order conditions are, by analogous arguments to those given in the unconstrained case:

(a) d^2z positive definite and $dG = 0$ imply a minimum, and
(b) d^2z negative definite and $dG = 0$ imply a maximum.

The conditions for positive and negative definiteness again are derived from the second-order total differential expressed as a quadratic form. The argument will be developed for the case of two independent variables and one constraint. The more general formulation will be given later.

Given $z = f(x, y)$ and $G(x, y) = 0$. Then

(1) $$dz = f_x \, dx + f_y \, dy$$

(2) $$dG = G_x \, dx + G_y \, dy = 0$$

Equation (2) establishes a fixed relation between dy and dx, which means that we can no longer treat them as independent. For each selection of dx, Equation (2) determines a specific value of dy. (Cf. the discussion following Theorem 5.4–4.) This will be reflected in the form of d^2z as follows:

$$d^2z = \frac{\partial}{\partial x}(f_x \, dx + f_y \, dy) \, dx + \frac{\partial}{\partial y}(f_x \, dx + f_y \, dy) \, dy$$

$$= \left[f_{xx} \, dx + f_x \frac{\partial(dx)}{\partial x} + f_{yx} \, dy + f_y \frac{\partial(dy)}{\partial x} \right] dx$$

$$+ \left[f_{xy} \, dx + f_x \frac{\partial(dx)}{\partial y} + f_{yy} \, dy + f_y \frac{\partial(dy)}{\partial y} \right] dy$$

One of the derivatives, $\partial(dx)/\partial y$ or $\partial(dy)/\partial x$, will be zero depending on whether x or y is treated as the independent variable. Suppose we choose x. Then dx is arbitrary (a constant) and $\partial(dx)/\partial y = 0$. The expression for d^2z then reduces to

$$d^2z = \left[f_{xx} \, dx + f_{yx} \, dy + f_y \frac{\partial(dy)}{\partial x} \right] dx + \left[f_{xy} \, dx + f_{yy} \, dy + f_y \frac{\partial(dy)}{\partial y} \right] dy$$

However,

$$f_y \left[\frac{\partial(dy)}{\partial x} \, dx + \frac{\partial(dy)}{\partial y} \right] = f_y \, d^2y$$

so the expression simplifies to

(3) $\qquad d^2z = f_{xx} \, (dx)^2 + 2f_{xy} \, dx \, dy + f_{yy} \, (dy)^2 + f_y \, d^2y$

This is not a quadratic form, since the term $f_y \, d^2y$ is of first degree. However, the constraint can be used to solve for d^2y. Writing the second-order total differential of $G(x, y) = 0$, we have

$$d^2G = G_{xx} \, (dx)^2 + 2G_{xy} \, dx \, dy + G_{yy} \, (dy)^2 + G_y \, d^2y = 0$$

(The reader should verify this.) Solving for d^2y,

$$d^2y = -\left[\frac{G_{xx} \, (dx)^2 + 2G_{xy} \, dx \, dy + G_{yy} \, (dy)^2}{G_y} \right]$$

When this expression is substituted for d^2y in (3) we obtain, after simplification:

$$d^2z = \left(f_{xx} - \frac{f_y}{G_y} G_{xx} \right)(dx)^2 + 2\left(f_{xy} - \frac{f_y}{G_y} G_{xy} \right) dx \, dy$$
$$+ \left(f_{yy} - \frac{f_y}{G_y} G_{yy} \right)(dy)^2$$

which is, as the reader can verify, a quadratic form.

Consider the Lagrangean expression for this problem:

$$L = f(x, y) + \lambda G(x, y)$$

Taking the second-order partial derivatives of L we obtain

$$L_{xx} = f_{xx} + \lambda G_{xx}$$
$$L_{xy} = f_{xy} + \lambda G_{xy}$$
$$L_{yy} = f_{yy} + \lambda G_{yy}$$

If we solve the expression for L_y for λ we have

$$L_y = f_y + \lambda G_y = 0 \quad \text{or} \quad \lambda = -\frac{f_y}{G_y}$$

Substituting this result for λ in the expressions for the second-order derivatives, the second-order total differential can be written as

$$d^2z = L_{xx}\,(dx)^2 + 2L_{xy}\,dx\,dy + L_{yy}\,(dy)^2$$

This gives the Hessian determinant

$$H = \begin{vmatrix} L_{xx} & L_{xy} \\ L_{xy} & L_{yy} \end{vmatrix}$$

which, were it not for the constraint $dG = 0$, could be used to check the second-order conditions. This constraint implies that $dy = -(G_x/G_y)\,dx$. Substituting into the expression for d^2z and simplifying,

$$d^2z = (dx)^2 \left[L_{xx} - 2L_{xy}\frac{G_x}{G_y} + L_{yy}\left(\frac{G_x}{G_y}\right)^2 \right]$$

The positive or negative definiteness of this expression depends solely on the sign of the term in the square brackets. Factoring out $1/(G_y)^2$, which is obviously positive, we obtain

$$d^2z = \frac{(dx)^2}{(G_y)^2}\,[L_{xx}(G_y)^2 - 2L_{xy}G_xG_y + L_{yy}(G_x)^2]$$

The sign of d^2z depends only on the term in square brackets. Adding a new first row $(0,\ Gx,\ Gy)$ and first column

$$\begin{bmatrix} 0 \\ G_x \\ G_y \end{bmatrix}$$

to the Hessian determinant we obtain the **bordered Hessian, H^B**:

$$H^B = \begin{vmatrix} 0 & G_x & G_y \\ G_x & L_{xx} & L_{xy} \\ G_y & L_{xy} & L_{yy} \end{vmatrix}$$

Expanding H^B by the elements of column 1 we obtain

$$H^B = -G_x(G_xL_{yy} - G_yL_{xy}) + G_y(G_xL_{xy} - G_yL_{xx})$$

$$= -L_{xx}(G_y)^2 + 2L_{xy}G_xG_y - L_{yy}(G_x)^2$$

The value of H^B is thus the negative of the value of the term on which the sign of d^2z depends. Thus if $H^B > 0$, $d^2z < 0$ and vice versa.

The second-order conditions can thus be stated as follows for the two-variable, one-constraint problem:

(a) If $H^B > 0$, d^2z is negative definite, which leads to a maximum.
(b) If $H^B < 0$, d^2z is positive definite, which leads to a minimum.

In the case of n independent variables $x_1, x_2, \ldots, x_n$ and one constraint, the second-order conditions center around the bordered Hessian,

$$
H^B = \begin{vmatrix}
0 & G_{x_1} & G_{x_2} & \cdots & G_{x_n} \\
G_{x_1} & L_{x_1 x_1} & L_{x_1 x_2} & \cdots & L_{x_1 x_n} \\
\vdots & & & & \\
G_{x_n} & L_{x_n x_1} & & \cdots & L_{x_n x_n}
\end{vmatrix}
$$

and the signs of its $n - 1$ principal minors $H_2^B, \ldots, H_n^B$, where

$$
H_2^B = \begin{vmatrix}
0 & G_{x_1} & G_{x_2} \\
G_{x_1} & L_{x_1 x_1} & L_{x_1 x_2} \\
G_{x_2} & L_{x_2 x_1} & L_{x_2 x_2}
\end{vmatrix}
$$

and so on, and $H_n^B = H^B$. For $d^2 z$ to be positive definite (minimum) $H_2^B, H_3^B, \ldots, H_n^B < 0$. For $d^2 z$ to be negative definite (maximum) the principal minors must alternate in sign beginning with $H_2^B > 0$; that is, $H_2^B > 0$, $H_3^B < 0$, $H_4^B > 0$, and so on.

For the case of n independent variables and m constraints ($m \leq n$) the second-order conditions involve the determinant

$$
\begin{vmatrix}
L_{11} & L_{12} & \cdots & L_{1n} & G_{1_1} & G_{2_1} & \cdots & G_{m_1} \\
\vdots & & & & & & & \\
L_{n1} & L_{n2} & \cdots & L_{nn} & G_{1_n} & G_{2_n} & \cdots & G_{m_n} \\
G_{1_1} & G_{1_2} & \cdots & G_{1_n} & 0 & 0 & \cdots & 0 \\
\vdots & & & & & & & \\
G_{m_1} & G_{m_2} & \cdots & G_{m_n} & 0 & 0 & \cdots & 0
\end{vmatrix}
$$

where L is the Lagrangean expression. If the number of constraints is even, the associated quadratic form will be positive definite if all the principal minors are positive. If m is odd, all the principal minors must be negative to assure positive definiteness. For negative definiteness the principal minors must alternate in sign, with the first having sign $(-1)^{m+1}$. The principal minors to be examined in this case are

$$
M_1 = \begin{vmatrix}
L_{ij} & G_{ki} \\
G_{lj} & 0
\end{vmatrix}
$$

where i and $j = 1, 2, \ldots, r$; k and $l = 1, 2, \ldots, m$; 0 represents a zero subdeterminant of appropriate dimension; and $m + 1 \leq r \leq n$. The first minor is obtained by setting $r = m + 1$, the second by $r = m + 2$, and the last by $r = n$. This procedure obviously can be followed only if $m < n$. Assuming the constraints are functionally independent, if $m = n$, there will either be one unique solution, no solution, or an infinite number of solutions. In none of these cases do the second-order conditions need to be checked.

Example 3. Application of Maximization Techniques: The Slutsky Equation
Consider the following individual utility function, where x and y are the amounts of the two consumption goods:

$$U = U(x, y)$$

The first-order condition for utility maximization is

(1) $$U_x = U_y = 0$$

while the second-order condition is

(2) $$d^2U = U_{xx} (dx)^2 + 2U_{xy} dx dy + U_{yy} (dy)^2 < 0$$

which implies that

(3) $$U_{xx} < 0 \quad \text{and} \quad U_{xx}U_{yy} - (U_{xy})^2 > 0$$

must hold for a maximum (see Table 5.4–1).

Since U_x and U_y are the marginal utilities of x and y, (1) says that for an unconstrained maximum of utility, both marginal utilities must be zero. If for a commodity bundle $(\bar{x}, \bar{y})$, (1) and (2) hold, the consumer has reached a point of complete satiation, that is, he is indifferent between $(\bar{x}, \bar{y})$ and any bundle (x_j, y_j), where $x_j \geq \bar{x}$ and $y_j \geq \bar{y}$.[12] In standard utility theory the assumption of nonsatiety is made. In our terms this assumption means that U_x and U_y are strictly positive for all values of x. As a result there is no unconstrained maximum of utility, since the first-order condition can never be satisfied.

If the assumption of nonsatiety is dropped, an unconstrained maximum may exist. If one does, how are the second-order conditions for a maximum interpreted?

U_{xx} negative means the marginal utility of x is decreasing around $\bar{x}$. Since $U_{xx} < 0$, U_{yy} must also be negative, since $U_{xx}U_{yy}$ must be positive in (3). Thus the marginal utility of y is also decreasing around $\bar{y}$. The sign of U_{xy} tells us in what direction U_x changes, x constant, given changes in the consumption of y. In a two-commodity world x and y must be substitute goods. Does this fact enable us to make a definite statement about the sign of U_{xy}?

Since a maximum exists by assumption, we know that both U_x and U_y must be positive for $x < \bar{x}$ and $y < \bar{y}$. This fact, coupled with the signs of U_{xx} and U_{yy}, leads us to conclude that increasing the quantities of x and y

---

[12] Or possibly, he prefers $(\bar{x}, \bar{y})$ to any (x_j, y_j). In the latter case U_x and $U_y < 0$ for $x > \bar{x}$ and $y > \bar{y}$. Otherwise, U_x and $U_y = 0$ for all x and y greater than $\bar{x}$ and $\bar{y}$.

beyond $\bar{x}$ and $\bar{y}$ actually reduces total utility. [Everyone has eaten one hamburger too many and had the "disasterous" fourth (or fifth) martini.] Thus we have a situation where $(\bar{x}, \bar{y})$ is preferred to *every* other commodity bundle if the marginal utility functions are monotonic.

Suppose we retain the assumption of nonsatiety (i.e., U_x and $U_y > 0$). Then we are lead to seek a constrained maximum of

(1) $$U = U(x, y)$$

The typical constraint is the budget equation

(4) $$Z \geq P_x x + P_y y$$

where Z is the consumer's income. Equation (4) is stated as an inequality–the consumer may spend all, or only a part, of his income on the two goods. However, the assumption of nonsatiety and the utility function we have specified ensure that we can treat (4) as a strict equality.[13] (Why?). Our problem then becomes

$$\text{maximize:} \quad U = U(x, y)$$

$$\text{subject to:} \quad Z = P_x x + P_y y$$

This is a straightforward application of constrained maximization using Lagrangean multipliers. Form the Lagrangean expression

$$L = U(x, y) + \lambda(P_x x + P_y y - Z)$$

where λ is the Lagrangean multiplier and we have rewritten the constraint to conform to Theorem 5.4–5. L is now differentiated with respect to x, y, and λ. This yields

(5) $$\frac{\partial L}{\partial x} = \frac{\partial U}{\partial x} + \lambda P_x = 0$$

(6) $$\frac{\partial L}{\partial y} = \frac{\partial U}{\partial y} + \lambda P_y = 0$$

(7) $$\frac{\partial L}{\partial \lambda} = P_x x + P_y y - Z = 0$$

The first-order condition forces (5), (6), and (7) to be zero. Rearranging terms:

(5') $$U_x = -\lambda P_x$$

(6') $$U_y = -\lambda P_y$$

(7') $$Z = P_x x + P_y y$$

---

[13] For the more general case where the inequality may hold, see the discussion of mathematical programming in Chapter 11.

Solving for λ from (5') and substituting the result into (6') we have

$$(8) \qquad U_y = \frac{U_x}{P_x} P_y \quad \text{or} \quad \frac{U_y}{P_y} = \frac{U_x}{P_x}$$

Equation (8) simply says that the change in total utility per unit of expenditure change must be equal for x and y.

The second-order conditions for a maximum are $d^2 U$ negative definite and $d(P_x x + P_y y - Z) = 0$. First calculate the second-order derivatives of L:

$$L_{xx} = U_{xx}$$

$$L_{yy} = U_{yy}$$

$$L_{xy} = L_{yx} = U_{xy} = U_{yx}$$

The Hessian determinant is therefore

$$H = \begin{vmatrix} U_{xx} & U_{xy} \\ U_{xy} & U_{yy} \end{vmatrix}$$

The bordered Hessian is

$$H^B = \begin{vmatrix} 0 & P_x & P_y \\ P_x & U_{xx} & U_{xy} \\ P_y & U_{xy} & U_{yy} \end{vmatrix}$$

Expanding H^B by the elements of the first column we have

$$-(P_x)^2 U_{yy} + 2 P_x P_y U_{xy} - (P_y)^2 U_{xx} > 0$$

for a maximum. There are many ways this requirement can be satisfied. Suppose, for example, that U_{yy} and U_{xx} are both negative while $U_{xy} > 0$. Thus, if both marginal utilities are positive but decreasing and the marginal utility of $x(y)$ increases when $y(x)$ is increased, the second-order conditions will be satisfied.

Suppose the first- and second-order conditions for a maximum are satisfied. Then the first-order conditions can be used to derive the demand functions for x and y. U_x and U_y are, in general, functions of both x and y. Therefore (5) and (6) can be viewed as a system of two equations in the unknowns x and y. Solving these equations simultaneously for x and y yields relations in the form

$$x = f(P_x, P_y, y)$$

and

$$y = g(P_x, P_y, x)$$

which are the demand equations for x and y.

The previous analysis has enabled us to find the optimum (maximizing) quantities of x and y given a particular level of income, and fixed prices of x and y. The first-order condition for this case also serves as the basis for examining how the purchases of x and y change when income and prices are allowed to vary, since the purchases of x and y made after these changes must also satisfy the first-order conditions[14]

(5″)
$$U_x - \lambda P_x = 0$$

(6″)
$$U_y - \lambda P_y = 0$$

(7″)
$$-P_x x - P_y y + Z = 0$$

To analyse these changes we now treat P_x, P_y, and Z as variables and take the total differentials of (5″), (6″), and (7″). This yields

$$U_{xx}\, dx + U_{xy}\, dy - \lambda\, dP_x - P_x\, d\lambda = 0$$

$$U_{yy}\, dy + U_{yx}\, dx - \lambda\, dP_y - P_y\, d\lambda = 0$$

$$-P_x\, dx - x\, dP_x - P_y\, dy - y\, dP_y + dZ = 0$$

Rearranging terms we have

$$U_{xx}\, dx + U_{xy}\, dy - P_x\, d\lambda = \lambda\, dP_x$$

(9)
$$U_{yy}\, dy + U_{yx}\, dx - P_y\, d\lambda = \lambda\, dP_y$$

$$-P_x\, dx - P_y\, dy = -dZ + x\, dP_x + y\, dP_y$$

The system (9) can now be solved simultaneously for the variables dx, dy, and $d\lambda$ if we treat the terms on the right as constants. In effect we are attempting to find the changes in x and y that preserve the first-order conditions given that we know the magnitudes of dP_x, dP_y, and dZ.

Using Cramer's rule to solve (9) for dx and dy we obtain

(10)
$$dx = \frac{\begin{vmatrix} \lambda\, dP_x & U_{xy} & -P_x \\ \lambda\, dP_y & U_{yy} & -P_y \\ -dZ + x\, dP_x + y\, dP_y & -P_y & 0 \end{vmatrix}}{\begin{vmatrix} U_{xx} & U_{xy} & -P_x \\ U_{yx} & U_{yy} & -P_y \\ -P_x & -P_y & 0 \end{vmatrix}}$$

[14] The difference in the signs of the double-primed equations arises because we assume the Lagrangean expression to be $L = U(x, y) + \lambda(Z - P_x X - P_y Y)$. The reader should convince himself that the change in the sign of the Lagrangean multiplier makes no difference in the analysis.

$$(11) \qquad dy = \frac{\begin{vmatrix} U_{xx} & \lambda\, dP_x & -P_x \\ U_{yx} & \lambda\, dP_y & -P_y \\ -P_x & -dZ + x\, dP_x + y\, dP_y & 0 \end{vmatrix}}{\begin{vmatrix} U_{xx} & U_{xy} & -P_x \\ U_{xy} & U_{yy} & -P_y \\ -P_x & -P_y & 0 \end{vmatrix}}$$

Call the determinant in the denominator of (10) and (11) D. Then, expanding the numerators of (10) and (11) by elements of the third column:

$$\text{numerator of } dx = -P_x \begin{vmatrix} \lambda\, dP_y & U_{yy} \\ -dZ + x\, dP_x + y\, dP_y & -P_y \end{vmatrix}$$

$$+ P_y \begin{vmatrix} \lambda\, dP_x & U_{xy} \\ -dZ + x\, dP_x + y\, dP_y & -P_y \end{vmatrix}$$

Evaluating these determinants and collecting terms:

(12)

$$dx = \frac{(\lambda P_x P_y)\, dP_y - (\lambda P_y P_y)\, dP_x + (-dZ + x\, dP_x + y\, dP_y)(P_x U_{yy} - P_y U_{xy})}{D}$$

As the reader can verify, this can be written as

$$(13) \qquad dx = \frac{\lambda D_{11}\, dP_x - \lambda D_{21}\, dP_y + D_{31}(-dZ + x\, dP_x + y\, dP_y)}{D}$$

where D_{ij} is the minor of the element in the ith row and jth column of D.
  In a similar manner it follows that

$$(14) \qquad dy = \frac{-\lambda D_{12}\, dP_x + \lambda D_{22}\, dP_y + D_{32}(-dZ + x\, dP_x + y\, dP_y)}{D}$$

Equations (13) and (14) tell us how much x and y change given the changes in P_x, P_y, and Z.
  Divide the expression for dx by dP_x and assume that dP_y and dZ are zero. Then we obtain

$$(15) \qquad \frac{\partial x}{\partial P_x} = \frac{\lambda D_{11}}{D} + \frac{x D_{31}}{D}$$

This partial derivative measures the rate of change of purchases of x when P_x changes, P_y and income constant.

Assume that dP_x and dZ are zero. Then from (13) we obtain

(16) $$\frac{\partial x}{\partial P_y} = -\frac{\lambda D_{21}}{D} + \frac{y D_{31}}{D}$$

the rate of change in x with respect to P_y, P_x and Z constant. In a similar manner we obtain

(17) $$\frac{\partial x}{\partial Z} = -\frac{D_{31}}{D}$$

for P_x and P_y constant.

When only one price or income is allowed to vary, the consumer will be on a different indifference curve after the change. Suppose we allow one price to vary and at the same time change the consumer's income in such a way that the level of utility is not affected—he is on the same indifference curve before and after the price and income change. Given $dP_x \neq 0$, we require a dZ such that $dPy = 0$ and $dU = U_x\, dx + U_y\, dy = 0$. From the first-order condition developed earlier, that is, $U_x/P_x = U_y/P_y$, it follows that $U_x/U_y = P_x/P_y$ (the marginal rate of substitution equals the price ratio) and therefore $dU = 0$ can be rewritten as $P_x\, dx + P_y\, dy = 0$. Then, from the last equation in (9), it follows that $-dZ + x\, dP_x + y\, dP_y = 0$ is equivalent to $dU = 0$. Consequently, (13) becomes, upon dividing through by dP_x,

(18) $$\left.\frac{\partial x}{\partial P_x}\right|_{U=\bar{U}} = \frac{\lambda D_{11}}{D}$$

where the notation is designed to underscore the fact that this expression for the rate of change of x with respect to P_x is valid only under the assumption that $dU = 0$.

Using (18) and (17) we have a restatement of (15):

(19) $$\frac{\partial x}{\partial P_x} = \left.\frac{\partial x}{\partial P_x}\right|_{U=\bar{U}} - x \left.\frac{\partial x}{\partial Z}\right|_{\text{prices constant}}$$

Equation (19) is the **Slutsky equation** and says that the total change in x when P_x changes is equal to the sum of two effects: (a) the income effect,

$$-x \left.\frac{\partial x}{\partial Z}\right|_{\text{prices constant}}$$

and (b) the substitution effect,

$$\left.\frac{\partial x}{\partial P_x}\right|_{U=\bar{U}}$$

The graphical analysis of these effects is well known.[15]

---

[15] An excellent graphical treatment of the income and substitution effects is given in Ferguson (1969). Also see Henderson and Quandt (1971).

Problems

5.4–1 Find the maximum, minimum, and inflection points (if any) for the following functions:

(a) $y = x - x^2$

(b) $y = 4x^3 - x^2$

(c) $y = \dfrac{x + 1}{x - 1}$

(d) $y = x + 2x^{-1}$

(e) $y = (x + 1)(x - 1)^2$

(f) $y = 6 - x^{1/3}$

(g) $y = e^{2x} + x^2$

(h) $y = \ln (x + 1)$

5.4–2 Expand the following functions in Taylor's series using the Lagrange form of the remainder for $n > 3$.

(a) $f(x) = x^3 - 2x^2$ and $\bar{x} = 0$ (b) $f(x) = \dfrac{x - 1}{(x + 1)^2}$ and $\bar{x} = 0$

5.4–3 Find the extreme values and saddle points (if any) for the following functions. Be sure to check the second-order conditions for each.

(a) $z = xy - 3x^2y^2$

(b) $z = y^2 - 2xy + x^2$

(c) $z = \dfrac{xy}{x - y}$

(d) $z = 3x + 2y^3$

(e) $z = 4x_1x_2 + 3x_3x_1^2 + x_2x_3$

(f) $z = \dfrac{x^2y}{w} + \dfrac{y}{z}$

(g) $z = 3xw^2y^{1/2}$

(h) $z = 2x + 4y - 7w^2$

5.4–4 Show that the bordered Hessian

$$\begin{bmatrix} 0 & G_x & G_y \\ G_x & L_{xx} & L_{xy} \\ G_y & L_{xy} & L_{yy} \end{bmatrix}$$

is equal to the "ordinary" Hessian

$$\begin{bmatrix} L_{\lambda\lambda} & L_{\lambda x} & L_{\lambda y} \\ L_{x\lambda} & L_{xx} & L_{xy} \\ L_{y\lambda} & L_{yx} & L_{yy} \end{bmatrix}$$

in the problem maximize $f(x, y)$ subject to $G(x, y) = 0$.

5.4–5 Solve the following constrained optimization problems. Check the second-order conditions.

(a) maximize $f = 5x + 3y$ subject to $x + y = 3$

(b) maximize $f = 3x^2 - 2xy + y^2$ subject to $xy = -2$

(c) minimize $f = 3x^2 - 2xy + y^2$ subject to $xy = -2$

(d) maximize $f = x^2 + 2xy$ subject to $x = 3y - 1$

(e) maximize $f = x^2 + 2y^2$ subject to $x + y = 1$ and $x^3 = y - 1$

(f) minimize $f = 10x + 7y$ subject to $Ax^\alpha y^\beta = 100$, where A, α, and β are positive constants.

References

1. ALLEN, R. G. D. (1938), *Mathematical Analysis for Economists*, London: Macmillan.
2. CHEMICAL RUBBER COMPANY (1964), *Mathematical Tables from the Handbook of Chemistry and Physics*, Cleveland.
3. COURANT, R. (1937), *Differential and Integral Calculus* (tr. by E. J. McShane), New York: Wiley-Interscience.
4. FERGUSON, C. E. (1969), *Microeconomic Theory*, Homewood, Ill.: Irwin.
5. HENDERSON, J. M., and R. E. QUANDT (1971), *Microeconomic Theory*, New York: McGraw-Hill.
6. JOHNSON, R. E., and F. L. KIOKEMEISTER (1969), *Calculus with Analytic Geometry*, 4th ed., Boston: Allyn & Bacon.
7. REKTORYS, KAREL (ed.) (1969), *Survey of Applicable Mathematics* (tr. by Rudolf Vyborny), Cambridge, Mass.: M.I.T. Press.
8. THOMAS, GEORGE (1968), *Calculus and Analytical Geometry*, 4th ed., Reading: Mass.: Addison-Wesley.
9. WIDDER, DAVID (1961), *Advanced Calculus*, Englewood Cliffs, N.J.: Prentice-Hall.

Chapter 6

Integration

6.1   RIEMANN INTEGRALS

Differentiation of a function yields a derived function, the derivative whose properties were examined in Chapter 5. Integration is essentially the reverse of differentiation. Given the derived function, the process of integration allows us to find an original function whose derivative is equal to the initial function. In other words, integration is the process of finding a function whose derivative is given.

Suppose we are given that $dy/dx = f(x)$. This is a simple example of a differential equation, the topic of the Chapter 7. A function $y = F(x)$ is a solution to this equation if $F(x)$ is differentiable and if

$$\frac{dF(x)}{dx} = f(x)$$

DEFINITION 6.1–1 $F(x)$ is the **Riemann integral** of $f(x)$ with respect to x, written

$$F(x) = \int f(x)\, dx$$

Furthermore, if $F(x)$ is a solution to the differential equation then $F(x) + C$, where C is an arbitrary constant, is also a solution. This follows immediately from the elementary observation that $dC/dx = 0$ for all C. Thus we can write more accurately $\int f(x)\, dx = F(x) + C$.

Integration is essentially a process of guessing the function that yields the given derivative. Some of the most basic rules of integration are given in Theorem 6.1–1.

Theorem 6.1–1   Given that u and v are differentiable functions and a, n, and C are constants:

(a) $\int du = u + C;$

(b) $\int (du + dv) = \int du + \int dv = u + C + v + C_1 = u + v + C_2$

(c) $\int a\ du = a \int du = a(u + C) = au + C_1$

(d) $\int u^n\ du = \dfrac{u^{n+1}}{n + 1} + C \quad (n \neq -1)$

(e) $\int u^{-1}\ du = \ln |u| + C$

(f) $\int e^u\ du = e^u + C$

(g) $\int f(u) \dfrac{du}{dv}\ dv = \int f(u)\ du = F(u) + C$

(h) $\int a^u\ du = \dfrac{a^u}{\ln a} + C$

The proof of any part of the theorem follows by taking the differential of the last term on the right. For example,

$$d\left(\frac{u^{n+1}}{n + 1} + C \right) = \frac{n + 1}{n + 1} u^n\ du = u^n\ du$$

This proves part (d).

Part (g) of the theorem is the integral calculus counterpart to the chain rule. Its proof follows by applying the chain rule to $F(u)$, where $u = u(v)$. Much more complete rules of integration ("integral tables") are readily available.[1]

In many cases, however, the simple rules of Theorem 6.1–1 and even the most complete integral table are not sufficient for solving integration problems. In some cases no solution exists. There are a multitude of methods available for solving integration problems. We shall present a few of the most frequently used below.[2]

Method 1: Integration by Parts

From the rule for finding the differential of a product of two functions, we have

$$d(uv) = u\ dv + v\ du$$

or

(1) $$u\ dv = d(uv) - v\ du$$

---

[1] See the mathematical tables in the Chemical Rubber Company's *Mathematical Tables from the Handbook of Chemistry and Physics*.

[2] For a more complete description of integration methods see Thomas (1968), Chapters 4–7.

Integrating both sides of (1):

(2) $$\int u \, dv = uv - \int v \, du + C$$

Equation (2) is the formula for integration by parts. Successful application of this method depends on the proper selection of the two functions u and v (and thus dv).

Example 1.   Find $\int \ln x \, dx$. To fit this to our formula, let $u = \ln x$ and $dv = dx$. Then $du = (1/x) \, dx$ and $v = x$. We have

$$\int \ln x \, dx = (\ln x)x - \int x \left(\frac{1}{x} \right) dx = x \ln x - x + C = x(\ln x - 1) + C$$

Example 2.   Find $\int x^2 e^x \, dx$. It is not the case that the integral of the product of two functions is the product of the integrals, as our formula for integration by parts illustrates. In this case, integration by parts must be repeated twice. Let $u = x^2$, $du = 2x \, dx$, $dv = e^x \, dx$, and $v = e^x$. Then

$$\int x^2 e^x \, dx = x^2 e^x - \int 2x e^x \, dx$$

$$= x^2 e^x - 2 \int x e^x \, dx$$

Applying integration by parts to the last integral, let $u = x$, $du = dx$, $dv = e^x \, dx$, and $v = e^x$. Then

$$-2 \int x e^x \, dx = -2 \left(x e^x - \int e^x \, dx \right) + C_1$$

$$= -2x e^x + 2 e^x + C_2 + C_1$$

Therefore

$$\int x^2 e^x \, dx = x^2 e^x - 2x e^x + 2 e^x + C,$$

where C is a composite constant of integration equal to C_1 and C_2.

As these examples show, the object of integration by parts is to select u and v in such a way that $\int v \, du$ is easier to evaluate than the original $\int u \, dv$.

Method 2: Substitution

The substitution method is based on part (g) of Theorem 6.1–1 and involves simplifying the integrand (the expression to be integrated) by substitution. A few examples should make the procedure clear.

Example 3.   Find $\int (x^4 + x^2)(3x^5 + 5x^3 + 2) \, dx$. One way to solve this problem is to perform the multiplication and then apply part (b) of Theorem

6.1–1. Rather than do that, let $u = 3x^5 + 5x^3 + 2$. Then $du = (15x^4 + 15x^2) \, dx$ or, solving for dx,

$$dx = \frac{du}{15(x^4 + x^2)}$$

Substituting for dx and $3x^5 + 5x^3 + 2$ in the original integral, we obtain

$$\int (x^4 + x^2)(3x^5 + 5x^3 + 2) \, dx = \int (x^4 + x^2)u \, \frac{du}{15(x^4 + x^2)} = \int \frac{u}{15} \, du$$

$$= \frac{u^2}{30} + C = \frac{(3x^5 + 5x^3 + 2)^2}{30} + C$$

Example 4. Find $\int e^{5x} \, dx$. Let $u = 5x$. Then $du = 5 \, dx$, or $dx = du/5$. Thus

$$\int e^{5x} \, dx = \int \frac{e^u \, du}{5} = \frac{e^u}{5} + C = \frac{e^{5x}}{5} + C$$

Example 5. Find

$$\int \frac{4x^2}{x^3 + 9} \, dx$$

Let $u = x^3 + 9$. Then $du = 3x^2 \, dx$ or $dx = du/3x^2$. Thus

$$\int \frac{4x^2}{x^3 + 9} \, dx = \int \frac{4x^2}{u} \frac{du}{3x^2} = \frac{4}{3} \int \frac{du}{u} = \frac{4}{3} \ln u + C = \frac{4}{3} \ln |x^3 + 9| + C$$

Note that the absolute value signs must be included, since if $x < -3$, $x^3 + 9 < 0$ and natural logarithms of negative numbers are not defined.

The reader should verify that these substitutions are in fact applications of part (g), Theorem 6.1–1, by identifying $f(u)$ and du/dx for each example. This method is so powerful that it should be tried in actual problems before attempting other methods.

Method 3: Partial Fractions

Adding fractions by finding a common denominator is known to every grade-school student. This method is essentially the reverse of that procedure. Given a fraction, we decompose it into the sum of two or more fractions to provide a method for solving some integration problems of the form

$$\int \frac{f(x)}{g(x)} \, dx$$

Suppose we wish to express $f(x)/g(x)$ as a sum of partial fractions. To be able to do so: (1) the degree of $f(x)$ must be less than the degree of $g(x)$, if not perform the division and work with the remainder, and (2) all the factors of $g(x)$ must be known. Consider

$$\frac{x + 1}{x^2 - 2x - 8}$$

The factors of the denominator are $(x - 4)$ and $(x + 2)$. Thus we want to find an A and B such that

$$\frac{x + 1}{(x - 4)(x + 2)} = \frac{A}{(x - 4)} + \frac{B}{(x + 2)}$$

Multiplying this expression through by $(x - 4)(x + 2)$ we obtain

$$x + 1 = A(x + 2) + B(x - 4)$$

or

$$x + 1 = x(A + B) + 2A - 4B$$

For the right and left sides to be equal, the coefficients of x on both sides must be equal, as must the constant terms. Thus we have

$$A + B = 1 \qquad \text{(coefficients of } x\text{)}$$

and

$$2A - 4B = 1 \qquad \text{(constant terms)}$$

This system of two equations can be solved for A and B, yielding $A = \frac{5}{6}$ and $B = \frac{1}{6}$. Thus

$$\frac{x + 1}{x^2 - 2x - 8} = \frac{\frac{5}{6}}{x - 4} + \frac{\frac{1}{6}}{x - 2}$$

The application of this procedure to integration should be clear.

$$\int \frac{x + 1}{x^2 - 2x - 8}\, dx$$

cannot be found by simple substitution or by integration by parts. However, from the preceding we know that

$$\int \frac{x - 1}{x^2 - 2x - 8}\, dx = \int \left(\frac{\frac{5}{6}}{x - 4} + \frac{\frac{1}{6}}{x + 2} \right) dx$$

$$= \int \frac{\frac{5}{6}}{x - 4}\, dx + \int \frac{\frac{1}{6}}{x + 2}\, dx$$

$$= \frac{5}{6} \int \frac{dx}{x - 4} + \frac{1}{6} \int \frac{dx}{x + 2}$$

These two integrals can be solved easily by substitution. In the first let $u = x - 4$. Then $du = dx$, and

$$\frac{5}{6} \int \frac{dx}{x - 4} = \frac{5}{6} \int \frac{du}{u} = \frac{5}{6} \ln |u| - C_1 = \frac{5}{6} \ln |x - 4| + C_1$$

Similar substitution shows that

$$\frac{1}{6} \int \frac{dx}{x + 2} = \frac{1}{6} \ln |x + 2| + C_2$$

Thus, combining these results,

$$\int \frac{x + 1}{x^2 - 2x - 8} \, dx = \frac{5}{6} \ln |x - 4| + \frac{1}{6} \ln |x + 2| + C$$

where $C = C_1 + C_2$.

Returning to the method of partial fractions itself, suppose that $x = \alpha$, where α is a constant, is a linear factor of $g(x)$. If $(x - \alpha)^n$ is the highest power of $x - \alpha$ that is also a factor of $g(x)$ [which implies that $(x - \alpha)^2$, $(x - \alpha)^3, \ldots$, and $(x - \alpha)^{n-1}$ are also factors of $g(x)$], then the following sum of n partial fractions corresponds to the factor $x - \alpha$:

$$\frac{A_1}{x - \alpha} + \frac{A_2}{(x - \alpha)^2} + \frac{A_3}{(x - \alpha)^3} + \cdots + \frac{A_n}{(x - \alpha)^n}$$

If $x^2 + bx + c$ is a quadratic factor of $g(x)$, and $(x^2 + bx + c)^m$ is its highest power that also is a factor, then the following sum of m partial fractions corresponds to this factor:

$$\frac{B_1 x + C_1}{x^2 + bx + c} + \frac{B_2 x + C_2}{(x^2 + bx + c)^2} + \cdots + \frac{B_m x + C_m}{(x^2 + bx + c)^m}$$

Example 6. Express

$$\frac{-4x - 7}{(x^2 + 2)(x + 1)^3}$$

as a sum of partial fractions.

$$\frac{-4x - 7}{(x^2 + 2)(x + 1)^3} = \frac{Ax + B}{x^2 + 2} + \frac{C_1}{x + 1} + \frac{C_2}{(x + 1)^2} + \frac{C_3}{(x + 1)^3}$$

Thus

$$-4x - 7 = (Ax + B)(x + 1)^3 + C_1(x^2 + 2)(x + 1)^2$$
$$+ C_2(x^2 + 2)(x + 1) + C_3(x^2 + 2)$$

Performing the multiplications and collecting terms:

$$-4x - 7 = x^4(A + C_1) + x^3(3A + B + 2C_1 + C_2)$$
$$+ x^2(3A + 3B + 3C_1 + C_2 + C_3)$$
$$+ x(A + 3B + 4C_1 + 2C_2) + (B + 2C_1 + 2C_2 + 2C_3)$$

Equating coefficients of like powers of x, we obtain the following simultaneous equation system:

$$A + C_1 = 0$$
$$3A + B + 2C_1 + C_2 = 0$$
$$3A + 3B + 3C_1 + C_2 + C_3 = 0$$
$$A + 3B + 4C_1 + 2C_2 = -4$$
$$B + 2C_1 + 2C_2 + 2C_3 = -7$$

Writing the system in matrix form and applying Cramer's rule[3]:

$$\begin{bmatrix} 1 & 0 & 1 & 0 & 0 \\ 3 & 1 & 2 & 1 & 0 \\ 3 & 3 & 3 & 1 & 1 \\ 1 & 3 & 4 & 2 & 0 \\ 0 & 1 & 2 & 2 & 2 \end{bmatrix} \begin{bmatrix} A \\ B \\ C_1 \\ C_2 \\ C_3 \end{bmatrix} = \begin{bmatrix} 0 \\ 0 \\ 0 \\ -4 \\ -7 \end{bmatrix}$$

$$A = \frac{\begin{vmatrix} 0 & 0 & 1 & 0 & 0 \\ 0 & 1 & 2 & 1 & 0 \\ 0 & 3 & 3 & 1 & 1 \\ -4 & 3 & 4 & 2 & 0 \\ -7 & 1 & 2 & 2 & 2 \end{vmatrix}}{\begin{vmatrix} 1 & 0 & 1 & 0 & 0 \\ 3 & 1 & 2 & 1 & 0 \\ 3 & 3 & 3 & 1 & 1 \\ 1 & 3 & 4 & 2 & 0 \\ 0 & 1 & 2 & 2 & 2 \end{vmatrix}} \quad (=D)$$

$$B = \frac{\begin{vmatrix} 1 & 0 & 1 & 0 & 0 \\ 3 & 0 & 2 & 1 & 0 \\ 3 & 0 & 3 & 1 & 1 \\ 1 & -4 & 4 & 2 & 0 \\ 0 & -7 & 2 & 2 & 2 \end{vmatrix}}{D}$$

$$C_1 = \frac{\begin{vmatrix} 1 & 0 & 0 & 0 & 0 \\ 3 & 1 & 0 & 1 & 0 \\ 3 & 3 & 0 & 1 & 1 \\ 1 & 3 & -4 & 2 & 0 \\ 0 & 1 & -7 & 2 & 2 \end{vmatrix}}{D}$$

$$C_2 = \frac{\begin{vmatrix} 1 & 0 & 1 & 0 & 0 \\ 3 & 1 & 2 & 0 & 0 \\ 3 & 3 & 3 & 0 & 1 \\ 1 & 3 & 4 & -4 & 0 \\ 0 & 1 & 2 & -7 & 2 \end{vmatrix}}{D}$$

$$C_3 = \frac{\begin{vmatrix} 1 & 0 & 1 & 0 & 0 \\ 3 & 1 & 2 & 1 & 0 \\ 3 & 3 & 3 & 1 & 0 \\ 1 & 3 & 4 & 2 & -4 \\ 0 & 1 & 2 & 2 & -7 \end{vmatrix}}{D}$$

[3] See Section 4.3.

We have $A = 1$, $B = 1$, $C_1 = -1$, $C_2 = -2$, and $C_3 = -1$. Thus

$$\frac{-4x - 7}{(x^2 + 2)(x + 1)^3} = \frac{x + 1}{x^2 + 2} - \frac{1}{x + 1} - \frac{2}{(x + 1)^2} - \frac{1}{(x + 1)^3}$$

DEFINITION 6.1–2   The integrals discussed above are examples of **indefinite integrals,** which are integrals that cannot be assigned a specific numerical value but are expressed only as functions.

DEFINITION 6.1–3   **Definite integrals** are integrals that have a specific numerical value.

Theorem 6.1–2   *Fundamental Theorem of Integral Calculus*   Given a function $y = f(x)$ is continuous in the closed interval $a_1 \leq x \leq b_1$. Then:
  (a) $\int f(x)\, dx$ exists in that interval; and
  (b) for any two points a and b in the interval, the definite integral

$$\int_a^b f(x)\, dx = F(b) - F(a)$$

where $\int f(x)\, dx = F(x) + C$. a and b are the lower and upper limits of integration, respectively.

Example 7.   Find $\int_3^5 (x^3 + 3x^{-2})\, dx$.

$$\int_3^5 (x^3 + 3x^{-2})\, dx = \frac{x^4}{4} - 3x^{-1} \Big]_3^5$$

(the symbol $\cdots\,]_3^5$ means that the expression is to be evaluated at the limits 3 and 5)

$$= \frac{(5)^4}{4} - 3(5)^{-1} - \left[\frac{(3)^4}{4} - 3(3)^{-1} \right]$$

$$= \frac{625}{4} - \frac{3}{5} - \frac{81}{4} + 1 = 136\tfrac{2}{5}$$

The proof of Theorem 6.1–2 depends on another theorem basic to many of the results in calculus, the mean value theorem.

Theorem 6.1–3   *Mean Value Theorem*   Given that $y = f(x)$ is continuous in the closed interval $a \leq x \leq b$ and is differentiable in the open interval $a < x < b$. Then there is at least one number c, $a < c < b$, such that

$$f(b) - f(a) = f'(c)(b - a)$$

PROOF   See Figure 6.1–1. The function is the curved line ACB while the straight line AB is the chord connecting the two end points. The mean value theorem states that there is at least one point, C, where the slope of the curve

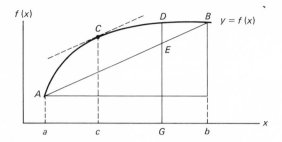

Figure 6.1–1   *The mean value theorem.*

is equal to the slope of the chord AB. This is equivalent to saying that if we slide the chord upward in a parallel way there will be at least one point where the displaced chord is tangent to the graph of the function.

The distance ED is the distance between the chord and the function. Clearly,

$$ED = GD - GE$$

GD is, however, just $f(x)$ while GE may be found from the equation for the chord:

$$y - f(a) = \frac{f(b) - f(a)}{b - a} (x - a)$$

[This is simply the point-slope equation of the chord using the point $(a, f(a))$ and calculating the slope to be $f(b) - f(a)/(b - a)$.] Thus

$$GE = f(a) + \frac{f(b) - f(a)}{b - a} (x - a)$$

and we can write

(1) $$ED = f(x) - f(a) - \frac{f(b) - f(a)}{b - a} (x - a)$$

the distance between the chord and the graph of the function for any x between a and b. Call this function $F(x)$; that is,

$$F(x) = f(x) - f(a) - \frac{f(b) - f(a)}{b - a} (x - a)$$

Then clearly,

$$F(a) = f(a) - f(a) - \frac{f(b) - f(a)}{b - a} (a - a) = 0$$

and

$$F(b) = f(b) - f(a) - \frac{f(b) - f(a)}{b - a} (b - a) = 0$$

since the distance between the chord and the graph is zero at a and b. Both $f(x)$ and $(x - a)$ are continuous and differentiable for the intervals $a \leq x \leq$

b and $a < x < b$ by hypothesis. Thus the function $F(x)$ satisfies the hypotheses of Rolle's theorem,[4] which means that there is some value of x, say $x = c$, between a and b for which $F'(c) = 0$. Differentiating the definition of $F(x)$ we obtain

$$F'(x) = f'(x) - \frac{f(b) - f(a)}{b - a}$$

By Rolle's theorem,

$$F'(c) = 0 = f'(c) - \frac{f(b) - f(a)}{b - a}$$

or

$$f'(c) = \frac{f(b) - f(a)}{b - a}$$

from which it is a short step to

$$f(b) - f(a) = f'(c)(b - a) \qquad \text{QED}$$

PROOF OF THE FUNDAMENTAL THEOREM   Imagine that we divide the interval between a and b into n equal subintervals of length $\Delta x = (b - a)/n$. In each of these subintervals select a value of x, c_i, $i = 1, 2, \ldots, n$, and form the sum

$$f(c_1)\,\Delta x + f(c_2)\,\Delta x + \cdots + f(c_n)\,\Delta x = \sum_{i=1}^{n} f(c_i)\,\Delta x$$

Then, if $F(x) = \int f(x)\,dx$, we need to show that

$$\lim_{n \to \infty} \sum_{i=1}^{n} f(c_i)\,\Delta x = F(b) - F(a)$$

See Figure 6.1–2. Here we have divided the interval $a \le x \le b$ into four equal subintervals by selecting x_1, x_2, and x_3 such that $x_1 - a = \Delta x = (b - a)/4$, and so on. We now proceed to choose the numbers c_1, c_2, c_3, and c_4 in each subinterval by applying the mean value theorem to the function $F(x)$ in each subinterval. (Are the hypotheses of the mean value theorem satisfied here?) Thus we obtain

$$F(x_1) - F(a) = F'(c_1)(x_1 - a) = f(c_1)\,\Delta x$$
$$F(x_2) - F(x_1) = F'(c_2)(x_2 - x_1) = f(c_2)\,\Delta x$$
$$F(x_3) - F(x_2) = F'(c_3)(x_3 - x_2) = f(c_3)\,\Delta x$$
$$F(b) - F(x_3) = F'(c_4)(b - x_3) = f(c_4)\,\Delta x$$

[4] Thomas (1968).

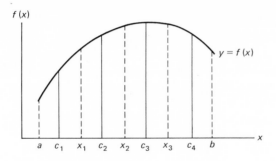

Figure 6.1–2   *The Fundamental theorem.*

since $F'(x) = f(x)$ by definition of $F(x)$. Adding these equations together we obtain

$$F(b) - F(a) = \sum_{i=1}^{4} f(c_i) \, \Delta x$$

Since the left side does not depend on n, as we take the limit as $n \to \infty$ of the right side we obtain the desired result:

$$F(b) - F(a) = \lim_{n \to \infty} \sum_{1}^{n} f(c_i) \, \Delta x = \int_{a}^{b} f(x) \, dx \qquad \text{QED}$$

The proof of the fundamental theorem leads directly to the interpretation of the definite integral as the area under a curve. See Figure 6.1–3. Here the

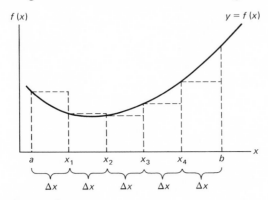

Figure 6.1–3   *Area under a curve.*

interval (a, b) is divided into five equal subintervals. If we let $c_1 = a, c_2 = x_1$, and so on, then the sum $f(a) \, \Delta x + f(x_1) \, \Delta x + \cdots + f(x_4) \, \Delta x$ gives the sum of the areas of the rectangles shown. Since

$$\int_{a}^{b} f(x) \, dx = \lim_{n \to \infty} \sum_{i} (c_i) \, \Delta x$$

as we let $n \to \infty$ (increase the number of subintervals without bound), the sum of the areas of the rectangles will approach the actual area under the curve from a to b. Calculated with a as the lower limit and b as the upper limit of integration, the area in Figure 6.1–3 will be positive, since each $\Delta x > 0$ and every y value is also positive. Areas calculated by integration will be negative (1) for portions of the curve lying below the x axis ($y < 0$) and (2) if the curve lies above the x axis and the lower limit is greater than the upper limit of integration ($\Delta x < 0$). Thus in Figure 6.1–3, $\int_a^b f(x)\,dx = -\int_b^a f(x)\,dx$.

In Figure 6.1–4, $\int_a^b f(x)\,dx = \int_a^{a_1} f(x)\,dx + \int_{a_1}^{a_2} f(x)\,dx + \int_{a_2}^b f(x)\,dx = A_1 + A_2 + A_3$, where areas A_1 and A_3 are negative while A_2 is positive. This expression also illustrates how a definite integral can be broken down into a sum of two or more "smaller" integrals by appropriate changes of the limits of integration.

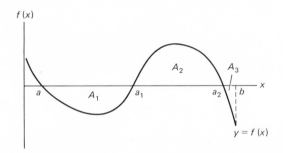

Figure 6.1–4   *Negative areas.*

Besides finding areas under curves, the definite integral has many other uses. We shall mention and briefly illustrate some of these.

Example 8.   Area Between Two Curves

Suppose we have $y = f(x)$ and $y = g(x)$, two continuous, differentiable functions, and we wish to calculate the area enclosed by these curves and two x values. See Figure 6.1–5. This area is given by $\int_a^b [f(x) - g(x)]\,dx$. We shall make an intuitive argument for this. $\int_a^b [f(x) - g(x)]\,dx = \int_a^b f(x)\,dx - \int_a^b g(x)\,dx$. As we know, the first integral gives us the (positive) shaded area in Figure 6.1–5. The second integral can be written as $-[\int_a^{a_1} g(x)\,dx + \int_{a_1}^b g(x)\,dx] = -(A_1 + A_2)$. However, A_1 is itself negative so $-A_1 > 0$, while A_2 is positive so $-A_2 < 0$. Clearly then, subtracting $A_1 + A_2$ from the shaded areas gives the area between the two curves.

Example 9.   Volume

See Figure 6.1–6. Here the volume of the figure can be thought of as being composed of the volumes of many "slices" through the figure, each with volume ΔV. If $A(x)$ is the area of the base of the slice shown in the figure, then

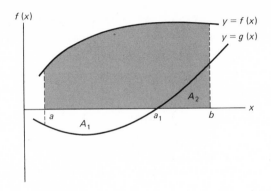

Figure 6.1–5   *Area between two curves.*

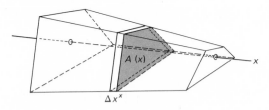

Figure 6.1–6   *Volume by integration.*

$\Delta V = A(x)\,\Delta x$ and the total volume is $V \approx \sum_a^b A(x)\,\Delta x$. As $\Delta x \to 0$, $\sum_a^b A(x)\,\Delta x$ becomes $\int_a^b A(x)\,dx$, an exact measure of the volume. In the case of a cylinder, $A(x) = \pi r^2$, where r is the radius of the cylinder, so that $V = \int_a^b \pi r^2\,dx = \pi r^2 \int_a^b dx = \pi r^2 x]_a^b$. The volume of many other solids may be found by this method of "slicing." In this case r was constant. In many others it may be a function of x.

Example 10.   Length of a Curve

Suppose we are asked to calculate the length of the curve $y = f(x)$ from a to b in Figure 6.1–7. Again we apply the general technique of successively

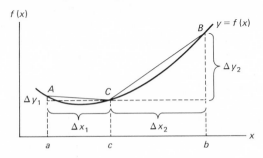

Figure 6.1–7   *Length of a curve.*

closer approximations used above. As a first approximation consider the lines *AC* and *CB*. By Pythagoras' theorem the length of such lines is equal to $\sqrt{(\Delta y)^2 + (\Delta x)^2}$. By increasing the number of such lines, we approximate the length by $\sum_{i=1}^{n} \sqrt{(\Delta y_i)^2 + (\Delta x_i)^2}$ and the length is given exactly by

$$\lim_{n \to \infty} \sum_{i=1}^{n} \sqrt{(\Delta y_i)^2 + (\Delta x_i)^2}$$

when this limit exists. By the mean value theorem, there is some value of x, say $x = c$, for which $\Delta y_i = f'(c)\, \Delta x_i$. Substituting into the expression for the length we obtain:

$$\lim_{n \to \infty} \sum_{i=1}^{n} \sqrt{[f'(c)\, \Delta x_i]^2 + (\Delta x_i)^2} = \lim_{n \to \infty} \sum_{i=1}^{n} \sqrt{[f'(c)]^2\, \Delta x + 1}$$

Or, if the limit exists, the length is given by

$$\int_a^b \sqrt{1 + \left(\frac{dy}{dx}\right)^2}\, dx$$

Certain types of definite integrals are called **improper integrals.**

DEFINITION 6.1–4   A definite integral is **improper** if: (1) the integrand is infinite at one of the limits of integration or at a value between the limits or (2) the lower limit is $-\infty$ and/or the upper limit is $+\infty$.

Special care must be taken to identify integrals of the first type. In either case, evaluation involves the use of limits.

Case 1.   Given $\int_a^b f(x)\, dx$ and $f(x) = \infty$ when $x = b$. Direct application of the rule for evaluating definite integrals fails. Define a new variable w and let $g(w) = \int_a^w f(x)\, dx$. The improper integral $\int_a^b f(x)\, dx$ is said to **converge** if $\lim_{w \to b^-} g(w) = \lim_{w \to b^-} \int_a^w f(x)\, dx$ exists. If not, $\int_a^b f(x)\, dx$ **diverges.** The test for convergence (finding the value of the integral) involves finding $\lim_{w \to b^-} F(x)]_a^w$, where $F(x) = \int f(x)\, dx$. A similar procedure involving $\lim_{w \to a^+} F(x)]_a^b$ is used if $f(x) = \pm\infty$ at $x = a$.

Case 2. $f(x) = \pm\infty$ at a value of x between a and b, say $x = c$. In this case the improper integral is written as the sum of two integrals and the limit process described above is applied to each of them. Specifically, $\int_a^b f(x)\, dx = \int_a^c f(x)\, dx + \int_c^b f(x)\, dx$. Both of these integrals are still improper, but are now of the first form discussed. Thus $\int_a^c f(x)\, dx = \lim_{w \to c^-} \int_a^w f(x)\, dx = \lim_{w \to c^-} F(x)]_a^w$ and $\int_c^b f(x)\, dx = \lim_{w \to c^+} F(x)]_w^b$. Both of these limits must exist for the proper integral to converge, that is, to have a finite value.

Case 3.   One or both of the limits is infinite. Suppose we have $\int_a^\infty f(x)\,dx$. Calculate $\lim_{b\to\infty} F(x)]_a^b$ to test for convergence. Similarly, given $\int_{-\infty}^b f(x)\,dx$, calculate $\lim_{a\to-\infty}\int_a^b f(x)\,dx = \lim_{a\to-\infty} F(x)]_a^b$.

To this point we have discussed only integration of functions of one independent variable. It is also possible to define integrals of functions of two or more independent variables. Suppose we are given $z = f(x, y)$ and we want to find two functions $F(x, y)$ and $G(x, y)$ such that $\partial F/\partial x = f$ and $\partial G/\partial y = f$. F and G can be found, as before, by integrating f with respect to x and y. Thus $F(x, y) + C = \int f(x, y)\,dx$ and $\int f(x, y)\,dy = G(x, y) + C$. When integrating with respect to x, y is treated as a constant and vice versa.

Example 11.   Suppose $z = 5xy^2 + 3x^2y + y$. Then $\int (5xy^2 + 3x^2y + y)\,dx = y^2 \int 5x\,dx + y \int 3x^2\,dx + y \int dx = \frac{5}{2}y^2x^2 + yx^3 + yx + C = F$ (verify that $\partial F/\partial x = f$). $\int (5xy^2 + 3x^2y + y)\,dy = 5x \int y^2\,dy + 3x^2 \int y\,dy + \int y\,dy = \frac{5}{3}xy^3 + \frac{3}{2}x^2y^2 + \frac{1}{2}y^2 + C$. This method, which might be called "partial integration," extends in an obvious manner to functions of more than two independent variables.

For $z = f(x, y)$ it is also possible to calculate the **double integral** over a certain region A, $\iint_A f(x, y)\,dA$. In the xy plane, we imagine the region A to be enclosed by continuous curves of finite length as in Figure 6.1–8. Here A is bounded above and below by two functions of x, f and g, and by the constant functions $x = a$ and $x = b$. Imagine that we divide A by a grid formed by lines parallel to the x and y axes into small pieces of area, denoted by ΔA as shown in Figure 6.1–8. Obviously, $\Delta A = \Delta x\,\Delta y = \Delta y\,\Delta x$. As Δx and $\Delta y \to 0$, $\sum \Delta A$ approaches the area enclosed by the curves f, g, $x = a$, and $x = b$. The function $z = f(x, y)$ lies above the xy plane as shown in Figure 6.1–9. For the particular ΔA shown, $f(\bar{x}, \bar{y})\,\Delta A$ gives the volume of the projection of ΔA up to the function $f(x, y)$, where $\bar{x}$ and $\bar{y}$ are in ΔA. The volume of the figure under $z = f(x, y)$ and above the region A is thus given by $\lim_{\Delta A\to 0} \sum_{i=1}^n f(x_i, y_i)\,\Delta A_i$, where x_i and y_i are values of x and y

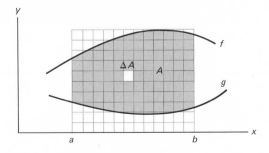

Figure 6.1–8   *Regions A and ΔA.*

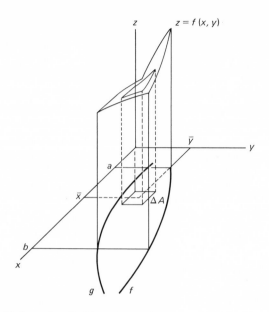

Figure 6.1–9 *Volume by double integration.*

determining a point in area ΔA_i. Furthermore, this is the definition of $\iint_A f(x, y)\, dA$. More formally, we have Definition 6.1–5.

DEFINITION 6.1–5 The **double integral**

$$\iint_A f(x,\, y)\, dA = \lim_{\Delta A \to 0} \sum_{i=1}^{n} f(x_i,\, y_i)\, \Delta A_i$$

Calculating double integrals as the limit of sums would try the patience of Job and the life span of Methusalah. Fortunately, we have the following theorem:

Theorem 6.1–4 The double integral $\iint_A f(x,\, y)\, dA$ over the region A: (a) exists if $f(x,\, y)$ is continuous and the region A is defined by continuous curves of finite length and (b) is equal to

(1) $$\iint_A f(x,\, y)\, dx\, dy$$

or

(2) $$\iint_A f(x,\, y)\, dy\, dx$$

Integrals (1) and (2) are **iterated integrals.** Taking the region A as shown in Figures 6.1–8 and 6.1–9, these integrals are calculated as follows:

$$\iint_A f(x, y)\, dy\, dx = \int_a^b \left[\int_{g(x)}^{f(x)} f(x, y)\, dy \right] dx$$

where first the integration is performed with respect to y, treating x as a constant between the limits $g(x)$ and $f(x)$. The resulting expression is then integrated with respect to x, treating y as a constant, and is evaluated between the limits a and b.

Example 12. Suppose $g(x) = x$ (i.e., $y = x$), $f(x) = -x + 1$, $a = 0$, and $b = \frac{1}{2}$. The region of integration, A, is shown in Figure 6.1–10. In addition,

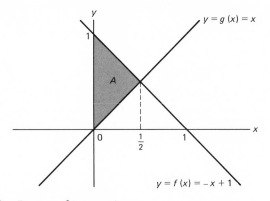

Figure 6.1–10   *Region of integration.*

suppose that $z = x + y$. Then $\iint_A (x + y)\, dA = \int_0^{1/2} \left[\int_x^{-x+1} (x + y)\, dy \right] dx$. Evaluating the inside integral:

$$\int_x^{-x+1} (x + y)\, dy = xy + \frac{y^2}{2} \Bigg]_x^{-x+1}$$

$$= x(-x + 1) + \frac{(-x + 1)^2}{2} - x^2 - \frac{x^2}{2} = -2x^2 + \frac{1}{2}$$

Thus

$$\iint_A f(x, y)\, dA = \int_0^{1/2} \left(-2x^2 + \frac{1}{2} \right) dx = -\frac{2}{3} x^3 + \frac{x}{2} \Bigg]_0^{1/2}$$

$$= -\frac{2}{3}\left(\frac{1}{8}\right) + \frac{1}{4} = \frac{1}{6}$$

If we wish to perform the integration of $f(x, y)$ with respect to x first, it is necessary to alter the limits of integration. It is not true that

$$\iint_A f(x, y)\, dA = \int_x^{-x+1} \left[\int_0^{1/2} (x + y)\, dx \right] dy$$

as calculation of this iterated integral shows. Examining Figure 6.1–8 shows that y can be treated as varying between 0 and 1, while x varies from y to $-y + 1$. Thus

$$\iint_A f(x, y)\, dA = \int_0^1 \left[\int_{-y+1}^y (x + y)\, dx \right] dy$$

Calculation of this iterated integral also shows that the volume contained between A and $z = x + y$ is $\frac{1}{6}$. Note that the limits of integration on the integral with respect to x have been transposed to ensure that the answer has the correct sign.

In many cases, reversing the order of integration involves breaking the region into two or more subregions. Consider the example shown in Figure 6.1–11, where the region of integration is bounded by $x = a$, $x = b$, $y = x$, and $y = 0$. When integrating first with respect to y,

$$\iint_A f(x, y)\, dA = \int_a^b \left[\int_0^x f(x, y)\, dy \right] dx$$

When integrating with respect to x first, A must be treated as being composed of two subregions, A_1 and A_2. In the rectangle A_1, as y varies from 0 to a, x varies from a to b. Thus for A_1 we have the iterated integral

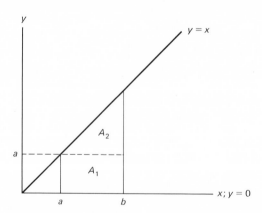

Figure 6.1–11 A_1 *and* A_2.

$\int_0^a \left[\int_a^b f(x, y) \, dx \right] dy$. In region A_2, as y varies from a to b, x varies from y to b. For this region we have the iterated integral $\int_a^b \left[\int_y^b f(x, y) \, dx \right] dy$. Over the entire region

$$\iint_A f(x, y) \, dA = \int_0^a \left[\int_a^b f(x, y) \, dx \right] dy + \int_a^b \left[\int_y^b f(x, y) \, dx \right] dy$$

$$= \int_a^b \left[\int_0^x f(x, y) \, dy \right] dx$$

Particular care must be taken to analyze the region of integration when writing the double integral as iterated integrals and when changing the order of integration.[5]

Double integrals have many applications. Their use in finding volumes has already been illustrated. They can also be used to find areas. See Figure 6.1–12. Here we are asked to find the area enclosed by $x = h(y)$, $x = g(y)$, $y = a$, and $y = b$. Since the total area is the limit of the sum of blocks of areas, equal to $\Delta y \, \Delta x$, as Δy and $\Delta x \to 0$, the total area is given by

$$\iint_A dx \, dy \quad \text{or} \quad \iint_A dy \, dx$$

In this particular case the best iterated integral to use is $\int_a^b \left[\int_{h(y)}^{g(y)} dx \right] dy$. Note that evaluating this integral leads to the expression for the area we could obtain by using a single integral, where the integration is performed with respect to y. The reader should attempt to write the equivalent iterated integral where the first integration is performed with respect to y rather than x.

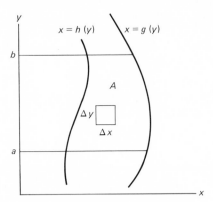

Figure 6.1–12   *Area by double integration.*

[5] A more complete discussion of the procedure for changing the limits of integration will be found in Widder (1961), Chapters 6 and 7.

Example 13.   Evaluate $\int_0^1 \int_1^{e^x} dy\, dx$. Performing the integration with respect to y:

$$\int_0^1 \left[y \Big|_1^{e^x} \right] dx = \int_0^1 (e^x - 1)\, dx$$

Integrating with respect to x:

$$\int_0^1 (e^x - 1)\, dx = e^x - x \Big|_0^1 = (e^1 - 1) - (e^0 - 0) = e - 2$$

Express the original integral in alternative form by reversing the order of integration. First sketch the region of integration (see Figure 6.1–13). This is

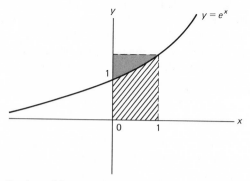

Figure 6.1–13   *Region of integration.*

done to help determine the limits of integration for the new double integral. When integrating with respect to x first, x can vary from $\ln y$ to 1, since with x as the "independent" variable, $y = e^x$ becomes $x = \ln y$. y, on the other hand, varies from 1 to e over the region of integration, since $e^0 = 1$ and $e^1 = e$. Thus the new double integral is

$$\int_1^e \int_{\ln y}^1 dx\, dy = \int_1^e \left[x \Big|_{\ln y}^1 \right] dy = \int_1^e (1 - \ln y)\, dy = \int_1^e dy - \int_1^e \ln y\, dy$$

The last integral can be evaluated by applying the rule for integration by parts. This yields

$$-\int_1^e \ln y\, dy = -(y \ln y - y) \Big|_1^e$$

so that the double integral becomes

$$y - (y \ln y - y) \Big|_1^e = e - (e \ln e - e) - [1 - (1 \ln 1 - 1)]$$

As the reader can verify, this expression is equal to $e - 2$. This shows the equivalence of the two double integrals.

Query: Which of the shaded areas in Figure 6.1–13 is the region of integration?

Example 14. Milton Friedman's permanent income hypothesis contains several interesting economic applications of single and multiple integration.[6] Friedman develops the following individual consumption function:

(1) $$c_p = k(i, w, u)y_p$$

where c_p is permanent consumption, y_p is permanent income, i is a representation of the interest rates on borrowing and lending, w is the ratio of non-human wealth to permanent income, and u is a variable reflecting the consumer's taste. The function $k(i, w, u)$, therefore, is the proportion of the individual's permanent income spent on permanent consumption in any one time period.

If Equation (1) applies to every member of a particular group of consumers, how can the aggregate level of permanent consumption, c_p^*, be calculated? $k(i, w, u)$ will vary between different consumers because (1) different groups may face a different structure of interest rates, (2) w will vary between groups, and (3) u will also, in general, be different for different consumers. Thus the ratio of c_p^* to y_p will differ between consumers. Obviously, the absolute level will also differ because of differences in permanent income. Consequently, aggregate consumption depends on the distribution of consumers by the variables i, w, and u.

Friedman defines

$$f(i, w, u, y_p) \, di \, dw \, du \, dy_p$$

as the number of consumers for whom the "interest rate," i, is between i and $i + di$, w is between w and $w + dw$, u is between u and $u + du$, and y_p is between y_p and $y_p + dy_p$. Consequently, c_p for this particular subgroup of consumers is

$$f(i, w, u, y_p) \, di \, dw \, du \, dy_p \, k(i, w, u)y_p$$

For all consumers, for all ranges of i, w, u, and y_p, aggregate consumption is the multiple integral:

(2) $$c_p^* = \int_i \int_w \int_u \int_{y_p} f(i, w, u, y_p)k(i, w, u)y_p \, di \, dw \, du \, dy_p$$

The notation $\int_i$, and so on, simply means that the limits of integration with respect to i include all the values of i, and so on.

---

[6] Friedman (1957).

If the distribution of consumers by income does not depend on i, u, and w, then

(3)
$$f(i, w, u, y_p) = g(i, w, u)h(y_p)$$

and the aggregate consumption function can be written as

(4)
$$c_p^* = \left[\int_i \int_w \int_u g(i, w, u)k(i, w, u) \, di \, dw \, du \right] y_p^*$$

where y_p^* is aggregate permanent income. To show this, substitute (3) into (2):

$$c_p^* = \int_i \int_w \int_u \int_{y_p} g(i, w, u)h(y_p)k(i, w, u)y_p \, di \, dw \, du \, dy_p$$

Rearranging terms,

$$c_p^* = \int_i \int_w \int_u g(i, w, u)k(i, w, u) \, di \, dw \, du \int_{y_p} h(y_p)y_p \, dy_p$$

This step is permissible since none of the terms in the brackets are functions of y_p and thus can be treated as constants when performing the integration with respect to y_p. Since $h(y_p)y_p$ represents the total permanent income of all consumers with income between y_p and $y_p + dy_p$, $\int_{y_p} h(y_p)y_p \, dy_p$ must be equal to aggregate permanent income, y_p^*. This demonstrates the validity of Equation (4).

This example illustrates one use in economics of multiple integration—that of building up functions that attempt to describe aggregate behavior from functions purporting to describe the behavior of individuals when there is more than one variable that influences behavior.

Friedman's functions for estimating permanent income serve as a good illustration of the use of single integration in economic theory. His estimate is based on the hypothesis that permanent income is a weighted average of income in previous years, where the weights themselves decline the further one moves into the past; for example, the weight associated with last year's income is larger than the weight applied to income 10 years ago. In his formulation both the weights themselves and the number of years to be included in the calculation are determined statistically. Let measured aggregate income, y^*, be a function of time: $y^*(t)$ is thus measured income in time t. Permanent income in time $\bar{i}$ is then estimated by

(5)
$$y_p^*(\bar{i}) = \int_{-\infty}^{\bar{i}} w(t - \bar{i})y^*(t) \, dt$$

where $w(t - \bar{i})$ is a weighting function with the necessary property that

(6)
$$\int_{-\infty}^{\bar{i}} w(t - \bar{i}) \, dt = 1$$

that is, the weights sum to one. One specific weighting function Friedman suggests is

$$w(t - \bar{t}) = \beta e^{\beta(t - \bar{t})}$$

where β is a positive constant. Let us prove that this function has the proper characteristics.

$$1 \stackrel{?}{=} \int_{-\infty}^{\bar{t}} \beta e^{\beta(t-\bar{t})} \, dt = \beta \int_{-\infty}^{\bar{t}} e^{\beta t} e^{-\beta \bar{t}} \, dt$$

$$= \beta e^{-\beta \bar{t}} \int_{-\infty}^{\bar{t}} e^{\beta t} \, dt$$

Now let $u = \beta t$ so that $dt = du/\beta$. The last integral is then

$$\beta e^{-\beta \bar{t}} \int_{-\infty}^{\bar{t}} \frac{e^u \, du}{\beta} = e^{-\beta \bar{t}} e^u = e^{-\beta \bar{t}} e^{\beta t} \Big]_{-\infty}^{\bar{t}}$$

$$= e^{-\beta t} e^{\beta t} - e^{-\beta t} e^{\beta(-\infty)}$$

$$= 1 - e^{-\beta \bar{t}} \lim_{a \to -\infty} e^{\beta a} = 1 - e^{-\beta \bar{t}}(0) = 1$$

So the weights sum to one. It is easy to verify that $\beta e^{\beta(t-\bar{t})}$ declines as t moves further away from $\bar{t}$.

With this specific function, the estimate becomes

$$y_p^*(\bar{t}) = \beta \int_{-\infty}^{\bar{t}} e^{\beta(t-\bar{t})} y^*(t) \, dt$$

In this formulation β is a constant to be estimated statistically.[7]

Problems

6.1–1   Calculate the following indefinite integrals:

(a) $\int (x^3 + 3x) \, dx$

(f) $\int (e^x + 1) \, dx$

(b) $\int (x^{-2} + 5) \, dx$

(g) $\int (e^{3x} - x^3) \, dx$

(c) $\int (x + 1)^2 \, dx$

(h) $\int \sin x \, dx$

(d) $\int \frac{dx}{x}$

(i) $\int \frac{x^3(x - 1)}{x^5 - (5x^4/4) + 1} \, dx$

(e) $\int \left(\frac{x^2 + 1}{x} \right) dx$

[7] See Friedman (1957), page 142.

6.1–2 Find the following integrals using the method of partial fractions:

(a) $\displaystyle\int \frac{x \, dx}{x^2 + 4x - 5}$

(c) $\displaystyle\int \frac{dx}{x(x + 1)^2}$

(b) $\displaystyle\int \frac{x^2 \, dx}{x^2 + 2x + 1}$

6.1–3 Find the following integrals using integration by parts:

(a) $\displaystyle\int x \ln x \, dx$

(b) $\displaystyle\int \ln (x + 1) \, dx$

6.1–4 Find the following definite integrals:

(a) $\displaystyle\int_0^1 (x^2 + x) \, dx$

(d) $\displaystyle\int_{-1}^1 2x^{-1} \, dx$

(b) $\displaystyle\int_{-5}^3 (x - 1)^2 \, dx$

(e) $\displaystyle\int_{-1}^2 \ln x \, dx$

(c) $\displaystyle\int_0^\infty x^2 \, dx$

6.1–5 Suppose a monopolist's demand curve is given by $P = -2x + 15$. Find the monopolist's total revenue by integration if he sells six units of good x.

6.1–6 Suppose a firm's total cost is given by $TC = 5Q + 3$ and its total revenue by $TR = 6Q - Q^2$. Find its profit by integration if the firm sells five units. Where is profit maximized?

6.1–7 If the equation of a highway is $y = 5x + 3$, how far does a truck travel in going from $x = 0$ to $x = 5$?

6.1–8 Find the following double integrals:

(a) $\displaystyle\int_0^1 \int_y^{y^2} dx \, dy$

(c) $\displaystyle\int_{-3}^0 \int_{x^2+2x}^{3x+1} dy \, dx$

(b) $\displaystyle\int_1^2 \int_0^{\ln y} e^{x+y} \, dx \, dy$

6.2 STIELTJES INTEGRALS

The Stieltjes integral is a generalization of the "ordinary" (Riemann) integral. In the Riemann integral the integration is performed with respect to a single variable; in the Stieltjes integral, integration is performed with respect to a function of a single variable.

DEFINITION 6.2–1   The **Stieltjes integral** of $f(x)$ with respect to $s(x)$ from $x = a$ to $x = b$ is

$$\int_a^b f(x)\, ds(x) = \lim_{\|\Delta\| \to 0} \sum_{i=1}^n f(c_i)[s(x_i) - s(x_{i-1})]$$

where c_i is a value of x between x_i and x_{i-1}.

As before we subdivide the interval from a to b into a series of subintervals, determined by the selection of the x_i, $i = 1, 2, \ldots, n$. The notation $\|\Delta\|$ stands for the norm of the subintervals, Δ, where $\|\Delta\|$ is the largest of the subintervals. Thus taking $\lim_{\|\Delta\| \to 0}$ forces the largest subinterval, and thus all subintervals, to approach zero. This limit need not exist, depending on the functions $f(x)$ and $s(x)$. If it does not, the Stieltjes integral does not exist.

Theorem 6.2–1   Given $f(x)$ is continuous in $a \le x \le b$ and $s(x)$ is either a strictly increasing or a strictly decreasing function in the same interval, then the Stieltjes integral $\int_a^b f(x)\, ds(x)$ exists.

Definition 6.2–1 and Theorem 6.2–1 give no convenient way to evaluate a Stieltjes integral. The following theorem shows that under certain conditions a Stieltjes integral may be expressed and evaluated as a Riemann integral.

Theorem 6.2–2   Given that $f(x)$ is continuous in $a \le x \le b$ and that $s(x)$ is continuous and has a continuous first derivative in the same interval. Then[8]

$$\int_a^b f(x)\, ds(x) = \int_a^b f(x) s'(x)\, dx$$

Example 1.   Find $\int_0^1 (x^2 + 2)\, d(3x^2)$. Here $s(x) = 3x^2$. Both $s(x)$ and $s'(x) = 6x$ are continuous in $(0, 1)$ as is $(x^2 + 2)$. Thus $\int_0^1 (x^2 + 2)\, d(3x^2) = \int_0^1 (x^2 + 2)6x\, dx = \int_0^1 6x^3\, dx + \int_0^1 12x\, dx = \frac{3}{2}x^4 + 6x^2|_0^1 = \frac{15}{2}$.

If the hypotheses of Theorem 6.2–2 are not satisfied, the value of the integral (if it exists) must be found by calculating the limit in Definition 6.2–1.[9]

Theorem 6.2–3 lists some of the most common properties of Stieltjes integrals. The reader should compare these with the properties of the Riemann integral discussed in the previous section.

Theorem 6.2–3   Given that k is a constant and that the functions $f_i(x)$ and $s_j(x)$ have the properties of Theorem 6.2–1, then:

(a) $\displaystyle\int_a^b ds(x) = s(b) - s(a)$;

[8] The proof is left as an exercise for the reader.

[9] For examples of this procedure see Widder (1961), Chapter 5.

(b) $\displaystyle\int_a^b f(x)\,d[s(x) + k] = \int_a^b f(x)\,ds(x);$

(c) $\displaystyle\int_a^b [f_1(x) + f_2(x)]\,ds(x) = \int_a^b f_1(x)\,ds(x) + \int_a^b f_2(x)\,ds(x);$

(d) $\displaystyle\int_a^b f(x)\,d[s_1(x) + s_2(x)] = \int_a^b f(x)\,ds_1(x) + \int_a^b f(x)\,ds_2(x);$ and

(e) $\displaystyle\int_a^b f(x)\,ds(x) = \int_a^c f(x)\,ds(x) + \int_c^b f(x)\,ds(x)\,[\text{provided that } \lim_{x \to c^+} f(x) =$

$\lim_{x \to c^-} f(x)].$

Stieltjes integrals can also be evaluated by a procedure analogous to integration by parts for Riemann integrals.

Theorem 6.2–4   Given that $f(x)$ is a nondecreasing function and that $s(x)$ is continuous in $a \leq x \leq b$. Then[10]

$$\int_a^b f(x)\,ds(x) = s(b)f(b) - s(a)f(a) - \int_a^b s(x)\,df(x)$$

Example 2.   Find $\int_0^1 x\,dx^3$ by integration by parts.

$$\int_0^1 x\,dx^3 = (1)^3(1) - (0)^3(0) - \int_0^1 x^3\,dx = 1 - \left.\frac{x^4}{4}\right|_0^1 = \tfrac{3}{4}$$

By Theorem 6.2–2, $\int_0^1 x\,dx^3 = \int_0^1 3x^3\,dx = \tfrac{3}{4}x^4|_0^1 = \tfrac{3}{4}$ and thus both methods give the same answer.

The existence of the Stieltjes integral does not depend on the continuity of the integrating function $s(x)$. The integral exists if $s(x)$ is discontinuous as long as it is either nonincreasing or nondecreasing between the limits of integration. It is this fact that accounts for the usefulness of the Stieltjes integral in physical and economic applications. The Riemann integral is suitable only in applications involving continuous distributions. In discrete cases, summation rather than Riemann integration must be used. Stieltjes integrals, on the other hand, can be used if the distribution is discrete, continuous, or a combination of the two.

Suppose that $s(x)$ is a step function on the interval $a \leq x \leq b$, with discontinuities at $x = k_1, k_2, \ldots, k_n$. The size of any jump of $s(x)$ is given by

$$j_{k_i} = \lim_{x \to k_i^+} s(x) - \lim_{x \to k_i^-} s(x)$$

[10] For a proof see Widder (1961).

if $s(x)$ is monotonically increasing or

$$j_{k_i} = \lim_{x \to k_i^-} s(x) - \lim_{x \to k_i^+} s(x)$$

if $s(x)$ is monotonically decreasing. If $f(x)$ is continuous on $a \leq x \leq b$, then

$$\int_a^b f(x) \, ds(x) = \sum_{i=1}^n j_{k_i} f(k_i)$$

Furthermore, if $s(x)$ is continuous on $c \leq x \leq a$,

$$\int_a^b f(x) \, ds(x) = \int_c^a f(x)s'(x) \, dx + \sum_{i=1}^n j_{k_i} f(k_i)$$

This relation is the basis for our previous statement.

Example 3. Consider the demand and marginal revenue functions in Figure 6.2–1. Suppose only two prices higher than P_a are changed—P_0 and P_1—and only two prices lower than P_b are charged—P_{b+1} and P_{b+2}—while every possible price between P_a and P_b is charged. If we are asked to calculate the total revenue of selling X_{b+2} units we can write

(1)
$$\mathrm{TR}_{X_{b+2}} = \int_0^{X_{b+2}} \mathrm{MR} \, dx$$

only if we interpret the integral as a Stieltjes integral with $s(x) = x$. Calculating (1) as a Riemann integral would obviously overstate total revenue.

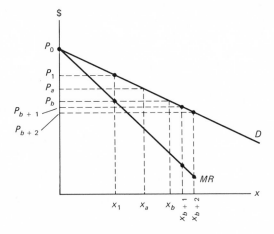

Figure 6.2–1 *Demand and marginal revenue.*

Evaluating (1) we have

(2)

$$TR_{X_{b+2}} = MR(0) + MR(X_1) + \int_a^b MR\ dx + MR(X_{b+1}) + MR(X_{b+2})$$

$\int_a^b MR\ dx$ is a Riemann integral of the form $\int f(x)s'(x)\ dx$. In this case $s'(x) = 1$ since $s(x) = x$. This illustrates the compactness of notation achieved by the use of Stieltjes integrals and the greater degree of generalization of such integrals. It also illustrates that the rules for their evaluation correspond to our common sense notions.

Problems

6.2–1   Find the following Stieltjes integrals:

(a) $\int x^3\ dx^2$ (c) $\int (x^2 + 1)^3\ dx^2$

(b) $\int (x + 1)\ d(x^2 + x)$

References

1. ALLEN, R. G. D. (1938), *Mathematical Analysis for Economists*, London: Macmillan.
2. CHEMICAL RUBBER COMPANY, *Mathematical Tables from the Handbook of Chemistry and Physics*, Cleveland.
3. COURANT, R. (1937), *Differential and Integral Calculus* (tr. by E. J. McShane), New York: Wiley-Interscience.
4. FRIEDMAN, MILTON (1957), *A Theory of the Consumption Function*, Princeton, N.J.: Princeton University Press.
5. HENSTOCK, R. (1963), *Theory of Integration*, London: Butterworths.
6. JOHNSON, R. E., and F. L. KIOKEMEISTER (1969), *Calculus with Analytic Geometry*, 4th ed., Boston: Allyn & Bacon.
7. REKTORYS, KAREL (ed.) (1969), *Survey of Applicable Mathematics* (tr. by Rudolf Vyborny), Cambridge, Mass.: M.I.T. Press.
8. THOMAS, GEORGE (1968), *Calculus and Analytical Geometry*, 4th ed., Reading, Mass.: Addison-Wesley.
9. WIDDER, DAVID (1961), *Advanced Calculus*, Englewood Cliffs, N.J.: Prentice-Hall.

Chapter 7

Differential Equations

7.1 ORDINARY DIFFERENTIAL EQUATIONS

Differential equations are simply equations involving one or more derivatives of various sorts. Equivalently, they are equations involving differentials.

DEFINITION 7.1–1 **Ordinary differential equations** contain only ordinary derivatives, although they may be of any order or degree.

Ordinary differential equations are the most frequently encountered in economics and the easiest to solve. This section will be devoted to them, while partial differential equations will be discussed in Section 7.2.

Differential equations are also classified by order.

DEFINITION 7.1–2. The **order** of a differential equation is the order of the highest-order derivative it contains.

DEFINITION 7.1–3 The **degree** of a differential equation is the highest power to which any of the derivatives in the equation is raised.

Thus

$$\frac{d^2y}{dx^2} + 5\left(\frac{dy}{dx}\right)^3 = 5$$

is a second-order, third-degree, ordinary differential equation.

The simplest type of differential equation to solve is a first-order, linear (first-degree), ordinary differential equation. Such an equation can be written in general form as

$$(1) \qquad\qquad y' + f(x)y = g(x)$$

where y is a function of x. The solution to (1) is a function $y = y(x)$ such that $y'(x) = g(x) - f(x)y$.

Let

$$F(x) = \int f(x)\, dx$$

199

Multiply both sides of (1) by $e^{F(x)}$:

(2) $$y'e^{F(x)} + f(x)ye^{F(x)} = g(x)e^{F(x)}$$

The left side of (2) can be written as[1]

(3) $$\frac{d[e^{F(x)}y(x)]}{dx}$$

so that:

$$[e^{F(x)}y(x)]' = g(x)e^{F(x)}$$

Let $G(x) = \int g(x)e^{F(x)}\, dx$. Then, integrating both sides of (3),

(4) $$\int [e^{F(x)}y(x)]'\, dx = G(x)$$

or $e^{F(x)}y(x) = G(x) + C$. Dividing through by $e^{F(x)}$ yields

(5) $$y(x) = e^{-F(x)}[G(x) + C]$$

Theorem 7.1–1 Every function of form (5) is a solution to the linear, first-order differential equation (1).

PROOF   Differentiate (5) with respect to x:

$$y' = \frac{d}{dx}\left\{\exp\left[-\int f(x)\, dx\right]\left[\int g(x)\exp\left[\int f(x)\, dx\right]dx + C\right]\right\}$$

$$= \frac{d[\exp(-\int f(x)\, dx)]}{dx}\left[\int g(x)\exp\left[\int f(x)\, dx\right]dx + C\right]$$

$$+ \left(\exp\left[-\int f(x)\, dx\right]\right)\frac{d[\int g(x)\exp(\int f(x)\, dx)\, dx]}{dx}$$

$$= \left[-f(x)\exp\left(-\int f(x)\, dx\right)\right]\left\{\int g(x)\exp\left[\int f(x)\, dx\right]dx + C\right\}$$

$$+ \exp\left[-\int f(x)\, dx\right]\left[g(x)\exp\left(\int f(x)\, dx\right)\right]$$

$$= g(x) - f(x)\left\{\exp\left[-\int f(x)\, dx\right]\left[\int g(x)\exp\left[\int f(x)\, dx\right]dx + C\right]\right\}$$

---

[1] Since

$$d[e^{F(x)}y(x)] = y'e^{F(x)} + y(x)\frac{de^{F(x)}}{dx}$$

by the chain rule, and

$$\frac{de^{F(x)}}{dx} = \frac{dF(x)}{dx}e^{F(x)} = \frac{d[\int f(x)\, dx]}{dx}e^{F(x)} = f(x)e^{F(x)}$$

By (5) the term in curly brackets is y. Thus we have

$$y' = g(x) - f(x)y \qquad \text{QED}$$

Equation (5) describes a whole family of functions with the required derivative because of the presence of the integration constant C.

DEFINITION 7.1–4   (a) Equation (5) is the **general solution** to the differential equation (1). (b) The **specific solution** selects one curve from the family (5) based on an **initial condition.**

An initial condition is simply knowledge of the x and y coordinants of one point on the curve $y = y(x)$. Suppose we know the value of y when $x = 0$, that is, $y(0)$. Then the specific solution is obtained by substituting these values of x and y into (5):

$$y(0) = e^{-F(0)}[G(0) + C]$$

Solving for C, $C = y(0)e^{F(0)} - G(0)$. This value of C is then substituted into (5), obtaining the specific solution

(6) $$y(x) = e^{-F(x)}\{G(x) + [y(0)e^{F(0)} - G(0)]\}$$

Equation (6) not only has the proper derivative, but passes through the point $(0, y(0))$, thus satisfying the initial condition.

The function $e^{F(x)}$ is known as the **integrating factor.** We shall now illustrate how the integrating factor and the procedure of Theorem 7.1–1 can be used to solve specific first-order, linear differential equations:

Case 1. $f(x) = k$, where k is a constant and $g(x) = 0$. Equation (1) becomes $y' + ky = 0$. Then $F(x) = \int k \, dx = kx$. Thus the general solution becomes

$$y(x) = Ce^{-kx}$$

while the specific solution is, in terms of $y(0)$,

$$y(x) = y(0)e^{-kx}$$

Differential equations of this sort are called **homogeneous, constant-coefficient** equations.

Case 2. $f(x) = k$, $g(x) = j$, where k and j are constants. $F(x) = kx$, $G(x) = \int je^{kx} \, dx = (j/k)e^{kx}$ so that the general solution is

$$y(x) = e^{-kx}\left(\frac{j}{k}e^{kx} + C\right) = \frac{j}{k} + Ce^{-kx}$$

The specific solution, again in terms of $y(0)$, is

$$y(x) = \left[y(0) - \frac{j}{k} \right] e^{-kx} + \frac{j}{k}$$

as the reader can verify by solving for C. Equations of this sort are **non-homogeneous, constant-term** equations.

Case 3. $f(x) = x^2$ and $g(x) = 2x^2$. Equation (1) is

$$y' + x^2 y = 2x^2$$

an example of a **variable-term, variable-coefficient** equation. In this case $F(x) = x^3/3$ and $G(x) = \int 2x^2 e^{x^3/3} \, dx$. Thus

$$y(x) = e^{-x^3/3} \left(\int 2x^2 e^{x^3/3} \, dx + C \right)$$

In $\int 2x^2 e^{x^3/3} \, dx$, let $u = x^3/3$. Then $du = x^2 \, dx$ and the integral becomes $2 \int e^u \, du = 2e^u = 2e^{x^3/3}$. Thus $y(x) = e^{-x^3/3}(2e^{x^3/3} + C) = 2 + Ce^{-x^3/3}$. The specific solution is $y(x) = 2 + [y(0) - 2]e^{-x^3/3}$.

Any first-order, linear differential equation of form (1) can be solved by the method of Theorem 7.1–1. In practice, however, some of the integrals involved cannot be solved exactly but must be approximated.

DEFINITION 7.1–5 **Separable, first-order differential equations** are equations of the form

(7) $$y' = \frac{f(x)}{g(y)}$$

Thus $g(y)y' = f(x)$. Let $G(y) = \int g(y) \, dy$ and $F(x) = \int f(x) \, dx$. Then $g[y(x)]y'(x) = G'[y(x)]y'(x) = (d/dx)G[y(x)]$. Consequently, y is a solution to (7) if and only if

(8) $$\frac{d}{dx} \{G[y(x)] - F(x)\} = 0$$

Equivalent to (8) we have

(9) $$G[y(x)] - F(x) = C$$

where C is an arbitrary constant.

Theorem 7.1–2   Solving (9) for $y(x)$ provides the general solution to separable differential equations of form (7).

The proof follows immediately by differentiating (9).

Example 1.   Let $f(x) = x + 1$ and $g(y) = y + 1$. Then (7) becomes $y' = (x + 1)/(y + 1)$. $F(x) = (x^2/2) + x$ and $G(y) = (y^2/2) + y$. Thus (9) becomes

$$\frac{y(x)^2}{2} + y(x) - \left(C + \frac{x^2}{2} + x\right) = 0$$

or

$$y(x)^2 + 2y(x) - 2\left(C + \frac{x^2}{2} + x\right) = 0$$

Solving this equation for $y(x)$ by the quadratic formula,

$$y(x) = \frac{-2 \pm \sqrt{4 + 8[C + (x^2/2) + x]}}{2}$$

which is the general solution. Another way to solve this example is to treat y' as a ratio of differentials. Thus $dy/dx = (x + 1)/(y + 1)$ or $(y + 1)\, dy = (x + 1)\, dx$. Integrating both sides, $(y^2/2) + y = (x^2/2) + x + C$, and we have the same quadratic equation as before. The specific solution is obtained as before.

Another method of wide application in solving first-order differential equations is change of variable or substitution. Since there are many possible substitutions depending on the particular equation, this is really not a single method. We shall illustrate some of the more simple, frequently encountered substitutions.

Case 1. $y' = f(y/x)$. Let $z = y/x$. Then $y = zx$ and $dy/dx = z + x\, dz/dx$. Thus $z + x\, dz/dx = f(z)$. $[f(z) - z]^{-1}\, dz = x^{-1}\, dx$ is a separable equation and can be solved by the method of Theorem 7.1–2 for z as a function of x. The solution $y(x)$ is obtained by resubstituting $z = y/x$.

Case 2.   Bernoulli equations.

DEFINITION 7.1–6   A differential equation of the form $(dy/dx) + f(x)y - g(x)y^n = 0$ is called a **Bernoulli equation.**

Bernoulli equations may be solved by a change of variable. Let $z = y^{1-n}$. Dividing through by y^n yields $y^{-n}\, dy/dx + f(x)y^{1-n} = g(x)$. Since dz/dx is, by the chain rule, $(1 - n)y^{-n}\, dy/dx$, we have

$$\frac{1}{1 - n}\frac{dz}{dx} + f(x)z = g(x)$$

This is a first-order, linear differential equation that can be solved by the methods at our disposal for $z(x)$. $z(x)$ can be transformed into $y(x)$ by substitution.

Some first-order differential equations are *exact differential equations*. Even though they can be solved by the use of the integrating factor of Theorem 7.1–1, there is a special method available for such equations.

DEFINITION 7.1–7   An **exact differential equation** is one that can be written in the form $A\,dy + B\,dx = 0$ and where $\partial A/\partial x = \partial B/\partial y$. [Use Young's theorem (Theorem 5.2–1) to show how this definition is based on the expression for the total differential of a function of two independent variables.]

Theorem 7.1–3   The general solution to an exact differential equation $A\,dy + B\,dx = 0$ is

$$\int A\,dy + \int B\,dx - \int\left(\frac{\partial}{\partial x}\int A\,dy\right)dx = C$$

where C is an arbitrary constant.

PROOF   Since $A\,dy + B\,dx = 0$ is an exact differential equation, it corresponds to a function $F(x, y)$, where $dF(x, y) = 0$. The general solution thus must be of the form $F(x, y) = k$, where k is a constant. Since $dF(x, y) = (\partial F/\partial x)\,dx + (\partial F/\partial y)\,dy = 0$, it follows that $A = \partial F/\partial y$ and $B = \partial F/\partial x$. Thus we can write $F(x, y) = \int A\,dy + \theta(x)$, where $\theta(x)$ is an unknown function of x. Now $B = \partial F/\partial x = (\partial/\partial x)[\int A\,dy + \theta(x)]$, from which it follows that

$$\theta'(x) = B - \frac{\partial}{\partial x}\int A\,dy$$

Integrating this expression with respect to x,

$$\theta(x) = \int\left(B - \frac{\partial}{\partial x}\int A\,dy\right)dx$$

Substituting into the earlier expression for $F(x, y)$ we have

$$F(x, y) = \int A\,dy + \int B\,dx - \int\left(\frac{\partial}{\partial x}\int A\,dy\right)dx \qquad \text{QED}$$

Example 2. $(dy/dx) + (y^2x/x^2y) = 0$ is an exact differential equation, where $A = x^2y$ and $B = y^2x$, since $\partial A/\partial x = 2xy = \partial B/\partial y$. Thus the general solution can be written as

$$F(x, y) = \int (x^2y)\, dy + \int (y^2x)\, dx - \int \left[\frac{\partial}{\partial x} \int (x^2y)\, dy\right] dx = C$$

$$= \frac{x^2y^2}{2} + \frac{y^2x^2}{2} - \int \left[\frac{\partial}{\partial x}\left(\frac{x^2y^2}{2}\right)\right] dx = C$$

$$= x^2y^2 - \int (xy^2)\, dx = C$$

$$= x^2y^2 - \frac{x^2y^2}{2} = C$$

$$= \frac{x^2y^2}{2} = C$$

The general solution is

$$y^2 = \frac{2C}{x^2} \quad \text{or} \quad y(x) = \frac{\sqrt{2C}}{x}$$

The reader should verify that if a differential equation is inexact it can be transformed to an exact differential equation by the integrating factor and procedure of Theorem 7.1–1.

The following theorem describes a procedure for evaluating linear differential equations of first and higher orders.

DEFINITION 7.1–8   A **linear nth-order** differential equation is an equation of the form

(1) $$y^{(n)} + x_{n-1}y^{(n-1)} + \cdots + x_1 y' + x_0 y = k$$

where x_i, $i = 0, 1, 2, \ldots, n - 1$ and k are functions of x, and $y^{(i)}$ is the ith derivative of y.

Define the function $Y(y) = y^{(n)} + \sum_{i=0}^{n-1} x_i y^{(i)}$, where $y^{(0)} \equiv y$. Then (1) is simply $Y(y) = k$.

Theorem 7.1–4   Let $\bar{y}$ be a solution to Equation (1). Then $Y(\bar{y}) = k$. Then all solutions to (1) are of the form

$$y = \bar{y} + y^*$$

where $Y(y^*) = 0$. Conversely, every $y = \bar{y} + y^*$ is a solution to (1).

PROOF If $Y(y) = k$, let $y^* = y - \bar{y}$. Then $Y(y^*) = Y(y - \bar{y}) = k - k = 0$, so that y^* is a solution to the homogeneous version of (1), that is, $Y(y^*) = 0$. If $y = \bar{y} + y^*$ and $Y(y^*) = 0$, then $Y(y) = Y(\bar{y}) + Y(y^*) = k + 0 = k$.   QED

This theorem says to find the general solution to (1) find:

(a) *any one* solution $\bar{y}$ to (1). This is called the **particular solution;** and
(b) all solutions, y^*, to the homogeneous version of (1) [i.e., (1) with $k = 0$]. Then y, the **general solution,** is equal to $\bar{y} + y^*$.

Example 3. Let $dy/dx = x^3 y - x^3$. Suppose that y is a constant. Then $dy/dx = 0$ and $y = x^3/x^3 = 1$. Thus $\bar{y} = 1$ for this example. The homogeneous version is $dy/dx = -x^3 y$ or $dy/y = -x^3 \, dx$. Integrating both sides gives $\ln y = -x^4/4$, so that $y = Ce^{-(x^4/4)} + 1$.

With these methods in mind for solving first-order differential equations, we turn to the solution techniques for second-order differential equations. We consider first the solution to second-order linear differential equations with constant coefficients and a constant term, that is,

(1) $$y''(x) + a_1 y'(x) + a_2 y = k$$

where a_1, a_2, and k are constants. By Theorem 7.1–4 the solution to (1) is the sum of $\bar{y}$ [any solution to (1)] and y^* [the solution to the homogeneous version of (1)]. $\bar{y}$, the particular solution, is easy to find. First try $\bar{y}$ equal to a constant. Then $y'' = y' = 0$ and $\bar{y} = k/a_2$, where $a_2 \neq 0$. If $a_2 = 0$ this solution will not work. In such a case try $\bar{y} = jx$, where j is a constant. Then $y' = j$ and $y'' = 0$ and we have $a_1 j + a_2 \bar{y} = k$ or $a_1 j = k$, since $a_2 = 0$ by assumption. Thus $j = k/a_1$ or $jx = (k/a_1)x = \bar{y}$. If both a_1 and a_2 are zero this particular solution will not work either. In this case try $\bar{y} = jx^2$, where j is a constant. Then $y' = 2jx$ and $y'' = 2j$. Then we have, on substitution into (1) and since $a_1 = a_2 = 0$, $j = k/2$. Since $\bar{y} = jx^2$, $\bar{y} = (k/2)x^2$. These particular solutions exhaust the possibilities for the type of equation being considered.

To find y^*, the solution to $y'' + a_1 y' + a_2 y = 0$, try a solution of the form $y^* = Ae^{rx}$ based on our experience with solutions to homogeneous first-order differential equations. Then $y' = rAe^{rx}$ and $y'' = r^2 Ae^{rx}$ and (1) becomes

(2) $$r^2 Ae^{rx} + a_1 rAe^{rx} + a_2 Ae^{rx} = 0$$

Factoring Ae^{rx} from (2):

(3) $$Ae^{rx}(r^2 + a_1 r + a_2) = 0$$

Ae^{rx} is nonzero (why?) so Equation 3) can be reduced to

(4) $$r^2 + a_1 r + a_2 = 0$$

As long as we select values of r that satisfy (4), $y = Ae^{rx}$ will be a solution to (1).

DEFINITION 7.1–9 Equation (4) is the **characteristic equation** of the differential equation (1).[2]

Solving (4) by the quadratic formula,

$$(5) \qquad r = \frac{-a_1 \pm \sqrt{a_1^2 - 4a_2}}{2}$$

or

$$r_1 = \frac{-a_1 + \sqrt{a_1^2 - 4a_2}}{2}$$

and

$$r_2 = \frac{-a_1 - \sqrt{a_1^2 - 4a_2}}{2}$$

DEFINITION 7.1–10 r_1 and r_2 are the **characteristic roots** of the differential equation (1).

Thus we have two solutions: $y_1^*(x) = A_1 e^{r_1 x}$ and $y_2^*(x) = A_2 e^{r_2 x}$. Thus $y^* = y_1^* + y_2^* = A_1 e^{r_1 x} + A_2 e^{r_2 x}$. Note that by using both y_1^* and y_2^*, we have ensured that the general solution to (1) will contain two arbitrary constants, A_1 and A_2. Since two constants are lost in the process of finding the second derivative, y'', it is necessary to have two arbitrary constants in the general solution to (1). The reader should convince himself that $y_1^* + y_2^*$ is indeed a solution to the homogeneous version of (1) by performing the necessary differentiation of $y_1^* + y_2^*$ with respect to x and substituting the result into (1) with $k = 0$.

If, in Equation (5), $a_1^2 > 4a_2$, both r_1 and r_2 will be real numbers and $r_1 \neq r_2$. In this case $y^* = A_1 e^{r_1 x} + A_2 e^{r_2 x}$ as before. If, however, $a_1^2 = 4a_2$, then r_1 and r_2 will be equal real numbers. In this case $y^* = A_1 e^{r_1 x} + A_2 x e^{r_2 x}$ is still a solution to the homogeneous equation and contains two arbitrary constants, A_1 and A_2. A third possibility exists. If $a_1^2 < 4a_2$ in (5), r_1 and r_2 will be unequal complex numbers. In this case $r_1 = (-a_1/2) + (\frac{1}{2}\sqrt{4a_2 - a_1^2})i$ and $r_2 = (-a_1/2) - (\frac{1}{2}\sqrt{4a_2 - a_1^2})i$, where $i = \sqrt{-1}$. Letting u and v represent $-\frac{1}{2}a_1$ and $\frac{1}{2}\sqrt{4a_2 - a_1^2}$, respectively, r_1 and r_2 are the conjugate pair of complex numbers, $u \pm vi$. Thus y^* can be written as $A_1 e^{(u+vi)x} + A_2 e^{(u-vi)x}$ or as $e^{ux}(A_1 e^{vix} + A_2 e^{-vix})$.

The Euler relations allow us to write y^* in a more useful form.

[2] Cf. Definition 4.5–1 for the characteristic equation of a matrix.

Theorem 7.1-5 *Euler Relations* The complex numbers e^{vix} and e^{-vix} are equal to (a) cos $(vx) + i$ sin (vx), and (b) cos $(vx) - i$ sin (vx), respectively.

PROOF   The proof centers around the following infinite series expressions for e^w, sin w, and cos w:

$$(6) \qquad e^w = 1 + w + \frac{w^2}{2!} + \frac{w^3}{3!} + \cdots$$

$$(7) \qquad \sin w = w - \frac{w^3}{3!} + \frac{w^5}{5!} - \frac{w^7}{7!} + \cdots$$

$$(8) \qquad \cos w = 1 - \frac{w^2}{2!} + \frac{w^4}{4!} - \frac{w^6}{6!} + \cdots ^3$$

We shall prove relation (a) of the theorem. Let $w = vix$. The (6) becomes

$$(9) \qquad e^{vix} = 1 + vix + \frac{(vix)^2}{2!} + \frac{(vix)^3}{3!} + \cdots$$

By the definition of i,

$$i^{4n} = 1, \quad i^{4n+1} = i, \quad i^{4n+2} = -1, \quad \text{and} \quad i^{4n+3} = -i$$

for any positive integer n. Consequently, (9) can be written

(10)
$$e^{vix} = 1 + i(vx) - \frac{(vx)^2}{2!} - \frac{i(vx)^3}{3!} + \frac{(vx)^4}{4!} + \frac{i(vx)^5}{5!} - \frac{(vx)^6}{6!} - \frac{i(vx)^7}{7!} + \cdots$$

Replacing w with vx in (7) and multiplying by i we have, on adding this expression to (8) with $w = vx$,

$$(11) \quad \cos (vx) + i \sin (vx) = \left[1 - \frac{(vx)^2}{2!} + \frac{(vx)^4}{4!} - \frac{(vx)^6}{6!} + \cdots \right]$$
$$+ \left[i(vx) - \frac{i(vx)^3}{3!} + \frac{i(vx)^5}{5!} - \frac{i(vx)^7}{7!} + \cdots \right]$$

Rearranging terms in (11) to conform with their order in (10) proves relation (a). The proof of relation (b) is left as an exercise.

Then, by Theorem 7.1-5, $y^* = e^{ux}[A_1(\cos vx + i \sin vx) + A_2(\cos vx - i \sin vx)]$. Define two new arbitrary constants B_1 and B_2, where $B_1 = A_1 + A_2$ and $B_2 = (A_1 - A_2)i$. Then $y^* = e^{ux}(B_1 \cos vx + B_2 \sin vx)$. This sinusoidal function is the general solution to the homogeneous version of (1).

---

³ For proofs of validity of (1), (2), and (3) see Thomas (1968).

The specific solution is obtained from the general solution through the use of initial conditions. The following example illustrates how to find both the general and specific solutions.

Example 4. Solve $y''(x) - y'(x) + 2y(x) = 1$. $\bar{y}$ is any solution. Try $\bar{y} = k$, which implies that $y'' = y' = 0$. Thus $\bar{y} = \frac{1}{2}$ is the particular solution. The characteristic equation for this equation is

$$r^2 - r + 2 = 0$$

This gives

$$r_1 = \frac{1}{2} + \frac{i\sqrt{7}}{2} \qquad r_2 = \frac{1}{2} - \frac{i\sqrt{7}}{2}$$

Thus, in our earlier notation, $u = \frac{1}{2}$ and $v = \sqrt{7}/2$. Then

$$y^* = e^{x/2}\left[B_1 \cos\left(\frac{\sqrt{7}}{2}x\right) + B_2 \sin\left(\frac{\sqrt{7}}{2}x\right)\right]$$

Thus the general solution is $y(x) = y^* + \bar{y}$ or

$$y(x) = e^{x/2}\left[B_1 \cos\left(\frac{\sqrt{7}}{2}x\right) + B_2 \sin\left(\frac{\sqrt{7}}{2}x\right)\right] + \frac{1}{2}$$

The specific solution is obtained by evaluating the constants B_1 and B_2. To do this we must have two initial conditions. Suppose $y(0) = 0$ and $y'(0) = 1$. Then we have

$$y(0) = 0 = e^{0/2}\left[B_1 \cos\left(\frac{\sqrt{7}}{2}0\right) + B_2 \sin\left(\frac{\sqrt{7}}{2}0\right)\right] + \frac{1}{2}$$

$$= 1(B_1 \cos 0 + B_2 \sin 0) + \frac{1}{2}$$

or $0 = B_1 + \frac{1}{2}$. Thus $B_1 = -\frac{1}{2}$. To use the second initial condition we must first differentiate the general solution. This yields

$$y'(x) = \frac{1}{2}e^{x/2}\left[B_1 \cos\left(\frac{\sqrt{7}}{2}x\right) + B_2 \sin\left(\frac{\sqrt{7}}{2}x\right)\right]$$

$$+ e^{x/2}\left[-\frac{\sqrt{7}}{2}B_1 \sin\left(\frac{\sqrt{7}}{2}x\right) + \frac{\sqrt{7}}{2}B_2 \cos\left(\frac{\sqrt{7}}{2}x\right)\right]$$

Evaluating y' at $x = 0$:

$$y'(0) = 1 = \frac{1}{2}B_1 + \frac{\sqrt{7}}{2}B_2$$

Since $B_1 = -\frac{1}{2}$, we have

$$\frac{\sqrt{7}}{2} B_2 = \frac{5}{4}$$

or

$$B_2 = \frac{5}{2\sqrt{7}}$$

The specific solution is therefore

$$y(x) = e^{x/2}\left[-\frac{1}{2}\cos\left(\frac{\sqrt{7}}{2}x\right) + \frac{5}{2\sqrt{7}}\sin\left(\frac{\sqrt{7}}{2}x\right)\right] + \frac{1}{2}$$

The reader should notice that the imaginary number i that appears in the constant B_2 does not appear in the specific solution, which is strictly a real-valued function. No problem of "interpretation" of imaginary-valued functions describing economic phenomena arises.

Suppose that in (1) k is not a constant, but a function of x, $k(x)$. Thus we have a linear, constant-coefficient, variable-term, second-order differential equation to solve. The only problem this modification creates is in finding the particular solution, $\bar{y}$. The procedure for finding y^* is not affected. $\bar{y}$ is found by using the method of undetermined coefficients. If $k(x)$ is a polynomial in x, say $k(x) = k_0 + k_1 x + \cdots + k_n x^n$, for k_i constants, then try $\bar{y} = A_0 + A_1 x + \cdots + A_n x^n$, where the A_i are the undetermined coefficients. Calculate $\bar{y}' = A_1 + 2A_2 x + \cdots + nA_n x^{n-1}$ and $\bar{y}'' = 2A_2 + 6A_3 x + \cdots + n(n-1)A_n x^{n-2}$. Then we have $[2A_2 + 6A_3 x + \cdots + n(n-1)A_n x^{n-2}] + a_1(A_1 + 2A_2 x + \cdots + nA_n x^{n-1}) + a_2(A_0 + A_1 x + \cdots + A_n x^n) = k_0 + k_1 x + \cdots + k_n x^n$. For this to be an equality, coefficients of like powers of x must be equal. Thus, for example,

$$k_0 = 2A_2 + a_1 A_1 + a_2 A_0$$

$$k_1 = 6A_3 + 2a_1 A_2 + a_2 A_1$$

and so on

This procedure yields a system of $n + 1$ simultaneous equations that can be solved for the coefficients A_i of $\bar{y}$.

Example 5. Solve $y'' + 2y' + y = 3x^2 + x + 5$. Thus $\bar{y} = A_0 + A_1 x + A_2 x^2$, $\bar{y}' = A_1 + 2A_2 x$, and $\bar{y}'' = 2A_2$. Substituting into the differential equation,

$$2A_2 + 2(A_1 + 2A_2 x) + A_0 + A_1 x + A_2 x^2 = 3x^2 + x + 5$$

Collecting terms,

$$A_2 x^2 + (4A_2 + A_1)x + (2A_2 + 2A_1 + A_0) = 3x^2 + x + 5$$

Equating coefficients of like powers of x we arrive at the following system of equations:

$$A_2 = 3$$

$$4A_2 + A_1 = 1$$

$$2A_2 + 2A_1 + A_0 = 5$$

Thus $A_2 = 3$, $A_1 = -11$, $A_0 = 21$, and $\bar{y} = 21 - 11x + 3x^2$.

If k is a polynomial of degree p, $\bar{y}$ is a polynomial of degree $p + n$, where

(a) $n = 0$ if $a_2 \neq 0$ in (1)

(b) $n = 1$ if $a_2 = 0$ and $a_1 \neq 0$ in (1)

(c) $n = 2$ if $a_1 = a_2 = 0$ in (1)

If k is an exponential function of form Ae^{rx}, there will be a solution of the form $\bar{y} = B(x)e^{rx}$, where $B(x)$ will be a polynomial of degree ≤ 2. The degree of $B(x)$ is determined by the procedure in the preceding paragraph. Try the substitution $y = ze^{rx}$. Then $y^{*\prime} = z'e^{rx} + rze^{rx}$ and $y'' = z''e^{rx} + rz'e^{rx} + r(z'e^{rx} + rze^{rx})$. Thus we have

$$e^{rx}(z'' + 2rz' + r^2z) + a_1 e^{rx}(z' + rz) + a_2 ze^{rx} = Ae^{rx}$$

or, dividing through by e^{rx},

$$z'' + (2r + a_1)z' + (r^2 + a_1r + a_2)z = A$$

The particular solution for this differential equation can be obtained by the methods outlined earlier, since A is by assumption a constant. Thus, if $r^2 + a_1r + a_2 \neq 0$, $z = A/(r^2 + a_1r + a_2)$. Transforming back to y, since $y = ze^{rx}$,

$$\bar{y} = \left(\frac{A}{r^2 + a_1r + a_2} \right) e^{rx}$$

In addition to the general methods outlined above, it is also possible in many cases to solve second-order homogeneous equations by substitution, reducing them to first-order equations. If the dependent variable, y, does not appear explicitly, try the substitution $p = dy/dx$ and $dp/dx = d^2y/dx^2$.

Example 6. Solve $y'' + y' = 0$ by substitution. This becomes a simple first-order equation: $(dp/dx) + p = 0$. Integrating both sides we have $\ln p = -x + c$ or $p = e^{-x+c} = Ae^{-x}$. Since $p = y'$, $y' = Ae^{-x}$, and integrating both sides yields the solution $y(x) = -Ae^{-x} + c$.

Another substitution that may be useful will be possible if the independent variable does not appear explicitly. In such a case let $q = dy/dx$ so that, by the chain rule; $d^2y/dx^2 = q\, dq/dy$.

Example 7. Solve $y'' + y = 0$ by substitution. This equation becomes $q \, (dq/dy) + y = 0$ or $q \, dq = -y \, dy$. By integrating both sides, $q^2/2 = -y^2/2 + C$ (or $q = \pm\sqrt{-y^2 + C_1}$). Then since $q = dy/dx$, we have $dy/\sqrt{C_1 - y^2} = \pm \, dx$. Integrating both sides of this expression we obtain

$$\sin^{-1} \frac{y}{C_1} = \pm(x + C_2) \quad \text{or} \quad y = \pm C_1 \sin(x + C_2)$$

The $\pm$ sign can be dropped, since C_1 is an arbitrary constant. Thus

$$y = C_1 \sin(x + C_2)$$

is the general solution.

We turn now to the solution to higher-order differential equations, beginning with the case of constant-coefficient, homogeneous equations of the general form

(1) $$y^{(n)} + a_{n-1}y^{(n-1)} + \cdots + a_0 y = 0$$

The general solution centers around the characteristic polynomial of (1):

(2) $$r^n + a_{n-1}r^{n-1} + \cdots + a_1 r + a_0 = 0$$

When $n = 2$ we have the second-order case, where the general solution is given by

(3) $$y = A_1 e^{r_1 x} + A_2 e^{r_2 x}$$

or by

(4) $$y = A_1 e^{r_1 x} + A_2 x e^{r_2 x}$$

where r_1 and r_2 are the roots of (2) [$r_1 = r_2$ by assumption in (4)]. For $n > 2$, suppose the characteristic polynomial can be factored and written as a sum of linear factors:

(5) $$(r - p_0)^{k_0}(r - p_1)^{k_1}(r - p_2)^{k_2} \cdots (r - p_m)^{k_m}$$

where the p_i are constants, as are the k's. Furthermore, the product $\prod_{j=1}^{m} k_j < n$. Then the roots of the characteristic polynomial are $p_0, p_1, \ldots, p_m$, where p_0 has multiplicity k_0, p has multiplicity k_1, and so on.[4] Thus the general solution can be written, in a manner analogous for the case $n = 2$, as

$$y = A_1 e^{p_0 x} + (A_2 + A_3 x + \cdots + A_{k_1+1}x^{k_1-1})e^{p_1 x} + (A_{k_1+2} + A_{k_1+3}x + \cdots$$

$$+ A_{k_1+k_2+1}x^{k_2-1})e^{p_2 x} + \cdots$$

$$+ (A_{(\sum_{j=1}^{} k_j) + 2} + \cdots + A_{(\sum_{j=1}^{} k_j) + 1}x^{k_m-1})e^{p_m x}$$

[4] The multiplicity of a root is the number of times it appears as a solution. p_1 appears k_1 times, etc.

Example 8.   Find the general solution to

$$y^{(4)} + 5y^{(3)} + 9y'' + 7y' + 2y = 0$$

The characteristic polynomial is

$$r^4 + 5r^3 + 9r^2 + 7r + 2 = 0$$

which factors into

$$(r + 1)^3(r + 2) = 0$$

Thus there are two distinct roots, $r_1 = -1$ and $r_2 = -2$, where r_1 has multiplicity 3 and r_2 has multiplicity 1. Thus the general solution is

$$y(x) = (A_1 + A_2x + A_3x^2)e^{-x} + A_4e^{-2x}$$

If the nth-order equation is nonhomogeneous, the problem becomes that of finding the particular solution $\bar{y}$. y^* can be found by the preceding method. If k is a constant, a polynomial, or an exponential function, $\bar{y}$ may be found by the methods described for the case where $n = 2$. No new theory is required, although the procedure becomes more computationally tedious.

Examples 9 and 10 illustrate two uses of ordinary differential equations in economic theory.

Example 9.   Suppose that the demand for a certain commodity is $D(p) = 20 - p$ and the supply is $S(p) = 15 + p$, where p is the price of the commodity. Suppose further that the rate of change of the price over time depends on the excess demand for the commodity: $dp/dt = f[D(p) - S(p)]$. Explicitly, suppose

$$\frac{dp}{dt} = D(p) - S(p) = 20 - p - 15 - p = 5 - 2p$$

Solve for p as a function of t.

$$\frac{dp}{dt} = 5 - 2p$$

or

$$\frac{dp}{5 - 2p} = dt$$

Integrating both sides,

$$-\tfrac{1}{2} \ln (5 - 2p) = t + c$$

or

$$5 - 2p = e^{-2(t+c)} = Ae^{-2t}$$

Thus the general solution is

$$p(t) = \frac{5}{2} - \frac{A}{2} e^{-2t}$$

If $p(0) = 1$, then

$$1 = \frac{5}{2} - \frac{A}{2}$$

or

$$A = \frac{3}{2}$$

and the specific solution is

$$p(t) = \tfrac{5}{2} - \tfrac{3}{4}e^{-2t}$$

as $t \to \infty$, $p(t) \to \frac{5}{2}$.[5] As the reader can verify, $p = \frac{5}{2}$ is indeed the equilibrium price. Furthermore, for all $p < 2\frac{1}{2}$, $dp/dt > 0$ while if $p > 2\frac{1}{2}$, $dp/dt < 0$. In both cases, the market price converges to equilibrium over time.

Example 10.   Suppose that there are only two consumer goods, x and y, and that a consumer's marginal rate of substitution of x for y is given by

$$\text{MRS}_{x/y} = \frac{ax + b}{ey + f}$$

where a, b, e, and f are constants. Find the general form of his utility function, $U = U(x, y)$.

$$\text{MRS}_{x/y} = -\frac{dy}{dx} = \frac{ax + b}{ey + f}$$

Thus $dy(ey + f) = -(ax + b)\, dx$. Integrating both sides,

$$\frac{e}{2} y^2 + fy = -\left(\frac{a}{2} x^2 + bx + C \right)$$

or

$$\frac{e}{2} y^2 + fy + \frac{a}{2} x^2 + bx = C$$

Replacing C, the arbitrary constant, by U, the level of utility, we have

(1) $$U = \frac{e}{2} y^2 + fy + \frac{a}{2} x^2 + bx$$

---

[5] No matter what the sign of A is, since e^{-2t} approaches 0 as to $t \to \infty$.

To show that (1) is indeed the utility function, calculate dU:

$$dU = (ey + f)\, dy + (ax + b)\, dx$$

Along an indifference curve, $dU = 0$, so

(2) $$(ey + f)\, dy + (ax + b)\, dx = 0$$

must hold along every indifference curve. Solving (2) for dy/dx,

$$\frac{dy}{dx} = -\frac{ax + b}{cy + b}$$

Since, by definition $\mathrm{MRS}_{x/y} = -dy/dx$, (1) yields the appropriate marginal rate of substitution and must therefore be a representation of the utility function.

Problems

7.1–1   Solve the following first-order differential equations using $y(0)$ as the initial condition.

(a) $\dfrac{dy}{dx} = x\sqrt{y}$

(h) $(x^2 + y)\, dy + (2yx)\, dx = 0$

(b) $2y' = 6y + 3$

(i) $\dfrac{y - x}{x + y}\dfrac{dy}{dx} = 1$

(c) $y' - 2x^2 + x = 5$

(j) $x^2\, dy = -(x^3 - x^2 y)\, dx$

(d) $y' + 2xy = 3x$

(k) $y' + \dfrac{(y^2 - x^2)}{2xy} = 0$

(e) $y' = e^{x-y}$

(l) $y' + 2y = e^{-x}$

(f) $\sqrt{xy}\,\dfrac{dy}{dx} = 3$

(m) $x\, dy + y\, dx = y\, dy$

(g) $xy^2\, dy + dx = 0$

(n) $2y' - y = e^{x/2}$

7.1–2   Solve the following second-order differential equations using $y(0)$ and $y'(0)$ as the initial conditions.

(a) $y'' + 2y' = 3$

(e) $y'' + 3y' + 2y = 0$

(b) $y'' + y' + y = x$

(f) $y'' + y' + 2y = e^x$

(c) $y'' + y = -5$

(g) $2y'' - y' + 3y = x + 1$

(d) $y'' - y = 1$

(h) $y'' + y = x^2$

7.1–3   Solve the following higher-order differential equations.

(a) $\dfrac{d^3x}{dx^3} = 0$

(c) $2\dfrac{d^4y}{dx^4} + y'' = x^5$

(b) $\dfrac{d^3y}{dx^3} - y' = 1$

(d) $\dfrac{d^3y}{dx^3} - 2y'' + y' = 0$

7.2   PARTIAL DIFFERENTIAL EQUATIONS

DEFINITION 7.2–1   **Partial differential equations** involve two or more independent variables $x, y, \ldots$, a function of these variables $f(x, y, \ldots)$, and various first- and higher-order partial derivatives.

We shall consider only equations with two independent variables containing only first-order partial derivatives.[6] Specifically we shall treat equations of the form

(1) $$af_x + bf_y = c$$

where a, b, and c may be any functions of x and y.

As in the case of ordinary differential equations, we may be asked to find both the general and the specific solution to a partial differential equation. As before, the general solution is the family of all solutions to the equation, while the specific solution is obtained from the general solution by use of some initial conditions. Obtaining the specific solution to an ordinary differential equation is a relatively easy matter. That is not the case for partial differential equations, as the following example illustrates.

Example 1.   Find the general solution to $f_x = y^2x$. Simply integrate both sides with respect to x, treating y as a constant. This yields

$$f(x, y) = \frac{y^2x^2}{2} + g(y)$$

where $g(y)$ is an arbitrary function of y. This is indeed the general solution, as differentiation with respect to x shows.

To obtain the specific solution we must find the *function* $g(y)$ from the initial conditions rather than simply evaluate one or more constants as in ordinary differential equations. The ease with which this can be done depends on both the nature of the original equation and the form of the initial conditions. In many cases, finding the specific solution may be more difficult than obtaining the general solution.

[6] For a fuller treatment the reader is referred to Berg and McGregor (1966).

Example 1 also illustrates that, in principle, the general solution to partial differential equations of any order that contain partial derivatives of f with respect to *only one* independent variable can be obtained by repeated integration.

Another easy type of partial differential equation to solve is the homogeneous equation with constant coefficients, that is, one of the general form

$$(2) \qquad\qquad af_x + bf_y = 0$$

Following the same general procedure as for ordinary differential equations, let $f(x, y) = e^{rx+sy}$. Performing the partial differentiation,

$$f_x = re^{rx+sy} \quad \text{and} \quad f_y = se^{rx+sy}$$

Substituting into (2) and collecting terms,

$$(ar + bs)e^{rx+sy} = 0$$

Consequently, $f = e^{rx+sy}$ will be a solution to (2) if $ar + bs = 0$. Solving this equation for s in terms of r,

$$s = -\frac{a}{b}r$$

We now try $f(x, y) = e^{rx-(a/b)ry}$ as a solution to (2). As the reader can verify by differentiation and substitution, this is indeed the general solution. To obtain the specific solution, r must be evaluated using the initial conditions. This technique can also be used for higher-order, *linear* equations.

Happily, there are general methods available to solve nonhomogeneous, linear partial differential equations with constant coefficients in two independent variables. (All the adjectives show how very little we have to be happy about!) These involve some type of change of variables. Consider the general equation

$$(3) \qquad\qquad af_x + bf_y + cf = g(x, y)$$

Define new variables, α and β, by

$$(4) \qquad\qquad x = A_1\alpha + B_1\beta \quad \text{and} \quad y = A_2\alpha + B_2\beta$$

and set

$$(5) \qquad\qquad f(x, y) = \gamma(\alpha, \beta)$$

$A_1, A_2, B_1,$ and B_2 are constants to be determined later. From (4) and (5) it follows that

$$\frac{\partial \gamma}{\partial \alpha} = f_x \frac{\partial x}{\partial \alpha} + f_y \frac{\partial y}{\partial \alpha} = A_1 f_x + A_2 f_y$$

If we let $A_1 = a$ and $A_2 = b$, Equation (3) can be written as

$$(6) \qquad \frac{\partial \gamma}{\partial \alpha} + c\gamma = G(\alpha, \beta)$$

$G(\alpha, \beta)$ is obtained from $g(x, y)$ through use of (4). Equation (6) is now solved as though it were an ordinary differential equation with β treated as a constant. This general solution will contain unknown functions of β rather than arbitrary constants. The general solution to (3) is obtained by transforming back to the original variables, x and y.

Example 2. Find the general solution to $f_x + 2f_y = 3$. In this case $A_1 = 1$ and $A_2 = 2$ and the equation reduces to

$$\frac{\partial \gamma}{\partial \alpha} = 3$$

Integrating, treating β as a constant, we obtain $\gamma(\alpha, \beta) = f(x, y) = 3\alpha + h(\beta)$, where $h(\beta)$ is an unknown function of β. To satisfy what turns out to be a standard initial condition,[7] we set $B_2 = 0$ and $B_1 = 1$. This enables us to solve for α and β from the pair of equations

$$(7) \qquad x = \alpha + \beta \quad \text{and} \quad y = 2\alpha$$

From (7) it follows that $\beta = x - \alpha = x - y/2$. Subtracting the first relation in (7) from the second we obtain

$$\alpha = y - x + \beta = y - x + \left(x - \frac{y}{2}\right)$$

or

$$\alpha = \frac{y}{2}$$

Substituting these results into (6) yields

$$(8) \qquad f(x, y) = \frac{3y}{2} + H\left(x - \frac{y}{2}\right)$$

the general solution. Here the unknown function $h(\beta)$ is replaced by H, an arbitrary constant times $x - y/2$. To show that (8) is indeed the general solution, one need only perform the differentiations and substitute the results into the original equation.

The foregoing will enable the reader to solve the most commonly encountered types of partial differential equations even though the discussion has barely scratched the surface.

---

[7] See Berg and McGregor (1966), pages 19–21.

Example 3. Consider a world of two commodities, x and y, and an individual consumer with income z attempting to maximize $U = U(x, y)$ subject to his budget constraint, z. From the first-order conditions we have[8]:

$$U_x - \lambda P_x = 0$$

and

$$U_y - \lambda P_y = 0$$

Solving for λ, this system can be reduced to a single first-order, homogeneous partial differential equation:

(1)
$$\frac{\partial U}{\partial x} - \frac{\partial U}{\partial y} \frac{P_x}{P_y} = 0$$

This equation can be solved for the individual utility function, $U(x, y)$. The general solution will be of the form

$$U(x, y) = e^{rx+sy}$$

Specifically we have, since $s = (P_y/P_x)r$,

(2)
$$U(x, y) = e \exp\left[r\left(x + \frac{P_y}{P_x} y\right)\right]$$

the general solution (where the notation e exp [ ] means that the term in brackets is the exponent of e). To find the specific solution suppose we have the initial condition

(3)
$$U(1, 1) = \alpha, \qquad \alpha \text{ a positive constant.}$$

Then we have

(4)
$$\alpha = e \exp\left[r\left(1 + \frac{P_y}{P_x}\right)\right]$$

Solving for r,

$$r\left(1 + \frac{P_y}{P_x}\right) = \ln \alpha$$

or

(5)
$$r = \frac{(\ln \alpha)P_x}{P_x + P_y}$$

Substituting (5) into (2) and simplifying, we obtain the specific solution

(6)
$$U(x, y) = e \exp\left[\ln \alpha \left(\frac{P_x x + P_y y}{P_x + P_y}\right)\right]$$

[8] See Section 5.4.

However, $P_x x + P_y y = z$, so (6) can be written

(7) $$U(x, y) = e \exp\left(\frac{z \ln \alpha}{P_x + P_y}\right) = \alpha^{z/P_x + P_y}$$

a form that shows the functional dependence of utility on both prices and income. The reader should examine the properties of (7) and convince himself that it is a "reasonable" utility function.

Problems

7.2–1   Solve the following partial differential equations.

(a) $\dfrac{\partial f}{\partial x} - \dfrac{\partial f}{\partial y} = 0$

(c) $\dfrac{\partial f}{\partial x} - \dfrac{\partial f}{\partial y} = 1$

(b) $2\dfrac{\partial f}{\partial x} + 3\dfrac{\partial f}{\partial y} = 0$

(d) $2\dfrac{\partial f}{\partial x} + 3\dfrac{\partial f}{\partial y} = 2$

7.3   DIFFERENTIAL EQUATION SYSTEMS[9]

In this section we consider the solutions to systems of linear, first-order differential equations.

Suppose we have a system of two equations in three unknowns:

(1)
$$a_{11}\frac{dy}{dx} + a_{12}\frac{dz}{dx} + a_{13}y + a_{14}z = b_1$$

$$a_{21}\frac{dy}{dx} + a_{22}\frac{dz}{dx} + a_{23}y + a_{24}z = b_2$$

where y and z are functions of x. b_1, b_2, and the a_{ij}'s are constants. Define the following matrices:

$$A_1 = \begin{bmatrix} a_{11} & a_{12} \\ a_{21} & a_{22} \end{bmatrix} \quad A_2 = \begin{bmatrix} a_{13} & a_{14} \\ a_{23} & a_{24} \end{bmatrix} \quad B = \begin{bmatrix} b_1 \\ b_2 \end{bmatrix}$$

$$C = \begin{bmatrix} \dfrac{dy}{dx} \\ \dfrac{dz}{dx} \end{bmatrix} \quad D = \begin{bmatrix} y \\ z \end{bmatrix}$$

The system (1) can then be written as:

(2) $$A_1 C + A_2 D = B$$

[9] This topic is covered in more detail in Chapter 14, within the discussion of control theory.

Once again, the general solution to this system can be expressed as the sum of the particular solution and the solution to the homogeneous version of (1). To find the particular solution try y and z constants. Then $C = 0$ and we have

$$A_2 D = B$$

or

$$\begin{bmatrix} \bar{y} \\ \bar{z} \end{bmatrix} = \bar{D} = A_2^{-1} B$$

We thus obtain two particular solutions, $\bar{y}$ and $\bar{z}$.

To find the solution to the homogeneous version, try solutions in the form

$$y^* = ae^{rx} \quad \text{and} \quad z^* = be^{rx}$$

Thus C becomes

$$\begin{bmatrix} rae^{rx} \\ rbe^{rx} \end{bmatrix} = \begin{bmatrix} a \\ b \end{bmatrix} re^{rx}$$

while D is

$$\begin{bmatrix} ae^{rx} \\ be^{rx} \end{bmatrix} = \begin{bmatrix} a \\ b \end{bmatrix} e^{rx}$$

Thus we have

$$A_1 \begin{bmatrix} a \\ b \end{bmatrix} re^{rx} + A_2 \begin{bmatrix} a \\ b \end{bmatrix} e^{rx} = \begin{bmatrix} 0 \\ 0 \end{bmatrix}$$

or

(4)
$$[rA_1 + A_2] \begin{bmatrix} a \\ b \end{bmatrix} = \begin{bmatrix} 0 \\ 0 \end{bmatrix}$$

The system (4) is then solved for a and b. One solution, $a = b = 0$, is immediately apparent. This trivial solution however provides us with no information. For a nontrivial solution for a and b to exist, it is necessary that the determinant $|rA_1 + A_2|$ vanish[10]; that is,

(5)
$$|rA_1 + A_2| = 0$$

Equation (5) is the characteristic equation of the system (4) written as a determinant. It can be solved for the characteristic roots which in turn enable

[10] $|rA_1 + A_2| = 0$ implies that $[rA_1 + A_2]^{-1}$ does not exist, so that the trivial solution

$$\begin{bmatrix} a \\ b \end{bmatrix} = [rA_1 + A_2]^{-1} \begin{bmatrix} 0 \\ 0 \end{bmatrix} = \begin{bmatrix} 0 \\ 0 \end{bmatrix}$$

cannot be obtained. (Cf. Section 4.2).

us to find a and b. Suppose the characteristic roots are r_1 and r_2. Then substituting into (4),

(6)

$$[r_1A_1 + A_2]\begin{bmatrix} a_1 \\ b_1 \end{bmatrix} = 0$$

$$[r_2A_1 + A_2]\begin{bmatrix} a_2 \\ b_2 \end{bmatrix} = 0$$

This system allows us to determine the ratio between the constants a_i and b_i. They cannot be determined uniquely since $[rA_1 + A_2]^{-1}$ does not exist.

Note that there are now four constants, two for each characteristic root, since our trial solutions are now of the form

$$y^* = a_1e^{r_1x} + a_2e^{r_2x}$$

$$z^* = b_1e^{r_1x} + b_2e^{r_2x}$$

Suppose we find $a_1 = nb_1$ and $a_2 = mb_2$ by solving (6). We can then define two new arbitrary constants, say $b_1 = A_1$ and $b_2 = A_2$. Thus $a_1 = nA_1$ and $a_2 = mA_2$ and the solution to the homogeneous version is

$$\begin{bmatrix} y^* \\ z^* \end{bmatrix} = \begin{bmatrix} nA_1e^{r_1x} + mA_2e^{r_2x} \\ A_1e^{r_1x} + A_2e^{r_2x} \end{bmatrix}$$

$$\begin{bmatrix} y \\ z \end{bmatrix} = \begin{bmatrix} y^* \\ z^* \end{bmatrix} + \begin{bmatrix} \bar{y} \\ \bar{z} \end{bmatrix}$$

yields the general solution. A_1 and A_2 are evaluated by using initial conditions.

Example 1. Solve:

$$y' + 2y + z = 5$$

$$z' + y + 2z = 3$$

where $y(0) = 1$ and $z(0) = 2$. Here

$$A_1 = \begin{bmatrix} 1 & 0 \\ 0 & 1 \end{bmatrix} \quad A_2 = \begin{bmatrix} 2 & 1 \\ 1 & 2 \end{bmatrix} \quad B = \begin{bmatrix} 5 \\ 3 \end{bmatrix} \quad C = \begin{bmatrix} y' \\ z' \end{bmatrix} \quad D = \begin{bmatrix} y \\ z \end{bmatrix}$$

The characteristic equation, $|rA_1 + A_2| = 0$, is

$$\begin{vmatrix} r & 0 \\ 0 & r \end{vmatrix} + \begin{vmatrix} 2 & 1 \\ 1 & 2 \end{vmatrix} = 0$$

or

$$\begin{vmatrix} r + 2 & 1 \\ 1 & r + 2 \end{vmatrix} = 0$$

Expanding this determinant, we have

$$r^2 + 4r + 3 = 0$$

or

$$(r + 3)(r + 1) = 0$$

Thus $r_1 = -3$ and $r_2 = -1$. Then, for r_1,

$$[r_1 A_1 + A_2]\begin{bmatrix} a_1 \\ b_1 \end{bmatrix} = \begin{bmatrix} -1 & 1 \\ 1 & -1 \end{bmatrix}\begin{bmatrix} a_1 \\ b_1 \end{bmatrix} = 0$$

From which it follows that $a_1 = b_1$.

For r_2,

$$[r_2 A_1 + A_2]\begin{bmatrix} a_2 \\ b_2 \end{bmatrix} = \begin{bmatrix} 1 & 1 \\ 1 & 1 \end{bmatrix}\begin{bmatrix} a_2 \\ b_2 \end{bmatrix} = 0$$

from which it follows that $a_2 = -b_2$.

Letting $b_1 = A_1$, we have $a_1 = A_1$. If $b_2 = A_2$, then $a_2 = -A_2$. Thus the solution to the homogeneous system is

$$\begin{bmatrix} y^* \\ z^* \end{bmatrix} = \begin{bmatrix} A_1 e^{-3x} - A_2 e^{-x} \\ A_1 e^{-3x} + A_2 e^{-x} \end{bmatrix}$$

The particular solution is given by

$$\begin{bmatrix} \bar{y} \\ \bar{z} \end{bmatrix} = A_2^{-1} B$$

$$A_2^{-1} = \begin{bmatrix} \frac{2}{3} & -\frac{1}{3} \\ -\frac{1}{3} & \frac{2}{3} \end{bmatrix}$$

so that

$$\begin{bmatrix} \bar{y} \\ \bar{z} \end{bmatrix} = \begin{bmatrix} \frac{2}{3} & -\frac{1}{3} \\ -\frac{1}{3} & \frac{2}{3} \end{bmatrix}\begin{bmatrix} 5 \\ 3 \end{bmatrix}$$

or

$$\begin{bmatrix} \bar{y} \\ \bar{z} \end{bmatrix} = \begin{bmatrix} \frac{7}{3} \\ \frac{1}{3} \end{bmatrix}$$

The general solution is therefore

$$\begin{bmatrix} y \\ z \end{bmatrix} = \begin{bmatrix} A_1 e^{-3x} - A_2 e^{-x} + \frac{7}{3} \\ A_1 e^{-3x} + A_2 e^{-x} + \frac{1}{3} \end{bmatrix}$$

Using the initial conditions, $y(0) = 1$ and $z(0) = 2$, we obtain the following system to solve for A_1 and A_2:

$$1 = A_1 - A_2 + \tfrac{7}{3}$$
$$2 = A_1 + A_2 + \tfrac{1}{3}$$

or $A_1 = \tfrac{1}{6}$, $A_2 = \tfrac{4}{3}$. The specific solution is therefore

$$\begin{bmatrix} y(x) \\ z(x) \end{bmatrix} = \begin{bmatrix} \tfrac{1}{6}e^{-3x} - \tfrac{3}{2}e^{-x} + \tfrac{7}{3} \\ \tfrac{1}{6}e^{-3x} + \tfrac{3}{2}e^{-x} + \tfrac{1}{3} \end{bmatrix}$$

Problems

7.3–1   Solve the following systems of differential equations [use $y(0)$ and $z(0)$ as the initial conditions].

(a) $\dfrac{dy}{dx} + 2\dfrac{dz}{dx} + y - z = 1$

    $2\dfrac{dy}{dx} + \dfrac{dz}{dx} + 2y = 4$

(b) $y' + 3z' + y + z = 1$

    $-z' - 2z = 3$

References

1. AGNEW, R. P. (1960), *Differential Equations*, New York: McGraw-Hill.
2. ALLEN, R. G. D. (1958), *Mathematical Economics*, London: Macmillan.
3. BAUMOL, W. J. (1970), *Economic Dynamics: An Introduction*, 3rd. ed., London: Macmillan.
4. BECKENBACK, E. F. (ed.) (1961), *Modern Mathematics for the Engineer*, 2nd series, New York: McGraw-Hill.
5. BERG, P. W., and J. L. MCGREGOR (1966), *Elementary Partial Differential Equations*, San Francisco: Holden-Day.
6. CODDINGTON, E. A., and N. LEVINSON (1955), *Theory of Ordinary Differential Equations*, New York: McGraw-Hill.
7. KAPLAN, WILFRED (1961), *Ordinary Differential Equations*, Reading, Mass.: Addison-Wesley.
8. PONTRYAGIN, L. S. (1962), *Ordinary Differential Equations*, Reading, Mass.: Addison-Wesley.
9. REKTORYS, KAREL (ed.) (1969), *Survey of Applicable Mathematics* (tr. by Rudolf Vyborny), Cambridge, Mass.: M.I.T. Press.
10. SAATY, T. (1967), *Modern Nonlinear Equations*, New York: McGraw-Hill.
11. ————, and J. BRAM (1964), *Nonlinear Mathematics*, New York: McGraw-Hill.
12. THOMAS, GEORGE (1968), *Calculus and Analytical Geometry*, 4th ed., Reading, Mass.: Addison-Wesley.

Chapter 8

Difference Calculus: Difference Equations

8.1 INTRODUCTION

Physical and economic phenomena are observed at discrete points in time. Based on discrete data, scientists generalize to a theoretical construct that usually involves continuity and/or differentiability assumptions. These simplifying assumptions allow us to apply the tools of the differential and integral calculus discussed in the previous chapters as well as other mathematical techniques to be discussed later in the book. The usefulness of these assumptions in a wide variety of cases cannot be doubted.

Since the continuous version of a problem is only a generalization of the phenomena observed in discrete time, the validity of the continuous formulation depends on the validity of a (the) discrete formulation. The purposes of this chapter are to examine the techniques of discrete analysis and to illustrate their close relation to the techniques of continuous analysis. In many cases the discrete version may itself yield all the information the economist wants, obviating the necessity of conversion to continuous form.

Another important reason for studying and understanding the discrete approach to economic problems is a result of the nature of computers. With few exceptions, all computers carry out their calculations using discrete techniques. Thus a thorough knowledge of these techniques is valuable for a complete understanding of computer programming and for interpreting computer output.

8.2 THE DIFFERENCE CALCULUS

Suppose we have a function, $y = f(x)$, that is defined only at n points, $x_i, i = 1, 2, \ldots, n$. For convenience it is assumed that the distance between any two adjacent points is the same; that is $x_{i+1} - x_i = h$ for all i. $y = f(x)$ is a discrete function with equally spaced data points. (Later in the section we shall relax the assumption of equal spacing.)

DEFINITION 8.2–1   The **first forward difference** of $y = f(x)$, written Δy, is given by

$$\Delta y = f(x + h) - f(x)$$

where h is the distance between any two adjacent data points. [1]

The close similarity between the first difference of a discrete function and the first derivative of a differentiable function should be obvious. The derivative is defined as the limit of the difference quotient, $\Delta y / \Delta x$, as $\Delta x \to 0$. Δy in the definition of the derivative is, in a formal sense, simply the first difference $f(x + \Delta x) - f(x)$, where h is replaced by Δx.

Theorem 8.2–1

(a) $\Delta[af(x) \pm bg(x)] = a \, \Delta f(x) \pm b \, \Delta g(x)$, where a and b are constants;

(b) $\Delta[f(x)g(x)] = f(x + h)g(x + h) - f(x)g(x)$;

(c) $\Delta \left[\dfrac{f(x)}{g(x)} \right] = \dfrac{f(x + h)}{g(x + h)} - \dfrac{f(x)}{g(x)}$; and

(d) $\Delta x^n = (x + h)^n - x^n$. [2]

The process of finding differences ("differencing") is closely analogous to differentiation. From part (a) of Theorem 8.2–1, differencing is a linear operator as is differentiation:

$$\frac{d}{dx}[af(x) \pm bg(x)] = af'(x) \pm bg'(x)$$

Adding and subtracting $f(x + h)g(x)$ to (b) yields $f(x + h)g(x + h) - f(x + h)g(x) + f(x + h)g(x) - f(x)g(x)$. Collecting terms and factoring:

$$f(x + h)[g(x + h) - g(x)] + g(x)[f(x + h) - f(x)]$$

The terms in the square brackets are simply $\Delta g(x)$ and $\Delta f(x)$, respectively. Thus

$$\Delta[f(x)g(x)] = f(x + h) \, \Delta g(x) + g(x) \, \Delta f(x)$$

Compare this with the formula for the derivative of a product of two functions:

$$\frac{d}{dx}[f(x)g(x)] = f(x)g'(x) + g(x)f'(x)$$

---

[1] Beside the forward difference Δy, the backward difference $\nabla y = f(x) - f(x - h)$ can be defined. This is essentially a notational change useful to mathematicians, but not particularly useful in practical applications. When we refer to differences, we shall mean forward differences unless otherwise specified.

[2] The proof of Theorem 8.2–1 is based on the definition of first difference and is left as an exercise for the reader.

In part (c) of Theorem 8.2–1, combining the fractions yields

$$\frac{f(x + h)g(x) - f(x)g(x + h)}{g(x)g(x + h)}$$

Then, adding and subtracting $f(x)g(x)$ to the numerator gives

$$\frac{f(x + h)g(x) - f(x)g(x) + f(x)g(x) - g(x + h)f(x)}{g(x)g(x + h)}$$

This expression simplifies to

$$\frac{g(x)\,\Delta f(x) - f(x)\,\Delta g(x)}{g(x)g(x + h)}$$

Compare this to the corresponding formula in the differential calculus:

$$\frac{d}{dx}\left[\frac{f(x)}{g(x)}\right] = \frac{g(x)f'(x) - f(x)g'(x)}{[g(x)]^2}$$

By the binomial theorem when n is an integer, part (d) of the theorem can be written as

$$\sum_{j=0}^{n}\binom{n}{j}h^{n-j}x^j - x^n$$

Writing out the binomial coefficients and performing the subtraction, we have

$$\Delta x^n = nhx^{n-1} + \frac{n(n - 1)h^2}{2}x^{n-2} + \cdots + h^n$$

For the case where $h = 1$, we have

$$\Delta x^n = nx^{n-1} + \frac{n(n - 1)}{2}x^{n-2} + \cdots + 1$$

This expression is much messier than its differential calculus counterpart, $(d/dx)x^n = nx^{n-1}$ since we have, instead of one term, a polynomial of degree $n - 1$ with $n - 1$ terms. Differencing does, however, reduce the degree of the original expression by one, as does differentiation.

Example 1. Calculate $\Delta 2^x$. $\Delta 2^x = 2^{x+h} - 2^x = 2^x(2^h - 1)$. Note that if $h = 1$, this reduces to $\Delta 2^x = 2^x$. The number 2 in the difference calculus is analogous to e in the differential calculus, since for $h = 1$, $\Delta 2^x = 2^x$, and $(d/dx)e^x = e^x$.

It is possible to list more difference formulas as we did in the chapter on the differential calculus. The reader is encouraged to construct his own list of difference formulas. This should help to underline both the similarities and the differences between differencing and differentiation.

Second- and higher-order differences are defined analogously to the definition of higher-order derivatives.

DEFINITION 8.2–2   The **second difference** of $y = f(x)$, written $\Delta^2 y$, is simply the difference of the first difference of y; that is,

$$
\begin{aligned}
\Delta^2 y &= \Delta[\Delta y] \\
&= \Delta[f(x + h) - f(x)] \\
&= f(x + 2h) - f(x + h) - [f(x + h) - f(x)] \\
&= f(x + 2h) - 2f(x + h) + f(x)
\end{aligned}
$$

Higher-order differences are defined in the same way. The third difference, $\Delta^3 y$, is simply the difference of the second difference, and so on. This corresponds to the definition of the second derivative as the derivative of the first derivative, and so on.

Example 2.   Find the first, second, third, and fourth differences of $y = 3x^2 + 2x - 1$.

$$
\begin{aligned}
\Delta y &= 3(x + h)^2 + 2(x + h) - 1 - (3x^2 + 2x - 1) \\
&= 3x^2 + 6xh + 3h^2 + 2x + 2h - 1 - 3x^2 - 2x + 1 \\
&= 6xh + 2h + 3h^2 \\
\Delta^2 y &= \Delta(6xh + 2h + 3h^2) \\
&= 6(x + h)h + 2h + 3h^2 - 6xh - 2h - 3h^2 \\
&= 6h^2 \\
\Delta^3 y &= \Delta(6h^2) \\
&= 6h^2 - 6h^2 = 0 \\
\Delta^4 y &= \Delta 0 = 0
\end{aligned}
$$

Example 2 is an illustration of the fundamental theorem of difference calculus.

Theorem 8.2–2   *Fundamental Theorem of Difference Calculus*   The nth difference of a polynomial of degree n,

$$
y = a_0 + a_1 x + a_2 x^2 + \cdots + a_n x^n
$$

is a constant, $a_n n! h^n$, and the $(n + 1)$st difference is zero.

PROOF   By Theorem 8.2–1(d), if y is a polynomial of degree n, Δy is a polynomial of degree $n - 1$. Using this property n times, the nth difference of a polynomial of degree n is a polynomial of degree zero (a constant) and, as we have seen in Example 2, the difference of a constant (like the derivative of a constant) is zero. That the nth difference is $a_n n!\, h^n$ is proven by induction. Note that, in Example 2, $n = 2$ and $a_n = 3$ so that $\Delta^2 y = 3(2 \cdot 1)h^2 = 6h^2$ as before.

Example 3. Compute the fifth difference of $y(x) = 3x^5 - 4x^4 + 10x^3 - 2x + 5$. Computing $\Delta^5 y$ by first finding Δy, $\Delta^2 y$, and so on, is very tedious. However, by the fundamental theorem we have

$$\Delta^5 y = 3(5!)h^5 = 3(120h^5) = 360h^5$$

The fundamental theorem, useful as it is, gives no direct method of computing differences of order less than the degree of the polynomial function. Theorem 8.2–3 presents such a method.

Theorem 8.2–3 *Lagrange Form of the Difference* For $h = 1$ and the general function $y(x)$, the kth difference, $\Delta^k y$, is given by[3]

$$\Delta^k y(x) = \sum_{j=0}^{k} (-1)^{k-j} \binom{k}{j} y(x + j)$$

Example 4. Calculate the third difference of $y(x) = 3x^5 - 4x^4 + 10x^3 - 2x + 5$.

$$\Delta^3 y(x) = \sum_{j=0}^{3} (-1)^{3-j} \binom{3}{j} y(x + j)$$

$$= (-1)^3 \binom{3}{0} (3x^5 - 4x^4 + 10x^3 - 2x + 5)$$

$$+ (-1)^2 \binom{3}{1} [3(x + 1)^5 - 4(x + 1)^4 + 10(x + 1)^3$$
$$- 2(x + 1) + 5]$$

$$+ (-1) \binom{3}{2} [3(x + 2)^5 - 4(x + 2)^4 + 10(x + 2)^3$$
$$- 2(x + 2) + 5]$$

$$+ (-1)^0 \binom{3}{3} [3(x + 3)^5 - 4(x + 3)^4 + 10(x + 3)^3$$
$$- 2(x + 3) + 5]$$

$$= -[3x^5 - 4x^4 + 10x^3 - 2x + 5]$$
$$+ 3[3(x + 1)^5 - 4(x + 1)^4 + 10(x + 1)^3 - 2(x + 1) + 5]$$
$$- 3[3(x + 2)^5 - 4(x + 2)^4 + 10(x + 2)^3 - 2(x + 2) + 5]$$
$$+ [3(x + 3)^5 - 4(x + 3)^4 + 10(x + 3)^3 - 2(x + 3) + 5]$$

[3] For proof see Hamming (1962), pages 11–13.

Table 8.2–1   A Difference Table

x	y	Δy	$\Delta^2 y$	$\Delta^3 y$	$\cdots$
0	$y(0)$				
		$\Delta y(0)$			
1	$y(1)$		$\Delta^2 y(0)$		
		$\Delta y(1)$		$\Delta^3 y(0)$	
2	$y(2)$		$\Delta^2 y(1)$		
		$\Delta y(2)$			
3	$y(3)$				
$\vdots$					

The Lagrange formula for the difference allows us to write the expression for the kth difference but does not perform all the tedious algebra necessary to evaluate it.

Higher-order differences can often be calculated efficiently by using a device known as a **difference table**. Table 8.2–1 shows a portion of such a table. The values of the independent variable are written in the first column with the corresponding functional values written in the second. The next columns contain the first- and higher-order differences. The way the table is laid out is suggestive of how the differences are computed; for example, $\Delta y(0) = y(1) - y(0)$ (we assume $h = 1$), $\Delta^2 y(0) = \Delta y(1) - \Delta y(0)$, $\Delta^3 y(0) = \Delta^2 y(1) - \Delta^2 y(0)$, and so on. Table 8.2–2 is an actual difference table for $y = 2x^2 - 3x + 5$ for $x = 0, 1, \ldots, 5$.

Note first that Table 8.2–2 illustrates the fundamental theorem, since the second difference is constant for all values of x while the third difference is identically equal to zero. This is what we expect when differencing a polynomial of degree 2. Second, there are two ways to construct a difference table. We might calculate all the y values and then find the first differences by subtraction. From the first differences the second differences are again found by subtraction, and so on. Alternatively, we might calculate only the top value in each column and fill in the rest of the table by addition. Calculating $y(0)$, $\Delta y(0)$, $\Delta^2 y(0)$, and $\Delta^3 y(0)$ would allow us to calculate $y(1) = y(0) + \Delta y(0)$, $\Delta y(1) = \Delta y(0) + \Delta^2 y(0)$, $\Delta^2 y(1) = \Delta^2 y(0) + \Delta^3 y(0)$, and so on. The entire table can be built up in this manner. Third, there is an easy way to check for arithmetic mistakes in a difference table. The sum of the entries in any column of differences plus the first entry in the next column on the left must be equal to the last entry in the column on the left. In Table 8.2–2 the sum of column 4 ($\Delta^2 y$) is 16. Then $16 + (-1) = 15$, the last element in

Table 8.2–2 $y = 2x^2 - 3x + 5$

x	y	Δy	$\Delta^2 y$	$\Delta^3 y$
0	5			
		−1		
1	4		4	
		3		0
2	7		4	
		7		0
3	14		4	
		11		0
4	25		4	
		15		
5	40			

column 3. Similarly, the sum of column 3 is 35. $35 + 5 = 40$, the last element in column 2. (The reader should attempt to prove this property.)

In constructing Table 8.2–2 we knew the exact form of the function $y = f(x)$. In many cases we may have only the values of some unknown function at a series of values of x. In such a case it is natural to look for an approximation to the function $y = f(x)$. There are, of course, many methods, including a wide variety of statistical techniques, available. One useful technique based on the difference calculus is known as *Newton's interpolation formula*.

DEFINITION 8.2–3 For a polynomial of degree n, **Newton's interpolation formula** is

$$f(x) = \sum_{j=0}^{n} \frac{\Delta^j f(0)}{j!} x^{(j)}$$

The notation $x^{(j)}$ is read "x to the j factorial" and stands for the factorial function $x^{(j)} = x(x - 1)(x - 2) \cdots (x - j + 1)$.

Thus, for example, $x^{(3)}$ (x to the 3 factorial) is equal to $x(x - 1)(x - 2)$. Factorial functions in the difference calculus are analogous to expressions such as x^n in ordinary calculus, since $(d/dx)x^n = nx^{n-1}$ and $\Delta x^{(n)} = nx^{(n-1)}$, as the reader can verify by differencing the definition of $x^{(n)}$.

To illustrate the use of Newton's formula, suppose we had only the information in columns 1 and 2 of Table 8.2–1. We could then calculate columns 3, 4, and 5 as before. Since the $\Delta^3 y$ column is all zero, we know that our unknown function can be approximated by a polynomial of degree 2. Thus, in this example $n = 2$. Writing out the terms in Newton's formula,

$$f(x) = \frac{\Delta^0 f(0)}{0!} x^{(0)} + \frac{\Delta^1 f(0)}{1!} x^{(1)} + \frac{\Delta^2 f(0)}{2!} x^{(2)}$$

By convention $\Delta^0 f(0) \equiv f(0)$, $0! \equiv 1$, and $x^{(0)} \equiv 1$. Thus, since we know $f(0)$, $\Delta f(0)$, and $\Delta^2 f(0)$ from the table, we can write

$$f(x) = 5 + \frac{(-1)}{1} x + \frac{4}{2} x(x - 1)$$

$$= 5 - x + 2(x^2 - x)$$
$$= 2x^2 - 3x + 5$$

which is the desired result. In this case the "approximation" is exact. In empirical applications the approximating polynomial obtained by this method evaluated at each data point will be exactly equal to the observed value $y(x)$. For values of x between the data points, the approximating polynomial will, in general, not be equal to the exact relation between y and x.[4]

The formula given above is applicable *only* for the case of equally spaced data. To generalize this technique to the case of arbitrarily (unevenly) spaced data, suppose we have $n + 1$ data points $(x_i, y(x_i))$, and we want the approximating polynomial to pass through each of these points. This will be a polynomial of degree n. Call it $\hat{f}_n(x)$, where the n subscript denotes the degree and the hat reminds us that it is an approximation to some "true" relation between y and x. Then we can write

$$(1) \qquad \hat{f}_n(x) = y(x_1) + (x - x_1)\hat{f}_{n-1}(x)$$

where $\hat{f}_{n-1}$ is a polynomial of degree $n - 1$. This follows since $\hat{f}_n(x_1) = y(x_1) + (x_1 - x_1)\hat{f}_{n-1}(x_1) = y(x_1)$, which conforms to the requirement that $\hat{f}_n(x)$ passes through each data point. Rearranging (1) we obtain

$$(2) \qquad \hat{f}_{n-1}(x) = \frac{\hat{f}_n(x) - y(x_1)}{x - x_1}$$

or, by the immediately preceding argument,

$$(3) \qquad \hat{f}_{n-1}(x) = \frac{\hat{f}_n(x) - \hat{f}_n(x_1)}{x - x_1}$$

For a particular value of x, say x_j, (3) becomes

$$(4) \qquad \hat{f}_{n-1}(x_j) = \frac{\hat{f}_n(x_j) - \hat{f}_n(x_1)}{x_j - x_1} = \frac{\hat{f}(x_j) - y(x_1)}{x_j - x_1}$$

[4] For a discussion of the error between data points, see Hamming (1962).

Thus, to ensure that $\hat{f}_n(x_j) = y(x_j)$ it is necessary that

$$\hat{f}_{n-1}(x_j) = \frac{y(x_j) - y(x_1)}{x_j - x_1}$$

Substituting (4) into (1):

$$\hat{f}_n(x_j) = y(x_1) + (x_j - x_1)\frac{y(x_j) - y(x_1)}{x_j - x_1} = y(x_1) + y(x_j) - y(x_1) = y(x_j)$$

DEFINITION 8.2–4   The terms

$$\frac{y(x_j) - y(x_1)}{x_j - x_1}$$

are called **first divided differences,** abbreviated as $[x_j, x_1]$ or as $[x_1, x_j]$, since these two expressions are equivalent.

Thus

$$\hat{f}_{n-1}(x_j) = [x_j, x_1]$$

Next, by an argument similar to the above:

(5) $$\hat{f}_{n-1}(x) = [x_1, x_2] + (x - x_2)\hat{f}_{n-2}(x)$$

where $\hat{f}_{n-2}(x)$ is a polynomial of degree $n - 2$, or

(6) $$\hat{f}_{n-2}(x) = \frac{\hat{f}_{n-1}(x) - [x_1, x_2]}{x - x_2}$$

For $x = x_j$,

(7) $$\hat{f}_{n-2}(x_j) = \frac{\hat{f}_{n-1}(x_j) - [x_1, x_2]}{x_j - x_2}$$

Since $\hat{f}_{n-1}(x_j) = [x_j, x_1]$, (7) becomes

(8) $$\hat{f}_{n-2}(x_j) = \frac{[x_j, x_1] - [x_1, x_2]}{x_j - x_2}$$

DEFINITION 8.2–5   Equation (8) is the **second divided difference** (the divided difference of the divided difference), written $[x_1, x_2, x_j]$.

In general, higher-order divided differences are defined as

$$[x_1, x_2, x_3, \ldots, x_j] = \frac{[x_1, x_2, \ldots, x_{j-2}, x_{j-1}] - [x_1, x_2, \ldots, x_{j-2}, x_j]}{x_{j-1} - x_j}$$

The values of the higher-order divided differences are also independent of the order in which the x entries are written, for example $[x_1, x_j, x_2] \equiv [x_j, x_2, x_1]$.

Thus we have $\hat{f}_{n-2}(x_j) = [x_1, x_2, x_j]$. If we have $n + 1$ data points, it is necessary to calculate the n divided differences $[x_1, x_2]$, $[x_1, x_2, x_3], \ldots,$ $[x_1, x_2, \ldots, x_n]$. Then by substitution we find that

$$(9) \quad \hat{f}_n(x) = y(x_1) + (x - x_1)$$
$$\times [[x_1, x_2] + (x - x_2)\{[x_1, x_2, x_3] + (x - x_3)$$
$$\times \{[x_1, x_2, x_3, x_4] + (x - x_4)\{\cdots\}\}\}]$$

which is equal to

$$(10) \quad \hat{f}_n(x) = y(x_1) + (x - x_1)[x_1, x_2] + (x - x_1)(x - x_2)[x_1, x_2, x_3]$$
$$+ (x - x_1)(x - x_2)(x - x_3)[x_1, x_2, x_3, x_4] + \cdots$$
$$+ (x - x_1)\cdots(x - x_n)[x_1, x_2, \ldots, x_n, x_{n+1}]$$

To illustrate both Newton's formula for unequally spaced data and the calculation of divided differences, suppose we started with the data (observations) given in Table 8.2–3.

Table 8.2–3

$x_1 = 0$	$x_2 = 2$	$x_3 = 5$	$x_4 = 6$
$y_1 = 1$	$y_2 = 3$	$y_3 = 0$	$y_4 = 2$

Since we have four data points, we must calculate the third-order divided difference. Table 8.2–4 is a divided difference table with the specific numbers of this example filled in.[5]

Table 8.2–4

x	y	$[,]$	$[,,]$	$[,,,]$
$x_1 = 0$	1			
		$[x_1, x_2] = 1$		
$x_2 = 2$	3		$[x_1, x_2, x_3] = -\frac{6}{15}$	
		$[x_2, x_3] = -1$		$[x_1, x_2, x_3, x_4] = \frac{23}{120}$
$x_3 = 5$	0		$[x_2, x_3, x_4] = \frac{3}{4}$	
		$[x_3, x_4] = 2$		
$x_4 = 6$	2			

[5] This is only one of an equivalent number of ways to construct a divided difference table. For others see Hamming (1962), pages 97–101.

The calculations in constructing Table 8.2–4 are given below.

$$[x_1, x_2] = \frac{y(x_1) - y(x_2)}{x_1 - x_2} = \frac{1 - 3}{-2} = 1$$

$$[x_2, x_3] = \frac{3 - 0}{2 - 5} = \frac{3}{-3} = -1$$

$$[x_3, x_4] = \frac{0 - 2}{5 - 6} = \frac{-2}{-1} = 2$$

$$[x_1, x_2, x_3] = \frac{[x_1, x_2] - [x_1, x_3]}{x_2 - x_3} = \frac{1 - (1 - 0)/(0 - 5)}{-3} = \frac{6/5}{-3} = -\frac{6}{15}$$

$$[x_2, x_3, x_4] = \frac{[x_2, x_3] - [x_2, x_4]}{x_3 - x_4} = \frac{-1 - (3 - 2)/(2 - 6)}{-1}$$

$$= \frac{-1 + \frac{1}{4}}{-1} = \frac{3}{4}$$

$$[x_1, x_2, x_3, x_4] = \frac{[x_1, x_2, x_3] - [x_1, x_2, x_4]}{x_3 - x_4}$$

$$= \frac{-6/15 - ([x_1, x_2] - [x_1, x_4])/(x_2 - x_4)}{-1}$$

$$= \frac{-\frac{6}{15} - [(1 - \frac{1}{6})/-4]}{-1} = \frac{23}{120}$$

Thus the Newton formula becomes

$$\hat{f}_3(x) = 1 + (x - 0)(1) + (x - 0)(x - 2)(-\tfrac{6}{15}) + (x - 0)(x - 2)(x - 5)(\tfrac{23}{120})$$

This reduces to

$$\hat{f}_3(x) = 1 + \tfrac{223}{60}x - \tfrac{209}{120}x^2 + \tfrac{23}{120}x^3$$

As the reader can verify, this unlikely looking polynomial does indeed pass through the four data points in Table 8.2–3. Note that the first divided differences are approximations of the first derivative of the true relation, the second divided differences approximations of the second derivative, and so on.

Figure 8.2–1 illustrates the approximating polynomial and the true relation between y and x for an unspecified function $y = y(x)$. Here the solid line, $y(x)$, is the true relation while the dotted line, $\hat{y}(x)$, is the approximating polynomial. Note that $\hat{y}(x_i) = y(x_i)$, $i = 1, 2, \ldots, 5$, while $\hat{y}(x)$ is not equal to $y(x)$ for values of x between data points.

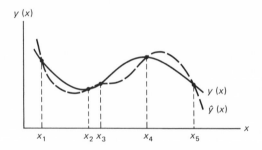

Figure 8.2–1 *The true relation and the approximating polynomial—five unequally spaced data points.*

There are many additional ways to calculate the approximating polynomial for a given set of data based on the requirement that it pass through each data point. There is a uniqueness theorem that assures that all of these alternate approaches give the same polynomial.[6]

One additional method using determinants is worth discussing, since it allows us to build in more conditions on the approximating polynomial than the Newton formula. Again we begin with a set of $n + 1$ arbitrarily spaced data points, $\{x_1, x_2, \ldots, x_{n+1}\}$. We seek an approximating polynomial of the form

$$(1) \qquad\qquad P(x) = \sum_{j=0}^{n} a_j x^j$$

where $P(x_i) = y(x_i)$ for $i = 1, 2, \ldots, n + 1$. This requirement corresponds to the system of equations

$$
\begin{aligned}
a_0 + a_1 x_1 + a_2 x_1^2 + \cdots + a_n x_1^n &= y(x_1) \\
a_0 + a_1 x_2 + a_2 x_2^2 + \cdots + a_n x_2^n &= y(x_2) \\
&\ \ \vdots \\
a_0 + a_1 x_{n+1} + a_2 x_{n+1}^2 + \cdots + a_n x_{n+1}^n &= y(x_{n+1})
\end{aligned}
$$

(2)

In matrix notation, the system (2) can be written as

$$(3) \qquad\qquad AV' = Y$$

where

$$A = [a_0, a_1, \ldots, a_n]$$

$$V = \begin{bmatrix} 1 & x_1 & x_1^2 & \cdots & x_1^n \\ 1 & x_2 & x_2^2 & \cdots & x_2^n \\ & \vdots & & & \\ 1 & x_{n+1} & x_{n+1}^2 & \cdots & x_{n+1}^n \end{bmatrix}$$

[6] Cf. Hamming (1962).

and

$$Y = \begin{bmatrix} y(x_1) \\ y(x_2) \\ \vdots \\ y(x_{n+1}) \end{bmatrix}$$

DEFINITION 8.2–6 V is the **Vandermonde matrix** of the polynomial $P(x)$. We can solve (3) for the elements of A by Cramer's rule:

$$a_j = \frac{|V_j|}{|V|} \quad \text{for } j = 0, 1, \ldots, n$$

where V_j is the matrix formed by replacing the jth column of V by Y. Thus we can write $P(x)$ as

(4) $$P(x) = \frac{|V_0|}{|V|} + x\frac{|V_1|}{|V|} + x^2\frac{|V_2|}{|V|} + \cdots + x^n\frac{|V_n|}{|V|}$$

Using $P(x) = y(x)$, Equation (4) can be written as

(5) $$y(x)|V| - |V_0| - x|V_1| - \cdots - x|V_n| = 0$$

Writing (5) out in full we obtain

(6) $$y(x)\begin{vmatrix} 1 & x_1 & \cdots & x_1^n \\ 1 & x_2 & \cdots & x_2^n \\ \vdots & \vdots & & \\ 1 & x_{n+1} & \cdots & x_{n+1}^n \end{vmatrix} - \begin{vmatrix} y(x_1) & x_1 & \cdots & x_1^n \\ y(x_2) & x_2 & \cdots & x_2^n \\ \vdots & \vdots & & \\ y(x_{n+1}) & x_{n+1} & \cdots & x_{n+1}^n \end{vmatrix}$$

$$- x\begin{vmatrix} 1 & y(x_1) & x_1^2 & \cdots & x_1^n \\ 1 & y(x_2) & x_2^2 & \cdots & x_2^n \\ \vdots & \vdots & & \\ 1 & y(x_{n+1}) & x_{n+1}^2 & \cdots & x_{n+1}^n \end{vmatrix} \cdots$$

$$- x^n\begin{vmatrix} 1 & x_1 & x_1^2 & \cdots & y(x_1) \\ 1 & x_2 & x_2^2 & \cdots & y(x_2) \\ \vdots & & & \\ 1 & x_{n+1} & x_{n+1}^2 & \cdots & y(x_{n+1}) \end{vmatrix} = 0$$

By an elementary theorem of matrix algebra, interchanging rows or columns of a determinant changes the determinant's sign.[7] We now move the column $y(x_1), \ldots, y(x_{n+1})$ in each of the determinants in (6) to the first column. For the determinants of odd powers of x, this requires an odd number of column transpositions, thus changing the sign of those terms in (6). For even powers

[7] Theorem 4.3–1.

of x, an even number of transpositions are made, leaving the sign of the terms unchanged. By this procedure (6) becomes

$$
(7) \quad y
\begin{vmatrix}
1 & x_1 & \cdots & x_1^n \\
\vdots & & & \\
1 & x_{n+1} & \cdots & x_{n+1}^n
\end{vmatrix}
-
\begin{vmatrix}
y(x_1) & x_1 & \cdots & x_1^n \\
\vdots & & & \\
y(x_{n+1}) & x_{n+1} & \cdots & x_{n+1}^n
\end{vmatrix}
$$

$$
+ x
\begin{vmatrix}
y(x_1) & 1 & x_1^2 & \cdots & x_1^n \\
\vdots & \vdots & \vdots & & \\
y(x_{n+1}) & 1 & x_{n+1}^2 & \cdots & x_{n+1}^n
\end{vmatrix}
$$

$$
- x^2
\begin{vmatrix}
y(x_1) & 1 & x_1 & x_1^3 & \cdots & x_1^n \\
\vdots & \vdots & \vdots & \vdots & & \vdots \\
y(x_{n+1}) & 1 & x_{n+1} & x_{n+1}^3 & \cdots & x_{n+1}^n
\end{vmatrix}
+ \cdots
$$

$$
+ (-1)^{n+1} x^n
\begin{vmatrix}
y(x_1) & 1 & x_1 & x_2^2 & \cdots & x_1^{n-1} \\
\vdots & \vdots & \vdots & \vdots & & \vdots \\
y(x_{n+1}) & 1 & x_{n+1} & x_{n+1}^2 & \cdots & x_{n+1}^{n-1}
\end{vmatrix}
= 0
$$

System (7) is simply the expansion of the following determinant by cofactors, as the reader can verify:

$$
(8) \quad
\begin{vmatrix}
y(x) & 1 & x & x^2 & \cdots & x^n \\
y(x_1) & 1 & x_1 & x_1^2 & \cdots & x_1^n \\
y(x_2) & 1 & x_2 & x_2^2 & \cdots & x_2^n \\
\vdots & \vdots & \vdots & & & \\
y(x_{n+1}) & 1 & x_{n+1} & x_{n+1}^2 & \cdots & x_{n+1}^n
\end{vmatrix}
= 0
$$

Expanding (8) by the cofactors of the first row yields the approximating polynomial. Note that the system (8) is obtained by bordering the Vandermonde determinant, $|V|$, with a first row: $y(x), 1, x, x^2, \ldots, x^n$, and a first column $y(x), y(x_1), \ldots, y(x_{n+1})$. For the example in Table 8.2–3 the system is

$$
\begin{vmatrix}
y(x) & 1 & x & x^2 & x^3 \\
1 & 1 & 0 & 0 & 0 \\
3 & 1 & 2 & 4 & 8 \\
0 & 1 & 5 & 25 & 125 \\
2 & 1 & 6 & 36 & 216
\end{vmatrix}
= 0
$$

Expanding this by the cofactors of row 1 yields our previous answer.

We indicated earlier that the determinantial form provided more flexibility. Specifically, it allows us to build additional restrictions on the approximating polynomial. Suppose that, in addition to the $n + 1$ data points, we also know the value of the first derivative at each of these points. Now, not only do we want the polynomial to pass through each data point, but we also want it to have the appropriate slope at each of these points. If $y'(x_1), y'(x_2), \ldots, y'(x_{n+1})$ are the required slopes at each data point, the polynomial is obtained by expanding the following determinant by the cofactors of the first row and equating the result to zero:

$$(9) \quad \begin{vmatrix} y(x) & 1 & x & x^2 & x^3 & \cdots & x^{2n+1} \\ y(x_1) & 1 & x_1 & x_1^2 & x_1^3 & \cdots & x_1^{2n+1} \\ \vdots & & & & & & \\ y(x_{n+1}) & 1 & x_{n+1} & x_{n+1}^2 & x_{n+1}^3 & \cdots & x_{n+1}^{2n+1} \\ y'(x_1) & 0 & 1 & 2x_1 & 3x_1^2 & \cdots & (2n+1)x_1^{2n} \\ y'(x_2) & 0 & 1 & 2x_2 & 3x_2^2 & \cdots & (2n+1)x_2^{2n} \\ \vdots & & & & & & \\ y'(x_{n+1}) & 0 & 1 & 2x_{n+1} & 3x_{n+1}^2 & \cdots & (2n+1)x_{n+1}^{2n} \end{vmatrix}$$

In this case the total number of conditions imposed on the approximating polynomial is $2n + 2$ ($n + 1$ data points plus $n + 1$ values of the first derivatives). As a result, the approximating polynomial will be of degree $2n + 1$. If we knew the second derivative at each data point, (9) could be expanded in a similar manner. We would then have an approximating polynomial of degree $3n + 2$.

Example 5. Given

x	1	2	4
y	1	0	2

and $y'(x_1) = 0$, $y'(x_2) = 1$, and $y'(x_3) = 0$. Find the approximating polynomial. The determinant form is

$$(10) \quad \begin{vmatrix} y(x) & 1 & x & x^2 & x^3 & x^4 & x^5 \\ 1 & 1 & 1 & 1 & 1 & 1 & 1 \\ 0 & 1 & 2 & 4 & 8 & 16 & 32 \\ 2 & 1 & 4 & 16 & 64 & 256 & 1024 \\ 0 & 0 & 1 & 2 & 3 & 4 & 5 \\ 1 & 0 & 1 & 4 & 12 & 32 & 80 \\ 0 & 0 & 1 & 8 & 48 & 256 & 1280 \end{vmatrix}$$

The determinant (10) is not something one would normally like to evaluate by hand. The large number of calculations involved in this case with only three data points and two requirements to be met per observation is a compelling reason to handle such problems by computer. In any actual empirical application the number of observations will obviously be much larger, with a corresponding increase in the number of computations involved.

Problems

8.2–1 Find the first and second differences of

(a) $y = 2x^2 - 3$

(b) $y = \dfrac{x + 1}{x - 1}$

(c) $y = x^{(n)} + x^{(m)}$

(d) $y = (2x - 1)^2$

8.2–2 Find the third difference of the following functions, using Theorem 8.2–3:

(a) $y = x^5 - 2x^3 + 1$

(b) $y = (x - 1)^4$

(c) $y = \left(\dfrac{x + 1}{x - 1}\right)^2$

8.2–3 Construct difference tables for the following (let $x = 0, 1, \ldots, 5$):

(a) $y = 2x^2 + 3x^3$

(b) $y = (3x^2 + 2)^2$

(c) $y = \dfrac{x + 2}{1 + x}$

8.2–4 Find an approximating polynomial for the following data points:

(a)

x	0	1	2	3	4	5
y	-1	2	3	1	-1	0

(c)

x	0	1	3	7	8
y	0	-2	-1	0	1

(b)

x	2	4	6	8
y	-10	8	20	11

(d)

x	-1	3	5	9
y	1	5	8	11

8.2–5 Find the approximating polynomial for the following set of data points, using the Vandermonde matrix:

x	0	2	3	5
y	1	-1	3	2

8.2–6 In addition to the data points in Problem 8.2–5, suppose we knew that $y'(0) = 1$, $y'(2) = -\frac{1}{2}$, $y'(3) = 0$, and $y'(5) = -2$. Write the determinant from which we could find the approximating polynomial.

8.3 DIFFERENCE EQUATIONS

In Section 8.2 we noted the close similarity between the difference and the derivative. Not surprisingly, the solutions to difference equations are found by methods similar to the methods used for solving differential equations.

Before attempting any explicit definitions note that, by the definition of the first difference, the following two equations are equivalent:

(1) $$a \, \Delta y(x) = b$$

and

(2) $$y(x + 1) - y(x) = \frac{b}{a}$$

Furthermore, if (2) holds for $y(x + 1)$ and $y(x)$, it must hold for all adjacent y values. Thus (2) is also equivalent to

(3) $$y(x + i + 1) - y(x + i) = \frac{b}{a}$$

for i a positive or negative integer. In this section we shall always assume that $h = 1$.

DEFINITION 8.3–1   A **first- (nth)-order difference equation** is an equation involving the first- (nth)-difference of a function.

Besides being classified by order, difference equations are also classified by degree, by whether or not they are homogeneous, and by whether there are any variable terms other than $y(x + i)$ terms in the equation.[8]

DEFINITION 8.3–2   The **degree of a difference equation** is the highest power to which a $y(x + i)$ term is raised.

Thus (2) is a linear, first-order, first-degree difference equation since both of the $y(x + i)$ terms, $y(x + 1)$ and $y(x)$, are raised to the first power.

Example 1. $y(x + 1)^2 - 4y(x) + 5 = 0$ is an example of a first-order, second-degree difference equation. Write it in the same form as (1).

DEFINITION 8.3–3   A difference equation is **homogeneous** if the constant term is zero. If there is a nonzero constant term or a variable term, the equation is **nonhomogeneous.**

The equation in Example 1 is therefore a nonhomogeneous, first-order, second-degree difference equation. If b were zero in (1), it would be an example of a homogeneous difference equation. Homogeneity of a difference equation is the same concept as homogeneity of a differential equation.

---

[8] In some cases the coefficients of the $y(x + i)$ terms may be variables, such as powers of x, etc. Such equations are, in general, very difficult to solve. For some of the techniques involved see Saaty and Bram (1964). For this reason we shall assume that all the coefficients of the $y(x + i)$ terms are constants.

First-order, linear (first-degree) difference equations are the easiest to solve. The general form of such an equation is

(4) $$ay(x + 1) + by(x) = c$$

If a is not equal to 1, the first step is to normalize this equation by dividing through by a, obtaining

(5) $$y(x + 1) + fy(x) = e$$

where $f = b/a$ and $e = c/a$. Just as with differential equations, the solution to the simplified version (5) is composed of two portions—the particular solution [any solution to (5)] and the solution to the homogeneous version of (5), that is, $y(x + 1) + fy(x) = 0$. In keeping with the notation of Chapter 7, denote these components as $\bar{y}$ and y^*, respectively. The general solution (disregarding initial values) to (5) is simply $\bar{y} + y^*$ as for differential equations.

Let us begin by finding $\bar{y}$. Since this is any solution to (5), try $y(x) = k$, an arbitrary constant. Then (5) becomes

$$k + fk = e$$

Solving for k,

$$k = \frac{e}{1 + f}$$

Thus $\bar{y} = e/(1 + f)$ if $f \neq -1$. If $f = -1$ we employ the trick used in Section 7.1 and try $y(x) = kx$. Then (5) becomes

$$k(x + 1) + fkx = e$$

or, solving again for k,

$$k = \frac{e}{x + fx + 1}$$

This reduces to $k = e$, since $f = -1$ by assumption. In this case $\bar{y} = kx = ex$.

To find y^*, suppose we start with an initial value $y(0)$. Then we can write

$$y(1) = -fy(0)$$
$$y(2) = -fy(1) = -f[-fy(0)] = (-f)^2 y(0)$$
$$y(3) = -fy(2) = (-f)^3 y(0)$$
$$\vdots$$
$$y(n) = -fy(n - 1) = (-f)^n y(0)$$

From this it follows that we can write $y(x) = (-f)^x y(0)$, as a solution. There are infinitely many solutions of the form

$$y^* = y(x) = A(-f)^x$$

where A is an arbitrary constant. Since $y(0)$ is itself a constant, it has been lumped into the arbitrary constant A. To prove this statement, substitute $y(x) = A(-f)^x$ into $y(x + 1) + fy(x) = 0$. This yields

(7) $$A(-f)^{x+1} + fA(-f)^x = 0$$

The left side of (7) is zero. If x is an odd integer, the first term is positive while the second term is the negative of the first. If x is an even integer, the opposite is true. This argument holds for all values of A. Thus $y^* = A(-f)^x$ and the general solution to (5) is

$$y(x) = A(-f)^x + \frac{e}{1 + f} \qquad \text{if } f \neq -1$$

or

$$y(x) = A(-f)^x + ex \qquad \text{if } f = -1$$

This solution is general because of the presence of the arbitrary constant A. The specific solution, based on a known initial value, is obtained by substitution as was the case of differential equations. Suppose we know that $y(0) = 5$. Then

$$y(0) = 5 = A(-f)^0 + \frac{e}{1 + f}$$

or

$$A = 5 - \frac{e}{1 + f}$$

Substituting this solution for A into the general solution yields the specific solution

$$y(x) = \left(5 - \frac{e}{1 + f}\right)(-f)^x + \frac{e}{1 + f}$$

Example 2. Solve the difference equation

$$\Delta y(x) = 3y(x + 1) + 2 \qquad \text{with } y(0) = 1$$

First, this equation must be converted to the form of (2) by using the definition of the first difference:

$$y(x + 1) - y(x) = 3y(x + 1) + 2$$

or

$$2y(x + 1) + y(x) = -2$$

This expression must then be normalized by dividing by 2:

$$y(x + 1) + \tfrac{1}{2}y(x) = -1$$

This expression is now in the form of (5), with $f = \frac{1}{2}$ and $e = -1$. Since $f \neq -1$, $\bar{y} = -1/(1 + \frac{1}{2}) = -\frac{2}{3}$ while $y^* = A(-\frac{1}{2})^x$. The general solution is simply $\bar{y} + y^*$ or

$$y(x) = A(-\tfrac{1}{2})^x - \tfrac{2}{3}$$

Since $y(0) = 1$ is our initial condition, solving for A yields

$$A = 1 - \left(\frac{-1}{1 + \frac{1}{2}}\right) = \tfrac{5}{3}$$

The specific solution is therefore

$$y(x) = \tfrac{5}{3}(-\tfrac{1}{2})^x - \tfrac{2}{3}$$

The reader can verify that this is indeed the solution by substituting back into the original equation.

Before examining solution techniques for higher-order linear difference equations, we shall treat the case of nonlinear first-order difference equations. The general form of such an equation is

(1) $$y(x + 1) = f[y(x)]$$

where f is not an explicit function of x. There is no general method for solving equations of this type as there is for linear first-order equations. The most useful approach is through construction of what is usually called a "phase diagram." Since the value of $y(x + 1)$ is determined by (1) if the value of $y(x)$ is known, it is possible to graph $y(x + 1)$ as a function of $y(x)$. See Figure 8.3–1. The 45° line contains all points for which $y(x + 1) = y(x)$, while the curve represents the actual relation between $y(x)$ and $y(x + 1)$. It is the "phase line" and is simply the graph of the function $f[y(x)]$. The 45° line is used to construct the phase line as illustrated in Figure 8.3–1. Given an initial value of x, say $x = 0$, $y(0)$ is known. Thus $y(1)$ can be calculated from (1). The point $(y(0), y(1))$ is one point on the phase line. $y(1)$ is then used to calculate $y(2)$ to

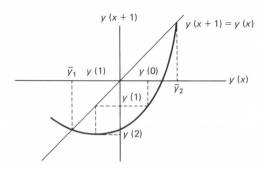

Figure 8.3–1 *Phase diagram.*

give a second point on the phase line, $(y(1), y(2))$. Graphically, this corresponds to drawing a line from $y(1)$ on the $y(x + 1)$ axis to the 45° line and then perpendicularly to the $y(x)$ axis. From this point on the $y(x)$ axis a line is extended to the phase line and then to the $y(x + 1)$ axis, thus determining $y(2)$. The same procedure is then repeated.

Once the phase line is constructed, a great deal of information about the behavior of the difference equation can be obtained from it and its relation to the 45° line. Intersections of the phase line and the 45° line represent equilibrium values of y, since at these points $y(x + i + 1) = y(x + i)$ for all values of x. The phase line also enables us to determine whether the equilibria are stable or unstable and the nature of oscillations about equilibria (if any). Before discussing these points, note that if the phase line and the 45° line do not intersect $y(x)$ goes to $+\infty$ or $-\infty$ as $x \to \infty$. (Why?)

Whether the equilibrium is stable or unstable depends on the slope of the phase line at the intersection. If the absolute value of the slope is less than one at the intersection, the equilibrium point it represents is stable; if the absolute value is greater than one, the equilibrium is unstable. Furthermore, if the slope is positive there are no oscillations. There is either a steady movement toward (stable) or away from (unstable) the intersection point. If the slope is negative, there are either damped oscillations towards equilibrium (stable) or explosive oscillations away from equilibrium (unstable). Figure 8.3–2 illustrates these four possibilities. The arrows indicate the direction of

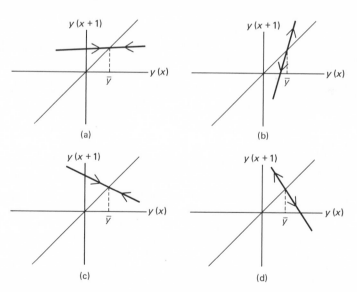

Figure 8.3–2 (a) $0 < f'(\bar{y}') < 1$. (b) $f'(\bar{y}') > 1$. (c) $-1 < f'(\bar{y}) < 0$. (d) $f'(\bar{y}) < -1$.

movement for $y \neq \bar{y}$ in each of the graphs. The reader should verify, using similar graphs, that the situations in parts (c) and (d) give rise to oscillation while those in parts (a) and (b) do not. What types of equilibria are illustrated by $\bar{y}_1$ and $\bar{y}_2$ in Figure 8.3–1? The reader should examine what happens if the slope of the phase line is either $+1$ or -1 at the intersection point.

As mentioned earlier, there are no general methods for solving nonlinear difference equations. However, there are techniques available for approximating the solution in various cases.[9]

The solution techniques for higher-order difference equations are similar to those for higher-order differential equations. The easiest case is that of second-order linear equations with constant coefficients and constant term. The general form of such an equation is

$$(1) \qquad\qquad y(x + 2) + ay(x + 1) + by(x) = c$$

where a, b, and c are constants. As before, the solution to (1) is the sum of any solution to (1), $\bar{y}$, and the solution to the homogeneous version, y^*.

Following our previous procedure, try $\bar{y} = k$ as a solution. Then (1) becomes $k + ak + bk = c$. Solving for k, and thus $\bar{y}$.

$$(2) \qquad\qquad \bar{y} = \frac{c}{1 + a + b}$$

This is indeed $\bar{y}$ if $a + b \neq -1$. If $a + b = -1$ then try $\bar{y} = kx$. Equation (1) becomes

$$k(x + 2) + ak(x + 1) + bkx = c$$

Solving for k,

$$k = \frac{c}{a + 2}$$

since $a + b = -1$ by assumption. Thus

$$(3) \qquad\qquad \bar{y} = kx = \left(\frac{c}{a + 2}\right) x$$

Equation (3) is the solution if $a + b = -1$ and if $a \neq -2$. If $a = -2$ this solution also breaks down and it is necessary to try a solution in the form $\bar{y} = kx^2$. In this case we obtain

$$k(x + 2)^2 + ak(x + 1)^2 + bkx^2 = c$$

or

$$k = \frac{c}{x^2(1 + a + b) + x(4 + 2a) + 4 + a}$$

[9] For an introduction to such techniques and further references, see Saaty (1967).

which simplifies to $k = c/2$.

(4)
$$\bar{y} = \left(\frac{c}{2}\right) x^2$$

Equations (2), (3), and (4) represent the only three possibilities for $\bar{y}$ for an equation of the form (1).

To find y^* we start with the homogeneous version of (1):

(5)
$$y(x + 2) + ay(x + 1) + by(x) = 0$$

Our previous treatment of differential equations suggests that we should try a solution of the form

(6)
$$y(x) = Ar^x$$

Equation (5) thus becomes

$$Ar^{x+2} + aAr^{x+1} + bAr^x = 0$$

Factoring and simplifying:

(7)
$$r^2 + ar + b = 0$$

Equation (7) is the **characteristic equation** of (5).[10] The characteristic equation of a second-order difference equation will be a quadratic equation with two solutions, or roots. Solving (7) by the quadratic formula,

$$r_1 = \frac{-a + \sqrt{a^2 - 4b}}{2}$$

$$r_2 = \frac{-a - \sqrt{a^2 - 4b}}{2}$$

As in the case of differential equations, both of these roots must appear in the solution. There are three posibilities for r_1 and r_2:

  (1) if $a^2 = 4b$, $r_1 = r_2$ are repeated real roots;
  (2) if $a^2 > 4b$, r_1 and r_2 are unequal real numbers; and
  (3) if $a^2 < 4b$, r_1 and r_2 are imaginary numbers.

In case 1, $r_1 = r_2 = -a/2$. For this situation,

(8)
$$y^* = A\left(-\frac{a}{2}\right)^x + Bx\left(-\frac{a}{2}\right)^x$$

where A and B are arbitrary constants. Equation (8) points out the fact that the solution to a second-order difference equation must contain two distinct

---

[10] See Definition 4.5–1 and Definition 7.1–9.

constants. In this case we are forced to introduce the x term in (8) to ensure that there are in fact two constants. To prove that (8) is indeed the solution, simply substitute into (5):

$$A\left(-\frac{a}{2}\right)^{x+2} + B(x+2)\left(-\frac{a}{2}\right)^{x+2} + a\left[A\left(-\frac{a}{2}\right)^{x+1} + B(x+1)\left(-\frac{a}{2}\right)^{x+1}\right]$$

$$+ b\left[A\left(-\frac{a}{2}\right)^{x} + Bx\left(-\frac{a}{2}\right)^{x}\right] \overset{?}{=} 0$$

which simplifies to

$$A\left(-\frac{a}{2}\right)^{x}\left[\frac{a^2}{4} - \frac{a^2}{2} + b\right] + B\left(-\frac{a}{2}\right)^{x}\left[\frac{xa^2}{4} - \frac{xa^2}{2} + bx\right] \overset{?}{=} 0$$

Both terms in square brackets reduce to zero, since $b = a^2/4$ by hypothesis. This proves that (8) is indeed the solution to (5).

In case 2, y^* is given by

$$y^* = A_1 r_1^x + A_2 r_2^x$$

where A_1 and A_2 are distinct constants, as the reader can easily verify by the previous procedure.

For the case of imaginary roots, r_1 and r_2 are a conjugate pair of complex numbers that as before,[11] we represent by

$$r_1 = h + vi \quad \text{and} \quad r_2 = h - vi$$

where h and v are real numbers given by

$$h = -\frac{a}{2} \quad \text{and} \quad v = \frac{\sqrt{4b - a^2}}{2}$$

Consequently, $y^* = A(h + vi)^x + B(h - vi)^x$. Following the procedure developed for differential equations, this expression can be written in trigonometric terms as[12]

$$y^* = R^x(\cos \theta x \pm i \sin \theta x)$$

where $R = \sqrt{b}$, $\cos \theta = h/\sqrt{b}$, and $\sin \theta = v/\sqrt{b}$. Thus y^* becomes

$$A_1(\sqrt{b})^x(\cos \theta x + i \sin \theta x) + B_1(\sqrt{b})^x(\cos \theta x - i \sin \theta x)$$

$$= (\sqrt{b})^x(A_2 \cos \theta x + B_2 \sin \theta x)$$

where $A_2 = A_1 + B_1$ and $B_2 = (A_1 - B_1)i$. A_2 and B_2 are the arbitrary constants that must be evaluated using two initial conditions to arrive at the specific solution.

---

[11] Cf. Section 7.1.

[12] See Theorem 7.1–5.

Example 3. Find the general and specific solutions for $y(x + 2) + y(x + 1) + \frac{1}{4}y(x) = 1$, with initial values $y(0) = 1$ and $y(1) = 3$. Here $a = 1$ and $b = \frac{1}{4}$, so $a^2 = 4b$ and we shall have repeated real roots. To see this, note that the characteristic equation is $r^2 + r + \frac{1}{4} = 0$, which factors to $(r + \frac{1}{2})(r + \frac{1}{2}) = 0$. Thus $r_1 = r_2 = r = -\frac{1}{2}$, which is, of course, equal to $-a/2$. Consequently,

$$y^* = A(-\tfrac{1}{2})^x + Bx(-\tfrac{1}{2})^x$$

Since $a + b \neq -1$, $\bar{y}$ can be written immediately as

$$\bar{y} = \frac{1}{1 + a + b} = \frac{1}{9/4} = \frac{4}{9}$$

The general solution is then

$$y(x) = A(-\tfrac{1}{2})^x + Bx(-\tfrac{1}{2})^x + \tfrac{4}{9}$$

To find the specific solution the constants A and B are evaluated from the simultaneous equations

$$1 = A(-\tfrac{1}{2})^0 + B(0)(-\tfrac{1}{2})^0 + \tfrac{4}{9}$$

and

$$3 = A(-\tfrac{1}{2})^1 + B(1)(-\tfrac{1}{2})^1 + \tfrac{4}{9}$$

which reduce to

$$A = \tfrac{5}{9}$$

and

$$-\frac{A}{2} - \frac{B}{2} = \frac{23}{9}$$

Thus $A = \tfrac{5}{9}$ and $B = -\tfrac{51}{9}$. The specific solution is therefore

$$y(x) = \tfrac{5}{9}(-\tfrac{1}{2})^x - \tfrac{51}{9}x(-\tfrac{1}{2})^x + \tfrac{4}{9}$$

The reader can check that this does indeed satisfy both the original equation and the initial conditions.

Example 4. Solve $y(x + 2) - 3y(x + 1) + 2y(x) = 3$, with initial values $y(0) = 0$ and $y(1) = 1$. Since $(-3)^2 > (4)(2)$, this is an example of unequal real roots. The characteristic equation is

$$r^2 - 3r + 2 = 0$$

which factors into $(r - 2)(r - 1) = 0$, yielding $r_1 = 2$ and $r_2 = 1$. Therefore

$$y^* = A_1(2)^x + A_2$$

Since $a + b = -1$ but $a \neq -2$, we can write $\bar{y}$ as

$$\bar{y} = \frac{c}{a + b} = \frac{3}{-1} = -3$$

The general solution is then

$$y(x) = A_1 2^x + A_2 - 3$$

To evaluate A_1 and A_2, solve the equation system derived from the initial conditions

$$0 = A_1 + A_2 - 3$$

and

$$1 = 2A_1 + A_2 - 3$$

Simplifying,

$$A_1 + A_2 = 3$$

and

$$2A_1 + A_2 = 4$$

or $A_1 = 1$ and $A_2 = 2$. The specific solution is therefore

$$y(x) = 2^x - 1$$

Example 5. Solve $y(x + 2) + y(x + 1) + y(x) = 5$, with initial values $y(0) = 0$ and $y(1) = 1$. This is a case of imaginary roots, since $a^2 < 4b$. r_1 and r_2 are given by

$$r_1 = -\frac{a}{2} + \frac{\sqrt{4b - a^2}}{2} i = -\frac{1}{2} + \frac{\sqrt{3}}{2} i$$

and

$$r_2 = -\frac{1}{2} - \frac{\sqrt{3}}{2} i$$

Therefore

$$y^* = A \left(-\frac{1}{2} + \frac{\sqrt{3}}{2} i \right)^x + B \left(-\frac{1}{2} - \frac{\sqrt{3}}{2} i \right)^x$$

or

$$y^* = \sqrt{1}^x (\cos \theta x \pm i \sin \theta x)$$

or

$$y^* = A_2 \cos \theta x + B_2 \sin \theta x$$

To evaluate θ, we use the relations $\cos \theta = h/\sqrt{b}$ and $\sin \theta = v/\sqrt{b}$. In this particular example we have $\cos \theta = -1/2$ and $\sin \theta = \sqrt{3}/2$. From a table of trigonometric functions this corresponds to an angle of $\pi/3$ radians; that is, $\theta = \pi/3$. Thus

$$y^* = A_2 \cos\left(\frac{\pi}{3}x\right) + B_2 \sin\left(\frac{\pi}{3}x\right)$$

Since $a + b \neq -1$, we can again write

$$\bar{y} = \frac{c}{1 + a + b} = \frac{5}{3}$$

The general solution can then be written as

$$y(x) = A_2 \cos\left(\frac{\pi}{3}x\right) + B_2 \sin\left(\frac{\pi}{3}x\right) + \frac{5}{3}$$

The solution for A_2 and B_2 comes from the equation system

$$0 = A_2 \cos\left[\left(\frac{\pi}{3}\right)(0)\right] + B_2 \sin\left[\left(\frac{\pi}{3}\right)(0)\right] + \frac{5}{3}$$

and

$$1 = A_2 \cos\left[\left(\frac{\pi}{3}\right)(1)\right] + B_2 \sin\left[\left(\frac{\pi}{3}\right)(1)\right] + \frac{5}{3}$$

These equations reduce to

$$0 = A_2 + \frac{5}{3}$$

and

$$1 = A_2 \cos\frac{\pi}{3} + B_2 \sin\frac{\pi}{3} + \frac{5}{3}$$

or

$$A_2 = -\frac{5}{3}$$

and

$$1 = A_2\left(\frac{1}{2}\right) + B_2\left(\frac{\sqrt{3}}{2}\right) + \frac{5}{3}$$

which yields

$$A_2 = -\frac{5}{3} \quad \text{and} \quad B_2 = \frac{2}{\sqrt{3}} - \frac{5}{3\sqrt{3}}$$

The reader is encouraged to verify this solution.

If the constant term is replaced by some function of x, we have a variable-term difference equation. We shall consider two types of variable-term equations: those with a variable term in the form kp^x and those with a variable term in the form kx^p, where k and p are constants. In either of these cases, the methods for finding y^* are the same as before. To find $\bar{y}$ it is necessary to use, as in the case of differential equations with variable terms, the method of undetermined coefficients.

Case 1: Variable term kp^x

Try Dp^x as a solution, where D is an unknown constant. If we have a first-order difference equation,

$$y(x + 1) + ay(x) = kp^x$$

we get, by substitution,

$$Dp^{x+1} + aDp^x = kp^x$$

Factoring,

$$D(p + a)p^x = kp^x$$

or, since the coefficients of p^x must be equal,

$$D = \frac{k}{p + a}$$

Therefore

(1)
$$\bar{y} = Dp^x = \left(\frac{k}{p + a}\right)p^x$$

is the solution as long as $p + a \neq 0$. This situation will be treated later.

If we start with a second-order difference equation,

$$y(x + 2) + ay(x + 1) + by(x) = kp^x$$

we again try $\bar{y} = Dp^x$. By substitution and factoring, this leads to

$$D(p^2 + ap + b)p^x = kp^x$$

or

$$D = \frac{k}{p^2 + ap + b}$$

from which it follows that

(2)
$$\bar{y} = \left(\frac{k}{p^2 + ap + b}\right)p^x$$

if

$$p^2 + ap + b \neq 0$$

If the denominator in either (1) or (2) is zero, we must try a solution in the form Dxp^x. To illustrate, suppose we start with $y(x + 1) + 2y(x) = 5(-2)^x$.

Here $p + a = 0$ so (1) will not work. Making the indicated substitution,

$$D(x + 1)(-2)^{x+1} + 2[Dx(-2)^x] = 5(-2)^x$$

Factoring,

$$D(-2)^x[x(-2)^1 + (-2)^1 + 2x] = 5(-2)^x$$

or

$$-2D(-2)^x = 5(-2)^x$$

from which it follows that

$$D = -\tfrac{5}{2}$$

Thus $\bar{y} = Dxp^x = -\tfrac{5}{2}x(-2)^x$ is the desired solution. The reader should work through an example for a second-order difference equation.

In the case that a solution in the form Dxp^x does not work, try Dx^2p^x. If this also fails, try Dx^3p^x, and so on until a solution for $\bar{y}$ is obtained.

Case 2: Variable term kx^p

Try a solution in the form $D_0 + D_1x + D_2x^2 + \cdots + D_px^p$. If this fails to work try $x(D_0 + D_1x + \cdots + D_px^p)$, and so on until a solution for $\bar{y}$ is obtained. In this case $D_0, D_1, \ldots, D_p$ are the undetermined coefficients. We shall illustrate this technique with a specific example. Find $\bar{y}$ for

$$y(x + 2) + 2y(x + 1) + 3y(x) = x^2$$

Here $k = 1$ and $p = 2$. Thus our trial solution is $\bar{y}(x) = D_0 + D_1x + D_2x^2$. Substituting into the original equation,

$$D_0 + D_1(x + 2) + D_2(x + 2)^2 + 2[D_0 + D_1(x + 1) + D_2(x + 1)^2]$$
$$+ 3[D_0 + D_1x + D_2x^2] = x^2$$

Carrying out the algebraic dogwork and collecting terms,

$$6D_0 + 4D_1 + 6D_2 + x(6D_1 + 8D_2) + x^2(6D_2) = x^2$$

This leads to the following three simultaneous equations by equating coefficients of like powers of x:

$$6D_0 + 4D_1 + 6D_2 = 0$$
$$6D_1 + 8D_2 = 0$$
$$6D_2 = 1$$

Solving this system simultaneously yields

$$D_0 = -\tfrac{1}{54} \qquad D_1 = -\tfrac{2}{9} \qquad D_2 = \tfrac{1}{6}$$

Thus $\bar{y} = -\tfrac{1}{54} - \tfrac{2}{9}x + \tfrac{1}{6}x^2$ is the solution.

Suppose that the variable term had been $x^2 + 5x$. The same trial solution should be used. Now the simultaneous system used to solve for D_0, D_1, and D_2 becomes

$$6D_0 + 4D_1 + 6D_2 = 0$$
$$6D_1 + 8D_2 = 5$$
$$6D_2 = 1$$

or $D_0 = -\frac{31}{54}$, $D_1 = \frac{11}{18}$, and $D_2 = \frac{1}{6}$. In this case $\bar{y} = -\frac{31}{54} + \frac{11}{18}x + \frac{1}{6}x^2$ is the solution.

Higher-order difference equations can be solved with relative ease if their characteristic equation is easy to solve. Since the characteristic equations will be of degree 3 or higher, they are sometimes very difficult to solve.

The general linear nth-order difference equation with constant coefficients and constant term can be written as

$$y(x + n) + a_{n-1}y(x + n - 1) + a_{n-2}y(x + n - 2) + \cdots + a_0 y(x) = b$$

The associated characteristic equation is

$$r^n + a_{n-1}r^{n-1} + a_{n-2}r^{n-2} + \cdots + a_0 = 0$$

which has n characteristic roots, $r_1, r_2, \ldots, r_n$. If all the roots are real and distinct,

(1) $$y^* = \sum_{i=1}^{n} A_i r_i^x$$

which is analogous to our previous result. If all the roots are real but k of them are identical, (1) must be modified to

(2) $$y^* = A_1 r_1^x + A_2 x r_1^x + A_3 x^2 r_1^x + \cdots + A_k x^{k-1} r_1^x + \sum_{i=k+1}^{n} A_i r_i^x$$

Since the numbering of the roots is purely arbitrary, we have placed the identical roots in the first k slots and referred to them all as r_1. Equation (2) is also analogous to our previous results. If there are a pair of complex roots (they will, of course, always occur in pairs) then (2) becomes

$$y^* = R^x(A_1 \cos \theta x + A_2 \sin \theta x) + \sum_{i=3}^{n} A_i r_i^x$$

with R and θ defined as before. If two pairs of complex roots are identical, we have

$$y^* = R^x(A_1 \cos \theta x + A_2 \sin \theta x) + xR^x(A_3 \cos \theta x + A_4 \sin \theta x) + \sum_{i=5}^{n} A_i r_i^x$$

Thus the only theoretical problem in finding y^* is finding all the roots of the characteristic equation. In many cases this can be a problem of great difficulty.

The solution to the homogeneous version of the nth-order difference equation is found using exactly the same procedures as before. The general solution is again simply $\bar{y} + y^*$. To find the specific solution there will be n constants to evaluate, thus necessitating n initial conditions. Otherwise, finding the specific solution is simply an exercise in algebra (perhaps a very tedious one).[13]

Problems

8.3-1 Write the following difference equations in an equivalent form:
  (a) $\Delta(x^2 + 3x - 5) + 2\Delta^2(x^2 + 3x - 5) = 10$
  (b) $y(x + 2) - 3y(x + 1) - 2 = 0$
  (c) $y(x + 1) - 2y(x) + 3y(x - 1) + 2 = 0$
  (d) $\Delta^2 y(x) = 2y(x) + y(x + 1) - 3$
  (e) $\Delta y(x + 1) = y(x) - 2y(x + 1) + 3$

8.3-2 Solve the following first-order difference equations, using the given initial condition given:
  (a) $3y(x + 1) - 2y(x) = 0; y(0) = 1$
  (b) $-y(x + 1) + y(x) = -3; y(0) = 0$
  (c) $y(x + 1) + 5y(x) = 2; y(0) = 2$
  (d) $4y(x + 2) - 3y(x + 1) = 4; y(0) = -1$

8.3-3 Construct a phase diagram for the following difference equations. Is the equilibrium stable or unstable? Are there oscillations? Are they damped or explosive?
  (a) $y(x + 1) = [y(x)]^2 + 2y(x) + 1$
  (b) $y(x + 1) = [y(x)]^3 + [y(x)]^2 - 2y(x) - 2$

8.3-4 Solve the following higher-order difference equations:
  (a) $y(x + 2) - y(x + 1) + y(x) = 0; y(0) = 1, y(1) = 2$
  (b) $y(x + 2) + 3y(x + 1) - 2y(x) = 5; y(0) = 0, y(1) = \frac{1}{2}$
  (c) $y(x + 2) - 2y(x + 1) + y(x) = 3; y(0), y(1)$
  (d) $3y(x + 2) - y(x) = 5$
  (e) $2y(x + 2) - y(x + 1) = 7; y(0) = 5, y(1) = -2$
  (f) $4y(x + 2) - 3y(x) = 0; y(0) = 0, y(1) = 1$
  (g) $y(x + 2) - 2y(x + 1) + y(x) = 1; y(0) = 0, y(1) = 1$
  (h) $y(x + 2) + 4y(x + 1) + 4y(x) = 0$
  (i) $2y(x + 2) + 2y(x + 1) + y(x) = 5; y(0), y(1) = 1$

8.3-5 Solve the following variable-term difference equations for $\bar{y}$:
  (a) $y(x + 1) - 2y(x) = 3^x$
  (b) $y(x + 1) - 2y(x) = 5(2^x); y(0) = 5$
  (c) $y(x + 2) + y(x + 1) + y(x) = 2^x$
  (d) $y(x + 2) + y(x + 1) - y(x) = 2x^2$
  (e) $y(x + 2) - 3y(x + 1) + y(x) = x^3 - 2x$
  (f) $y(x + 2) - 2y(x) = x + x^2$

8.3-6 Solve the following higher-order difference equations:
  (a) $y(x + 3) + 3y(x + 2) - y(x + 1) - 3y(x) = 0$
  (b) $y(x + 4) - 3y(x + 3) + 2y(x + 2) = 0$
  (c) $y(x + 4) - 5y(x + 2) + 4y(x) = 0$
  (d) $y(x + 4) + 7y(x + 3) + 5y(x + 2) - 7y(x + 1) - 6y(x) = 0$

---

[13] This topic is covered again in more detail in Chapter 9.

8.4   EXISTENCE AND STABILITY OF SOLUTIONS TO DIFFERENTIAL AND DIFFERENCE EQUATIONS

This section is designed to treat explicitly some important topics either only hinted at or omitted from our previous discussion of differential and difference equations. In particular we are interested in the interpretation of the two parts of the general solution, $\bar{y}$ and y^*.

We know already that $\bar{y}$ represents *any* solution to the complete differential or difference equation, while y^* represents the family of solutions to the homogeneous version of the equation. By Theorem 7.1–1, $\bar{y} + y^*$ is the general solution to the equation.

Theorem 8.4–1   Given a general differential or difference equation and its general solution $y(x) = \bar{y}(x) + y^*(x)$. Then $\bar{y}(x)$ is a function of x such that either:

(a) $\lim\limits_{x \to \infty} |y(x) - \bar{y}(x)| = k, 0 < k < \infty$;

(b) $\lim\limits_{x \to \infty} |y(x) - \bar{y}(x)| = 0$; or

(c) $\lim\limits_{x \to \infty} |y(x) - \bar{y}(x)|$ does not exist.

PROOF   Since $y(x) - \bar{y}(x) = y^*(x)$, parts (a), (b), and (c) correspond to $\lim_{x \to \infty} |y^*(x)| = k, 0 < k < \infty$; $\lim_{x \to \infty} |y^*(x)| = 0$; and $\lim_{x \to \infty} |y^*(x)| = \pm \infty$. This exhausts the possibilities for $\lim_{x \to \infty} |y^*(x)|$.   QED

While this is certainly a candidate for the world's most trivial theorem, our reasons for stating it are not. This theorem is the rationale for considering $\bar{y}(x)$ to be the equilibrium value of $y(x)$ and $y^*(x)$ to be a measure of the deviation of $y(x)$ from its equilibrium level. Let us translate parts (a), (b), and (c) of the "theorem" to more common-sense terms. If (a) holds, there are perpetual oscillations about $\bar{y}(x)$. $y(x)$ may reach temporarily its "equilibrium" value, but never stay there for more than one value of x. Figure 8.4–1 illustrates such a situation. If (b) holds, there are two possibilities: Either $y(x)$ approaches $\bar{y}(x)$ directly or there are damped oscillations about $\bar{y}(x)$. Figure 8.4–2 illustrates such a situation. If (c) holds $y(x)$ "explodes away from" $\bar{y}(x)$. Again there are two possibilities, illustrated in Figure 8.4–3. On the basis of this discussion we have Definition 8.4–1.

DEFINITION 8.4–1   The general solution to a differential or difference equation is said to be **dynamically stable** if $\lim_{x \to \infty} |y^*(x)| = 0$.

In the previous diagrams we have graphed $\bar{y}(x)$ as though it were a constant. In general, of course, this need not be the case. If $\bar{y}(x)$ is a true function of x rather than a constant, the previous discussion holds. Now, however, we are

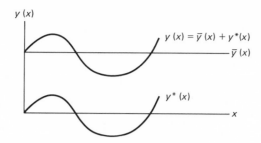

Figure 8.4–1 *Perpetual oscillations about "equilibrium."*

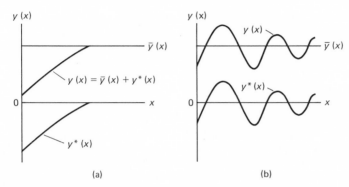

Figure 8.4–2 (a) $y(x) \to \bar{y}(x)$ as $x \to \infty$, no oscillations. (b) Damped oscillations about $\bar{y}(x)$.

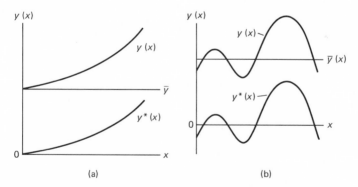

Figure 8.4–3 (a) No oscillations. (b) Explosive oscillations.

dealing with moving rather than stationary equilibria. Figure 8.4–4 illustrates a dynamically stable, moving equilibrium. Note that in the figure $\bar{y}(x)$ is assumed to be a linear function of x. Other functions are, of course, encountered.

Since $\lim_{x \to \infty} |y^*(x)|$ plays the central role in this analysis, Table 8.4–1 summarizes our results for both differential and difference equations and

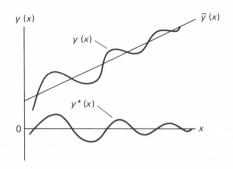

Figure 8.4-4   *Dynamically stable, moving equilibrium.*

indicates on what convergence to equilibrium, (i.e., $\lim_{x \to \infty} |y(x)| = 0$) depends. The reader should work out any relation in the table of which he is unsure.

Having discussed the stability of equilibrium for types of equations we can solve directly, we now consider two theorems that give us some information

Table 8.4–1

	Differential	*Difference*
First order	$y(x) = Ae^{-ax}$ converges if $|a| < 1$, oscillates perpetually if $|a| = 1$, diverges if $|a| > 1$	$y(x) = A(-f)^x$ converges if $|f| < 1$, oscillates perpetually if $|f| = 1$, diverges if $|f| > 1$
Second order, equal real roots	$y(x) = A_1e^{rx} + A_2xe^{rx}$ converges if $r < 0$, diverges if $r > 0$	$y(x) = A_1r^x + A_2xr^x$ converges if $|r| < 1$, diverges if $|r| > 1$
Second order, unequal real roots	$y(x) = A_1e^{r_1x} + A_2e^{r_2x}$ converges if r_1 and $r_2 < 0$, diverges if either r_1 or $r_2 > 0$	$y(x) = A_1r_1^x + A_2r_2^x$ converges if $|r_1|$ and $|r_2| < 1$, diverges if either $|r_1|$ or $|r_2| > 1$
Second order, imaginary roots	$y(x) = e^{ux}(A_1e^{vix}$ $\qquad + A_2e^{-vix})$ converges if $v < 0$ oscillates constantly if $v = 0$, diverges if $v > 0$	$y(x) = R^x(A_1 \cos \theta x$ $\qquad + A_2 \sin \theta x)$ converges if $R < 1$ (i.e., $|r_1|$ and $|r_2| < 1$) (why?)

about the nature of the solutions to higher-order equations without having actually to solve them.

Theorem 8.4–2 *Schur Theorem* Given an nth-order difference equation with characteristic equation $a_n r^n + a_{n-1} r^{n-1} + \cdots + a_1 r + a_0 = 0$. The absolute value of each root is less than one, and thus $y(x)$ converges to $\bar{y}(x)$ if and only if all n of the following determinants are positive:

$$D_1 = \begin{vmatrix} a_n & a_0 \\ a_0 & a_n \end{vmatrix}$$

$$D_2 = \begin{vmatrix} a_n & 0 & a_0 & a_1 \\ a_{n-1} & a_n & 0 & a_0 \\ a_0 & 0 & a_n & a_{n-1} \\ a_1 & a_0 & 0 & a_n \end{vmatrix}, \ldots,$$

$$D_n = \begin{vmatrix} a_n & 0 & \cdots & 0 & a_0 & a_1 & \cdots & a_n \\ a_{n-1} & a_n & \cdots & 0 & 0 & a_0 & \cdots & a_{n-1} \\ \vdots & & & & \vdots & & & \\ a_1 & a_2 & \cdots & a_n & 0 & 0 & \cdots & a_0 \\ a_0 & 0 & \cdots & 0 & a_n & a_{n-1} & \cdots & a_1 \\ a_1 & a_0 & \cdots & 0 & 0 & a_n & \cdots & a_2 \\ \vdots & & & & \vdots & & & \\ a_n & a_{n-1} & \cdots & a_0 & 0 & 0 & \cdots & a_n \end{vmatrix}$$

Notice that the opposite corners of the determinants are symmetric.

Theorem 8.4–3 *Routh–Hurwitz Theorem*[14] Given an nth-order differential equation with the characteristic equation $a_n r^n + a_{n-1} r^{n-1} + \cdots + a_1 r + a_0 = 0$. The real parts of the roots of this equation will be negative and thus $y(x)$ converges to $\bar{y}(x)$ if and only if the following determinants are all positive:

$$D_1 = |a_{n-1}|$$

$$D_2 = \begin{vmatrix} a_{n-1} & a_{n-3} \\ a_n & a_{n-2} \end{vmatrix}$$

$$D_3 = \begin{vmatrix} a_{n-1} & a_{n-3} & a_{n-4} \\ a_n & a_{n-2} & a_{n-3} \\ 0 & a_{n-1} & a_{n-2} \end{vmatrix}$$

$$D_4 = \begin{vmatrix} a_{n-1} & a_{n-3} & a_{n-5} & a_{n-7} \\ a_n & a_{n-2} & a_{n-4} & a_{n-6} \\ 0 & a_{n-1} & a_{n-3} & a_{n-5} \\ 0 & a_n & a_{n-2} & a_{n-4} \end{vmatrix}, \ldots$$

[14] Cf. Theorem 9.4–2.

These two theorems provide means for testing higher-order equations for convergence when their general solution is difficult to obtain. The reader may care to apply them to second-order equations whose convergence properties are already known.

Example 1.   Test $y(x + 3) + 2y(x + 2) + 5y(x + 1) + y(x) = 10$ for convergence. Using the Schur theorem, the determinants to be evaluated are

$$D_1 = \begin{vmatrix} 1 & 1 \\ 1 & 1 \end{vmatrix} \qquad D_2 = \begin{vmatrix} 1 & 0 & 1 & 5 \\ 2 & 1 & 0 & 1 \\ 1 & 0 & 1 & 2 \\ 5 & 1 & 0 & 1 \end{vmatrix} \qquad D_3 = \begin{vmatrix} 1 & 0 & 0 & 1 & 5 & 2 \\ 2 & 1 & 0 & 0 & 1 & 5 \\ 5 & 2 & 1 & 0 & 0 & 5 \\ 1 & 0 & 0 & 1 & 2 & 5 \\ 5 & 1 & 0 & 0 & 1 & 2 \\ 2 & 5 & 5 & 0 & 0 & 1 \end{vmatrix}$$

However, $D_1 = 0$, which violates the condition that all the determinants be positive. Thus the equation does not converge.

Example 2.   Test $2y''' + 5y'' + y' = 0$ for convergence. The Routh–Hurwitz determinants for this equation are

$$D_1 = \begin{vmatrix} 5 \end{vmatrix} \qquad D_2 = \begin{vmatrix} 5 & 0 \\ 2 & 1 \end{vmatrix} \qquad D_3 = \begin{vmatrix} 5 & 0 & 0 \\ 2 & 1 & 0 \\ 0 & 5 & 0 \end{vmatrix}$$

D_1 and D_2 are positive, but $D_3 = 0$. Thus the equation does not converge.

Before ending this section, let us note that the phase-diagram approach outlined in the previous section can be applied just as well to differential equations as difference equations. It serves as another method for ascertaining the properties of the solutions to differential and difference equations without actually solving them. In some cases it may be a more fruitful approach than the methods of the previous two theorems.

Problems

8.4–1   Do the difference equations in Problems 8.3–2 and 8.3–4 converge to or diverge from equilibrium? If there are oscillations, are they damped or explosive?

8.4–2   Same question for the differential equations in Problem 7.1–2

8.4–3   Use the Schur theorem to test the following difference equations for convergence:

(a) $y(x + 3) - y(x + 2) + 7y(x + 1) - 3y(x) = 0$

(b) $y(x + 4) - y(x + 2) + 8y(x + 1) - 2y(x) = 0$

(c) $y(x + 3) + 5y(x + 2) + 7y(x) = 0$

8.4–4   Use the Routh–Hurwitz theorem to test the following differential equations for convergence:

(a) $3 \dfrac{d^3 y}{dx^3} - 2 \dfrac{d^2 y}{dx^2} + 5 \dfrac{dy}{dx} = 3$ (c) $4 \dfrac{d^4 y}{dx^4} + \dfrac{d^3 y}{dx^3} + 3 \dfrac{d^2 y}{dx^2} - 2 \dfrac{dy}{dx} = 5$

(b) $\dfrac{d^3 y}{dx^3} + \dfrac{d^2 y}{dx^2} + 5 \dfrac{dy}{dx} = 0$

8.5   THE SUMMATION CALCULUS AND INFINITE SERIES

The general technique for finding expressions for the sum of series with either a finite or an infinite number of terms is known as the summation calculus. It is analogous to the integral calculus. In the first part of this section we shall examine some of the techniques for summing series with a finite number of terms (finite series) and in the latter part we shall examine the concept and some applications for testing convergence of a series with an infinite number of terms (infinite series).

DEFINITION 8.5–1   The **sum of** $f(x)$ from $x = a$ to $x = b$, written $\sum_a^b f(x)$, is

$$f(a) + f(a + 1) + f(a + 2) + \cdots + f(b)$$

where $b > a$.

Before examining some specific summation methods, we note the following important property of the summation operator, $\sum$.

Theorem 8.5–1   *Linearity of Summation*   Given any two constants, c and d, and two functions of x, $f(x)$ and $g(x)$, then

$$\sum_a^b [cf(x) + dg(x)] = c \sum_a^b f(x) + d \sum_a^b g(x)$$

PROOF   The fact that the constants c and d may be "taken outside" the summation sign follows immediately, since $\sum_a^b cf(x) = cf(a) + cf(a + 1) + \cdots + cf(b) = c[f(a) + f(a + 1) + \cdots + f(b)] = c \sum_a^b f(x)$. This portion of the theorem is analogous to $\int cf(x)\, dx = c \int f(x)\, dx$. To prove the other part of the theorem, note that $\sum_a^b [f(x) + g(x)] = f(a) + g(a) + f(a + 1) + g(a + 1) + \cdots + f(b) + g(b)$. By simply changing the order of addition and applying Definition 8.5–1, this is equal to $f(a) + f(a + 1) + \cdots + f(b) + g(a) + g(a + 1) + \cdots + g(b) = \sum_a^b f(x) + \sum_a^b g(x)$. QED.

This corresponds to the linearity of the integration operator; that is, $\int [f(x) + g(x)]\, dx = \int f(x)\, dx + \int g(x)\, dx$.

Theorem 8.5–2 contains another result of the summation calculus that is closely analogous to a basic result of the integral calculus.

Theorem 8.5–2 $\sum_a^{b-1} \Delta f(x) = f(b) - f(a)$.

This, of course, is analogous to $\int_a^b f'(x)\, dx = f(b) - f(a)$, the key result for evaluating definite integrals.

PROOF   By definition, $\Delta f(x) = f(x + 1) - f(x)$. Thus $\sum_a^{b-1} \Delta f(x) = \sum_a^{b-1} [f(x + 1) - f(x)]$. Applying the definition of the sum, we can write

$$\sum_a^{b-1} [f(x + 1) - f(x)] = \left\{ \begin{array}{l} f(a + 1) - f(a) \\ + \quad f(a + 2) - f(a + 1) \\ + \quad f(a + 3) - f(a + 2) \\ \vdots \\ + \quad f(b) - f(b - 1) \end{array} \right\} = f(b) - f(a)$$

Note that every term except $f(a)$ and $f(b)$ appears twice, once with a positive sign and once with a negative sign.   QED

It is important to note that the upper limit of summation is $b - 1$ and not b. However, it is easy to show that $\sum_a^b \Delta f(x) = f(b + 1) - f(a)$.

The result of Theorem 8.5–2, combined with the concept of factorial functions defined in Section 8.2, provide a useful technique for summing series. Factorial functions were defined in such a way that

(1) $$\Delta x^{(n)} = n x^{(n-1)}$$

Dividing (1) by n and letting $m = n - 1$, we have

(2) $$x^{(m)} = \frac{\Delta x^{(n)}}{n} = \frac{\Delta x^{(m+1)}}{m + 1}$$

Equation (2) permits us to write $\sum_a^b x^{(m)}$ as

$$\sum_a^b \frac{\Delta x^{(m+1)}}{m + 1}$$

which, by Theorem 8.5–1, is equal to

$$\frac{1}{m + 1} \sum_a^b \Delta x^{(m+1)}$$

By Theorem 8.4–2, this expression is equal to

$$\frac{1}{m + 1} [b^{(m+1)} - a^{(m+1)}]$$

Combining these results we have

(3)
$$\sum_{a}^{b-1} x^{(m)} = \frac{b^{(m+1)} - a^{(m+1)}}{m + 1}$$

This result allows us to sum series of powers of x by converting the polynomial to factorial functions. One of the easiest conversion methods is through use of Stirling numbers of the second kind.[15]

DEFINITION 8.5–2 **Stirling numbers,** $S(m, k)$, satisfy

$$x^m = \sum_{k=0}^{m} S(m, k)x^{(k)}$$

Consider the case where $m = 1$. Then we have

(4)
$$x = S(1, 0)x^{(0)} + S(1, 1)x^{(1)}$$

Since $x^{(0)} = 1$ and $x^{(1)} = x$, Equation (4) becomes

$$x = S(1, 0) + S(1, 1)x$$

from which it follows that $S(1, 0) = 0$ and $S(1, 1) = 1$. In the case where $m = 2$ we have

$$x^2 = S(2, 0) + S(2, 1)x + S(2, 2)x(x - 1)$$

From which it follows that $S(2, 0) = 0$, $S(2, 1) = 1$, and $S(2, 2) = 1$. If we were to proceed in this manner, it would become apparent that $S(m, 0) = 0$ and $S(m, m) = 1$ for all m. Furthermore, this procedure would yield the following recurrence relation from which the Stirling numbers can be calculated:

(5)
$$S(m + 1, k) = S(m, k - 1) + kS(m, k)$$

Equation (5) has been used to tabulate the partial listing of Stirling numbers in Table 8.5–1.

As an example of the use of Stirling numbers, consider the problem of finding $\sum_{x=1}^{p} x^3$. Here $m = 3$, so we can write

$$\sum_{x=1}^{p} x^3 = \sum_{1}^{p} (x^{(3)} + 3x^{(2)} + x^{(1)})$$

which, by Equation (3) can be written as

$$\frac{(p + 1)^{(4)} - 1^{(4)}}{4} + 3\left[\frac{(p + 1)^{(3)} - 1^{(3)}}{3}\right] + \frac{(p + 1)^{(2)} - 1^{(2)}}{2}$$

[15] For a discussion of Stirling numbers of the first kind, see Hamming (1962), pages 18–19. In the rest of this section, when we refer to Stirling numbers we mean Stirling numbers of the second kind.

Table 8.5–1 Stirling Numbers

m \ k	1	2	3	4	5	6
1	1	—	—	—	—	—
2	1	1	—	—	—	—
3	1	3	1	—	—	—
4	1	7	6	1	—	—
5	1	15	25	10	1	—
6	1	31	90	65	15	1

By the definition of factorial functions, this can be written as

$$\frac{(p + 1)(p)(p - 1)(p - 2) + 4(p + 1)(p)(p - 1) + 2(p + 1)(p)}{4}$$

By some rather tedious algebra, this expression can be shown to be equal to

$$\left[\frac{(p + 1)p}{2}\right]^2$$

Thus we have $\sum_{x=1}^{p} x^3 = [(p + 1)(p)/2]^2$. If $p = 5$, then $\sum_{1}^{5} x^3 = [(6)(5)/2]^2 = 15^2 = 225$.

This technique can also be used to sum more complicated polynomial, as well as other types of series.

Example 1. Find $\sum_{x=1}^{p} (3x^3 + 2x^2 - 10x)$. Without carrying out all the actual algebra involved, we proceed in the following manner. First, by Theorem 8.5–1, this is equal to $3 \sum_{1}^{p} x^3 + 2 \sum_{1}^{p} x^2 - 10 \sum_{1}^{p} x$, which in turn can be written as $3 \sum_{1}^{p} (x^{(3)} + 3x^{(2)} + x^{(1)}) + 2 \sum_{1}^{p} (x^{(2)} + x^{(1)}) - 10 \sum_{1}^{p} x^{(1)}$. Collecting terms, we have $3 \sum_{1}^{p} x^{(3)} + 11 \sum_{1}^{p} x^{(2)} - 5 \sum_{1}^{p} x^{(1)}$. By relation (3) this expression is

$$3\left[\frac{(p + 1)^{(4)} - 1^{(4)}}{4}\right] + 11\left[\frac{(p + 1)^{(3)} - 1^{(3)}}{3}\right] - 5\left[\frac{(p + 1)^{(2)} - 1^{(2)}}{2}\right]$$

or, since $1^{(4)} = 1^{(3)} = 1^{(2)} = 0$,

$$\tfrac{3}{4}(p + 1)(p)(p - 1)(p - 2) + \tfrac{11}{3}(p + 1)(p)(p - 1) - \tfrac{5}{2}(p + 1)(p)$$

Further simplification involves only algebraic manipulations.[16]

Before turning to an examination of infinite series, we shall briefly examine the summation calculus counterpart to integration by parts, summation by parts. This technique is sometimes useful in converting series that are hard to sum to ones easier to sum.

---

[16] For a more complete discussion of summation techniques for finite series the reader is referred to Hamming (1962) or to Jolley (1925). These references discuss techniques using synthetic division, present more complete tables of Stirling numbers of the first and second kind, and provide lists of various summation formulas.

The technique itself is based on the formula for the difference of a product of two functions, that is,

$$\Delta[f(x)g(x)] = f(x)\,\Delta g(x) + g(x + 1)\,\Delta f(x)$$

Suppose we were asked to find $\sum_0^p f(x)\,\Delta g(x)$. From the preceding expression, this is equal to $\sum_0^p \{\Delta[f(x)g(x)] - g(x + 1)\,\Delta f(x)\}$. By the linearity of the operator and Theorem 8.5–1, this expression is

$$f(p + 1)g(p + 1) - f(0)g(0) - \sum_0^p g(x + 1)\,\Delta f(x)$$

If the last sum in this expression is easier to evaluate than the original series, summation by parts is worthwhile. In general, the type of series to which summation by parts can be applied profitably are the same expressions that can be integrated by parts were they to appear in an integration problem.

Example 2. Find $\sum_{x=0}^9 xe^x$. To put this in the form $\sum f(x)\,\Delta g(x)$, let $f(x) = x$ and $\Delta g(x) = e^x$. Then $\Delta f(x) = 1$, while $g(x) = e^x/(e - 1)$. Therefore

$$\sum_{x=0}^9 xe^x = 10\left(\frac{e^{10}}{e - 1}\right) - 0\left(\frac{1}{e - 1}\right) - \sum_{x=0}^9 \frac{e^{x+1}}{e - 1}$$

However,

$$\sum_0^9 \frac{e^{x+1}}{e - 1} = \frac{e}{e - 1}\sum_0^9 e^x$$

Since $e^x = \Delta e^{x+1}/(e - 1)$, by Theorem 8.5–2,

$$\frac{e}{e - 1}\sum_0^9 e^x = \left(\frac{e}{e - 1}\right)\frac{e^{11} - e}{e - 1} = \frac{e^2(e^{10} - 1)}{(e - 1)^2}$$

Thus we have the result:

$$\sum_{x=0}^9 xe^x = \frac{10e^{10}}{e - 1} - \frac{e^2(e^{10} - 1)}{(e - 1)^2}$$

We turn now to an examination of infinite series.

DEFINITION 8.5–3 A **sequence** is a collection of ordered pairs, (i, s_i), where the i's are positive integers and the s_i are numbers, one associated with each positive integer i. The notation $\{s_i\}$ denotes a sequence.

DEFINITION 8.5–4 A sequence, $\{s_i\}$, is said to have a **limit** L, written $\lim_{i \to \infty} s_i = L$, if there exists a positive number δ for every positive number ε, such that whenever i is greater than δ, $|L - s_i| < \varepsilon$.

Intuitively, $\{s_i\}$ has a limit L if its values tend to cluster around L as i increases. See Figure 8.5–1. If a sequence $\{s_i\}$ has a limit, the sequence is said to converge; if it has no limit, the sequence diverges. The concept of the limit of a sequence is important in understanding what is meant by the limit of an infinite series.

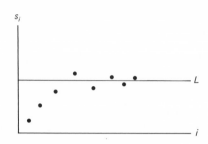

Figure 8.5–1   *Limit of a sequence.*

Consider the infinite series $\sum_{i=1}^{\infty} a_i$. Define the following sequence constricted from the series:

$$s_1 = a_1$$
$$s_2 = a_1 + a_2$$
$$s_3 = a_1 + a_2 + a_3$$
$$\vdots$$
$$s_n = \sum_{i=1}^{n} a_i$$

The sequence $\{s_i\}$ formed in this way is called the sequence of partial sums of the series $\sum_{i=1}^{\infty} a_i$.

DEFINITION 8.5–5   If the sequence of partial sums $\{s_i\}$ converges to a limit L as $i \to \infty$, then the **series converges** and its sum is L, written

$$\sum_{i=1}^{\infty} a_i = \lim_{n \to \infty} \sum_{i=1}^{n} a_i = L$$

If the sequence of partial sums has no limit, the **series diverges.**

Theorem 8.5–3 is obvious from the preceding discussion.

Theorem 8.5–3   *Necessary Condition for Convergence*   If the infinite series $\sum_{i=1}^{\infty} a_i = a_1 + a_2 + \cdots + a_n + \cdots$ converges, it must be true that $\lim_{i \to \infty} a_i = 0$.

The proof follows directly from what has been said about the convergence of the sequence of partial sums of $\sum_{i=1}^{\infty} a_i$.

Note that Theorem 8.5-3 is not a sufficient condition for a series to converge. Consider the series

$$1 + \tfrac{1}{2} + \tfrac{1}{2} + \tfrac{1}{4} + \tfrac{1}{4} + \tfrac{1}{4} + \tfrac{1}{4} + \tfrac{1}{8} + \tfrac{1}{8} + \tfrac{1}{8} + \tfrac{1}{8} + \tfrac{1}{8} + \tfrac{1}{8} + \tfrac{1}{8} + \tfrac{1}{8}$$

$$+ \cdots + \underbrace{\tfrac{1}{2}k + \tfrac{1}{2}k + \cdots + \tfrac{1}{2}k}_{2^k \text{ terms}} + \cdots$$

This series obviously does not converge (sum) even though $\lim_{i \to \infty} a_i = 0$.

Testing for convergence and finding the sum of an infinite series thus involves evaluation of limits. We shall illustrate how this can be done for some special types of series and some general techniques for "atypical" series.

DEFINITION 8.5–6   A **geometric series** is one in which the ratio of any two "adjacent" terms is a constant; that is, a geometric series is one of the form

$$a + ar + ar^2 + ar^3 + \cdots + ar^n + \cdots$$

The ratio of any two adjacent terms is r.

Theorem 8.5–4   A geometric series, $\sum_{i=0}^{\infty} ar^i$, converges to $a/(1 - r)$ if $|r| < 1$ and diverges if $|r| \geq 1$.

PROOF   The nth partial sum of the series is

(1) $$s_n = a + ar + ar^2 + \cdots + ar^{n-1}$$

Multiply (1) by r. Then

(2) $$rs_n = ar + ar^2 + \cdots + ar^n$$

Subtracting (2) from (1) we obtain

(3) $$(1 - r)s_n = a(1 - r^n)$$

Dividing (3) through by $(1 - r)$, which is permissible as long as r is not equal to 1,

(4) $$s_n = \frac{a(1 - r^n)}{1 - r}$$

Thus

$$\lim_{n \to \infty} s_n = \lim_{n \to \infty} \frac{a(1 - r^n)}{1 - r} = \frac{a}{1 - r}$$

since $r^n \to 0$ as $n \to \infty$ if $|r| < 1$. This proves the theorem for $|r| < 1$. If $|r| > 1$ then the series diverges, since $\lim_{n\to\infty} r^n = \infty$. The reader should persuade himself that the series diverges for $r = +1$ or -1.   QED

Example 3.   Find $\sum_{i=0}^{\infty} 10/2^i$. This is a geometric series with $a = 10$ and $r = \frac{1}{2}$. Its sum is $10/(1 - \frac{1}{2}) = 10/\frac{1}{2} = 20$.

The following theorem is the basis for most of the techniques for testing a positive series (one whose terms are all positive) for convergence.

Theorem 8.5–5   *Comparison Test 1*   Given that $\sum_{i=0}^{\infty} s_i$ converges to a limit S. Then $\sum_{i=0}^{\infty} t_i$ converges to a limit $T \leq S$ if $t_i \leq s_i$ for all i. (s_i and $t_i \geq 0$ for all i.)

The proof of this theorem is left as an exercise.

The theorem simply says that a given series converges if there is another series that is term-by-term larger than the given series that converges. Many of the tests for convergence are thus comparison tests. A series whose convergence property is not known is compared term by term to a series that is known to converge. We also have a companion theorem to Theorem 8.5–5.

Theorem 8.5–6   *Comparison Test 2*   Given that $\sum_{i=0}^{\infty} s_i$ diverges, then $\sum_{i=0}^{\infty} t_i$ diverges if $t_i \geq s_i$ for all i. (t_i and $s_i \geq 0$ for all i.)

Two of the more useful test series are the geometric series and the "p series."

DEFINITION 8.5–7   A series of the form

$$\sum_{i=1}^{\infty} \frac{1}{i^p} = 1 + \frac{1}{2^p} + \frac{1}{3^p} + \cdots$$

is called a p **series.**

Theorem 8.5–7   The p series converges for values of $p > 1$ and diverges for all other values of p.[17]

Theorem 8.5–8   A series of the form $\sum_{i=2}^{\infty} 1/i(\log i)^p$ converges for $p > 1$ and diverges for all other values of p.[17]

Thus Theorems 8.5–4, 8.5–7, and 8.5–8 provide us with three general test series with which the convergence of some series may be determined using the results of Theorems 8.5–5 and 8.5–6.

Some other useful tests for the convergence of positive series are given in the following theorems.

Theorem 8.5–9   *D'Alembert's Ratio Test*   A series $\sum_{i=1}^{\infty} s_i$ converges if $s_i > 0$ for all i and if $\lim_{i\to\infty} s_{i+1}/s_i = L < 1$. If $L > 1$, $\sum_{i=1}^{\infty} s_i$ diverges

---

[17] For proofs of these theorems see Widder (1961), pages 289–290.

and if $L = 1$, D'Alembert's ratio test fails, that is, $\sum_{i=1}^{\infty} s_i$ may either diverge or converge.

PROOF   With $L < 1$, we have $s_{i+1}/s_i < r$, where $L < r < 1$. Since this holds for any two adjacent terms we have $s_{i+k} < r^k s_i$ for $k = 1, 2, \ldots$. s_i is one particular term of the series and the right side of the previous inequality is a representative term from a convergent geometric series, since $|r| < 1$. By comparison test 1, $\sum_{i=1}^{\infty} s_i$ converges for $L < 1$. The reader should satisfy himself that the series diverges for $L > 1$. (Hint: Apply Theorem 8.5–3.)

Theorem 8.5–10   *Cauchy's Test*   The series $\sum_{i=1}^{\infty} s_i$ converges if $s_i > 0$ for all i and if $\lim_{i \to \infty} \sqrt[i]{s_i} = L < 1$. If $L > 1$ the series diverges. For $L = 1$, Cauchy's test fails.

The proof of Cauchy's test follows the proof of the previous theorem.

Theorem 8.5–11   *Maclaurin's Integral Test*   Given $y = f(x)$ is a continuous, nonnegative, nonincreasing function of x. Then $\sum_{i=1}^{\infty} f(i)$ converges if $\lim_{b \to \infty} \int_1^b f(x)\, dx$ is finite. If $\lim_{b \to \infty} \int_1^b f(x)\, dx$ is infinite (does not exist), $\sum_{i=1}^{\infty} f(i)$ diverges.[18]
Maclaurin's integral test is used to prove that the p series and the third test series developed above converge.

Thus far we have restricted ourselves to a discussion of the convergence of series of all positive terms. Another important type of series is the alternating series, whose terms alternate in sign. These series, and negative series (ones whose terms are all negative), require the concepts of absolute and conditional convergence.

DEFINITION 8.5–8   The series $\sum_{i=1}^{\infty} s_i$ **converges absolutely** if and only if $\sum_{i=1}^{\infty} |s_i|$ converges ($s_i \gtrless 0$).

DEFINITION 8.5–9   The series $\sum_{i=1}^{\infty} s_i$ **converges conditionally** if and only if it converges and $\sum_{i=1}^{\infty} |s_i|$ diverges absolutely ($s_i \gtrless 0$).

For $\sum_1^{\infty} s_i$ to converge absolutely, $\sum_1^{\infty} |s_i|$ must converge. On the other hand, if $\sum_1^{\infty} s_i$ converges while the series of absolute values diverges, then $\sum_1^{\infty} s_i$ is said to converge conditionally. Thus if the series of absolute values converges, we can be assured that the original series converges (absolutely). If, however, $\sum_1^{\infty} |s_i|$ diverges, it does not necessarily follow that $\sum_1^{\infty} s_i$ diverges. The following theorem is useful for testing for conditional convergence when a series diverges absolutely.

[18] Widder (1961), page 289.

Theorem 8.5–12   *Convergence of Alternating Series*   Given a series $\sum_1^\infty (-1)^i s_i$. If:

(1) each term alternates in sign;

(2) $s_i \geq s_{i+1}$ for all i (each term is strictly nonincreasing); and

(3) $\lim_{i\to\infty} s_i = 0$

then the series converges.

Note that if $\sum_1^\infty |s_i|$ diverges, the series of Theorem 8.5–12 converges conditionally. If $\sum_1^\infty |s_i|$ converges the series $\sum_1^\infty (-1)^i s_i$ converges absolutely.[19]

Example 4.   Suppose the banking system is composed of a large number of independent banks. Reserve requirements are $r\%$ and apply to all types of deposits. Each bank holds $e\%$ of its total deposits in excess reserves. In addition, only $c\%$ of every check written is redeposited in another bank in the system. Suppose $100 in currency is deposited in bank A. By how much does the level of bank deposits increase? As we shall see, answering this question depends on being able to find the limit of an infinite series.

Deposits in bank A increase by $100. Required reserves and excess reserves increase by $100r$ and $100e$, respectively. Thus, of the original increase in deposits $(1 - e - r)(100)$ can be used to increase either loans or investments. Suppose the bank loans out the entire amount.[20] This amount is credited to the borrower's account. He subsequently uses the loan to make a purchase of $(1 - e - r)100$ and writes a check for this amount. Under our assumption, the person receiving the check will deposit only $c(1 - e - r)100$ in his bank. The rest will be held either in currency or deposited in a nonbank financial institution.

Now deposits in a second bank have increased by $(c - ce - cr)100$. Required and excess reserves increase by $(e + r)(c - ce - cr)100$, while loans increase by $(1 - e - r)(c - ce - cr)100$. Thus deposits in still another bank increase by $c(1 - e - r)(c - ce - cr)100 = (c - ce - cr)^2 100$. This leads to an increase in deposits in yet another bank of $(c - ce - cr)^3 100$.

Thus, after four banks, the increase in deposits is

$$\$100 + \$(c - ce - cr)100 + (c - ce - cr)^2 100 + (c - ce - cr)^3 100$$

or

$$\$100 + \sum_{i=1}^{3} \$(c - ce - cr)^i 100$$

[19] Again see Widder (1961) for a proof.

[20] The reader should convince himself that the results of the analysis would be the same whether banks increase loans or investments as a result of increase in deposits.

The total increase in deposits is given by

$$(1) \qquad \$100 + \sum_{i=1}^{\infty} (c - ce - cr)^i 100$$

As is easily verified, (1) is a geometric series, where $c - ce - cr$ is less than 1. Thus we have an infinite series to which we can apply Theorem 8.5–4. Consequently (1) converges to

$$\$100 + \frac{1}{1 - (c - ce - cr)} (100) = \$100 + \frac{100}{1 + ce + cr - c}$$

Suppose $r = 20\%$, $c = 10\%$, and $e = 25\%$. The total increase in deposits is

$$\$100 + \frac{\$100}{1 + \frac{1}{10}\frac{1}{4} + \frac{1}{10}\frac{1}{5} - \frac{1}{10}} = \$100 + \frac{\$100}{\frac{189}{200}} = \$205.81$$

This same general technique can be used to develop many of the "multipliers" in economic theory.

Problems

8.5–1 Sum the following series using Stirling numbers:

(a) $\displaystyle\sum_{1}^{p} x^2$

(b) $\displaystyle\sum_{1}^{p} (x + 1)^3$

8.5–2 Sum the following series by parts:

$$\sum_{0}^{3} x^2 e^x$$

8.5–3 Which of the following series converge? Diverge? Find the limit for those that converge.

(a) $\displaystyle\sum_{i=0}^{\infty} \frac{2i + 1}{1 - 3i}$

(e) $\displaystyle\sum_{i=1}^{\infty} \frac{1}{5^i}$

(b) $\displaystyle\sum_{i=0}^{\infty} 2 + \frac{(-1)^i}{i}$

(f) $\displaystyle\sum_{i=1}^{\infty} \frac{i^2}{2^i}$

(c) $\displaystyle\sum_{i=0}^{\infty} 2 + (-1)^i$

(g) $\displaystyle\sum_{i=1}^{\infty} \frac{1}{1 + \ln i}$

(d) $\displaystyle\sum_{i=0}^{\infty} e^{-i} + i$

8.5–4   The following series all converge absolutely for some range of values of x. Find that range.

(a) $\displaystyle\sum_{i=0}^{\infty} x^i$

(b) $\displaystyle\sum_{i=1}^{\infty} i^3 x^i$

8.5–5   Do the following alternating series converge, diverge, converge conditionally, or converge absolutely?

(a) $\displaystyle\sum_{i=0}^{\infty} (-1)^i x^i$ (b) $\displaystyle\sum_{i=0}^{\infty} (-1)^i (i + 1)(x - 1)^i$

References

1. ALLEN, R. G. D. (1958), *Mathematical Economics*, London: Macmillan.
2. BAUMOL, W. J. (1970), *Economic Dynamics: An Introduction*, 3rd ed. London: Macmillan.
3. HAMMING, R. W. (1962), *Numerical Methods for Scientists and Engineers*, New York: McGraw-Hill.
4. JOLLEY, L. B. W. (1925), *Summation of Series*, London: Chapman-Hall.
5. JORDAN, C. (1939), *Calculus of Finite Differences*, New York: Chelsea.
6. MILNE-THOMPSON, L. M. (1951), *Calculus of Finite Differences*, London: Macmillan.
7. RICHARDSON, C. R. (1954), *An Introduction to the Calculus of Finite Differences*, New York: Van Nostrand Reinhold.
8. SAATY, T. (1967), *Modern Nonlinear Equations*, New York: McGraw-Hill.
9. SAATY, T., and J. BRAM (1964), *Nonlinear Mathematics*, New York: McGraw-Hill.
10. WIDDER, DAVID (1961), *Advanced Calculus*, Englewood Cliffs, N.J.: Prentice-Hall.

Chapter 9

Existence and Stability of Solutions to Static Models

9.1 INTRODUCTION

In this chapter we shall be concerned with the problem of the existence and stability of solutions to a set of functional relations. In earlier chapters we discussed the solution techniques for single equations. Here we want to extend this analysis to several functions. The relevant questions are: (1) Do sets of equations have a common solution? (2) Is it unique or one of many? (3) Is it stable?

A simple example, which will pave the way for much more involved and complicated problems, is that of supply and demand. Equations (1) and (2) below represent the functional relation between the quantity supplied and the market price and the quantity demanded and the market price. The problems are: (a) Is there a $(\bar{q}, \bar{p})$ that will simultaneously satisfy (1) and (2)? (b) Is there only one such pair? (c) Is any such solution stable? (d) In what sense is it stable?

$$q^s = q^s(p) \tag{1}$$

$$q^d = q^d(p) \tag{2}$$

In Figure 9.1–1 we have a graphical representation of the ordinary upward-sloping supply and downward-sloping demand with a unique solution $(\bar{q}, \bar{p})$. In Figure 9.1–2 there is no solution and in Figure 9.1–3 there are more than one.

The question of stability requires more information than is contained in Equations (1) and (2), namely, what determines the independent variable, price. One definition of stability (many are possible) is simply whether or not $(\bar{p}, \bar{q})$ would ever exist in the real-world counterpart of the two equations. Another definition of stability is a system that would return to $(\bar{p}, \bar{q})$ if perturbed. We shall reserve a more detailed discussion of stability for Section 9.4. In the next sections we shall turn our attention to the first question: the

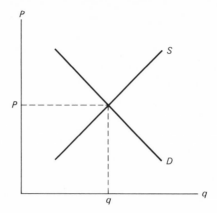

Figure 9.1–1   *Ordinary supply and demand schedules.*

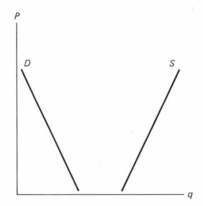

Figure 9.1–2   *No solution.*

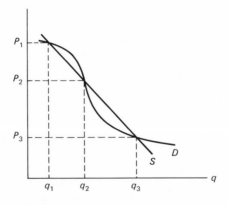

Figure 9.1–3   *Several solutions.*

existence of a solution. More particularly, in the following section we focus our attention on a special topic from abstract algebra, fixed-point theorems. Fixed-point theorems are quite useful in proving that a set of simultaneous equations has at least one solution. Of course, we have already considered a special case of simultaneous linear equations and their solution under the discussion of matrix algebra in Chapter 4. And quite properly, matrix algebra is a portion of the question of existence. Having discussed matrices, we now shall take a different, more abstract approach to the question of existence. Following that, stability will be discussed.

9.2 SPERNER'S LEMMA, BROUWER'S FIXED-POINT THEOREM, AND KAKUTANI'S FIXED-POINT THEOREM

Fixed-point theorems, at least in the simplified applications, are formal proofs of things that are almost intuitively obvious. For example, consider a sphere, S, which is collapsed into a smaller sphere, S', such that every point in S is also in S'. Further assume that the sphere does not tear or break so that points close together in S are also close together in S'. What is almost obvious is that the position of at least one point in S' must be in the same position in S; that is, through the collapsing process one point will remain fixed. (This is illustrated in Figures 9.2–1 and 9.2–2.) In other words, if we connect a line between every point $s \in S$ and its new position $s' \in S'$, for at least one $s \in S$ the length of this line must be zero.

In Figure 9.2–2 any point such as s_4 or s_5 could be a fixed point, depending upon the way the sphere was collapsed.

As another example, suppose that the unit interval (all the real numbers between zero and one) is mapped into itself, $f : [0, 1] \to [0, 1]$, in such a

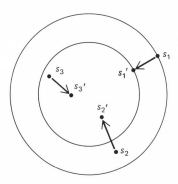

Figure 9.2–1 *S collapsed into S'.*

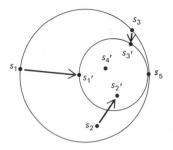

Figure 9.2–2   *S collapsed into S'.*

manner that *f* is continuous. Then a fixed-point theorem would assert that for at least one $x \in [0, 1]$, $f(x) = x$. This is illustrated in Figure 9.2–3.

From the examples we can observe that there are many fixed-point theorems that can be proven depending upon the particular mapping involved. In this section we wish to cover three principal developments in fixed-point theorems: Sperner's lemma, Brouwer's fixed-point theorem, and Kakutani's fixed-point theorem.[1]

Sperner's lemma deals with simplexes, their subdivisions, and the admissable labelings of the vertices of these subdivisions.

DEFINITION 9.2–1   An *n*-**dimensional simplex**, S^n, is the smallest[2] convex set with given $n + 1$ vertices that contains points in *n*-dimensional space.

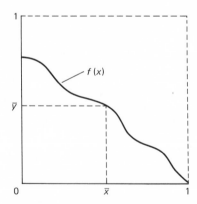

Figure 9.2–3 $f(x) = x$ *for at least one* $x \in [0, 1]$, *where* $f: [0, 1] \to [0, 1]$.

[1] Here we draw heavily upon an article by Tompkins (1964) for the discussion of Sperner's lemma and Brouwer's fixed-point theorem, and Kakutani (1941).

[2] Here "smallest" means in terms of area or volume enclosed in the vector space for a given set of points. For example, a triangle in 2-space through three points is a "smaller" convex set than a circle through the same three points.

Thus, if $n = 2$, a simplex in two-dimensional space is a triangle (i.e., the smallest convex set in 2-space with $n + 1 = 3$ vertices). In three-dimensional space a simplex would be a tetrahedron with four faces. Likewise, a (0)-dimensional simplex is a single point and a (-1)-dimensional simplex contains no points.

An n-dimensional simplex, S^n, is composed of $2^{n+1} - 1$ lower-dimensional simplexes from -1 to $n - 1$ that have vertices in common with S^n. Thus, for S^2 there are $2^3 = 8$ simplexes with common vertices. In Figure 9.2–4, they are the triangle itself, the three sides (one-dimensional simplexes), the three vertices (zero-dimensional), and one (-1)-dimensional simplex for a total of 8. We shall let the symbol S^n_i, $-1 \leq i < n$, be an ith-dimensional simplex contained in S^n with vertices in common with S^n.

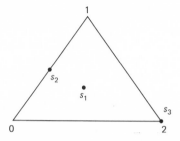

Figure 9.2–4   *Two-dimensional simplex $= S^2$.*

DEFINITION 9.2–2   A **carrier** of a point $s_i \in S^n$ is the lowest-dimensional simplex composing S^n (naturally associated with S^n) that contains s_i.

In other words, a carrier of $s_i \in S^n = \min_j S^n_j$ such that $s_i \in S^n_j$.

In Figure 9.2–4, the carrier of the point s_1 is S^n itself. (What are the carriers for the points s_2 and s_3?)

DEFINITION 9.2–3   Any set of points, $\{s_i\} \in S^n$ is an **admissibly labeled set** by $f: \{s_i\} \to I_n = \{0, 1, \ldots, n\}$ if:

(1) all vertices v_i of S^n are contained in $\{s_i\}$;

(2) $f(v_i) = i \in I_n$ and $f(v_i) \neq f(v_j)$ if $i \neq j$; and

(3) $f(s_i) = f(v_j)$, where v_j is any vertex of the carrier of s_i.

In other words, an admissibly labeled set of points associated with a simplex S^n must have each vertex labeled with a different integer and if a point is contained in a lower-dimensional simplex, S^n_j, naturally associated with S^n, then it must carry the label of some vertex of S^n_j. In Figure 9.2–4, for example, S_2 could have the label zero or one.

[If an admissably labeled point, s_i, is not contained in the boundary of S^n, then what are the admissible values for $f(s_i)$?]

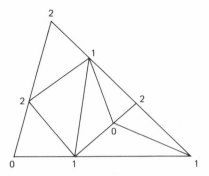

Figure 9.2–5 *A subdivision of a two-dimensional simplex properly labeled.*

DEFINITION 9.2–4   **A subdivision** of S^n is a finite set, $\{\sigma_i\}$, of n-dimensional simplexes such that:

(1) $\sigma_j \subset S^n$;

(2) for each $s_i \in S^n$, $s_i \in \{\sigma_j\}$;

(3) $\sigma_i \cap \sigma_j$ contains no interior points of σ_i or σ_j; and

(4) if $v_i^{\sigma_j}$ is a vertex of ~~σ_j~~ $\{\sigma_i\}$, then it is a vertex of each simplex $\sigma_k \in \{\sigma_i\}$ to which it is incident.

In Figure 9.2–5, the definition of a subdivision of a two-dimensional simplex is illustrated and labeled in accord with Definition 9.2–3. In Figure 9.2–6 the two-dimensional simplex does not have a proper subdivision nor is the set of points illustrated an admissibly labeled set. Why?

With the aid of Definitions 9.2–3 and 9.2–4 we can now state Sperner's lemma.

Theorem 9.2–1   Sperner's lemma   For any admissible labeling of the set of vertices of any subdivision of an n-dimensional simplex, S^n, there exists at least one simplex σ_j of the subdivision with its vertices carrying a complete

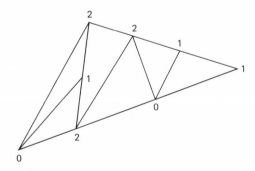

Figure 9.2–6 *An improperly labeled simplex.*

set of labels; that is, for at least one $\sigma_j \in \{\sigma_i\}$, $f(v_i^{\sigma_j}) \neq f(v_k^{\sigma_j})$ for any two vertices of the n-dimensional simplex σ_j.

PROOF   It is mathematically convenient to prove a stronger proposition, *viz.*, the number of simplexes satisfying Sperner's lemma is odd.[3] (Why does this prove Sperner's lemma?)

If $n = 0$, S^0 is a point and the lemma is trivial. Next consider S^1, a line segment, one end labeled zero, the other labeled one. Assume it to be punctuated with a finite number of points, n, thus creating $n + 1$ subdivisions σ_i of S^1. Suppose that the number of subsegments carrying a label zero at both ends is k, and the number carrying a label zero at only one vertex is j. Thus the number of end points labeled zero is equal to $2k + j$. Since the number of zero labels on the interior of the total line segment is $2k + j - 1$, these must account for $2(2k + j - 1)$ subsegments on the interior. Adding the subsegment that starts with the end of the line labeled zero, $2(2k + j - 1) + 1$ subsegments are odd. Therefore $2(2k + j - 1)$ is even, $2k + j - 1$ is even, and hence $2k + j$ is an odd number. Therefore j is odd. But since j is the number of subsegments carrying a full set of labels in this case, the lemma is proven for S^1.[4]

Next we show that if the lemma holds for S^{n-1}, it must hold for S^n as well thus proving the theorem by induction.

Let the number of n-dimensional subdivisional simplexes, σ_j^n, that carry all labels but n be equal to a; that is, the number of σ_j^n labeled $(0, \ldots, n - 1, i)$ is equal to a, where i is any integer $1, 2, \ldots, n - 1$. Any σ_j has $n + 1$ vertices, and for those making up a: $f(v_k^{\sigma_j}) = f(v_i^{\sigma_j})$ for some i and k, and $f(v_g^{\sigma_j}) \neq f(v_i^{\sigma_j})$ all $g \neq i$ and k. Therefore the number of $n - 1$ subdimensional simplexes associated with those in a must be equal to $2a$.

Let the number of fully labeled σ_j^n, subdivisional simplexes be b. Since each of these is fully labeled, there must be b $(n - 1)$-dimensional simplexes associated with b. Consequently, the number of fully labeled simplexes σ_j^{n-1} is $2a + b$.

Of these lower-dimensional simplexes, σ_j^{n-1}, some are inside S^n and some are on the boundary. Those that are inside are incident to two simplexes of the subdivision. Those on the boundary are incident to only one simplex of the subdivision. Assuming the lemma holds for $n - 1$, the total of those on the boundary must be odd. Since the sum of an odd and an even number is odd, $2a + b$ must be odd. Hence b is odd. Since b is the number of fully labeled σ_j^n, the lemma is proved.   QED

The immediate application of Sperner's lemma is to prove Brouwer's fixed-point theorem, which we now state.

[3] This technique of inductive proof is interesting in and of itself and is discussed more fully by Tompkins (1964).

[4] Illustrate this portion of the proof by drawing an example.

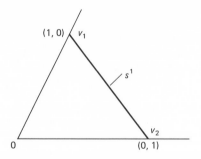

Figure 9.2–7   *Barycentric coordinate system of one-dimensional simplex.*

Theorem 9.2–2 *Brouwer's Fixed-Point Theorem*   Any continuous function from an n-dimensional simplex to itself leaves at least one fixed point.

PROOF   To prove the theorem we must show first that a continuous function of a simplex into itself implies that some subdivision and its vertices, which are labeled by the continuous function, satisfy Sperner's lemma. Second, we must show that an arbitrarily small subdivision can be found satisfying the lemma, which further implies the existence of a fixed point.

Points in S^n are labeled in the following manner. We construct a coordinate system of $n + 1$ dimensions such that each axis passes through one vertex of the simplex S^n and the distance from the origin to the vertex is one. Hence the coordinate of each vertex, v_i, is an $n + 1$-tuple of n zeros with one in the ith position; that is, $v_1 = (1, 0, \ldots, 0), \ldots, v_i = (0, \ldots, 1, \ldots, 0)$, and so on. This is illustrated in Figures 9.2–7 and 9.2–8 for S^1 and S^2. These systems are termed **barycentric** coordinate systems and the axes need not be perpendicular.

By construction, the sum of the barycentric coordinates of any one point is equal to one. For example, for $p \in S^n$ such that $p = (p_1, p_2, \ldots, p_{n+1})$,

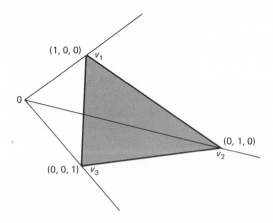

Figure 9.2–8   *Barycentric coordinate system for S^2.*

$\sum_{i=1}^{n+1} p_i = 1$. Therefore, if we label each point with a continuous function, $(f: S^n \rightarrow S^n$, then $f: p \rightarrow q$, for p and $q \in S^n$), in the following manner: $f(p) = j$ if j is the smallest coordinate index such that $q_j \leq p_j \neq 0$.

$f: p \rightarrow q$ represents the mapping of the point p into q, while $f(p)$ is the label of the image of p under the map f. For example, suppose $p = (\frac{1}{2}, \frac{1}{2})$ and $q = (\frac{1}{3}, \frac{2}{3})$, then $f(p) = \frac{1}{3}$ since $q_1 \leq p_1$. For the points $p^* = (\frac{1}{3}, \frac{2}{3})$ and $q^* = (\frac{3}{4}, \frac{1}{4})$, $f(p^*) = \frac{1}{4}$. On inspection we see that such a labeling procedure satisfies the admissable labeling condition, Definition 9.2–3.

By taking arbitrarily fine subdivisions, choosing the simplex from each subdivision with a full set of labels, and choosing a single point from each simplex, we shall generate an infinite sequence of points in S^n. Also, we can choose some subsequence of points that converge to a single point. Now, since by our labeling rule $q_j \leq p_j$ for each j, in the limit the barycentric coordinates of q_j cannot exceed the barycentric coordinate of p_j. And since the barycentric coordinates of any point must sum to one, there must be a sequence such that the coordinates of p and q are equal. Hence p equals q or $f: p \rightarrow p$.   QED

Example 1.   Brouwer's Fixed-Point Theorem and the Existence of an Equilibrium in a Single Market   We shall now use Brouwer's fixed-point theorem to prove the existence of an equilibrium price and quantity in a single market. In spite of the analogy of firing a cannon at a fly, the illustration is useful for more involved questions to follow.

Consider a market as illustrated in Figure 9.2–9, where over some region the average absolute values of the slopes of the supply and demand equations are equal.[5] The intervals $[p_1, p_2]$ and $[q_1, q_2]$ are one-dimensional simplexes and, consequently, if we define the mappings $m_0: f(p^s) \rightarrow p^d$ and $m_1: q(q^d) \rightarrow q^s$, we shall have continuous single-valued mappings of the interval $[p_1, p_2]$

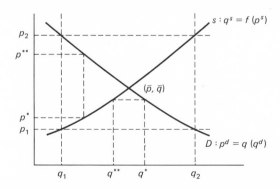

Figure 9.2–9   *Brouwer's fixed-point theorem applied to supply and demand.*

[5] This assumption ensures the continuity of the mappings when the supply and demand are monotonically increasing and decreasing, respectively.

into itself and the interval $[q_1, q_2]$ into itself, respectively. In Figure 9.2–9, m_0 maps p^* into p^{**}, while m_1 maps q^* into q^{**}. Applying Brouwer's fixed-point theorem twice, we have that for m_0 there must exist a p^s such that $p^s = p^d = \bar{p}$ and for m_1, $q^d = q^s = \bar{q}$. That is, there is an equilibrium $\bar{p}$ and $\bar{q}$ that simultaneously satisfies the supply and demand equations.

Kakutani's fixed-point theorem represents an immediate generalization of Brouwer's fixed-point theorem and, more important, makes it applicable to a variety of economic problems of existence. Applications will follow the principal results of Kakutani's article. First, we need some additional definitions that generalize the concepts of Sperner's lemma and Brouwer's fixed-point theorem.

DEFINITION 9.2–5   A **point-to-set mapping** is a mapping from a point, p, to a set that is a function of p, that is, $f: p \to \phi(p)$.

DEFINITION 9.2–6   A point-to-set mapping $f: x \to \phi(x)$, such that $\phi(x) \in R(S^n)$, where $R(S^n)$ is the family of closed convex subsets of S^n, an n-dimensional simplex, is **upper semicontinuous** if for a sequence of points in x from x_n to x_0 and if $y_n \in \phi(x_n)$, then for a sequence of points from y_n to y_0 it must be true that $y_0 \in \phi(x_0)$.

The definition of upper semicontinuity states that the graph of $\phi(x)$: $\sum_{x \in S} x \times \phi(x)$ is a closed subset of the Cartesian product $S^n \times S^n$. An upper semicontinuous function is illustrated in Figure 9.2–10.

Theorem 9.2–3   Kakutani's Fixed-Point Theorem   If $f: x \to \phi(x)$ is an upper semicontinuous point-to-set mapping of an n-dimensional closed simplex S^n into $R(S^n)$, the family of subsets of S^n, then there exists an $x_0 \in S^n$ such that $x_0 \in \phi(x_0)$.

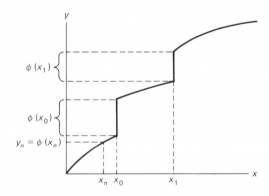

Figure 9.2–10   *An upper semicontinuous point-to-set mapping.*

PROOF To prove the theorem we make use of Brouwer's fixed-point theorem in the following manner. From σ_j^n, the jth subdivision of S^n, take an arbitrary point $y_i \in \phi(v_i^{\sigma j})$, where $v_i^{\sigma j}$ is a vertex of σ_j^n. Then the linear mapping, $f^*: x \rightarrow y_i$, between vertices is a continuous point-to-point mapping. By Brouwer's fixed-point theorem there exists a v_i^{σ} such that $f^*(v_i^{\sigma}) = v_i^{\sigma}$. Now, by taking a subsequence of points $\{v_i^{\sigma j}\}$, $(j = 1, 2, \dots)$ of $\{v_i^{\sigma}\}$, for $i = (1, 2, \dots)$, which converges to a point $x_0 \in S^n$ and since the mapping is upper semicontinuous, an x_0 can be found that satisfies the theorem.[6]   QED

This generalization permits the supply and demand equations of Example 1 to have horizontal or vertical sections as illustrated in Figure 9.2–11. (Why and where in Figure 9.2–11 is the mapping described in Example 1 now a point-to-set mapping?)

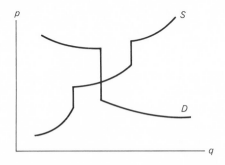

Figure 9.2–11 *Supply and demand curves with flat portions.*

An immediate consequence of the foregoing theorem is a corollary that leads to two more theorems further generalizing the usefulness of Theorem 9.2–3.

Corollary to Theorem 9.2–3 Theorem 9.2–3 is also valid even if S, the set mapped into itself, is an arbitrary, bounded, closed convex set in a Euclidean space.

PROOF Consider S^n, a closed simplex that contains S as a subset (cf. Figure 9.2–10), and consider also a continuous point-to-point mapping of S^n into S, $\psi: S^n \rightarrow S$. Then $f: x \rightarrow \phi[\psi(x)]$ is an upper semicontinuous point-to-set mapping of S^n into $R(S) \subseteq R(S^n)$. By Theorem 9.2–3, there exists an $x_0 \in S^n$ such that $x_0 \in \phi[\psi(x_0)]$, and since $\phi[\psi(x_0)] \subseteq S$, then $x_0 \in S$. Therefore it follows that $x_0 \in \phi(x_0) \subseteq S$.   QED

Theorem 9.2–4 Let $K \subset R^m$ and $L \subset R^n$ be two bounded, closed convex sets in Euclidean space with the Cartesian product $K \times L \subset R^{m+n}$. If U and

---

[6] For further details see Kakutani (1941).

V are two closed subsets of $K \times L$ such that: (1) for any $x_0 \in K$ the set $U_{x_0} = \{y \in L \mid (x_0, y) \in U\}$ is nonempty, closed, and convex; and (2) for any $y_0 \in L$ the set $V_{y_0} = \{x \in K \mid (x, y_0) \in V\}$ is nonempty, closed, and convex; then U and V have a common point.

PROOF   Let $S = K \times L$ and define the mapping $f: z \to \phi(z)$ for $z \in S$ and $\phi(z) \subseteq R(S)$ as follows: If $z = (x, y)$ then $\phi(z) = V_y \times U_x$. Since U and V are closed, the mapping is upper semicontinuous. By the preceding corollary there exists a $z_0 \in K \times L$ such that $z_0 \in f(z_0)$, which means that $z_0 = (x_0, y_0)$ for some $z_0 \in U$ and $z_0 \in V$.   QED

Theorem 9.2–4 has applications in programming theory and game theory that will be developed in Chapters 11, 12, and 13. For completeness here, we present the following application, Theorem 9.2–5.

Theorem 9.2–5   If $f(x, y)$ is a continuous, real-valued function defined for $x \in K$ and $y \in L$, where K and L are arbitrary, bounded, closed convex sets in Euclidean spaces R^m and R^n; and if $f(x, y)$ is such that for every $x_0 \in K$, $y_0 \in L$, α and $\beta \in R$, the sets $\{y \in L \mid f(x_0, y) \leq \alpha\}$ and $\{x \in K \mid f(x, y_0) \geq \beta\}$ are convex sets, then

$$\max_{x \in K} \min_{y \in L} f(x, y) = \min_{y \in L} \max_{x \in K} f(x, y)$$

PROOF   If we let U and V be the sets of all $z_0 = (x_0, y_0) \in K \times L$ such that

$$f(x_0, y_0) = \min_{y \in L} f(x_0, y) \quad \text{and} \quad f(x_0, y_0) = \max_{x \in K} f(x, y_0)$$

then U and V satisfy Theorem 9.2–4 and thus U and V have some point in common. By the definition of U and V,

$$f(x_0, y_0) = \min_{y \in L} f(x_0, y) = \max_{x \in K} f(x, y_0)$$

Therefore

$$\min_{y \in L} \max_{x \in K} f(x, y) \leq \max_{x \in K} f(x, y_0) = f(x_0, y_0)$$

$$= \min_{y \in L} f(x_0, y) \leq \max_{x \in K} \min_{y \in L} f(x, y)$$

However, since it is also true that the minimum of the maximums must be greater than or equal to the maximum of the minimums, it must be true that the strict equality holds; that is,

$$\min_{y \in L} \max_{x \in K} f(x, y) = \max_{x \in K} \min_{y \in L} f(x, y)   \text{QED}$$

This is an alternative proof of the "minimax" theorem proven first by John von Neumann. Further details of its uses will be developed in Chapters 11, 12, and 13.

Example 2.   Existence of a General Equilibrium Solution   In many areas of economic analysis it is of interest to show that a system of equations (say, representing the actions of individual decision units) has a simultaneous solution. For example, does there exist a vector of prices that will satisfy suppliers and demanders of all commodities and clear all markets? This question may seem trivial, obvious, or both. It is somewhat analogous to questioning whether the real world exists. However, existence theory is actually more useful than it may appear. First, it provides a check for the consistency and completeness of a model purporting to encompass all aspects of the economic system. Second, the existence of a general equilibrium solution permits further analysis of uniqueness and stability of the solution. Suppose that the economic and social system were structured so that there was no equilibrium point, no mixture of interpersonal exchanges that would satisfy everyone. This implies in some sense that conflict is not being reconciled and that there is no hope that it will be. The point is that the analysis of questions such as stability is greatly affected by definite answers of existence.[7]

Leon Walras (1954) first formulated a rigorous mathematical model of general equilibrium in the latter 1800's. Walras dismissed the questions of existence and uniqueness by demonstrating very carefully that his general equilibrium model contained the same number of equations as unknowns. Clearly, as illustrated in Figures 9.1–1, 9.1–2, and 9.1–3, this is not sufficient to ensure either. Abraham Wald (1935) presented the first rigorous analysis of existence of such a general equilibrium solution. In what follows we shall discuss the Walras model, Wald's approach to the question of existence, and a proof of a generalized Walras–Wald model incorporating the Kakutani fixed-point theorem.[8] This particular approach is useful for several reasons: first, it possesses a certain historical value by demonstrating the theoretical progress and isolation of the relevant questions and second, it demonstrates the power of fixed-point theorems in obtaining answers to what have appeared, at times, to be insoluble questions.

Suppose we have an economy with m resources and n commodities produced. Let b_i represent the fixed amount of the ith resource available for use

[7] The example is, in a sense, artificial since any system can be sufficiently expanded to obtain some kind of potential solution. The real question is the scope of the model necessary to attain an equilibrium solution, i.e., existence theory serves primarily as a check on the sufficiency of a model.

[8] There have appeared several models in the literature that generalize Wald's analysis. These include Arrow and Debreu (1954), Debreu (1959), Gale (1955), McKenzie (1959) (first application of the Kakutani fixed-point theorem). Later texts that contain a fuller discussion of general equilibrium are Kuenne (1963) and Quirk and Saposnik (1968).

and q_j represent the amount of the jth commodity produced. We shall assume that the relation between commodities produced and resources used is linear and that all resources need not be fully utilized. Thus the following "technological" equations describe the production possibilities:

(1)
$$
\begin{aligned}
a_{11}q_1 + a_{12}q_2 + \cdots + a_{1n}q_n &\leq b_1 \\
&\vdots \\
a_{m1}q_1 + a_{m2}q_2 + \cdots + a_{mn}q_n &\leq b_m
\end{aligned}
\qquad \text{or} \quad Ax \leq b
$$

In (1) the a_{ij}'s represent the technological coefficients. a_{11}, for example, is the amount of the first resource, b_1, used per unit of the first commodity produced, q_1. Furthermore, the equations require the resources to be combined in *fixed* proportions. That is, to produce one unit of q_1, one *must* use a_{11} units of b_1, a_{21} units of $b_2, \ldots$, and, a_{m1} units of the mth resource. As well, there are constant returns to scale. The maximum quantity of q_1 that can be produced is determined by its most limiting resource, $\min_i b_i/a_{i1}$. For any amount of q_1 between that and zero, the relation is linear.[9]

The equations in (2) are the demand equations for each commodity and depend upon the relative price of each commodity, p_i, and the relative price of each resource, y_j. Since prices are only exchange ratios, any one price is arbitrary and the demand equations are homogeneous of degree zero. If all prices are doubled, tripled, or cut in half, the exchange ratios will be unaffected. Further, we shall assume that the demand equations are continuous.

(2)
$$
\begin{aligned}
q_1 &= f_1(p_1, \ldots, p_n, y_1, \ldots, y_m) \\
&\vdots \\
q_n &= f_n(p_1, \ldots, p_n, y_1, \ldots, y_m)
\end{aligned}
$$

Since we are dealing with a competitive economy, the factors are paid according to their productivity. Namely, the amount of the first resource used in the per unit production of the first commodity, a_{11}, times its price, y_1, plus the amount of the second resource used in the per unit production of the first commodity, a_{21}, times its price, y_2, and so on for all resources used in production of the first commodity is equal to its price if the first commodity is produced. If the cost of resources is greater than the commodity's price, the commodity is unprofitable and not produced. The possibility of the price

---

[9] The apparent overly restrictive nature of this assumption can be ameliorated by interpreting each q as a process rather than a commodity and thus allowing some variation in the factor proportions used to produce a commodity. However, to do so would involve a great many additional equations and variables and the results would not differ significantly from the above. Consequently, in the interest of simplicity the assumption of one process per commodity will be retained.

being more than the cost of resources used is ruled out since we are in competitive equilibrium where resource owners maximize their incomes. Equations (3) and (4) describe this relation between costs and prices and all n commodities:

$$a_{11}y_1 + a_{21}y_2 + \cdots + a_{m1}y_m \geq p_1$$

(3) $\vdots$

$$a_{1n}y_1 + a_{2n}y_2 + \cdots + a_{mn}y_m \geq p_n$$

and

(4)   if $a_{1i}y_1 + a_{2i}y_2 + \cdots + a_{mi}y_m > p_i$, then $q_i = 0$ for any i

Similarly, with respect to the inequalities of Equation (1), if any resource is not fully used, it will become, in a competitive economy, a free good. Thus we have

(5)   if $a_{j1}q_1 + a_{j2}q_2 + \cdots + a_{jn}q_n < b_j$, then $y_j = 0$

Statements (1)–(5) represent the basic ideas of Walras' analysis of general equilibrium. Wald's solution to the question of existence was based on a more restrictive model than that above in that he assumed strict equalities rather than the more general inequalities. In addition, Wald assumed that each good had positive (and diminishing) marginal utility and was perfectly divisable. Consequently, every individual possessed some amount of each and every good. However, since these assumptions are not necessary to prove the existence of an equilibrium set of prices, we have generalized Wald's approach.

Theorem 9.2–6   For the system (1)–(5), there exist equilibrium vectors $q^* = (q_1, \ldots, q_n)$, $p^* = (p_1, \ldots, p_n)$, and $y^* = (y_1, \ldots, y_m)$ such that $p^*q^* = \max pq$ subject to Equation (1) and $p^*q^* = y^*b$.

That is, if firms maximize profits subject to the technology and resource availabilities and if a budget constraint is imposed on the demand equations, then the value paid for commodities equals the value paid for resources, that is, $p^*q^* = y^*b$.

PROOF   Although there are many ways of proving Theorem 9.2–6, and many slight variations of the theorem itself, we shall use two theorems of Kakutani, *viz.*, Theorems 9.2–3 and 9.2–5.

Consider an arbitrary price vector for commodities p^0 and a price vector y^0 for resources. Given p^0 and y^0, producers will maximize profits $= f(q, y^0) = p^0q - y^0b$, subject to $q \in K = \{q \mid Ax \leq b\}$. $f(q, y^0)$ must be nonnegative, since they will not produce if unprofitable. On the other hand, for a given p^0 and q^0, consumers maximize their incomes. Thus they will minimize $f(q^0, y) = p^0q^0 - yb$ subject to $y \in \{yA \geq p\}$. By Theorem 9.2–5 these two must be equal and, furthermore, equal to zero; that is, $p^0q^0 = y^0b$. Thus for every p there is an associated y such that $pq = yb$. All that remains to be shown is that for some p and y the demand equations (2) are satisfied. Since the demand equations are homogeneous of degree zero, we can impose any single restriction we wish. By letting $\sum p_i + \sum y_i = 1$, the vector (p, y) is an $(n + m)$-dimensional simplex. Now define the composite mapping $\theta\colon (p, y) \to \phi(p, y)$, where for each (p, y) the resulting output vector, q, is mapped into the demand equations, (2), giving a set of possible prices $\phi(p, y)$, where p, y, and q now satisfy Theorem 9.2–2.[10] Thus θ is a point-to-set mapping of the simplex (p, y) into itself and hence, by Theorem 9.2–3, there exists at least one fixed point that is an equilibrium vector.   QED

As one can see by the premises of Kakutani's theorems, the proof of the existence of a general equilibrium solution can be easily generalized. For example, the assumptions of fixed coefficients of production and continuous demand equations can be replaced with more general concepts.[11]

Problems

9.2–1 If a line is divided into segments by points labeled alternatively 1 and 0, then:

   (a) If the ends of the line are labeled 1 and 0, is the number of segments odd or even?

   (b) If the ends of the line are both labeled 1 (or 0), is the number of segments odd or even?

   (c) If there is an odd number of two segment ends (interior points of the line) labeled 0, is the number of segments odd or even?

   (d) Prove (a), (b), and (c).

9.2–2 If a triangle is divided into smaller triangles by points interior to the original triangle and vertices of all the smaller triangles labeled 0, 1, or 2, then:

   (a) If there are an odd number of edges on the border of the original triangle that are labeled 0 and 1, then is the number of smaller triangles carrying a complete set of labels odd or even?

   (b) What difference would it make in (a) if we replace 0 and 1 with 0 and 2?

   (c) What would be the outcome of (a) if there were an even number of edges on the border labeled 1 and 2?

9.2–3 For a circle punctuated with an arbitrary number of points labeled 0, 1, 2, or 3, what is the relation between the number of segments with end labels 1 and 2 and the number labeled 2 and 3?

---

[10] Define the simple maps that make up θ.

[11] For these other examples, the interested reader should refer to the following literature. Debreu (1959), Koopmans (1957), McKenzie (1959), Arrow and Debreu (1954), and Gale (1955) prove the existence of competitive equilibria under similar, but different assumptions. For two excellent reviews of the literature on existence see Dorfman, Samuelson, and Solow (1958), Chapter 13, and Quirk and Saposnik (1968), Chapter 3.

9.2–4   The following functions are defined for the unit interval, $x \in [0, 1]$. Find a fixed point for each.

(a) $f(x) = \dfrac{x^2 + x}{2}$ (c) $f(x) = e^{x-1}$

(b) $f(x) = (x - \frac{1}{2})^2$ (d) $f(x) = 0.7 - 0.7x$

9.2–5   What is the dimension of the following simplexes?
(a) straight line (c) rectangular cube
(b) null set

9.2–6   For S^3, how many lower-dimensional simplexes have verticies in common with S^3? Give the number of each lower-dimensional simplex.

9.2–7   In two-dimensional space draw a convex set and illustrate a mapping that would transform the convex set into a two-dimensional simplex.

9.3   UNIQUENESS OF SOLUTIONS

Uniqueness amounts to proving that no other alternative solution exists for a system of equations. This question has not been considered particularly important, mainly for two reasons. First, in most static economic applications it does not make any difference whether more than one solution exists. Second, the assumptions and postulates necessary to prove uniqueness are often overly restrictive on the real-world counterpart. For example, in the case of supply and demand analysis, the usual question is whether the market is cleared, rather than whether alternative price-quantity combinations clear the market.

Furthermore, there is little that can be said in general about uniqueness. Since this problem cannot be given a very abstract treatment, the answer to whether a system is unique or not will vary with the particulars of that system. For this reason the following discussion will be quite limited. We return to this topic in Section 9.5, where the question of stability is considered.

Unique Linear Systems

A system of n linear equations in n unknowns has a unique solution if and only if the coefficient matrix A, of the system $Ax = b$, is nonsingular. This was proved in Theorem 4.2–2. When the number of unknowns is not equal to the number of equations, the rank of the coefficient matrix must be equal to the number of unknowns (cf. Theorem 4.2–4.). Therefore, if the number of equations is less than the number of unknowns, the system cannot possess a unique solution. There will either be an infinite number of possible solutions or the system will be inconsistent. Alternatively, if the number of equations is greater than the number of unknowns, the system will either not possess a solution, possess a unique solution, or possess an infinite number of solutions depending upon the rank of the coefficient matrix and the number of unknowns.

Unique Nonlinear Systems

The fixed-point theorems developed in Section 9.2 do not imply uniqueness. For uniqueness it is necessary to show that if two solutions exist they are equivalent. As alluded to above, this generally requires more information than existence proofs. For example, two strictly convex sets with only boundary points in common will have a single element common to both. Convex sets with boundary points in common may have more than a single element in common. These are illustrated in Figure 9.3–1.

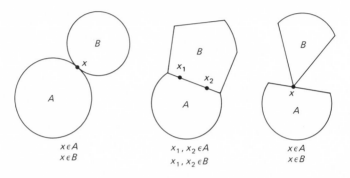

Figure 9.3–1 *Strictly convex and convex sets having unique and multiple solutions.*

Example 1.[12]   Every Competitive Equilibrium is a Pareto Optimum and Every Pareto Optimum is a Competitive Equilibrium   An example of the confusion and misleading conclusions that can arise in economic analysis due to a failure to consider the question of uniqueness is the relation between a competitive equilibrium and a Pareto optimum.

DEFINITION 9.3–1   A **Pareto optimum** is an existing distribution of economic goods and services such that there exists no other feasible distribution of goods and services where at least one individual is made better off and no one is made worse off.

There are several proofs demonstrating that a competitive equilibrium is Pareto optimum as well as proofs that any Pareto optimum can be attained by a competitive equilibrium. This had led to statements such as, "Every Pareto optimum is a competitive equilibrium."[13] However, such statements

[12] Cf. Example 6 in Section 2.8.

[13] See, for example, Dorfman, Samuelson, and Solow (1958), page 410.

are misleading to say the least. The difficulty is that proofs of the latter are proofs of existence only and not uniqueness. For every Pareto optimum, there *exists* some competitive equilibrium. However, this does not preclude a Pareto optimum from being achieved by other kinds of economic systems.

The following is an example of a Pareto optimum being achieved by an economy with monopoly elements. Suppose there are three individuals, A, B, and C, and they initially possess the amounts of steak and beer shown in Table 9.3–1. Suppose that A, being an alcoholic, prefers one beer to two

Table 9.3–1   Initial Holdings

	Steak	Beer
A	2	0
B	0	5
C	0	1

steaks, while B and C prefer a steak to their initial holdings of beer. If competition exists in the sense of a single exchange ratio between steak and beer, then one steak will exchange for one beer and the distribution given in Table 9.3–2 will occur after trade. However, if A is a perfectly discriminating

Table 9.3–2   Competitive Distribution

	Steak	Beer
A	0	2
B	1	4
C	1	0

monopolist, then he will be able to charge B and C different "beer" prices and end up with all of the beer (see Table 9.3–3). Clearly Table 9.3–3 is Pareto optimal as well as Table 9.2–2.

Table 9.3–3   Discriminating Monopoly Distribution

	Steak	Beer
A	0	6
B	1	0
C	1	0

This example illustrates the specific nature of existence theorems: They say nothing about uniqueness nor do they say anything about the possibility of attaining such a state. For these questions one needs more information as to the dynamic or adjustment processes of the system. These questions are discussed further in the next section.

Problems

9.3-1 Given the following supply and demand functions:

$$p^s = q^2 + 2$$
$$p^d = 8q - q^2 - 4$$

(a) Is the solution unique?

(b) What conditions could you impose on the supply price, p^s, and the demand price, p^d, functions to ensure a unique equilibrium market price?

9.3-2 For a two-good economy construct a production possibility frontier that has a unique equilibrium output for any given price ratio. Construct a production possibility frontier in two-dimensional space that has multiple solutions for some price ratios.

9.3-3 In a two-person, Edgeworth-box trading diagram, is the Pareto optimum unique? Describe some conditions that would lead to a unique point on the contract curve.

9.4 STABILITY OF SOLUTIONS

The study of stability of a system of simultaneous equations implies recourse to additional properties implicit in the simultaneous equations. Specifically, the question of stability is concerned with what happens to values of some specified parameters when the system is not in equilibrium. Suppose, for example, that the market price is not the equilibrium price, that is, it does not satisfy the supply and demand equations. What happens in the market? Do the dynamic properties of this sytem ensure that the market price converges to or diverges from equilibrium? Further, what is the length of time required for the equilibrium price to be established? Both of these questions are crucial to a relevant characterization of the economic system. Since scientific analysis is a mixture of simplicity and realism, as we have argued in more detail above, analyzing some empirical phenomenon as a set of simultaneous equations implies a qualitative judgment of the stability properties. Clearly, if a system is unstable so that the equilibrium state is never attained, it is hardly useful to characterize an empirical phenomenon as being in equilibrium. On the other hand, if the system does possess stability properties such that it will eventually converge to an equilibrium solution, but only over a very long period, then it may be more *useful* or *realistic* to analyze the system as being in perpetual disequilibrium.

A full or complete analysis of stability is simply a fuller or more complete specification of the properties of an empirical system. If x is a relevant variable of the system, then for a precise specification of stability one would need to formulate the functional change of x over time dependent upon some other parameters of the system; for example,

$$\frac{dx}{dt} = f(y_1, \ldots, y_n)$$

or

$$\frac{\Delta x}{\Delta t} = f(y_1, \ldots, y_n)$$

Since this requires more information, stability is a "higher-order" analysis—a more detailed analysis. The general properties of such a system of differential or difference equations are discussed in Chapter 7 (differential equations), in Chapter 8 (difference equations), and in Chapter 14 (control theory).

This is all very well if the requisite data and information are available to specify the particular equations. However, in many cases such data is not available, or not available in sufficient detail or accuracy to make such complete specification possible. For this reason there has been substantial consideration of what might be called **qualitative stability analysis.** By qualitative stability analysis we mean a consideration of the implicit stability properties in enough detail to give the conditions under which the assumption of equilibrium is relevant. The remainder of this chapter will be devoted to some of the main types of qualitative stability analysis. The first, **static stability,** covers Walras' and Marshall's consideration of dynamics and stability.[14]

Static Stability Analysis

Static stability is a statement of the conditions necessary for a set of simultaneous equations to be stable, but with no explicit formulation of how the variables change over time. As Samuelson (1947) noted in his *Foundations of Economic Analysis*, this procedure is, in a word, wrong—but by assuming static stability one can derive conclusions about the equilibrium system itself. In other words, there is a sufficient correspondence between static stability and dynamic stability, albeit implicit, to make a study of static stability useful. The following definitions are examples of types of static stability.

DEFINITION 9.4–1   A market is **stable** in the **Marshallian sense** if when quantity supplied exceeds (is less than) the equilibrium level, the supply price exceeds (is less than) the demand price.

---

[14] Walras (1954) and Marshall (1920).

DEFINITION 9.4–2 A market is **stable** in the **Walrasian sense** if when the market price is greater (less) than the equilibrium price, the quantity supplied exceeds (is less than) the quantity demanded.

If the supply and demand curves are respectively upward and downward sloping to the right, then the market is stable by both definitions. If, however, the supply schedule is downward sloping, then by one definition the market is stable and by the other it is unstable. In Figure 9.4–1 we have a market that is stable in the Marshallian sense. When q_s is the quantity supplied, the supply price is greater than the demand price, that is, $p^s > p^d$. However, by the second definition, the market is unstable since when the market price, p_m, exceeds the equilibrium price, the quantity demanded is less than the quantity supplied.

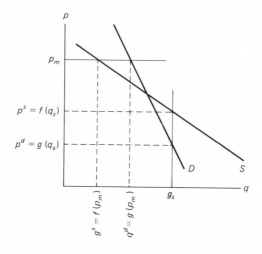

Figure 9.4–1 *Marshallian stable–Walrasian unstable market.*

The difference in the two definitions is the implicit, intuitive notion of the operation of the market mechanism. Behind the Marshallian definition is the argument that when there is an excess of equilibrium supply, producers will reduce output, resulting in a movement toward the equilibrium level. However, the implicit Walrasian dynamics argue that if the market price is such that a shortage exists, demanders will bid up the price further, moving away from equilibrium. (Are all markets with a downward-sloping supply and demand unstable in the Walrasian sense?)

Hicks (1936), in *Value and Capital*, extended the notion of Walrasian stability from the single market to multiple markets and derived properties of an equilibrium system from the stability properties of a corresponding dynamic system. Hicks argued that static analysis implies dynamic stability, and he derived conditions that were independent of the speed of response and compatible with some dynamic stability conditions, but not all. As we shall see, the problem in the Hicksian definition is a lack of a specific dynamic system.

DEFINITION 9.4-3   Hicksian Stability   (a) Equilibrium for multiple markets is **imperfectly stable** if an increase above the equilibrium price in a market creates an excess supply in that market after all other market prices have adjusted themselves so that all other markets are in equilibrium.

(b) Equilibrium for multiple markets is **perfectly stable** if an increase above the equilibrium price in a market creates an excess supply in that market after any subset of the other markets adjust themselves.

(c) Equilibrium for n multiple markets is **partially stable of order m** $(m < n)$ if an increase above the equilibrium price in a market creates an excess supply in that market after m other markets have adjusted.

If we let x_i be the excess demand in the ith market, that is, $x_i = D_i(p_1, \ldots, p_n) - S_i(p_1, \ldots, p_n)$, then Hicks' stability condition for imperfect stability requires $dx_i/dp_i < 0$. Since

$$\begin{bmatrix} a_{11} & \cdots & a_{1n} \\ \vdots & & \vdots \\ a_{n1} & \cdots & a_{nn} \end{bmatrix} \begin{bmatrix} dp_1/dp_i \\ \vdots \\ 1 \\ \vdots \\ dp_n/dp_i \end{bmatrix} = \begin{bmatrix} dx_1/dp_i \\ \vdots \\ dx_i/dp_i \\ \vdots \\ dx_n/dp_i \end{bmatrix} = \begin{bmatrix} 0 \\ \vdots \\ dx_i/dp_i \\ \vdots \\ 0 \end{bmatrix}$$

where $a_{ij} = \partial x_i/\partial p_j$, by Cramer's rule,

$$\frac{dx_i}{dp_i} = \frac{|A|}{|A_{ii}|} < 0$$

The numbering of commodities is arbitrary. Therefore the condition for imperfect stability requires that all principal minor determinants of order $n - 1$, $|A_{ii}|$, have the opposite sign of $|A|$. Perfect stability requires that principal minors alternate in sign.

Notice that the Hicks conditions are stated entirely in terms of the slopes of the excess demand functions (i.e., a_{ij}). But as Samuelson (1941) and Lange (1945) pointed out, these conditions are not derived from an explicit dynamic system. When such a system is introduced, the stability depends also upon the relative speed of adjustment in the individual markets.

Dynamic Stability

Dynamic stability analysis *does* involve an explicit consideration of the adjustment mechanism. There are several different kinds of stability that may be identified. The main kinds follow:

DEFINITION 9.4–4 **Global stability** means that the variables of the system approach some equilibrium value in the limit as time becomes infinite. That is, if $\phi(X, t)$ denotes the path of variables $X = (x_1, \ldots, x_n)$ over time, then global stability implies that for a particular equilibrium value $\overline{X}$, $\lim_{t \to \infty} \phi(X, t) = \overline{X}$, regardless of the initial value of X.

DEFINITION 9.4–5 **Quasistability** means that the variables converge to a set of equilibrium values; that is, the limit of every dynamic process is an equilibrium. If the equilibrium is unique, quasistability implies global stability.

DEFINITION 9.4–6 **Local stability** means that the variables, X, approach some equilibrium value, $\overline{X}$, in the limit as time becomes infinite if the initial values of X are in a sufficiently small neighborhood of $\overline{X}$.

DEFINITION 9.4–7 **Lyapunov stability** means that the variables of a system when perturbed slightly remain within some neighborhood of the equilibrium without necessarily converging to it.

DEFINITION 9.4–8 **Orbital stability** means that the variables converge not to an equilibrium point, but to an equilibrium path of periodic motion.

The familiar cobweb theorem for a single market can be utilized to illustrate all these types. In the cobweb model the system begins at a nonequilibrium price. The suppliers base their output decisions for the subsequent marketing period on that price. When the output is sold, the market price corresponds to that required to clear the market, that is, that given by the demand curve. This establishes a new market price on which suppliers base their next period's output, and this process continues to repeat itself. The type of stability of such a market, if any, will depend upon the relative slopes of the supply and demand curves. (What about the speed of market response in the cobweb model?) Two types of stability are illustrated in Figure 9.4–2. In part (a) the market possesses local stability, since if the initial price is such as p_s, the market price will converge to equilibrium. It is not globally stable as an initial price such as p_u results in an increasing divergence from the equilibrium price. In part (b) the market possesses orbital stability about the prices p_{o_1} and p_{o_2}. If the initial price is p_1, price over time will diverge and oscillate between p_{o_1} and p_{o_2}; given an initial price p_2, price will converge and oscillate between p_{o_1} and p_{o_2}.

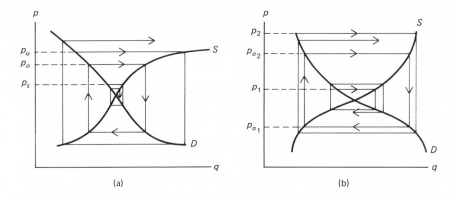

Figure 9.4-2   *The cobweb theorem illustrating (a) a market that is locally stable and not globally stable, and (b) a market that has orbital stability.*

When a *specific* dynamic mechanism is introduced in a multimarket adjustment process, the Hicksian conditions turn out to be necessary but not sufficient conditions for stability. In other dynamic models, the Hicksian conditions are not even necessary for stability. Samuelson (1941) presented an example of a system that fulfilled the Hicks conditions for perfect stability but that was dynamically unstable. On the other hand there are systems that do not conform to the Hicks definition for perfect stability but that are dynamically stable. For example, (Metzler, 1945), let $n = 2$ and suppose

$$\frac{dp_1}{dt} = -\alpha_1(p_1 - \bar{p}_1) - \alpha_1(p_2 - \bar{p}_2)$$

$$\frac{dp_2}{dt} = 2\alpha_2(p_1 - \bar{p}_1) + \alpha_2(p_2 - \bar{p}_2)$$

This system is stable or unstable depending on the relative values of α_1 and α_2, the speeds of adjustment in market 1 and market 2. If α_1 is greater than (less than) α_2 the system is stable (unstable). Lange (1945) and Metzler (1945) proved the following Theorem 9.4–1 relating the Hicks conditions to a dynamic system where the "speed of adjustment" is constant in each market.

Let $x_i = D_i(p_1, \ldots, p_n) - S_i(p_1, \ldots, p_n)$ be the excess demand in the ith market for $i = 1, \ldots, n$.

Then if $dp_i/dt = f_i(x_i)$ for all i we have, by dropping the higher-order terms in a Taylor's series:[15]

(1)
$$\frac{dp_i}{dt} = f_i(x_i)\Big|_{x_i=0} + f'_i \sum_{j=1}^{n} a_{ij}(p_j - \bar{p}_j)$$

[15] See Definition 5.3–4.

where $\bar{p}$ is the equilibrium price in the ith market, $a_{ij} = \partial x_i / \partial p_j$, a_{ij} is evaluated at $(\bar{p}_1, \ldots, \bar{p}_n)$, and $f_i' = \partial f_i / \partial x_i$. By assumption, the speed of adjustment with zero excess demand is zero,

$$f_i(x_i)\Big|_{x_i = 0} = 0$$

Therefore $dp_i/dt = f_i' \sum_{j=1}^{n} a_{ij}(p_i - \bar{p}_i)$, or for the entire system,

(2)
$$\begin{bmatrix} f_1' a_{11} & \cdots & f_1' a_{1n} \\ \vdots & & \vdots \\ f_n' a_{n1} & \cdots & f_n' a_{nn} \end{bmatrix} \begin{bmatrix} (p_1 - \bar{p}_1) \\ \vdots \\ (p_n - \bar{p}_n) \end{bmatrix} = \begin{bmatrix} dp_1/dt \\ \vdots \\ dp_n/dt \end{bmatrix}$$

or

$$[A][P - \bar{P}] = \left[\frac{dP}{dt}\right]$$

Theorem 9.4–1   If a market system is stable for all possible sets of adjustment speeds, then the Hicks conditions for perfect stability are satisfied.

PROOF   From Section 7.1 the solution to each differential equation is

(3)
$$(p_i - \bar{p}_i) = k_i e^{\lambda t}, \quad \text{for} \quad i = 1, \ldots, n$$

where k_i and λ are constants. Thus, if the $\lim_{t \to \infty} (p_i - \bar{p}_i) = 0$, the real part of λ must be negative.

Substituting (3) in (2) and factoring out $e^{\lambda t}$, we have

(4)
$$\begin{bmatrix} f_1' a_{11} - \lambda & \cdots & f_1' a_{1n} \\ \vdots & & \\ f_n' a_{n1} & \cdots & f_n' a_{nn} - \lambda \end{bmatrix} \begin{bmatrix} k_1 \\ \vdots \\ k_n \end{bmatrix} = \begin{bmatrix} 0 \\ \vdots \\ 0 \end{bmatrix}$$

or

$$[A^*][k] = [0]$$

For a nontrivial solution this means that $|A^*| = 0$, but $|A^*|$ is the characteristic equation for $[A]$ in (2), where λ is the vector of characteristic roots. Since (4) must be satisfied for all values of f_1', if $f_2', \ldots, f_n' = 0$, then $f_1' a_{11} = \lambda < 0$ or $a_{11} < 0$. This is the first condition for Hicksian perfect stability. On the other hand, for very large f_i' the diagonal product will dominate the sign of the determinant; that is, sign $|A^*| = \text{sign} (-1)^n$. This in turn requires that sign $|A| = \text{sign} (-1)^n$ since, if sign $|A| = \text{sign} (-1)^{n+1}$, then $|A^*| = 0$ for some real positive value of λ. This is the last Hicksian condition. Taking any number of $f_i' = 0$ produces similar results for the remaining Hicksian conditions for perfect stability.   QED

The concept of a stable matrix as used in Theorem 9.4–1 can be stated explicitly and the following two theorems proven.

DEFINITION 9.4–9   For a square ($n \times n$) matrix A, if every characteristic root has a negative real part then A is a **stable matrix.**

Theorem 9.4–2   *Routh-Hurwitz Theorem*   A real matrix A is stable if and only if:

$$
(1) \qquad\qquad a_i = (-1)^1 \sum_j a_j^i > 0
$$

for all $i = 1, \ldots, n$, where $\sum_j a_j^i$ is the sum of all ith order principal minor determinants of A^{16} and

$$
(2) \quad
\begin{vmatrix} a_1 & a_3 \\ 1 & a_2 \end{vmatrix} > 0
\quad
\begin{vmatrix} a_1 & a_3 & a_5 \\ 1 & a_2 & a_4 \\ 0 & a_1 & a_3 \end{vmatrix} > 0 \cdots
\begin{vmatrix} a_1 & a_3 & \cdots & 0 \\ 1 & a_2 & \cdots & 0 \\ \vdots & & & \\ 0 & 0 & \cdots & a_n \end{vmatrix} > 0
$$

Example 1.   Let

$$
A = \begin{bmatrix} -2 & 2 \\ -10 & 8 \end{bmatrix}
$$

For A to be a stable matrix it is necessary that the sum of the first-order principal minors be greater than zero. Since $-2 + 8 > 0$, this condition is satisfied. The value of the second-order determinant or $|A|$ is 4, also positive. If A is stable it is also necessary that

$$
\begin{vmatrix} 6 & 0 \\ 1 & 4 \end{vmatrix} > 0
$$

a_3 is zero since A has no third-order determinants. Thus A is a stable matrix by Theorem 9.4–2.

Theorem 9.4–3   *Lyapunov Theorem*   A real matrix A is stable if and only if there exists a symmetric matrix B such that:

(1) $x'Bx > 0$ for any vector x with not all $x_i = 0$; and

(2) $x'[BA + A'B]x < 0$ for any vector x with not all $x_i = 0$ (i.e., B is a positive definite matrix and $[BA + A'B]$ is a negative definite matrix).[17]

An immediate corollary to the Lyapunov theorem follows by letting $B = I$, the identity matrix.

---

[16] a_3, for example, is (-1) times all third-order principal minor determinants and also if $i > n$, then $a_i = 0$. Cf. Theorem 8.4–3. For proof see Gantmacher (1960).

[17] For proof see Gantmacher (1960). Also refer to Theorem 9.5–4.

Corollary to Theorem 9.4–3 If, for a real $n \times n$ matrix A, $A + A'$ is negative definite, then A is stable.

Example 2. If

$$A = \begin{bmatrix} -3 & 1 \\ 2 & -1 \end{bmatrix}$$

then

$$A + A' = \begin{bmatrix} -6 & 3 \\ 3 & -2 \end{bmatrix}$$

-2 and $-6 < 0$,

$$\begin{vmatrix} -6 & 3 \\ 3 & -2 \end{vmatrix} = 12 - 9 = 3 > 0$$

Thus, A is negative quasidefinite (i.e., $A + A'$ is negative definite) and A is a stable matrix.

If we test the 2×2 matrix A used for the Routh–Hurwitz theorem in Example 1, the test fails (i.e., $A + A'$ is not negative definite). However, the corollary to the Lyapunov theorem only provides us with sufficient conditions for a stable matrix.

Although an economist may not have the precise values for every entry in a particular matrix, he may be able to deduce certain qualitative information or formulate hypotheses concerning the entries of the matrix. (For example, if the matrix is an input–output model, the sum of the entries in any row must be less than or equal to one.) The possibility of generating such information makes the following theorems useful in stability analysis.

Theorem 9.4–4 (McKenzie, 1960) A real $n \times n$ matrix A is stable if it has a negative and quasidominant diagonal.

DEFINITION 9.4–10 A real $n \times n$ matrix A has a **quasidominant diagonal** if there exist positive numbers $c_1, \ldots, c_n$ such that $c_i|a_{ii}| > \sum_{j \neq i} c_j|a_{ij}|$ for every i, or if there exist positive numbers $d_1, \ldots, d_n$ such that $d_i|a_{ii}| > \sum_{j \neq i} d_j|a_{ji}|$, for all i.

PROOF   A matrix is either singular or nonsingular. If A is singular then there exists a nonzero vector c such that $c'A = 0$, or that $\sum_{j=1}^{n} c_j a_{ji} = 0$ for all i. Let

$$c^* = \max_j |c_j|$$

Then $c_k^* a_{kk} = -\sum_{j \neq k} c_j a_{jk}$. Taking absolute values, this means that $c_k^*|a_{kk}| \leq \sum_{j \neq k} |c_j||a_{jk}| \leq \sum c_k^*|a_{jk}|$, which contradicts the assumption of a quasidominant diagonal. Hence A is nonsingular. Now consider an element $a_{ii} - \lambda$. Then for $R(\lambda)$ and $I(\lambda)$, the real and imaginary parts of λ, we have

$$|a_{ii} - \lambda| = \sqrt{[a_{ii} - R(\lambda)]^2 + I(\lambda)^2} \leq |a_{ii} - R(\lambda)|$$

Since $a_{ii} < 0$, if the real part of λ, $R(\lambda)$, is ≥ 0, then

$$|a_{ii} - R(\lambda)| \geq |a_{ii}|$$

Thus the matrix $A - \lambda I$ has also a quasidominant diagonal and $A - \lambda I$ must also be nonsingular. Consequently, a λ such that $R(\lambda) \geq 0$ cannot be a characteristic root. Therefore, for the characteristic root of A, $R(\lambda) < 0$, and hence A is stable.   QED

As a corollary to Theorem 9.4–4, if the absolute values of all the elements along the diagonal are greater than the sum of the absolute values of its row or column, then A is stable. If this is true, we can let $c_i = 1$ (or $d_i = 1$) for all i and satisfy the theorem.

Problems

9.4–1   Given the following supply and demand functions:

$$q^s = 100 - 2p$$
$$q^d = 75 - p$$

(a) What is the static equilibrium price–quantity combination?

(b) If excess supply (demand) causes prices to be bid down (bid up) according to

$$\frac{\Delta p}{\Delta t} = \tfrac{1}{2}(q^d - q^s)$$

is the above market stable for $q^d > q^s$? For $q^d < q^s$? Is this Walrasian or Marshallian stability?

(c) If excess supply (demand) causes producers to reduce (increase) the quantity supplied in the next period according to

$$\frac{\Delta q^s}{\Delta t} = \tfrac{1}{2}(q^d - q^s)$$

is the above market stable when $q^d \neq q^s$? Is it Walrasian or Marshallian stability?

9.4–2   Give an example of a market that is
(a) locally stable but not globally stable
(b) quasistable but not locally stable
(c) quasistable and locally stable but not globally stable

9.4–3   Given the following relation between price changes and excess demand in the ith market, x_i, $i = 1, 2, 3$:

$$5 + \frac{dp_2}{dp_1} + \frac{dp_3}{dp_1} = \frac{dx_1}{dp_1}$$

$$-1 - 3\frac{dp_2}{dp_1} = \frac{dx_2}{dp_1}$$

$$1 - 4\frac{dp_2}{dp_1} - \frac{dp_3}{dp_1} = \frac{dx_3}{dp_1}$$

(a) Write the above system in matrix notation.
(b) Does the above system satisfy the Hicks condition for imperfect stability? Explain why.
(c) Does it satisfy the Hicks condition for perfect stability? Why?

9.4–4   For a two-commodity world, we have the following equations for price adjustment:

$$\frac{dp_1}{dt} = -3(p_1 - 50) - 3(p_2 - 100)$$

$$\frac{dp_2}{dt} = 4(p_1 - 50) + 2(p_2 - 100)$$

(a) If $p_1 < 50$ and $p_2 < 100$, what will be the signs of dp_1/dt and dp_2/dt?
(b) Does the above system satisfy the Hicks conditions for perfect stability?
(c) Explain in words why the above system is dynamically stable.

9.4–5   If

$$A = \begin{bmatrix} 1 & 1 \\ -5 & 4 \end{bmatrix}$$

(a) How many first-order principal minor determinants are there? Second-order?
(b) Find the sum of all first-order principal minor determinants.
(c) Find the sum of all second-order principal minor determinants.
(d) Is A a stable matrix?

9.4–6   Which of the following matrices are stable?

(a) $\begin{bmatrix} -5 & 4 \\ -3 & 2 \end{bmatrix}$

(b) $\begin{bmatrix} -3 & 5 \\ -6 & -1 \end{bmatrix}$

(c) $\begin{bmatrix} -2 & -3 \\ -5 & -2 \end{bmatrix}$

(d) $\begin{bmatrix} -1 & -3 & 4 \\ 0 & -2 & -1 \\ -1 & 1 & -2 \end{bmatrix}$

(e) $\begin{bmatrix} -4 & 0 & 0 \\ -2 & -6 & 1 \\ -1 & 5 & -3 \end{bmatrix}$

9.4–7   Using the corollary to Theorem 9.4–3, which of the following matrices can definitely be said to be stable matrices?

(a) $\begin{bmatrix} -4 & -2 \\ 2 & -1 \end{bmatrix}$

(b) $\begin{bmatrix} -3 & 2 \\ 1 & -1 \end{bmatrix}$

(c) $\begin{bmatrix} -3 & 0 \\ -10 & -6 \end{bmatrix}$ 　　　　　(e) $\begin{bmatrix} -4 & -1 \\ -1 & 3 \end{bmatrix}$

(d) $\begin{bmatrix} -3 & -2 \\ 1 & -4 \end{bmatrix}$

9.4-8　If possible, find c_1 and c_2 such that the matrices in Problem 9.4–7 can be shown to be stable by Theorem 9.4–4.

9.5　MORE ECONOMIC EXAMPLES OF STABILITY ANALYSIS[18]

Gross Substitutes and Local Stability

Theorem 9.4–4 can be applied to a market where all commodities are gross substitutes and local stability can be proved. Note that the qualitative hypothesis of the following theorem, while restrictive and perhaps unrealistic, leads to some meaningful statements about the solution of a system of simultaneous equations.

Theorem 9.5–1　If all commodities in an n-commodity world of exchange (where the excess demand functions are $x_i = x_i(p_1, \ldots, p_n)$ with $\partial x_i/\partial p_i < 0$) have the property of gross substitutatility, that is, $\partial x_i/\partial p_j = a_{ij} > 0$, for all $i \neq j$, then the equilibrium price vector, $\bar{P} = (\bar{p}_1, \ldots, \bar{p}_n)$, is locally stable for all speeds of adjustment.

PROOF　We shall show that the hypotheses of the theorem satisfy the requirements of a negative quasidominant diagonal, and thus the resulting A matrix, is stable by Theorem 9.4–4, which implies that the equilibrium is locally stable.

Since the excess demand functions represent a willingness and ability to exchange commodities and the prices represent relative exchange ratios, $\sum_{i=1}^{n} p_i x_i + x_m = 0$, for any P (i.e., Walras' law for purely competitive exchange holds). x_m is the excess demand for "money."[19] Differentiating with respect to p_j yields

$$\sum_{i=1}^{n} p_i a_{ij} + x_j = -a_{mj} \qquad \text{for } j = 1, \ldots, n$$

Evaluating the expression at $\bar{P}$ and remembering that $a_{mj} > 0$, we have $\sum_{i=1}^{n} \bar{p}_i a_{ij} < 0$ or $-\bar{p}_j a_{jj} > \sum_{i \neq j} \bar{p}_i a_{ij}$.

---

[18] This section largely follows Quirk and Saposnik (1968).

[19] "Money" here may either exist as coins and currency, a numeraire commodity, or merely ledger entries.

Since $a_{jj} < 0$ and $a_{ij} > 0$ for all $i \neq j$, the $n \times n$ matrix A has a negative quasidominant diagonal. Hence, by Theorem 9.4–4, A is stable and the equilibrium is locally stable.   QED

Global stability requires a stronger assumption about the properties of the excess demand equations. Theorem 9.4–5 proves only local stability, since the hypotheses apply only to the partial derivatives of the x_i functions. Before giving some examples of conditions that imply global stability, for completeness we present the following two theorems due to Quirk and Ruppert (1965) and Morishima (1952). These give additional conditions under which A will be stable. These are purely qualitative theorems, because all they require is information as to the sign of the elements in the matrix A.

Theorem 9.5–2   If A is an $n \times n$, indecomposable, real matrix such that;

(1) $a_{ij}a_{ji} \leq 0$ for all $i \neq j$;

(2) for any i, j, and k such that $i \neq j \neq k$, $a_{ij} \neq 0$ and $a_{jk} \neq 0$ imply $a_{ki} = 0$;

(3) $a_{ii} \leq 0$ for all i and $a_{jj} < 0$ for at least one j; and

(4) in the expansion of $|A|$ not all terms are zero;

then A is a stable matrix. Furthermore, it is called a **sign-stable matrix,** since any matrix with the sign pattern satisfying the conditions is a stable matrix. Hence, if the marginal adjustments to equilibrium satisfy the above qualitative conditions the equilibrium is locally stable.

Theorem 9.5–3   If A is a real, $n \times n$ matrix such that:

(1) $a_{ij} \neq 0$ for all i and j;

(2) $a_{ii} < 0$ for all i;

(3) sign $a_{ij} =$ sign a_{ji} for all i and j; and

(4) sign $a_{ij}a_{jk} =$ sign a_{ik} for $i \neq j \neq k$;

then A is a stable matrix if and only if A satisfies the Hicks conditions for perfect stability.

Unique and Globally Stable Equilibrium
    The theorems that follow concerning unique and globally stable equilibria utilize the following theorem of Lyapunov for proving stability.[20]

---

[20] For more details see Hahn (1963).

Theorem 9.5–4 *Lyapunov's Fundamental Theorem for Stability.*[21]   Let $\bar{x}$ denote an equilibrium solution vector of the vector of equations $F(x)$, where $F(\bar{x}) = 0$. The equilibrium $\bar{x}$ is globally stable if there exists a distance function $D(x - \bar{x})$ such that

$$\frac{dD(x - \bar{x})}{dt} < 0 \qquad \text{for any } x \neq \bar{x}$$

or if there exists a distance function $D^*[F(x)]$ such that

$$\frac{dD^*[F(x)]}{dt} < 0 \qquad \text{for any } x \neq \bar{x}$$

A typical example of a distance function is a Euclidean distance function $D(x - \bar{x}) = [\sum_{i=1}^{n} (x_i - \bar{x}_i)^2]^{1/2}$ and $D^*[F(x)] = \{\sum_{i=1}^{n} [F_i(x)]^2\}^{1/2}$. Of course, these are not the only kind of distance function that may be used.[22] The theorem asserts that all we need to do to establish stability properties is to find any distance function such that either the distance between x and $\bar{x}$ is diminishing over time *or* that some measure of the degree that the distance functions are from being zero is diminishing over time. While this theorem is intuitively appealing and relatively simple, it has a great many applications. In fact, Theorem 9.5–4 and Theorem 9.4–3 have a good deal in common. The following theorem relates the Lyapunov theorem to a negative quasi-definite matrix A.

Theorem 9.5–5 (Arrow–Hurwicz, 1958) If A, an $n \times n$, real matrix, is negative quasidefinite [i.e., if $x'[A + A']x < 0$ for any real $x \neq 0$], then A is a stable matrix. Hence, for the system of simultaneous equations $F(x)$, where $F(\bar{x}) = 0$, and the change in x when not equal to $\bar{x}$ is

(1) $$\frac{\partial F_i}{\partial x_j} = a_{ij}$$

and

(2) $$\frac{dx_i}{dt} = k_i F_i \qquad \text{where } k_i > 0$$

then this equilibrium is globally stable.

PROOF   By Theorem 9.5–4 it suffices to show that negative quasidefiniteness implies the existence of a distance function $D[F(x)]$ such that $dD[F(x)]/dt <$

[21] This is a more general statement of Theorem 9.4–3.

[22] Cf. Section 10.3, especially Definition 10.3–3.

0 unless $F(x) = 0$. Define $D[F(x)] = \frac{1}{2} \sum_{i=1}^{n} F_i(x)^2$. Then

$$(3) \qquad \frac{dD}{dt} = \sum_{i=1}^{n} \sum_{j=1}^{n} F_i \frac{\partial F_i}{\partial x_j} \frac{dx_j}{dt}$$

Since we are dealing with global stability, it involves no loss in generality to choose the unit of x_i such that $k_i = 1$. Then substituting (2) into (3) we have

$$(4) \qquad \frac{dD}{dt} = F'[A]F$$

where F' is an $1 \times n$ vector and A is an $n \times n$ matrix. It immediately follows that if A is negative quasidefinite,

$$\frac{dD}{dt} = F'[\tfrac{1}{2}(A + A')]F < 0 \qquad \text{QED}$$

Theorem 9.5–5 is analogous to Theorem 9.4–3. A similar analogy exists for Theorem 9.4–4. In Theorem 9.5–6, we consider a matrix A with a negative quasidominant diagonal, relate such a matrix to the dynamic adjustment process, and deduce global stability.

Theorem 9.5–6 (Arrow, Block, and Hurwicz, 1959) For a system of simultaneous equations $F(x)$, where $F(\bar{x}) = 0$, suppose the adjustment process of $x \neq \bar{x}$ is defined by the differential equation system

$$(1) \qquad \frac{dx_j}{dt} = a_j f_j(x) \qquad \text{for all } j$$

where a_j is a positive constant, and

$$(2) \qquad \bar{x} > 0$$

Then the system is globally stable if there exists a set of positive constants $c_1, \ldots, c_n$ such that

$$(3) \qquad f_{jj} < 0$$

and

$$(4) \qquad c_j |f_{jj}| > \sum_{i \neq j} c_i |f_{ji}|$$

If the matrix A has a negative quasidominant diagonal the system possesses global stability.

PROOF   The proof consists of showing that $dD/dt < 0$ for the distance function

$$D = \max_j \frac{|a_j f_j|}{c_j}$$

wherever dD/dt exists except at equilibrium $\bar{x}$. Let

(5)
$$\frac{|a_k f_k|}{c_k} \geq \frac{|a_j f_j|}{c_j} \qquad \text{for all } j$$

Then

$$D = \frac{|a_k f_k|}{c_k}$$

Thus

$$\frac{dD}{dt} = \left(\frac{a_k}{c_k}\right)(\text{sign } f_k)\sum_{i=1}^{n} f_{ki}\frac{dx_i}{dt}$$

From (1) we have

$$\frac{dD}{dt} = \frac{a_k}{c_k}(\text{sign } f_k)\sum_{i=1}^{n} f_{ki}f_i a_i$$

which we must show to be negative. If $x \neq \bar{x}$, then $f_j \neq 0$ for some j. Hence $|f_k| > 0$. From (4),

$$c_k|f_{kk}\|f_k| > \sum_{i \neq k}^{n} c_i|f_{ki}\|f_k|$$

Further, from (5) it follows that

(6)
$$c_k|f_{kk}\|f_k| > \sum_{i \neq k} c_i|f_{ki}|\left(\frac{a_i c_k}{a_k c_i}\right)|f_i|$$

Since $f_{kk} < 0$, then by multiplying both sides of (6) by a_k/c_k we have

$$-f_{kk}(\text{sign } f_k)f_k a_k > \sum_{i \neq k}^{n} |f_{ki}\|f_i|a_i \geq (\text{sign } f_k)\sum_{i \neq k}^{n} f_{ki}f_i a_i$$

Thus

$$\frac{dD}{dt} = (\text{sign } f_k)\sum_{i=1}^{n} f_{ki}f_i a_i < 0 \qquad \text{QED}$$

Before turning to the next section on qualitative models, the correspondence principle, and comparative static analysis, we state a final exemplary theorem that demonstrates some conditions producing a unique and globally stable equilibrium. This is similar to Theorem 9.5–1. It is also due to Arrow, Block, and Hurwicz (1959) and utilizes a more general concept of gross substitutability.

Theorem 9.5–7 If all commodities in an n-commodity world of exchange are gross substitutes in the sense that for all excess demand equations $x_i(P)$ for $i = 1, \ldots, n$ and two price vectors P' and P'', where $p_i' = p_i''$, for all $i \neq j$ and $p_j' > p_j''$, then it is true that $x_i(P') > x_i(P'')$ for all $i \neq j$, and the equilibrium is unique and globally stable.

The conditions of Theorem 9.5–7 and its conclusion assert that if the price of the jth commodity increases, the excess demand for the ith commodity will increase. This will bid up the price in the ith market and consequently produce a dynamic interaction that will bring the system into equilibrium. It should be reiterated that the likelihood of all commodities possessing such properties is small for any economic system. Theorem 9.5–7 represents some sufficient conditions that are not necessary. Fuller utilization of the foregoing properties of systems of market adjustment equations await the development of conditions that are both necessary and sufficient.

Problems

9.5–1   Which of the following matrices are sign stable?

(a) $\begin{bmatrix} -5 & -1 \\ 2 & -2 \end{bmatrix}$

(c) $\begin{bmatrix} -1 & 2 & 3 & -5 \\ 0 & -1 & -6 & 3 \\ -7 & 4 & -2 & 1 \\ 2 & 3 & 0 & -2 \end{bmatrix}$

(b) $\begin{bmatrix} -2 & -1 & 4 \\ 3 & -1 & -2 \\ -1 & 2 & -3 \end{bmatrix}$

(d) $\begin{bmatrix} - & + & - & - \\ - & - & + & - \\ + & 0 & - & + \\ 0 & + & - & - \end{bmatrix}$

9.5–2   For the system of excess demand equations

$$F_1 = 50 - 4x_1 - x_2 - x_3$$
$$F_2 = 80 - 4x_1 - 8x_2 + x_3$$
$$F_3 = 100 - 2x_1 - x_2 - 4x_3$$

where $F_i = \dot{x}_i$:
(a) Find $\bar{x}$.
(b) Find $A = [a_{ij}]$, $a_{ij} = \partial F_i / \partial x_j$.
(c) Find $A + A'$.
(d) Is the system of equations globally stable? Why?
(e) Find $\dot{x}$ at (10, 5, 15) and $\dot{x}$ at (20, 0, 0). Explain these answers.

9.6 QUALITATIVE MODELS, COMPARATIVE STATICS, AND THE CORRESPONDENCE PRINCIPLE

A typical principle of economics taught to beginning students is the following: Suppose that the market for bread is in equilibrium and one night the bread fairy comes along and increases everyone's preference for bread. This causes an outward shift to the right in the demand for bread. If supply is upward sloping, the quantity of bread sold will increase and the price of bread will rise.

Such a statement as illustrated in Figure 9.6–1 is an example of comparative static analysis. Such a comparative static analysis implicitly assumes that the adjustment process is dynamically stable and further that the market price and quantity will move from (p^0, q^0) to (p', q') in some fashion. Thus, for a comparative static statement to be meaningful, there must be a direct correspondence between the two equilibrium values and a stable dynamic adjustment process. This is a bit of a rub, as the obvious advantage of comparative static analysis is its simplicity and omission of the details of minute and explicit changes in the variables. Now, it seems that the only way to meaningfully use a simple comparative static analysis is to have information of the more complex, dynamic adjustment process.

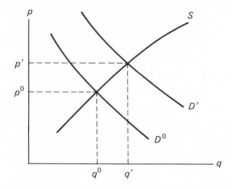

Figure 9.6–1 *A principle of comparative static analysis.*

Before proceeding, let us define more explicitly the following terms.

DEFINITION 9.6–1 **Comparative statics** is that branch of economic theory whose task it is to show the effects on equilibrium values of given variables resulting from changes in some specified data (or parameters).

DEFINITION 9.6–2 The **correspondence principle**[23] is the direct connection between useful comparative static statements and the underlying stability of equilibrium.

DEFINITION 9.6–3 **Comparative static information** is available from an economic model when one is able to determine the qualitative change in a variable due to a change in a parameter. **Complete comparative static information** is available if one is able to determine the qualitative change in all variables of the model.

[23] Samuelson (1947).

The thesis put forward by Samuelson (1947) in his *Foundations of Economic Analysis* is that comparative static information can be obtained by three basic means:

(1) viewing each equilibrium position as a regular maximum of some functional relation;
(2) by assuming stable equilibria exist and using the properties of stability to infer such comparative static conclusions; or
(3) by having certain qualitative information available concerning the dynamic adjustment process.

Of course one can deduce comparative static theorems without recourse to a dynamic system, but the meaningfulness, predictiveness, and relevance of such statements is nil without some consideration of stability. There are two alternatives possible: (1) stability may be hypothesized or (2) since comparative statics involve *qualitative* conclusions, these conclusions may be achieved with *only* qualitative information of the underlying dynamic system. Thus the first tenet of Samuelson's thesis is not relevant unless all such behavior (i.e., microeconomic maximization) implies stability. The second tenet uses stability to derive qualitative information, while the third is just reversed, that is, *only qualitative* dynamic information is used to derive further comparative static theorems. Either of the latter two cases turns out to be less imposing, since only qualitative information rather than precise quantitative data is required.

This has led to the development of qualitative economic models and the associated necessary and sufficient conditions on the sign patterns of these qualitative models, so that comparative static conclusions may be reached.

Suppose we have a system of n equations and n unknowns $(x_1, \ldots, x_n)$ and m shift parameters, $a_1, \ldots, a_m$. The a_i are the "data" specified in the model. Thus we have

$$f_1(x_1, \ldots, x_n; a_1, \ldots, a_m) = 0$$
$$\vdots$$
$$f_n(x_1, \ldots, x_n; a_1, \ldots, a_m) = 0$$

For comparative statics we have known changes in the data, da_i. Thus

$$\frac{\partial f_1}{\partial x_1} d\bar{x}_1 + \cdots + \frac{\partial f_1}{\partial x_n} d\bar{x}_n = -\sum_{i=1}^{m} \frac{\partial f_1}{\partial a_i} da_i$$
$$\vdots$$
$$\frac{\partial f_n}{\partial x_1} d\bar{x}_1 + \cdots + \frac{\partial f_n}{\partial x_n} d\bar{x}_n = -\sum_{i=1}^{m} \frac{\partial f_n}{\partial a_i} da_i$$

or in matrix notation, $A \, d\bar{x} = b$, where

$$A = \left[\frac{\partial f_i}{\partial x_j} \right], \ d\bar{x} = [d\bar{x}_i], \text{ and } b = \left[-\sum_{i=1}^{m} \frac{\partial f_j}{\partial a_i} \, da_i \right]$$

$d\bar{x}_i$ is the change in the equilibrium value of the ith variable.

DEFINITION 9.6–4 A **purely qualitative model**, $A \, d\bar{x} = b$, is one where A is a matrix of partial derivatives, $d\bar{x}$ is a vector of changed equilibrium values, b is a vector of parameter shift effects, and the only knowledge of A and b is the signs of their elements.

Although this approach was initiated by Samuelson (1947), Lancaster (1962, 1964) and Gorman (1964) generated the necessary and sufficient conditions for the solution of a qualitative model.

Theorem 9.6–1 *Lancaster–Gorman Theorem* A purely qualitative model $A \, d\bar{x} = b$ may be solved to obtain complete comparative static information if the matrix $C = [A, b]$ can be brought into *partitionable* form.

DEFINITION 9.6–5 For the system $A \, d\bar{x} = b$ let $C = [A, b]$. C can be brought into **partitionable form** if by interchanging the rows and columns of C or multiplying a row or column by -1, C can be brought into the form

$$\begin{bmatrix} a_1 & a_2 \\ A_1 & 0_1 \\ 0_2 & A_2 \end{bmatrix}$$

where a_1 is a $(1 \times k)$-dimensional vector, such that $a_1 \geq 0$ (i.e., $a_{1i} \geq 0$ and $a_{1j} > 0$ for some j); a_2 is a $(1 \times n + 1 - k)$-dimensional vector, such that $a_2 \leq 0$ (i.e., $a_{2i} \leq 0$ and $a_{2j} < 0$ for some j); A_1 is a $(k - 1 \times k)$ matrix; A_2 is an $(n - k \times n + 1 - k)$ matrix; 0_1 is a $(k - 1 \times n + 1 - k)$ matrix of all zeros; and 0_2 is an $(n - k \times k)$ matrix of all zeros. Furthermore, A_1 and A_2 can be partitioned into the same pattern until rows with only one positive and one negative element are reached.[24]

Example 1. Suppose we have the following qualitative information for the system $A \, d\bar{x} = b$:

$$\begin{bmatrix} - & - & + \\ 0 & 0 & - \\ - & + & 0 \end{bmatrix} \begin{bmatrix} d\bar{x}_1 \\ d\bar{x}_2 \\ d\bar{x}_3 \end{bmatrix} = \begin{bmatrix} + \\ + \\ 0 \end{bmatrix}$$

---

[24] The proof of Theorem 9.6–1 follows from a series of lemmas and the interested reader should consult Lancaster (1962, 1964) and Gorman (1964) for full details.

The matrix $C = [A, b]$ is

$$C = \begin{bmatrix} - & - & + & + \\ 0 & 0 & - & + \\ - & + & 0 & 0 \end{bmatrix}$$

C can be put into partitional form by rearranging columns 1 and 2 with columns 3 and 4. That is, we shall then obtain

$$\begin{bmatrix} + & + & \vdots & - & - \\ + & - & \vdots & 0 & 0 \\ 0 & 0 & \vdots & + & - \end{bmatrix}$$

which conforms to Definition 9.6–5. That $A\,d\bar{x} = b$ can be qualitatively solved is verified by applying Cramer's rule. For example,

$$d\bar{x}_1 = \frac{|A_1|}{|A|} = \frac{\begin{vmatrix} + & - & + \\ + & 0 & - \\ 0 & + & 0 \end{vmatrix}}{\begin{vmatrix} - & - & + \\ 0 & 0 & - \\ - & + & 0 \end{vmatrix}} = \frac{+}{-} < 0$$

In other words, given the qualitative information in $A\,d\bar{x} = b$, the equilibrium value of x_1 will decrease. Furthermore, since C can be put in partitional form, we can obtain unambiguous results for $d\bar{x}_2$ and $d\bar{x}_3$ as well. (What will be the change in $d\bar{x}_2$ and $d\bar{x}_3$, $\gtreqless 0$?)

Comparative Static Economic Theorems

The following comparative statics theorem is due to Basset, Maybee, and Quirk (1968).

Theorem 9.6–2 For an economic system of n commodities, where x_i is the excess demand for commodity i, $A = [\partial x_i / \partial p_j]$, and each excess demand equation has one shift parameter α_i, if A is stable and $dx_i / d\alpha_i > 0$, then there exists a k such that $d\bar{p}_k / d\alpha_k > 0$.

PROOF   Since A is stable, $|A_{ii}|/|A| < 0$, and for $A^{-1} = [a_{ij}^{-1}]$, $a_{ii}^{-1} = |A_{ii}|/|A| < 0$. Thus, since at least one diagonal element of A^{-1} is negative and

$$\left[\frac{d\bar{p}}{d\alpha} \right] = A^{-1} \begin{bmatrix} 0 \\ \vdots \\ -1 \\ 0 \end{bmatrix}$$

for at least one k, $d\bar{p}_k / d\alpha_k > 0$.   QED

Theorem 9.6–2 asserts that if A is stable and if $dx_i/d\alpha_i > 0$, then the effect on the price of the kth commodity by a positive change in its shift parameter, α_k, must be to increase p_k. Suppose, for example, that income is a shift parameter in every excess demand equation. If i is a normal good $dx_i/d\alpha_i > 0$, then the price of all commodities cannot decrease to a stable equilibrium. That is, if A is stable the new equilibrium must have at least one commodity with a higher price.

Similar comparative static theorems can be proven using the results of Section 4.2. Hicks' "laws" of comparative statics are an example.

Theorem 9.6–3 If all commodities are gross substitutes, then a shift in demand away from x_0 (the numeraire commodity where $p_0 \equiv 1$), to commodity x_i, all other excess demands being unchanged, will cause:

(1) $d\bar{p}_i > 0$;
(2) $d\bar{p}_j > 0$ for all $j \neq 0$; and
(3) $d\bar{p}_i > d\bar{p}_j$ for $j \neq 0$ and $j \neq 1$.

PROOF Since

$$dx_i = \frac{\partial x_i}{\partial p_1} dp_1 + \cdots + \frac{\partial x_i}{\partial p_n} dp_n > 0$$

and $dx_j = 0$ for $j \neq i$, we have the system

$$[A][dp] = \begin{bmatrix} 0 \\ \vdots \\ + \\ \vdots \\ 0 \end{bmatrix}$$

Define the matrix A^* such that $A = sI - A^*$, where the scalar $s > r^*$, the maximal characteristic root of A^*. By Theorem 4.5–9, $A^{-1} > 0$. Therefore

$$dp_i > 0 \quad \text{and} \quad dp_j > 0$$

This proves (1) and (2). Furthermore, by Theorem 4.5–10, $|A_{ii}| > |A_{ij}|$. Thus, since

$$dp_i = \frac{|A_{ii}|}{|A|} \quad \text{and} \quad dp_j = \frac{|A_{ij}|}{|A|}$$

we have $dp_i > dp_j$. QED

These results can be even further generalized by what is termed the "Morishima case."[25]

[25] Morishima (1952).

DEFINITION 9.6–6 An indecomposable matrix[26] M is a **Morishima matrix** if by moving like rows and columns, it can be put into the following form:

$$M = \begin{bmatrix} M_{11} & M_{12} \\ M_{21} & M_{22} \end{bmatrix}$$

where M_{11} and M_{22} are square and contain no negative elements (M_{11} and $M_{22} \geq 0$), while M_{12} and M_{21} contain no positive elements (M_{12} and $M_{21} \leq 0$).

Theorem 9.6–4 (Morishima, 1952) If M is a Morishima matrix, then there exists a maximal characteristic root, r^*, of M such that:

(1) r^* is real and positive;
(2) $r^* \geq |r|$, where r is any characteristic root of M; and
(3) $r^* > m_{ii}$, the diagonal elements of M.

Further, if $M^* = [M - sI]^{-1}$, where the scalar $s > r^*$, then for

$$M^* = \begin{bmatrix} M_{11}^* & M_{12}^* \\ M_{21}^* & M_{22}^* \end{bmatrix}$$

(1) M_{11}^* and $M_{22}^* < 0$

and

(2) M_{12}^* and $M_{21}^* > 0$

This leads immediately to the following generalization of Theorem 9.6–3.

Theorem 9.6–5 (Morishima, 1952) Given an $(n + 1)$-commodity world, where x_0 is the numeraire commodity ($p_0 \equiv 1$); $A = M - sI$, where M is a Morishima matrix, $A = [\partial x_i / \partial p_j]$; x_i is the excess demand for the ith commodity; and A is stable. If there is a shift in demand from the numeraire commodity to the ith commodity while all other excess demand functions are unchanged, then:

(1) $d\bar{p}_i > 0$;
(2) if $\partial x_j / \partial p_i > 0$ for $i \neq j$, then $d\bar{p}_j > 0$ (i.e., if i and j are substitutes p_j will increase); and
(3) if $\partial x_j / \partial p_i < 0$ for $i \neq j$, then $d\bar{p}_j < 0$ (i.e., if i and j are complements, p_j decreases).

Unfortunately, the comparative static conclusions of Theorem 9.6–5 are not likely to be relevant, as the Morishima assumptions do not ensure stability. In fact, it can be shown that if all commodities follow the Morishima

[26] Definition 4.5–4.

conditions and we eliminate the gross substitutes, the equilibrium is not locally stable. Even if some goods are gross substitutes, stability cannot be demonstrated.

Problems

9.6–1   For the following qualitative model, determine whether or not $C = [A, b]$ can be brought into partitional form.

$$\begin{bmatrix} - & + & + \\ 0 & - & + \\ + & 0 & 0 \end{bmatrix}\begin{bmatrix} d\bar{x}_1 \\ d\bar{x}_2 \\ d\bar{x}_3 \end{bmatrix} = \begin{bmatrix} - \\ 0 \\ - \end{bmatrix}$$

9.6–2   To verify your results in Problem 9.6–1, solve for $d\bar{x}_1$ by Cramer's rule and show whether $d\bar{x}_1$ is qualitatively determinable or not.

9.6–3   Suppose we have a four-commodity world: food, clothing, shelter, and a numeraire commodity, money, and that, further, all commodities are gross substitutes.
   (a) If one individual has a change in preferences such that he decides to hold less money and buy more food, all other preferences unchanged, what must be the change in the price of food, clothing, and shelter?
   (b) What must be the change in the price of food relative to clothing? Of food relative to shelter?
   (c) Is the model such that a new equilibrium will be reached?

9.7 RELEVANCE OF SIMULTANEOUS EQUATIONS AND THEIR SOLUTIONS TO ECONOMIC THEORY

We conclude this chapter with a comment on the relevance of simultaneous equations and their solutions to economic theory. Suppose that we have an economic model of simultaneous equations for which we are able to demonstrate the existence and uniqueness of an equilibrium solution. Further, with a few more theorems we are able to prove global, dynamic stability. Everything would appear to be a bed of roses.

This is not quite correct. Clearly, if the models contain restrictive assumptions, such as the gross substitute assumptions of Theorems 9.5–1 and 9.5–7, the predictive properties and meaningfulness of the model will be reduced. However, suppose that we have succeeded in establishing a most general model, with assumptions and conditions so innocuous that it would fit most any economic environment. Can we now retire from our analytical endeavors? Alas, no, even this is not sufficient to guarantee an economic solution to social ills. Still it is a necessity, for the model to be fruitful, that the corresponding real-world economy be in equilibrium within a reasonable period of time. Even though the model has a unique and stable equilibrium solution, the length of time required for the economy to attain that equilibrium must be relatively short. If the economy requires 2000 years to reach the equilibrium, the model is hardly going to be of much value.

This means that in addition to the foregoing problems, we have another: namely, a quantitative or qualitative evaluation of the time necessary for adjustment and some assurance that there are no induced "parametric" shifts. This latter problem implies a misspecification of parameters and variables, an improper or unusable mix of simplicity and realism.

The reader should bear in mind that none of the foregoing theorems and examples have considered this problem rigorously. As one might expect, this further question requires even more data and more detail concerning the interrelationships of economic agents and their environment. To some extent this question will be considered in Chapter 14 on control theory. However, to a larger extent, the answers to such further problems are little known beyond an intuitive or subjective evaluation of the length of the adjustment period and what the relevant variables are.

References

1. ARROW, K. J., and G. DEBREU (1954), "Existence of an Equilibrium for a Competitive Economy," *Econometrica*, **22**:265–290.
2. ARROW, K. J., and L. HURWICZ (1958), "The Stability of Competitive Equilibrium I," *Econometrica*, **26**:522–552.
3. ARROW, K. J., H. BLOCK, and L. HURWICZ (1959), "The Stability of Competitive Equilibrium II," *Econometrica*, **27**:82–109.
4. BASSETT, L., J. MAYBEE, and J. QUIRK (1968), "Qualitative Economics and the Scope of the Correspondence Principle," *Econometrica*, **36**:544–563.
5. DEBREU, G. (1959), *Theory of Value*, New York: Wiley.
6. DORFMAN, R., P. SAMUELSON, and R. SOLOW, (1958), *Linear Programming and Economic Analysis*, New York: McGraw-Hill.
7. GALE, DAVID (1955), "The Law of Supply and Demand," *Mathematica Scandinavia*, **3**:155–169 [reprinted in Newman (1958), pages 87–101].
8. GANTMACHER, F. R. (1960), *The Theory of Matrices*, New York: Chelsea.
9. GORMAN, W. M. (1964), "More Scope for Qualitative Economics," *Review of Economic Studies*, **31**:65–68.
10. HAHN, W. (1963), *Theory and Application of Lyapunov's Direct Method*, Englewood Cliffs, N.J.: Prentice-Hall.
11. HICKS, J. R. (1936), *Value and Capital*, London: Oxford University Press.
12. KAKUTANI, S. (1941), "A Generalization of Brouwer's Fixed Point Theorem," *Duke Mathematical Journal*, **8**:457–459 [reprinted in Newman (1968), pages 33–35].

13. KOOPMANS, T. (1957), *Three Essays on the State of Economic Science*, New York: McGraw-Hill.
14. KUENNE, R. E. (1963), *The Theory of General Economic Equilibrium*, Princeton, N.J.: Princeton University Press.
15. LANCASTER, K. J. (1962), "The Scope of Qualitative Economics," *Review of Economic Studies*, **29**:99–123.
16. LANCASTER, K. J. (1964), "Partitional Systems and Qualitative Economics," *Review of Economic Studies*, **31**:69–72.
17. LANGE, O. (1945), *Price Flexibility and Employment*, Bloomington, Ind.: Principia Press [appendix reprinted in Newman (1968), pages 178–196].
18. MCKENZIE, L. W. (1959), "On the Existence of a Competitive Equilibrium for a Competitive Market," *Econometrica*, **27**:54–71.
19. MCKENZIE, L. W. (1960), "The Matrix with Dominant Diagonal and Economic Theory," *Symposium on Mathematical Methods in the Social Sciences*, Palo Alto, Calif.: Stanford University Press.
20. MARSHALL, JOHN (1920), *Principles of Economics*, 8th ed., London: Macmillan.
21. METZLER, L. A. (1945), "Stability of Multiple Markets: The Hicks Conditions," *Econometrica*, **13**:277–292 [reprinted in Newman (1968), pages 197–212].
22. MORISHIMA, M. (1952), "On the Laws of Change of the Price System in an Economy Which Contains Complementary Commodities," *Osaka Economic Papers*, **1**:101–113.
23. NEWMAN, PETER (1968), *Readings in Mathematical Economics*, Baltimore, Md.: Johns Hopkins Press.
24. QUIRK, J., and R. RUPPERT (1965), "Qualitative Economics and the Stability of Equilibrium," *Review of Economics and Statistics*, **32**:311–326.
25. QUIRK, J., and R. SAPOSNIK (1968), *An Introduction to General Equilibrium Theory and Welfare Economics*, New York: McGraw-Hill.
26. SAMUELSON, P. A. (1941), "The Stability of Equilibrium: Comparative Statics and Dynamics," *Econometrica*, **9**:97–120.
27. SAMUELSON, P. A. (1947), *Foundations of Economic Analysis*, Cambridge, Mass.: Harvard University Press.
28. TOMPKINS, C. B. (1964), "Sperner's Lemma and Some Extensions" in E. P. Beckenbach (ed.), *Applied Combinatorial Mathematics*, New York: Wiley [reprinted in Newman (1968), pages 20–32].
29. WALD, ABRAHAM (1935), "On Some Systems of Equations of Mathematical Economics" (English translation), *Econometrica*, **19**:368–403 (1951).
30. WALRAS, LEON (1954), *Elements of Pure Economics* (tr. by W. Jaffe), Homewood, Ill.: Irwin.

Chapter 10

Calculus of Variations

10.1 INTRODUCTION: FUNCTIONALS

Before attempting a definition of the calculus of variations and a treatment of its most important techniques, we consider for illustrative purposes the classical problem in the calculus of variations. The brachistochrone problem (from two Greek words meaning "shortest time") was formulated and solved by J. Bernoulli in 1696.

The basic problem is this: Given two points in the xy plane, (a, y_a) and (b, y_b), where $y_b < y_a$ and $a \neq b$, find the curve with continuous first derivatives that minimizes the time it takes for a point of mass to roll from (a, y_a) to (b, y_b) in a frictionless system. If t is the time taken to roll from point 1 to point 2, the solution to the problem is the function selected from the infinitely many functions with continuous first derivatives that joins the points and minimizes t.

The formulation of this problem underlines the basic difference between the calculus of variations and ordinary calculus. In ordinary calculus the standard problem is, given a particular function, find the values of the independent variable(s) that maximize or minimize the value of the given function. The calculus of variations is also a technique for finding maxima and minima. Here we are dealing with a set of functions and are asked to select one element (one function) of the set that either maximizes or minimizes a particular objective function (usually an integral). The functional plays the same role in the calculus of variations as the function does in ordinary calculus.

DEFINITION 10.1–1 Let S be a set of functions and let R be the set of real numbers. A mapping, F, from S to R is a **functional** on S.

A functional thus associates one real number with every function in a particular set of functions. In the calculus of variations, the goal is to select a function that has either the smallest or largest image under a particular functional. What is the corresponding statement for ordinary calculus?

To return to the brachistochrone problem, let s be the distance along the

318

curve $y = y(x)$ measured from the initial point. Then velocity, v is equal to ds/dt. In our frictionless system with an initial velocity of zero, we have

$$(1) \qquad \tfrac{1}{2}mv^2 = mgy$$

where m is the mass of the particle, g is the gravitational constant, and y is the vertical distance of the particle from the initial point.[1] Then

$$v = \sqrt{2gy} = \frac{ds}{dt}$$

and

$$dt = \frac{ds}{\sqrt{2gy}}$$

or, by the definition of the distance, s,

$$ds = \sqrt{1 + \left(\frac{dy}{dx}\right)^2}\, dx$$

so that

$$(2) \qquad dt = \frac{\sqrt{1 + (dy/dx)^2}}{\sqrt{2gy}}\, dx$$

Integrating both sides of (2) yields

$$(3) \qquad t = \int_a^b \frac{\sqrt{1 + [y'(x)]^2}}{\sqrt{2gy(x)}}\, dx$$

Thus, of all the functions $f = \sqrt{1 + [y'(x)]^2}/\sqrt{2gy(x)}$ with continuous first derivatives, the problem is to select the particular function $\bar{f}$ for which $\int_a^b \bar{f}\, dx$ is a minimum. Equivalently, the problem may be viewed as finding the function $y = y(x)$ for which $\int_a^b \bar{f}\, dx$ is a minimum. The set of functions y is described by

$$(4) \qquad y(a) = y_a$$

$$(5) \qquad y(b) = y_b$$

(y passes through both endpoints), and

$$(6) \qquad \frac{dy}{dx} \text{ is continuous}$$

[1] Most introductory calculus books present this formula. See, e.g., Thomas (1968).

The functional in this case is the mapping that assigns to each function y^i satisfying (4)–(6) the image $t^i \in R$, where

$$t^i = \int_a^b f^i \, dx$$

Problems

10.1–1 Show that

$$F[y] = \int_a^b f(x, y(x), y'(x)) \, dx$$

is a functional for all x, $y(x)$, and $y'(x)$ if $f(x, y(x), y'(x))$ is continuous.

10.1–2 Show that the functional in Problem 10.1–1 includes all Riemann integrals as special cases.

10.1–3 Explain why a functional is sometimes referred to as a "function of functions."

10.2 GENERAL TYPES OF PROBLEMS

The brachistochrone problem is an example of the **fixed point–fixed point problem,** since both initial and terminal points are fixed. In many cases, one or both points are free to vary (usually along curves with continuous derivatives). Such problems are referred to as either (1) fixed point–variable point, (2) variable point–fixed point, or (3) variable point–variable point problems. In general, the solutions to these types are more difficult to obtain than the solutions to fixed point–fixed point problems. The types usually encountered in economic applications are fixed point–fixed point and fixed point–variable point problems. Examples of these and the other types will be encountered later.

Another classification of problem types that sheds additional light on the nature of the calculus of variations is:

(1) Brachistochrone problems (fixed point–fixed point).
(2) Minimum surfaces of revolution (fixed point–fixed point). Given two points, we are to select from the set of functions passing through each point with continuous derivatives, the function that produces a surface with minimum area when rotated about the horizontal axis.
(3) Isoperimetric problems (fixed point–fixed point). Given two points and a curve of fixed length passing through each, find the curve that encloses the largest possible area.
(4) "Navigation" problems (any of the types noted above). Given a river of certain width and current, find the path that will allow a boat with

constant speed to cross the river in the shortest period. Initial and terminal points need not be specified.

(5) Optimum control problems. Control theory will be discussed in detail in Chapter 14.

Another classification scheme could obviously be built around the number of independent variables in the functions under consideration. Both the case of one independent variable and the general case of $n(n \geq 2)$ independent variables will be considered.

Problem

10.2–1   Formulate economic examples of as many of the various types of problems as you can.

10.3   NORMED LINEAR SPACES AND THE DIFFERENTIAL OF A FUNCTIONAL

In this section and the ones that follow, we turn our attention to the theory of the calculus of variations. Our goal is to develop necessary and sufficient conditions for the various types of problems mentioned above.

DEFINITION 10.3–1   Given a set of elements S and a field F.[2] S is a **linear space over** F if:

(1) for all x and $y \in S$, $x + y$ is defined and $x + y$ is an element of S (S is closed under addition);
(2) addition is commutative and associative;
(3) $0 \in S$ is an additive identity;
(4) there is an additive inverse for every $x \in S$, denoted by $-x$;
(5) scalar multiplication of elements of S by elements of F is defined; if $s \in S$ and $f \in F$, then $fs \in S$;
(6) scalar multiplication is both associative and distributive; and
(7) the element $1 \in F$ is the multiplicative identity for scalar multiplication.

DEFINITION 10.3–2   Let S be a linear space over the field of real numbers, R. $\|x\|$ is called the **norm** of $x \in S$ if

(1) $\|x\| > 0$ for all $x \neq 0$ and $x \in S$;
(2) $\|x\| = 0$ if $x = 0$;
(3) $\|\lambda x\| = \lambda \|x\|$ for all $x \in S$ and $\lambda \in R$; and
(4) $\|x + y\| \leq \|x\| + \|y\|$. (This is usually referred to as the triangle inequality.)

---

[2] See Definition 2.7–5.

The concept of a norm is a generalization of the concept of the distance between two points in Euclidean space. Its importance here is that when a norm is defined on a linear space, it serves as the measure of the "distance" between two functions in that space.

DEFINITION 10.3–3 S is a **normed linear space over** R if S is a linear space over R and if a norm, $\|x\|$, is defined for all $x \in S$ that satisfies Definition 10.3–2.

Note that for a given linear space there may be several different norms defined, each of which satisfy Definition 10.3–2. At least one norm must exist for S to be a normed linear space.

The concepts of an open subset of a normed linear space and of a neighborhood of an element of S play roles in the calculus of variations analogous to those played by the open interval and the neighborhood of a point in the ordinary calculus.

DEFINITION 10.3–4   Let T be a subset of the normed linear space S. Then T is an **open subset** of S if for every $t \in T$ there is a number $\delta > 0$ such that $t + h \in T$ for all elements h of S for which $\|h\| < \delta$.[3]

DEFINITION 10.3–5 S is a normed linear space. Then the ε **neighborhood** of $s_0 \in S$, written $N^\varepsilon(s_0)$, is the open subset of S whose elements are $s_0 + h$, for $h \in S$, where $\|h\| < \varepsilon$.[4]

In other words, $N^\varepsilon(s_0)$ is the set of all elements of S such that $\|s - s_0\| < \varepsilon$. Intuitively, $N^\varepsilon(s_0)$ is the set of all functions in S lying within an ε distance of s_0.

Given the concepts of a normed linear space and an ε neighborhood of an element of the space, the concept of the differential of a function is easily generalized to the concept of the variation of a functional. As the differential of a function is crucial to the development of necessary and sufficient conditions for extreme values in ordinary calculus,[5] the variation of a functional is basic to the development of such conditions in the calculus of variations.

DEFINITION 10.3–6   Given that $F[y]$ is a functional and S is a normed linear space over R, the set of real numbers. $\delta F[h]$ is called the **first variation** of $F[y]$ at $y = y_0$ if for $r \in R$:

$$\delta F[h] = \frac{d}{dt} F[y_0 + th]\Big|_{t=0}$$

exists for all $h \in S$.

---

[3] Cf. Definitions 2.2–1 and 2.2–4.
[4] See the discussion of interior, exterior, and boundary points in Section 2.8.
[5] See Section 5.3.

An equivalent definition of $\delta F[h]$ that underscores its similarity to the ordinary differential is

$$\delta F[h] = \lim_{r \to 0} \frac{F[y_0 + rh] - F[y_0]}{r}$$

DEFINITION 10.3–7 The **total variation** of $F[y]$ at $y = y_0$ is $F[y_0 + h] - F[y_0]$, for $h \in S$. Furthermore, $F[y_0 + h] - F[y_0] = \delta F[h] + \varepsilon[h]$, where $\varepsilon[rh]/r \to 0$ as $r \to 0$, for $r \in R$.

We state the following properties of $\delta F[h]$ without proof[6]:

Theorem 10.3–1 $\delta F[h]$ is homogeneous of degree 1.

Theorem 10.3–2 $\delta F[h]$, if it exists, is unique.

All the elements of a given normed linear space S will not, in general, satisfy the initial conditions (boundary conditions) of a given problem. The subset of S whose elements are functions that satisfy the boundary conditions (pass through both the initial and terminal points in a fixed point–fixed point problem) is called the space of competing functions, denoted by Σ.

DEFINITION 10.3–8 Let S be a normed linear space, and let $\Sigma \subset S$ be a space of competing functions. Then $y_0 \in \Sigma$ yields a **relative minimum (maximum)** of $F[y]$ if

$$F[y] - F[y_0] \geq 0 \,(\leq 0)$$

for all $y \in \Sigma$ for which $\| y - y_0 \| < \delta$ for some constant $\delta > 0$.

This definition is closely analogous to the definition of relative maxima (minima) points in the ordinary calculus. (See Figure 10.3–1). Here $f(x)$

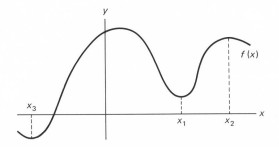

Figure 10.3–1 *Extreme points in ordinary calculus.*

[6] For proofs of these theorems see Sagan (1969).

attains a relative minimum at both x_1 and x_3, since $f(x) - f(x_1) > 0$ for all x in a sufficiently small interval about x_1. The same is true for $f(x) - f(x_3)$ for all $x \in (x_3 - \varepsilon, x_3 + \varepsilon)$ and $\varepsilon > 0$. Similarly, x_2 is a relative maximum, since $f(x) - f(x_2) \leq 0$ for all x in an ε neighborhood (interval) about x_2. The requirement that $\|y - y_0\| < \delta$ in Definition 10.3–8 corresponds to the ε-neighborhood requirement in the ordinary calculus. (Why is this condition imposed in both cases?)

The following theorem follows in an obvious way from Definition 10.3–8.

Theorem 10.3–3 A necessary condition for $F[y]$ to be at a relative minimum (maximum) at $y_0 \in \Sigma$ is that

$$F[y_0 + h] - F[y_0] \geq 0 \ (\leq 0)$$

for all $h \in H$, the space of admissible variations.[7]

Thus, by the previous theorem and the definition of the first variation, we have

$$F[y_0 + h] - F[y_0] = \delta F[h] + \varepsilon[h] \geq 0 \ (\leq 0)$$

for a relative minimum (maximum).

Theorem 10.3–4 *First Necessary Condition for a Relative Maximum or Minimum* For the functional $F[y]$ to possess a relative maximum or minimum at $y = y_0 \in \Sigma$, it is necessary that

$$\delta F[h] = 0$$

for all $h \in H$, the space of admissible variations.

PROOF   Previously, we had

$$F[y_0 + h] - F[y_0] = \delta F[h] + \varepsilon[h] \geq 0 \ (\leq 0)$$

for a relative minimum (maximum). Consider the case of a relative minimum. Then

$$\delta F[h] + \varepsilon[h] \geq 0$$

For an arbitrary h_0 in the space of admissible variations, H,

$$\delta F[h_0] + \varepsilon[h_0] \geq 0$$

By the homogeneity of $F[h_0]$, we have for some $r \in R$, $\delta F[rh_0] = r \, \delta F[h_0]$. Since H is a linear space, if $h_0 \in H$, then $rh_0 \in H$ for all $r \in R$. Thus

$$r \, \delta F[h_0] + \varepsilon[rh_0] \geq 0$$

---

[7] The space of admissible variations is defined as the set of all functions h such that for all $y \in \Sigma$, $h + y \in \Sigma$.

If $0 < r \leq 1$, then

$$\delta F[h_0] + \frac{\varepsilon[rh_0]}{r} \geq 0$$

If $-1 \leq r < 0$, then

$$\delta F[h_0] + \frac{\varepsilon[rh_0]}{r} \leq 0$$

since dividing by a negative number reverses the sign of the inequality. Since $\lim_{r \to 0} \varepsilon[rh_0]/r = 0$ (Definition 10.3–7), $\delta F[h_0] \gtreqless 0$ must be satisfied simultaneously, and thus $\delta F[h_0] = 0$. Since h_0 was an arbitrary element of H, $\delta F[h] = 0$ for all $h \in H$.   QED

Interpretation of the first necessary condition and attempts to translate it into "operational" forms fall into what is called the theory of the first variation. Before exploring this area, we shall examine the second variation.

Problems

10.3–1 Show that the three-dimensional vector space and the field of real numbers form a linear space.

10.3–2 Show that $\|x\|$ in Definition 10.3–2 is a functional.

10.3–3 Define an explicit norm that makes the linear space in Problem 10.3–1 a normed linear space.

10.3–4 Verify Theorem 10.3–1.

10.3–5 Prove Theorem 10.3–3.

10.3–6 Given that the functional

$$F[y] = \int_a^b f(x, y(x), y'(x)) \, dx$$

is to be minimized for boundary conditions $y(a) = 0$, $y(b) = 1$.
(a) What is the space of competing functions, Σ?
(b) Show that $H = \{h \mid h \text{ and } h' \text{ are continuous in } [0, 1] \text{ and } h(a) = h(b) = 0\}$ is the space of admissible variations.
(c) Write the general expression for $\delta F[h]$.
(d) What condition must $\delta F[h]$ satisfy? Why?

10.4 SECOND VARIATION AND THE SECOND NECESSARY CONDITION

DEFINITION 10.4–1 $\delta^2 F[h]$ is the **second variation** of $F[y]$ at $y = y_0$, if, for $r \in R$,

$$\delta^2 F[h] = \frac{d^2}{dr^2} F[y_0 + rh]\bigg|_{r=0}$$

exists for all $h \in S$.

The total variation $F[y_0 + h] - F[y_0]$ can be expressed in terms of the first and second variations as

$$F[y_0 + h] - F[y_0] = \delta F[h] + \tfrac{1}{2}\delta^2 F[h] + \varepsilon_1[h]$$

if $\delta^2 F[h]$ exists and is continuous in a neighborhood of $r = 0$. Furthermore,

$$\lim_{r \to 0} \frac{\varepsilon_1[rh]}{r^2} = 0$$

The expression is derived from the Taylor series expansion of $F[y_0 + h] - F[y_0]$.

As a direct consequence of the first necessary condition for a relative maximum (minimum), we have the second necessary condition:

Theorem 10.4–1 *Second Necessary Condition* If $F[y]$ is at a relative maximum (minimum) at $y = y_0 \in \Sigma$ and if $\delta^2[h] = (d^2/dr^2)F[y_0 + rh]$ exists and is continuous in a neighborhood about $r = 0$ for all $h \in H$, then it is necessary that $\delta F[h] = 0$ (Theorem 10.3–4) and $\delta^2 F[h] \le 0 (\ge 0)$ for all $h \in H$.

The proof of this theorem is based on the fact that

$$\lim_{r \to 0} \varepsilon_1 \left[\frac{rh}{r^2} \right] = 0$$

Example 1. Let $F[y] = \int_a^b f[x, y(x), dy/dx]\, dx$ and all continuity and other requirements are satisfied. Then at $y = y_0$

$$\delta F[h] = \frac{d}{dr} F[y_0 + rh] \Big|_{r=0}$$

$$= \frac{d}{dr} \int_a^b \left[f\left(x, y_0(x) + rh(x), \frac{dy_0}{dx} + r\frac{dh}{dx} \right) \right] dx \Big|_{r=0}$$

$$= \int_a^b \left[\frac{\partial f}{\partial y} h(x) + \frac{\partial f}{\partial(dy/dx)} \frac{dh}{dx} \right] dx$$

$$= \int_a^b \left[f_y h(x) + f_{y'} h'(x) \right] dx$$

where the subscript notation is used to indicate the partial derivatives and the prime notation to indicate ordinary derivatives. The second variation is given by

$$\frac{d^2}{dr^2} F[y_0 + rh] \Big|_{r=0}$$

or by

$$\frac{d}{dr}\left[\int_a^b [f_y h(x) + f_{y'} h'(x)]\, dx\right]_{r=0}$$

$$= \int_a^b [f_{yy}(x, y_0(x), y_0'(x))h(x)^2 + 2f_{yy'}(x, y_0(x), y_0'(x))h(x)h'(x)$$

$$+ f_{y'y'}(x, y_0(x), y_0'(x))h'(x)^2]\, dx$$

Finding the function $y(x)$ that maximizes or minimizes integrals of the form $\int_a^b f(x, y(x), y'(x))\, dx$ is often referred to as the simplest problem in the calculus of variations.

Problems

10.4–1   Verify the second necessary condition (Theorem 10.4–1).

10.4–2   Verify that the brachistochrone problem is an example of the simplest problem in the calculus of variations.

10.4–3   Write the first and second variations for $F[y] = \int_a^b f(x, y(x), y'(x))\, dx$ if
(a) $f(x, y, y') = 3x^2 y - (5y')^2$
(b) $f(x, y, y') = \sqrt{y' - 2x}$

10.4–4   Write the total variation for the same functional and functions as in Problem 10.4–3.

10.5   PRACTICAL NECESSARY CONDITIONS

For the simplest variational problem $F[y] = \int_a^b f(x, y(x), y'(x))\, dx$, we have, as in Example 1 in Section 10.4,

$$\delta F[y] = \int_a^b [f_y(x, y_0(x), y_0'(x))h(x) + f_{y'}(x, y_0(x), y_0'(x))h'(x)]\, dx = 0$$

for a relative minimum (maximum). Let $\int_a^x f_y(z, y_0(z), y_0'(z))\, dz = \phi(x)$. Then $\int_a^b f_y(x, y_0(x), y_0'(x))h(x)\, dx = \int_a^b h(x)\phi'(x)\, dx$. Integrating the second expression by parts yields

$$\int_a^b f_y(x, y_0(x), y_0'(x))h(x)\, dx = h(x)\phi(x)\Big|_a^b - \int_a^b \phi(x)h'(x)\, dx$$

But $h(a) = h(b) = 0$, so the first necessary condition becomes

$$\int_a^b h'(x)\{f_{y'}[x, y_0(x), y_0'(x)] - \phi(x)\}\, dx = 0$$

Let $f_{y'}(x, y_0(x), y_0'(x)) - \phi(x) = M(x)$. For an integral of the form $\int_a^b M(x)h'(x)\,dx$ to be zero, it is necessary that $M(x) = C$, where C is a constant. By this result and the definition of $\phi(x)$ we have

$$(1) \qquad f_{y'}[x, y_0(x), y_0'(x)] = \int_a^x f_y[z, y_0(z), y_0'(z)]\,dz + C$$

Equation (1) must be satisfied by $y = y_0(x)$ for all $x \in [a, b]$ for $F[y]$ to have a relative maximum or minimum at $y = y_0$. This condition will not hold at points where y_0' is discontinuous (more on this point later).

DEFINITION 10.5–1   Equation (1) is the **Euler–Lagrange equation in integrated form.**

DEFINITION 10.5–2   The **Euler– Lagrange equation** is

$$f_y(x, y, y') - \frac{d}{dx} f_{y'}(x, y, y') = 0$$

The Euler–Lagrange equation is obtained by total differentiation of (1) and must hold for all continuous portions of $y = y_0$ if y_0 minimizes $F[y]$.

DEFINITION 10.5–3   The **Euler–Lagrange equation in explicit form** is

$$f_y - f_{y'x} - f_{y'y}y' - f_{y'y'}y'' = 0$$

The explicit form is obtained by completing the differentiation in Definition 10.5–2. This is, of course, a second-order differential equation (usually non-linear). It is important to remember that the Euler–Lagrange equation (1) is a necessary but not sufficient condition and (2) will not be satisfied at points of discontinuity of y'.

At points of discontinuity of y', the **Weierstrass–Erdmann corner** conditions must hold. These conditions are derived from the Euler–Lagrange equation.

DEFINITION 10.5–4   The **Weierstrass–Erdmann conditions** require that at every point where y' is discontinuous:

$$(1) \qquad (f_{y'})_{c-0} = (f_{y'})_{c+0}$$

and

$$(2) \qquad (y'f_{y'} - f)_{c-0} = (y'f_{y'} - f)_{c+0}$$

where the notation $(\ )_{c-0}$ and $(\ )_{c+0}$ indicate that the expression in parentheses is to be evaluated as x approaches c from the left $(c - 0)$ and from the right $(c + 0)$.

Equations (1) and (2) require that the left and right limits of the given expressions be equal at the points of discontinuity. For portions of y with y' continuous, the **continuous** Euler–Lagrange equation must be satisfied.

Both the Euler–Lagrange equation and the Weierstrass–Erdmann corner conditions are readily generalized for problems with more than one unknown function to be determined. Consider the general problem

$$F[y_1, y_2, \ldots, y_n]$$

$$= \int_a^b f[x; y_1(x), y_2(x), \ldots, y_n(x); y_1'(x), y_2'(x), \ldots, y_n'(x)] \, dx$$

We must find n functions of x, $y_1, y_2, \ldots, y_n$ that either maximize or minimize $F[y_1, \ldots, y_n]$. A bar over a letter will indicate a vector; thus $\bar{y}(x) = (y_1(x), y_2(x), \ldots, y_n(x))$, and so on. Our problem is to find $\bar{y}_0$ yielding critical values for $F[\bar{y}] = \int_a^b f(x, \bar{y}(x), \bar{y}'(x)) \, dx$. In three-dimensional space this problem is illustrated in Figure 10.5–1. The fixed points are $(a, y_1(a), y_2(a))$ and $(b, y_1(b), y_2(b))$. The solution is the curve $\bar{y} = (y_1(x), y_2(x))$. The individual functions y_1 and y_2 are simply the projections of $\bar{y}$ onto the xy_1 and xy_2 planes, respectively.

For $\bar{y}_0$ to be a solution to such a problem, the Euler–Lagrange equations

$$f_{y_j}(x, \bar{y}, \bar{y}') - \frac{d}{dx} f_{y_j'}(x, \bar{y}, \bar{y}') = 0 \qquad \text{for } j = 1, 2, \ldots, n$$

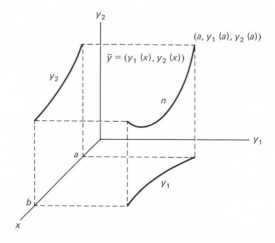

Figure 10.5–1 $n = 2$.

must be satisfied. We now have a system of n simultaneous second-degree differential equations to be solved. For $n = 2$ the equations are

(1) $$f_{y_1}(x, \bar{y}, \bar{y}') - \frac{d}{dx} f_{y_1'}(x, \bar{y}, \bar{y}') = 0$$

and

(2) $$f_{y_2}(x, \bar{y}, \bar{y}') - \frac{d}{dx} f_{y_2'}(x, \bar{y}, \bar{y}') = 0$$

Notice that each of these equations has the same form as the Euler–Lagrange equation for one unknown function.

The Weierstrass–Erdmann corner conditions in the n-function case are

$$f_{y_j'}(c, \bar{y}, \bar{y}')_{c-0} = f_{y_j'}(c, \bar{y}, \bar{y}')_{c+0}$$

and

$$f(c, \bar{y}, \bar{y}')_{c-0} - \sum_{i=1}^{n} (\bar{y}_i')_{c-0} f_{y_i'}(c, \bar{y}, \bar{y}')_{c-0}$$

$$= f(c, \bar{y}, \bar{y}')_{c+0} - \sum_{i=1}^{n} (\bar{y}_i')_{c+0} f_{y_i'}(c, \bar{y}, \bar{y}')_{c+0}$$

where $x = c$ is the point at which $\bar{y}'(x)$ is discontinuous. The notations $c - 0$ and $c + 0$ again denote left and right limits.

Another obvious generalization is to consider problems with either one or more unknown functions with more than one independent variable. For one unknown function with two independent variables $W = (w_1, w_2)$, we have

$$F[W] = \iint_R f[w_1, w_2, W(w_1, w_2), W_{w_1}(w_1, w_2), W_{w_2}(w_1, w_2)] \, dw_1 \, dw_2$$

where R is the region of integration defined by the boundary conditions. For this problem the Euler–Lagrange equation is

$$f_W - \frac{\partial}{\partial w_1} f_{w_1} - \frac{\partial}{\partial w_2} f_{w_2} = 0$$

a second-order partial differential equation.

For the more general problem of m unknown functions, W_i ($i = 1, 2, \ldots, m$), in n independent variables, w_j ($j = 1, 2, \ldots, n$), the Euler–Lagrange equations are

$$f_{W_i} - \sum_{j=1}^{n} \frac{\partial}{\partial w_j} f_{W_i w_j} = 0 \qquad \text{for } i = 1, 2, \ldots, m$$

where $f = f(\bar{w}, \overline{W}, \overline{W}_{w_1}, \ldots, \overline{W}_{w_n})$. Again bars denote vectors.

Problems

10.5-1 Write the Euler–Lagrange equations in explicit form for

(a) $f(x, y, y') = x^2 y' - y^3 y'^2$ (c) $f(x, y, y') = \dfrac{x^3 y'}{y^2}$

(b) $f(x, y, y') = \dfrac{x}{y - y'}$ (d) $f(x, y, y') = xy^3(y')^2 - \dfrac{y'y}{x}$

10.5-2 Write the Euler–Lagrange equations for

(a) $F[y_1, y_2, y_3] = \displaystyle\int_a^b (xy_1 y_2 y_3' - y_1' y_2' y_3^2)\, dx$

(b) $F[y_1, y_2] = \displaystyle\int_a^b \left(\dfrac{x^2 y_1'}{y_2} - \dfrac{3x^3 y_2}{(y_1')^2} \right) dx$

10.5-3 Write the Weierstrauss–Erdmann corner conditions for the functionals in Problems 10.5–1(a) and 10.5–2(a).

10.5-4 Write the Euler–Lagrange equations for

(a) $F[W] = \displaystyle\iint_R \left[W^2 w_1 \dfrac{\partial W}{\partial w_2} - 2W w_2 \left(\dfrac{\partial W}{\partial w_1} \right)^2 \right] dw_1\, dw_2$

(b) $F[W_1, W_2] = \displaystyle\iint_R \left[w_1^2 w_2 \dfrac{\partial W_1}{\partial w_1} W_2 + W_1^2 \dfrac{\partial W_2}{\partial w_1} \left(\dfrac{\partial W_1}{\partial w_2} \right)^2 \right] dw_1\, dw_2$

10.6 BOUNDARY CONDITIONS

Thus far we have developed necessary conditions that must be satisfied along interior points in the maximizing or minimizing function. No explicit mention has been made of the conditions imposed by the initial and terminal points through which the functions must pass. These conditions that serve to constrain the problem are called boundary conditions. Such conditions obviously vary depending on the nature of the problem.

Fixed Point–Fixed Point Problems

Let the fixed initial point be $P_1 = (a, y(a))$ and the fixed terminal point be $P_2 = (b, y(b))$. For the maximizing (minimizing) function $y_0(x)$ to pass through these points, $y_0(a) = y(a)$ and $y_0(b) = y(b)$.

Variable Point–Variable Point Problems

Suppose both end points may fall anywhere on the parallel lines $x = a$ and $x = b$. Only the x coordinates of the end points are fixed while the y coordinates are free to vary. It can be shown that in such a problem the natural boundary conditions must be satisfied.

DEFINITION 10.6–1   The **natural boundary conditions** are

$$f_{y'}(a, y_0(a), y_0'(a)) = 0$$

and

$$f_{y'}(b, y_0(b), y_0'(b)) = 0$$

Suppose that both end points are free to vary along continuous curves that possess continuous first derivatives. Let these curves be $c_1(x)$ and $c_2(x)$. In such a case the following transversality conditions must hold.

DEFINITION 10.6–2   The **transversality conditions** are

$$f_{y'}[a, y_0(a), y_0'(a)][c_1'(a) - y_0'(a)] + f(a, y_0(a), y_0'(a)) = 0$$

and

$$f_{y'}[b, y_0(b), y_0'(b)][c_2'(b) - y_0'(b)] + f(b, y_0(b), y_0'(b)) = 0$$

where $(a, c_1(a))$ is the point at which the function leaves the initial curve $c_1(x)$ and $(b, c_2(b))$ is the point at which the function crosses (transverses) the curve $c_2(x)$.[8]

Fixed Point–Variable Point and Variable Point–Fixed Point Problems

In these cases the boundary conditions are obtained by combining those discussed above in an obvious manner. For example, if the initial point is fixed at $(a, y(a))$ while the terminal point is free to vary along the curve $c_2(x)$ (assumed to be continuous and possess a continuous first derivative), the boundary conditions are

$$y_0(a) = y(a)$$

and

$$f_{y'}[b, y_0(b), y_0'(b)][c_2'(b) - y_0'(b)] + f(b, y_0(b), y_0'(b)) = 0$$

The boundary conditions discussed above hold for only the simplest case of one unknown function with one independent variable. They are, however, readily generalized to cases involving more than one unknown function with or without more than one independent variable.

More than One Unknown Function

With fixed end points $(a, y_1(a), \ldots, y_n(a))$ and $(b, y_1(b), \ldots, y_n(b))$, the boundary conditions are

$$y_{0i}(a) = y_i(a) \qquad \text{for } i = 1, 2, \ldots, n$$

and

$$y_{0i}(b) = y_i(b) \qquad \text{for } i = 1, 2, \ldots, n$$

[8] This is covered again in the context of control theory in Section 14.4. Cf. Definition 14.4–2.

With variable end points, the generalization of the transversality conditions is, for the case of two unknown functions y_1 and y_2,

$$\frac{\partial u}{\partial y_1} f + \left(1 - \frac{\partial u}{\partial y_1} y'_{10} - \frac{\partial u}{\partial y_2} y'_{20}\right) f_{y_1'}\bigg|_{x=u} = 0$$

and

$$\frac{\partial u}{\partial y_2} f + \left(1 - \frac{\partial u}{\partial y_1} y'_{10} - \frac{\partial u}{\partial y_2} y'_{20}\right) f_{y_2'}\bigg|_{x=u} = 0$$

where the end points are free to vary on the surface $x = u(y_1, y_2)$. The 0 subscripts are used to indicate the extremal functions. For n unknown functions whose end points can vary along parallel lines $x = a$ and $x = b$, the natural boundary conditions generalize to

$$f_{y'_j}(a, \bar{y}_0(a), \bar{y}'_0(a)) = 0$$

and

$$f_{y'_j}(b, \bar{y}_0(b), \bar{y}'_0(b)) = 0 \qquad \text{for } j = 1, 2, \ldots, n$$

Figure 10.6–1 illustrates the typical boundary condition for one unknown function, W, in two independent variables, w_1 and w_2. The surface A represents the boundary conditions. Its equation in implicit form is $Z(w_1, w_2) = 0$. Let α be the boundary of A. Suppose that $\overline{W}(w_1, w_2)$ is the critical function obtained from the Euler–Lagrange equation for this type of problem. The boundary conditions require that $\overline{W}(\bar{w}_1, \bar{w}_2) = Z(\bar{w}_1, \bar{w}_2)$ for all $(\bar{w}_1, \bar{w}_2) \in \alpha$; that is, the optimizing function $\overline{W}$ passes through all points in the boundary

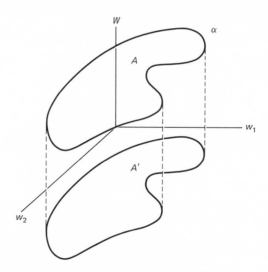

Figure 10.6–1   *Typical boundary condition.*

of A. Since the function $Z(w_1, w_2)$ is given, checking that the boundary conditions are satisfied by $\overline{W}$ presents no conceptual difficulties.

The boundary conditions for problems of this type may be given in other forms.[9]

Problems

10.6–1   Write the transversality conditions for the problem min $F[y] = \int_a^b (1 - y'^2)^{1/2} \, dx$.

10.6–2   Write the boundary conditions for the problem min $F[y] = \int_a^b y\sqrt{1 + y'^2} \, dx$ if $y(a) = y_a$ and the terminal point lies on the curve $x = 3$.

10.6–3   Same as Problem 10.6–2, with $y(a)$ free to vary along $c_1(x) = e^x$ and $y(b)$ free to vary along $c_2(x) = 2x - 2$.

10.7   ADDITIONAL NECESSARY CONDITIONS AND SOME SUFFICIENT CONDITIONS

Consider the simplest problem in the calculus of variations: Find the function $y_0(x)$ that minimizes (maximizes)

$$F[y] = \int_a^b f(x, y(x), y'(x)) \, dx$$

where the initial and terminal points, $(a, y(a))$ and $(b, y(b))$ are fixed. For $y_0(x)$ with $y_0'(x)$ continuous, we have the following necessary conditions:

Euler–Lagrange equation:

(1) $$f_y(x, y_0(x), y_0'(x)) - \frac{d}{dx} f_{y'}(x, y_0(x), y_0'(x)) = 0$$

DEFINITION 10.7–1   **Legendre Condition** requires

(2) $$f_{y'y'}[x, y_0(x), y_0'(x)] \geq 0 \ (\text{min})$$
$$\leq 0 \ (\text{max})$$

DEFINITION 10.7–2   **Strengthened Legendre Condition**[10] requires

(3) $$f_{y'y'}[x, y_0(x), y_0'(x)] > 0 \ (\text{min})$$
$$< 0 \ (\text{max})$$

For the two Legendre conditions, $f_{y'y'} = \partial^2 f/\partial y'^2$ and this second-order partial derivative is to be evaluated at x, $y_0(x)$, and $y_0'(x)$.

---

[9] For a discussion of an alternative representation see Sagan (1969) pages 125ff.

[10] Other necessary conditions, such as Weierstrass' necessary condition and the Jacobi condition, depend on the so-called "embedding theorems" and the concept of conjugate points, which we shall not discuss. See Section 14.7 and Sagan (1969).

For the function $y(x)$ to yield a relative minimum (maximum) of $F[y]$, in general it is necessary that condition (1) and either condition (2) or condition (3) be satisfied.

DEFINITION 10.7–3   Equation (1) in conjunction with either (2) or (3) constitutes the **complete necessary condition.**

The usual sufficient conditions formulated in the theory of the calculus of variations also depend on the concepts of embeddibility and conjugate points (see footnote 10). Intuitively, sufficient conditions are derived from conditions that ensure the second variation is positive for y_0 that equated the first variation to zero for a minimum, or a negative second variation with zero first variation for a maximum, given that these variations are "admissible." ($F[y_0 + h]$ for $h \in H$).

We propose the following crude method to ensure that a y_0 satisfying the necessary conditions does, in fact, lead to a relative maximum or minimum: Let $F[y_0]$ be the value of the integral for $y = y_0$. If $F[y_0] - F[y_0 + h] \geq 0$ for a function h arbitrarily "close" to y_0, then y_0 maximizes $F[y]$, provided that it fulfills the necessary conditions for a maximum. If $F[y_0] - F[y_0 + h] \leq 0$ for h arbitrarily close to y_0, then y_0 minimizes $F[y]$, again provided the necessary conditions are fulfilled.

Such a procedure lacks any vestige of mathematical elegance. It has, however, the advantage of letting us sidestep some of the more complex questions in the calculus of variations. In what follows, we shall either assume that the sufficient conditions hold or present them explicitly as examples.

Example 1.   Consider the problem of finding the curve with the shortest length between the points $(0, 0)$ and $(1, 1)$. The answer to this rather trivial problem can be written immediately as $y = x$. This problem can also be solved (more laboriously) by the calculus of variations. The length of the curve is given by $\int_0^1 f(x, y, y')\, dx$ where $f = \sqrt{1 + (y')^2}$ and where $(0, 0)$ and $(1, 1)$ are the fixed end points. The Euler–Lagrange equation, $f_y - (d/dx)f_{y'} = 0$, must be satisfied for the integral to be a minimum. Since $(d/dx)f_{y'} = f_{y'x} + f_{y'y}y' + f_{y'y'}y''$, we must have $f_y = f_{y'x} - f_{y'y}y' - f_{y'y'}y'' = 0$. Evaluating each of these derivatives yields

(1)
$$f_y = \frac{\partial f}{\partial y} = 0$$

(2)
$$f_{y'} = \frac{2y'}{\sqrt{1 + y'^2}}$$

(3)
$$\frac{d}{dx}\left(\frac{2y'}{\sqrt{1 + y'^2}}\right) = \frac{2(\sqrt{1 + (y')^2})y'' - 2y'[\frac{1}{2}(1 + y'^2)^{-1/2}(2y'y'')]}{1 + y'^2}$$

Thus the Euler–Lagrange equation becomes

$$0 - \sqrt{1 + y'^2}\, y'' + \frac{y'^2 y''}{\sqrt{1 + y'^2}} = 0$$

which simplifies to $y'' = 0$.

The solution to this second-order differential equation is $y = c_1 x + c_2$, where c_1 and c_2 are arbitrary constants that are evaluated by using the boundary conditions. Thus, for the initial point, $(0, 0)$,

$$0 = c_1(0) + c_2 \quad \text{implies} \quad c_2 = 0$$

For the terminal point, $(1, 1)$,

$$1 = c_1(1) + 0 \quad \text{implies} \quad c_1 = 1$$

Thus we obtain the solution $y = x$.

The Legendre sufficient condition ($f_{y'y'} \geq 0$ implies a minimum and ≤ 0 implies a maximum) can be readily checked. Since $f_{y'} = 2y'/\sqrt{1 + (y')^2}$,

$$f_{y'y'} = \frac{2}{[1 + y'^2]^{1/2}} - \frac{2y'^2}{[1 + y'^2]^{3/2}}$$

Since $y' = 1$,

$$f_{y'y'} = \frac{2}{\sqrt{2}} - \frac{2}{2^{3/2}} = \frac{1}{\sqrt{2}} > 0$$

Thus the Legendre condition for a minimum is met.

Example 2. Let $f = y' + x^2 y'^2$. Write the Euler–Lagrange equation and solve it for y.

(1) $\qquad\qquad\qquad\qquad f_y = 0$
(2) $\qquad\qquad\qquad\qquad f_{y'} = 1 + 2x^2 y'$
(3) $\qquad\qquad\qquad\qquad f_{y'y'} = 2x^2$
(4) $\qquad\qquad\qquad\qquad f_{y'x} = 4xy'$
(5) $\qquad\qquad\qquad\qquad f_{y'y} = 0$

Thus $f_y - [f_{y'x} + f_{y'y}y' + f_{y'y'}y''] = 0 = 0 - 4xy' - 0y' - 2x^2 y''$. The Euler–Lagrange equation is

$$x^2 y'' + 2xy' = 0$$

or

$$y'' + \frac{2}{x} y' = 0$$

This second-order differential equation can be solved by a substitution that reduces it to a first-order differential equation.

Let $p = dy/dx$. Then $d^2y/dx^2 = dp/dx$. Our equation becomes $dp/dx + (2/x)p = 0$. This is a first-order differential equation in p and x and can be solved by separating variables.

$$\frac{dp}{p} + \frac{2}{x} dx = 0$$

Solving this equation yields

$$\ln |p| = -2 \ln |x| + c$$

Taking antilogs,

$$p = \frac{dy}{dx} = e^c e^{-2\ln|x|} = \frac{c_1}{x^2} \qquad \text{where } c_1 = e^c$$

Solving this first-order differential equation yields

$$y = -\frac{c_1}{x} + c_2$$

which is the solution to the Euler–Lagrange equation. For the functional given, the solution is an hyperbola. The values of c_1 and c_2, of course, depend on the boundary conditions.

It is important to remember that, as these examples illustrate, y and y' are functions of x alone; that is, derivatives such as $\partial y/\partial y'$, $\partial y'/\partial y''$, and so on are zero. These examples also clearly underline the dependence of the calculus of variations on the theory of differential equations.

Problem

10.7–1 Write the Legendre and strengthened Legendre conditions for the brachistochrone problem. In addition, write the Euler–Lagrange equation.

10.8 ADDITIONAL CONSTRAINTS, THE PROBLEM OF LAGRANGE, AND LAGRANGEAN MULTIPLIERS

The technique of Lagrangean multipliers is well known in the ordinary calculus for problems of constrained maxima and minima.[11] This technique can be generalized for problems in the calculus of variations with additional constraints over and above the boundary conditions.

We shall begin the discussion with problems involving one constraint and proceed to generalize the technique to multiconstraint, multiunknown

[11] See Section 5.4.

function problems. Constrained problems are classified by the nature of the constraints.

DEFINITION 10.8–1   When the constraints are differential equations, the problem is a **Lagrange problem.**

DEFINITION 10.8–2   If the constraints are integrals, the problem is generally an **isoperimetric problem.**

DEFINITION 10.8–3   A **Mayer problem** is one where there are n unknown functions and m constraints that are either differential or ordinary equations. For the Mayer problem, m is less than n.

Since, as we shall show, these problems can be treated as general Lagrange problems we shall begin with a discussion of the Lagrange problem:

$$\max\ (\min): F[y] = \int_a^b f(x,\ y,\ y')\ dx$$

subject to

$$\phi(x,\ y,\ y') = 0$$

This is the simplest Lagrange problem with one unknown function, y, and one constraint, ϕ. In many cases the problem may be solved without using multipliers simply by substituting ϕ into f and solving the resulting unconstrained problem. To solve the problem using multipliers, define a new function $G = f + \lambda(x)\phi$, where $\lambda(x)$ is an unknown function of x, the Lagrangean multiplier. The problem is reduced to finding the functions y and λ that minimize or maximize $\int_a^b G\ dx$. The Euler–Lagrange equation becomes

(1)
$$G_y - \frac{d}{dx} G_{y'} = 0$$

or in terms of f,

(2)
$$f_y + \phi_y \lambda(x) - \frac{d}{dx} [f_{y'} + \phi_{y'}\lambda(x)] = 0$$

Equation (2) and the constraint

$$\phi(x,\ y,\ y') = 0$$

form a system of two equations in the two unknown functions $y(x)$ and $\lambda(x)$. Solving them simultaneously yields the solution to the original problem.

Consider a Lagrange problem with two unknown functions, y_1 and y_2, and one constraint $\phi(x,\ y_1,\ y_2,\ y_1',\ y_2') = 0$. Then $G = f(x,\ y_1,\ y_2,\ y_1',\ y_2') + \lambda(x)\phi$. The Euler–Lagrange equations are

$$G_{y_1} - \frac{d}{dx} G_{y_1'} = 0$$

and

$$G_{y_2} - \frac{d}{dx} G_{y_2'} = 0$$

or

(3) $$f_{y_1} + \phi_{y_1}\lambda(x) - \frac{d}{dx} [f_{y_1'} + \phi_{y_1'}\lambda(x)] = 0$$

and

(4) $$f_{y_2} + \phi_{y_2}\lambda(x) - \frac{d}{dx} [f_{y_2'} + \phi_{y_2'}\lambda(x)] = 0$$

We now have a system of three simultaneous equations [(3), (4), and ϕ] to solve for the three unknown functions $y_1(x)$, $y_2(x)$, and $\lambda(x)$. The generalization to higher numbers of unknown functions (given one constraint) should be clear.

Suppose there were two constraints, ϕ_1 and ϕ_2, in the preceding problem. Then $G = f + \lambda_1(x)\phi_1 + \lambda_2(x)\phi_2$. The Euler–Lagrange equations are

$$f_{y_1} + \phi_{1y_1}\lambda_1(x) + \phi_{2y_1}\lambda_2(x) - \frac{d}{dx} [f_{y_1'} + \phi_{1y_1'}\lambda_1(x) + \phi_{2y_1'}\lambda_2(x)] = 0$$

and

$$f_{y_2} + \phi_{1y_2}\lambda_1(x) + \phi_{2y_2}\lambda_2(x) - \frac{d}{dx} [f_{y_2'} + \phi_{1y_2'}\lambda_1(x) + \phi_{2y_2'}\lambda_2(x)] = 0$$

These two equations together with the two constraints are then solved simultaneously for y_1, y_2, λ_1, and λ_2.

The isoperimetric problem may be written as

$$\text{max (min):} \quad F_1[y] = \int_a^b f(x, y, y') \, dx$$

$$\text{subject to:} \quad F_2[y] = \int_a^b g(x, y, y') \, dx = k$$

where k is a constant. To reduce such a problem to a Lagrange problem let

(5) $$\rho(x) = \int_a^x g \, dx$$

Then $\rho'(x) = g(x, y, y')$. The new function G is given by $G = f + \lambda(x)(\rho' - g)$. The Euler–Lagrange equations are

(6) $$G_y - \frac{d}{dx} G_{y'} = 0$$

and

(7) $$G_\rho - \frac{d}{dx} G_{\rho'} = 0$$

Performing the differentiation in (7) yields

$$- \frac{d\lambda(x)}{dx} = 0$$

Thus, for the isoperimetric problem in Lagrange form, the Lagrangean multiplier, $\lambda(x)$, is a constant. Here (6), the new constraint $\rho'(x) = g(x, y, y')$, and the fact that $\lambda(x)$ is a constant are used to solve for y and $\rho(x)$.

A Mayer problem has n unknown functions and m constraints, $m < n$. To connect such a problem to a general Lagrange problem, define $n - m$ new functions $z_i(x)$ by $z_i = y_i'$. The problem is then

$$\text{max (min):} \qquad F[z] = \int_a^b (z_1 + z_2 + \cdots + z_{n-m}) \, dx$$

subject to the original constraints, $\phi_1, \phi_2, \ldots, \phi_m = 0$. The general technique developed earlier can then be applied.

Example 1. Given two points $\rho_1 = (x_1, 0)$ and $\rho_2 = (x_2, 0)$. Find the curve $y(x)$, with given length l that connects ρ_1 and ρ_2 and encloses the greatest area along with the line segment $\rho_1\rho_2$. This is an isoperimetric problem:

(1) $$\text{max:} \qquad \int_{x_1}^{x_2} y(x) \, dx$$

subject to:

(2) $$\int_{x_1}^{x_2} [1 + y'^2]^{1/2} \, dx = k \qquad (k \text{ a constant})$$

and the boundary conditions $y(x_1) = y(x_2) = 0$. Equation (1) is simply an expression for the area under the curve $y(x)$, while (2) constrains the curve to a length k.

Applying the rule developed earlier,

$$G = y + \lambda_0[1 + y'^2]^{1/2}$$

since $f = y$ and $g = [1 + y'^2]^{1/2}$. The Euler–Lagrange equation is

$$G_y - \frac{d}{dx} G_{y'} = 0$$

Writing this out in full:

$$G_y - G_{y'x} - G_{y'y}y' - G_{y'y'}y'' = 0 \quad \text{where} \quad G_{y'} = \frac{\lambda_0 y'}{[1 + y'^2]^{1/2}}$$

Since $G_{y'}$ is not an explicit function of x, $G_{y'x} = 0$. The Euler–Lagrange equation can then be written as

(3) $$G_y - G_{y'y}y' - G_{y'y'}y'' = 0$$

Multiplying each term of (3) by y' yields

$$G_y y' - G_{y'y}y'^2 - G_{y'y'}y'y'' = 0$$

Consider the expression

(4) $$\frac{d}{dx}[G - y'G_{y'}]$$

Performing the differentiation of (4) yields

(5) $$G_x + G_y y' + G_{y'}y'' - y''G_{y'} - y'[G_{y'x} + G_{y'y}y' + G_{y'y'}y'']$$

But G_x and $G_{yx} = 0$, so (5) reduces to (3) and the Euler–Lagrange equation becomes

(6) $$\frac{d}{dx}[G - y'G_{y'}] = 0$$

Integrating (6) yields the "first integral" of the Euler–Lagrange equation:

(7) $$G - y'G_{y'} = C_1 \qquad \text{where } C_1 \text{ is a constant}$$

In terms of our problem, the explicit version of (7) is

$$y + \lambda_0(1 + y'^2)^{1/2} - \frac{\lambda_0 y'^2}{[1 + y'^2]^{1/2}} = C_1$$

which simplifies to

$$y + \lambda_0\left[(1 + y'^2)^{1/2} - \frac{y'^2}{[1 + y'^2]^{1/2}}\right] = C_1$$

or to

(8) $$y = C_1 - \frac{\lambda_0}{(1 + y'^2)^{1/2}}$$

Squaring both sides of (8) yields

$$(y - C_1)^2 = \frac{\lambda_0^2}{1 + y'^2}$$

Solving this differential equation leads to

(9) $$(y - C_1)^2 + (x - C_2)^2 = \lambda_0^2$$

the general equation of a circle with radius λ. The constant terms in (9) (C_1, C_2, and λ_0) can be solved for from the boundary condition and the constraint. Figure 10.8–1 shows the graphical solution to this problem.

One important aspect of the problem considered in Example 1 is that it illustrates one way in which the Euler–Lagrange equation may be simplified when G is not an explicit function of x. Some other useful simplifications of the Euler–Lagrange equation can be made if:

(1) G is not an explicit function of y;
(2) G is an explicit function only of y'; and
(3) $G_{y'y'} = 0$ for all values of x.

In case (1), $G_y = 0$ and the equation reduces to $(d/dx)G_{y'} = 0$. This implies that $G_{y'}$ is a constant. Thus y' is a function of x and it follows that y can then be expressed as an integral.

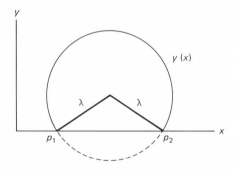

Figure 10.8–1 *A graphical solution.*

In case (2), again the Euler–Lagrange equation is $(d/dx)G_{y'} = 0$. In this case $G_{y'}$ and $G_{y'y}$ must also be zero. Thus $y'' = 0$ and the solution will have the form $y = ax + b$, where a and b are constants. The extreme functions in such a case will, therefore, always be straight lines.

In case (3), for $G_{y'y'}$ to be zero it must be true that either G is not an explicit function of y', or is in the form $G_1 = G(x, y) + G_2(x, y)y'$. Such functions are **degenerate**. Solutions to degenerate problems will not be considered here.[12]

Problems

10.8–1   Write the first integral of the Euler–Lagrange equation for the brachisto-chrone problem.

[12] See Sagan (1969).

10.8–2 Write the Euler–Lagrange equations for

(a) min: $F[y] = \int_a^b (y'^2 + yx^2)\, dx$

subject to: $yx^2 - y' = 0$

(b) min: $F[y] = \int_a^b \left(\dfrac{y'y^2}{x}\right) dx$

subject to: $x + 2y' = 5$

10.8–3 Write the Euler–Lagrange equations for

min: $F[y_1, y_2] = \int_a^b (y_1' y_2 x^2 - y_2^2 y_2')\, dx$

subject to: $y_1' y_2' - y_1 y_2 = 0$

10.8–4 Solve the following problem:

max: $\int_0^1 y(x)\, dx$

subject to: $\int_0^1 (1 + y'^2)\, dx = 5$

10.9 APPROXIMATE METHODS

The lack of easily formulated, readily computable sufficient conditions is not such a serious problem as might appear. Suppose only one function, y_0, satisfies the necessary conditions and the boundary conditions. Then y_0 must then either maximize or minimize $F[y]$. Whether y_0 yields a maximum or minimum can be read from the Legendre or strengthened Legendre conditions. Suppose n functions, y_i, satisfy the necessary and boundary conditions. Computation and comparison of $F[y_i]$, for all i, will show which y_i yield relative maxima and minima.

Furthermore, there are several algorithms available for numerical approximation of y_0. Two of them discussed below fall into the general category of dynamic programming.[13] Simple versions of these techniques in nonprogramming terminology are as follow: Given $F[y] = \int_a^b f(x, y, y')\, dx$ with fixed terminal and initial points. Suppose $y_0(x)$ is the exact solution to this problem with $F[y_0] = k$. The object in this technique is to construct a sequence of functions $\bar{y}_i$, $i = 1, 2, \ldots, n$, such that $F[\bar{y}_i] \to k$ as $i \to n$. As

[13] See Bellman (1957) and Bellman and Dreyfus (1962). Also See Sections 12.3, 14.6, and 14.7 for additional discussion.

n becomes sufficiently large $F[y_n]$ is made arbitrarily close to $F[y_0]$. Thus $\bar{y}_n$ approximates the true solution, y_0.

Method 1: Euler's Method or the Method of Broken Lines

Divide the interval from a to b (the initial and terminal values of x) into n equal segments. (See Figure 10.9–1). Construct a curve consisting of straight line segments connecting $(a, y(a))$ and $(b, y(b))$. An example of one such curve is drawn in Figure 10.9–1. The y coordinates of the points where the curve crosses a subdivision of (a, b) are denoted $b_0, b_1, \ldots, b_n$. Since b_0 and b_6 are fixed by the boundary conditions, such a curve is a function of the coordinates $b_1, b_2, \ldots, b_{n-1}$ (in Figure 10.9–1, b_1, b_2, b_3, b_4, and b_5). The problem is then to select these coordinates so as to make the curve approximate y_0. In other words, we select the b_j ($j = 1, 2, \ldots, n - 1$) so the integrals of the curve are at a minimum (or maximum, depending on the nature of the original problem). For the example given in Figure 10.9–1, this integral is

$$\sum_{i=0}^{5} \left\{ \int_{a+ih}^{a+(i+1)b} \left[\left(\frac{b_{i+1} - b_i}{h} \right) (x - a + ih) + b_i \right] dx \right\} - (b - a)b_0$$

Call this integral I. Then we have for the b_j that minimize I, $\partial I/\partial b_j = 0$, for $j = 1, 2, \ldots, 5$, which is a system of five equations in the five unknown b_j. This system solves for the b_j. By increasing n (the subdivision between the initial and terminal points), the value of I_n can be made arbitrarily close to k. n can be made very large and the calculations involved can be done very rapidly by computer.[14]

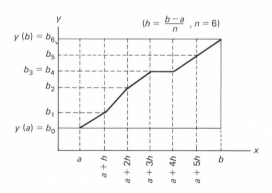

Figure 10.9–1   *Euler's Method.*

[14] An example of the method of dynamic programming is given in Example 4 in Section 12.1. Also see Sections 14.6 and 14.7 for a discussion of control theory, mathematical programming, and the calculus of variations.

Method 2: Linear Combinations of Functions

Again let y_0 be the function that minimizes $\int_a^b f(x, y, y')\, dx$. This approximation method begins by picking any function, $\beta_0(x)$ that satisfies the boundary conditions; that is, $\beta_0(a) = y(a)$ and $\beta_0(b) = y(b)$. Next select a sequence of functions, $\beta_1(x), \beta_2(x), \ldots, \beta_n(x)$, with the property that $\beta_i(a) = \beta_i(b) = 0$ for $i = 1, 2, \ldots, n$. Then form the linear combination

$$B_n = \beta_0 + a_1\beta_1 + a_2\beta_2 + \cdots + a_n\beta_n$$

B_n is the candidate chosen to approximate y_0. Substitute B_n in $I = \int_a^b f(x, y, y')\, dx$. After calculating B_n and performing the integration we obtain a function of the constants $a_1, a_2, \ldots, a_n$. The problem then boils down to choosing these a's so that the integral has the smallest possible value. In other words, we have a system of n equations,

$$\frac{\partial}{\partial a_i} I(B_n) = 0 \qquad \text{for } i = 1, 2, \ldots, n$$

in the n unknown a's. If we denote the values of the a's obtained by solving this system as $\bar{a}_i$, then

$$\bar{B}_n = \beta_0 + \bar{a}_1\beta_1 + \bar{a}_2\beta_2 + \cdots + \bar{a}_n\beta_n$$

is an approximation to y_0. As before the larger is n, in general, the better the approximation $\bar{B}_n$ will be to y_0. This technique is obviously done most expediently on a computer.[15]

10.10   ECONOMIC APPLICATIONS

Optimal control theory is based on the calculus of variations, as we shall see in the Chapter 14. Consequently, economic applications of control theory also serve as one of the most important areas of application of the calculus of variations. In this section we shall explore some of the economic applications of the calculus of variations without reference to control theory.

Efficient Paths of Capital Accumulation[16]

Given an economy that produces two goods, capital (K) and a consumption good (C). Let the instantaneous production function for capital be

(1) $$\dot{K}(t) = g[K(t), C(t); \dot{C}(t) + c(t)] - k(t)$$

where $\dot{C}$ and $\dot{K}$ are time derivatives and $c(t)$ and $k(t)$ are the consumption of the consumption goods and the capital goods at time t. $\dot{K}(t)$ is thus net

---

[15] For additional approximation methods and a more complete discussion of the previous methods, the reader is referred to Gunnowski and Mira (1968).

[16] See Samuelson (1960).

investment in time t. Suppose that, given an initial time period t_0 and a terminal period t_1, the goal of the economy is to maximize the capital stock in period t_1. This objective may be written as

$$\max K(t_1) - K(t_0) = \int_{t_0}^{t_1} \dot{K}(t)\, dt$$

subject to the production function (1). It is assumed that the functions $c(t)$ and $k(t)$ are known. This is a problem in the calculus of variations with two unknown functions $K(t)$ and $C(t)$ and one constraint, which is a differential equation. Here f is of the general form

$$f[t,\, K(t),\, C(t);\, \dot{K}(t),\, \dot{C}(t)]$$

Explicitly, $f = \dot{K}(t)$. The constraining equation is

$$G = g[K(t),\, C(t);\, \dot{C}(t) + c(t)] - \dot{K}(t) - k(t) = 0$$

Form the new function $H = \dot{K}(t) + \lambda(t)G$. The problem then becomes

$$\max: \quad \int_{t_0}^{t_1} H\, dt$$

The Euler–Lagrange equations are

$$H_C - \frac{d}{dt}\, H_{\dot{C}} = 0$$

and

$$H_K - \frac{d}{dt}\, H_{\dot{K}} = 0$$

Alternatively,

(2) $$\frac{d}{dt}[1 - \lambda(t)] = \lambda(t)\,\frac{\partial G}{\partial K}$$

and

(3) $$\frac{d}{dt}\left[\lambda(t)\,\frac{\partial G}{\partial \dot{C}}\right] = \lambda(t)\,\frac{\partial G}{\partial C}$$

Performing the differentiation on the left-hand sides of (2) and (3) yields

(4) $$-\dot{\lambda} = \lambda(t)G_K$$

and

(5) $$\dot{\lambda}G_{\dot{C}} = \lambda(t)G_C$$

Substituting (4) into (5):

$$\lambda(t)G_C + \lambda(t)G_K G_{\dot{C}} = 0$$

or, since $\lambda(t) \neq 0$,

(6) $$G_C + G_K G_{\dot{C}} = 0$$

The functions C and K must, therefore, satisfy (6) as well as (1) for $K(t_1) - K(t_0)$ to be a maximum; or, since $g \equiv \dot{K}$,

(7) $$\frac{\partial \dot{K}}{\partial C} + \frac{\partial \dot{K}}{\partial K}\frac{\partial \dot{K}}{\partial \dot{C}} = 0$$

Equation (7) is an alternative version of what Samuelson calls the "fundamental efficiency condition" and must hold along any efficient path of capital accumulation. Samuelson's version,

(8) $$\frac{d}{dt}\frac{\partial \dot{K}}{\partial \dot{C}} = \frac{\partial \dot{K}}{\partial C} + \frac{\partial \dot{K}}{\partial K}\frac{\partial \dot{K}}{\partial \dot{C}}$$

is derived simply by noting that $(d/dt)G_{\dot{C}} = 0$ by the definition of G.

Equation (4) leads to the economic interpretation of the Lagrangean function $\lambda(t)$. Dividing (4) by $\lambda(t)$ yields

$$\frac{-d}{dt}\frac{\lambda(t)}{\lambda(t)} = G_K = \frac{\partial \dot{K}}{\partial K}$$

$\partial \dot{K}/\partial K$ is the own rate of interest of capital; thus $\lambda(t)$ must be a discounting function. The fundamental efficiency condition, (8) can be interpreted as follows. Let $r_k = \partial \dot{K}/\partial K$ and r_c (the own rate of interest on the consumption good) $= \partial \dot{C}/\partial C$. Let P_c be the flow price of the consumption good with capital taken as the numeraire. Then $P_c = -\partial \dot{K}/\partial \dot{C}$ and P_k, the flow price of capital, is 1. (8) then can be written as

(9) $$r_k = r_c + \frac{1}{P_c}\left(\frac{dP_c}{dt}\right)$$

Equation (9) simply says that to be on an efficient path of capital accumulation, the own rate of interest of capital must be equal to the own rate of interest of the consumption good plus the percentage change in the flow price of the consumption good. If prices are constant, the own rates must be equal.

Equation (9) is derived in the following manner. Divide (8) by $\partial \dot{K}/\partial \dot{C}$:

$$\frac{(d/dt)(\partial \dot{K}/\partial \dot{C}) - \partial \dot{K}/\partial C}{\partial \dot{K}/\partial \dot{C}} = \frac{\partial \dot{K}}{\partial K}$$

Then

(10) $$\frac{((dP_c/dt)/P_c) - \partial \dot{K}/\partial C}{\partial \dot{K}/\partial \dot{C}} = \frac{\partial \dot{K}}{\partial K}$$

By the implicit function rule,

$$\frac{\partial \dot{C}}{\partial C} = -\frac{\partial \dot{K}/\partial C}{\partial \dot{K}/\partial \dot{C}}$$

so (10) becomes

$$\frac{d}{dt}(P_c)\frac{1}{P_c} + r_c = r_k$$

which is (9).

Thus, without solving explicitly for $K(t)$ and $C(t)$, it is possible to obtain a great deal of information by interpreting the Euler–Lagrange equations. Often, it is more valuable to know what properties optimizing functions must satisfy than to be able to display the particular optimizing function or functions. In this example, all the functions were unspecified, which naturally precludes solving for the K and C functions explicitly. Nonetheless, a great deal of information about the properties of efficient growth paths has been derived.

Optimal Growth and Turnpike Theorems

In the previous example we considered an application of calculus of variations to the problem of maximizing the capital stock of an economy in some terminal period. In this example we want to consider some of the general aspects of optimal growth theory and turnpike theorems. Since there is a voluminous literature in these closely related fields, we shall review some of the important concepts of optimal growth theory and discuss some "typical" turnpike theorems with particular regard to illustrating the use of techniques from the calculus of variations.

We begin with some basic definitions and concepts from optimal growth theory. To simplify matters we assume that we are dealing with an economy where:

(1) There are m outputs, denoted by the m-dimensional vector $q = (q_1, q_2, \ldots, q_m)$, where q_i is the output of the ith good. $p = (p_1, p_2, \ldots, p_m)$ is the vector of output prices.

(2) There are n inputs, denoted by the n-dimensional vector $f = (f_1, f_2, \ldots, f_n)$, where f_i is the amount of the ith input (factor). $e = (e_1, e_2, \ldots, e_n)$ is the vector of input prices.

(3) Every good is produced by only one activity.

(4) Every activity requires the positive input of at least one factor.

(5) The production function is homogeneous of degree 1.

(6) No subset of outputs can be produced without using some good not in the subset.[17]

With these simplifying assumptions we are ready to define some basic terms.

---

[17] In von Neumann's terminology, such an economy is said to be *indecomposable*. Cf. Definition 4.5–4.

DEFINITION 10.10–1 **Balanced growth** is a regime where all possible ratios of quantities of inputs and outputs are constant over time.

Thus, if balanced growth is achieved only the size and not the composition of the economy changes over time. There may be many different rates of balanced growth possible for a given economy. Of these many possibilities a highest rate must exist.

DEFINITION 10.10–2 The **von Neumann path** is the path the economy traces out over time when it is growing at the highest possible rate of balanced growth.[18]

What relation does the von Neumann path have to optimal growth paths and to efficient growth paths? What is the relation between optimal growth and efficient growth? We shall attempt to answer these questions by taking the last first.

The concept of efficient growth is based on the notion of efficient production. In a static (single-period) sense we can say that production is efficient if and only if it is possible to produce more of any one good by (1) reducing the output of another good or (2) increasing the amounts of inputs used. This concept leads to the following definition of efficient growth.

DEFINITION 10.10–3 A growth path is **efficient** if production in every time period (or at every point in time if we have a continuous model) is efficient.[19]

The term "optimal" implies some optimizing problem (e.g., maximizing an objective function subject to constraints).

DEFINITION 10.10–4 An **optimal growth path** (optimal growth) is one that optimizes some objective function subject to any constraints imposed on it.

Thus, a path that is optimal for some objective function with certain constraints in general would not be optimal for another objective function with different constraints (or perhaps even the same objective function with different constraints). It is useful to distinguish between two general types of optimal growth paths.

---

[18] See von Neumann (1945). A detailed discussion and elaboration of the von Neumann model is also contained in Gale (1960). For an extension of the von Neumann model see Morishima (1969).

[19] This definition is obviously not rigorous in any mathematical sense. Specific efficiency conditions should be developed for each specific model or problem encountered. The previous example spelled out specific efficiency conditions for the problem of efficient capital accumulation.

DEFINITION 10.10–5   A **terminally optimal** growth path is one that optimizes an objective function that depends only on the terminal stocks of goods.

DEFINITION 10.10–6   A **continuously optimal** growth path is one that optimizes an objective function that depends upon some measure of utility or welfare at each point in time.

The path in the previous example was terminally optimal. It should be obvious that, from a theoretical point of view, continuously optimal growth is a more important concept than terminally optimal growth unless one takes the position that we produce goods for their own sake rather than for the welfare they make possible. Unfortunately, most work has been done on terminally optimal paths. One of the most important reasons for this is the lack of any generally accepted dynamic utility function, not to mention the many problems of welfare economics. Consequently, from now on, when we refer to optimal growth we shall mean terminally optimal growth.

The relation between optimal and efficient paths should be fairly obvious from the preceding discussion:

(1) every optimal growth path is an efficient growth path; and

(2) every inefficient growth path is nonoptimal.

(1) and (2) leave one unanswered question—can an efficient growth path be nonoptimal? Suppose production in every period is efficient, but that social welfare could be increased by a redistribution of the output in one, or more than one period. Such a path may not be continuously optimal. Would all such paths be terminally optimal?

Before tackling our first question, we state the following theorem.

Theorem 10.10–1   *Bellman's Optimality Principle*[20]   For a policy to be optimal it must be true that no matter what the initial state is and no matter what initial decision is made, each subsequent decision must be optimal with respect to the state resulting from the decision made immediately preceding it.

As far as optimal growth is concerned, Bellman's optimal principle means that if a path is optimal from time 0 to time T, then any portion of the path, say from times n to m, must be terminally optimal with respect to m ($0 \leq n < m \leq T$). What can be said about portions of efficient growth paths?

We are now ready to consider our first question—the relation between optimal growth paths and the von Neumann path. Dorfman, Samuelson, and Solow were responsible for giving theorems concerned with this relation the name "turnpike theorems." As we shall see, the von Neumann path is not, in general, an optimal growth path. It is, however, the "turnpike". Heuristically, let us think of the initial state as the beginning point on a long auto trip and

---

[20] See Bellman (1957) and Bellman and Dreyfus (1962).

the value of the stocks in the terminal period as the destination. What is the best way to get to our destination? In most cases, this would be to get on the turnpike as soon as possible and stay on it as long as possible.[21]

This analogy is somewhat misleading, since the optimal path may never actually reach the von Neumann path and will not run along it unless the terminal point is actually on the von Neumann path. Although many different turnpike theorems have been proven, they all attempt to describe the relation of the optimal growth path to the von Neumann ray with particular emphasis on the distance between the two.

R. Radner (1961) is generally regarded as the "father" of turnpike theorems. His original model and theorem have since been modified and generalized by Nikaido (1964) and Morishima (1969) among others. We shall present the Nikaido version of Radner's basic theorem as an illustration of the general nature of turnpike theorems. No calculus of variations is employed in this case. Subsequently, we shall review Lancaster's turnpike example,[22] which does employ calculus of variations techniques.

We shall first develop Radner's original result and then indicate how it has been modified by Nikaido. The economy is closed and characterized by constant returns to scale. There are m goods. Time is discrete, which is to say production takes place during well-defined periods. At the end of each period a vector $y = (y_1, y_2, \ldots, y_m)$ is produced as output and is available for use as inputs at the beginning of the next period. At the beginning of each period a vector $x = (x_1, x_2, \ldots, x_m)$ is used as an input. x is completely used up in each period. Radner denotes the technology as T, where

$$T = \{(x, y) \mid (x, y) \text{ is technologically feasible}\}$$

Furthermore if N is the terminal period, there is a function $U(x_N)$ that is to be maximized. U is a preference function over terminal stocks.

The following assumptions (A) and definitions (D) are crucial to the model:

A1 (Continuous technology and constant returns to scale) T is a closed
      cone in the nonnegative orthant of $2m$-dimensional space.
A2 (Something cannot be produced from nothing) $(0, y) \in T$ implies $y = 0$.
A3 (a) U is nonnegative and continuous over commodity space.
      (b) There exists at least one x such that $U(x) > 0$.
A4 U is a homogeneous of degree 1.
A5 (Costless disposal) If $(x, y) \in T$ and $x' \geq x$ and $y' \leq y$, then $(x', y') \in T$.
A6 (Every good can be produced) There is at least one $(x, y) \in T$ for which
      $y_i > 0, i = 1, 2, \ldots m$.
D1 x is *balanced* if there is a number $\rho > 0$ such that $(x, \rho x) \in T$. ρ is called
      the growth factor. $\rho - 1$ is the growth rate.

---

[21] A better name might be "interstate theorems" for several reasons.

[22] See Lancaster (1968), pages 190–194.

D2 The *coefficient of expansion*, λ, of any $(x, y) \in T$ is

$$\lambda = \max\{c \mid y \geq cx, \text{ and } (x, y) \in T\}.$$

D3 A sequence $\{x_n\}_{n=0}^{N}$ of commodity vectors is feasible if, given x_0, the initial stocks, $(x_n, x_{n+1}) \in T$ for all n.

Before proceeding to the rest of Radner's definitions and assumptions, it is necessary to introduce profit and prices into the system. Consider the following relation[23]:

$$p \cdot (y - \mu x)$$

where p is an m-dimensional vector, μ is a scalar > 0, and $(x, y) \in T$. This expression can clearly be interpreted as profit if we interpret p as a price vector and μ as an interest factor. y is the physical output resulting from an input x. μ, which is 1 plus the interest rate, times x represents the next best use of input vector x. The difference between y and μx is profit in physical terms, in the best opportunity cost tradition. This relation leads to the following definitions.

D4 (p, μ) is an *equilibrium price-interest pair* if:
(a) $p \cdot (y - \mu x) \leq 0$ for all $(x, y) \in T$; and
(b) $p \geq 0$ and $\mu > 0$.

D4(a) requires the economy to be perfectly competitive by forcing all profits to be strictly nonpositive. D4(b) rules out negative (but not zero) prices and nonpositive interest rates.

We now state von Neumann's basic result as a theorem.

Theorem 10.10-2 (von Neumann) Given A1–A6[24,25] there exists $\hat{x}, p$, and ρ such that:

(a) $\hat{x}$ is balanced with growth factor ρ; and
(b) (p, ρ) is an equilibrium price-interest pair.

Furthermore, any triple $(\hat{x}, p, \rho)$ satisfying (a) and (b) is a von Neumann growth path.

Additionally, it can be shown that ρ is the maximum coefficient of expansion, that is, $\rho = \max \lambda$. This is the big link between the optimal growth path

[23] This is the scalar product of two vectors p and $y - \mu x$.

[24] It can be shown that all these assumptions are not needed for the theorem; see Radner (1961).

[25] The reader interested in a proof of this theorem should refer to von Neumann's original work and to Karlin (1959).

and the von Neumann path. Before presenting Radner's basic results we need the definition of the angular distance between two vectors, $d(x, y)$.

D5
$$d(x, y) = \left| \frac{x}{|x|} - \frac{y}{|y|} \right|$$

where $|x|$ is the square root of the scalar product of x with itself (i.e., $\sqrt{x \cdot x}$).

We are ready to state Radner's turnpike theorem:

Theorem 10.10–3 *Radner's Turnpike Theorem* If A1–A4 hold and if:

(a) $(\hat{x}, p, \rho)$ is a von Neumann growth path;
(b) $p \cdot (y - \rho x) < 0$ for all $(x, y) \in T$ that are not scalar multiples of $(\hat{x}, \rho\hat{x})$;
(c) there is a number $K > 0$ such that for all vectors x, $U(x) \leq Kp \cdot x$;
(d) an initial commodity vector x_0 is given such that for some $L > 0$, $(x_0, Lx_0) \in T$; and
(e) $U(\hat{x}) > 0$;

then for any $\delta > 0$ there exists a number S such that for any number N and any optimal sequence $\{x_n\}_{n=0}^N$, the number of periods in which $d(x_n, \hat{x}) \geq \delta$ cannot exceed S, where S is independent of N.

How are the additional assumptions of Theorem 10.10–3 to be interpreted? (b) simply means that for any input-output combination (x, y) not on the von Neumann path, "shadow profit" calculated by using the von Neumann growth rate ρ as the interest factor will be negative, since the von Neumann rate is greater than any other rate. (c) requires the utility associated with any x to be finite and, more important, implies that elements of x with zero prices do not have any impact on utility. (d) simply says that a balanced bundle can be reached no matter what the initial stocks are.

The proof of Theorem 10.10–3 is based on the following lemma:

Theorem 10.10–4 *Radner's Lemma* Given A1 and A2 and (a) and (b) from Theorem 10.10–3, for any $\delta > 0$ there exists a $\gamma > 0$ such that for any $(x, y) \in T$ for which $d(x, \hat{x}) \geq \delta$, $p \cdot y \leq (\rho - \gamma)p \cdot x$.

PROOF Rather than reproduce Radner's mathematical proof, we shall present a somewhat intuitive version. From Theorem 10.10–3(b) we have $p \cdot y < \rho p \cdot x$ for (x, y) not scalar multiples of $(\hat{x}, \rho\hat{x})$. Furthermore, for all x such that $d(x, \hat{x}) > 0$ it follows that $(x, y) \in T$ is not proportional to $(\hat{x}, \rho\hat{x})$. Consequently, $d(x, \hat{x}) > 0$ implies $p \cdot y < \rho p \cdot x$. Thus we can find a positive number γ such that $p \cdot y \leq (\rho - \gamma)p \cdot x$.   QED

PROOF OF THEOREM $10.10–3$ The basic technique is to develop a "comparison" sequence that itself may or may not be optimal and to show that this comparison sequence is better than any other sequence that is either "too far" from the von Neumann growth path or stays away from it for "too long."

Define a feasible sequence $\{x_n\}_{n=0}^N$ by

(1)
$$\tilde{x}_0 = x_0$$
$$\tilde{x}_1 = L\hat{x}$$
$$\tilde{x}_n = L\rho^{n-1}\hat{x}$$

For any $\varepsilon > 0$ and any feasible sequence $\{x_n\}_{n=0}^N$ it follows by Theorem 10.10–4 that

(2)
$$p \cdot x_{t+1} \leq (\rho - \gamma)p \cdot x_t$$

for any period t where $d(x_t, \hat{x}) \geq \varepsilon$. Simultaneously, it must be true that

(3)
$$p \cdot x_{t+1} \leq \rho p \cdot x_t$$

since $\{x_n\}_0^N$ need not be a von Neumann growth path. In particular we can write

(4)
$$p \cdot x_1 \leq \rho p \cdot x_0$$

where x_0 is the vector of initial stocks. Now, suppose that $d(x_t, \hat{x}) \geq \varepsilon$ for R periods. Then we can write

(5)
$$p \cdot x_N \leq (\rho - \gamma)^R \rho^{N-R} p \cdot x_0$$

where $N - R$ is, of course, the number of periods for which $d(x_t, \hat{x}) \leq \varepsilon$. By Theorem 10.10–3(c) it must be true that

(6)
$$U(x_N) \geq K(\rho - \gamma)^R \rho^{N-R} p \cdot x_0$$

The utility of the final stocks in our comparison series (1) is simply[26]

(7)
$$U(\tilde{x}_N) = L\rho^{N-1} U(\hat{x})$$

Furthermore, by Theorem 10.10–3(e), (7) is strictly positive. To compare the utility of the two sequences, divide (6) by (7):

$$\frac{U(x_N)}{U(\tilde{x}_N)} \geq \frac{K(\rho - \gamma)^R \rho^{N-R} p \cdot x_0}{L\rho^{N-1} U(\hat{x})}$$

or

(8)
$$\frac{U(x_N)}{U(\tilde{x}_N)} \geq \frac{K\rho p \cdot x_0}{LU(\hat{x})} \left(\frac{\rho - \gamma}{\rho}\right)^R$$

---

[26] What role does A4 play in this result?

For the arbitrary sequence $\{x_0\}_0^N$ to be optimal, it must be true that it yields at least as much utility as any other feasible sequence, that is, that

$$\frac{U(x_N)}{U(\tilde{x}_N)} \geq 1$$

Thus we have, for optimality,

(9)
$$\frac{K\rho p \cdot x_0}{LU(\hat{x})} \left(\frac{\rho - \gamma}{\rho} \right)^R \geq 1$$

Solving (9) for R, for optimality it must be true that

(10)
$$R \leq \frac{\log \left[(K\rho p \cdot x_0)/LU(\hat{x}) \right]}{\log \left[\rho/(\rho - \gamma) \right]}$$

The theorem is proven by setting S, the number of periods for which $d(x_N, \hat{x}) \geq \varepsilon$, equal to

$$\max \left[1, \frac{\log \left[(K\rho p \cdot x_0)/LU(\hat{x}) \right]}{\log \left[\rho/(\rho - \gamma) \right]} \right]$$

Thus, for $N - S$ periods the optimal path is within ε of the von Neumann path. Also, S is clearly finite and independent of N.   QED

Figure 10.10–1 illustrates the Radner theorem in 2-space. Note that the theorem does not preclude the situation shown where one of the periods for which $d(x_n, \hat{x}) \geq \varepsilon$ (e.g., x_3) occurs in the "middle" of the path. We are not guaranteed that they all occur at the "ends" of the path.

We turn now to a brief discussion of Nikaido's extensions of Radner's theorem.

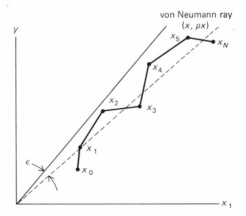

Figure 10.10–1   *Radner's theorem.*

With some additional restrictions on the model, Nikaido showed that Theorem 10.10–3 can be generalized to include the following:

(a) If the terminal stocks lie on the von Neumann path, the optimal path gets closer to the von Neumann path in every period, becoming asymptotic to it.
(b) If there are two points on the optimal path that are the same distance from the von Neumann path, every point between them must be closer to the von Neumann path.

Figure 10.10–2 illustrates the Nikaido extensions. The reader should compare Figures 10.10–1 and 10.10–2.

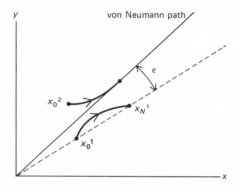

Figure 10.10–2   *Nikaido's extensions.*

We turn now to Lancaster's specific example, where there are two inputs, x_1 and x_2, and two outputs, y_1 and y_2. The specific transformation function he used is

$$a^2(\dot{y}_1)^2 + (\dot{y}_2)^2 - b^2\dot{x}_1^2\left[f\left(\frac{\dot{x}_2}{\dot{x}_1}\right)^2\right] = 0$$

where dots indicate time derivatives and a and b are constants. By assumption, $f > 0$, $df/dt > 0$, and $d^2f/dt^2 < 0$. Furthermore, $\dot{x}_1(t) = k_1 y_1(t)$ and $\dot{x}_2(t) = k_2 y_2(t)$.

Define new variables u and v by $y_1 = (1/a)e^u \cos v$ and $y_2 = e^u \sin v$. After appropriate substitutions, the transformation function can be written as

(1) $$\dot{u} = [1 + (v')^2]^{-1/2}[\phi(v)]^{-1}$$

where

$$[\phi(v)]^{-1} = \left\{\left(\frac{bk_1}{a}\right)\cos v + \left[\frac{ak_2}{k_1}\tan v\right]\right\}^2$$

Notice that $v' = dv/du$ and v itself depends only on the ratio y_1/y_2. Thus, for balanced growth, $v' = 0$ and the rate of balanced growth is simply[27]

$$\dot{u} = [\phi(v)]^{-1}$$

Equation (1) can be written as

$$\frac{du}{dt} = [1 + (v')^2]^{-1/2}[\phi(v)]^{-1}$$

or

(2) $$dt = [1 + (v')^2]^{1/2}\phi(v) \, du$$

Solving (2) for t,

(3) $$t = \int [1 + (v')^2]^{1/2}\phi(v) \, du$$

The right side of (3) is a functional with one unknown function, v, in one independent variable, u. Given the initial and terminal stocks (which establish the limits of integration in this fixed point–fixed point problem) we can solve (3) for v, obtaining the general form of the optimum growth path. Since the independent variable u does not appear explicitly in (3) (see Section 10.8), the first integral of the Euler equation becomes

(4) $$G - v'G_{v'} = C$$

Since $G = [1 + (v')^2]^{1/2}\phi(v)$, we have $G_{v'} = [1 + (v')^2]^{-1/2}v'\phi(v)$. Equation (4) can then be shown to be

(5) $$C = [1 + (v')^2]^{-1/2}\phi(v)$$

Solving (5) for v',

(6) $$v' = \left[\frac{(\phi(v))^2}{C^2} - 1\right]^{1/2}$$

Equation (6) enables us to determine the slope of the optimal path, v', in terms of the stocks (v is the ratio of the stocks) and the constant C.

Let v^* be the von Neumann proportions. Then the maximum growth rate is $[\phi(v^*)]^{-1}$. Consequently, $\phi(v)/\phi(v^*)$ must be ≥ 1 for all v. We can use this relation to explore the implications of possible values of C in (6). We also need an expression for v'' to describe the shapes of optimal paths. Differentiating (6) we obtain

(7) $$v'' = \frac{\phi(v)\phi'(v)}{C^2\left\{\left[\dfrac{\phi(v)}{C^2}\right]^2 - 1\right\}^{1/2}}$$

----

[27] It can be shown that $u = \ln [a^2 y_1^2 + y_2^2]$ and $v = \arctan (y_2/ay_1)$ in this example.

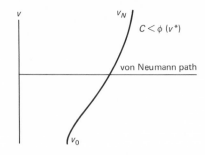

Figure 10.10–3 $C < \phi(v^*)$.

Consider the expression for v''. $\phi(v)$ has a minimum at v^*, since v^* maximizes $[\phi(v)]$. Thus, at $v = v^*$, $\phi'(v) = 0$ and $v'' = 0$ at the von Neumann ray. If $v > v^*$, $\phi'(v) > 0$ and $v'' > 0$. If $v < v^*$ it follows in a similar manner that $v'' < 0$.

Consequently, we can conclude from this sign pattern on v'' that all optimum paths are convex toward the von Neumann path both from above and from below. Equations (6) and (7) together enable us to describe the optimal paths for various values of C. Three different cases arise:

(1) $C < \phi(v^*)$
(2) $C > \phi(v^*)$
(3) $C = \phi(v^*)$

In case (1) we know that $\phi(v)^2/C^2$ must be strictly greater than one in (6). Thus v' is real valued for all v. Since $\phi(v)^2/C^2 \neq 1$, v' cannot be zero in this case. Thus the optimal path cannot be tangent to any ray from the origin. At the von Neumann ray however, $v'' = 0$, since $\phi(v) = 0$ only if $v = v^*$. The optimum path crosses the von Neumann ray at an angle and has an inflection point there. From our previous remarks on the convexity of optimal paths, it should be clear that Figure 10.10–3 shows the general shape for $C < \phi(v^*)$.

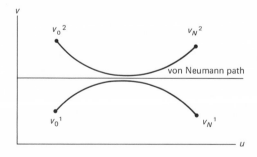

Figure 10.10–4 $C > \phi(v^*)$.

In case (2) v' is an imaginary number for v sufficiently close to v^*. Consequently, the optimal path does not touch the von Neumann path. There will, however, be a v for which $v' = 0$. This is the nearest point to the von Neumann path. Such a path is shown in Figure 10.10–4. In this case the optimal path is called a **catenary**.

In case (3) $v' = 0$ only if $v = v^*$. However, once $v = v^*$, v'' is also zero, so that the optimal path corresponds to the von Neumann path if it ever reaches it. In this case the optimal path is asymptotic to the von Neumann path, as shown in Figure 10.10–5.

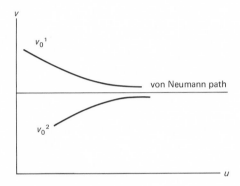

Figure 10.10–5 $C = \phi(v^*)$.

In summary, if the initial and terminal stocks lie on the same side of the von Neumann ray but neither one on the ray, the optimal growth path will be a catenary as in Figure 10.10–4, that is, $C > \phi(v^*)$. If the terminal and initial points are on opposite sides of the von Neumann path, the optimal path will be shaped like the one illustrated in Figure 10.10–3. If the terminal point is on the von Neumann ray, the optimal path approaches the von Neumann path asymptotically. If the initial point is on the von Neumann path, the optimal path corresponds to the von Neumann path.

References

1. BELLMAN, R. E. (1957), *Dynamic Programming*, Princeton, N.J.: Princeton University Press.
2. BELLMAN, R. E., and S. E. DREYFUS (1962), *Applied Dynamic Programming*, Princeton, N.J.: Princeton University Press.
3. BLISS, G. A. (1935), *Calculus of Variations*, LaSalle, Ill.: Open Court.

4. BLISS, G. A. (1946), *Lectures on the Calculus of Variations*, Chicago: University of Chicago Press.
5. BOLZA, O. (1961), *Lectures on the Calculus of Variations*, New York: Dover.
6. DREYFUS, S. E. (1965), *Dynamic Programming and the Calculus of Variations*, New York: Academic.
7. EL'SGOL'C, L. E. (1962), *Calculus of Variations*, Reading, Mass.: Addison-Wesley.
8. FOX, C. (1950), *An Introduction to the Calculus of Variations*, London: Oxford University Press.
9. GALE, D. (1960), *The Theory of Linear Economic Models*, New York: McGraw-Hill.
10. GUMOWSKI, I., and C. MIRA (1968), *Optimization in Control Theory and Practice*, Cambridge, Mass.: Harvard University Press.
11. HESTENES, M. R. (1966), *Calculus of Variations and Optimal Control Theory*, New York: Wiley.
12. KARLIN, S. (1959), *Mathematical Methods and Theory in Games; Programming, and Economics*, Reading, Mass.: Addison-Wesley.
13. LANCASTER, K. (1968), *Mathematical Economics*, New York: Macmillan.
14. MORISHIMA, M. (1969), *Equilibrium, Stability, and Growth*, London: Oxford University Press.
15. NIKAIDO, H. (1964), "Persistence of Continual Optimal Growth Near the von Neumann Ray: A Strong Version of the Radner Turnpike Theorem," *Econometrica*, **32**:151–162.
16. PARS, L. A. (1963), *An Introduction to the Calculus of Variations*, New York: Wiley.
17. RADNER, R. (1961), "Paths of Economic Growth That Are Optimal with Regard Only to Final States: A Turnpike Theorem," *Review of Economic Studies*, **28**:98–104.
18. SAGAN, H. (1969), *Introduction to the Calculus of Variations*, New York: McGraw-Hill.
19. SAMUELSON, P. A. (1960), "Efficient Paths of Capital Accumulation in Terms of the Calculus of Variations," in K. J. Arrow, S. Karlin, and P. Suppes (eds.), *Mathematical Methods in the Social Sciences*, Palo Alto, Calif.: Stanford University Press.
20. THOMAS, GEORGE B. (1968), *Calculus and Analytical Geometry*, 4th ed., Reading, Mass.: Addison-Wesley.
21. VON NEUMANN, J. (1945), "A Model of General Economic Equilibrium," *Review of Economic Studies*, **13**:1–9.
22. YOUNG, L. C. (1969), *Calculus of Variations and Optimal Control Theory*, Philadelphia: Saunders.

Chapter 11

Mathematical Programming: Theory

11.1 INTRODUCTION: GENERALIZATION OF THE CONSTRAINED MAXIMUM PROBLEM

As we discussed in some detail in Chapter 5, the problem of finding a constrained maximum in ordinary calculus assumes that the constraints hold with equality. For example, in Figure 11.1–1 we have a graphical representation (positive quadrant only) of finding the maximum of $f(x_1, x_2)$ subject to $g(x_1, x_2) = 0$. The solution is constrained to the curve $g(x_1, x_2) = 0$. In Figure 11.1–2 we have three variables and two constraints, and thus the solution must occur along the line ab. In the case of two variables and two linearly independent constraints,[1] the maximizing problem is trivial (i.e., there is only one solution), while with two linearly dependent equations, the system is inconsistent (cf. Figures 11.1–3 and 11.1–4). The point of this discussion is

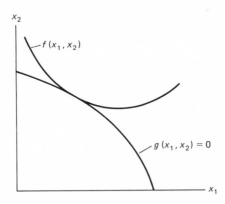

Figure 11.1–1 *Two variables and one constraint:* $g(x_1, x_2) = 0$.

[1] That is, two constraints that are not coincident with each other.

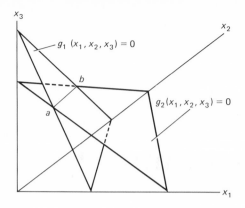

Figure 11.1–2   *Three variables and two constraints:* $g_1(x_1, x_2, x_3) = 0$, $g_2(x_1, x_2, x_3) = 0$.

that this ordinary approach is restrictive and often, in economic applications, not quite realistic.

For example, consider the usual approach to demand theory:

$$\text{max:} \qquad U(x_1, x_2)$$

$$\text{subject to:} \qquad p_1x_1 + p_2x_2 = M$$

Using Lagrangean multiplier techniques as developed in Chapter 5, we have

$$\phi = U(x_1, x_2) + \lambda(M - p_1x_1 - p_2x_2) = 0$$

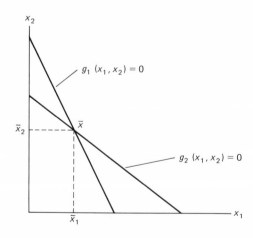

Figure 11.1–3   *One value,* $(\bar{x}_1, \bar{x}_2)$, *feasible.*

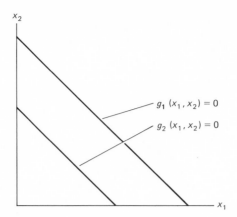

Figure 11.1–4 *Inconsistent system.*

where λ is the Lagrangean multiplier. Taking partial derivatives of ϕ with respect to each variable, x_1, x_2, and λ, we have

$$\frac{\partial U}{\partial x_1} - \lambda p_1 = 0$$

$$\frac{\partial U}{\partial x_2} - \lambda p_2 = 0$$

and

$$M - p_1 x_1 - p_2 x_2 = 0$$

However, this analysis is unrealistic in the sense that there is no constraint requiring x_1 or x_2 to be nonnegative, and a negative quantity of a good or service is usually not very meaningful. The analysis above precludes a "corner" solution (Figure 11.1–5), which could occur if the variables x_1 or x_2 are implicitly assumed to be greater than or equal to zero. This approach explicitly assumes that the budget constraint is the only constraint on the activities of the individual. It suggests that the individual has an infinite amount of time, for example, to consume the goods or else that they require no time for consumption. Also, this usual approach of utility theory implies that there are no social constraints of any kind that impinge upon the consumption of x_1 or x_2.

In a more general sense, the budget constraint does not have to hold with equality but is a limitation, an inequality that the individual cannot exceed. Further, there are a number of other constraints that may or may not be effective on the decision calculus of the individual, such as social taboos against particular consumption combinations.

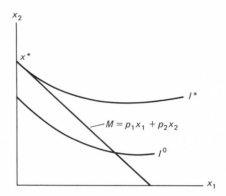

Figure 11.1–5   *Corner solution to utility maximizing problem,* x_1, $x_2 \geq 0$.

The more general problem of finding a maximum subject to inequalities rather than strict equalities is termed mathematical programming. In Section 11.2 we present the fundamental theorem of mathematical programming developed by Kuhn and Tucker (1951), which gives the necessary conditions for a maximum. In Section 11.3 we discuss the Arrow and Enthoven (1961) generalization of Kuhn and Tucker's sufficient conditions for a maximum. The remainder of the chapter is devoted to a special application of general mathematical programming theory: linear programming. In Chapter 12 we discuss various techniques for solving and analyzing mathematical programming problems.

Problems

11.1–1   Given a maximization problem with n independent variables, how many constraints, which must hold with equality, can there be without the problem being inconsistent?

11.1–2   State the intuitive properties of a maximization problem with two constraints that are inequalities, where one constraint is "redundant."

11.1–3   Given a maximization problem with three variables and one constraint, what would be the characteristics of the variables if the maximum were a "corner" solution?

11.2   KUHN–TUCKER NECESSARY CONDITIONS FOR A MAXIMUM

As noted in the introduction, a general mathematical programming problem is a constrained maximum problem, where the constraints are inequalities.

DEFINITION 11.2–1 A **general mathematical programming problem** is one
of finding an n-dimensional vector x so as to

$$\begin{aligned}
\text{max:} \quad & f(x_1, \ldots, x_n) \\
\text{subject to:} \quad & g_1(x_1, \ldots, x_n) \geq 0 \\
& \quad\vdots \\
& g_m(x_1, \ldots, x_n) \geq 0 \\
& x_1, \ldots, x_n \geq 0
\end{aligned}$$

or, as expressed in vector notation:

$$\begin{aligned}
\text{max:} \quad & f(x) \\
\text{subject to:} \quad & g(x) \geq 0 \\
& x \geq 0
\end{aligned}$$

where $f(x)$ and $g_j(x)$, for $j = 1, \ldots, m$, are assumed to be differentiable functions.

DEFINITION 11.2–2 A function $f(x)$ of several variables is **differentiable**
if $f(x + h) = f(x) + ch + eh$, where c is a vector dependent upon x but not
upon h, and $e \to 0$ as $h \to 0$.

If a function is differentiable, then its partial derivatives exist, and $\partial f/\partial x = c$;
however, the existence of partial derivatives is not sufficient to guarantee
differentiability.[2]
Virtually all constrained maximization or minimization problems can be
put in the above form by one of the following five standard transformations:

I. (a) Original problem:

$$\begin{aligned}
\text{min:} \quad & f^*(x) \\
\text{subject to:} \quad & g(x) \geq 0 \\
& x \geq 0
\end{aligned}$$

   (b) Transformation:

$$f(x) = -f^*(x)$$

II. (a) Original problem:

$$\begin{aligned}
\text{max:} \quad & f(x) \\
\text{subject to:} \quad & g^*(x) \leq 0 \\
& x \geq 0
\end{aligned}$$

   (b) Transformation:

$$g(x) = -g^*(x)$$

[2] Cf. Definition 5.1–5.

III. (a) Original problem:

$$\begin{aligned}\text{max:} \quad & f(x^*) \\ \text{subject to:} \quad & g(x^*) \geq 0 \\ & x^* \leq 0\end{aligned}$$

(b) Transformation:

$$x = -x^*, f(x) = f(x^*) \quad \text{and} \quad g(x) = g(-x^*)$$

IV. (a) Original problem:

$$\begin{aligned}\text{max:} \quad & f(x) \\ \text{subject to:} \quad & g^*(x) = 0 \\ & x \geq 0\end{aligned}$$

(b) Transformation:

$$g(x) = \begin{bmatrix} g^*(x) \\ -g^*(x) \end{bmatrix}$$

V. (a) Original problem:

$$\begin{aligned}\text{max:} \quad & f(x) \\ \text{subject to:} \quad & g(x) \geq 0 \\ & x \gtreqless 0\end{aligned}$$

(b) Transformation:

$$x = x^+ - x^-$$
$$x^+ \geq 0, x^- \geq 0$$

where if $x_i^+ > 0$, then $x_i^- = 0$ or if $x_i^- > 0$, $x_i^+ = 0$.

To develop the necessary conditions for a maximum for a general mathematical programming problem, we shall utilize the notion of a saddle value function.[3]

DEFINITION 11.2–3   A differentiable function $\phi(x_1, \ldots, x_n, \lambda_1, \ldots, \lambda_m) = \phi(x, \lambda)$ is a **saddle-value function** if and only if $\phi(x, \lambda^0) \leq \phi(x^0, \lambda^0) \leq \phi(x^0, \lambda)$ for all $x \geq 0$ and $\lambda \geq 0$. The point $\phi(x^0, \lambda^0)$ is termed the **saddle point**.

The following necessary conditions follow directly from the definition.

Theorem 11.2–1   If $\phi(x^0, \lambda^0)$ is a saddle point, then:[4]

(1) $\qquad \left.\dfrac{\partial \phi}{\partial x}\right|_0 \leq 0 \quad \text{and} \quad \left.\dfrac{\partial \phi}{\partial x}\right|_0 x^0 = 0 \qquad \text{for } x^0 \geq 0$

---

[3] Cf. Section 5.4 and Figure 5.4–4b.

[4] $\partial \phi / \partial x|_0$ reads "the partial of ϕ with respect to x evaluated at the point (x^0, λ^0). Since x is a vector of variables, $\partial \phi / \partial x$ is a vector of partial derivatives.

and

(2) $\left.\dfrac{\partial\phi}{\partial\lambda}\right|_0 \geq 0$ and $\left.\dfrac{\partial\phi}{\partial\lambda}\right|_0 \lambda^0 = 0$ for $\lambda^0 \geq 0$

where

$$\left.\frac{\partial\phi}{\partial x}\right|_0 = \left[\left.\frac{\partial\phi}{\partial x_1}\right|_0, \ldots, \left.\frac{\partial\phi}{\partial x_n}\right|_0\right]'$$

and

$$\left.\frac{\partial\phi}{\partial\lambda}\right|_0 = \left[\left.\frac{\partial\phi}{\partial\lambda_1}\right|_0, \ldots, \left.\frac{\partial\phi}{\partial\lambda_m}\right|_0\right]'$$

PROOF   Suppose that

$$\left.\frac{\partial\phi}{\partial x_i}\right|_0 > 0   \text{for some } i$$

and

$$\left.\frac{\partial\phi}{\partial x_j}\right|_0 = 0   \text{for all } j \neq i$$

Then $\phi(x_1^0, \ldots, x_i^0 + \delta x_i, \ldots, x_n^0, \lambda_1^0, \ldots, \lambda_m^0) > \phi(x^0, \lambda^0)$. Thus $\phi(x^0, \lambda^0)$ is not a saddle point.

Suppose that

$$\left.\frac{\partial\phi}{\partial x_i}\right|_0 < 0   \text{where } x_i^0 > 0 \text{ for some } i$$

and

$$\left.\frac{\partial\phi}{\partial x_j}\right|_0 = 0   \text{for all } j \neq i$$

Then $\phi(x^0, \lambda^0) < \phi(x_1^0, \ldots, x_i^0 - \delta x_i^0, \ldots, x_n^0, \lambda_1^0, \ldots, \lambda_m^0)$. Thus $\phi(x^0, \lambda^0)$ is not a saddle point. This proves (1). A similar argument follows for (2). QED

In words, Theorem 11.2–1 says that if ϕ is a saddle-value function, then at the saddle point (x^0, λ^0) if x_i is positive (i.e., $x^0 > 0$) then

$$\left.\frac{\partial\phi}{\partial x_i}\right|_0 = 0$$

If x_i is zero at the saddle point, then the partial derivative of ϕ with respect to x_i is less than or equal to zero. A similar statement applies for the variables λ at (x^0, λ^0). It must be, however, that the products

$$\left.\frac{\partial\phi}{\partial x_i}\right|_0 x_i^0   \text{and}   \left.\frac{\partial\phi}{\partial\lambda_j}\right|_0 \lambda_j^0$$

are zero for all values of i and j.

A slight reflection on Theorem 11.2–1 shows that (1) and (2) only describe a neighborhood of x^0. Something stronger is needed for a true saddle point.

Theorem 11.2–2   If (1) and (2) hold and if

$$(3) \qquad \phi(x, \lambda^0) \leq \phi(x^0, \lambda^0) + \frac{\partial \phi}{\partial x}\bigg|_0 (x - x^0) \qquad \text{for all } x \geq 0$$

and

$$(4) \qquad \phi(x^0, \lambda) \geq \phi(x^0, \lambda^0) + \frac{\partial \phi}{\partial \lambda}\bigg|_0 (\lambda - \lambda^0) \qquad \text{for all } \lambda \geq 0$$

then $\phi(x^0, \lambda^0)$ is a saddle point.

PROOF   By (1),

$$\frac{\partial \phi}{\partial x}\bigg|_0 x \leq 0 \quad \text{and} \quad \frac{\partial \phi}{\partial x}\bigg|_0 x^0 = 0$$

Thus if (3) holds, $\phi(x, \lambda^0) \leq \phi(x^0, \lambda^0)$.
   Similarly, by (2),

$$\frac{\partial \phi}{\partial \lambda}\bigg|_0 \lambda \geq 0 \quad \text{and} \quad \frac{\partial \phi}{\partial \lambda}\bigg|_0 \lambda^0 = 0$$

Thus, if (4) holds, $\phi(x^0, \lambda) \geq \phi(x^0, \lambda^0)$. Combining, we have $\phi(x, \lambda^0) \leq \phi(x^0, \lambda^0) \leq \phi(x^0, \lambda)$.   QED

Kuhn and Tucker's main theorem of the necessary conditions for a maximum to mathematical programming problem relates the objective function and constraint functions to a saddle value function. Hence the necessary conditions for a saddle point to exist become equivalent to the necessary conditions for a maximum to a general mathematical programming problem. However, in order to do this, a qualification is needed on the constraint equations.

DEFINITION 11.2–4   For the constraint equations $g_1(x) \geq 0, \ldots, g_m(x) \geq 0$ and any x^0 on the boundary of the constraint set, let:

$$G_1 = \begin{cases} g_1(x^0) = 0 \\ \quad \vdots \\ g_r(x^0) = 0 \end{cases}$$

that is, G_1 is the set of constraints that are an equality at x^0;

$$G_2 = \begin{cases} g_{r+1}(x^0) > 0 \\ \quad \vdots \\ g_m(x^0) > 0 \end{cases}$$

that is, G_2 is the set of constraints that are a strict inequality at x^0; and I is an $n \times n$ identity matrix partitioned into $I = [I_1, I_2]$ such that the columns of I_1 correspond to all $x_i^0 = 0$ and the columns of I_2 correspond to all $x_i^0 > 0$. Thus we have

$$G_1(x^0) = 0$$
$$I_1 x^0 = 0$$
$$G_2(x^0) > 0$$
$$I_2 x^0 > 0$$

The **Kuhn–Tucker constraint qualification** is as follows: For each x^0 on the boundary of the constraint set and for any dx such that if

(5)
$$\left.\frac{\partial G_1}{\partial x}\right|_0 dx > 0$$

and

(6)
$$I_1\, dx > 0$$

then $(\partial G_1/\partial x)|_0\, dx$ is tangent to an arc, $a(\theta)$, contained in the constraint set where $0 \le \theta \le 1$, and $a(0) = x^0$.

What the Kuhn–Tucker constraint qualification does is to eliminate "cusps" in the constraint set. In Figure 11.2–1 a constraint is illustrated where the qualification holds. At the point x^0 the equation $(\partial G_1/\partial x)|_0\, dx = 0$, where $I_1\, dx = 0$ is the tangent to $g(x_1, x_2) = 0$ at the point x^0. $a(\theta)$ is an arc contained in the constraint set. In Figure 11.2–2 we have a cusp and there exists no arc $a(\theta)$ contained in $g(x) \ge 0$ that is tangent to $(\partial G_1/\partial x)|_0\, dx$. We are now ready to state and prove the Kuhn–Tucker Theorem 1.

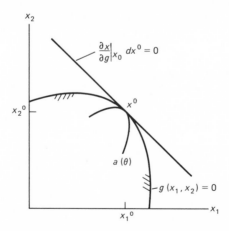

Figure 11.2–1   *Kuhn–Tucker constraint qualification holds.*

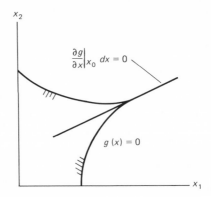

Figure 11.2–2   *Kuhn–Tucker constraint qualification does not hold.*

Theorem 11.2–3   *Kuhn–Tucker Theorem 1*   If x^0 is a solution to a mathematical programming problem [if max $f(x) = f(x^0)$, subject to $g(x) \geq 0$, $x \geq 0$], and if the constraint qualification holds, then x^0 and λ^0, an m-dimensional vector of Lagrangean multipliers, must satisfy:

(1)
$$\left.\frac{\partial \phi}{\partial x}\right|_0 \leq 0 \quad \text{and} \quad \left.\frac{\partial \phi}{\partial x}\right|_0 x^0 = 0 \quad \text{for } x^0 \geq 0$$

and

(2)
$$\left.\frac{\partial \phi}{\partial \lambda}\right|_0 \geq 0 \quad \text{and} \quad \left.\frac{\partial \phi}{\partial \lambda}\right|_0 \lambda_0 = 0 \quad \text{for } \lambda^0 \geq 0$$

where $\phi(x, \lambda) = f(x) + \lambda' g(x)$.

Before proving Theorem 11.2–3 it is worthwhile to do two things. The first is to give an example demonstrating that the constraint qualification is needed. In Figure 11.2–3 we have one constraint, $g(x_1, x_2) \geq 0$, and two variables, x_1

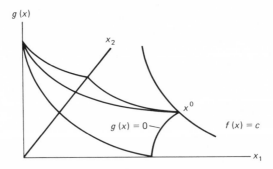

Figure 11.2–3   *A violation of the postulates and conclusions in Theorem 11.2–3.* x^0 *maximizes* $f(x)$ *subject to* $g(x) \geq 0$ *and* $x \geq 0$, *but* $\partial \phi / \partial x > 0$.

and x_2. At the point x^0, $\partial g/\partial x_1 = 0$ and $\partial g/\partial x_2 = 0$. The "isovalue" curve $f(x) = c$, a constant, is such that $\partial f/\partial x_1^0 > 0$ and $\partial f/\partial x_2^0 > 0$. Therefore (1) does not hold; that is,

$$\left.\frac{\partial\phi}{\partial x}\right|_0 = \left.\frac{\partial f}{\partial x}\right|_0 + \lambda'\left.\frac{\partial g}{\partial x}\right|_0 = \left.\frac{\partial f}{\partial x}\right|_0 > 0$$

but x^0 is indeed a maximum solution.

The second item is to state and explain Farkas' lemma, which is used in the proof.

Theorem 11.2–4 *Farkas' Lemma* For the vectors y $(1 \times m)$, b $(m \times 1)$, and x $(n \times 1)$, and the $m \times n$ matrix A:
Either there exists a y such that:

$$yA \geq 0 \quad \text{and} \quad yb < 0$$

or there exists an x such that:

$$Ax = b \quad \text{and} \quad x \geq 0$$

An alternative way of stating Farkas' lemma is as follows: If for any y, it is true that $yA \geq 0$ and $yb \geq 0$, then there exists an x such that $Ax = b$ and $x \geq 0$. In other words, if any point y makes a nonobtuse angle with the columns of A and also makes a nonobtuse angle with the point b, then $Ax = b$ for some $x \geq 0$. That is, b must be some nonnegative weighted average of the columns of A. This idea is expressed graphically in Figure 11.2–4, where $m = 2$ and $n = 4$. In the figure any vector y that makes a nonobtuse angle with all the columns of A also forms a nonobtuse angle with b. Thus b is some average of the columns of A.

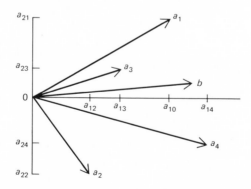

Figure 11.2–4 *A graphical interpretation of Farkas' lemma: $A = (a_1, a_2, a_3, a_4)$.*

PROOF OF THEOREM *11.2–3*   Let x^0 be a solution to the mathematical programming problem. Then for dx that satisfies (5) and (6) of the constraint qualification, it must be true that

(7)
$$\frac{\partial f}{\partial x}\bigg|_0 dx \le 0$$

This is shown in Figure 11.2–5. dx is such that $(\partial G_1/\partial x)\, dx = 0$, and for any

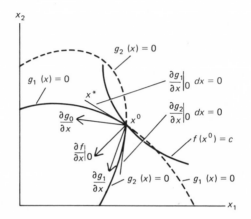

Figure 11.2–5   *A feasible space bounded by two constraints,* $g_1(x) \ge 0$, *and* $g_2(x) \ge 0$. *The maximum of* $f(x)$ *occurs at* x^0.

point along that line, for example, x^*, the value of $f(x^*) \le f(x^0)$. The line labeled $-(\partial f/\partial x)|_0$ is the negative of the normal[5] to the point x^0. It also follows by the constraint qualification and Farkas' lemma that:

(8) $$-\frac{\partial f}{\partial x}\bigg|_0 = \frac{\partial G_1}{\partial x}\bigg|_0 \lambda_1^0 + I_1' w_1^0 \qquad \text{for some } \lambda_1^0 \ge 0 \text{ and } w_1^0 \ge 0$$

To see this let:

$$-\frac{\partial f}{\partial x}\bigg|_0 = b$$

$$\frac{\partial G_1}{\partial x}\bigg|_0 = (a_1, \ldots, a_r) = A_1$$

$$A = [A_1, I_1'] = (a_1, \ldots, a_r, u_1, \ldots, u_{n-r})$$

$$dx = y$$

[5] The normal at x^0 is simply a vector, v, which is orthogonal at x^0 to the vector of partial derivatives, the gradient Δ, i.e., $v \cdot \Delta = 0$. In two dimensions the normal to a point on a curve is perpendicular to the tangent to the curve at that point.

Then, by (7), $yb \geq 0$. By the constraint qualification, $yA \geq 0$. Therefore there exists an x such that $Ax = b$, and $x \geq 0$.

Letting $Ax = [(\partial G_1/\partial x)|_0]' \lambda_1^0 + I_0' w_1^0$ for $\lambda_1^0 \geq 0$ and $w_1^0 \geq 0$, then (8) follows.

By adding zeros as components to λ_1^0 and w_1^0 to form λ^0 and w^0, (8) becomes

$$(9) \qquad -\frac{\partial f}{\partial x}\bigg|_0 = \left[\frac{\partial g}{\partial x}\bigg|_0\right]' \lambda^0 + w^0$$

and thus

$$(10) \qquad \frac{\partial f}{\partial x}\bigg|_0 + \lambda^0 \frac{\partial g}{\partial x}\bigg|_0 + w^0 = 0$$

Since $w^0 \geq 0$,

$$\frac{\partial \phi}{\partial x}\bigg|_0 = \frac{\partial f}{\partial x}\bigg|_0 + \lambda^0 \frac{\partial g}{\partial x}\bigg|_0 \leq 0$$

Since $w^{0'}x^0 = w_1 I_1 x^0 = 0$, multiplying (10) by x^0 gives

$$\frac{\partial \phi}{\partial x}\bigg|_0 x^0 = \frac{\partial f}{\partial x}\bigg|_0 x^0 + \lambda^0 \frac{\partial g}{\partial x}\bigg|_0 x^0 = 0$$

By definition we have

$$(11) \qquad \frac{\partial \phi}{\partial \lambda}\bigg|_0 = g(x^0) \geq 0$$

and multiplying (11) by λ^0:

$$\lambda^0 \frac{\partial \phi}{\partial \lambda}\bigg|_0 = \lambda^0 g(x^0) = \lambda^0 \frac{\partial G_1(x)}{\partial x}\bigg|_0 = 0 \qquad \text{QED}$$

The next Kuhn–Tucker theorem generates a set of sufficient conditions for a maximum to a general mathematical programming problem. This theorem also is couched in terms of the conditions for a saddle value function to exist as we used above.

Theorem 11.2–5   *Kuhn–Tucker Theorem 2*   If x^0 and some λ^0 satisfy (1), (2), and (3) of Theorems 11.2–1 and 11.2–2 for $\phi(x, \lambda) = f(x) + \lambda g(x)$, then x^0 is a solution to

$$\begin{aligned} \text{max:} \quad & f(x) \\ \text{subject to:} \quad & g(x) \geq 0 \\ & x \geq 0 \end{aligned}$$

PROOF By (3):

$$f(x) + \lambda^0 g(x) = \phi(x, \lambda^0) \leq \phi(x^0, \lambda^0) + \frac{\partial \phi}{\partial x}\bigg|_0 (x - x^0)$$

since $(\partial \phi / \partial x)|_0 x \leq 0$. Also, $(\partial \phi / \partial x)|_0 x^0 = 0$ by (1). Therefore

$$f(x) + \lambda^0 g(x) \leq \phi(x^0, \lambda^0)$$

However, by Theorem 11.2–1, $\lambda^0 g(x^0) = 0$. Thus we have $\phi(x^0, \lambda^0) = f(x^0) + \lambda^0 g(x^0) = f(x^0)$; hence $f(x) \leq f(x^0)$.   QED

Theorem 11.2–5 assures us that by dealing with programming problems whose objective and constraint functions satisfy (1)–(3) of Theorems 11.2–1 and 11.2–2 and the constraint qualification, we shall know the necessary and sufficient conditions for a solution to the problem. For example, if $f(x)$ and $g(x)$ are concave functions, then (1) and (2) of Theorem 11.2–1 are necessary and sufficient conditions for a maximum solution, which we shall demonstrate in Theorem 11.2–6.

DEFINITION 11.2–5 $f(x)$ is a **concave function** if

(a) $f[\theta x + (1 - \theta)x^0] \geq \theta f(x) + (1 - \theta)f(x^0)$ for $0 \leq \theta \leq 1$

Alternatively, if $f(x)$ is also differentiable,[6]

(b) $$f(x) \leq f(x^0) + \frac{\partial f}{\partial x}\bigg|_{x^0} (x - x^0)$$

The two equivalent definitions of a concave function are illustrated in Figures 11.2–6 and 11.2–7. A production function with decreasing marginal product throughout is an example of a concave function.

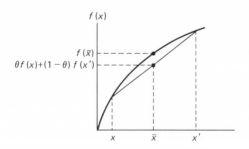

Figure 11.2–6 $f(x)$ *is concave by Definition 11.2–5(a) and* $\bar{x} = \theta x + (1 - \theta)x^0$.

---

[6] If the inequalities in the definition are reversed, then $f(x)$ is a *convex* function.

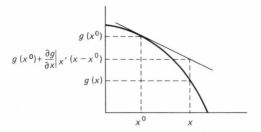

Figure 11.2–7 *g(x) is concave by Definition 11.2–5(b).*

Theorem 11.2–6   If:

(a) $f(x)$ is concave;
(b) $g(x)$ is concave; and
(c) x^0 and λ^0 satisfy (1) and (2) of Theorem 11.2–1

then x^0 is a solution to max $f(x)$ subject to $g(x) \geq 0$ and $x \geq 0$.

PROOF   The theorem is easily proved by showing that $\phi(x, \lambda^0) = f(x) + \lambda^0 g(x)$ satisfies (3) in Theorem 11.2–2 if $f(x)$ and $g(x)$ are concave. From Definition 11.2–5 we have

$$f(x) \leq f(x^0) + \frac{\partial f}{\partial x}\bigg|_0 (x - x^0)$$

and

$$g(x) \leq g(x^0) + \frac{\partial g}{\partial x}\bigg|_0 (x - x_0)$$

Therefore

$$\phi(x, \lambda^0) = f(x) + \lambda^0 g(x) \leq f(x^0) + \frac{\partial f}{\partial x}\bigg|_0 (x - x^0) + \lambda^0\left[g(x^0) + \frac{\partial g}{\partial x}\bigg|_0 (x - x^0)\right]$$

Combining $f(x^0)$ and $\lambda^0 g(x^0)$, we have

$$\phi(x, \lambda^0) \leq \phi(x^0, \lambda^0) + \left[\frac{\partial f}{\partial x}\bigg|_0 + \frac{\partial g}{\partial x}\bigg|_0\right](x - x^0)$$

or

$$\phi(x, \lambda^0) \leq \phi(x^0, \lambda^0) + \frac{\partial \phi}{\partial x}\bigg|_0 (x - x^0)$$

which is (3) and Theorem 11.2–5 can now be applied.

For completeness, we also note that if $f(x)$ and $g(x)$ are concave functions, then (4) holds.

Since

$$\phi(x^0, \lambda) = \phi(x^0, \lambda^0) + \frac{\partial \phi}{\partial \lambda}\bigg|_0 (\lambda - \lambda^0)$$

that is, $\phi(x^0, \lambda)$ is linear in the λ's, (4) holds.   QED

We could now derive theorems for a variety of special programming problems whose objective and constraint functions are concave, including the well-known case of linear programming. Before going into these special cases and examples, we present Arrow and Enthoven's (1961) generalization of the Kuhn–Tucker sufficient conditions. This generalization makes the Kuhn–Tucker necessary conditions, (1) and (2) in Theorem 11.2–1, applicable to a wide variety of economic problems.

Problems

11.2–1   Transform the following problems into standard form for a general mathematical programming problem:

(a)   min: $-x_1^2 + x_1 x_2 - x_2^2$
        subject to: $100 - 10x_1 - 20x_2 \geq 0$
        $x_1, x_2 \geq 0$

(b)   max: $\frac{1}{2} \log x_1 + \frac{3}{4} \log x_2$
        subject to: $5x_1 + 10x_2 \leq 50$
        $x_1, x_2 \geq 0$

(c)   max: $x_1^2 - x_1 x_2 + x_2^2$
        subject to: $-x_1 x_2 + 20 \geq 0$
        $x_1, x_2 \leq 0$

(d)   max: $e^{x_1 + x_2}$
        subject to: $x_1 + x_2 = 40$
        $x_1, x_2 \geq 0$

(e)   max: $x_1^2 - x_2 + x_3^2 - x_4$
        subject to: $x_1 - x_2 - x_3 - x_4 \leq 50$
        $x_i \gtreqless 0, i = 1, 2, 3, 4$

(f)   min: $0.2x_1^2 x_2^4 - 6x_1 x_2^2$
        subject to: $5x_1 + 7x_2 \leq 50$
        $x_1, x_2 \geq 0$

11.2–2   Illustrate why the function

$$\phi = x_1^{1/2} x_2^{1/2} + 50\lambda - 10x_1\lambda - 5x_2\lambda$$

is a saddle-value function about the point $(x^0, \lambda^0) = (2.5, 5, 0.0707)$ in the following way:
(a) Find $\phi(x^0, \lambda^0)$.
(b) Let $\lambda = 0.07, 0.08$ and show that $\phi(2.5, 5, 0.07) \geq \phi(x^0, \lambda^0) \leq \phi(2.5, 5, 0.08)$.

(c) Let $x_1 = 2$, 3 and show that $\phi(2, 5, 0.0707) \le \phi(x^0, \lambda^0) \ge \phi(3, 5, 0.0707)$.

(d) Let $x_2 = 4$, 6 and show that $\phi(2.5, 4, 0.0707) \le \phi(x^0, \lambda^0) \ge \phi(2.5, 6, 0.0707)$.

11.2–3   Find $(\partial\phi/\partial x)|_0$ and $(\partial\phi/\partial\lambda)|_0$ for the function in Problem 11.2–2. Does it conform to the necessary conditions for $\phi(x^0, \lambda^0)$ to be a saddle point?

11.2–4   Given:

$$\begin{aligned} \text{max:} \quad & x_1 x_2 + 5x_2 \\ \text{subject to:} \quad & 2x_2 + 10x_1 \le 20 \\ & x_1, x_2 \ge 0 \end{aligned}$$

(a) Graphically sketch the locus of points where the objective function has a value of 25, 50, and 75, respectively.

(b) Draw in the constraint and find the approximate value of x_1 and x_2 at the maximum.

(c) Is

$$\phi(x, \lambda) = x_1 x_2 + 5x_2 + 20\lambda - 10x_1\lambda - 2x_2\lambda$$

a saddle-value function about the point $(x_1^0, x_2^0, \lambda^0) = (0, 10, 2.5)$? Why?

(d) Find $(\partial\phi/\partial x)|_0$ and $(\partial\phi/\partial\lambda)|_0$ and show that $(\partial\phi/\partial x)|_0 x^0 = (\partial\phi/\partial\lambda)|_0 \lambda^0 = 0$

11.2–5   Is $g(x) = 20 - 2x_2 - 10x_1$ a concave function? Verify your conclusions by using both methods indicated in Definition 11.2–5.

11.2–6   Which of the following are concave functions?

(a) $f(x) = \ln x + 5$ (d) $f(x) = 10x - x^2$

(b) $f(x) = ax + b$ (e) $f(x) = \dfrac{x^2}{7x^3 + 3x}$

(c) $f(x) = x^{1/3}$

11.2–7   Generalize Equations (1) and (2) in Theorem 11.2–1 for the case where $g_i(x) \ge 0$, $i = 1, \ldots, k$; $g_i(x) \le 0$, $i = k + 1, \ldots, l$; and $g_i(x) = 0$, $i = l + 1, \ldots, m$.

11.2–8   Generalize Equations (1) and (2) in Theorem 11.2–1 for the case where $x_i \ge 0$, $i = 1, \ldots, k$; $x_i \le 0$, $i = k + 1, \ldots, l$; and $x_i \gtreqless 0$, $i = l + 1, \ldots, n$.

11.3   ARROW AND ENTHOVEN'S QUASICONCAVE PROGRAMMING THEOREMS

A quasiconcave function is a generalized notion of a concave function.

DEFINITION 11.3–1 $f(x)$ is a **quasiconcave function** for some specified domain for x if either:

(a) for each real number c, the set $\{x \mid f(x) \ge c\}$ is a convex set, or

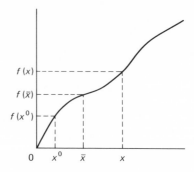

Figure 11.3–1 $f(x) \geq f(x^0)$ *implies that* $f(\bar{x}) \geq f(x^0)$, *where* $\bar{x} = \theta x + (1 - \theta)x^0$ *for* $0 \leq \theta \leq 1$.

(b) $f(x) \geq f(x^0)$ implies that $f(\theta x + (1 - \theta)x^0) \geq f(x^0)$ for $0 \leq \theta \leq 1$,
   or
(c) $f(x) \geq f(x^0)$ implies that $(\partial f/\partial x)|_0(x - x^0) \geq 0$ if $f(x)$ is differentiable.[7]

The three alternative definitions are equivalent.

Clearly, all concave functions are quasiconcave. In fact, any monotonic nondecreasing function of a concave function is quasiconcave. For a single variable a convex function is also quasiconcave. For more than one variable a convex function may or may not be quasiconcave. In Figures 11.3–1 and 11.3–2, a quasiconcave function of a single variable is illustrated.

A function that is quasiconcave over some specified domain need not be

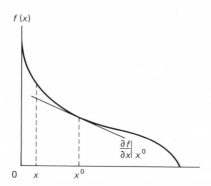

Figure 11.3–2 $f(x) \geq f(x^0)$ *implies that* $\partial f/\partial x|_0(x - x^0) \geq 0$; *that is,* $\partial f/\partial x|_0 \leq 0$ *and* $(x - x)^0 \leq 0$.

---

[7] A quasiconvex function is one where the set $\{x \mid f(x) \leq x\}$ is a convex set.

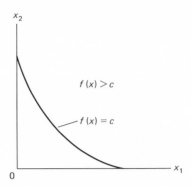

Figure 11.3–3 $f(x)$ *is quasiconcave.*

quasiconcave outside this domain. For example, $f(x_1, x_2) = x_1 x_2$ is quasi-concave for x_1 and $x_2 \geq 0$ but not for negative values of x_1 and x_2.

For a quasiconcave function, if $\partial f/\partial x \geq 0$ and $x \geq 0$, then the isovalue curves must be convex to the origin to satisfy Definition 11.3–1(a). Alternatively, if $\partial f/\partial x \leq 0$ and $x \geq 0$, then the isovalue curves must be concave to the origin. This is usually the case in economic theory, for example, indifference curves and a production possibility frontier as illustrated in Figures 11.3–3 and 11.3–4. (Is the single variable function in Figure 11.3–5 quasiconcave? Why?)

The first theorem proven by Arrow and Enthoven is analogous to Theorem 11.2–6 where concavity requirements for $f(x)$ and $g(x)$ are replaced with quasiconcavity. This alone is not quite sufficient to make the Kuhn–Tucker necessary conditions sufficient conditions for a maximum, as one of four other mild criteria must be met.

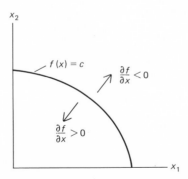

Figure 11.3–4 $f(x)$ *is quasiconcave.*

Figure 11.3–5 *Is $f(x)$ quasiconcave?*

Theorem 11.3–1 (Arrow–Enthoven, 1961) If:

(1) $f(x)$ is quasiconcave;
(2) $g(x)$ is quasiconcave;
(3) x^0 and λ^0 satisfy (1) and (2) of Theorem 11.2–1; and
(4) either:

    (a) $\left.\dfrac{\partial f}{\partial x_i}\right|_0 < 0$, for at least one x_i^0;

    (b) $\left.\dfrac{\partial f}{\partial x_i}\right|_0 > 0$, for an x_i such that $g(x_i) \geq 0$ if $x_i > 0$;

    (c) $\left.\dfrac{\partial f}{\partial x}\right|_0 \neq 0$ and $f(x)$ is twice differentiable in the neighborhood of x^0;

or

    (d) $f(x)$ is concave;

then

$$f(x^0) = \quad \begin{aligned} &\text{max:} \quad && f(x) \\ &\text{subject to:} \quad && g(x) \geq 0 \\ & && x \geq 0 \end{aligned}$$

Before proving the theorem, we give an example that shows that quasi-concavity is not sufficient to guarantee a maximum. A further condition, such as 4(a)–(d) is needed.

Example 1. Consider the problem:

$$\begin{aligned} &\text{max:} \quad && f(x) = (x - 1)^3 \\ &\text{subject to:} \quad && g(x) = 2 - x \geq 0 \\ & && x \geq 0 \end{aligned}$$

Since $f(x)$ is a monotonically increasing function of one variable, it is quasiconcave (cf. Figure 11.3–6). Also, $g(x)$ is linear and therefore a quasiconcave function. The Kuhn–Tucker necessary conditions are

$$\phi = (x - 1)^3 + \lambda(2 - x)$$

$$\frac{\partial \phi}{\partial x} = 3(x - 1)^2 - \lambda \leq 0$$

$$\frac{\partial \phi}{\partial x} x = 0$$

$$\frac{\partial \phi}{\partial \lambda} = 2 - x \geq 0$$

$$\frac{\partial \phi}{\partial \lambda} \lambda = 0$$

Therefore, if we let $\lambda = 0$ and $x = 0$, the conditions are satisfied, but the maximum solution to the problem is clearly at $x = 2$ and $\lambda = 3$. The problem with such a cubic function is that $(\partial f/\partial x)|_{x=1} = 0$ and thus $f(x)$ does not satisfy any of conditions 4(a)–4(d) (or some similar condition).

If all variables can be positive and still fulfill the constraint equations; that is, if $g(x) \geq 0$ and $x_i \geq 0$, then conditions 4(a) and 4(b) can be combined into condition 4(e):

(4) (e) $\left.\dfrac{\partial f}{\partial x}\right|_0 \neq 0$ where for each variable x_i there is some point in the

constraint set where $x_i > 0$.

PROOF OF THEOREM *11.3–1*   To prove the first part of the theorem we need to show that for any other x' in the constraint set, $f(x') \leq f(x^0)$.

Assume that 4(a) holds: $(\partial f/\partial x_i)|_0 < 0$, for some i, and that x^0 satisfies the Kuhn–Tucker necessary conditions (1) and (2) of Theorem 11.2–1.

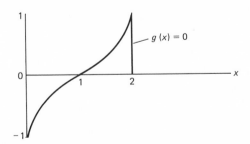

Figure 11.3–6 $f(x) = (x - 1)^3$ *is a monotonically increasing function and quasiconcave.*

Let $x^* = x^0 + u$, where $u =$ the unit vector in the ith direction. Then

(1)
$$\left.\frac{\partial f}{\partial x}\right|_0 (x^* - x^0) = \left.\frac{\partial f}{\partial x}\right|_0 u = \left.\frac{\partial f}{\partial x_i}\right|_0 < 0$$

For some x' in the constraint set, that is, $g(x') \geq 0$, define:
(2)

$$x'(\theta) = (1 - \theta)x' + \theta x^* \quad \text{and} \quad x^0(\theta) = (1 - \theta)x^0 + \theta x^* = x^0 + \theta(x^* - x^0)$$

Combining these two, we have

(3)
$$x'(\theta) - x^0(\theta) = (1 - \theta)(x' - x^0)$$

Now, for $(\partial f/\partial x)|_0[x^0(\theta) - x^0]$, substitute from (2), and use (1) for $\theta > 0$ to obtain (4):

(4)
$$\left.\frac{\partial f}{\partial x}\right|_0 [x^0(\theta) - x^0] = \left.\frac{\partial f}{\partial x}\right|_0 \theta(x^* - x^0) + \left.\frac{\partial f}{\partial x}\right|_0 x^0 - \left.\frac{\partial f}{\partial x}\right|_0 x^0$$

$$= \left.\frac{\partial f}{\partial x}\right|_0 \theta(x^* - x^0) < 0 \qquad \text{if } \theta > 0$$

Also, by using (3) note that

(5)
$$\left.\frac{\partial f}{\partial x}\right|_0 [x'(\theta) - x^0(\theta)] = \left.\frac{\partial f}{\partial x}\right|_0 (1 - \theta)(x' - x^0)$$

Equation (5) must be less than or equal to zero. To show this, consider

$$\left.\frac{\partial f}{\partial x}\right|_0 (x' - x^0) \equiv \left(\left.\frac{\partial f}{\partial x}\right|_0 + \lambda^0 \left.\frac{\partial g}{\partial x}\right|_0\right)(x' - x^0) - \lambda^0 \left.\frac{\partial g}{\partial x}\right|_0 (x' - x^0)$$

The first term must be ≤ 0, since $x' \geq 0$ and, by (1) in Theorem 11.2–1, $(\partial \phi/\partial x)|_0 x^0 = 0$. Thus $\lambda^0 \geq 0$. If all $\lambda^0_j = 0$, then

$$\left.\frac{\partial f}{\partial x}\right|_0 (x' - x^0) \leq 0$$

If some $\lambda^0_i > 0$ then, by (2) in Theorem 11.2–1, $g_i(x^0) = 0$. Therefore, for any x' in the constraint set, $g_i(x') \geq g_i(x^0)$. Further, since $g_i(x)$ is quasiconcave by assumption, this implies that $(\partial g_i/\partial x)|_0(x' - x^0) \geq 0$ for all $\lambda_i > 0$. Therefore (5) becomes

$$\left.\frac{\partial f}{\partial x}\right|_0 (1 - \theta)(x' - x^0) \leq 0 \qquad \text{for } 0 \leq \theta \leq 1$$

Adding (4) and (5), we have

(6) $\dfrac{\partial f}{\partial x}\Big|_0 [x^0(\theta) - x^0] + \dfrac{\partial f}{\partial x}\Big|_0 [x'(\theta) - x^0(\theta)]$

$= \dfrac{\partial f}{\partial x}\Big|_0 [x'(\theta) - x^0]$

$= \dfrac{\partial f}{\partial x}\Big|_0 \theta(x^* - x^0) + \dfrac{\partial f}{\partial x}\Big|_0 (1 - \theta)(x' - x^0) < 0 \qquad \text{for } 0 < \theta \le 1$

Since $x'(\theta) = (1 - \theta)x' + \theta x^*$ by (2), (6) can be written as

$$\dfrac{\partial f}{\partial x}\Big|_0 x'(\theta) - \dfrac{\partial f}{\partial x}\Big|_0 x^0 < 0$$

or

(7) $$\dfrac{\partial f}{\partial x}\Big|_0 [x'(\theta) - x^0] < 0$$

Since $f(x)$ is quasiconcave, and since (7) must hold in the limit as $\theta \to 0$, this implies that $f(x') \le f(x^0)$, which proves the theorem for case 4(a).

Assume that 4(b) is true: $(\partial f/\partial x_i)|_0 > 0$, for some x_i such that $g(x_i) \ge 0$ if $x_i > 0$ and x^0 satisfies the Kuhn–Tucker necessary conditions, (1) and (2) in Theorem 11.2–1.

Since we have proved case 4(a), where $(\partial f/\partial x_j)|_0 < 0$, for some j, we can assume that $(\partial f/\partial x)|_0 x^0 > 0$.

As was proved in 4(a) for any $x' \ne x^0$, where x' is contained in the constraint set, $g(x)$ is quasiconcave; that is,

$$\dfrac{\partial f}{\partial x}\Big|_0 (x' - x^0) \le 0$$

Since $f(x)$ is quasiconcave, $f(x') \le f(x^0)$ which proves case 4(b).

The proofs of cases 4(c) and 4(d) are too lengthy to be included here and complete details can be found in Arrow and Enthoven (1961).

Theorem 11.3–1 states that if the objective and constraint functions are quasiconcave and any *one* of the conditions 4(a)–4(d) holds as well, then the *necessary conditions of Kuhn–Tucker* are *sufficient* for a maximum. However, Theorem 11.3–1 does not employ the notion of a constraint qualification. A careful review of the theorem will also indicate that the theorem *does not* prove that (1) and (2) of Theorem 11.2–1, that is,

(1) $$\dfrac{\partial \phi}{\partial x}\Big|_0 \le 0, \quad \dfrac{\partial \phi}{\partial x}\Big|_0 x^0 = 0$$

(2) $$\dfrac{\partial \phi}{\partial \lambda}\Big|_0 \ge 0, \quad \dfrac{\partial \phi}{\partial \lambda}\Big|_0 \lambda^0 = 0$$

are *necessary* for a maximum when $f(x)$ and $g(x)$ are quasiconcave and one of 4(a)–4(d) are satisfied. That is, it is feasible that the constraint equations be quasiconcave and the Kuhn–Tucker constraint qualification not be satisfied. The following is an illustration of such a case.

All that is necessary is to have quasiconcave functions in the specified domain and a cusp formed. Therefore, if a constraint function has an inflection point on the x surface, the function can be quasiconcave in the positive orthant and $\partial g_i / \partial x_j = 0$. Such a case is illustrated in Figures 11.3–7 and

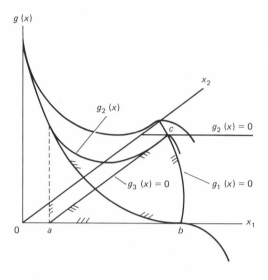

Figure 11.3–7 *Feasible space for two variables and three constraints that are quasiconcave and form a "cusp" at point c.*

11.3–8. We have two variables, x_1 and x_2 and three constraints, g_1, g_2, and g_3. g_1 is a function of both x_1 and x_2, and also

$$\frac{\partial g_1}{\partial x_1} = \frac{\partial g_1}{\partial x_2} = 0$$

for any x_1 and x_2 such that $g_1(x_1, x_2) = 0$. That is, for any x on the boundary, the partial derivatives of g_1 are zero. Also, it is assumed that constraint g_2 is solely dependent upon x_2 and has an inflection point at x_2^0. Therefore

$$\frac{\partial g_2}{\partial x_1} = \frac{\partial g_2}{\partial x_2}\bigg|_0 = 0$$

g_3 only varies with x_1, and consequently,

$$\frac{\partial g_3}{\partial x_2} = 0$$

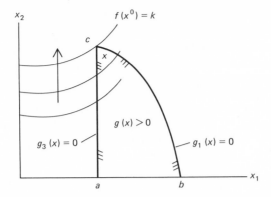

Figure 11.3–8 *Feasible space for two variables and three constraints shown in two dimensions, at x_0, $\partial f/\partial x_2 > 0$, $\partial g_1/\partial x_2 = 0$, $\partial g_2/\partial x_2 = 0$, $\partial g_3/\partial x_2 = 0$, yet $x^0 = \max f(x)$, $g(x) \geq 0$, $x \geq 0$.*

This creates the feasible space *abcd* in three dimensions in Figure 11.3–7 or the space *abc* in two dimensions in Figure 11.3–8.

Also in Figure 11.3–8 are isovalue lines for $f(x)$. At every point in the feasible space or the constraint set, $\partial f/\partial x_1 < 0$ and $\partial f/\partial x_2 > 0$. Clearly, x^0 is a maximum and we have

$$\frac{\partial \phi}{\partial x_1}\bigg|_0 \leq 0$$

and

$$\frac{\partial \phi}{\partial x_2}\bigg|_0 > 0$$

In fact, for every x such that $g(x) \geq 0$, it is true that $\partial \phi/\partial x_2 > 0$. Thus, the Kuhn–Tucker conditions are not necessary even though they *would be* sufficient *if* there existed an x^0 and λ^0 to so satisfy them.

The fact that the first partial derivative vanishes for the constraint function suggests the following theorem proved by Arrow, Hurwicz, and Uzawa (1962).

Theorem 11.3–2 (Arrow–Hurwicz–Uzawa) If:

(1) $g(x)$ is a quasiconcave function;
(2) $g(x^*) > 0$ for some $x^* \geq 0$; and
(3) if *either*
   (a) $g_j(x)$ is concave for all j
   or
   (b) for each x^* such that $g(x^*) \geq 0$,

$$\frac{\partial g_j}{\partial x}\bigg|_{x^*} \neq 0 \qquad \text{for all } j$$

then the Kuhn–Tucker constraint qualification is satisfied. Thus if both hypotheses of Theorems 11.3–1 and 11.3–2 are fulfilled, then

(1)
$$\left.\frac{\partial \phi}{\partial x}\right|_0 \leq 0, \quad \left.\frac{\partial \phi}{\partial x}\right|_0 x^0 = 0$$

and

(2)
$$\left.\frac{\partial \phi}{\partial \lambda}\right|_0 \geq 0, \quad \left.\frac{\partial \phi}{\partial \lambda}\right|_0 \lambda^0 = 0$$

for

$$\phi(x, \lambda) = f(x) + \lambda g(x)$$

are both necessary and sufficient conditions for a maximum to a general mathematical programming problem.

Another aspect that has been apparent in establishing sufficient conditions, and that was present in our graphical discussion of quasiconcave functions, is that of a convex constraint set.[8] This was a "flaw" in the constraint set of Figures 11.3–7 and 11.3–8. This suggests another possible sufficient condition for finding a maximum. Arrow and Enthoven have proven the following theorem, which places no specific conditions on the functions $g(x)$ and which also generalizes the nonnegativity requirements on x.[9]

Theorem 11.3–3   (Arrow–Enthoven) If:

(1) $f(x)$ is a quasiconcave function defined in the closed, convex domain D;

(2) $g(x)$ is defined in D such that for all $\{x\} \subseteq D$, where $g(x) \geq 0$, the set $\{x\}$ is convex;

(3) any one of the following hold:

(a) $\left.\dfrac{\partial f}{\partial x}\right|_0 (x^* - x^0) < 0$, for some $x^* \in D$;

(b) $\left.\dfrac{\partial f}{\partial x}\right|_0 (x^* - x^0) \neq 0$, for some $x^* \in D$ and $f(x)$ is twice differentiable

in a neighborhood of x^0; or

(c) $f(x)$ is concave; and

---

[8] A convex set $\{x\}$ (Definition 2.8–8) is one such that if x^0 and $x^* \in \{x\}$, then $[\theta x^0 + (1 - \theta)x^*] \in \{x\}$.

[9] Obviously, if the constraint set is convex the Kuhn–Tucker constraint qualification is satisfied. Thus, (1) and (2) of Theorem 11.2–1 are necessary conditions. Kuhn and Tucker assumed that $g(x)$ is concave, while Arrow and Enthoven established sufficient conditions without the constraint qualification. Theorem 11.3–3 is a mix of the two.

(4) for x^0 and $\lambda^0 \geq 0$;

(a) $\left(\dfrac{\partial f}{\partial x}\bigg|_0 + \lambda^0 \dfrac{\partial g}{\partial x}\bigg|_0 \right) (x^* - x^0) \leq 0$ for all $x^* \in D$ and

(b) $\lambda^0 g(x^0) = 0$;

then x^0 maximizes $f(x)$, subject to $g(x) \geq 0$ and $x \in D$.

Even though the foregoing theorems do not give necessary conditions for a maximum (unless the constraint qualification is satisfied), the sufficient conditions presented are adequate for most problems in economic analysis. The following two examples should clarify both the generality and the nature of the fundamental theorems for mathematical programming problems.

Example 2. Generalized Approach to Consumer Demand Theory Suppose that an individual's preference ordering over a consumption space is such that it is characterized by a single-valued, differentiable utility function that is quasiconcave:

$$U(x) = U(x_1, \ldots, x_n)$$
$$x \geq 0$$

This implies that the individual's indifference curves are convex to the origin (i.e., diminishing marginal rate of substitution) and implies neither increasing nor diminishing marginal utility of income (it could be either or both in different regions of the commodity space).

Assume that the individual is constrained by his social environment not to spend more than he receives through the sale of goods and services and also that the individual possesses some initial stock of commodities, $\bar{x} \geq 0$, where some $\bar{x}_i > 0$. Thus we have

$$g_1(x) = \sum_{i=1}^{n} p_i \bar{x}_i - \sum_{i=1}^{n} p_i x_i \geq 0$$

$g_1(x)$ is illustrated in Figure 11.3–9 for three commodities: $x_1 =$ labor, $x_2 =$ food, and $x_3 =$ clothes. The initial stock is $(\bar{x}_1, 0, 0)$, which, given the market prices, determines the budget-constrained space, *oabc*. If the individual were at x^0, he would have the commodity basket (x_1^0, x_2^0, x_3^0) and would have worked the amount $\bar{x}_1 - x_1^0$.

Additionally, the individual is constrained by the amount of time that he has available. The consumption of commodities, whether food or labor, takes time, which is a physical limitation on the feasible consumption space. Thus the second constraint is

$$g_2(x) = T_0 - g_2^*(x_1, \ldots, x_n) \geq 0$$

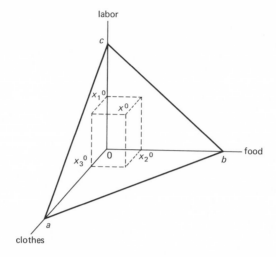

Figure 11.3–9 *Feasible consumption space from initial stock of* $(\bar{x}_1, 0, 0)$ *and three commodities:* x_1, x_2, x_3.

where T_0 is the amount of time available. In any social milieu the individual finds a host of mores, ethics, customs, laws, and various other social institutions that impinge upon his decision calculus. For example, in the United States there are social limits on the relative amounts of tea consumed by the Ladies' Aid Society and marijuana smoked. People who choose to give up a quantity of labor in the form of salesmanship may not be permitted to collect garbage. People who choose to be prostitutes in Nevada may not be patrons of art. And the list could be extended to cover all such social "rules and regulations." We shall assume that these can be specified as follows:

$$g_3(x_1, \ldots, x_n) \geq 0$$
$$\vdots$$
$$g_m(x_1, \ldots, x_n) \geq 0$$

If the constraint set $g(x) \geq 0$ is a convex set and nonsatiation is assumed, then since $f(x)$ is quasiconcave, the hypotheses of Theorems 11.2–3 and 11.3–1 are satisfied. Thus, (1) and (2) in Theorem 11.2–3 are both necessary and sufficient for a maximum solution to the individual's decision process:

$$\begin{aligned} \text{max:} \quad & U(x) \\ \text{subject to:} \quad & g(x) \geq 0 \\ & x \geq 0 \end{aligned}$$

For the solution x^0 and

$$\phi(x, \lambda) = U(x) + \lambda_1 g_1(x) + \cdots + \lambda_m g_m(x)$$

we have

$$\left.\frac{\partial \phi}{\partial x_i}\right|_0 = \left.\frac{\partial U}{\partial x_i}\right|_0 + \lambda_1^0 \left.\frac{\partial g_1}{\partial x_i}\right|_0 + \cdots + \lambda_m^0 \left.\frac{\partial g_m}{\partial x_i}\right|_0 \leq 0$$

for all $i = 1, \ldots, n$;

$$\left.\frac{\partial \phi}{\partial x_i}\right|_0 x_i^0 = \left.\frac{\partial U}{\partial x_i}\right|_0 x_i^0 + \lambda_1^0 \left.\frac{\partial g_1}{\partial x_i}\right|_0 x_i^0 + \cdots + \lambda_n^0 \left.\frac{\partial g_n}{\partial x_i}\right|_0 x_i^0 = 0$$

for all $i = 1, \ldots, n$;

$$\left.\frac{\partial \phi}{\partial \lambda_j}\right|_0 = g_j(x^0) \geq 0$$

for all $j = 1, \ldots, m$; and

$$\left.\frac{\partial \phi}{\partial \lambda_j}\right|_0 \lambda_j^0 = \lambda_j^0 g_j(x^0) = 0$$

for all $j = 1, \ldots, m$. Which is to say, if $x_i^0 > 0$ in the optimum commodity bundle, then $(\partial \phi/\partial x_i)|_0 = 0$, and for all constraints j that are relevant or effective on x^0, then $\lambda_j^0 > 0$. Therefore, if we have two goods at positive level, say x_i^0 and $x_j^0 > 0$, and letting $R = \{\lambda i_i^0 \mid \lambda_i^0 > 0\}$ then at the optimum,

Marginal rate of substitution (MRS$_{i:j}$) $= \dfrac{(\partial U/\partial x_i)|_0}{(\partial U/\partial x_j)|_0} = \dfrac{\sum_{k \in R} \lambda_k(\partial g_k/\partial x_i)}{\sum_{k \in R} \lambda_k(\partial g_k/\partial x_j)}$

Or at equilibrium, the marginal trade-off between two goods is equal to the ratio of what can be interpreted as the value of marginal resource usage by x_i and x_j at x^0. This is a generalization of MRS$_{i:j} = p_i/p_j$ in ordinary demand theory.

Example 3.   A Production Problem and Mathematical Programming The reader may have been lead into a notion that quasiconcave programming is a panacea for every economic problem. This example taken from Arrow and Enthoven illustrates a very simple case where reasonable economic assumptions fail to meet the hypotheses of the theorems above.

Suppose that a firm's production function is a Cobb–Douglas function with increasing returns to scale, that is,

$$q = \alpha_0 K^{\alpha_1} L^{\alpha_2} \qquad \text{where} \quad \alpha_1 + \alpha_2 > 1$$

This function is not concave but it is quasiconcave. However, the simple problem of maximizing profits:

$$\begin{aligned} \text{max:} \quad & \pi = pq - (rK + wL) \\ \text{subject to:} \quad & K, L \geq 0 \end{aligned}$$

where p is the price of output, r is the cost of capital, and w is the wage rate for labor, does not meet the hypotheses of Theorem 11.3–1 because the objective function

$$\pi = p\alpha_0 K^{\alpha_1} L^{\alpha_2} - rK - wL$$

is not quasiconcave. (Why?)

Problems

11.3–1   Determine, by using (a), (b), or (c) of Definition 11.3–1, which of the following functions are quasiconcave.

(a) $f(x) = ax + b$

(b) $f(x) = ax^2 + bx + c$

(c) $f(x) = ax_1^2 + bx_2^2 + cx_1x_2$

(d) $f(x) = 10x_1x_2 - x_1^2x_2^2$

11.3–2   Given the following mathematical programming problem:

$$\text{max:} \quad f(x) = \frac{\ln x_1x_2}{2} + 100$$

$$\text{subject to:} \quad g_1(x) = 100 - x_1^2 - x_2^2 \geq 0$$
$$g_2(x) = 400 - x_1^2 - 16x_2^2 \geq 0$$
$$x \geq 0$$

(a) Is $f(x)$ quasiconcave?

(b) What is the shape of an isovalue curve for $f(x)$?

(c) Graphically construct the constraint set. Is it a convex set?

(d) From the graph, at approximately what value of x_1 and x_2 does the maximum occur?

(e) If the constraint set is convex and the function $f(x)$ is quasiconcave, the Kuhn–Tucker conditions are sufficient providing other minor conditions are met. Is any one of these met for this problem? Which?

(f) Use the Kuhn–Tucker Equations (1) and (2) of Theorem 11.2–1 to solve this problem.

11.3–3   A firm can potentially produce m products, $q_1, \ldots, q_m$, which require k resources $x_1, \ldots, x_k$; that is,

$$q_i = q_i(x_1, \ldots, x_k)$$

is the production function for each output, q_i. The price of each output depends upon the entire product line of the firm and its use of "sales" resources, $x_{k+1}, \ldots, x_n$; that is,

$$p_i = p_i(q_1, \ldots, q_m, x_{k+1}, \ldots, x_n) \qquad i = 1, \ldots, m$$

The price of each resource is $v_i, i = 1, \ldots, n$. The firm is faced with two additional constraints, sales personnel and plant managers, which are given by the following functions:

$$g_1(q_1, \ldots, q_m) \leq M$$
$$g_2(x_{k+1}, \ldots, x_n) \leq S$$

Negative quantities of resources $x_1, \ldots, x_n$ are not meaningful.

(a) Set up the problem in general mathematical programming form.
(b) What assumptions are necessary to use the Kuhn–Tucker theorems as sufficient conditions for a maximum?
(c) What assumptions are needed to use the Arrow–Enthoven generalization theorems for sufficiency of a maximum?
(d) Solve the problem analytically and interpret your results.

11.4 THE SPECIAL CASE OF LINEAR PROGRAMMING

The development of mathematical programming commenced with linear programming during the 1940's and subsequently expanded to more general problems. The most notable pioneer in the field of linear programming is George B. Dantzig, who developed the technique to solve problems of planning distribution and other activities for the U.S. Air Force.[10]

Prior to this time, two other economic techniques, which possess many characteristics similar to linear programming, had begun to develop. As early as 1928, John von Neumann[11] had proved a central theorem for game theory and Wassily Leontief[12] by 1936 had published an article on the method of input–output analysis. All three approaches employ linear relations. Game-theory problems can be transformed into linear programming problems. Thus game theory is formally equivalent to linear programming, although the relationship is not obvious at a glance. Input–output analysis interprets economic activity in much the same way that linear programming does when applied to the firm or to an economy. Of these three branches, linear programming and the development of mathematical programming have become the most significant and most fruitful.

This section considers the fundamental theorems of linear programming and what linear programming means, or implies, when applied to economic problems. The reader will probably feel that using the preceding theory for the case of a linear programming problem is somewhat analogous to building Hoover Dam to light a small bulb, but it is a very efficient way to proceed.

[10] See Dorfman, Samuelson, and Solow (1958) for more details.
[11] von Neumann (1928).
[12] Leontief (1936).

In linear programming, as the name implies, all equations are linear. That is, the objective function $f(x)$ is linear and the constraints $g(x)$ are linear.

DEFINITION 11.4–1   A **linear programming problem** is one of finding a vector x that maximizes a linear function subject to linear constraints:

$$\text{max:} \quad f(x) = p_1 x_1 + \cdots + p_n x_n$$
$$\text{subject to:} \quad a_{11} x_1 + a_{12} x_2 + \cdots + a_{1n} x_n \leq b_1$$
$$\vdots$$
$$a_{m1} x_1 + a_{m2} x_2 + \cdots + a_{mn} x_n \leq b_m$$
$$x_i \geq 0, \quad \text{for } i = 1, \ldots, n;$$

or, in matrix notation,

$$\text{max:} \quad px$$
$$\text{subject to:} \quad Ax \leq b$$
$$x \geq 0$$

where $p = (p_1, \ldots, p_n)$, $b = (b_1, \ldots, b_m)'$, and

$$A = \begin{bmatrix} a_{11} & \cdots & a_{1n} \\ \vdots & & \\ a_{m1} & \cdots & a_{mn} \end{bmatrix}$$

are constants.

Since $f(x)$ and $g(x) \geq 0$ are linear, they are both concave (convex as well) and quasiconcave. Furthermore, the constraint set is a convex set since it is bounded by linear segments. Therefore we have, by Theorems 11.2–3 and 11.2–5, that (1) and (2) are both necessary and sufficient for a maximum:

$$\phi = px + \lambda(b - Ax)$$

(1)   (a) $\left. \dfrac{\partial \phi}{\partial x} \right|_0 = p - \lambda^0 A \leq 0 \quad \text{or} \quad \lambda^0 A \geq p$

(b) $\left. \dfrac{\partial \phi}{\partial x} \right|_0 x^0 = px^0 - \lambda^0 A x^0 = 0 \quad \text{or} \quad px^0 = \lambda^0 A x^0$

(2)   (a) $\left. \dfrac{\partial \phi}{\partial \lambda} \right|_0 = b - Ax^0 \geq 0 \quad \text{or} \quad Ax^0 \leq b$

(b) $\left. \dfrac{\partial \phi}{\partial \lambda} \right|_0 \lambda^0 = \lambda^0 b - \lambda^0 A x^0 = 0 \quad \text{or} \quad \lambda^0 b = \lambda^0 A x^0$

Combining (1b) and (2b);

(3) $$px^0 = \lambda^0 A x^0 = \lambda^0 b$$

Consider another linear programming problem:

$$\text{min:} \quad \beta y$$
$$\text{subject to:} \quad ay \geq \pi$$
$$y \geq 0$$

where y is the vector of variables, β and π are vectors of constants, and a is a matrix of constants. Again the Kuhn–Tucker conditions are necessary and sufficient for a maximum, where $\phi = (-\beta y) + \mu[ay - \pi]$. μ is the vector of Lagrangean multipliers. And we have

(4) (a) $\left.\dfrac{\partial \phi}{\partial y}\right|_{(y^0,\mu^0)} = -\beta + \mu^0 a \leq 0 \quad \text{or} \quad \mu^0 a \leq \beta$

(b) $\left.\dfrac{\partial \phi}{\partial y}\right|_{(y^0,\mu^0)} y^0 = -\beta y^0 + \mu^0 a y^0 = 0 \quad \text{or} \quad \mu^0 a y^0 = \beta y^0$

(5) (a) $\left.\dfrac{\partial \phi}{\partial \mu}\right|_{(y^0,\mu^0)} = a y^0 - \pi \geq 0 \quad \text{or} \quad a y^0 \geq \pi$

(b) $\left.\dfrac{\partial \phi}{\partial \mu}\right|_{(y^0,\mu^0)} \mu^0 = \mu^0 a y^0 - \mu^0 \pi = 0 \quad \text{or} \quad \mu^0 a y^0 = \mu^0 \pi$

Combining (4b) and (5b):

(6) $$\beta y^0 = \mu^0 a y^0 = \mu^0 \pi$$

Taking the transposes of the matrices in (6):

(7) $$y^{0\prime}\beta' = y^{0\prime}a'\mu^{0\prime} = \pi'\mu^{0\prime}$$

Now, if one compares (1)–(3) with (4)–(7), the two problems have the same *necessary and sufficient conditions* if we let

$$\pi' = p, \; \beta' = b, \; a' = A$$
$$\mu^0 = x^0 \quad \text{and} \quad \lambda^0 = y^{0\prime}$$

Therefore, in this case the solution to either the first maximization problem or the second minimization problem is the same. This is the notion of duality in linear programming—which we state formally as a theorem:

Theorem 11.4–1 For every linear programming problem (called the primal), there exists an equivalent problem called the dual, where if the primal is

$$\text{max:} \quad px$$
$$\text{subject to:} \quad Ax \leq b$$
$$x \geq 0$$

the dual is

$$\begin{aligned} \min: & \quad yb \\ \text{subject to}: & \quad yA \geq p' \\ & \quad y \geq 0 \end{aligned}$$

and the solutions of the two problems are equivalent. That is, x^0 and λ^0 in the primal are equal to μ^0 and y^0 in the dual.

Example 1.   Linear Programming Problems in the Theory of the Firm: Tricycles or Wagons?   It is instructive to work through an example of a simple linear programming problem to highlight what the assumptions imply when applied to the theory of the firm.

Suppose a firm's present facilities are capable of producing either wagons or tricycles. The firm's plant consists of four departments: metal stamping (M), wheel manufacturing (W_h), assembly (A), and painting (P). The maximum capacities per week of operation are given in Table 11.4–1. If there are no

Table 11.4–1

Department	Tricycles	Wagons
Metal stamping (M)	500	200
Wheel mfg. (W_h)	300	250
Assembly (A)	250	500
Painting (P)	400	400

economies or diseconomies of scale in the operation of any department for either of the two products, then the trade-off between tricycle and wagon production in any one department will be linear. For example, if we were to run tricycles through the assembly line for one-half week and wagons for the other half, we would have assembled 125 tricycles and 250 wagons. This means that we can calculate the percentage of each department used per tricycle and per wagon as given in Table 11.4–2.

If the price of tricycles is \$30 and each "trike" requires 5 man-hours of labor at \$2 per hour, while the price of wagons is \$20 and each wagon requires $2\frac{1}{2}$ man-hours of labor at \$2 per hour, then the net prices to the firm, after labor is paid, are

$$\begin{aligned} \text{Net price/tricycle} &= P_T = \$20 \\ \text{Net price/wagon} &= P_W = \$15 \end{aligned}$$

Table 11.4-2

	% used per:	
	Tricycle	Wagon
M	0.20	0.50
W_h	0.33	0.40
A	0.40	0.20
P	0.25	0.25

We now have a linear programming problem for the firm:

$$\text{max:} \quad f(x) = 20T + 15W$$

subject to:

$$\{Ax \leq b\} = \begin{cases} 0.2T + 0.5W \leq 100 = M \\ 0.33T + 0.4W \leq 100 = W_h \\ 0.4T + 0.2W \leq 100 = A \\ 0.25T + 0.25W \leq 100 = P \end{cases}$$

$$x' = (T, W) \geq 0$$

The feasible production space is shown in Figure 11.4–1 as *oabc*. As one can see, it is impossible to use the painting department to capacity. (Why?)

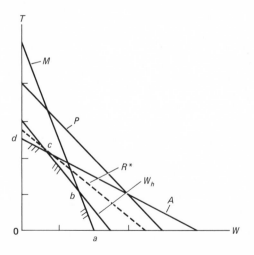

Figure 11.4–1 *Feasible production space for firm with two outputs, T and W, and four constraints, M, P, W_h, and A.*

Since the net prices to the firm are $20 and $15, this means that an iso-revenue line (combinations of T and W yielding an equal amount of net revenue) will have a slope of $-\frac{3}{4}$. R^* in Figure 11.4–1 is the highest attainable isorevenue line. At c two departments will be running at full capacity, while the other two will not. (What about a solution that occurs at point a? b? d? What departments will be fully utilized? What is necessary for such solutions to occur?)

Knowing which resources will be used to capacity, those inequalities can be turned into equalities and the system solved. One finds that the maximum revenue at c is

$$R^* = \$5357.14$$

and

$$T = 214\tfrac{2}{7}$$
$$W = 71\tfrac{3}{7}$$

Now, by Theorem 11.4–1 every linear programming problem has an equivalent dual: Find a vector y that solves:

min: $\quad yb = y_m M + y_w W_h + y_a A + y_p P$

subject to: $\quad yA \geq p = \begin{cases} 0.2y_m + 0.33y_w + 0.4y_a + 0.25y_p \geq 20 \\ 0.5y_m + 0.4y_w + 0.2y_a + 0.25y_p \geq 15 \end{cases}$

$$y = (y_m, y_w, y_a, y_p) \geq 0$$

From the theory in Section 11.3 we know that the y's are the Lagrangean multipliers to the original problem and the Lagrangean multiplier must be zero for any constraint that does not hold with equality; that is,

$$\left. \frac{\partial \phi}{\partial \lambda} \right|_0 \lambda^0 = 0 = g(x^0)\lambda^0$$

Therefore, since we know that $y_p = 0$ and $y_m = 0$ and some of both T and W will be produced at point c, both inequalities above can be turned into equalities and y_w and y_a solved for. Doing so, we find that the minimum yb is equal to $5357.14, where $y_a = \$32\tfrac{1}{7}$ and $y_w = \$21\tfrac{3}{7}$.

To interpret the dual, we notice that the left-hand sides of the constraint equations are the sums of the amount of each resource used per unit produced times the value or price, y, of that resource. Thus the dual finds the value to the firm of its resources according to the productivity of those resources at the margin of production. The dual imputes the net revenue from production back to the resources in such a manner that the resulting price, y, is the value of marginal product of that resource. In other words, each y tells the rate that revenue would increase if that resource were increased. For example, if the assembly department were increased by 1%, the revenue would go up by

$32.14. If the paint shop were expanded, revenue would not increase, since it is not being used to capacity as it is.

Example 2. Linear Programming and Cost Curves In the foregoing example, the firm could produce two products and there was only one way of producing each, that is, each required a particular percentage of each factor or department. It is possible that a firm could have various methods of producing a single product. In other words, there might be three (or n) different processes available to produce a product. If there is only a single process for each product, then there is only one way of combining factors of production to produce output (i.e., fixed as opposed to variable proportions). In Figure 11.4–2 we show such a case, with the isoquants being right angles. This means that the marginal product of either factor is zero. Given L_0 an increase in capital, K, will not increase output.

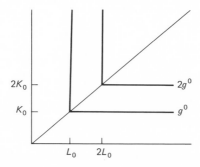

Figure 11.4–2   *One process or method of combining K and L.*

However, if we have several linear processes or methods of producing output, the resulting isoquants begin to take on the more conventional shape. Alternatively, since the definition of a "product" is somewhat arbitrary, one could define the product as being revenue and have several ways of producing revenue. In other words, prices would serve as a common denominator to equate different products.

Suppose we have a firm with three processes, or ways, of combining capital, K, and labor, L, where the subscripts denote the process:

(1) $$K_1 = 2L_1$$
(2) $$K_2 = L_2$$
(3) $$K_3 = \tfrac{1}{3}L_3$$

The relation between factor input and output is as follows:

(1) $$q_1 = 10K_1$$
(2) $$q_2 = 12K_2$$
(3) $$q_3 = 15K_3$$

Now, if the output of three processes is homogeneous, $q_1 = q_2 = q_3$, then we have sufficient information to derive the isoquants in Figure 11.4–3.

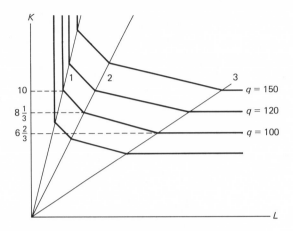

Figure 11.4–3   *Three processes for combining K and L.*

The more processes the firm has at its disposal, the more the isoquants become the traditional, smooth, convex (to the origin) curves. In fact, such isoquants imply an infinite number of ways of combining K and L to produce q. If both factors are variable, since the relation between input and output is linear and homogeneous, only one process will be used (depending upon relative factor prices) and marginal cost will equal average cost, a constant. However, if one of the factors is fixed in the short run, then the firm will have increasing marginal cost and average cost after some level of output. For example, if K is fixed at 10, then to minimize cost the firm would use the most capital intensive process, process 1. But the capacity of process 1, with $K = 10$, is 100 units. Therefore, to produce between 100 and 120 units of q the firm would use a combination of processes 1 and 2. Since process 2 uses more labor per unit of output, the marginal cost of production will be higher between 100 and 120 than between 0 and 100 units of output. The result is a step-shaped marginal cost function and an average variable cost curve with linear segments. This is illustrated in Figure 11.4–4, where $w = \$6$. This means that marginal cost between 0 and 100 will be

$$\text{MC}_1 = \frac{w(\Delta L_1)}{\Delta q_1} = 6\left(\frac{1}{20}\right) = \$0.30$$

Between 100 and 120, the firm must switch over from 1 to 2 as it moves along the line $K = 10$ in Figure 11.4–3. Thus

$$\text{MC}_2 = \frac{w(\Delta L_1 + \Delta L_2)}{\Delta q_1 + \Delta q_2} = \frac{\$6(-\frac{1}{2} + 1)}{(-10 + 12)} = 6\left(\frac{1}{4}\right) = \$1.50$$

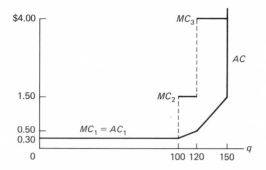

Figure 11.4–4   *Marginal and average cost curves for three processes.*

while between 120 and 150, we have

$$MC_3 = \frac{w(\Delta L_2 + \Delta L_3)}{\Delta q_2 + \Delta q_3} = \frac{\$6(-1 + 3)}{(-12 + 15)} = 6\left(\frac{2}{3}\right) = \$4.00$$

We are now ready to prove formally the observations in Examples 1 and 2. For the following theorems, it is easier to transform[13] the linear programming problem

$$
\begin{array}{lll}
\text{(I)} & \text{max:} & p^*x^* \\
& \text{subject to:} & A^*x^* \leq b \\
& & x^* \geq 0
\end{array}
$$

into

$$
\begin{array}{lll}
\text{(II)} & \text{max:} & px \\
& \text{subject to:} & Ax = b \\
& & x \geq 0
\end{array}
$$

where to each constraint inequality, a variable x_i is added and each such "slack" variable has a zero price in the objective function. For example, the first constraint would change from

$$a_{11}x_1 + \cdots + a_{1n}x_n \leq b_1$$

to

$$a_{11}x_1 + \cdots + a_{1n}x_n + x_{n+1} = b_1$$

where $x_{n+1} \geq 0$. If x_{n+1} has a zero price in the objective function, $p_{n+1} = 0$, then the two forms are equivalent; that is, $x_{n+1} > 0$ implies that $a_{11}x_1 + \cdots + a_{1n}x_n < b_1$, while $x_{n+1} = 0$ implies that $a_{11}x_1 + \cdots + a_{1n}x_n = b_1$.

The first theorem proves formally the statement that the feasible constraint set is a convex set.

---

[13] See the five standard transformations in Section 11.2.

Theorem 11.4–2   For the problem

$$\text{max:} \quad px$$
$$\text{subject to:} \quad Ax = b$$
$$x \geq 0$$

the set $X_F = \{x \mid Ax = b\}$ is convex; that is, if $x^0 \in X_F$ and $x^* \in X_F$, then $[\theta x^0 + (1 - \theta)x^*] \in X_F$ for $0 \leq \theta \leq 1$.

PROOF   For any x^0 and $x^* \in X_F$,

$$Ax^0 = b \quad \text{and} \quad Ax^* = b$$

Then, to show that $A[\theta x^0 + (1 - \theta)x^*] = b$, simply complete the multiplication:

$$A[\theta x^0 + (1 - \theta)x^*] = \theta Ax^0 + (1 - \theta)Ax^* = \theta b + (1 - \theta)b = b.$$
QED

The next theorem proves formally that a maximum solution must occur on one (or more) corner point if a solution exists.[14] First we generalize the notion of a corner point.

DEFINITION 11.4–2   An **extreme feasible point** is one that is not a weighted average of any other two feasible points. That is, if $y = \theta x_i + (1 - \theta)x_j$ for $0 < \theta < 1$ and where $x_i, x_j \in \{Ax = b\}$, then y is not an extreme feasible point.

Theorem 11.4–3   For any linear programming problem one and only one of the following is true:

(1) there is no feasible point;
(2) some extreme feasible point is a maximum; or
(3) the maximum is unlimited.

PROOF   The theorem will be proved in three parts. In each, two of the three statements will be assumed false and then it will be shown that the third statement must hold.
Part I: Assume (1) and (2) false; then (3) must be true. If (2) is false, there must exist a y, not an extreme point such that $py > px$ for all $x \in \{$extreme points$\}$. Therefore the maximum must be unlimited unless it is on an axis. That is, $y = (y_1, \ldots, y_n)$ with some $y_i = 0$, but that is an extreme point. QED
Part II: Assume (2) and (3) false; then (1) must be true. Every feasible point is either an extreme feasible point or a linear combination of feasible extreme

---

[14] Cf. Figure 11.4–1.

points. Since $Ax = b$ is an $n + m - 1$ dimensional hyperplane, every nonextreme feasible point is $x = \sum_{i=1}^{n+m} \theta_i x^i$, where $0 \le \theta_i < 1$ for all i and $x^i \in \{\text{extreme feasible points}\}$. Therefore, if no extreme point is a maximum and the maximum $p\bar{x}$, is finite, then, assuming $\bar{x}$ is a feasible point: $p\bar{x} = p \sum_{i=1}^{n+m} \theta_i x^i$, where $\sum \theta_i = 1$, $0 \le \theta_i < 1$ for all i and $x^i \in \{\text{extreme points}\}$, and $p\bar{x} > px_i$, for all i. But $p\bar{x} = p \sum_{i=1}^{n+m} \theta_i x^i$ and all $\theta_i < 1$ implies that $p\bar{x} < px^i$ for at least one i, which is a contradiction. Therefore there is no feasible point.   QED

Part III: Assume (1) and (3) false; then (2) must be true. If (1) and (3) are false, this implies that a feasible and finite maximum exists, x^*, such that $px^* \ge px$, for any $x \in \{x \mid Ax = b\}$ and $x \ge 0$.

(IIIa) Assume that $px^* > px$. Suppose that x^* is not an extreme point. Then $x^* = \sum_{i=1}^{n+m} \theta_i x^i$ where $0 \le \theta_i < 1$ for all i and $x^i \in \{\text{extreme feasible points}\}$. Therefore $px^* = p \sum \theta_i x^i$, but since $\theta_i < 1$,

$$px^* < px^i \text{ for some } i, \text{ which is a contradiction.}$$

(IIIb) Assume that $px^* = px$ for some $x \in \{x \mid Ax = b\}$. Since $x^* = \sum \theta_i x^i$ for $\sum \theta_i = 1$, $0 \le \theta_i \le 1$ where $x^i \in \{\text{extreme feasible points}\}$. $px^* = p \sum \theta_i x^i$ can hold if $\theta_i = 1$ and $\theta_j = 0$ for all $j \ne i$ or $px^* = px^i = px$ for all θ_i and $\theta_j > 0$. Therefore, if x^* is a maximum, at least one extreme point must be a maximum. If $\theta_i = 1$ and $\theta_j = 0$ for all $j \ne i$, then x^* is the extreme point x^i. If more than one $\theta_i > 0$, then x^* is a linear combination of those x^i and each of those x^i is also a maximum. That is, if x^* is not an extreme point, then two or more extreme points must be maxima.   QED

The next theorem relates an extreme point to a basic feasible solution and is fundamental to the development of the simplex algorithm.

DEFINITION 11.4–3 x is a **basic feasible solution** for $Ax = b$, where $A = (a_1, \ldots, a_m, \ldots, a_n)$, a_i is the column vector of the $m \times n$ matrix A, and $x = (x_1, \ldots, x_m, \ldots, x_n)$, if:

(1) $a_1, \ldots, a_m$ are linearly independent,[15] and
(2) $x_{m+1}, \ldots, x_n = 0$.

Theorem 11.4–4   An extreme feasible point is a basic feasible solution.

PROOF   For $\bar{x}$, an extreme feasible point, assume $x_i > 0$, for $1 \le i \le m$ and $x_i = 0$ if $i > m$.

If $a_1, \ldots, a_m$ are linearly dependent, then

$$\sum_{i=1}^{n} a_j \theta_j = 0 \quad \text{and} \quad \text{some } \theta_j \ne 0$$

[15] $(a_1, \ldots, a_m)$ are linearly independent, when $\sum_{j=1}^{m} \theta_j a_j = 0$ if and only if $\theta_j = 0$ for all j. Cf. Definition 4.2–4.

But for all feasible x, $Ax = b$ implies

$$\sum_{j=1}^{m} a_j x_j = b \quad \text{and} \quad x \neq 0$$

Therefore, for an extreme point $x = (x_1, \ldots, x_n)$ with all $x_j > 0$, the corresponding columns of A must be linearly independent. That is, an extreme feasible point must be a basic feasible solution.   QED

Corollary to Theorems 11.4–3 and 11.4–4 Some basic feasible solution must be the maximum for a linear programming problem.

Problems

11.4–1 The following table relates the maximum production possible from four given resources for a farmer with two possible crops: avocadoes and coffee.

		Maximum Production	
Resources	Amount	Avocadoes	Coffee (lb)
Land	50 acres	8000	4000
Spraying time	100 hours	20,000	10,000
Fertilizing time	37.5 hours	6000	∞
Harvesting time	80 hours	16,000	3200

(a) If avocadoes sell for $1.00 each and coffee for $1.50 per pound and the resource usage by avocadoes and coffee is linear, set up a linear programming problem to maximize revenue subject to the given constraints.
(b) Construct the production possibility surface and label each constraint.
(c) Draw in the isorevenue line that is the maximum attainable.
(d) Which resources will be used to capacity?
(e) What will be the amounts of each crop produced and the total revenue?
(f) State the dual linear programming problem.

11.4–2 Consider the following diet problem. An individual needs 8 units of vitamin A and 10 units of vitamin B, which are available from four foods as follows:

$1 worth of	Vitamin A	Vitamin B
Food 1	1	0.2
Food 2	0.8	0.4
Food 3	0.3	0.6
Food 4	0.2	1

(a) Assuming the relation is linear for dollars of food and vitamins received, on a graph with vitamin A on the horizontal axis and vitamin B on the vertical axis draw in the rays that relate the proportions of vitamins A and B for the four foods.

(b) Next draw an isocost curve for a $10 expenditure. That is, connect all points on the rays showing the amounts of the vitamins purchased for $10.

(c) A food will be an "inefficient" way of attaining vitamins A and B if the isocost curve constructed by its omission lies above the isocost curve with it included. Explain why. Are there any inefficient foods in this problem? Which?

(d) For a minimum-cost diet, which foods should be purchased?

(e) Set up the implied linear programming problem and solve it using your graphical information.

(f) State the dual to this problem and interpret its meaning.

11.4-3   Tru-Trail Mfg., Inc., has three plants of various vintage: one built in 1940, one in 1950, and one in 1970. For every unit of steel run through the plants, it requires 3 units, 2 units, and 1 unit of labor, respectively. The labor available is fixed in supply and equal to 100 units, while steel is available on the market at $30 per unit.

(a) With steel on one axis and labor on the other, construct the three process rays for the three plants.

(b) If the output is a linear function of steel in the following way:

$$q_{40} = 1.5S_{40}$$
$$q_{50} = 1.25S_{50}$$
$$q_{70} = S_{70}$$

where q_i = output from plant built in i, and S_i = steel used in plant built in i:

   (i)   What is the maximum production from the 1940 plant? The 1950 plant? The 1970 plant?
   (ii) Draw in the isoproduct curves for each maximum.

(c) Given the fixed factor of labor and the price of steel, what is the marginal cost of production in the three plants?

(d) Graphically show the following cost curves:
   (i)   marginal cost
   (ii) average variable cost
   (iii) average fixed cost, where labor is a fixed cost of $20 per unit
   (iv) average total cost

11.4-4   (a) Construct a graph of two outputs and three linear constraints.

(b) Label the extreme feasible points beginning with $A, B, \ldots$ that are on the graph.

(c) Are there other extreme feasible points? Explain why.

(d) As the price ratio between the two outputs varies from 0 to ∞, how does the solution to a linear programming problem vary in your graph?

References

1. ARROW, K. J., and A. C. ENTHOVEN (1961), "Quasi-concave Programming," *Econometrica*, **29**: 779–800.
2. ARROW, K. J., L. HURWICZ, and H. UZAWA (1962), "Constraint Qualifications in Maximization Problems," *Naval Research Logistics Quarterly*.
3. DANTZIG, G. B. (1951), "Maximization of a Linear Function of Variables Subject to Linear Inequalities" in T. Koopmans (ed.), *Activity Analysis of Production and Allocation*, New York: Wiley.
4. DORFMAN, R., P. A. SAMUELSON, and R. SOLOW (1958), *Linear Programming and Economic Analysis*, New York: McGraw-Hill.
5. HADLEY, G. (1961), *Linear Algebra*, Reading, Mass.: Addison-Wesley.
6. HADLEY, G. (1962), *Linear Programming*, Reading, Mass.: Addison-Wesley.
7. HADLEY, G. (1964), *Nonlinear and Dynamic Programming*, Reading, Mass.: Addison-Wesley.
8. KUHN, H.W., and A. W. TUCKER (1951), "Nonlinear Programming" in J. Neyman (ed.), *Proceedings of the Second Berkeley Symposium on Mathematical Statistics and Probability*, Berkeley: University of California Press.
9. LEONTIEF, WASSILY (1936), "Quantitative Input and Output Relations in the Economic System of the United States," *Review of Economics and Statistics*, **18**: 108–125.
10. LEONTIEF, WASSILY (1951), *The Structure of the American Economy, 1919–1929*, Cambridge, Mass.: Harvard University Press.
11. VAJDA, S. (1961), *Mathematical Programming*, Reading, Mass.: Addison-Wesley.
12. VON NEUMANN, JOHN (1928), "Zur Theorie der Gesellschaftsspiele" *Mathematische Annalen*, **100**: 295–320.

Chapter 12

Mathematical Programming: Techniques of Solution

12.1 THE SIMPLEX METHOD

Even though we know both the necessary and sufficient conditions for a maximum to a general mathematical programming problem, finding such a point may be quite a task. If we have to test every point in the constraint set to see if it satisfies our conditions for a maximum, a trial-and-error process, the task may be infinitely time consuming and only a slight improvement over testing every point.

In the case of a linear programming problem, we have shown in Section 11.4 that the solution must be a basic feasible solution. However, if there are more than a few variables and constraints, the number of basic feasible solutions to test rapidly becomes forbidding. The simplex method or algorithm is a technique of solution that guarantees an answer in a finite number of steps. The simplex also has several other advantages. First, the rules of simplex application are simple and easily applied, and the method is quite adaptable to computers. In addition, during the early development of programming theory, a major portion of the literature was devoted solely to the simplex method. So much so that linear programming and the simplex method became almost synonomous. A final reason for including a section on the simplex algorithm is that other types of programming problems can be transformed or altered so that the simplex can be applied and a solution obtained.

The simplex is based upon a tableau, a rectangular array of numbers, which is defined in the following way. For the linear programming problem

$$\begin{aligned} \max: \quad & px \\ \text{subject to:} \quad & Ax = d \\ & x \geq 0 \end{aligned}$$

where A is an $m \times n$ matrix, assume that the rank of A equals m. Then, for a basic feasible solution, there will be m linearly independent columns from A whose associated variables $x_1, \ldots, x_m$ will be positive, while for the remaining $n - m$ columns of A, the variables $x_{m+1}, \ldots, x_n$ will be zero. Thus we can partition $Ax = d$ into $Bx_b + Nx_N = d$, where $A = (a_1, \ldots, a_n)$, and a_i is the ith column of A; $B = (b_1, \ldots, b_m)$, the m linearly independent columns from A that form a basis (basic feasible solution); x_b, the m variables in the basis; and x_N, those variables not in the basis and equal to zero. Since every column a_j of A is a linear combination of a basis for A, we may write

$$a_j = \sum_{i=1}^{m} \tau_{ij} b_i$$

Consequently, we may form a tableau of these coefficients by putting the columns of B on the vertical side and the columns of A on the top:

$$
\begin{array}{c|ccccc}
 & a_1 & \cdots & a_j & \cdots & a_n \\
\hline
b_1 & \tau_{11} & \cdots & \tau_{1j} & \cdots & \tau_{1n} \\
\vdots & \vdots & & \vdots & & \vdots \\
b_i & \tau_{i1} & \cdots & \tau_{ij} & \cdots & \tau_{in} \\
\vdots & \vdots & & \vdots & & \vdots \\
b_m & \tau_{m1} & \cdots & \tau_{mj} & \cdots & \tau_{mn}
\end{array} = T
$$

Tableau 12.1–1

Since each column of B is a column of A, the τ_{ij}'s associating a column with itself will form a unit vector, $(0, \ldots, 1, \ldots, 0)$. For example, suppose b_f is the column a_g, then $\tau_{fg} = 1$ and $\tau_{ig} = 0$ for all $i = 1, \ldots, m$ and $i \neq f$. Thus in the tableau there will be m unit column vectors.

Finding an initial basic feasible solution is accomplished very easily. If the A matrix contains an $m \times m$ identity matrix, we have immediately a basic feasible solution and the values for the tableau T are equal to A. For example, if one slack variable is added to every constraint, transforming $A^*x^* \leq b$ into $Ax = b$, then the m slack variables constitute an initial basic feasible solution. If some constraints hold with a strict equality, then artificial variables can be added in the constraint equations and an arbitrarily large negative price can be associated with them in the objective function. This provides an initial basic feasible solution, and the large negative price ensures that the optimal solution will not contain an artificial variable.

Theorem 12.1–1 provides the rules for changing the basis, while Theorem 12.1–2 gives the rule that guarantees that the new basis is feasible.

Theorem 12.1–1 If $\tau_{rs} \neq 0$, then the vectors $b_1, \ldots, b_{r-1}, a_s, b_{r+1}, \ldots,$ b_m form a basis for A and the entries in the new tableau T' are given by the rules:

(1)
$$\tau'_{ij} = \tau_{ij} - \frac{\tau_{is}}{\tau_{rs}} \tau_{rj} \qquad \text{for all } i \neq r$$

(2)
$$\tau'_{rj} = \frac{\tau_{rj}}{\tau_{rs}} \text{ for all } j$$

PROOF   First we need to show that $b_1, \ldots, a_s, \ldots, b_m$ is a basis, or that $b_1, \ldots, a_s, \ldots, b_m$ are linearly independent. To do this we shall assume that

(3)
$$\sum_{i \neq r}^{m} \lambda_i b_i + \mu_s a_s = 0$$

and show that all λ_i and $\mu_s = 0$. From T, Tableau 12.1–1, we have

(4)
$$a_s = \sum_{i=1}^{m} \tau_{is} b_i$$

and thus (3) becomes

$$\sum_{i \neq r}^{m} \lambda_i b_i + \mu_s \sum_{i=1}^{m} \tau_{is} b_i = 0$$

or

$$\sum_{i \neq r}^{m} (\lambda_i + \mu_s \tau_{is}) b_i + \mu_s \tau_{rs} b_r = 0$$

By assumption $\sum_{j=1}^{m} \theta_j b_j = 0$, if and only if $\theta_j = 0$ for all j. Therefore $\mu_s = 0$, since $\tau_{rs} \neq 0$. Since $\mu_s = 0$, $\lambda_i = 0$ for $i \neq r$, by the same argument. Therefore $b_1, \ldots, a_s, \ldots, b_m$ is also a basis for A.

Second, we must show that the new tableau, T', formed by the rules (1) and (2) is such that

(5)
$$a_j = \sum_{i \neq r}^{m} \tau'_{ij} b_i + \tau'_{rj} a_s$$

We do this by working backward.

Substituting (1) and (2) into (5),

$$a_j = \sum_{i \neq r}^{m} \left(\tau_{ij} - \frac{\tau_{is}}{\tau_{rs}} \tau_{rj} \right) b_i + \frac{\tau_{rj}}{\tau_{rs}} a_s$$

But $a_s = \sum_{i=1}^{m} \tau_{is} b_i$, so

$$a_j = \sum_{i \neq r}^{m} \left(\tau_{ij} - \frac{\tau_{is}}{\tau_{rs}} \tau_{rj} \right) b_i + \frac{\tau_{rj}}{\tau_{rs}} \sum_{i=1}^{m} \tau_{is} b_i$$

Combining common terms:

$$a_j = \sum_{i \neq r}^{m} \left(\tau_{ij} - \frac{\tau_{is}}{\tau_{rs}} \tau_{rj} + \frac{\tau_{rj}}{\tau_{rs}} \tau_{is} \right) b_i + \frac{\tau_{rj}}{\tau_{rs}} \tau_{rs} b_r$$

and

$$a_j = \sum_{i \neq r}^{m} \tau_{ij} b_i + \tau_{rj} b_r = \sum_{i=1}^{m} \tau_{ij} b_i \qquad \text{QED}$$

Theorem 12.1–2   For $\tau_{rs} > 0$, the new level of the variables $\bar{x}_b$ with the new basis $b_1, \ldots, a_s, \ldots, b_m$, is given by

(1)
$$\bar{x}_{bk} = \left(x_{bk} - x_{br} \frac{\tau_{ks}}{\tau_{rs}} \right)$$

and

(2)
$$\bar{x}_{bs} = \frac{x_{br}}{\tau_{rs}}$$

If, in addition,

(3)
$$\frac{x_{br}}{\tau_{rs}} = \min_{k} \left\{ \frac{x_{bk}}{\tau_{ks}} \right\} \qquad \text{for } \tau_{ks} > 0$$

then the new basis formed by Theorem 12.1–1 is feasible.

PROOF   Since for the original basis we have

$$B x_b = d \quad \text{or} \quad \sum_{k=1}^{m} x_{bk} b_k = d$$

d is a linear combination of the columns in B just as it is of the columns of A. Hence Theorem 12.1–1 applies to establish (1) and (2).

Thus we just have to show that under (1), (2), and (3) the transformed basic solution remains feasible. For the new basis to be feasible,

$$\sum_{k \neq r} \bar{x}_{bk} b_k + \bar{x}_{bs} a_s = d$$

Since $x_i \geq 0$, by (1) and (2) we have

$$\bar{x}_{bk} = x_{bk} - x_{br} \left(\frac{\tau_{ks}}{\tau_{rs}} \right) \geq 0 \qquad \text{for } k \neq r$$

and

$$\bar{x}_{bs} = \frac{x_{br}}{\tau_{rs}} \geq 0 \quad \text{since} \quad \tau_{ks} > 0 \text{ and } \tau_{rs} > 0$$

Substituting, we have

$$\frac{x_{bk}}{\tau_{ks}} \geq \frac{x_{br}}{\tau_{rs}} > 0$$

which is (3).   QED

Of course, it does no good to move from one basic feasible solution to another unless the objective function is increasing. Since $z = p_b x_b$, the value of the objective function when x_b is the basis, and $\bar{z} = \bar{p}_b \bar{x}_b$, the new value of the objective function, then the change in the objective function is given by $\bar{z} - z$, which, if positive, represents an improvement. Substituting $\bar{x}_{bk} = x_{bk} - x_{br}(\tau_{ks}/\tau_{rs})$ and $\bar{x}_{bs} = x_{br}/\tau_{rs}$ in $\bar{z}$, we have

$$\bar{z} = \sum_{\substack{k \neq r}}^{n} p_{bk} \left(x_{bk} - x_{br} \frac{\tau_{ks}}{\tau_{rs}} \right) + p_s \frac{x_{br}}{\tau_{rs}}$$

Add and subtract $x_{br} = x_{br}(\tau_{rs}/\tau_{rs})$:

$$\bar{z} = \sum_{k=1}^{m} p_{bk} x_{bk} - \sum_{k=1}^{m} p_{bk} x_{br} \frac{\tau_{ks}}{\tau_{rs}} + p_s \frac{x_{br}}{\tau_{rs}}$$

Therefore

$$\bar{z} - z = \sum_{k=1}^{m} p_{bk} x_{bk} - \sum_{k=1}^{m} p_{bk} x_{bk} + p_s \frac{x_{br}}{\tau_{rs}} - \sum_{k=1}^{m} p_{bk} x_{br} \frac{\tau_{ks}}{\tau_{rs}}$$

or

$$\bar{z} - z = \frac{x_{br}}{\tau_{rs}} \left(p_s - \sum_{k=1}^{m} p_{bk} \tau_{ks} \right)$$

Define $z_s = p_s - \sum_{k=1}^{m} p_{bk} \tau_{ks}$, the opportunity cost of not having process (column) s in the basis.

Theorem 12.1–3   If $z_s = p_s - \sum_{k=1}^{m} p_{bk} \tau_{ks} > 0$, the objective function will increase. If all $z_s \leq 0$, we have a maximum solution to the linear programming problem

$$\begin{aligned} \text{max:} \quad & px \\ \text{subject to:} \quad & Ax = d \\ & x \geq 0 \end{aligned}$$

We can now combine the foregoing three theorems to get the simplex algorithm for finding a solution to a linear programming problem.

DEFINITION 12.1–1   Simplex Rules

(1) Find an initial feasible basic solution and construct the tableau, T.
(2) Find the maximum $z_s > 0$; s is then the incoming column.

(3) Find the maximum level at which the new activity can be brought in:

$$\tau_{rs} = \min_{k} \left\{ \frac{x_{bk}}{\tau_{ks}} \right\} \quad \text{for } \tau_{ks} > 0$$

r is the outgoing column in the basis.

(4) Recompute the new tableau T' as follows:

$$\tau'_{rj} = \frac{\tau_{rj}}{\tau_{rs}} \quad \text{for all } j$$

and

$$\tau'_{ij} = \tau_{ij} - \frac{\tau_{is}}{\tau_{rs}} \tau_{rj} \quad \text{for all } i \neq r \text{ and all } j$$

(5) If some $z > 0$, continue with step 2; if all z's ≤ 0 a maximum is found.

Although the simplex is not the only method of finding a solution, its simplicity of application and computer adaptability have made it a widely used method of solving both linear and certain nonlinear programming problems.

Example 1. As an example of the simplex technique, let us solve the following linear programming problem:

$$\begin{array}{rl} \text{max:} & 1x_1 + 1.5x_2 \\ \text{subject to:} & 25x_1 + 50x_2 \leq 100{,}000 = R_1 \\ & 20x_1 + 40x_2 \leq 200{,}000 = R_2 \\ & 25x_1 \quad\quad\quad \leq 75{,}000 = R_3 \\ & 20x_1 + 10x_2 \leq 160{,}000 = R_4 \end{array}$$

(1) The first step is to add slack variables x_3, x_4, x_5, and x_6 to transform $Ax \leq d$ into $Ax = d$.

$$\begin{bmatrix} 25 & 50 & 1 & 0 & 0 & 0 \\ 20 & 40 & 0 & 1 & 0 & 0 \\ 25 & 0 & 0 & 0 & 1 & 0 \\ 20 & 10 & 0 & 0 & 0 & 1 \end{bmatrix} \begin{bmatrix} x_1 \\ x_2 \\ x_3 \\ x_4 \\ x_5 \\ x_6 \end{bmatrix} = \begin{bmatrix} 100{,}000 \\ 200{,}000 \\ 75{,}000 \\ 160{,}000 \end{bmatrix}$$

(2) The next step is to find an initial basic feasible solution. This is most easily found by using the slack variables. That is, $x_3 = x_4 = x_5 = x_6 = 1$ is a basic feasible solution. Therefore the tableau T is

	1	2	3	4	5	6
3	25	50	1	0	0	0
4	20	40	0	1	0	0
5	25	0	0	0	1	0
6	20	10	0	0	0	1

(3) The next step is to find the values z_s. Since

$$z_s = p_s - \sum_{k=1}^{4} p_{bk} \tau_{ks}$$

where $p_{bk} = 0$ (i.e., the prices of all slack variables in the initial basic solution are zero), initially, we have

$$z_s = p_s$$

Thus, since $p_2 = 1.5 > p_1 = 1$, column 2 is a new incoming column.

(4) To find the outgoing row we need to compute

$$\tau_{rs} = \min_{k} \left\{ \frac{x_{bk}}{\tau_{ks}} \right\}$$

for $\tau_{ks} > 0$. It is most convenient to do this alongside and beneath the tableau as follows. Add an additional column to the tableau for x_{bk}, the level of the variables in the basic feasible solution. The initial values in this column will be equal to the column d, since each slack variable is in a one-to-one relation with its resource. Now to compute x_{bk}/τ_{rs}, divide each element in column x_{bk} by the element in column 2, the incoming column. The results are shown in Tableau 12.1–2.

bk	x_{bk}		1	2	3	4	5	6	x_{bk}/τ_{ks}
3	100,000	1	25	(50)	1	0	0	0	2000
4	200,000	1	20	40	0	1	0	0	5000
5	75,000	1	25	0	0	0	1	0	∞
6	160,000	1	20	10	0	0	0	0	16,000

$$\min_{k} \left\{ \frac{x_{bk}}{\tau_{ks}} \right\} = 2000$$

	z_s		1	(1.5)	0	0	0	0

Tableau 12.1–2

Since the minimum is 2000, column 3 goes out of the basic solution and column 2 comes in. The new simplex tableau is found by dividing all elements of row 1 by 50, subtracting 40 times the new row 1 from row 2, and subtracting 10 times the new row 1 from row 4. At the same time, the same procedure may be applied to the column x_{bk} and the row z_s to find their new values. For example, 100,000 in the x_{bk} column is divided by 50, also giving 2000. Since 40 times the new row is subtracted from row 2, also subtract 40 times 2000 from 200,000 to obtain the second element in the new column $\bar{x}_{bk}$, 120,000. Similarly, 1.5 times the new first row is subtracted from row z_s to obtain the new opportunity costs. The results are shown in Tableau 12.1–3 along with new values of $\bar{x}_{bk}$, z_s, and $\bar{x}_{bk}/\tau_{ks}$.

bk	$\bar{x}_{bk}$	1	2	3	4	5	6	
2	2000	$\frac{1}{2}$	1	0.02	0	0	0	4000
4	120,000	0	0	−0.8	1	0	0	∞
5	75,000	(25)	0	0	0	1	0	3000
6	140,000	15	0	−0.2	0	0	1	9333
	z_s	(0.25)	0	−0.03	0	0	0	

Tableau 12.1–3

The most restrictive level for the next incoming column, 1 (since it has the highest positive price, i.e., $z_s = 0.25$) is 3000. Therefore that row is now divided by 25, the pivot element in that row. Then multiples of that row are added to the other rows to zero out column 1 in the tableau. Notice by the rules that this same procedure is carried out with the column x_{bk} and the row z_s. The result is given in Tableau 12.1–4.

bk	x_{bk}	1	2	3	4	5	6
2	500	0	1	0.02	0	−0.002	0
4	120,000	0	0	−0.8	1	0	0
1	3000	1	0	0	0	0.004	0
6	95,000	0	0	−0.2	0	−0.6	1
	z_s	0	0	−0.03	0	−0.001	0

Tableau 12.1–4

Since all $z_s \leq 0$, now we have the solution to the problem. The real variables x_1 and x_2 are at a level of 3000 units and 500, respectively. The maximum value of the objective function subject to the given constraints is 3750. The artificial or slack variables indicate how much of the resources are not being used. The first resource, available in the amount of 100,000 units, is being fully utilized, as is the third resource. For the second resource, only 80,000 of its given 200,000 units are being used. 95,000 units of the fourth resource are going unused, while 65,000 units are being used for the maximum solution.

Dual Simplex Algorithm

A similar technique to the simplex algorithm, which is often very useful, is the dual simplex algorithm. The dual simplex algorithm is used when one has a basic solution that is not feasible. For example, for the linear programming problem

$$\text{max:} \quad px$$
$$\text{subject to:} \quad Ax = b$$
$$x \geq 0$$

the dual problem is

$$\text{min:} \quad yb$$
$$\text{subject to:} \quad yA \geq p$$
$$y \geq 0$$

Since the solution to the dual is equivalent to the solution to the primal, we could solve the dual for values of the primal problem that will be given in the simplex tableau. However, by adding "slack" variables to the dual, we now have a basic solution that is not feasible. The rules of iteration then move from the basic nonfeasible solution to the optimal solution.

An initial basic nonfeasible solution will appear in the simplex tableau with negative values for some x_i and all $z_i \leq 0$. If we move from one basic solution to another while maintaining $z_i \leq 0$ for all i, then the first feasible solution will be the optimal solution.

DEFINITION 12.1–2   The **rules for the dual simplex algorithm** are as follows:

(1) The vector to leave the basis is the most negative x_{bi}; call that row r.
(2) The vector to enter the basis is

$$\min_{j} \frac{z_j}{\tau_{rj}} > 0 \text{ where } \tau_{rj} < 0.$$

(3) Change the simplex tableau according to the rules for the regular simplex method (Definition 12.1–1).
(4) If all $x_{bi} \geq 0$, it is the optimal solution. If some $x_{bi} < 0$, repeat the algorithm.

The second rule assures that all z_i will remain nonpositive, while rule 3 assures us that we move from one basic solution to another.[1]

The dual simplex algorithm applies to the dual of a "regular" linear programming problem. That is, the dual simplex algorithm applies specifically to a problem of the type

$$\text{min:} \quad px$$
$$\text{subject to:} \quad Ax \geq b$$
$$x \geq 0$$

---

[1] See Section 12.5, where the dual simplex algorithm is used to solve an integer linear programming problem.

Consider the following linear problem:

$$\begin{aligned}
\text{max:} \quad & 3x_1 + 2x_2 \\
\text{subject to:} \quad & 2x_1 + 3x_2 \geq 6 \\
& 4x_1 + 5x_2 \leq 40 \\
& 3x_1 + 2x_2 \leq 36 \\
& x_1, x_2 \geq 0
\end{aligned}$$

Since the first constraint is "greater than or equal to," if we add a slack variable to the first constraint we shall not add it but subtract it. The problem with slack variables added is

$$\begin{aligned}
\text{max:} \quad & 3x_1 + 2x_2 \\
\text{subject to:} \quad & 2x_1 + 3x_2 - x_3 = 6 \\
& 4x_1 + 5x_2 + x_4 = 40 \\
& 3x_1 + 2x_2 + x_5 = 36 \\
& x_i \geq 0 \qquad i = 1, 2, 3, 4, 5
\end{aligned}$$

If we construct the simplex table we shall not have a basic solution with the slack variables x_3, x_4, and x_5 because x_3 has a coefficient of -1. Therefore, let us multiply the first row by -1 and construct the corresponding simplex tableau:

bk	x_{bk}	1	2	3	4	5
3	-6	-2	-3	1	0	0
4	40	4	5	0	1	0
5	36	3	2	0	0	1

Tableau 12.1–5

We have a basic solution, but it is not feasible since in the x_{bk} column (the level of variables in the basic solution) $x_3 = -6 < 0$. Therefore, what we need to do is obtain a basic solution that is feasible. We may do this by bringing in column 1 or 2 in place of column 3. In other words, if we use either -2 or -3 as pivot elements, in the usual fashion, then the negative level of the basis variable in that row will become positive; that is, $-6/-2 = 3$ or $-6/-3 = 2$. In the process of bringing in a new column to replace a negative x_{bi}, other x_{bk} variables may become negative. Therefore the following simplex rules apply to a general linear programming problem:

DEFINITION 12.1–3 The **general rules for the simplex algorithm** are as follows:

(1) Change all constraints to the form $Ax \leq b$.
(2) Add slack variables.

(3) (a) If any $x_{bk} < 0$, the vector to leave the basis is the most negative x_{bk}. Call that row r. Go to step 4.

(b) If all $x_{bk} > 0$, proceed with the usual simplex algorithm as defined in Definition 12.1–1.

(4) The vector to enter the basis is

$$\min_{j} \frac{x_{br}}{\tau_{rj}}$$

(i.e., $\tau_{rj} < 0$; if no $\tau_{rj} < 0$ the problem has no feasible solution). Return to step 3.

Problems

12.1–1 Use the simplex method to solve the following problem:

$$\text{max:} \quad 5x_1 + 10x_2$$
$$\text{subject to:} \quad 2x_1 + 4x_2 \le 10$$
$$x_1 + 6x_2 \le 18$$
$$x_1, x_2 \ge 0$$

12.1–2 Use the simplex method to show that the maximum to the following problem is 48.

$$\text{max:} \quad x_1 + 2x_2 + 3x_3$$
$$\text{subject to:} \quad 10x_1 + 5x_2 + x_3 \le 100$$
$$6x_1 + 9x_2 + 3x_3 \le 90$$
$$4x_1 + 2x_2 + 6x_3 \le 84$$
$$x_i \ge 0, \, i = 1, 2, 3$$

12.1–3 Use the simplex method to solve Problem 11.4–1.

12.1–4 Use the simplex method to solve the dual to Problem 11.4–1.

12.1–5 Use the simplex method to solve the following problem:

$$\text{max:} \quad 4x_1 + 3x_2 + 4x_3$$
$$\text{subject to:} \quad x_1 + x_2 = 10$$
$$8 - x_1 \ge 0$$
$$x_3 + x_2 + x_1 \le 20$$
$$7 - x_2 \ge 0$$
$$4x_3 + x_2 \le 50$$
$$x_1 + 8x_3 \le 60$$
$$x_1, x_2, x_3 \ge 0$$

12.2 THE GRADIENT METHOD

Another technique of solution that may be used for linear programming problems and nonlinear problems is called the gradient method of solution. Basically, this amounts to climbing the objective function surface at the maximum rate. However, the steepest rate of assent up a mountain does not always lead to the peak. In Figure 12.2–1, where the objective function has

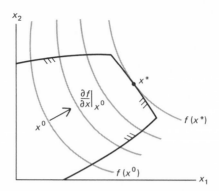

Figure 12.2–1 *Nonlinear programming problem with two variables and the gradient method of solution.*

"regular" properties, beginning at x^0 and moving in the direction of the gradient $(\partial f/\partial x)|_{x^0}$, we end up almost immediately at the true maximum, x^*. However, in Figure 12.2–2 the objective-function contours are such that the final solution attained by the gradient method depends upon the initial starting position. If, for example, we begin with an initial feasible solution such as x^{10}, we are first led to the boundary at point x^{11} and then along the boundary (to remain feasible) to the point x^1. $f(x^1)$ is not the maximum value of $f(x)$, subject to $g(x) \geq 0$, although $f(x)$ has a relative maximum in the neighbourhood of x^1. Likewise, beginning at x^{20} does not attain the true maximum. The final point is x^2, a "corner" solution and relative maximum of $f(x)$ in the neighborhood of x^2. Only by beginning at a point such as x^0 in Figure 12.2–2 does the gradient method arrive at the global maximum,

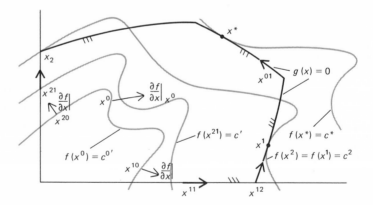

Figure 12.2–2 *Nonlinear programming problem with two variables and the gradient method of solution.*

x^*. Thus with the gradient method one can be assured only of finding a relative maximum unless concavity and/or convexity properties can be established that will guarantee a global maximum.

Let us now state more formally the rules for the gradient technique.

DEFINITION 12.2–1   The **rules for the gradient technique** are as follows:

(1) Find an initial feasible solution, x^0.
(2) Compute $(\partial f/\partial x)|_{x^0}$ and
    (a) if $(\partial f/\partial x)|_{x^0} = 0$, method terminates, or
    (b) if $(\partial f/\partial x)|_{x^0} \neq 0$, proceed to step 3.
(3) Find a new feasible x', defined in the following way:
    (a) If no $g_j(x^0) = 0$:
        (i) find the maximum λ such that:

$$(1) \quad x_i' = x_i^0 + \lambda \frac{\partial f}{\partial x_i} \geq 0$$

$$(2) \quad g(x') \geq 0$$

        (ii) move to $\displaystyle\max_{0 \leq k \leq 1} f\left(x^0 + k\lambda \left.\frac{\partial f}{\partial x}\right|_{x^0}\right)$. Go to step 4.

    (b) If some $g_j(x^0) = 0$, find the x' such that
        (i) $g_j(x') = 0, g(x') \geq 0, x' \geq 0$
        and either:
        (1) for $g_k(x^0) > 0, g_k(x') = 0$, that is, another constraint is encountered, or
        (2) for some $x_i^0 > 0, x_i' = 0$, that is, a new axis is encountered.
        (ii) Move to max $f(x)$, where $g_j(x) = 0$ and x is between x^0 and x'. Go to step 4.

(4) Return to step 2, letting the new value of x be called x^0.

In other words, if one begins at an initial point where no constraint is effective, $g(x^0) > 0$, and no variables are zero, $x^0 > 0$, move along the gradient until either some constraint becomes effective *or* some variable goes to zero. Then move along the constraint or the axis, as long as the objective function is increasing, until some other constraint becomes effective or until another axis is encountered.

As one can see, the gradient method as described above requires a great deal of trial and error. For example, a guess usually determines how fine the path between x^0 and x' is to be partitioned to ensure that the objective function is greatest at the final chosen x between x^0 and x'. If the constraints are nonlinear, then step B may be quite difficult to compute. If the objective function is quasiconcave and the constraint set is convex, then the gradient method can be used to find a true maximum.[2]

Example 1. As an example of the gradient method, consider the following nonlinear programming problem:

$$\begin{aligned}
\text{max:} \quad & f(x) = x_1 x_2 \\
\text{subject to:} \quad & x_1^2 + x_2^2 \leq 100 \\
& x_1^2 + 16x_2^2 \leq 400 \\
& x_1, x_2 \geq 0.
\end{aligned}$$

Since any initial feasible solution will do, try $x_1 = x_2 = 1$. Step 1 is to evaluate the partial derivatives:

$$\left. \frac{\partial f}{\partial x_1} \right|_{x^0} = x_2 = 1$$

and

$$\left. \frac{\partial f}{\partial x_2} \right|_{x^0} = x_1 = 1$$

Proceeding to step 2, we see that since neither constraint is binding, we must find the maximum value of λ. To solve for the maximum λ, substitute $x_1^0 + \lambda$ and $x_2^0 + \lambda$ in each constraint and solve as an equality. Doing that, we find that from $g_1(x) = 100 - x_1^2 - x_2^2$ that $\lambda \leq \sqrt{50} - 1$ and from $g_2(x)$, $\lambda \leq 20/\sqrt{17} - 1 = 3.85$. Therefore the maximum value of λ is 3.85.

Step 3 is to move to the maximum value of $f(x^0 + k\lambda(\partial f/\partial x|_{x^0}))$ for $0 \leq k \leq 1$. In this case the maximum is at $k = 1$.

Returning to step 2, we see that both partial derivatives are still positive and therefore move on to step 3. Since we are now at a position where one constraint is binding, that is, $g_2(x) = 0$, the rule is to move along $g_2(x)$ until either another constraint is encountered, that is, $g_1(x) = 0$, or an axis is encountered, that is, x_1 or $x_2 = 0$. If we move along $g_2(x) = 0$ such that $f(x)$ increases, we come to the point where $g_1(x) = 0$ also. Solving for the values of x_1 and x_2, we find $x_1 = \sqrt{80}$, $x_2 = \sqrt{20}$, and $f(x) = 40$. Since now both constraints are binding, there is no other feasible x_1 and x_2 that would increase the value of the objective function. Therefore we have a solution.

Two comments are in order concerning this example. First, it is quite cumbersome to carry out the calculations by hand even in a simple and contrived example. However, computers do not seem to tire as easily and thus the method is useful. Second, the fact that our solution occurred where both constraints were binding is not an indication that this will be the normal case.

[2] For additional discussion see Hadley (1964), Chapter 9, and Arrow, Hurwicz, and Uzawa (1958).

Problem

12.2–1   Use the gradient method to solve the following nonlinear programming problem, beginning with an initial feasible solution of $x_1^0 = x_2^0 = 1$. Graphically illustrate the steps of your calculations.

$$\text{max:} \quad f(x) = x_2 - (x_1 - 4)^2$$
$$\text{subject to:} \quad 0 \le x_2 \le 10$$
$$0 \le x_1 \le 8$$
$$x_1^2 + x_2^2 \le 125$$

12.3   DYNAMIC PROGRAMMING[3]

Another computational technique that may be employed to solve a variety of special linear and nonlinear programming problems is termed dynamic programming. The term is a misnomer. It refers not to a special kind of programming problem, but to a computational method of solution for a variety of programming problems. Furthermore, it is not dynamic. It was developed in the 1950's by Richard Bellman to solve sequential decision-making problems and thus acquired the name dynamic although the decision stages need not refer to any particular time sequence.

Dynamic programming amounts to breaking up a general programming problem into a series of n-stage programming problems that can be solved one at a time in some sequential fashion. This means that the objective of dynamic programming is to choose a set of parameters for the ith stage that may be used to solve the $(i + 1)$th stage. The variety of general programming problems that can be put in this form is so broad that dynamic programming cannot be given a specific formulation. It is only by a series of examples that one can gain an understanding of its applications. Due to space restrictions the number of such illustrative problems is limited. For further examples and discussion the reader is referred to Section 10.9, Section 14.6, and the selected references at the end of the chapter.

Example 1.   Stocking Spare Parts for a Submarine   Consider the nonlinear programming problem

$$\text{max:} \quad z = - \sum_{i=1}^{n} f_i(x_i)$$

$$\text{subject to:} \quad \sum_{i=1}^{m} a_i x_i \le b \qquad a_j > 0 \text{ for all } j$$

$$x \ge 0 \text{ and } x_i \text{ an integer for all } i$$

[3] This technique was discussed briefly in Section 10.9.

This type of problem could arise, for example, where one is trying to optimize the stocking of spare parts in a submarine. b is the volume of storage space and a_i is the amount of space taken up by each part, x_i. The negative of the cost function, z, is a separable (that is, $\partial^2 z/\partial x_i \, \partial x_j = 0$ for all i and j), nonlinear function dependent on the cost of each part, the cost of its failure, and the probability of failure on each spare part.

Given the nonlinearity of the objective functions $f_i(x_i)$ and the integer restrictions, no method of solution may be available other than comparing all possible combinations of values for x. If we assume for simplicity that all $a_i = 1$, then, even for small values of n and b, the number of comparisons that must be made can reach an incredible size. In such a case one may be able to reduce the number of computations a sizeable amount by converting the foregoing problem into a series of n different stages, that is, applying dynamic programming techniques.

For example, suppose we set the arbitrary unit of measure in the restriction so that all a_i and b are integers. Next solve $g_1(\xi)$ for $\xi = 0, \ldots, b$ where $g_1(\xi) = \max f_1(x_1)$ and $0 \le x_1 \le \xi/a_1$. Having $b + 1$ values for $g_1(\xi)$, next solve

$$g_2(\xi) = \max_{0 \le x_2 \le \xi/a_2} [f_2(x_2) + g_1(\xi - a_2 x_2)] \qquad \text{for } \xi = 0, \ldots, b$$

Continuing to iterate the above procedure for $g_i(\xi)$ for $\xi = 0, \ldots, b$ until $i = n - 1$, by solving

$$g_n(b) = \max_{0 \le x_n \le b/a_n} [f_n(x_n) + g_{n-1}(b - a_n x_n)]$$

we shall obtain the optimal value for x_n in the original problem. Further, if we have kept track of our previous calculations for $g_i(\xi)$ for $\xi = 0, \ldots, b$ and $i = 1, \ldots, n - 1$, we can then work backwards to obtain the optimal values for each x_i, $i = 1, \ldots, n - 1$. The efficiency of this dynamic programming technique over comparison of all possible values for the vector x in the case where $n = 5$ and $b = 10$ is 275 to 1001. That is, using dynamic programming, a little over $\frac{1}{4}$ of the computations are needed. As n and b increase, the efficiency increases as well.

Example 2. Dynamic Programming and the Calculus of Variations In Chapter 10, for the simplest variational problem in the calculus of variations, that is,

$$\max (\min) F[y] = \int_a^b f\left(x, y, \frac{dy}{dx}\right) dx$$

we found the first necessary condition (the Euler-Lagrange equation)[4] to be

(1)
$$\frac{\partial f}{\partial y} = \frac{d}{dx}\left[\frac{\partial f}{\partial(dy/dx)}\right]$$

[4] See Definition 10.5–2.

or, by completing the differentiation,[5]

(2) $$\frac{\partial f}{\partial y} = \frac{\partial^2 f}{\partial(dy/dx)\,\partial x} + \frac{\partial^2 f}{\partial(dy/dx)\,\partial y}\frac{dy}{dx} + \frac{\partial^2 f}{\partial(dy/dx)^2}\frac{d^2 y}{dx^2}$$

In general this second-order differential equation will be nonlinear and solvable only by numerical techniques. In this example we shall illustrate how the techniques of dynamic programming can be implemented to obtain a numerical solution.

Suppose that we have a firm whose objective is to maximize profits, π, over the period t_0 to t_n:

$$\max \pi = \int_{t_0}^{t_n} (p_t q_t - c_t)\, dt$$

where the quantity produced, q_t, is a function of the amount of capital on hand, K_t. The price at time t, p_t, is dependent upon the quantity produced at t. Costs at time t depend not only on the quantity of capital, K_t, but also upon the rate of investment, dK/dt. A rapid increase in the stock of capital entails additional costs in overtime, special deliveries, and so forth. A very slow increase in the stock of capital, on the other hand, results in additional costs due to natural deterioration and the like. In other words, everything else being equal, there is an optimal rate of investment—a rate $(dK/dt)^*$ that minimizes the cost of capital. This is illustrated in Figure 12.3–1.

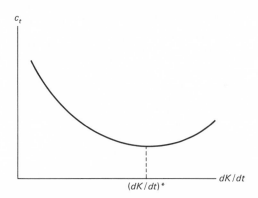

Figure 12.3–1   *Relation between cost and rate of investment.*

Incorporating this information into the profit function, the problem for the firm is to

$$\max \pi = \int_{t_0}^{t_n} \left\{ p(q(K_t))q(K_t) - c\left(K_t, \frac{dK}{dt}\right)\right\} dt + v \int_{t_0}^{t_n} K_t\, dt$$

where v is the market price for the firm's capital stock at t_n.

[5] See Definition 10.5–3.

The above can be written more simply as

$$\max \pi = \int_{t_0}^{t_n} f\left(t, K_t, \frac{dK}{dt}\right) dt$$

where $f(t, K_t, dK/dt) = p(q(K_t))q(K_t) - c(K_t, dK/dt) + vK_t$

A quick comparison of $f(t, K_t, dK/dt)$ and Equation (2) will show that the Euler-Lagrange equation will be nearly impossible to solve without resorting to numerical techniques. The dynamic programming approach does not yield an analytic expression for K_t but will give the value of K_t at a finite number of points.

Initially, the interval t_0 to t_n is divided into n subintervals of length Δt.[6] The subintervals are separated by grid points $t_i = t_0 + i \Delta t, i = 0, \ldots, n$. If Δt is small we can now approximate dK/dt by

$$\frac{dK}{dt} \simeq \frac{K_{ti} - K_{ti-1}}{\Delta t}$$

Also approximating the integral, we have

$$\pi \simeq \sum_{i=1}^{n} f\left(K_{ti}, \frac{K_{ti} - K_{ti-1}}{\Delta t}, t_i\right) \Delta t$$

Given an initial stock of capital K_0, our fixed point, variable end-point problem in the calculus of variations can now be viewed as one of finding the n values for K_i that maximize π. Therefore let

$$g_j(\xi) = \max_{(K_{j+1}, \ldots, K_n)} \sum_{i=j+1}^{n} f\left(K_i, \frac{K_i - K_{i-1}}{\Delta t}, t_i\right) \Delta t$$

where $K_j = \xi$.

Thus

$$g_{n-1}(\xi) = \max_{K_n} f\left(K_n, \frac{K_n - \xi}{\Delta t}, t_n\right) \Delta t$$

and

$$g_j(\xi) = \max_{K_{j+1}} \left[f\left(K_{j+1}, \frac{K_{j+1} - \xi}{\Delta t}, t_j\right) \Delta t + g_{j+1}(K_{j+2})\right]$$

We can solve the n-stage series of problems for various values of ξ. It would appear that since we have a variable end-point problem that there is no upper bound on ξ. However, if we make a couple of additional assumptions, we shall have an upper limit for ξ. First we shall assume that it is not profitable for the firm to acquire capital without producing. That is, the resale value of

---

[6] See the discussion of the Euler method in Section 10.9.

capital is less than the cost regardless of the rate of investment. Second, if $\partial c / [\partial (dK/dt)] > 0$, then we can solve for the optimal initial stock of capital, K^*. K^* is the quantity of capital that equates marginal revenue to marginal cost when the rate of investment is zero, that is, for K^*,

$$\frac{\partial (pq)}{\partial K} = \frac{\partial c}{\partial K}\bigg|_{dK/dt=0}$$

With $K_0 < K^*$ we have

$$K_0 \leq \xi \leq K^*$$

This interval can be divided into any number of finite intervals, depending upon the desired degree of accuracy, and the problem solved by comparisons as in Example 1.

Problem

12.3–1 A professor of archeology is planning an excursion into the desert in his jeep, which has 3 ft³ of storage space for spare parts. Spare tires, spare carburetors, and spare batteries take up 1 ft³, 0.5 ft³, and 0.5 ft³, respectively. The probability that $0, 1, 2, 3, 4, \ldots$ tires will fail is $0, \frac{1}{2}, \frac{1}{4}, \frac{1}{4}, 0, \ldots$. The probability that $0, 1, 2, 3, 4, 5, 6, 7, \ldots$ carburetors will fail is $\frac{1}{2}, \frac{1}{4}, \frac{1}{8}, \frac{1}{8}, 0, 0, 0, 0, \ldots$. The probability that $0, 1, 2, 3, 4, 5, 6, 7, \ldots$ batteries will fail is $\frac{1}{4}, \frac{1}{2}, \frac{1}{8}, \frac{1}{8}, 0, 0, 0, 0, \ldots$. If the professor runs out of tires, he will lose 1 day. If he runs out of carburetors or batteries, he will lose 2 days. What parts should he take along to minimize the expected number of days lost?

12.4   QUADRATIC PROGRAMMING

In this section we review a special kind of nonlinear programming problem, the quadratic programming problem. This technique has several economic applications, and, although it is nonlinear in the objective function, it can be solved by using the simplex method. It illustrates the use of programming theory to obtain a solution and also demonstrates that simple changes in a linear programming problem often create a great increase in the difficulty of solution.

DEFINITION 12.4–1 A **quadratic programming problem** is a general mathematical programming problem with a quadratic objective function and linear constraints:

$$\begin{aligned} \text{max:} \quad & f(x) = cx + x'Dx \\ \text{subject to:} \quad & Ax = b \\ & x \geq 0 \end{aligned}$$

where x is an $n \times 1$ vector of variables, c is a $1 \times n$ vector of constants, b is an $m \times 1$ vector, A is an $m \times n$ matrix of constants, and D is an $n \times n$ matrix of constants.

If D is a negative semidefinite matrix, that is, if $x'Dx \leq 0$ for all x,[7] then the objective function, $f(x)$, will be concave and since the constraints are linear (hence concave as well), the Kuhn–Tucker conditions [Equations (1) and (2) of Theorem 11.2–1] are both necessary and sufficient for a maximum.

First, let us briefly show $x'Dx \leq 0$, for all x, implies that $f(x) = cx + x'Dx$ is concave. Let $f_1(x) = cx$, $f_2(x) = x'Dx$. To show that $x'Dx$ is concave we refer to Definition 11.2–4: $f_2(x)$ is concave if $f_2(\bar{x}) \geq \lambda f_2(x) + (1 - \lambda)f_2(x^0)$ where $\bar{x} = \lambda x + (1 - \lambda)x^0$ and $0 \leq \lambda \leq 1$. By definition,

$$(1) \quad f_2(\bar{x}) = \bar{x}'D\bar{x} = [\lambda x + (1 - \lambda)x^0]'D[\lambda x + (1 - \lambda)x^0]$$

$$= [x^0 + \lambda(x - x^0)]'D[x^0 + \lambda(x - x^0)]$$

$$= x^{0'}Dx^0 + 2\lambda(x - x^0)'Dx^0 + \lambda^2(x - x^0)'D(x - x^0)$$

Since $0 \leq \lambda \leq 1$, $\lambda^2 \leq \lambda$ and since $x'Dx \leq 0$, for all x,

$$(2) \quad \lambda(x - x^0)'D(x - x^0) \leq \lambda^2(x - x^0)'D(x - x^0)$$

Using (2) and (1), we have

$$f_2(\bar{x}) \geq x^{0'}Dx^0 + 2\lambda(x - x^0)'Dx^0 + \lambda(x - x^0)'D(x - x^0)$$

or

$$f_2(\bar{x}) \geq x^{0'}Dx^0 + \lambda(x - x^0)'Dx^0 + \lambda(x - x^0)'Dx$$

or

$$f_2(\bar{x}) \geq f_2(x^0) - \lambda f_2(x^0) + \lambda f_2(x) = \lambda f_2(x) + (1 - \lambda)f_2(x^0).$$

Which is what we wished to show, and can state the following as a theorem:

Theorem 12.4–1 If D is a negative semidefinite matrix, then $f(x) = x'Dx$ is a concave function.

Now, using the fact that the sum of two concave functions is a concave function, we know that Equations (1) and (2) of Theorem 11.2–1 are necessary and sufficient conditions for a maximum solution.

Theorem 12.4–2 If $f_i(x)$, $i = 1, \ldots, n$, are concave (convex), then $f(x) = \sum_{i=1}^{n} f_i(x)$ is concave (convex).

[7] See Definition 4.4–1.

PROOF   For any x, x^0, and λ, $0 \leq \lambda \leq 1$

$$f[\lambda x + (1 - \lambda)x^0] = \sum_{i=1}^{n} f_i[\lambda x + (1 - \lambda)x^0]$$

$$\geq \sum_{i=1}^{n} \lambda f_i(x) + \sum_{i=1}^{n} (1 - \lambda)f_i(x^0)$$

$$= \lambda f(x) + (1 - \lambda)f(x^0) \qquad \text{QED}$$

By utilizing the necessary and sufficient conditions we can convert the given quadratic programming problem into an equivalent linear programming problem and find a solution using the simplex algorithm. The Lagrangean function and conditions are as follows:

(1) $$\phi = cx + x'Dx + \lambda[b - Ax]$$

(2) $$\left. \frac{\partial \phi}{\partial x} \right|_0 = c + 2x^{0\prime}D - \lambda^0 A \leq 0$$

(3) $$\left. \frac{\partial \phi}{\partial x} \right|_0 x^0 = cx^0 + 2x^{0\prime}Dx^0 - \lambda^0 Ax^0 = 0$$

(4) $$\left. \frac{\partial \phi}{\partial \lambda} \right|_0 = b - Ax^0 \geq 0$$

(5) $$\left. \frac{\partial \phi}{\partial \lambda} \right|_0 \lambda^0 = \lambda^0 b - \lambda^0 Ax^0 = 0$$

We now add slack variables $w = (w_1, \ldots, w_n) \geq 0$ and $v = (v_1, \ldots, v_m) \geq 0$ to convert (2) and (4) into (6) and (7), respectively:

(6) $$\lambda^0 A - 2x^{0\prime}D - wI = c$$

(7) $$Ax^0 + Iv' = b$$

Further, from Equations (3) and (5), at the maximum:

(8) $$x^0 w' = 0$$

and

(9) $$\lambda^0 v' = 0$$

Thus, using (6)–(9) an equivalent quadratic programming problem to the original is

$$\begin{aligned} \text{max:} \quad & -(xw' + \lambda v') \\ \text{subject to:} \quad & -wI + \lambda A - 2x'D = c \\ & Iv + Ax = b \end{aligned}$$

or, letting

$$\bar{q}' = (x', v, \lambda, w)$$
$$q' = (w, \lambda, v, x')$$

$$T = \begin{bmatrix} -I & A' & 0 & -2D' \\ 0 & 0 & I & A \end{bmatrix}$$

$$d = \begin{bmatrix} c' \\ b \end{bmatrix}$$

the problem becomes

$$\begin{aligned} \text{max:} &\quad -\tfrac{1}{2}\bar{q}'q \\ \text{subject to:} &\quad Tq = d \\ &\quad q \geq 0 \end{aligned}$$

Next, find any feasible value for q, say q^0, such that $Tq = d$, but not necessarily one where $-\tfrac{1}{2}\bar{q}'q = 0$, and define r_1 using the values of q^0. Now consider the following linear program:

$$\begin{aligned} \text{max:} &\quad -\tfrac{1}{2}r_1 q \\ \text{subject to:} &\quad Tq = d \\ &\quad q \geq 0 \end{aligned}$$

Solving this problem for q, say q_1, we can define another linear program by letting r_2 be defined from q_1 and then solve

$$\begin{aligned} \text{max:} &\quad -\tfrac{1}{2}r_2 q \\ \text{subject to:} &\quad Tq = d \\ &\quad q \geq 0 \end{aligned}$$

Since we know from Equations (8) and (9) that at the optimum $-\tfrac{1}{2}\bar{q}'q = 0$, the above iterative solving of linear programs can be terminated when max: $-\tfrac{1}{2}r_k q_k = 0$. This will be the solution to the original quadratic programming problem. For this method, developed by Frank and Wolfe (1956), it can be shown that the iterative solutions are such that $-\tfrac{1}{2}r_k q_k > -\tfrac{1}{2}r_{k-1} q_{k-1} > \ldots > -\tfrac{1}{2}r_1 q_1$ and that the procedure will converge ultimately to the optimal solution in a finite number of iterations.

Notice that the Frank and Wolfe method uses the fact that the Kuhn–Tucker conditions are necessary and sufficient for a solution. Thus, consider the following quadratic programming problem:

$$\begin{aligned} \text{max:} &\quad f(x) = cx + x'Dx \\ \text{subject to:} &\quad Ax = b \\ &\quad x \geq 0 \end{aligned}$$

Suppose that D is a positive definite matrix. By Theorem 12.4–2, $f(x) = cx + x'Dx$ is a convex function. Since convex functions are also quasi-concave functions, and given the set of linear constraints, it follows by the

Arrow–Enthoven generalizations (Theorem 11.3–3) that the Kuhn–Tucker conditions will be both necessary and sufficient.

Example 1.   As an illustration of solving a quadratic programming problem, consider the following:

$$\begin{aligned}
\text{max:} \quad & x_1 + x_2 - x_1 x_2 \\
\text{subject to:} \quad & 2x_1 + 4x_2 \le 10 \\
& 6x_1 + 2x_2 \le 12 \\
& x_1 \le 4 \\
& x_1, x_2 \ge 0
\end{aligned}$$

In vector notation, the problem is

$$\begin{aligned}
\text{max:} \quad & cx + x'Dx \\
\text{subject to:} \quad & Ax \le b \\
& x \ge 0
\end{aligned}$$

where

$$D = \begin{bmatrix} 0 & -\tfrac{1}{2} \\ -\tfrac{1}{2} & 0 \end{bmatrix}$$

The equivalent quadratic programming problem is

$$\begin{aligned}
\text{max:} \quad & -\tfrac{1}{2}\bar{q}'q \\
\text{subject to:} \quad & Tq = d \\
& q \ge 0
\end{aligned}$$

where

$$q' = (w_1, w_2, \lambda_1, \lambda_2, \lambda_3, v_1, v_2, v_3, x_1, x_2)$$
$$\bar{q}' = (x_1, x_2, v_1, v_2, v_3, \lambda_1, \lambda_2, \lambda_3, w_1, w_2)$$

$$T = \begin{bmatrix}
-1 & 0 & 2 & 6 & 1 & 0 & 0 & 0 & 0 & 1 \\
0 & -1 & 4 & 2 & 0 & 0 & 0 & 0 & 1 & 0 \\
0 & 0 & 0 & 0 & 0 & 1 & 0 & 0 & 2 & 4 \\
0 & 0 & 0 & 0 & 0 & 0 & 1 & 0 & 6 & 2 \\
0 & 0 & 0 & 0 & 0 & 0 & 0 & 1 & 1 & 0
\end{bmatrix}$$

$$d' = (1, 1, 10, 12, 4)$$

The initial feasible solution is easily found by letting the slack variables equal 10, 12, and 4, respectively, $\lambda_1 = 0.2$, $\lambda_2 = 0.1$, and all other variables set equal to zero. Thus

$$r_1 = (0, 0, 10, 12, 4, 0.2, 0.1, 0, 0, 0)$$

and the linear program to solve is

$$\begin{aligned}
\text{max:} \quad & -\tfrac{1}{2}r_1 q \\
\text{subject to:} \quad & Tq = d \\
& q \ge 0
\end{aligned}$$

This linear program is now solved for $q = q^*$ and then r_2 set by using q^* and the process repeated until $-\frac{1}{2}rq \simeq 0$. As one can see, from an initial 3×2 A matrix, we have a 5×10 T matrix and several iterations to perform, which is quite tedious to solve by hand.

The foregoing discussion illustrates the fact that finding a solution, finding a vector that satisfies known necessary and sufficient conditions, may be quite an arduous task. For a linear programming problem we have the simplex method. For a quadratic program the solution may be found by several iterations of the simplex, but how many depends upon the specific problem and it may be quite large. There are several other techniques[8] that have been developed for solving the quadratic programming problem just as there are methods other than the simplex for solving a linear program. However, no one particular technique for solving a quadratic programming problem appears to have such superiority over others as is the case with the simplex and linear programming problems.

Problems

12.4–1   Find the matrices c and D for the following objective functions for quadratic programming problems and determine whether or not D is negative semidefinite.
   (a) $x_1 + x_2 + 3x_1^2 + x_2^2 + 8x_1x_2$
   (b) $3x_1 + 6x_2^2 - 4x_1^2$
   (c) $3x_1 - 2x_2 + x_1x_2 - x_1^2 - x_2^2$
   (d) $x_1x_2 - x_1 - x_2$
   (e) $x_1 + 3x_2 - 2x_3 + x_1x_2 - x_1x_3 + x_2x_3 - x_1^2 - x_2^2$

12.4–2   For the linear programming problem used in the first step in Example 1 of this section to solve a quadratic problem, find r_2.

12.4–3   Given that the optimal solution to Example 1 of this section is $x_1 = 1$ and $x_2 = 1$ for the real variables, find:
   (a) the values for λ_1, λ_2, and λ_3;
   (b) the values for v_1, v_2, and v_3;
   (c) the values for w_1, and w_2; and
   (d) the value of $\bar{q}'q$ for these values.

12.5 INTEGER PROGRAMMING

In this section we review another special programming problem, the integer programming problem.

---

[8] See Hildreth (1957), Houthakker (1960), Lemke (1962), Wolfe (1959), Markowitz (1959), and Hadley (1964) for other methods of solving a quadratic programming problem.

DEFINITION 12.5–1 (a) An **integer programming problem** is a general mathematical programming problem where some or all of the variables are restricted to integer values.

(b) An **integer linear programming problem** is a nonlinear programming problem that would be a linear one if some or all of the variables were not restricted to integer values:

  (i) If all variables must be integers, it is an **all-integer linear programming problem**.

  (ii) If only a portion of the variables are limited to positive integers, it is termed a **mixed-integer problem.**

Since some variables are restricted to only integer values, this problem is very relevant to situations where economic goods come in lumps rather than in infinitely small bits. One may purchase one or two automobiles but the meaning of 1.6537 automobiles is questionable. A firm may purchase some whole number of computerized welding machines but $\frac{2}{3}$ of a machine does not exist. Also, the methods of solution for an integer programming problem are somewhat unique and interesting in and of themselves.

Of equal importance is that a method of solution for an integer programming problem would permit the solution of a variety of other problems as well. For example, a nonconvex feasible constraint set may be converted into, or at least approximated by, an integer programming problem. In Figure 12.5–1 we have two variables and a set of constraints that create the feasible set traced out by the points $0abcde$. This problem can be converted into a linear integer programming problem by adding another variable, x_3, which is restricted to a value of zero or one. The resulting feasible constraint set, if it were a linear programming problem, would be convex. Simply partition $0abcde$ into two rectangles $0abf$ and $0gde$, where $0gde$ is feasible if $x_3 = 0$ and $0abf$ is feasible if $x_3 = 1$ as illustrated in Figure 12.5–2.

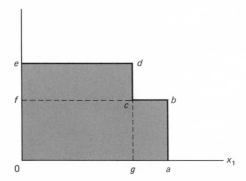

Figure 12.5–1 *Nonconvex constraint set.*

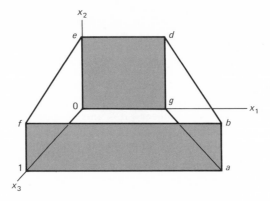

Figure 12.5–2   *Transforming a nonconvex constraint set into an integer linear program*

Methods of Solution

One possible method of solving an integer programming problem might seem to be to treat the problem as if it had no integer restrictions and rounding off to the nearest whole number. This sounds especially appealing since most mathematical and theoretical models are simplified approximations anyway. A cursory glance at Figure 12.5–3 will satisfy the reader that this will not, in general, provide the correct answer. With x_1 and x_2 required to take on only integer values and the constraint set $0abcde$, the optimum is $x^* = (3, 1)$. Solving the problem without the integer restrictions, $x^+ = (2.2, 2.7)$ is the optimum. Rounding off to the nearest integer values of x^+ we have $x' = (2, 3)$, which is not feasible. Rounding off x^+ to the nearest feasible x we have $x^0 = (2, 2)$, but clearly this is *not* the best solution. Not only does rounding off not work in general, but integer programming is a method of analysis utilized when the assumption of continuous variables is not sufficiently realistic to be useful.

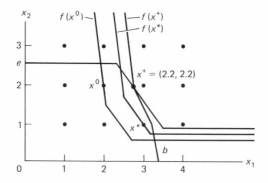

Figure 12.5–3   *An integer programming problem with x_1 and x_2 restricted to integral values and the feasible set $0abcde$.*

Gomory Algorithm

In the remainder of this section we shall summarize a method of solution developed by Gomory (1958, 1960a, 1960b, 1963) for integer linear programming problems. Formally, the problem is

$$\begin{aligned} \text{max:} \quad & cx \\ \text{subject to:} \quad & Ax = b \\ & x \geq 0 \end{aligned}$$

where x_j is an integer if $j \in J$, the set of indices for variables restricted to integer values.

First consider the case where $J = (1, \ldots, n)$; that is, we have an all-integer linear programming problem. Basically, the method of solution amounts to solving the linear programming problem without the integer restrictions and then "cutting" the feasible space, $Ax = b$, down until the correct integer optimum is attained. The Gomory method is a systematic method of introducing such "cuts" so as to converge to the optimal solution, if one exists, in a finite number of steps.

The initial step is to solve the linear program

$$\begin{aligned} \text{max:} \quad & cx \\ \text{subject to:} \quad & Ax = b \\ & x \geq 0 \end{aligned}$$

to obtain the solution (x_B, x_N), where x_B are the variables in the basis β, x_N those not in the basis. Letting $A = [B, N]$ we have

$$x_B = B^{-1}b - B^{-1}Nx_N$$

Then if we define

$$\begin{aligned} q_0 &= B^{-1}b \\ q_j &= B^{-1}a_j \end{aligned}$$

where $j \in \eta$, the index set of those variables not in the basic solution, then

$$x_B = q_0 - \sum_{j \in \eta} q_j x_j$$

or

$$x_{Bi} = q_{0i} - \sum_{j \in \eta} q_{ji} x_j$$

for $i \in \beta$, the index set of basic variables. For the solution x_B, three cases are possible:

(1) q_{0i} is an integer for all i;
(2) q_{0i} is not an integer for some $i \in \beta$ and q_{ji} is a noninteger for some $j \in \eta$;
(3) q_{0i} is not an integer value for any i and q_{ji} is an integer for all $j \in \eta$.

If (1) occurs the problem is solved. If (3) occurs the problem is not feasible. Thus (2) is the usual and most interesting case.

In case (2) we have some variables in the basic solution to the linear program that are not integers and therefore do not satisfy the full-integer program. This means that if $x_{Bi} = q_{0i} + \sum_{j \in \eta} q_{ji} x_j$ is to be an integer, some x_j for $j \in \eta$, will have to be positive (for the linear programming solution all $x_j = 0$ for $j \in \eta$). Furthermore, since x_j must also be an integer this means that $x_j \geq 1$. If we separate q_{0i} and q_{ij} into its integer and fractional components for an x_{Bi} not an integer we have

$$q_{0i} = k_{0i} + f_{0i}$$

where k_{0i} is an integer and $0 < f_{0i} < 1$, and

$$q_{ji} = k_{ji} + f_{ji}$$

where k_{ji} is an integer and $0 < f_{ji} < 1$. Then

$$x_{Bi} = k_{0i} + f_{0i} - \sum_{j \in \eta} (k_{ji} + f_{ji}) x_j$$

or

$$x_{Bi} = \left(k_{0i} - \sum_{j \in \eta} k_{ji} x_j \right) + \left(f_{0i} - \sum_{j \in \eta} f_{ji} x_j \right)$$

Since x_{Bi} must be an integer, it follows that

$$f_{0i} - \sum_{j \in \eta} f_{ji} x_j \leq 0$$

Therefore the Gomory method is to add another constraint. Let

$$s_i = -f_{0i} + \sum_{j \in \eta} f_{ji} x_j \geq 0$$

and add s_i to the linear programming problem as a slack variable (i.e., zero price in the objective function) and solve

$$\text{max:} \qquad cx$$

$$\text{subject to:} \qquad A^* \begin{bmatrix} x \\ s_i \end{bmatrix} = \begin{bmatrix} b \\ f_{0i} \end{bmatrix}$$

$$x \geq 0$$
$$s_i \geq 0$$

where A^* has one more column, the negative of the $n + 1$ unit vector, and one more row that is from the added constraint

$$\sum_{j \in \eta} f_{ji} x_j - s_i = f_{0i}$$

In other words, assuming that the last columns of A are not in the basis,

$$A^* \begin{bmatrix} x \\ s_i \end{bmatrix} = \begin{bmatrix} & & & 0 \\ & A & & \vdots \\ & & & 0 \\ 0 \cdots 0\, f_{m+1,i} \cdots f_{ni} & & -1 \end{bmatrix} \begin{bmatrix} x_1 \\ \vdots \\ x_n \\ s_i \end{bmatrix} = \begin{bmatrix} b_1 \\ \vdots \\ b_m \\ f_{0i} \end{bmatrix}$$

This additional constraint and slack variable, s_i, is a "cut" or a shrinkage of the feasible space $Ax = b$. With the additional slack variable, the solution to the linear program $Ax = b$ is not feasible; yet adding the row and column to the simplex tableau we shall have a basic solution. A new optimal solution is easily found by applying the dual simplex algorithm (cf. Section 12.1).

The method of solution now becomes one of iteration until the solution to one such linear program is such that all x_{Bi} are integers. The following example works through a simple integer linear programming problem.

Example 1. The Dust Bowl Air Service Corporation has (1) a fleet of two planes: a large plane, x_1, and a small plane, x_2; (2) seven service units: the large plane requires four per flight, the small plane, two; and (3) 15 man-hours to make a round trip flight per day: the large plane requires 3 hours for the trip, the small plane takes 10 hours. Each flight of the large plane generates $400 net revenue while the small plane brings in $100. If Dust Bowl Air Service wishes to maximize its net revenue, it is faced with an integer programming problem, since 0.75 of a round-trip flight would end somewhere in the nearby badlands. Consequently we have

$$\begin{aligned} \text{max:} \quad & 400x_1 + 100x_2 \\ \text{subject to:} \quad & 4x_1 + 2x_2 \le 7 \\ & 3x_1 + 10x_2 \le 15 \\ & x_1, x_2 \ge 0 \\ & x_1 \text{ and } x_2 \text{ are integers} \end{aligned}$$

Disregarding the integer restrictions the feasible space $0abc$ is shown in Figure 12.5–4. The initial solution is at point a for the problem

$$\begin{aligned} \text{max:} \quad & cx \\ \text{subject to:} \quad & Ax = b \\ & x \ge 0 \end{aligned}$$

where $x = (x_1, x_2, x_3, x_4)$; and x_3 and x_4 are slack variables.

Since 1.75 flights by the large plane does not satisfy the integer constraint, the following slack variable and restriction is added:

$$0x_1 - \tfrac{1}{2}x_2 - \tfrac{3}{4}x_3 + 0x_4 + 1s_1 = -\tfrac{3}{4}$$

where x_1 and x_4 are in the basic solution. This is the first Gomory cut. This iteration process is continued (in this case four slack variables were added

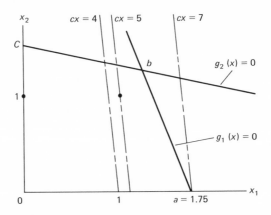

Figure 12.5–4 *Integer programming problem feasible space.*

and a total of five linear programs solved) until all x satisfy the integer requirements, the optimal solution occurs at $(x_1, x_2) = (1, 1)$, which is not the rounded-off solution to the initial linear program.

The solution to each successive linear program is found quite easily by using the dual simplex algorithm.[9] By adding the slack variable row to the simplex tableau of the solution to a linear programming problem, we shall have a basic but nonfeasible solution. It usually requires very few iterations (often only one) of the dual simplex algorithm to move from a basic non-feasible solution to a basic feasible solution that is also the optimal solution.

A similar Gomory algorithm is available for the mixed-integer linear programming problem that also can be shown to converge to the optimum in a finite number of steps. Also, other methods of solution for integer programs have been developed but none appear to have a significant advantage over the others.

Problems

12.5–1   State the following problem in integer programming form and identify each matrix and vector.

The objective of Broken Barge Co. is to maximize revenue with the given personnel and equipment, *viz.*, three barges, which can hold 400 tons, 500 tons, and 700 tons, respectively; 15 day laborers; three supervisory personnel; and four cranes. All trips down the river and back must be completed in 1 week. Time required for each barge trip is 2 days, 3 days, and 4 days, respectively. Day laborers required on each boat per trip are 5, 6, and 7, respectively. Each boat trip requires the full time of one of the supervisors. Each boat requires 1 crane-day per 100 tons of bulk loaded. The fare is $1 per ton moved down the river.

[9] See Section 12.1.

12.5–2   Solve Problem 12.5–1 for the optimum as if there were no integer restrictions on the number of boat trips per week. If the solution is all integers the problem is solved; if not, state the first cut using the Gomory method.

12.5–3   Use the dual simplex algorithm to solve Problem 12.5–2.

12.5–4   Use the simplex and dual simplex algorithms to verify the solution to the problem given in Example 1 of this section.

12.5–5   What is the optimal solution for Problem 12.5–1?

12.6   PARAMETRIC PROGRAMMING AND OTHER SENSITIVITY ANALYSES FOR PROGRAMMING PROBLEMS

In this section we take up the topic of parametric programming and other methods of analyzing the sensitivity of a solution to a programming problem. This topic, sensitivity analysis, is analogous to the questions of stability and comparative static analysis that were raised in Chapter 9. Here we are interested in questions such as: What is the difference in the optimal vector of variables and the value of the objective function if the parameters of the programming problem are varied slightly? How sensitive is the objective function to small variations in the variables in a neighborhood of the optimal solution? Given that our parameters and measures of variables are subject to error, what is the variance of alternative solutions to a programming problem? The answers to these and similar questions are quite useful in empirical applications as the parameters change over time and since our models are only an approximation to the real world.

Parametric Programming

Parametric programming is a comparative static analysis. The typical question is what happens to the optimal solution and/or dual variables if there is a change in some parameter in the model. For discussion purposes we shall limit the analysis of parametric programming to a standard linear programming problem.

For the linear programming problem,

$$
\text{(1)} \qquad
\begin{aligned}
\text{max:} \quad & px \\
\text{subject to:} \quad & Ax = b \\
& x \geq 0
\end{aligned}
$$

the parameters of the system of equations are the vectors p and b and the matrix A, and the possible parametric variations are δp, δb, and δA.[10]

First let us consider changes in the resource vector: $\delta b > 0$. This is very common in many linear programming problems. For example, what will

---

[10] δp, etc., is used here rather than dp, etc., because the variations are not infinitesimal.

happen to the value of the objective function with a change in some resource; that is, what is the marginal revenue product of a resource?

If x_B is the optimal basic solution for the linear program (1) then we have

$$Bx_B + Nx_N = b$$

where A is partitioned into $[B, N]$, or $x_B = B^{-1}b - B^{-1}Nx_N$.

From Theorem 12.1–3 and the discussion of the simplex method, x_B is the optimal basic feasible solution when

$$z_N = p_N - p_B B^{-1}N \leq 0$$

or

$$z_i = p_i - \sum_{k=1}^{m} p_{Bk}\tau_{ki} \leq 0 \quad \text{where } [B^{-1}N, B^{-1}B] = [\tau_{ij}]$$

Since this optimality criterion is not a function of b we have the following theorem.

Theorem 12.6–1 For a variational change in the resource vector b, $b + \delta b$, the variables in optimal basis x_B will remain in the new optimal basis, x_B^*, if and only if $x_B^* = B^{-1}(b + \delta b) \geq 0$. Furthermore, the change in the levels of those variables in the optimal solutions is given by

$$\delta x_B = x_B^* - x_B = B^{-1}\delta b$$

If the nonnegativity constraints for $\delta b_i > 0$ are violated, that is, if some $x_{Bj}^* < 0$, then some new variable will enter the basis and the slack variable for the ith resource will leave the basis. That resource will no longer impose a constraint on the optimal solution. In either case, the value of the objective function will increase. If the variables in the basis are unaltered, then

$$\delta z = z^* - z = p_B \delta x_B = p_B B^{-1} \delta b > 0$$

otherwise,

$$\delta z = z^* - z = p_B^* x_B^* - p_B x_B > 0 \quad B^* \neq B$$

For a change in the resource vector the shadow prices will change only if the variables in the basis change. In other words, if $x_B^* = B^{-1}(b + \delta b) \geq 0$, then $\delta y_B = 0$, where y_B are Lagrangean multipliers for the linear programming problem that are greater than zero.

For the initial optimal solution x_B, let b_B be the effective constraints[11] and let b_N be the noneffective constraints. Clearly, if $\delta b_N > 0$ then $\delta b_B = 0$ and $\delta y = 0$.

----

[11] Those constraints that hold with strict equality.

Suppose that $\delta b_{Bi} > 0$ and $\delta b_{Bj \neq i} = \delta b_N = 0$. Then if we let $\bar{z}$, $\bar{B}$, and $\bar{N}$ be analogous to z, B, and N from the simplex tableau of the *dual*, the optimality criterion for y_B will be

$$\bar{z}_N^* = -b_N + (b_B + \delta b_B)\bar{B}'^{-1}\bar{N}'$$

If $\bar{z}_N^* \leq 0$, that is, if the same y_B are in the basis of the dual problem, then it follows that $\delta y_B = 0$.

Further, if the constraints are normalized so that $b_i = 1$ for all i, then for $\delta b_i > 0$ and $\delta b_j = 0$, for $j \neq i$, it follows that

$$\delta y_{Bi} = \frac{\delta z}{\delta b_i} - y_{Bi} \leq 0$$

and if $\delta y_{Bi} < 0$, then $\delta x_{N_k} > 0$ for some $k \in \eta$.

This effect on the Lagrangean multipliers, or shadow prices, of the resources is illustrated in Figure 12.6–1. For two resources and three x_i, suppose that the initial solution is at (1); then x_2 and x_3 will be produced while $x_1 = 0$. Given a sufficient change in resource 1, $\delta b_1 > 0$, the optimal y's in the dual change from y_1 and y_2 to y_1^* and y_2^* and the solution moves from (1) to (2) in Figure 12.6–1. At (2), $x_3^* = 0$ where x_2^* and x_1^* are positive.

Change in $p = p + \delta p$, $\delta p > 0$

A change in the prices of the objective function will induce a change in the variables in the basis only if a nonbasic variable's opportunity price z_i changes. If $\delta p_N > 0$, $\delta p_B = 0$, and

$$z_N^* = p_N + \delta p_N - p_B B^{-1} N \leq 0$$

then there is no change in β, the index of variables in the basis and $z = z^*$.

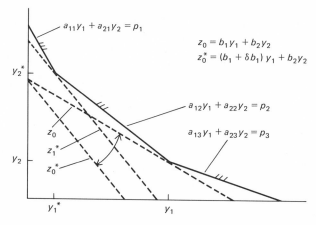

Figure 12.6–1   *Dual feasible space and change in y_B due to δb.*

If $\delta p_B > 0$, $\delta p_N = 0$, and $z_N^* \leq 0$, then there will be no change in the optimum levels of the basic variables, $\delta x_B = 0$, but there will be an increase in the optimum value of the objective function, that is, $\delta z > 0$.

If a basic variable's price changes, $\delta p_{Bi} > 0$ such that

$$z_N^* = p_N - (p_B + \delta p_B)B^{-1}N > 0$$

then the objective function can be increased by a change in the basic variables. The new variable to enter could be a real variable or a slack variable that would permit an increased level for x_{Bi}. In either case, $\delta x_{Bi} > 0$ and $\delta z > 0$.

The effect on the shadow prices or dual variables will depend upon the effect of δp on the optimality criterion. That is, if $z_N^* \leq 0$, so that $\beta = \beta^*$, $\delta yb = \delta p_B x_B$. If there is a change in the Lagrangean multipliers with zero values, some new variable (real or slack) must enter the basis. Of course, the effect of δp on y is analogous to the effect of δb on x.

Change in technological coefficient, $a_{ij} = a_{ij} + \delta a_{ij}$

First let us consider the effect of δa_{ij} on the optimality criterion, z_N:

$$z_N = p_N - p_B B^{-1}N \leq 0$$

Suppose that $j \in \eta$ for δa_{ij}. Then letting the columns of $N = (a_k, \ldots, a_j, \ldots, a_g)$ we have that

$$z_{j \in \eta} = p_j - p_B B^{-1}a_j$$

or

$$z_{j \in \eta}^* = p_j - p_B B^{-1}(a_j + \delta a_j)$$

$$= p_j - p_B B^{-1}a_j - p_B B^{-1}(0, \ldots, \delta a_{ji}, \ldots, 0)$$

Letting b_j^{-1} be the jth column of B^{-1}, that is, $B^{-1} = (b_1^{-1}, \ldots, b_m^{-1})$,

$$\delta z_{j \in \eta} = -p_B b_i^{-1} \delta a_{ij}$$

For there to be any effect on β, $z_{j \in \eta}$ must be greater than zero. If $\delta z_{j \in \eta} < -z_{j \in \eta}$, then $\delta x_B = 0$, and $\beta = \beta^*$. If $\delta z_{j \in \eta} > -z_{j \in \eta}$, then $\delta x_B \neq 0$, and $\beta \neq \beta^*$. Some variable must leave the basis and a new variable enter for the optimal solution.

If there is a change in a_{ij} for a variable in the basis, $j \in \beta$, then there may or may not be a change in the basis variables. It will depend upon the effects on z_N due to a change in B^{-1}. In Figure 12.6–2 part (a) shows a change in technology affecting only the levels of the basic variables, but not the variables in the basis, while in part (b), x_2 leaves the basis and is replaced by a slack variable.

Table 12.6–1 summarizes the results of parametric programming.

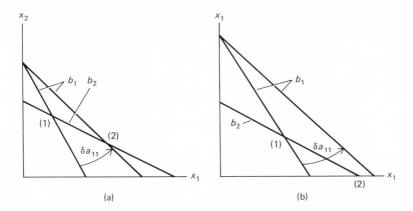

Figure 12.6–2 *A change in technology in* (*a*) *moves optimum from* (*1*) *to* (*2*);
in (*b*) *the slack variable for* b_1 *enters the basis and optimum moves from* (*1*)
to (*2*).

Example 1. In Example 1 of Section 12.1, we solved the following linear
programming problem:

$$\text{max:} \quad x_1 + 1.5x_2$$

subject to:

$$\begin{bmatrix} 25 & 50 & 1 & 0 & 0 & 0 \\ 20 & 40 & 0 & 1 & 0 & 0 \\ 25 & 0 & 0 & 0 & 1 & 0 \\ 20 & 10 & 0 & 0 & 0 & 1 \end{bmatrix} \begin{bmatrix} x_1 \\ x_2 \\ x_3 \\ x_4 \\ x_5 \\ x_6 \end{bmatrix} = \begin{bmatrix} 100{,}000 \\ 200{,}000 \\ 75{,}000 \\ 160{,}000 \end{bmatrix}$$

and found the solution for the real variables to be $x_1 = 3000$ and $x_2 = 500$.
Since resources 1 and 3 are used to capacity at the optimum,

$$B = \begin{bmatrix} 25 & 50 & 0 & 0 \\ 20 & 40 & 1 & 0 \\ 25 & 0 & 0 & 0 \\ 20 & 10 & 0 & 1 \end{bmatrix} \quad \text{and} \quad B^{-1} = \begin{bmatrix} 0 & 0 & 0.04 & 0 \\ 0.02 & 0 & -0.02 & 0 \\ -0.8 & 1 & 0 & 0 \\ -0.2 & 0 & -0.6 & 1 \end{bmatrix}$$

where $\beta = \{1, 2, 4, 6\}$.

Suppose that resource 1 increases from 100,000 units to 200,000. Is the
original basis still the optimal basis? Multiplying B^{-1} by $(b + \delta b)$ we find
that

$$\begin{bmatrix} x_1^* \\ x_2^* \\ x_4^* \\ x_6^* \end{bmatrix} = \begin{bmatrix} 3000 \\ 2500 \\ 40{,}000 \\ 75{,}000 \end{bmatrix} \geq 0$$

Table 12.6–1 Summary of the Results of Parametric Programming

	I	II	III
When: Change in:	$b^* = b + \delta b,\ \delta b > 0$ and (a) $x_B^* = B^{-1}(b + \delta b) \geq 0$ (b) $x_B^* < 0$	$p^* = p + \delta p,\ \delta p > 0$ and (a) $\delta p_N > 0,\ \delta p_B = 0$ (b) $\delta p_B > 0,\ \delta p_N = 0$	$a_{ij}^* = a_{ij} + \delta a_{ij}$ and (a) for $j \in \eta$ (b) for $j \in \beta$
Basis variables: β = index of old basis variables β^* = new basis variables η = old index of variables not in the basis η^* = new index of nonbasic variables	(a) $\beta = \beta^*$ (b) $\beta \neq \beta^*$	(a) if $z_N^* = p_N + \delta p_N - p_B B^{-1} N \leq 0$, then $\beta = \beta^*$; if $z_{N_i}^* > 0$, for some $i \in \eta$, then $\beta \neq \beta^*$ (b) if $z_N^* \leq 0$, then $\beta = \beta^*$; if $z_N^* > 0$, then $\beta \neq \beta^*$	(a) if $z_j^* = p_j - p_B b_i^{-1} \delta a_{ij} \leq 0$ then $\beta = \beta^*$ (b) if $z_N^* = p_N - p_B B^{*-1} N \leq 0$, then $\beta = \beta^*$
Variables: δx_B = a basic variable δx_N = nonbasic variables	(a) $\delta x_B = B^{-1}\,\delta b$ $\delta x_N = 0$ (b) $\delta x_B \neq 0$ $\delta x_N \neq 0$	(a) if $z_N^* \leq 0,\ \delta x_B = 0$ (b) if $z_N^* \leq 0,\ \delta x_B = 0$ if $z_N^* > 0,\ \delta x_{Bi} = -x_{Bi}$ for some i	(a) if $z_{j\in\eta}^* \leq 0,\ \delta x_B = 0$; if $z_{j\in\eta}^* > 0,\ \delta x_{Bi} = -x_{Bi}$ for some i (b) if $z_N^* \leq 0,\ \delta x_B = 0$ and $\delta x_N = 0$; if $z_N^* > 0,\ \delta x_{Bi} \neq 0$ and $\delta x_N \neq 0$

Table 12.6–1 (continued)

	I	II	III
Objective function:			
δz	(a) $\delta z = p_B B^{-1} \delta b$ (b) $\delta z \neq 0$	(a) if $z_N^* \leq 0$, then $\delta z = 0$; if $z_N^* > 0$, then $\delta z > 0$ (b) $\delta z > 0$	(a) if $z_j^* \leq 0$, then $\delta z = 0$; if $z_j^* > 0$, then $\delta z \neq 0$ (b) $\delta z \neq 0$
Dual variables:			
δy	(a) $\delta y = 0$ (b) if $\bar{z}_N^* \leq 0$; then $\delta y = 0$; if $\bar{z}_N^* > 0$, then $\delta y \neq 0$	(a) if $z_N^* \leq 0$, then $\delta y = 0$; if $z_N^* > 0$, then $\delta y_B = \bar{B}^{-1} \delta p$, if also $y_B^* \geq 0$ (b) if $z_N^* \leq 0$, then $\delta y_B b = \delta p_B x_B$ if $z_N^* > 0$, then $\delta y_B = \bar{B}^{-1} \delta p$ if also $y^* \geq 0$	(a) if $z_j^* \leq 0$, then $\delta y = 0$; if $z_j^* > 0$, then $\delta y \neq 0$ (b) $\delta y \neq 0$

and thus the answer is yes with the new optimum level of the real variables at $x_1^* = 3000$ and $x_2^* = 2500$. The slack variables x_4 and x_6 decrease in value, the slack variables x_3 and x_5 remain at zero, and the objective function increases by $3000 = p_B B^{-1} \delta b$.

Suppose that one of the basic variable's price changes; for example, $p_B^* = (1, 3, 0, 0) = p_B + \delta p_B$. To see what effect this has on the original optimal solution, we first calculate

$$z_N^* = p_N - (p_B + \delta p_B) B^{-1} N$$

$$= [0, 0] - [1, 3, 0, 0] \begin{bmatrix} 2 & 0 & 0.04 & 0 \\ 0.02 & 0 & -0.02 & 0 \\ -0.8 & 1 & 0 & 0 \\ -0.2 & 0 & -0.6 & 1 \end{bmatrix} \begin{bmatrix} 1 & 0 \\ 0 & 0 \\ 0 & 1 \\ 0 & 0 \end{bmatrix}$$

$$= [0, 0] - [0.06, -0.02] = [-0.06, 0.02]$$

Since $z_5^* = 0.02 > 0$, there will be a change in the variables in the basis and the level of those in the basis. As it turns out here, the new solution for the real variables is $x_1^* = 0$ and $x_2^* = 2000$ with the objective function at $z^* = 6000$. That is, the price change has caused x_2 to be its maximum possible value.

Perturbation Analysis

Perturbation analysis is basically similar to parametric programming, the difference being that parametric programming conclusions can be solved numerically from B^{-1} or the simplex tableau, while perturbation analysis is interested in qualitative results. In other words, the usual question in perturbation analysis is "Under what conditions can the parameters be perturbed without affecting the choice of the optimal basis?"

As one would expect, the results of the two approaches are similar as well. Suppose that for a linear programming problem

$$\begin{array}{lll} & \text{max:} & px \\ (1) & \text{subject to:} & Ax \le b \\ & & x \ge 0 \end{array}$$

(x^*, y^*) is the optimal solution to the linear programming problem and its dual. (x^*, y^*) fulfill the saddle-point function $\phi(x, y)$; that is,

$$\phi(x^*, y^*) = \max_x \phi(x, y^*) = \min_y \phi(x^*, y)$$

If the parameters of (1) are perturbed so that A goes to $A + \delta A$, b goes to $b + \delta b$, and p goes to $p + \delta p$ then if $(x^* + \delta x^*, y^* + \delta y^*)$ is the new solution to the perturbed problem and $\phi_\delta(x, y)$ is the saddle-point function for the perturbed problem, we have

$$\phi_\delta(x^* + \delta x^*, y^* + \delta y^*) = \max_x \phi_\delta(x, y^* + \delta y^*) = \min_y \phi_\delta(x^* + \delta x^*, y)$$

It therefore follows that

(1) $\phi(x^*, y^*) - \phi(x^* + \delta x^*, y^*) \geq 0$ and $-p\,\delta x^* + y^*A\,\delta x \geq 0$;

(2) $\phi(x^*, y^*) - \phi(x^*, y^* + \delta y^*) \leq 0$ and $\delta y^*b - \delta y^*Ax^* \geq 0$;

(3) $\phi_\delta(x^* + \delta x^*, y^* + \delta y^*) - \phi_\delta(x^*, y^* + \delta y^*) \geq 0$ and
$(p + \delta p)x^* - y^*(A + \delta A)\,\delta x^* - \delta y^*(A + \delta A)\,\delta x^* \geq 0$;

(4) $\phi_\delta(x^* + \delta x^*, y^* + \delta y^*) - \phi_\delta(x^* + \delta x^*, y^*) \leq 0$ and
$-\delta y^*(b + \delta b) + \delta y^*(A + \delta A)x^* + \delta y^*(A + \delta A)\,\delta x^* \geq 0$.

Combining $(1) + (2) + (3) + (4)$, we have

$$\delta p\,\delta x^* - y^*\,\delta A\,\delta x^* - \delta y^*\,\delta b + \delta y^*\,\delta Ax^* \geq 0$$

Now this implies that

(5) if δA and $\delta b = 0$, then $\delta p\,\delta x^* \geq 0$;

(6) if δp and $\delta A = 0$, then $\delta y^*\,\delta b \leq 0$;

(7) if $\delta A = 0$, then $\delta p\,\delta x^* \geq \delta y^*\,\delta b$; and

(8) if δp and $\delta b = 0$, then $\delta y^*\,\delta Ax^* - y^*\,\delta A\,\delta x^* \geq 0$, or if, in particular, $\delta a_{ij} < 0$ and $\delta a_{hk} = 0$, for all $h, k \neq i, j$, then $\delta y_i^*\,\delta a_{ij}\,x_j^* - y_i^*$ $\delta a_{ij}\,\delta x_j^* \geq 0$ or $\delta y_i^*/y_i^* \leq \delta x_j^*/x_j^*$.

Conclusions (5)–(8) are conformable to the results in Table 12.6–1, but perhaps (5)–(8) are easier to interpret in economic terms. (5) says that the change in an optimal basis variable will be in the same direction as its price. Likewise, in (6) the dual variable will vary in opposite direction of its parameter.

(7) states that the variation in x times the variation in price is greater than or equal to the variation in the dual vector times δb. (7) is also a combination of (5) and (6). For $\delta a_{ij} < 0$ in (8), this means that a technological change for x_j and resource b_i will change the optimal basis variable x_j in a greater percentage than the corresponding percentage change in the dual price y_i^*.

The obvious extension of the foregoing sensitivity analyses is to specify some probability function for $(\delta A, \delta b, \delta p)$ and to answer such questions as the variance of the optimal basis and objective function with respect to the probability distribution for $(\delta A, \delta b, \delta p)$. This general area of **reliability programming** (including chance constrained programming and stochastic programming), has come under increasing investigation in recent years. For further information the reader is referred to the selected references.

Problems

12.6–1 Find the following for Example 1 in this section.

(a) What is the maximum positive variation in resource 1 without causing a change in $\beta =$ index of basis variables? Resource 2?

(b) What is the maximum increase in p_2 that would leave both x_1 and x_2 in the basis at a positive level?

(c) What will be the effect of a 25% increase in both p_1 and p_2?

(d) What will be the effect if x_1 requires less of resource 1 per unit, from 25 to 20 (i.e., $a_{11}^* = a_{11} + \delta a_{11} = 25 - 5$ and $a_{ij}^* = a_{ij}$ for all other i and j)? If $a_{41}^* = 10$, $a_{ij}^* = a_{ij}$ for $ij \neq 41$?

12.6–2 For the linear programming problem (Problem 12.1–2):

max: $x_1 + 2x_2 + 3x_3$

subject to:
$$\begin{bmatrix} 10 & 5 & 1 \\ 6 & 9 & 3 \\ 4 & 2 & 6 \end{bmatrix}\begin{bmatrix} x_1 \\ x_2 \\ x_3 \end{bmatrix} \leq \begin{bmatrix} 100 \\ 90 \\ 84 \end{bmatrix}$$

$$x_i \geq 0, i = 1, 2, 3$$

What is the effect of the following parametric changes?

(a) $b + \delta b = (120, 90, 84)$ (d) $p + \delta p = (2, 2, 3)$
(b) $b + \delta b = (80, 100, 96)$ (e) $p + \delta p = (1, 4, 1)$
(c) $p + \delta p = (1.5, 3, 4.5)$

12.6–3 The relation between capital and labor in a small country is linear and fixed for each of six possible exports as follows:

$$x_1 + x_2 + x_3 + 4x_4 + 10x_5 + 3x_6 \leq K$$
$$15x_1 + 5x_2 + 2x_3 + 3x_4 + 4x_5 + 0.5x_6 \leq L$$

(a) If the world prices are 1, 2, 3, 1, 0.5, and 2, respectively for the six products and if $K = 7000$, $L = 20,000$, what products should be produced to maximize revenue?

(b) What will be the imputed price of capital and the price of labor (i.e., the dual variables y_K and y_L)?

(c) If the capital stock doubles, what will be the products produced? What will happen to the prices of capital and labor?

(d) If the capital stock increases to 100,000 and the labor force increases to 30,000, what products will be produced? What will happen to the price of capital and labor?

(e) If p_6 changes from 2 to 3, what will be the effect on both commodities produced and the shadow prices of capital and labor?

12.6–4 If the optimal solution for a linear programming problem and its dual varies from (x^*, y^*) to $(x^* + \delta x^*, y^* + \delta y^*)$ by perturbing the parameters A, b, and p, explain why:

(a) $-p\,\delta x^* + y^*A\,\delta x^* \geq 0$
(b) $\phi(x^*, y^*) - \phi(x^*, y^* + \delta y^*) \leq 0$
(c) $\delta y^*b - \delta y^*Ax^* \geq 0$
(d) $\phi_\delta(x^* + \delta x^*, y^* + \delta y^*) - \phi_\delta(x^*, y^* + \delta y^*) \geq 0$
(e) $(p + \delta p)\delta x^* - y^*(A + \delta A)\delta x^* - \delta y^*(A + \delta A)\delta x^* \geq 0$
(f) $\phi_\delta(x^* + \delta x^*, y^* + \delta y^*) - \phi_\delta(x^* + \delta x^*, y^*) \leq 0$
(g) $-\delta y^*(b + \delta b) + \delta y^*(A + \delta A)x^* + \delta y^*(A + \delta A)\delta x^* \geq 0$

12.6–5 Provide the qualitative answers available from perturbation analysis for the following:

(a) There is an increase in technology for producing x_1 in that x_1 requires less of every resource than before.

(b) There is an increase in the price of one variable that is not in the optimal basic solution.

(c) The quantity of two resources that were fully utilized increases.

(d) The price of one basic variable decreases and the price of another non-basic variable increases.

(e) Two resources decline and the prices of two variables decrease.

References

1. ARROW, K. J., L. HURWICZ, and H. UZAWA, (1958), *Studies in Linear and Nonlinear Programming*, Stanford, Calif.: Stanford University Press.

2. BELLMAN, RICHARD (1957), *Dynamic Programming*, Princeton, N.J.: Princeton University Press.

3. BELLMAN, RICHARD, and S. DREYFUS (1963), *Applied Dynamic Programming*, Princeton, N.J.: Princeton University Press.

4. CHARNES, A., and W. W. COOPER (1961), *Management Models and Industrial Applications of Linear Programming*, New York: Wiley.

5. DANTZIG, G. B. (1960), "On the Significance of Solving Linear Programming Problems with Some Integer Variables," *Econometrica*, **28**:30–44.

6. DORN, W. S. (1963), "Non-Linear Programming—A Survey," *Management Science*, **9**:171–208.

7. FRANK, M., and P. WOLFE (1956), "An Algorithm for Quadratic Programming," *Naval Research Logistics Quarterly*, **3**:95–110.

8. GOMORY, R. E. (1958), "Outline of an Algorithm for Integer Solutions to Linear Programs," *Bulletin of the American Mathematical Society*, **64**:275–278.

9. GOMORY, R. E. (1960a), "All Integer Programming Algorithm," *IBM Research Center, Research Report RC-189*.

10. GOMORY, R. E. (1960b), "An Algorithm for the Mixed Integer Problem," P-1885, The RAND Corp.

11. GOMORY, R. E. (1963), "An Algorithm for Integer Solutions to Linear Programs," in R. Graves and P. Wolfe (eds.), *Recent Advances in Mathematical Programming*, New York: McGraw-Hill.

12. HADLEY, G. (1964), *Nonlinear and Dynamic Programming*, Reading, Mass.: Addison-Wesley.

13. HILDRETH, C. (1957), "A Quadratic Programming Procedure," *Naval Research Logistics Quarterly*, **14**:79–85.

14. HOUTHAKKER, H. S. (1960), "The Capacity Method of Quadratic Programming," *Econometrica*, **28**:62–87.

15. LEMKE, C. E. (1962), "A Method of Solution of Quadratic Problems," *Management Science*, **8**:442–453.
16. MARKOWITZ, H. (1959), *Portfolio Selection*, New York: Wiley.
17. SENGUPTA, JATI K. (1965), "On the Sensitivity of Optimal Solution under Investment Planning and Programming," *Atlanities*, **8**:1–23.
18. SENGUPTA, JATI K. (1966), "The Stability of Truncated Solutions of Stochastic Linear Programming," *Econometrica* **34**:77–104.
19. SENGUPTA JATI K., and KARL FOX (1969), *Optimization Techniques in Quantitative Economic Models*, Amsterdam: North Holland.
20. SENGUPTA, JATI K., and T. K. KUMAR (1965), "An Application of Sensitivity Analysis to a Linear Programming Problem," *Unternehmungsforschung*, **9**:18–36.
21. VAJDA, S. (1961), *Mathematical Programming*, Reading, Mass.: Addison-Wesley.
22. WOLFE, FRANK (1959), "The Simplex Method for Quadratic Programming," *Econometrica*, **27**:382–398.

Chapter 13

Game Theory

13.1 CONCEPTS AND SCOPE OF GAME THEORY

Game theory is a maximization (minimization) problem where the outcome depends not only on the variables selected by one decision maker, but on the variables selected by one or more other decision makers as well. For example, the payoff to one individual who is matching pennies depends not only on whether he selects heads or tails but also on what the other player selects. The profit of General Motors depends explicitly upon the production, advertising, model changes, and so forth of Ford, Chrysler, American Motors, and various foreign automobile producers. The income of a farmer depends upon which crops he plants and fertilizers he uses but also upon the weather conditions (flood, drought, wind, hail, early snow, etc.). Thus the problem of maximization must include some analysis of what other decision makers will do. What is the best a player can receive if others are inimical to him (i.e., what is the best of a bad lot)? What is the "best" solution for all players?

The fact that decision makers' interactions determine the solution and each must make some estimate of what the opposing player(s) will do gives rise to the term **game theory**. The first definitive statement of game theory was by John von Neumann and Oskar Morgenstern (1947) in *The Theory of Games and Economic Behavior*. Although the concepts of strategy and payoff had been used prior to this time, von Neumann and Morgenstern's work was hailed as a landmark in economic theory. Its instant success and acceptance was accompanied by a plethora of articles and books on the subject. However, after a quarter of a century the applications of game theory have proved disappointing. It has not been the panacea for decision making and economic theory that it had promised to be. Still, the conceptual framework is useful for stating particular problems and their insolvability. In addition, it is possible that future research will rectify some of its current ills.

The simplest kind of a game, the two-person, constant-sum game, will be discussed in Section 13.2. The two-person, constant-sum game provides a concrete strategy and a determinant solution. This, of course, was the source of the original high expectations, but the process of generalization has not managed to maintain the attributes of the two-person, constant-sum game.

As was noted in Chapter 11, mathematical programming theory and game theory both originated at the end of World War II, were new techniques for solving maximization problems, and offered much for specific problems. Mathematical programming has contributed most, and in 1951 a correspondence between game theory and linear programming was demonstrated.[1] Both mathematical programming and some of the more recent developments in game theory (e.g., differential games, discussed in Section 13.5) appear to be heading toward the more general concepts of control theory, which is the subject of Chapter 14. In the next section we shall discuss the two-person, constant-sum game and its relation to linear programming. In Sections 13.3 and 13.4 we shall discuss some attempts to generalize the two-person game and the indeterminacy resulting therefrom.

13.2   TWO-PERSON, CONSTANT-SUM GAMES

The simplest kind of game is one in which there are two opposing players with a finite set of strategies and the total amount to be won or lost is constant. The first reason why this is the simplest is because the optimal decision by one player depends only on the actions of one other player. Second, since the total payoff is a constant, no collusion or cooperation is beneficial. This allows one to calculate what the other player will do if he plays optimally and is well informed.

We now state some definitions formally.

DEFINITION 13.2–1   An *n*-**person game** is a situation where *n* persons make decisions; that is, *n* decision makers select some alternative or strategy from their given choice sets, and the outcome or payoff to each player is dependent upon the selections of each player.

DEFINITION 13.2–2   A **constant-sum game** is a game in which the total payoff to be divided among players is invariant; that is, it does not depend upon the mix of strategies selected. If the constant is zero, it is a **zero sum game.**

DEFINITION 13.2–3   A **static game** is a game where each player may select one and only one element from a set of possible choices and the game then terminates.

DEFINITION 13.2–4   A **comparative static game** is a game where each player takes turns in selecting a strategy from his choice set (i.e., the strategy

---

[1] See Koopmans (1951), Chapters 19, 20, and 22.

choice alternatives for each player) and no time period between strategy changes is defined. The payoff to each player is the final equilibrium payoff, if one exists.

DEFINITION 13.2–5   A **dynamic game** is a game where the time interval between possible strategy selections is specified. If it is zero, that is, if strategies are continuously variable, then it is a **differential game.** The payoff in a dynamic game is the total payoffs over time and the end of the game is specified.

DEFINITION 13.2–6   A game with **pure strategies** is one where the choice set is finite. A game with **mixed strategies** is one where the choice set is infinite in that a player may choose any linear combination of his strategies.

The Two-Person, Constant-Sum Game with Pure Strategies

First we shall consider the case where only a finite choice set exists for each of two players. For example, in chess each player can move one of 10 pieces on his first move, but he cannot move a pawn part of a square and a knight $1\frac{2}{3}$ of a square. If there were two firms in a market and the choice set open to each was advertising, product change, and a midnight sale, then, under pure strategies, each firm would have to choose one of the three. They could not partially advertise and have a minor product change.

For a two-person, pure-strategy game with a constant sum, if player A has n strategies and player B has m strategies, there are mn possible outcomes for each player. These are arranged in the payoff matrix shown in Figure 13.2–1. The value a_{ij} is the payoff to A if A plays his ith strategy and B plays his jth strategy. Since there is a constant sum, C, the payoff to B corresponding to a_{ij} is $C - a_{ij}$.

First let us assume that we have a static game and that A must play first. Further, we shall assume that A and B have perfect knowledge as to what the various payoffs are and that both wish to maximize their respective payoffs. This means that B wants to minimize A's payoff and vice versa. Consequently, A knows exactly what B will do once A selects a strategy. B will

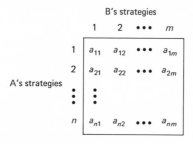

Figure 13.2–1   *A's payoff matrix.*

select a strategy that minimizes A's return. With A receiving only the minimum of each strategy, his best strategy is the one with the maximum minimum (**maximin**). The payoff for A will be the maximin, a_{ij}^*, and the payoff for B will be $C - a_{ij}^*$.

Let us suppose now that B must play first. After B picks a column from A's payoff matrix, A will select the largest column value; that is, A will choose $\max_i a_{ij}$ for a given j. This means that B should choose the column with the minimum maximum (**minimax**) to maximize his own returns. Upon slight reflection it becomes obvious that if the minimax equals the maximin, then the outcome of the game will be the same regardless of who plays first (c.f. Figures 13.2–2 and 13.2–3). If the minimax is greater than the maximin, the payoff to A will be the maximin if A plays first and the minimax if B plays first.

		B's strategies			$\min_j a_{ij}$
		1	2	3	
A's strategies	1	50	40	85	40
	2	75	35	20	20
	3	10	30	90	10 maximin = 40
$\max_i a_{ij}$		75	40	90	
				minimax = 40	

Figure 13.2–2   *A's payoff matrix, $C = 100$.*

If we have a comparative static game where the minimax equals the maximin, both players will select their best strategy and not change it, providing they both play optimally. If the game begins with A selecting a strategy at random and A playing optimally from then on, B playing optimally all the while, the game will converge to the equilibrium point (minimax = maximin) and stop. On the other hand, in a comparative static game where the minimax

		B's strategies				$\min_j a_{ij}$
		1	2	3	4	
A's strategies	1	50	30	80	60	30
	2	90	85	20	15	15
	3	20	45	50	90	20 maximin = 30
$\max_i a_{ij}$		90	85	80	90	
					minimax = 80	

Figure 13.2–3   *A's payoff matrix, $C = 100$.*

is greater than the maximin, the game will oscillate among strategies and have no equilibrium solution. (In Figure 13.2–3, what will be the sequence of play with A and B alternating moves?)

The Two-Person, Constant-Sum Game with Mixed Strategies

If mixed strategies are possible, that is, some linear combination of strategies and the resulting payoff is also the same linear combination as the payoffs of the two pure strategies, then the game will be strictly determined. The minimax always equals the maximin and if both players play optimally, each will select one combination of strategies and neither will have an incentive to change. (When will each player select a pure strategy when mixed strategies are possible?) This theorem was first proved by John von Neumann as early as 1928, using Brouwer's fixed-point theorem. The following proof is a corollary of Kakutani's fixed-point theorem (Theorem 9.2–5).

Theorem 13.2–1 If A chooses $\bar{S} = (\lambda_1 S_1, \ldots, \lambda_n S_n)$, where S_i is the ith pure strategy, $\lambda_i \geq 0$, and $\sum_{i=1}^{n} \lambda_i = 1$, so as to maximize $\phi(S, \bar{T})$ and B chooses $\bar{T} = (\mu_1 T_1, \ldots, \mu_m T_m)$, where T_j is the jth pure strategy, $\mu_j \geq 0$, and $\sum_{j=1}^{m} \mu_j = 1$, so as to minimize $\phi(\bar{S}, T)$, then

$$\max_{S} \phi(S, \bar{T}) = \min_{T} \phi(\bar{S}, T)$$

PROOF The proof follows directly from Theorem 9.2–5. ϕ is an upper semicontinuous mapping of a convex set into itself and therefore has a fixed point where

$$\min_{T} \max_{S} \phi(S, T) = \max_{S} \min_{T} \phi(S, T) \qquad \text{QED}$$

Converting the Two-Person, Constant-Sum Game into a Linear Programming Problem

It is easy to see a great deal of similarity between a two-person, constant-sum game with mixed strategies and the primal and dual in a linear programming problem. In a linear programming problem we maximize some linear objective function subject to a set of linear constraints.[2] The problem for player A with strategies $S_1, \ldots, S_n$ and corresponding payoffs $a_{1j}, \ldots, a_{nj}$, $j = 1, \ldots, m$, is to find λ_i, $i = 1, \ldots, n$, to maximize $V_j = \sum_i \lambda_i a_{ij}$. But j is unknown. We do know that B will choose j so that the value of the game to A, which is V, is $\min_j V_j$. Therefore, for any $\lambda_1, \ldots, \lambda_n$ selected, we know that $\sum_i \lambda_i a_{ij} \geq V$, for $j = 1, \ldots, m$. Since A's objective is to maximize the

[2] Cf. Section 11.4.

value of the game (it is also unknown until the problem is solved), define $\lambda_{n+1} = V$; then A's game theory problem is to find $\lambda_1, \ldots, \lambda_n, \lambda_{n+1}$ so as to

$$\text{max:} \quad \lambda_{n+1}$$

$$\text{subject to:} \quad \sum_{i=1}^{n} \lambda_i a_{i1} - \lambda_{n+1} \geq 0$$

$$\sum_{i=1}^{n} \lambda_i a_{i2} - \lambda_{n+1} \geq 0$$

$$\vdots$$

$$\sum_{i=1}^{n} \lambda_i a_{im} - \lambda_{n+1} \geq 0$$

$$\sum_{i=1}^{n} \lambda_i \leq 1$$

$$\lambda_i \geq 0 \quad \text{for } i = 1, \ldots, n+1$$

which is a linear programming problem. B's problem is equivalent to the dual problem: minimize y_{m+1} subject to $\sum_{j=1}^{m} y_j a_{ij} \leq y_{m+1}$, for $i = 1, \ldots, n$, $\sum_{j=1}^{m} y_j \geq 1$, and $y_j \geq 0$ for $j = 1, \ldots, m+1$.

The careful reader may have noticed that although the linear programming problem requires the value of the game, λ_{n+1}, to be nonnegative, there is no prior assurance in game theory that the solution is nonnegative. However, this minor problem is easily remedied where a game may have a negative solution by the addition of a constant to every a_{ij}. (Why does this not affect the optimal mix of strategies $\lambda_1, \ldots, \lambda_n$? Given the a_{ij}'s, what constant will ensure that the game has a positive payoff?)

Example 1.   Where to Locate a Firm Under Pure Strategies[3]   Suppose that A-1 Hamburgers (A) and Best Burgers (B) are contemplating locating in Story County, Iowa. There are six suitable sites available; A has options on three sites and B has options on the other three. Consumers in Story County appear to be quite indifferent to brand names and will all go to the store with the lowest price. If prices are the same, then they will go to the one that is closer. If all options are to expire on the same date, what should A do to maximize profits?

Since the demand curve for each firm will be kinked at a right angle at the going price, price will be the same for both firms and location is the only question. In Figure 13.2–4, two options are denoted as S_i for A and T_j for B. The payoff to A if he locates at S_i and B locates at T_j will be all the consumers' demands located above the line cd, which is the locus of all points equidistant from S_i and T_j. Therefore, if q_i is the demand of ith consumer we have

$$\text{Payoff } a_{ij} = \sum_{i \in \{cde\}} q_i$$

[3] An adaptation of an example given by Dorfman, Samuelson, and Solow (1958).

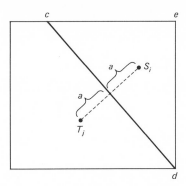

Figure 13.2–4   *Story County and two possible locations, S_i and T_j.*

After all entries in the payoff matrix have been calculated, if the minimax equals the maximin, A need not hesitate but can proceed at once to exercise his best strategy. (If A could locate anywhere and consumers are evenly distributed throughout Story County, where is his maximin location?) On the other hand, if the minimax is greater than the maximin, it would be better for A to let B locate first—but B would have the opposite incentive to let A locate first. Whoever locates first will depend upon a comparison of profits lost by waiting and profits lost by locating first.

Example 2.   Firm Location Under Mixed Strategies   In Example 1, if there are constant returns to scale on the size of hamburger stands, then by Theorem 13.2–1 we know that A can locate at some combination of his options and do so at once, since the minimax and maximin are equal under mixed strategies. Suppose that we have calculated the demand at each of the three locations for each player and that they appear in Figure 13.2–5 as A's payoffs.

A can find where to locate by solving the following linear program:

$$\begin{aligned}
\text{max:} \quad & \lambda_4 \\
\text{subject to:} \quad & -40\lambda_1 - 80\lambda_2 - 55\lambda_3 + \lambda_4 \leq 0 \\
& -70\lambda_1 - 30\lambda_2 - 60\lambda_3 + \lambda_4 \leq 0 \\
& -50\lambda_1 - 60\lambda_2 - 50\lambda_3 + \lambda_4 \leq 0 \\
& \lambda_1 + \lambda_2 + \lambda_3 \leq 1 \\
& \lambda_1, \lambda_2, \lambda_3, \lambda_4, \geq 0
\end{aligned}$$

Solving by the simplex method, we find that λ_4 is a maximum at 54 when $\lambda_1 = 0.6$, $\lambda_2 = 0.4$, and $\lambda_3 = 0$. (What are the corresponding mixed strategies for player B?)

Before moving to the next section, we note that the minimax solution under mixed strategies lies between the maximin and minimax solutions of the pure strategy game. Much more importantly, a mixed strategy minimax

	T_1	T_2	T_3	min
S_1	40	70	50	40
S_2	80	30	60	40
S_3	55	60	50	50
max	80	70	60	

A's options

Figure 13.2–5 *A's payoff matrix under pure strategies.*

solution is the maximum that A will receive if B plays optimally and both have complete information. The minimax solution under mixed strategies assures A of a minimum level of return no matter how B plays. However, if B does not play optimally then A will receive more. For example, in Figure 13.2–5 if B locates at T_1, then A will receive $0.6(40) + 0.4(80) = 24 + 32 = 56$, which is better than the value of the game, 54. However, had A known that B was to play nonoptimally, then A could have played the pure strategy S_2 and received 80. Thus, when we attempt to generalize to less than perfect information, the best solution to the game becomes one of second guessing as to just how badly B will play.

Problems

13.2–1   For the two-person, constant-sum games with A's payoff matrices shown in Figure 13.2–6, determine which are strictly determined when only pure strategies are possible.

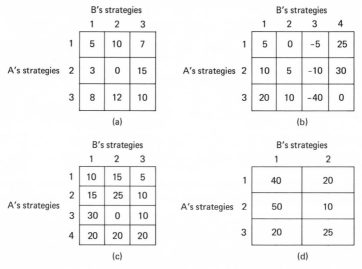

Figure 13.2–6

13.2–2   Give the value of the games to player A in Problem 13.2–1 if they are static games and A must play first. If B must play first, what is the value of the games to player A?

13.2–3   Convert the two-person, constant-sum games in Problem 13.2–1 that are not strictly determined under pure strategies into linear programming problems under mixed strategies.

13.2–4   Solve the first linear programming problem in Problem 13.2–3 for the optimal strategies for A and the value of the game.

13.2–5   Solve the dual to the primal problem solved in Problem 13.2–4 for the optimal strategies for player B. Is the value of the game to player B the same as that for A?

13.2–6   For the games in Problem 13.2–1, what is the value of a static game to A if B plays strategy 1? Is this more than the value of the game if B plays optimally in all cases? What is the value of the game to A if B plays half strategy 1 and half strategy 2 in the games in Problem 13.2–1?

13.3   GAMES AGAINST NATURE

In many cases where the payoff to an individual depends on the actions of others, it is not particularly realistic to assume that the other player is inimical or hostile. For example, when a man plants a garden the amount of produce he harvests will certainly depend upon the weather. The real income of an individual depends directly upon the prices of various commodities, which depend in turn on the total market demand and supply. An individual who sells ostrich eggs will have a higher real income if he lives near ostrich egg lovers than if he lives in western Kansas.

This generalization of the two-person, constant-sum game comes under the category of games against nature. In a two-person, constant-sum game it could be that the other player is a passive stoic and decides on strategies by contacting the cosmic reality. If the game is a nonconstant-sum game, so that B makes his decision on other criteria, then the game may appear to A as a game against nature. Or it could be a many-person game such that no one player concentrates his efforts against another particular player. Also, in certain cases where there is lack of information as to payoff values, the game may be analyzed as a game against nature. It might be that the play of nature is determined at random, such as the roll of dice or the spin of the roulette wheel. Or it actually could be a game against nature.

The question remains: Given the payoff matrix for A with strategies $S_1, \ldots, S_n$ and with strategies $T_1, \ldots, T_m$, for nature (N), what is the best play for A? The determinate answers derived in Section 13.2 are substantially vitiated. Instead of knowing what N will do we can only speculate.

Consider the farmer who can plant corn (C), wheat (W), and/or Brussels sprouts (B). His payoff matrix is shown in Figure 13.3–1, where nature can either rain (R), snow (S), or send out the locust hoards (L). What will nature play? Since all farmers are imbued with the Protestant ethic, it doesn't seem realistic to assume that N will minimize A's returns. There have been several criteria proposed to answer this question, all of which are deficient in one respect or another.

		Nature's strategies			
		R	S	L	min
	C	75	30	35	30
Farmer's strategies	W	40	55	40	40
	B	100	50	0	0

maximin = 40 (plant wheat)

Figure 13.3–1 *A payoff matrix for a farmer against nature.*

Savage (1951) suggested that the player look at the "regret" from each combination of strategies and minimax the regret, where the regret of payoff a_{ij} is $\max_k (a_{kj} - a_{ij})$. In other words, regret represents the loss of playing a nonoptimal strategy. For example, in Figure 13.3–1, if A plants all Brussels sprouts and it rains, he has made the correct decision and has no regret. However if it snows in August, he would have been better off to have planted wheat. His regret is $55-50 = 5$. In Figure 13.3–2 the regret matrix and the minimax criterion would advise the planting of corn.

Both the maximin payoff and minimax regret criteria are based on pessimism. Both aim at making the best out of the worst outcomes. In 1951 Hurwicz suggested an incorporation of the better aspects of each strategy with an optimism–pessimism (O–P) index, α.[4] Instead of looking at the

	R	S	L	max
C	25	25	5	25
W	60	0	0	60
B	0	5	40	40

minimax = 25 (plant corn)

Figure 13.3–2 *Regret matrix for a farmer against nature.*

[4] See Milnor (1954).

minimum payoff, the player might look at $[\alpha(\max_j a_{ij}) + (1 - \alpha) \min_j a_{ij}]$ for each strategy i, where α depends upon his optimism or pessimism. $\alpha = 0$ would be the "complete" pessimist, while $\alpha = 1$ would indicate the highest degree of optimism possible. Given these α-index payoff values for each-strategy, the player would then pick the maximum (cf. Figure 13.3–3).

As we can see, each of these criteria tend to give quite different answers. We have not, as yet, considered what plays by nature are likely or probable. Let us now turn to this consideration and see if this won't extricate us from some of the difficulties.

Jacob Bernoulli, in the seventeenth century, first formulated the "principle of insufficient reason." Essentially, this amounts to assigning equal probability to each possible event. Thus the farmer, not knowing the mechanism of producing rain, snow, or locusts, "should" consider them as equally probable.

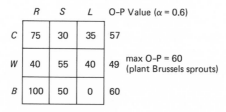

Figure 13.3–3 *Strategy values for C, W, and B when* $\alpha = 0.6$.

Milnor (1954) proposed that a "good" decision rule should satisfy certain reasonable conditions. That is, if a decision rule is applicable to all possible sets of problems where the probabilities are unknown, then it should obey the following conditions:

(1) *Completeness*—The rule should completely order all strategies.
(2) *Symmetry*—The rule should be independent of the numbering of the rows and columns of the payoff matrix.
(3) *Strong domination*—If for strategy j, all payoffs are greater than for strategy g, then strategy j is preferred to strategy g.
(4) *Continuity*—If a sequence of payoff matrices, A^i, converges to A^k and if for each payoff matrix in the sequence strategy j is preferred to strategy g, then in the limit at A^k strategy j should be preferred to strategy g.
(5) *Linearity*—The ordering of strategies by the rule should not change if each payoff is transformed by a positive linear transformation.
(6) *New strategies*—If a new strategy is added the ordering between old strategies should not change.

(7) *Column linearity*—The rule should not change the ordering among strategies if a constant is added to each element of a column.

(8) *Column duplication*—The ordering of strategies should not change if a new column is added to the payoff matrix.

(9) *Convexity*—If the rule orders strategy j as equal to strategy g, then neither is preferred to a strategy with payoffs of $\frac{1}{2}j + \frac{1}{2}g$.

(10) *Special new strategies*—The ordering between old strategies should not change if a new strategy is added with the property that for any given state of nature the new strategy is preferred to one of the old strategies.

Milnor then proved that the foregoing decision rules violates at least one of these 10 conditions. The principle of insufficient reason violates condition 8. The maximin criterion violates condition 7. The optimism–pessimism index of Hurwicz also violates 7, since it is a maximin criterion when $\alpha = 0$. In addition, the optimism–pessimism index violates condition 9. The generality of condition 6 is violated by the minimax regret criterion.

Attempting to formulate a good decision rule under the condition of unknown probabilities does not seem applicable to our example, since most farmers are amateur meteorologists. As such, they have a firm idea of the probability of each state of nature occurring. Thus, somehow a probabilistic or mixed strategy might be imputed to N.

The problems have merely begun, however. Unless the marginal utility of income (the payoff) is constant, the expected profit of each strategy will not, in general, produce the same ranking of strategies as will the expected utility. In general, then, one needs to calculate the utility of each payoff to determine the expected utility of each strategy.[5,6]

Just as before, a player could either maximize the expected utility or minimize the expected regret (in utility values). However, there is no particular reason for assuming that the utility function depends solely on the expected value (the first moment of the probability distribution). In many cases the variance and/or other parameters could be relevant to the decision maker. For example, suppose that the expected utility of planting Brussels sprouts is 50 while for wheat it is 45, but the variance of Brussels sprouts is 12 while the variance of wheat is 6. Is wheat or Brussels sprouts better? It depends upon the utility function.

That is, in general, each strategy selected by player A will have an associated probability distribution over utility outcomes. This probability distribution over utilities is a composition of the probability distribution over

[5] In this context, von Neumann and Morgenstern proved that if the individual maximizes expected utility, the utility function assumes a certain cardinality in that it is unique up to a linear transformation. Cf. Definition 3.2–8 and Theorem 3.2–5.

[6] Notice that the expected payoff or utility is a statistic with more information than the Hurwicz optimism–pessimism statistic, which is a weighted average of the greatest and the least. However, the mean requires the probability distribution to be known (guessed) while the optimism–pessisimism value does not.

physical outcomes and the utility of the outcomes. In other words, if U is utility and O is the outcome, then for a given probability distribution over the outcomes,

$$P(U) = P(O)$$

and

$$\int_{u(a)}^{u(b)} P(U)\, dU = \int_{a}^{b} P(O)\, dO$$

Graphically, this can be shown as in Figure 13.3–4, where we illustrate two cases. In (a), strategy A produces a normal distribution about its mean. In (b) strategy B produces a skewed probability distribution about its mean.

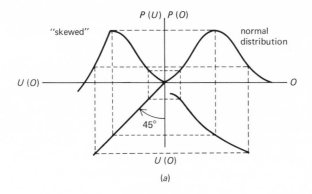

(a)

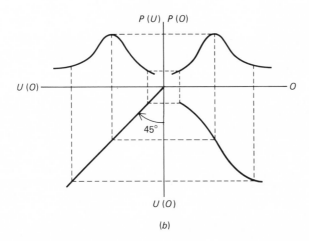

(b)

Figure 13.3–4 *Graphical representation of probability distributions over utility. (a) Probability distribution over utilities for strategy A. (b) Probability distribution over utilities for strategy B.*

Figure 13.3–4 is helpful in illustrating two things. First, the utility transformation does not change the frequency of a particular outcome and the utility resulting from it. That is, it does not change the height of the distribution but only affects the length by stretching or contracting the horizontal axis. Second, the choice of the individual is now properly a choice of **probability distributions** over outcomes rather than a choice over outcomes that produce a deterministic level of utility. Thus, to construct a utility index over probabilities, we need first to define the measures and dimension of the space and second, a set of axioms similar to those for a utility function over commodity or activity space. Alternatively, what we are looking for is a continuous, real-valued utility **functional**,[7] where for probability distributions $f_1(O)$ and $f_2(O)$, $U[f_1(O)] > U[f_2(O)]$ if and only if $f_1(O)$ is preferred to $f_2(O)$.

The difficulty encountered here is in defining the measures of probability distributions. There are at least two methods. The most popular is one that dates back to Daniel Bernoulli's *Exposition of a New Theory of the Measurement of Risk* in 1738 and is, therefore, termed the Bernoulli principle. This method relates probabilistic outcomes to certainty equivalents and assumes a particular indifference by individuals over specifically related probability distributions. The result is that the individual is characterized as maximizing expected utility. Essentially, this method was developed in Chapter 3 as a von Neumann–Morgenstern system of utility. Here we present a simplified version for expositional purposes.

Theorem 13.3–1   If for a set of finite outcomes $x_1, \ldots, x_n$ and a probability distribution $f(x)$ such that $f(x_i)$ is the probability of outcome x_i, the following axioms are satisfied:

(A1) there exists an $\bar{x}$ such that $U[f(x)] = U(\bar{x})$ (i.e., there exists a certainty equivalent);

(A2) for any binary probability distribution, $f_b(x)$, over x_i and x_j such that $f_b(x_i) = 1 - f_b(x_j)$, then as $f_b(x_j)$ goes from 0 to 1, $\bar{x}_b$ goes from x_i to x_j;

(A3) if $U(\bar{x}) = U[f(x)]$, then $U(\bar{x}) = U[f^*(x)]$, where f^* is a probability distribution over the outcomes $x_1, \ldots, x_{i-1}, x_{i+1}, \ldots, x_n$, where

$$f^*(x_1) = f(x_1) + f(x_i)[1 - f_b(x_i)]$$
$$f^*(x_n) = f(x_n) + f(x_i)f_b(x_i)$$
$$f^*(x_j) = f(x_j) \qquad \text{for } j \neq 1, i, n$$

then $U[f(x)] = \sum_{i=1}^{n} U(x_i)f(x_i)$. Furthermore, $U[f(x)]$ is unique up to a positive linear transformation.[8]

[7] Cf. Definition 10.1–1.

[8] Cf. Theorem 3.2–5.

Axiom (A3) in Theorem 13.3–1 is an axiom of linear indifference curves over probability distributions that have the following interpretation. If an individual is indifferent between $f(x)$ and $g(x)$, two probability distributions over outcomes $x_1, \ldots, x_n$, then he should be indifferent to a third prospect that will randomly select $f(x)$ or $g(x)$.

Graphically, axiom (A3) can be illustrated by an equilateral triangle where the vertices represent certainty outcomes of x_1, x_2, and x_3. Figure 13.3–5 is such a graph. Points interior to the triangle represent a probability distribution over the outcomes x_1, x_2, and x_3. The distance from the base measures the probability of one outcome. Thus the distance from a base to the opposite vertex is 1. For example, a point in the center of the triangle would represent a probability distribution where $f(x_i) = \frac{1}{3}$, $i = 1, 2, 3$. In Figure 13.3–5 there are indifference curves superimposed that correspond to axiom (A3) in Theorem 13.3–1. The indifference curves in Figure 13.3–6 do not follow axiom (A3).

While axiom (A3) imposes linear indifference curves over probability distributions, this is not nearly as restrictive as imposing linear indifference curves over commodity space. In fact, for many interpretations of probability, such as an outcome from a lottery, the axiom is a logical consequence of the probability concept. For other interpretations of $f(x)$ as a long-run frequency or a subjective belief, axiom (A3) is quite restrictive. Thus, in part, the simplification of Theorem 13.3–1 to the problem of a utility functional as the proper criterion for game-theoretic problems depends upon whether it is a static game or a comparative static game and the method by which the random states of "nature" are produced.

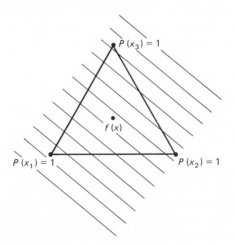

Figure 13.3–5 *Indifference curves over probability distributions with outcomes x_1, x_2, and x_3. $f(x)$ is a rectangular distribution over x_1, x_2, and x_3.*

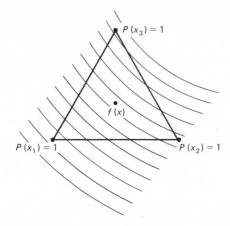

Figure 13.3–6 *Indifference curves over probability distributions that do not comply with axiom (A3) of Theorem 13.3–1.*

The second method is to postulate that individual preferences over probability distributions can be described by the first n moments of the distribution. This permits a probability distribution to be represented as a point in n-dimensional space. Then a complete, binary preference ordering is assumed to exist similar to the case of an n-dimensional commodity space.

Markowitz's (1952) analysis of portfolio selection is a special case of this second method, which assumes that only the first two moments, the mean and the variance, are relevant to an individual's choice. The usual assumption is that if two distributions have equal variance, then the one with a higher mean is preferred. If the means are equal, then the one with the lower variance is preferred. The relative trade-off between the mean value and the variance is a measure of risk aversion for the individual.

If only a finite number of strategies are available to the decision maker, all that is needed is to specify a binary preference ordering over the strategies with the usual properties of rationality, *viz.*, completeness and transitivity. For example, suppose that a decision maker is faced with 10 possible strategies in a game against nature. Then we need only assume that one strategy is preferred, equal, or inferior to another according to the individual's "preferences." One problem is that this method has no relation to the utility of deterministic outcomes. How these preferences were determined by the outcomes and probability of each state of nature remains a mystery. In itself, this is no problem until a preference ordering violates the logical properties of probability. For example, in Figure 13.3–7 we have five strategies and three states of nature. It would be inconsistent regardless of the probabilities attached to the states of nature for strategy 1 to be preferred to strategy 2,

States of nature

		1	2	3
	1	100	100	100
	2	0	0	100
A's strategies	3	0	100	100
	4	100	0	0
	5	100	100	0

Figure 13.3–7 *Game against nature.*

which is in turn preferred to strategy 3. Also, another inconsistency is revealed by a preference ordering of $4 > 2 > 3 > 5$. In this vein, Savage (1954) has proved the following theorem.

Theorem 13.3–2 For all preference orderings over a set of possible strategies that satisfy:

(1) consistency with respect to outcomes, that is, either more is preferred to less or less is preferred to more, and
(2) consistency with respect to implied probable states of nature, there exist:
    (a) a real-valued function over possible outcomes $U(O)$ that is unique up to a linear transformation and
    (b) a unique function P over the states of nature, S_i, such that
        (i) $P(S_i) \geq 0$ for all S_i,
        (ii) $P(S_i \cup S_j) = P(S_i) + P(S_j)$ if $S_i \cap S_j = 0$,
        (iii) $P(S_1 \cup \cdots \cup S_i \cup \cdots) = 1$
    such that strategy j is preferred to strategy g if and only if:

$$\sum_i P(S_i)U(O_{ji}) > \sum_i P(S_i)U(O_{gi})$$

where O_{ji} is the outcome if S_i occurs and strategy j is played.

This theorem implies that for a given preference ordering over a set of strategies in a game against nature, either the preferences are inconsistent or it is possible to specify an implied probability distribution and utility function such that the choice will be described by the Bernoulli principle.

However, we have moved from the two-person, constant-sum deterministic minimax equals maximin criterion, to a nearly tautological notion of maximizing utility. Granted we have a great deal of insight and perspective for specific problems, but no general conclusions can be drawn.

Problems

13.3–1 Find the best strategy for the game given in Figure 13.3–8 under the following criteria:
(a) maximin
(b) minimax regret
(c) maximize optimism–pessimism value, $\alpha = 0.3$
(d) maximize expected payoff under the principle of insufficient reason
(e) maximize expected payoff where $P(1) = 0.2$, $P(2) = 0.3$, and $P(3) = 0.5$
(f) minimize expected regret where $P(1) = 0.8$, $P(2) = 0.1$, and $P(3) = 0.1$
(g) go for broke (i.e., pick the strategy that has the highest return)

Nature's strategies

		1	2	3
	a	40	15	20
	b	50	25	0
A's strategies				
	c	60	0	5
	d	20	30	20

Figure 13.3–8 *A's payoff matrix.*

13.3–2 Given the following probability distribution for outcomes x_1, x_2, x_3, and x_4:

$$f(x_1) = 0.2 \quad f(x_2) = 0.4 \quad f(x_3) = 0.1 \quad f(x_4) = 0.3$$

and the following utilities for certainty outcomes:

$$U(x_1) = 20 \quad U(x_2) = 40 \quad U(x_3) = 50 \quad U(x_4) = 55$$

(a) What is the expected utility of $f(x)$?
(b) If the individual follows axioms (A1)–(A3) in Theorem 13.3–1 given the choice of x_2 with certainty and $f(x)$, which would he select?

13.3–3 Prove that a positive linear transformation of the utility indicator in Problem 13.3–2 does not affect the choice of $f(x)$ versus x_2 with certainty.

13.3–4 Give an example of a positive monotonic transformation of $U(x)$ in Problem 13.3–2 that will reverse the choice of $f(x)$ and x_2 with certainty.

13.3–5 Describe the difference in playing a game against nature with a known probability distribution over nature's strategies for 1000 times and for one time only.

13.3–6   For the game in Problem 13.3–1:
  (a) Illustrate that the principle of insufficient reason violates Milnor's condition 8.
  (b) Illustrate that the maximin criterion violates condition 7.
  (c) Give an example of an optimism–pessimism index that violates condition 9.
  (d) Give an example where the minimax regret criterion of Savage would violate Milnor's condition 6.

13.4   NONCONSTANT-SUM GAMES OF COOPERATION AND DECEPTION

As was the case when explicit opposition was eliminated, the conclusive results also vanish for a nonconstant-sum game. In this section we shall discuss two general kinds of games: the prisoner's dilemma and the battle of the sexes. The first is attributed to A. W. Tucker and possesses no solution, but it does illustrate the benefits of cooperation and/or collusion. The second is due to Luce and Raiffa (1957) and illustrates the incentive for concealing one's preferences and what might be termed "skillful play."

The Prisoner's Dilemma

There are many situations in life where the payoff to various individuals depends on the actions of others and, in addition, there are certain mixes of strategies that are better for all concerned. For example, two duopolists will have more to divide if they maximize their joint profits. However, it is a classic debate as to whether they will actually do so. Let us characterize the general properties of the prisoner's dilemma and then return to some economic interpretations.

Suppose that two prisoners are in jail awaiting trial. The county attorney can prosecute on either of two charges: a major crime or a minor offense. However, he does not have sufficient evidence to convict either on the major crime unless one or both confess. Conviction on the minor offense is assured. Suppose that he offers prisoner A immunity from prosecution if he confesses and helps convict B. However, if B also confesses, A will not be needed as county evidence and he will be tried as a confessed criminal. In Figure 13.4–1 A's payoff in terms of years in prison are depicted. The best possible outcome, assuming no interdependence of utility between A and B, would be for A to confess and B not to confess. The worst would be for B to confess and A not to confess.

First let us assume that A and B have made no prior arrangement and cannot communicate. What should A do? If B confesses, A is better off to confess. If B does not confess, A is better off to confess. Thus, the "confession" strategy dominates the "nonconfession" strategy. Regardless of what B does,

A's Years in Prison

If B:

		Confesses	Does not confess
If A:	Does not confess	5	0
	Confesses	50	1

Figure 13.4–1 *Prisoner A's payoffs in the prisoner's dilemma.*

A is better off to confess. However, if B has the same payoff matrix as A, he also has an incentive to confess. The result is that both confess and get 5 years in prison.

Clearly, they would both be better off if neither confesses. That way they would only get 1 year each. Thus there is strong incentive for prior collusion and bargaining. If binding, prior contracts are possible, neither A nor B will confess. However, in the case of criminals and nations there is no way to enforce a contract or agreement.[9] This brings forth a variety of possibilities. It now behooves A to establish a firm agreement with B not to confess and then to confess himself. B also has the same incentive as A. This combination of need for bargaining and incentives for deception result in the indeterminacy without additional information of the interaction between A and B.

There are many economic situations where collusion is better for all participants, but there is private incentive not to collude. For example, Davis and Palomba (1969) have recently likened the problem of the National Farmers' Organization (NFO) to that of the prisoner's dilemma. Suppose you are an individual farmer with two alternatives: (1) to produce or (2) not to produce. If all farmers do not produce, income to farmers will increase due to the inelasticity of demand. However, what is best for a single farmer is to produce while all others restrict their output. This gives him the benefit of current income *and* higher prices. This payoff is represented in Figure 13.4–2.

Such dilemma problems constitute a "fallacy of composition." What is reasonable and rational for the single individual to do acting in isolation is nonoptimal for all acting together. The final solution of these kinds of problems depends upon a variety of particulars that produce no general conclusions.

The Battle of the Sexes

There is another class of nonconstant-sum games that have incentives for a player to disguise his "true" preferences. These can by typified by the "battle of the sexes."

[9] In Schelling (1960) there is a much extended discussion of this particular aspect of non-constant-sum games.

A Single Farmer's Income

If all other farmers:

	Produce	Do not produce
Produces	50	200
Does not produce	0	100

If he:

Figure 13.4–2   *The farmer's dilemma.*

Suppose we have two lovers who would rather be with each other than apart. They have, however, somewhat different tastes. The male prefers football to concerts, while his female companion prefers the opposite. If their respective utility payoffs are as represented in Figure 13.4–3, there is a clear desire for both to go to the same event. However, which event they both attend will have different payoffs for the two players involved. The male will benefit more if they both go to the football game. She will benefit more if they both go to the concert.

As with the prisoner's dilemma, there are again a variety of possible "bargaining" processes and results. If the preferences of the woman are unknown to the man, but she knows his preferences, all she has to do is to assert that she will go to the concert regardless of what he does. If she is going to the concert, his choice will also be the concert. Alternatively, the man could make the assertion that he will go to the football game, and if she believes him, she will go along.

Whichever occurs, there is a strong incentive to conceal one's true preferences hoping for the best outcome. Much has been written about various methods of resolving the "battle of the sexes." One often-discussed method is that of money side payments. If one individual condescends to the wishes of

Man's Utility Level

If she goes to:

	Concert	Football
Concert	2	–10
Football	0	10

If he goes to:

Woman's Utility Level

If she goes to:

	Concert	Football
Concert	5	–20
Football	–10	3

If he goes to:

Figure 13.4–3   *Utility payoff matrices for the "battle of the sexes."*

another, he is compensated by the former with a monetary side payment. This amounts to another strategy or series of other strategies. Consequently, it may be possible to transform a nonconstant-sum game into a constant-sum game by adding strategies. However, the nonconstant-sum game will not, in general, possess a definite solution.

An example of a nonconstant-sum game that illustrates the problem embodied in the "battle of the sexes" occurs in the theory of public goods.

Example 1. Public Goods and the "Battle of the Sexes" Suppose an economy produces two goods, q and m. q is a purely public good in the sense that the amount consumed by each and every individual is equal to the total amount:

$$q^i = q \qquad \text{for } i = 1, \ldots, n$$

where q^i is the amount consumed by the ith individual and n is the total number of individuals. m is a purely private good in that the amount produced is equal to the sum of the individual amounts, m^i:

$$m = \sum_{i=1}^{n} m^i$$

First let us consider the "demand" curve for an individual if he is the only consumer in the market. For convenience we shall assume that individual I is endowed with m_0 of the private good and can purchase as much or as little of the public good, q, as he wishes at a constant price (the marginal cost of production). In Figure 13.4-4 we have depicted I's feasible consumption space with various prices and the corresponding quantities demanded. The individual's demand curve derived from Figure 13.4-4 is drawn in Figure 13.4-5.

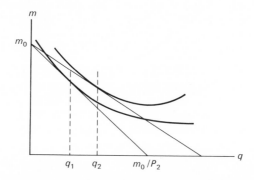

Figure 13.4-4 *Indifference curves and demand for an individual.*

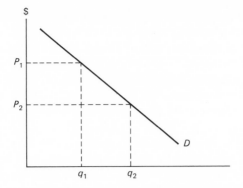

Figure 13.4–5 *Demand for the public good in a one-consumer world.*

Next, suppose that individuals I and J have demand curves D_I and D_J as shown in Figure 13.4–6. MC represents the constant marginal cost of production.

What quantity of q will be provided by this two-consumer economy? From Figure 13.4–6, we see that J would provide the quantity q^0 if he were the only consumer. However, since q is a purely public good, what is available to one is available to all. Hence with the addition of I to the economic system, several possibilities arise: (1) If J provides q^0 by himself, I's "demand" curve will shift since D_I was derived under the assumption that I was the only consumer. (2) I and J *could* contribute to a joint fund *as if* they were in

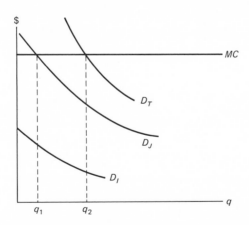

Figure 13.4–6 *Demand for public good with a two-consumer economy. Total demand D_T, is the vertical summation of isolated demand curves.*

isolation. Due to the characteristics of q, this would result in the quantity $q*$ being provided. (3) Any of an infinite number of other possible amounts of q and financing arrangements between I and J could occur.

The similarity between the final provision and the "battle of the sexes" is that J has an incentive *not* to reveal his true demand curve D_J, thus forcing I to help finance the provision of q. On the other hand, I may have a similar incentive. If he is better off with J providing q^0 and paying nothing (which may or may not be true, but is entirely possible), I would have an incentive to say he had no demand for q at any price. This is illustrated in Figure 13.4–7 as a nonconstant-sum game. In part (a) it is clear that if I believes that J will provide only part of the cost of q, then I will help. In part (b) it is equally clear that J will provide all the cost of q if J believes that I will pay nothing towards the financing of q.

The General Two-Person Game and the Nash Solution

As a criterion for a solution of a two-person, nonconstant-sum game Nash (1950) proposed the following general principle, which gives a unique solution to the bargaining problem.

DEFINITION 13.4–1   A **Nash solution** to a two-person, nonconstant-sum game is one that satisfies the following four conditions:

(1) If S_i and T_j are strategies with outcome O_{ij}, which is a solution given the utility functions $U^A(O)$ and $U^B(O)$, then O_{ij} is also a solution for the utility functions $\overline{U}^A(O) = \alpha U^A(O) + \beta$ and $\overline{U}^B(O) = \gamma U^B(O) + \delta$. That is, linear transformations of the utility functions leave the solution unaffected.

(2) If O_{ij} is a solution, then there exist no strategies g and h such that $U^A(O_{gh}) \geq U^A(O_{ij})$ and $U^B(O_{gh}) \geq U^B(O_{ij})$. That is, O_{ij} is Pareto optimal.

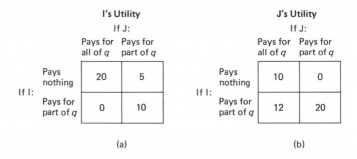

(a)   (b)

Figure 13.4–7 *The provision of the public good in a nonconstant-sum game framework.*

(3) If O_{ij} is a solution, then the elimination of outcomes that are not solutions leaves O_{ij} still a solution to the reduced problem.

(4) If $U^A(O_{ke}) = U^B(O_{ke})$, then the bargaining solution O_{ij} is such that the gain from cooperation is divided equally among the two players. That is, if O_{ke} is the minimax solution, then

$$U^A(O_{ij}) - U^A(O_{ke}) = U^B(O_{ij}) - U^B(O_{ke})$$

The only combination of strategies that satisfies the conditions of a Nash solution is one that maximizes the product of the gains in utility attained by cooperation. This theorem, proved by Nash (1950), is stated formally as Theorem 13.4–1.

Theorem 13.4–1 If O_{ij} is a Nash solution to a two-person, nonconstant-sum game and O_{ke} is a noncooperative or minimax solution, then:

$$O_{ij} = \max_{g,h} \{[U^A(O_{gh}) - U^A(O_{ke})][U^B(O_{gh}) - U^B(O_{ke})]\}$$

PROOF   The theorem is proved rather easily by first noting that conditions 1 and 4 imply that there exists some linear transformation of $U^A(O)$ and $U^B(O)$ such that $U^A(O_{ke}) = U^B(O_{ke})$, which in turn implies that $\Delta U^A = \Delta U^B$ for the cooperative bargain. Condition 3 implies that the set of outcomes is convex, and condition 2 implies the solution is on the northeast boundary of the convex set of outcomes. Since $\Delta U^A = \Delta U^B$, the slope of the boundary must equal -1 at the solution, or the Nash solution must satisfy

$$\max_{g,h} \{[U^A(O_{gh}) - U^A(O_{ke})][U^B(O_{gh}) - U^B(O_{ke})]\} \qquad \text{QED}$$

The Nash solution is illustrated in Figure 13.4–8.

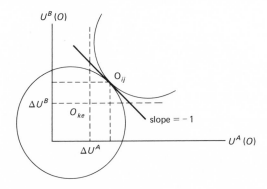

Figure 13.4–8 *Illustration of the Nash solution for a two-person, nonconstant-sum game.*

Problems

13.4–1   For a nonconstant-sum game we have the payoff matrices shown in Figure 13.4–9.

	A's Payoff Matrix					B's Payoff Matrix		

A's Payoff Matrix

B's strategies

A's strategies		1	2	3
	1	50	30	0
	2	60	40	5
	3	70	50	5

B's Payoff Matrix

B's strategies

A's strategies		1	2	3
	1	5	30	60
	2	10	40	50
	3	30	40	45

Figure 13.4–9

   (a) Which strategy is the best for player A in absence of any information of what B will do?
   (b) Which is the best strategy for B in absence of any information of what A will do?
   (c) Assuming that the payoff matrices are monetary values, which combination of pure strategies maximizes the joint return?
   (d) What is the minimum bribe or side payment from A to B necessary to move from the minimax solution to the optimal joint strategy?
   (e) What is the minimum bribe that B must pay A in order for A to change his strategy to make B best off while playing strategy 3.
   (f) What is the best and most equitable solution to this game? Why?

13.4–2   For the nonconstant-sum game shown in Figure 13.4–10:

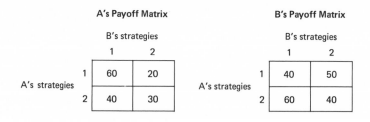

A's Payoff Matrix

B's strategies

A's strategies		1	2
	1	60	20
	2	40	30

B's Payoff Matrix

B's strategies

A's strategies		1	2
	1	40	50
	2	60	40

Figure 13.4–10

   (a) What is the solution for a static game with no cooperation if A knows B's payoff matrix?
   (b) Describe a solution that is better for both players.

13.5 DIFFERENTIAL GAME THEORY

Another generalization of the two-person, constant-sum game is the inclusion of a specific time dimension for strategy changes. Heretofore we have considered only static and comparative static games. A quick review of the preceding examples will show that by including possible rates of change of a strategy, we can significantly alter the scope and conclusions of static game theory. In this section we shall consider continuously variable strategies, within specified limits. This approach, developed by Isaacs (1965), generates differential equations and hence the name "differential game theory."

In differential game theory we first need to distinguish between two sets of variables: **state variables** and **control variables**. State variables, $x_1, \ldots, x_n$, completely describe the state of the game at any point in time. The value of all state variables is assumed to be known to the players at any particular point in time; that is, both players in a two-person game have full and accurate information of the correct state of the game. Consequently, they make decisions on the basis of the current values of $x_1, \ldots, x_n$.

For a two-person game, each player has a set of control variables— $S_1, \ldots, S_k$ for I and $T_1, \ldots, T_m$ for J—for which he chooses values within some specified limits. This means that the players have some control over the state variables over time.

All variables are assumed to be defined in n-dimensional Euclidean space and thus the state of the game at time t is some point in n-dimensional space. The game has some specified ending or terminating rules. For example, a certain length of time or values for the state variables may be specified. Definition 13.5–1 states these aspects of a differential game formally.

DEFINITION 13.5–1   A **two-person, zero-sum differential game** is a situation where, for two players I and J:

$$X = x_1, \ldots, x_n \text{ are } n \text{ state variables}$$
$$S = S_1, \ldots, S_k \text{ are } k \text{ control variables for player I}$$
$$T = T_1, \ldots, T_m \text{ are } m \text{ control variables for player J}$$

(1) The initial values of X, (X_0) are known.
(2) I chooses a value for S_i, $i = 1, \ldots, k$, at time t such that $a_i(t) \leq S_i \leq b_i(t)$, where $a_i(t)$ and $b_i(t)$ are constants at any point in time.
(3) J chooses a value for T_j, $j = 1, \ldots, m$, at time t such that $c_j(t) \leq T_j \leq d_j(t)$, where $c_j(t)$ and $d_j(t)$ are constants at any point in time.
(4) $dx_i/dt = \dot{x}_i = f_i(x_1, \ldots, x_n, S_1, \ldots, S_k, T_1, \ldots, T_m)$ or $\dot{X} = f(X, S, T)$.
(5) The **value of the game**, V, is given by

$$V = \int F(X, S, T) \, dt + G(\overline{X})$$

where $\overline{X}$ is the value of the state variables at the termination of the game

(6) The objective of I is to maximize V.

(7) The objective of J is to minimize V.

The following example illustrates the concepts of Definition 13.5–1.

Example 1.   A Simple Differential Game   (Isaacs, 1965) Suppose that we have an arsonist (A) and a sentry (S) initially located as in Figure 13.5–1. The enclosed area is the target of the arsonist, while the sentry would like to intercept the arsonist as far away from the target area as possible. Whenever the arsonist is intercepted he can detonate incendiary bombs and destroy part of the target area. If he reaches the boundary of the target he will destroy the entire area. Thus the value of the game is the distance away from the target area at the termination of the game. The game terminates when either (1) the sentry intercepts the arsonist or (2) the arsonist reaches the target.

If we assume that each player can travel at the same rate of speed and can change directions instantaneously, what is the best strategy for both players? That is, which way should each player move do the best he can for himself?

There are four state variables: (1) the direction of travel of A, (2) the direction of travel of S, (3) the distance of A from the target, and (4) the distance of A from S. The control variables for A and S are their change in direction at time t. If both players play optimally, the game has a determinate solution V^*. If A does not play optimally, V will be less than V^*, while if S does not play optimally the opposite is true.

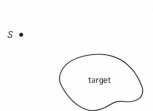

A •

S •

Figure 13.5–1   *The "arsonist-and-sentry" differential game.*

We can solve the problem in the following way. Suppose that A starts out straight toward S and does not change directions. Then S should proceed straight toward A and the game will terminate at a distance halfway between A and S (point y in Figure 13.5–2). Now suppose that A starts at an angle to S by moving straight toward the right end of the target and does not change directions. Then S should proceed at the same angle to A's initial position to intercept A at point W in Figure 13.5–2. In fact, for any unchanging direction by A, the points of interception will be given by the line that bisects the original distance between A and S.

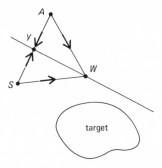

Figure 13.5–2 *Locus of interception points for optimal play by the sentry and an unchanged direction by the arsonist.*

The best that A can do, if S plays optimally, is to start out in a direction toward the point on the line of interception that is closest to the target area. This point, Z in Figure 13.5–3, is analogous to the minimax solution of static, two-person, constant-sum games. In other words, if both players play optimally, point Z is the best that both A and S can do. If S does not play optimally then A, by starting out toward point Z, can get closer to the target than Z. Similarly, if A does not play optimally, S can intercept A at a point farther from the target than Z. In other words, the optimal strategy for a player at any point in time is to proceed in the direction that intercepts the perpendicular bisector at its minimum distance from the target area.

In Figure 13.5–4 we have a case where the sentry does not play optimally while the arsonist does. The sentry starts out toward the initial spot of the arsonist and proceeds in that direction for one-quarter of the distance before playing optimally. The paths of the two players are sketched, showing that A comes closer to the target area at Z* than if S had played optimally. Figure 13.5–4 shows four representative corrections at the arrowheads, but A's optimal path under instantaneous correction would be a smooth curve as long

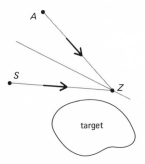

Figure 13.5–3 *The "minimax" solution for the "arsonist-and-sentry" game.*

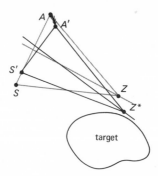

Figure 13.5–4 *An "arsonist-and-sentry" game solution in which the sentry does not play optimally.*

as S is between S and S' in Figure 13.5–4. At any point in time, the optimal path for A, knowing only where S is and not where S will be, is toward a point closest to the target area on the perpendicular bisector of the distance between the two players.

We now develop formally the general solution to a two-person differential game. From Definition 13.5–1 the value of the game is, in general,

$$V = \int F(X, S, T)\, dt + G(\overline{X})$$

V is composed of an integral portion and a terminal portion. If $G(\overline{X}) \equiv 0$, for all possible values of $\overline{X}$ (i.e., the final values of the state variables), the game has an **integral payoff.** If $F(X, S, T) \equiv 0$ the game is said to have a **terminal payoff.**

Theorem 13.5–1   All two-person differential games can be formulated as having a terminal payoff. That is, if $V = \int F(X, S, T)\, dt + G(\overline{X})$, then

$$V = G'(\overline{X}')$$

PROOF   The theorem is proved by defining an additional variable when $F(X, S, T)$ is not zero. Let x_{n+1} equal $F(X, S, T)$. Then it follows that $\overline{x}_{n+1} - x^0_{n+1} = \int F(X, S, T)\, dt$, where x^0_{n+1} is the initial value of x_{n+1} and $\overline{x}_{n+1}$ is the final value of x_{n+1}. Since the origin is arbitrary, we can define $x^0_{n+1} \equiv 0$ and define $G'(\overline{X}') = G(\overline{X}) + \overline{x}_{n+1}$. Thus $V = G'(\overline{X}')$.   QED

The objective for player I is to maximize the value of the game, given J's strategy. In other words, for any $\overline{T}$ and for $V = V(X, S, T)$, I wants to

$$\max_{S} V(X, S, \overline{T})$$

while for any $\bar{S}$, J wants to

$$\min_{T} V(X, \bar{S}, T)$$

To have a determinant solution to the game it is necessary that

$$\min_{T} \max_{S} V(X, S, T) = \max_{S} \min_{T} V(X, S, T)$$

Otherwise, we run into the same kind of indeterminancy associated with the "prisoner's dilemma" and the "battle of the sexes" games. Kakutani's third theorem (Theorem 9.2–5) presents some general sufficient conditions for the minimax to equal the maximin, and is restated here in terms of a two-person, differential game.

Theorem 13.5–2 If the sets of strategies $\{S\}$ and $\{T\}$ are bounded, closed, and convex and if the continuous, real-valued function $V(X, S, T)$ is such that for all $\bar{S} \in \{S\}$ and $\bar{T} \in \{T\}$, the sets

$$\{S \in \{S\} \mid V(X, S. \bar{T}) \geq \beta\} \qquad \beta \text{ a constant}$$

and

$$\{T \in \{T\} \mid V(X, \bar{S}, T) \leq \alpha\} \qquad \alpha \text{ a constant}$$

are convex sets; then

$$\min_{T} \max_{S} V(X, S, T) = \max_{S} \min_{T} V(X, S, T)$$

Assuming that

$$\min_{T} \max_{S} V(X, S, T) = \max_{S} \min_{T} V(X, S, T)$$

we can also solve for the optimal solution to a differential game, if both players play optimally.

Assuming that

$$\min_{T} \max_{S} V(X, S, T) = \max_{S} \min_{T} V(X, S, T)$$

it follows that the V function must satisfy a first-order partial differential equation.

Theorem 13.5–3 If

$$\min_{T} \max_{S} V(X, S, T) = \max_{S} \min_{T} V(X, S, T)$$

then $V(X, S, T) = \int F(X, S, T)\, dt + G(\bar{X})$ must satisfy

$$F(X, S, T) - \sum_{i=1}^{n} \frac{\partial V}{\partial x_i} f_i(X, S, T) = 0$$

where $f_i(X, S, T) = dx_i/dt$.

PROOF   Consider the value of the game between the points X and X^0 for $X^0 \neq \overline{X}$ and $X \neq \overline{X}$, where $\overline{X}$ is the vector of the final values of the state variables at the termination of the game. As the game moves from X to X^0 during the time interval t to $t + h$ we have

$$V(X) = \int_t^{t+h} F(X, S, T) \, dt + V(X^0)$$

Applying Taylor's expansion to the function $V(X)$ and dropping higher-order terms we have

$$V(X) - V(X^0) = \sum_{i=1}^n \frac{\partial V}{\partial x_i} \, dx_i$$

Also, by applying Taylor's expansion to the integral for small h, we have

$$\int_t^{t+h} F(X, S, T) \, dt \simeq hF(X, S, T)$$

Therefore

$$V(X) = hF(X, S, T) - \sum_{i=1}^n \frac{\partial V}{\partial x_i} \, dx_i + V(X)$$

and since

$$dx_i = f_i(X, S, T) \, dt = f_i(X, S, T)h$$

we have

$$F(X, S, T) - \sum_{i=1}^n \frac{\partial V}{\partial x_i} f_i(X, S, T) = 0 \qquad \text{QED}$$

Given $V(X, S, T)$, and assuming both players play optimally, $S_a \leq S \leq S_b$ and $T_a \leq T \leq T_b$, then

$$\frac{\partial V}{\partial \overline{S}} = 0 \text{ if } S_a < \overline{S} < S_b \qquad \frac{\partial V}{\partial \overline{T}} = 0 \text{ if } T_a < \overline{T} < T_b$$

$$\frac{\partial V}{\partial \overline{S}} \leq 0 \text{ if } \overline{S} = S_a \qquad \frac{\partial V}{\partial \overline{T}} \geq 0 \text{ if } \overline{T} = T_a$$

$$\frac{\partial V}{\partial \overline{S}} \geq 0 \text{ if } \overline{S} = S_b \qquad \frac{\partial V}{\partial \overline{T}} \leq 0 \text{ if } \overline{T} = T_b$$

This gives conditions that must hold for the unknowns $S_1, \ldots, S_k$ and $T_1, \ldots, T_m$. After solving for $\overline{S}$ and $\overline{T}$, the value for all state variables is given by $x_i = \int f_i(X, \overline{S}, \overline{T}) \, dt + x_i^0$ for any point in the game.

Problems

13.5–1 Given the following differential game, where x_1 is the only state variable:

$$V = x_1(5) = \int_0^5 \dot{x}_1(t)\, dt \qquad \text{since } x_1(0) = 0$$

$$\dot{x}_1 = S_1(t) + S_1(t)T_2(t) - T_1(t) - 2S_1(t)^2 + T_1(t)^2 - S_2(t)^2 + T_2(t)^2$$

S_1 and S_2, $0 \le S_1, S_2 \le 10$ control variables for I

T_1 and T_2, $0 \le T_1, T_2 \le 10$ control variables for J

(a) Show that the optimal values of the control variables for I and J are $S_1 = \frac{1}{4}$, $S_2 = T_2 = 0$, and $T_1 = \frac{1}{2}$.
(b) Show that if $T_2 = 1$ and $T_1 = \frac{1}{2}$, that I can select different values for S_1 and the value of the game increase. What is the optimal level of S_1 with J playing $T_2 = 1$?
(c) What would be the effect of limiting all control variables to being greater than or equal to $\frac{1}{2}$ and less than or equal to 1 in the answers to (a) and (b)?
(d) Show that the optimal values of the control variables in (a) satisfy the equation in Theorem 13.5–3.

13.5–2 For I find the optimal strategy $\bar{S}_1$, $0 \le S_1 \le 5$, for J find the optimal strategy, T_1, $-10 \le T_1 \le 10$, and find the value of the differential game if

$$V = \ln x$$
$$x(0) = 1$$
$$t_0 = 0,\ t_1 = 10$$
$$\dot{x} = S_1 T_1 + S_1 - 2T_1$$

13.5–3 In Problem 13.5–2, if I plays nonoptimally by letting $S_1 = 0$:
(a) What is the value of the game with no limit on T_1?
(b) What is the value of the game with T_1 limited to $0 \le T_1 \le 0.1$?

13.5–4 Solve for the optimal controls for I and J for the following two-person, differential game:

$$\begin{array}{ll} V = x_1 - x_2 & 0 \le S_1 \le 20 \\ \dot{x}_1 = 5S_1 - T_1 - \ln S_1 + \ln T_1 & \frac{1}{2} \le T_1 \le 5 \\ \dot{x}_2 = T_1^2 - 3S_1^2 & \end{array}$$

13.5–5 Why is it unimportant for I to know if J plays optimally in Problem 13.5–4?

13.6 *n-PERSON GAMES AND THE CORE*

In this section we shall make some general comments about many-person games, solutions to many-person games, discuss the concept of the core of a many-person game, and conclude with some theorems that relate the core to competitive equilibria.

When we have n persons playing a game, the relevant characteristics of the game change. In a two-person, zero-sum game we have, by definition, a situation of competition. In special nonzero-sum games of the "prisoner's dilemma" and the "battle of the sexes" types, we have cases where independent, self-maximizing strategies result in a nonoptimal solution. In an n-person, zero-sum game there are potential characteristics of both the two-person, zero-sum and the two-person, nonzero-sum game. When there are more than two players, it is possible that collusive action by some subset of players could result in more for that coalition than they would receive by acting independently. This possibility, or impossibility, has many economic implications. If there is no equilibrium solution to an n-person game where coalitions are better off, then the classic notion of independent competition is a better economic structure than mixtures of coalitions such as labor unions and cartels.

To discuss solutions to many-person games we first need some additional concepts. For an n-person game, there exists for each player a maximin return, $v(i)$, a particular level he can be certain of attaining, regardless of what other players do. If players i and j form a coalition, then this coalition acting in concert and applying maximin strategy has a minimum return $v(i, j)$. It seems reasonable that the two acting together cannot do worse than when acting independently; that is, $v(i, j) \geq v(i) + v(j)$. In general, if any subset S of the players 1, 2, ..., n form a coalition, then their joint maximin payoff is $v(S) \geq \sum_{i \in S} v(i)$. This leads to the following definition.

DEFINITION 13.6–1 $v(S)$ for all possible subsets S of players $1, \ldots, n$ in an n-person game is the **characteristic function** of the game and is real-valued and superadditive [i.e., $v(S) \geq \sum_{i \in S} v(i)$ for all subsets S].

It can be shown that the entire structure is contained in the characteristic function of the game. The characteristic function is based on the minimax theorem and, in general, there will be additional payoffs to all players, which would fall under the category of solutions.

DEFINITION 13.6–2   An **allocation** is a vector of any feasible set of outcomes to the n players $x = (x_1, \ldots, x_n)$. That is, x, an allocation, is a set of payments to each of the n players such that x_i is the amount received by the ith player

$$x_i \geq v(i)$$

and

$$\sum_{i=1}^{n} x_i = v(N)$$

The von Neumann–Morgenstern (1947) definition of a solution depends upon the concept of domination.

DEFINITION 13.6–3   An allocation $\bar{x}$ **dominates** the allocation x if there exists a coalition $S \subset \{1, \ldots, n\}$ such that

$$v(S) \geq \sum_{i \in S} \bar{x}_i$$

and

$$\bar{x}_i > x_i \qquad \text{for all } i \in S$$

DEFINITION 13.6–4   A **von Neumann–Morgenstern solution** to an *n*-person game is a set A of allocations such that (a) no allocation in A is dominated by any other allocation in A, and (b) every allocation not in A is dominated by some allocation in A.

Two aspects of Definition 13.6–4 should be emphasized. First, von Neumann and Morgenstern define a solution as a set of payoffs. Second, in general, a many-person game may have many solutions (i.e., many sets that satisfy Definition 13.6–4), a unique solution, or no solution.[10] The general character of the von Neumann–Morgenstern solution means that for many games, *any* allocation belongs to a set that is a solution.

An alternative definition of a solution was developed by Shapley (1953) which results in a unique payoff, based on probabilities.

DEFINITION 13.6–5   The **Shapley value** of an *n*-person game to player *i* is the expected outcome to player *i*. The number of outcomes depends upon the number of possible coalitions by player *i* and the outcome to player *i* from being in coalition S is his marginal addition to the coalition, that is, $v(S \cup \{i\}) - v(S)$. The probability of each coalition outcome is the relative number of ways such a coalition can be formed. That is, ϕ_i is the Shapley value when

$$\phi_i = \sum_{\text{all } S \subset N} \frac{s!(n - s - 1)!}{n!} \{v(S \cup \{i\}) - v(S)\}$$

where s is the number in coalition S, N is the total set of *n* players, and $v(S)$ is the characteristic function of the game.

For example, suppose that

$$V(0) = 0$$
$$V(1) = 5 \qquad V(2) = 10 \qquad V(3) = 0$$
$$V(1, 2) = 10 \qquad V(1, 3) = 20 \qquad V(2, 3) = 15$$
$$V(1, 2, 3) = 40$$

Player 1 has the following coalitions he can join:

$$S = \{0\} \qquad S = \{2\} \qquad S = \{3\} \qquad S = \{1, 2\}$$

[10] Lucus (1968) provides an example of a game with no solution.

Therefore

$$\phi_1 = \tfrac{2}{6}[v(1) - v(0)] + \tfrac{1}{6}[v(2, 1) - v(2)] + \tfrac{1}{6}[v(1, 3) - v(3)]$$
$$+ \tfrac{2}{6}[v(1, 2, 3) - v(2, 3)]$$

$$\phi_1 = \tfrac{2}{6}(5 - 0) + \tfrac{1}{6}(10 - 10) + \tfrac{1}{6}(20 - 0) + \tfrac{2}{6}(40 - 15) = \tfrac{80}{6}$$

Verify that $\phi_2 = \tfrac{80}{6}$, $\phi_3 = \tfrac{80}{6}$, and thus that $\phi_1 + \phi_2 + \phi_3 = v(1, 2, 3)$.

The Shapley value is somewhat the opposite of the von Neumann–Morgenstern solution. The Shapley value gives the expected payoff without stating anything about the outcomes possible. The von Neumann–Morgenstern solution is all possible solutions without any probability associated with each. A better construct would be a rule that assigns probabilities to the various allocations in a von Neumann–Morgenstern solution. This has been done (e.g., Aumann and Maschler, 1964), but necessarily requires additional assumptions about the interaction of the players and will not be gone into here.

The core of an n-person game was formally developed by Gillies (1953) and by Luce and Raiffa (1957) as a possible condition for equilibrium in an n-person game.

DEFINITION 13.6–6   An allocation is in the **core** of an n-person game if and only if the best that any coalition can do is not better than the amount received in total from allocation x by each acting independently. That is, an allocation is in the core if $v(S) \leq \sum_{i \in S} x_i$, for every subset $S \subset \{1, 2, \ldots, n\}$, where $v(S)$ is a characteristic function defined for all subsets S.

An alternative description of an allocation, x, which is in the core is that the allocation is **unblocked.** In such a case there is no coalition, or subset of the n players, that can profitably block the attainment of x if x is in the core. Although the formal concepts were not developed at the time, Edgeworth (1889) conjectured that the core of an economic game would reduce to a competitive equilibrium as the number of traders increased. This was proved formally by Scarf and Debreu (1963) and Aumann (1966).

The following example is a collection of definitions and theorems that relate the core of a market game to a competitive equilibrium.

Example 1.   The Core of a Marketing Game and Competitive Equilibria

(1) x is a vector of commodities consumed, where x_j is the total amount of the jth commodity consumed and x^i is the vector of commodities consumed by the ith individual. Thus x_j^i is the amount of the jth commodity consumed by the ith individual.

(2) y is a vector of commodities produced, where y_j is the total amount of the jth commodity produced.

(3) y^i is a vector of commodities produced by the ith individual.

(4) $x^i \in R^n$, the nth Cartesian product of R, the set of real numbers.

(5) Y^i is the feasible production set for the *i*th individual that is closed and convex.

(6) n is the number of players.

(7) $\gtrsim i$ is a complete, connected, and transitive binary preference ordering on R^n for the *i*th player such that:

   (a) $\{x^i \mid x^i \gtrsim_i x^{i*}\}$ is convex for all x^{i*} (i.e., indifference curves are convex to the origin), and

   (b) if $x_j^i \geq x_j^{i*}$ for all j and $x_j^i > x_j^{i*}$ for at least one j, then $x^i \gtrsim_i x^{i*}$ (i.e., more is preferred to less by everyone).

(8) t_i is a head tax levied on the *i*th player ($t_i < 0$ implies i receives a subsidy) such that $\sum_{i=1}^n t_i = 0$.

(9) P is a *n*-dimensional price vector.

(10) A market game is a game where each player selects (x^i, y^i) so as to obtain the most preferred x^i under the condition that $px^i \leq py^i - t_i$ (i.e., each player maximizes his utility given his budget constraint as determined by how much he chooses to produce, y^i).

(11) If $S \in \{1, \ldots, n\}$ is a coalition, then $(px)_S = \sum_{i \in S} py^i - t_i$ is the amount received by the coalition S.

(12) (x^*, y^*) is a **competitive equilibrium** if and only if:

   (a) $x^* = y^*$;

   (b) for some p and t, $py^{i*} \geq py^i$, $y^i \in Y^i$ for all i; and

   (c) if $x^i >_i x^{i*}$, then $px^i > py^{i*} - t_i$ (i.e., any other commodity bundle preferred by the *i*th player, exceeds the budget constraint).

(13) (x^*, y^*) is an **efficient allocation** if there does not exist another (x, y) such that:

   (a) $y = x$ and $y \in \sum_{i=1}^n Y^i$, that is, y is feasible; and

   (b) $x^i \gtrsim_i x^{i*}$ for all i and $x^i >_i x^{i*}$ for at least one i.

(14) (x^*, y^*) is a **core allocation** relative to p and t if there does not exist a blocking coalition, that is, a coalition $S \subset \{1, \ldots, n\}$ such that:

   (a) $\sum_{i \in S} y^i \in \sum_{i \in S} Y^i$;

   (b) $(px)_S \leq (py)_S - \sum_{i \in S} t_i$; and

   (c) $x^i \gtrsim_i x^{i*}$ for all $i \in S$ and $x^i >_i x^{i*}$ for some $i \in S$.

The interesting aspects of the foregoing definitions are their interrelationships. The following theorem proves Edgeworth's original conjecture that every core allocation is a competitive equilibrium under the given abstract definition of a competitive equilibrium.

Theorem 13.6–1

(a) Every core allocation is an efficient allocation.

(b) Every competitive equilibrium is in the core.

(c) Every efficient allocation is a competitive equilibrium.

(d) Every core allocation is a competitive equilibrium.

PROOF   Part (a) is proved by contradiction. Suppose a core allocation $(\bar{x}, \bar{y})$ is not efficient. Then there exists x and y such that $y = x$, y is feasible, and $x^i \gtrsim_i \bar{x}^i$ for all i and $x^i >_i \bar{x}^i$ for at least one i. Also, since $t = \sum t_i = 0$, $px = py - t$. Thus the coalition of $S = \{1, \ldots, n\}$, that is, all players, block $\bar{x}$ and $\bar{y}$, which is a contradiction that $(\bar{x}, \bar{y})$ is in the core.   QED

(b) Again the proof is by contradiction. First note that if $(\bar{x}, \bar{y})$ is a competitive allocation, then by definition, if $x^i \gtrsim_i \bar{x}^i$, then $px^i \geq p\bar{y}^i - t_i$. Suppose that some coalition S blocks $(\bar{x}, \bar{y})$, that is, $(\bar{x}, \bar{y})$ is not in the core. Then for some (x, y) we have

(1) $\sum_{i \in S} y^i \in \sum_{i \in S} Y^i$;
(2) $(px)_S \leq (py)_S - \sum_{i \in S} t_i$; and
(3) $x^i \gtrsim_i \bar{x}^i$ for all $i \in S$ and $x^i >_i \bar{x}^i$ for some $i \in S$.

Using (2), the fact that if $x^i \gtrsim_i \bar{x}^i$ then $px^i \geq p\bar{y}^i - t_i$, and if $x^i >_i \bar{x}^i$, then $px^i > p\bar{y}^i - t_i$, we have

$$(py)_S - \sum_{i \in S} t_i \geq (px)_S > (p\bar{y})_S - \sum_{i \in S} t_i$$

This implies

$$(py)_S > (p\bar{y})_S$$

However, this contradicts the definition that for a competitive allocation $p\bar{y}^i \geq py^i$ for all i, where $y^i \in Y^i$.   QED

Part (c) is proved by using the theorem of separating hyperplanes.[11] First define the "socially preferred" set $\mathring{X} = \sum \mathring{X}_j$, where $\mathring{X}_j = \{x_j \mid x_j >_i \bar{x}_j\}$; and the "socially preferred to or indifferent to" set $\tilde{X} = \sum \tilde{X}_i$, where $\tilde{X}_i = \{x^i \mid x^i \gtrsim_i \bar{x}^i\}$. The intersection of Y and $\mathring{X}$ is empty since both Y and X are convex. On the other hand, the intersection of Y and X is not empty since it contains $\bar{x} = \bar{y}$. Symbolically, we have

$$Y \cap \mathring{X} = \phi \quad \text{and} \quad \bar{x} = \bar{y} \in Y \cap X \neq \phi$$

Now, by Theorem 2.8–1 there exists a price vector p such that if $x \geq \bar{x}$, then $px \geq p\bar{x}$ and $p\bar{y} \geq py$. And also, if for any i, $x^i >_i \bar{x}^i$, then $px^i > p\bar{x}^i$. Finally, if we define $t_i = p\bar{y}^i - px^i$, we have a competitive equilibrium. QED

Part (d) is the converse of parts (a) and (c) combined. What we must show here is that for every $(\bar{x}, \bar{y})$ in the core there exists some p such that

(1) $p\bar{y}^i \geq py^i$ for all i and $y^i \in Y^i$;
(2) if $x^i >_i \bar{x}^i$, then $px^i > p\bar{y}^i - t_i$; and
(3) $\bar{x} = \bar{y}$.

---

[11] Cf. Theorem 2.8–1 and the following discussion.

Since each player must choose $(\bar{x}^i, \bar{y}^i)$ so that $p\bar{x}^i \leq p\bar{y}^i - t_i$ and if $(\bar{x}, \bar{y})$ is in the core it follows that $px^i > p\bar{x}^i$ if $x^i >_i \bar{x}^i$, since coalitions can be any subset of $\{1, \ldots, n\}$ including single individuals.

Next suppose that $py^i > p\bar{y}^i$ for some i and $py^j = p\bar{y}^j$ for all $j \neq i$, where $y^i \in Y^i$. Then by part (a) we have that $\bar{x} = \bar{y}$; that is, the core is efficient. In turn these two facts imply that $px = py > p\bar{y} = p\bar{x}$ or $px > p\bar{x}$. Thus for some i, $x^i >_i \bar{x}^i$, which contradicts the hypothesis that $(\bar{x}, \bar{y})$ is a core allocation.   QED

There have been several articles published that relate the core of an *n*-person game to economic theory.[12] As Foley (1970) notes, in addition to economic applications, the notion of the core of an *n*-person game appears to have a great deal of political relevance when applied to the real world. If, for example, a subset of individuals find it possible to achieve more by acting in concert, then they will withdraw from participation with the rest of the society. In such a case, it is not unrealistic to assume that this will create hostilities on the part of those not in the coalition to force them to participate. On the other hand, if society, in its allocation process, stays in the core, there is at least a minimum rationale for this social system to continue to stay together with all parties participating. There will, in general, still be conflict over initial distributions (e.g., resource ownership, advantages and dis-advantages to learning, etc.) but there is no advantage for a subset of the social system to withdraw unilaterally.

Problems

13.6–1 Suppose we have a two-person, nonconstant-sum game as given by the payoff matrices in Figure 13.6–1.

A's Payoff Matrix

		B's strategies	
		1	2
A's strategies	1	12	0
	2	0	4

B's Payoff Matrix

		B's strategies	
		1	2
A's strategies	1	8	0
	2	0	12

Figure 13.6–1

[12] For example, Shapley and Shubik (1969) show that totally balanced games (i.e., games whose subgames all have cores) are equivalent to market games and also discuss games that have no solution. Foley (1970) shows that some market games with public goods are also in the core of an *n*-person game.

(a) Assuming that mixed strategies are possible, what is A's return if he plays by the minimax criterion?

(b) What is B's minimax payoff?

(c) What is $v(1)$? $v(2)$? $v(1, 2)$?

(d) What conditions must an allocation satisfy for the above problem?

(e) What is the von Neumann–Morgenstern solution for the above problem?

13.6–2 Suppose that we have a three-person game with the following characteristic function:

$$v(1) = v(2) = v(3) = 0$$
$$v(1, 2) = v(1, 3) = v(2, 3) = 100$$
$$v(1, 2, 3) = 100$$

(a) For the allocation (50, 50, 0), find another allocation that dominates it.

(b) Find all other allocations such that they and (50, 50, 0) constitute a von Neumann–Morgenstern solution.

(c) For a given constant, k, explain why or why not the set

$$A_k = (k, x_2, x_3) \qquad 0 \le k \le 50$$

is a von Neumann–Morgenstern solution.

(d) What can you conclude from (b) and (c) about any arbitrary allocation?

13.6–3 Given the following characteristic function for a two-person game:

$$v(1) = 5, v(2) = 4, \quad \text{and} \quad v(1, 2) = 10$$

What is the Shapley value to player 1? To player 2?

13.6–4 What conditions must be met by the characteristic function $[v(1), v(2),$ and $v(1, 2)]$ for a two-person, zero-sum game?

13.6–5 Given the following characteristic function for a three-person game:

$$v(1) = 5 \qquad v(2) = 0 \qquad v(3) = 10$$
$$v(1, 2) = 15 \qquad v(1, 3) = 20 \qquad v(2, 3) = 10$$
$$v(1, 2, 3) = 20$$

Calculate the Shapley values.

13.6–6 Prove that $\sum \phi_i = v(N)$, i.e., prove the sum of the Shapley values equals the value of the characteristic function for the entire group.

References

1. AUMANN, R. J. (1966), "The Existence of a Competitive Equilibrium with a Continuum of Traders," *Econometrica*, **34**:1–17.
2. AUMANN, R. J., and M. MASCHLER (1964), "The Bargaining Set for Cooperative Games," *Annals of Mathematical Studies*, **52**:443–476.

3. BERKOVITZ, L. D. (1967), "A Survey of Differential Games," in A. V. Balrakrishnan and L. W. Neustadt (eds.), *Mathematical Theory of Control*, New York: Academic.

4. BORCH, K. H. (1968), *The Economics of Uncertainty*, Princeton, N.J.: Princeton University Press.

5. DAVIS, J. R., and N. PALOMBA (1969), "The National Farmers Organization and the Prisoners Dilemma," *Social Science Quarterly*, **50**:742–748.

6. DORFMAN, R., P. A. SAMUELSON, and R. SOLOW (1958), *Linear Programming and Economic Analysis*, New York: McGraw-Hill.

7. EDGEWORTH, F. Y. (1889), *Mathematical Psychics*, London: C. Kegan Paul.

8. FOLEY, DUNCAN (1970), "Lindahl's Solution and the Core of an Economy with Public Goods," *Econometrica*, **38**:66–72.

9. GILLIES, D. B. (1953), "Some Theorems on *n*-Person Games," Ph.D Dissertation, Princeton University, Princeton, N.J.

10. ISAACS, RUFUS (1965), *Differential Games*, New York: Wiley.

11. KOOPMANS, T. C. (1951) (ed.), *Activity Analysis of Production and Allocation*, New York: Wiley.

12. LUCE, R. D., and H. RAIFFA (1957), *Games and Decisions*, New York: Wiley.

13. LUCUS, W.F. (1968), "A Game with No Solution," *Bulletin of the American Mathematical Society*, **74**:237–239.

14. MARKOWITZ, H. M. (1952), "Portfolio Selection," *The Journal of Finance*, **7**:77–91.

15. MILNOR, J. (1954), "Games Against Nature," in R. M. Thrall, C. H. Coombs, and R. L. Davis (eds.), *Decision Processes*, New York: Wiley.

16. NASH, J. (1950), "The Bargaining Problem," *Econometrica*, **18**:155–162.

17. OWEN, G. (1966), *Game Theory*, Philadelphia: Saunders.

18. SAVAGE, L. J. (1951), "The Theory of Statistical Decision," *Journal of the American Statistical Association*, **46**:55–67.

19. SAVAGE, L. J. (1954), *The Foundation of Statistics*, New York: Wiley.

20. SCARF, H., and G. DEBREU (1963), "A Limit Theorem on the Core of an Economy," *International Economic Review*, **4**:235–246.

21. SCHELLING, T. C. (1960), *The Strategy of Conflict*, Cambridge, Mass.: Harvard University Press.

22. SHAPLEY, L. S. (1953), "A Value for *n*-Person Games," *Annals of Mathematics Studies*, **28**:307–317.

23. SHAPLEY, L. S., and M. SHUBIK (1969), "On Market Games," *Journal of Economic Theory*, **1**:9–25.

24. VON NEUMANN, JOHN, and OSKAR MORGENSTERN (1947), *The Theory of Games and Economic Behavior*, 2nd ed., Princeton, N.J.: Princeton University Press.

Chapter 14

Control Theory

14.1 INTRODUCTION: THE CONCEPTUAL FRAMEWORK OF CONTROL THEORY

Perhaps more than anything else, the most unique feature of control theory is its conceptual framework. The reader will notice, and be reminded of, many similarities between particular aspects of control theory and topics covered heretofore. For example, control theory can be viewed as a generalization of Lagrange's problem in the calculus of variations.[1] Also, problems in control theory can be formulated, at least conceptually, as mathematical programming problems. Alternative methods of solving "control theory problems" include both dynamic programming and Isaacs' solutions in differential game theory, which have been covered in previous chapters.[2] Details of how control theory is related to these other topics will be covered in more detail in Sections 14.6 and 14.7. First let us develop the conceptual framework of control theory.

Basically, modern control theory relies heavily on the concept of the state of a dynamical system and a set of parameters (controls) that determine the course of the state over time to best achieve specified ends. A system is understood to be any object that can be adequately characterized at any instant of time by n real numbers $x_1, \ldots, x_n$. This vector $x = (x_1, \ldots, x_n)$ is termed the state. The vector space X for the variable x is termed the phase space of the system. For example, if the object under study, that is, the system, were an automobile, then the state might consist of its coordinates, velocity, acceleration, change of direction, and so forth. If the system were an economy, the state might include output, unemployment, investment, change in the money supply, balance of payments, and so forth. How many variables x_i are included in the state? This will depend. What is necessary is that the state at $x(t_0)$ and the specification of a control vector $u(t) = [u_1(t), \ldots, u_m(t)]$, for all $t \geq t_0$, the initial time, must be sufficient to determine uniquely the entire future of all state variables, $x(t)$. In other words, the state is a sufficient

[1] See Definition 10.8–1.

[2] See Section 12.3 for a discussion of dynamic programming and Section 13.5 for a cursory view of Isaacs' models.

description of the system if no knowledge of the past history of the system is necessary to determine all future states.

This concept of the state presents no formal problems but may entail several practical difficulties. In the example of an automobile, if a prior accident were to have an impact on the future course of the automobile, then one of the state variables would perhaps include the condition of the frame at t. Or for a social system, a psychological trauma induced by a severe depression would perhaps be described in the state as a "trauma index."

The control vector u is contained in the control region U, which is a subset of m-dimensional Euclidean space. Also, u may be constrained by one or several equations $g(u) = 0$. However, these constraining relations can, in general, be included in the definition of the control region U.

Definition 14.1–1 formally defines a dynamical system and its associated components.[3]

DEFINITION 14.1–1 A **dynamical system,** S, is a composite of the sets T, X, U; the functions[4] $u(t)$ and $f^*[x(t), u(t), t]$; and variables $x(t)$ such that:

(a) X is the subset of n-dimensional Euclidean space, $X \subset R^n$, and U is a closed and bounded subset of m-dimensional Euclidean space.

(b) $x(t)$ is defined on T and takes on values in X.

(c) The function $u(t)$ is defined on T and takes on values in U, and each function $u(t)$ is piecewise continuous.[5]

(d) The function $f^*[x(t), u(t), t]$ maps $T \times X \times U$ into R^k (i.e., f^* is a real-valued k-dimensional function from the Cartesian product $T \times X \times U$ into k-dimensional space).

(e) For all $x(t_0) \in X$, all $t_0 \in T$, and all $t \in T$ such that $t \geq t_0$, if $u(t) = u^*(t)$, then $f^*[x(t_0), u^*(t_0), t] = f^*[x(t_0), u(t_0), t]$. That is, $u(t_0)$, a piecewise-continuous function defined for t, $t_0 \leq t < t_1$, uniquely determines f^* for a given $x(t_0)$.

(f) If t_0, t, and $t_1 \in T$, where $t_0 < t < t_1$ and $x(t_0) \in X$, then the intersection of the sets S_u is not empty, where

$$S_u = \{x(t_0), u(t_0), t \mid f^*[x(t_0), u(t_0), t] = f^*[x(t), u(t), t]\}$$

for $u \in U$; that is,

$$\bigcap_{u \in U} S_u \neq \varnothing$$

---

[3] This follows Athans and Falb (1966).

[4] The notation for a function will be as follows: $u(t)$ denotes a function defined through some period of time. The symbol $u(t)|t_0$ denotes the "value" of the function $u(t)$ at t_0. The symbol $u(t_0)$ will be used to denote a function that is defined beginning at t_0, i.e., $u(t_0)$ is defined for all t, where $t_0 \leq t < t_1$.

[5] That is, continuous except at a finite number of points.

This ensures that there is at least one $x \in X$ that accounts for any pair $\{u(t_0), f^*[x(t_0), u(t_0), t]\}$. In other words, (e) and (f) imply that there is a function ϕ such that $x(t) = \phi[t, u(t_0), x(t_0)]$.

(g) The functions f and ϕ are continuous in all arguments. In particular, this implies that for a small variation in the function u, the variation in the value of $f[x(t_0), u(t_0), t]$ for all t will be small.

(h) The function ϕ is such that:

   (i) $\lim_{t \to t_0} \phi[t, u(t_0), x(t_0)] = \phi[t_0, u(t_0), x(t_0)] = x(t_0)$ for all t, and $t_0 \in T$, $x(t_0) \in X$, and $u \in U$.

   (ii) $\phi[t, u(t_0), x(t_0)] = \phi[t, u(t_*), \phi(t_*, u(t_0), x(t_0))]$ for $t_0 < t_* \le t$, all t_0, t_*, and $t \in T$; $x(t_0) \in X$; and $u \in U$.

   (iii) $\phi[t, u(t_0), x(t_0)] = \phi[t, u^*(t_0), x(t_0)]$ for all $u(t_0) = u^*(t_0)$, and $t_0 \le t \le t_1$.

DEFINITION 14.1–2 X is the **state space** of the dynamical system S and $x(t)$ is the **state**.

DEFINITION 14.1–3 T is the **domain** of the system S.

DEFINITION 14.1–4 U is the **control space** and $u(t)$ is a **control** (or **input**) of the system S.

DEFINITION 14.1–5 $f^*[x(t_0), u(t_0), t]$ is the **output** of the system S, in general, a vector function.

DEFINITION 14.1–6 $\phi[t, u(t_0), x(t_0)]$ is the **transition function** of the system S.

DEFINITION 14.1–7   The subset $\{x(t) \mid x(t) = \phi[t, u(t_0), x(t_0)]\}$ is the **trajectory,** or **motion,** of the system generated by the control $u(t_0)$ and initial state $x(t_0)$.

It is useful now to interpret and illustrate the facets of a dynamical system given in Definitions 14.1–1–14.1–7. This will place the scope of control theory more firmly in mind, aid in noting its relation to other mathematical techniques, and illustrate its applicability.

Definition 14.1–1(e) states formally that the system is not dependent upon past history but is uniquely determined by a piecewise-continuous control $u(t) \in U \times T$. In Figure 14.1–1 we have sketched a piecewise-continuous control that is continuous except at the points t' and t^*. At points of discontinuity either a left derivative or right derivative can be defined. The left time derivative at t^* in Figure 14.1–1 is the slope of the tangent ss', while the right derivative is the slope of the tangent rr'.

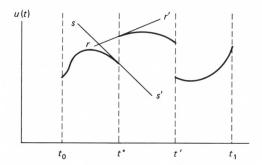

Figure 14.1–1   *A piecewise-continuous control function $u(t)$.*

Part (f) of the definition ensures that there is a state that corresponds to every control and output pair of the system. In addition, (f) requires that at any time t greater than t_0 there is a state that summarizes the past history of the system. Thus, specification of the initial state and a control determines all future states. For example, given an initial position of an automobile, its acceleration, change of direction, and so forth for all future time (i.e., a control function) determines all future positions of the automobile.

Part (g) is a "regularity" or smoothness condition. This guarantees that a small change in the control will cause a correspondingly small change in the output of the system. For example, an economic model must be sufficiently well structured so that a small change in the money supply would not create an infinite change in the level of employment, rate of investment, or the like.

Part (h) gives three conditions that the change in the state variables must meet. First the initial position, $x(t_0)$, must correspond to the starting point of the trajectory of the system under the influence of a specified control. Second, if $x(t_*)$ is a point on the trajectory of the system beginning at $x(t_0)$ under control $u(t_0)$, then the control $u(t_0)$ must transpose the state from $x(t_0)$ to $x(t_*)$ as t_0 goes to t_*. Third, future input or controls do not affect the current state. The current state does not depend upon the future of the control function $u(t)$.

Most work in control theory has dealt with differential systems, which are special dynamical systems.

DEFINITION 14.1–8   A dynamical system S is a **differential system** if

(1) in the transition equation, $\phi[t, u(t_0), x(t_0)] = x(t)$, ϕ is the solution of a system of differential equations; that is $\dot{x}(t) = dx/dt = f[x(t), u(t), t]$, where the functions are continuous in all arguments, have continuous partial derivations, and the solution ϕ is unique; and

(2) the output function $f^*[x(t_0), u(t_0), t]$ is a continuous function in all of its arguments.

DEFINITION 14.1–9   Two **dynamical systems,** S and S^*, **are equivalent** if there exists a nonsingular $n \times n$ matrix P such that

$$P^{-1}x(t) = z(t)$$

where $x(t)$ is the state variable for S and $z(t)$ is the state variable for S^*.

As in other areas of mathematics, the properties of a linear system often provide an analytic solution to the problem.[6] The same is true in control theory. In fact, unless the dynamical system is a linear system, it is quite likely that there will be no analytical solution and the problem can be solved only by numerical techniques.

DEFINITION 14.1–10   A differential system is a **linear differential system**[7] if:

(1) the differential equation for the state variable, $x(t)$, is a linear differential equation that is,

$$\dot{x}(t) = A(t)x(t) + B(t)u(t)$$

where $A(t)$ is an $n \times n$ matrix function of time and $B(t)$ is an $n \times m$ matrix function of time; and

(2) the output of the system is a linear function of $x(t)$ and $u(t)$, that is,

$$f^* = C(t)x(t) + D(t)u(t)$$

where $C(t)$ is a $k \times n$ matrix function of time and $D(t)$ is a $k \times m$ matrix function of time.

DEFINITION 14.1–11   A **time-invariant linear, autonomous,** or **stationary system** is one where the matrices A, B, C, and D in Definition 14.1–10 are invariant over time.

Thus far our efforts have been directed toward developing the conceptual framework of control theory and have not stated the "problem" of control. The problem of control theory is to minimize some performance function J. For example, the brachistochrone problem in the calculus of variations is a special case of a problem in control theory.[8] The state is the position and

---

[6] For example, linear programming in mathematical programming problems.

[7] Cf. Section 7.1.

[8] See Section 10.1.

acceleration of a ball due to the force of gravity, while the control is the shape of the path. The performance function is the elapsed time from point to point.

Formally, we have Definition 14.1–12.

DEFINITION 14.1–12   The **control problem** for a differential system (Definition 14.1–8) is to find the control $u^*(t) \in U$ such that the performance function J is a minimum, where

$$J = \int_{t_0}^{t_1} f^0[x(t), u(t), t]\, dt$$

t_1 may or may not be specified, and f^0 is part, all, or some transformation of the output f^* of the system.

If $u^*(t) = \min_{u(t)} J$, then $u^*(t)$ is termed the **optimal control.**

For example, if time were to be minimized, then

$$J = t - t_0 = \int_{t_0}^{t} f^0\, dt \quad \text{where} \quad f^0[x(t), u(t), t] \equiv 1$$

Several other typical performance functions will be presented in Section 14.4.

Pontryagin et al. (1962) give the solution to the above control problem in the form of the celebrated "maximum principle of Pontryagin," which will be be developed in Section 14.4. First we turn to some considerations of existence, uniqueness, stability, and methods of solution for differential equations.[9]

Problems

14.1–1   Suppose you wish to construct a dynamical system for an airplane.
  (a) How many state variables would you need to define? Give some examples.
  (b) How many control variables would you need to define? Give examples of control variables and their limits.
  (c) Give an example of the output of the system.
  (d) What might be a "control problem" for the aircraft if it is a fighter plane? Bomber? Commercial aircraft?

14.1–2   Illustrate the kinds of data and specified functional relations necessary to describe a firm as a dynamical system.

14.1–3   (a) How does the assumption that the system in Problem 14.1–1 is a differential system affect the relations described in that problem?
  (b) If the system in Problem 14.1–2 is a linear differential system, what will be the effect on the specified functional relations?

---

[9] The reader may skip the next two sections and proceed directly to Section 14.4 without loss in continuity.

14.2   SOME COMMENTS ON EXISTENCE, UNIQUENESS, STABILITY, AND SOLUTIONS FOR ORDINARY DIFFERENTIAL EQUATIONS

Before developing the maximum principle of Pontryagin, we shall review a few points of the existence, uniqueness, and stability of a differential system. This review and discussion is necessary to develop a "familiarity" or "sophistication" in dealing with the control problem.

A sufficient condition for an ordinary differential equation to possess a unique solution is that it satisfy the Lipschitz condition.

DEFINITION 14.2–1   For $\dot{x} = f(x)$, an ordinary differential equation, $f(x)$ satisfies the **Lipschitz condition** in an ε neighborhood of x^0, $N(x^0, \varepsilon) = \{x \mid \|x - x^0\| \leq \varepsilon\}$,[10] if there exists a constant $k > 0$ such that $\|f(x) - f(x^*)\| \leq k\|x - x^*\|$ for all x and $x^* \in R$.

If a function satisfies the Lipschitz condition, then it is continuous, but not all continuous functions satisfy the Lipschitz condition. For example, suppose $\dot{x} = f(x) = \sqrt{x}$. The Lipschitz condition requires that around the point $x^0 = 0$,

$$\sqrt{x} \leq kx$$

But for any $k > 0$, x can always be chosen small enough so that

$$\frac{1}{\sqrt{x}} > k$$

On the other hand, suppose that $f(x) = |x|$. The function $f(x)$ satisfies the Lipschitz condition, as is easily verified by letting $k = 1$. Thus the Lipschitz condition is more general than the requirement that the derivative be continuous.

Theorem 14.2–1   If $dx/dt = f(x)$ and $x(t_0) = x^0$ satisfy the Lipschitz condition in an ε neighborhood, $N(x^0, \varepsilon)$, then $x(t)$ exists and is unique in the interval $t_0 \leq t \leq t_0 + \varepsilon$.

PROOF   We only sketch the proof of the theorem following the development by Koppel (1968).

Define a sequence of functions $\{x^i(t) \mid i = 1, 2, \ldots\}$ by $x^{i+1}(t) = x^0 + \int_{t_0}^{t} f[x^i(t)]\, dt$. Then we have $x^0(t)$ is a constant and $x^1(t) = x^0 +$

---

[10] $\|x\|$ is the norm of x. The norm is a function such that $\|x\| \geq 0$, $\|x + x^*\| \leq \|x\| + \|x^*\|$, $\|ax\| = |a|\|x\|$, for all scalars a, and $\|x\| = 0$ if and only if $x = 0$. (Cf. Definition 10.3–2.)

$\int_{t_0}^{t} f[x^0(t)] \, dt$, and so on for all i. All such functions x^i are contained in $N(x^0, \varepsilon)$, since R is a compact point set[11] and $f(x)$ is continuous.

Since

$$x^2(t) - x^1(t) = \int_{t_0}^{t} \{f[x^1(t)] - f[x^0(t)]\} \, dt$$

or

$$\|x^2(t) - x^1(t)\| \le \int_{t_0}^{t} \|f[x^1(t)] - f[x^0(t)]\| \, dt$$

by definition of a norm, the Lipschitz condition states that

$$\|f[x^1(t)] - f[x^0(t)]\| \le k\|x^1(t) - x^0(t)\|$$

After substitution and integration, this becomes, for $i = 1$ and $i + 1 = 2$,

$$\|x^2(t) - x^1(t)\| \le k\varepsilon(t - t_0) \quad \text{where} \quad t_0 \le t \le t_0 + \delta$$

δ an arbitrarily small constant, and for any i,

$$\|x^{i+1}(t) - x^i(t)\| \le k \int_{t_0}^{t} \|x^i(t) - x^{i-1}(t)\| \, dt$$

or

$$\|x^{i+1}(t) - x^i(t)\| \le \varepsilon \frac{[k(t - t_0)]^i}{i!} \quad \text{where} \quad t_0 \le t \le t_0 + \delta$$

This implies that

$$\|x^{i+j}(t) - x^i(t)\| = \left\| \sum_{g=i}^{i+j-1} [x^{g+1}(t) - x^g(t)] \right\| \le \sum_{g=i}^{i+j-1} \|x^{g+1}(t) - x^g(t)\|$$

$$\le \varepsilon \sum_{g=i}^{i+j-1} \frac{[k(t - t_0)]^g}{g!}$$

$$\le \varepsilon \sum_{g=i}^{i+j-1} \frac{(k\delta)^g}{g!} \le \frac{\varepsilon(k\delta)^i}{i!} e^{k\delta}$$

The last inequality is obtained by Taylor's expansion of an exponential.

Since

$$\lim_{i \to \infty} \frac{\varepsilon(k\delta)^i}{i!} e^{k\delta} = 0$$

then

$$\lim_{i \to \infty} x^{i+1}(t) = x(t) = x^0 + \lim_{i \to \infty} \int_{t_0}^{t} f[x^i(t)] \, dt$$

or

$$x(t) = x^0 + \int_{t_0}^{t} f[x(t)] \, dt$$

---

[11] Cf. Definition 2.8–7.

which proves the existence of a solution. Uniqueness can be shown easily by letting $x(t)$ and $y(t)$ satisfy some initial conditions. Then $x(t) - y(t) = 0$ for all t.

The conditions of Theorem 14.2–1 can now be extended to a controllable system.

Corollary to Theorem 14.2–1   If the differential system is of the form

$$\dot{x} = f[x(t), u(t), t]$$

$$x(t_0) = x^0$$

then for a given $u(t)$ there exists a unique solution if $f[x(t), u(t), t]$ satisfies the Lipschitz condition.

Note that $u(t)$ changes $f[x(t), u(t), t]$ into $\tilde{f}[x(t), t]$. By extending the system into

$$\bar{x}(t) = \begin{bmatrix} x(t) \\ t - t_0 \end{bmatrix} \quad \text{and} \quad f(t) = \begin{bmatrix} \tilde{f}(t) \\ 1 \end{bmatrix}$$

then $\dot{\bar{x}}(t) = \tilde{f}(\bar{x})$ and Theorem 14.2–1 applies.

However, the Lipschitz condition is restrictive and the following, more general theorem can be proved:

Theorem 14.2–2[12]   If $x = f(x, t)$ is everywhere continuous in x and t in an ε neighborhood of $x(t_0) = x^0$ and if:

(1) $\|x(t) - x^0\| \le \alpha$ for all $x \in N$;
(2) $|t - t_0| \le \beta$ for all $x \in N$;
(3) $\|f(x, t)\| \le K(t)$ and $K(t)$ is integrable; and
(4) $\|f(x, t) - f(\bar{x}, t)\| \le k(t)\|x(t) - \bar{x}(t)\|$ and $k(t)$ is integrable;

then there exists a unique solution for $x(t)$ for $t_0 \le t \le t_0 + \delta$.

If the system is linear, existence and uniqueness are guaranteed.

Theorem 14.2–3   (Koppel, 1968) If $\dot{x} = A(t)x(t) + c(t)$, where $A(t)$ is a continuous matrix function of time and $c(t)$ is a continuous function of time for $t_0 \le t \le t_0 + \delta$, then there exists a unique solution $x(t)$ for the system.

PROOF   The proof of this theorem follows quite closely the lines of the proof of Theorem 14.2–1. Define a sequence of functions

$$x^{i+1} = x^0 + \int_{t_0}^{t} A(t)x^i(t) + c(t)\, dt \qquad \text{for } i = 1, 2, \ldots$$

[12] Struble (1962).

Then, since the norm of $A(t)x(t)$ satisfies

$$\|A(t)x(t)\| \leq \|A(t)\| \cdot \|x(t)\|$$

it follows that

$$\|x^{i+1}(t) - x^i(t)\| \leq \int_{t_0}^t [\|A(t)\| \cdot \|x^i(t) - x^{i-1}(t)\|]\, dt \qquad \text{for } i = 1, 2, \dots$$

Further, since $A(t)$ is continuous on the interval $t_0 \leq t \leq t_0 + \delta$, the norm of $A(t)$ must be bounded by nonnegative constants; that is, there exist positive numbers m and M such that

$$0 \leq m \leq A(t) \leq M \qquad \text{for all } t$$

Substituting, we have

$$\|x^{i+1}(t) - x^i(t)\| \leq M \int_{t_0}^t \|x^i(t) - x^{i-1}(t)\|\, dt$$

From which we establish by induction (cf. Theorem 14.2–1) that

$$\|x^{i+1}(t) - x^i(t)\| \leq \|x^0\| \frac{(M\delta)^{n+1}}{(n+1)!}$$

The proofs for existence and uniqueness follow from this as in the proof of Theorem 14.2–1.

A differential system is a set of simultaneous equations, thus questions of stability follow the development in Chapter 9. Here we shall review the basic concepts of stability and some special theorems that apply to control theory. For a more complete development the reader should refer to Chapter 9 and/or the references on stability.

There are various kinds of stability that can be defined. The most useful include total stability, asymptotic stability, and stability in the large. A system is **totally stable** at the origin if for every $\varepsilon > 0$ there exists a number $\delta > 0$ such that if the distance of $x(t_0)$ from the origin is less than or equal to δ, then the solution to the system is always within an ε distance from the origin. In short, if the state of a system begins anywhere less than an infinite distance from the origin, its value does not become infinite.

An **asymptotically stable system** is totally stable. In addition, there must exist an $r > 0$, such that if $x(t_0)$ is within an r distance from the origin, for every $\varepsilon > 0$, there exists a finite $t > 0$ such that the state of the system will be within an ε distance of the origin. In other words, the limit as time approaches infinity of the state variable is the origin. **Asymptotic stability in the large** guarantees that *every* motion will approach the origin instead of only those within an r neighborhood of the origin.

The following theorems give some sufficient conditions for stability, except Theorem 14.2–7 which gives some sufficient conditions for instability. Much of the dynamic stability theory utilizes a Lyapunov function, which is defined in Theorem 14.2–4.

Theorem 14.2–4[13]   If a Lyapunov function exists for the system $\dot{x} = f(x)$ and $f(0) = 0$, then the system is stable. A **Lyapunov function** $V(x)$ is a scalar function such that for all x, where $\|x\| \leq \varepsilon > 0$,

(1) $V(x) > 0$, if $x \neq 0$;
(2) $V(0) = 0$;
(3) $V(x)$ has continuous partial derivatives; and

(4)
$$\frac{dV}{dt} = \left(\frac{\partial V}{\partial x}\right)' f(x) \leq 0$$

Given a dynamical system, Theorem 14.2–4 assures us that all we need do to guarantee stability is to find a Lyapunov function. Asymptotic stability is guaranteed for a slightly more restricted Lyapunov function.

Theorem 14.2–5[13]   If a Lyapunov function exists for $x = f(x)$ such that

$$\frac{dV}{dt} = \left(\frac{\partial V}{\partial x}\right)' f(x) < 0$$

then the system is asymptotically stable.

Similarly, another slight restriction on the Lyapunov function gives sufficient conditions for asymptotic stability in the large.

Theorem 14.2–6   If

(1) a Lyapunov function exists for all x,

(2) $\dfrac{dV}{dt} = \left(\dfrac{\partial V}{\partial x}\right)' f(x) < 0$, and

(3) $V(x)$ becomes infinite as the distance of x from the origin becomes infinite,

then the system is asymptotically stable in the large.

By reversing the above argument for stability, we can find sufficient conditions for instability.

[13] Cf. Theorems 9.4–3 and 9.5–4. These ideas were given a precise definition by Lyapunov in 1892 and were translated from Russian into French in 1907. See Hahn (1966) for a further discussion of stability.

Theorem 14.2-7   If there exists a scalar function $V(x)$ for the region r such that

(1) $V(x) > 0$ for $0 < x \leq \varepsilon$,

(2) $V(0) = 0$,

(3) $\dfrac{dV}{dt} = \left(\dfrac{\partial V}{\partial x}\right)' f(x) > 0$, and

(4) $\dfrac{dV}{dt}$ is continuous,

then the system $\dot{x} = f(x)$ is unstable.

Given a linear differential system, we can find necessary and sufficient conditions for stability. The next two theorems give such conditions for asymptotic stability in the large.

Theorem 14.2-8   The linear homogeneous differential system $\dot{x} = Ax$ is asymptotically stable in the large if and only if for every negative definite matrix[14] Q there exists a positive definite matrix P such that[15]

$$A'P + PA = Q$$

Theorem 14.2-9   The linear differential system $\dot{x} = Ax + g(x)$ is asymptotically stable if and only if:

(1) the homogeneous system $\dot{x} = Ax$ is asymptotically stable in the large, and

(2) $\displaystyle\lim_{\|x\| \to 0} \left[\dfrac{\|g(x)\|}{\|x\|} \right] = 0$

The proofs are too lengthy to be presented here.[16]

As an aid in finding a Lyapunov function for nonlinear systems, we have the following two important theorems.[17]

Theorem 14.2-10   For the nonlinear homogeneous differential system $\dot{x} = f(x)$ and $f(0) = 0$, if the Jacobian[18] matrix $\partial f/\partial x$ is negative quasidefinite, that is, if $F(x) = \partial f/\partial x + [\partial f/\partial x]'$ is negative definite, then

---

[14] Definition 4.4–1.

[15] First proved by Lyapunov in 1892.

[16] For further details, see Hahn (1966) or Koppel (1968).

[17] See Kalman and Bertram (1960) or Hahn (1966) for further discussion.

[18] Definition 5.2–2.

$f(x)'f(x) = V(x)$ is a Lyapunov function. Since $dV/dt = (\partial V/\partial x)'f(x) < 0$, the system is asymptotically stable.

Theorem 14.2–11 For the nonlinear homogeneous differential system $\dot{x} = f(x)$ and $f(0) = 0$, if there exist constant, symmetric, positive definite matrices P and Q such that

$$F(x) = \left(\frac{\partial f}{\partial x}\right)'P + P\frac{\partial f}{\partial x} + Q$$

is positive definite, then $V(x) = f'Pf$ is a Lyapunov function and thus the system is asymptotically stable in the large.

Example 1. Consider the following simple nonlinear differential system:

$$\dot{x}_1 = -x_1^2 + x_2$$
$$\dot{x}_2 = -x_2^2 - x_1$$
$$x_1, x_2 \geq 0$$

The Jacobian matrix is

$$\frac{\partial f}{\partial x} = \begin{bmatrix} -2x_1 & 1 \\ -1 & -2x_2 \end{bmatrix}$$

and $(\partial f/\partial x)' + \partial f/\partial x$ is

$$\begin{bmatrix} -4x_1 & 0 \\ 0 & -4x_2 \end{bmatrix}$$

which is negative definite since the principal minor determinants alternate in sign $-$, $+$. Thus, by Theorem 14.2–10,

$$f(x)'f(x) = x_1^4 - 2x_1^2x_2 + 2x_1x_2^2 + x_1^2 + x_2^2 + x_2^4$$

is a Lyapunov function and the system is asymptotically stable in the large.

Example 2. Given the following differential system:

$$\dot{x}_1 = -x_2^2 - x_1$$
$$\dot{x}_2 = -x_2^2 - x_1^2$$
$$x_1, x_2 \geq 0$$

First evaluating the Jacobian, we find that

$$\frac{\partial f}{\partial x} = \begin{bmatrix} -1 & -2x_1 \\ -2x_1 & -2x_2 \end{bmatrix}$$

which is not negative quasidefinite. Therefore we next attempt to find constant, symmetric matrices P and Q such that

$$F(x) = \left(\frac{\partial f}{\partial x}\right)' P + P\frac{\partial f}{\partial x} + Q$$

is positive definite. If we let

$$P = \begin{bmatrix} 2 & -1 \\ -1 & 1 \end{bmatrix} \quad \text{and} \quad Q = \begin{bmatrix} 5 & 0 \\ 0 & 1 \end{bmatrix}$$

then $F(x)$ will be positive definite. Since P, Q, and $F(x)$ fulfill the premises of Theorem 14.2–11, we may conclude that the system is asymptotically stable in the large.

The foregoing theorems relate to properties of a dynamical system. They are "primary" properties in the sense that a system must possess a stable solution if there is to be any control problem. Furthermore, for a general nonlinear dynamical system, often the state equations do not possess an analytical solution. However, qualitative answers can be attained for questions of existence, uniqueness, and stability—precursors for numerical solutions. Next we review two methods of solving a system of ordinary differential equations, the Fourier and Laplace transforms.

Fourier and Laplace Transforms

A periodic function of time, $f(t)$, may be represented as a linear combination of sine and cosine waves by use of a Fourier series,

$$f(t) = \frac{1}{T}\int_{-T/2}^{T/2} f(\theta)\, d\theta + \frac{2}{T}\sum_{n=1}^{\infty} \cos\frac{2n\pi t}{T}\int_{-T/2}^{T/2} f(\theta)\cos\frac{2n\pi\theta}{T}\, d\theta$$

$$+ \frac{2}{T}\sum_{n=1}^{\infty}\sin\frac{2n\pi t}{T}\int_{-T/2}^{T/2} f(\theta)\sin\frac{2n\pi\theta}{T}\, d\theta$$

where T is the period of the function $f(t)$.

This expression can be simplified by defining the frequency $\omega_0 = 2\pi/T$. Since

$$\cos n\omega_0 t = \frac{e^{in\omega_0 t} + e^{-in\omega_0 t}}{2}$$

$$\sin n\omega_0 t = \frac{e^{in\omega_0 t} - e^{-in\omega_0 t}}{2}$$

where i is the imaginary number $\sqrt{-1}$, the Fourier series becomes

$$f(t) = \sum_{n=-\infty}^{\infty}\frac{e^{in\omega_0 t}}{T}\int_{-T/2}^{T/2} f(\theta)\, e^{-in\omega_0 t}\, d\theta$$

Any arbitrary function can be regarded as a periodic function with a period that becomes infinite. Thus define

$$\omega = n\omega_0 = \frac{2n\pi}{T}$$

Then

$$\frac{1}{T} = \frac{\omega_0}{2\pi} = \frac{\omega}{2n\pi}$$

Since $d\omega = \omega_0 \, dn = (2\pi \, dn)/T$ and since as T approaches infinity the summation portion becomes an integral, $viz.$,

$$\lim_{T\to\infty} \sum_{n=-\infty}^{\infty} \frac{e^{in\omega_0 t}}{T} = \int_{-\infty}^{\infty} \frac{e^{in\omega_0 t}}{T} \, dn$$

substituting, we have

$$\lim_{T\to\infty} \sum_{n=\infty}^{\infty} \frac{e^{in\omega_0 t}}{T} = \int_{-\infty}^{\infty} \frac{1}{2\pi} e^{i\omega t} \, d\omega$$

and the Fourier series becomes

$$f(t) = \frac{1}{2\pi} \int_{-\infty}^{\infty} F(i\omega)e^{i\omega t} \, d\omega$$

where

$$F(i\omega) = \int_{-\infty}^{\infty} f(t)e^{-i\omega t} \, dt$$

DEFINITION 14.2–2   The **Fourier transform** of $f(t)$ is

$$F(i\omega) = \int_{-\infty}^{\infty} f(t)e^{-i\omega t} \, dt$$

For many functions, the Fourier transform does not exist since the function must be absolutely integrable; that is,

$$\int_{-\infty}^{\infty} |f(t)| \, dt < \infty$$

For example, if $f(t) = t$, then the Fourier transform does not exist, since

$$\int_{-\infty}^{\infty} t \, dt = \frac{t^2}{2}\bigg|_{-\infty}^{\infty}$$

does not exist. For this reason the Laplace transform is a more general transformation. The Laplace transform requires the existence of a constant $\sigma \geq 0$ such that

$$\int_{-\infty}^{\infty} e^{-\sigma t}|f(t)| \, dt < \infty$$

The Laplace transform is the Fourier transform of $e^{-\sigma t} f(t)$ or a "discounted" Fourier transform. Since the Fourier transform of

$$e^{-\sigma t} f(t) = \int_{-\infty}^{\infty} f(t) e^{-(\sigma + i\omega)t} \, dt$$

letting $s = \sigma + i\omega$ we have

$$F(s) = \int_{0}^{\infty} f(t) e^{-st} \, dt$$

DEFINITION 14.2–3   The **Laplace transform** of $f(t)$ is

$$F(s) = \int_{0}^{\infty} f(t) e^{-st} \, dt$$

Example 3.   Suppose $f(t) = e^{at}$. The Laplace transform is

$$F(s) = \int_{0}^{\infty} e^{at} e^{-st} \, dt = \int_{0}^{\infty} e^{t(a-s)} \, dt$$

or

$$F(s) = \frac{1}{s - a}$$

s must be larger than a for the integral to exist. Hence the necessary value of σ depends upon a.

Since the Laplace transforms can be found in most standard mathematics tables, they are often quite useful in solving differential equations. For example, suppose we have the first-order differential equation

$$\dot{x}(t) + bx(t) + u(t) = 0$$

Taking the Laplace transform, we have

$$\int_{0}^{\infty} [\dot{x}(t) + bx(t) + u(t)] e^{-st} \, dt = 0$$

Letting $F(s) = L\{x(t)\}$, the Laplace transform of $x(t)$, and $U(s) = L\{u(t)\}$, the Laplace transform of $u(t)$, and since

$$\int_{0}^{\infty} \dot{x}(t) e^{-st} \, dt = -x(0) + s \int_{0}^{\infty} e^{-st} x(t) \, dt$$

we have $-x(0) + (b + s)F(s) - U(s) = 0$.
Solving for $F(s)$

$$F(s) = \frac{x(0) + U(s)}{b + s} = \frac{x(0)}{b + s} + \frac{U(s)}{b + s}$$

or, by inverting the Laplace transform,

$$x(t) = x(0)e^{-bt} + \alpha(t)$$

where

$$L\left\{\frac{x(0)}{b+s}\right\} = x(0)e^{-bt}$$

and[19]

$$L\{\alpha(t)\} = \frac{U(s)}{b+s}$$

An immediate extension is the solution for a system of n first-order differential equations that are time invariant.

Theorem 14.2–12   For a system of n first-order linear differential equations of the form $\dot{x}(t) = Ax(t) + Bu(t)$, where A is an $n \times n$ matrix, B is an $n \times m$ matrix, $\dot{x}(t)$ and $x(t)$ are n-dimensional vectors, and $u(t)$ is an m-dimensional vector, the solution is given by[20]

$$s(t) = e^{At}x(0) + \int_0^\infty e^{A(t-\tau)}Bu(\tau)\,d\tau$$

As another example of an application of Laplace transforms, consider a linear nth-order differential system:

(1) $$a_0\frac{d^n x(t)}{dt^n} + a_1\frac{d^{n-1}x(t)}{dt^{n-1}} + \cdots + a_{n-1}\frac{dx(t)}{dt} + a_n x(t) = u(t)$$

where $d^i x(0)/dt^i$ for $i = 0, \ldots, n$, are specified.

Taking the Laplace transform of (1), we have

(2) $$F(s) = \frac{U(s) + M^*(s)}{a_0 s^n + a_1 s^{n-1} + \cdots + a_{n-1}s + a_n}$$

where $F(s) = L\{x(t)\}$, $U(s) = L\{u(t)\}$, and $M^*(s)$ is a polynomial in s of degree less than n.

From a theoretical standpoint, all that remains is to find the inverse transformation of (2) and we shall have a solution. However, this usually is a very difficult task from a practical standpoint.

[19] As an exercise the reader should convince himself that the solution to the system $\dot{x}(t) + x(t) = 1$, $x(0) = 2$ is $x(t) = 1 + e^{-t}$ by using the Laplace transform method.

[20] Note that $Bu(t)$ could be replaced in Theorem 14.2–12 by $\bar{u}(t)$, an arbitrary n-dimensional vector function.

Often $U(s)$ can be "absorbed" into the polynomial $M*(s)$ so that $F(s)$ becomes a ratio of two polynomials itself; that is, letting

$$M(s) = U(s) + M*(s)$$

and

$$N(s) = a_0 s^n + \cdots + a_{n-1} s + a_n$$

then

(3)
$$F(s) = \frac{M(s)}{N(s)}$$

The next step is to find all roots of $N(s) = 0$, that is, $s_1, s_2, \ldots$, that contain real and conjugate complex values. The result is

(4)
$$N(s) = a_0(s - s_1)(s - s_2)(s - s_3) \cdots$$

which, after substitution into (3), results in a sum of fractions

$$F(s) = \sum_i \frac{M(s_i)}{N'(s_i)} \left\{ \frac{1}{s - s_i} \right\}$$

where i ranges over all roots, $s_1, s_2, \ldots$; $N'(s) = d[N(s)]/ds$; and $M(s_i)$ and $N(s_i)$ are the results of substituting the ith root into $M(s)$ and $N(s)$.

From this, inverting the Laplace transforms is immediate; that is,

$$x(t) = \sum_i \frac{M(s_i)}{N'(s_i)} e^{s_i t}$$

Problems

14.2–1 Which of the following functions satisfy the Lipschitz condition for all values of x?

(a) $f(x) = \sqrt[3]{x^2}$ (d) $f(x) = \ln x$
(b) $f(x) = x^2 - 1$ (e) $f(x) = tx^{1/4} - 5$
(c) $f(x) = |3x + 5|$

14.2–2 For (a)–(e) in Problem 14.2–1, what can be said about the solution $x(t)$, where $\dot{x} = f(x)$?

14.2–3 Which of the following satisfy the Lipschitz condition for all values of x and the given values of the control $u(t)$?

(a) $\dot{x} = x^{1/t} - tu$, $u = 2$, $t > 0$ (d) $\dot{x} = t^2 x^{1/2} + u$, $u = -5$, $t > 0$
(b) $\dot{x} = tx - ux$, $u = t/2$, $t > 0$ (e) $\dot{x} = t \ln x - \ln u$, $u = t$, $t > 0$
(c) $\dot{x} = t - 1 + u$, $u = t^2$, $t > 0$

14.2–4 Using Theorem 14.2–3, determine which of the following linear systems have unique solutions:

(a) $a_{11} t x_1(t) + a_{12} t^2 x_2(t) = \dot{x}_1$
     $a_{21} x_1(t) - a_{22} x_2(t) = \dot{x}_2$

(b) $\dfrac{a_{11}}{t} - x_1(t) + a_{12}^t x_2(t) = \dot{x}_1$

$a_{21} t x_1(t) - t x_2(t) = \dot{x}_2$

(c) $7t + (a_{11} + t)x_1(t) + (a_{12}t^2 - t)x_2(t) + a_{31}(t - 5t^2)x_3(t) = \dot{x}_1$

$3|t - 2| + a_{21}x_1(t) + \dfrac{a_{22}}{t - 5} x_2(t) + a_{23} \ln (t)x_3(t) = \dot{x}_2$

$\ln t + a_{31} \ln \left(\dfrac{1}{t}\right) x_1(t) + a_{32}x_2(t) + a_{33} + x_3(t) = \dot{x}_3$

14.2–5 By using Theorems 14.2–4–14.2–11, determine which of the following systems are unstable, stable, asymptotically stable, or asymptotically stable in the large. In each case explain which theorem was used and how.

(a) $\dot{x}_1 = -3x_1 + 2x_2$
    $\dot{x}_2 = -x_2^2 - x_1$

(b) $\dot{x}_1 = -7x_1 + x_2 + x_1^{-2}$
    $\dot{x}_2 = 3x_1 - x_2 + x_2^{1/2}$

(c) $\dot{x}_1 = -x_1 - x_2 + e^{-x_1} - x_2^2$
    $\dot{x}_2 = -x_1 - 2x_2 + x_2^{1/2}$

(d) $\dot{x}_1 = 3x_1 - 10x_2 + \ln x_1 x_2$
    $\dot{x}_2 = -x_1 - x_2 - x_2^3$

(e) $\dot{x}_1 = -x_1^2 - \ln x_2 + 7$
    $\dot{x}_2 = -x_2^2$

14.2–6 Find the Laplace transform for each of the following functions:

(a) $f(t) = 1$
(b) $f(t) = t$
(c) $f(t) = e^{5t}$

(d) $f(t) = (\pi t)^{-1/2}$
(e) $f(t) = te^{-t}$

14.2–7 Find the functions for the following Laplace transforms:

(a) $F(s) = \dfrac{1}{(s - a)^2}$

(b) $F(s) = \dfrac{1}{s^2}$

(c) $F(s) = \dfrac{1}{(s - 4)(s - 3)}$

14.2–8 Use the Laplace transform method to solve the following first-order differential equations:

(a) $\dot{x}(t) + 2x(t) - 1 = 0$
(b) $\dot{x}(t) = 3 - x(t)$

(c) $\dot{x}(t) = 5t - 2x(t)$

14.3   CONTROLLABLE AND OBSERVABLE SYSTEMS[21]

We now need to define what kinds of systems are controllable. This amounts to having a system that can be transposed from one specified state (x^0, t_0) to the origin, that is, $x(t_1) = 0$ for some $t_1 < \infty$. In a similar manner, before

[21] These concepts were introduced by Kalman (1961).

we can evaluate the functioning of a dynamical system, we must be able to observe the output of the system at some, if not all, points in time.

DEFINITION 14.3–1   A differential system is **controllable** at t_0 if for every state at t_0, $x(t_0)$, and for some t_1, where $t_0 < t_1 \leq \infty$, there exists a piecewise-continuous control, $u(t_0)$, such that

$$\phi[t_1, x(t_0), u(t_0)] = x(t_1) = 0$$

If the system is controllable for any initial time, the system is **controllable.**

DEFINITION 14.3–2   A differential system is **observable** at $x(t_0)$ if for any piecewise-continuous control, $u(t_0)$, the corresponding output $f^*[x(t_0), u(t_0), t_0]$ is sufficient to determine the value of the state variable $x(t_0)$. If the system is observable for any initial time, the system is **observable.**

Equivalent systems are either both controllable or both uncontrollable.

Theorem 14.3–1   If P is a nonsingular $n \times n$ matrix, where $z(t) = P^{-1}x(t)$, then the system

$$\dot{x}(t) = f[x(t), u(t), t]$$

$$f^*[x(t), u(t), t]$$

is controllable if and only if the equivalent system

$$\dot{z}(t) = P^{-1}f[Pz(t), u(t), t]$$

$$g^*[z(t), u(t), t] = f^*[Pz(t), u(t), t]$$

is controllable. (The same relation holds for observable equivalent systems.)

For linear differential systems we are able to demonstrate the following necessary and sufficient condition for controllability.

Theorem 14.3–2   An autonomous linear differential system

$$\dot{x}(t) = Ax(t) + Bu(t)$$

$$f^* = Cx(t) + Du(t)$$

is controllable if and only if the matrix K

$$K = (B \ AB \ A^2B \cdots A^{n-1}B)$$

has rank n. (K has n linearly independent columns or n independent rows.)

PROOF   *If:* By the Cayley–Hamilton theorem,[22] a square matrix, A, satisfies its own characteristic equation. This implies that the first $n - 1$ powers of a matrix are linearly independent. Therefore, since

$$(1) \qquad e^{At} = I + At + \frac{A^2 t^2}{2!} + \frac{A^3 t^3}{3!} + \cdots$$

there must exist scalar functions $g_i(t)$ such that

$$(2) \qquad e^{At} = \sum_{i=1}^{n-1} g_i(t) A^i$$

Now, by Theorem 14.2–12 the state $x(t)$ for a given x^0, $u(t_0)$, and $t_0 = 0$ is given by

$$x(t) = e^{At} x(0) + \int_0^t e^{A(t-\tau)} B u(\tau) \, d\tau$$

Therefore, if $x(t_1) = 0$ for some t_1,

$$(3) \qquad x(0) = -\int_0^{t_1} e^{-A\tau} B u(\tau) \, d\tau$$

Only if: Assume that the system is controllable and show that K has a rank of n. Using Equation (2) and letting $u(\tau) = u(\tau)I = \sum_{j=1}^m u_j(\tau) e_j$, where e_j is the jth unit vector, then (3) becomes

$$(4) \qquad x(0) = \sum_{i=1}^{n-1} \sum_{j=1}^m \left[\int_0^{t_1} g_i(\tau) u_j(\tau) \, d\tau \right] A^i B e_j$$

or

$$(5) \qquad x(0) = \left\{ \sum_{j=1}^m \left[\int_0^{t_1} g_i(\tau) u_j(\tau) \, d\tau \right] \right\} K$$

which is to say, every vector $x(0)$ is some linear combination of K; that is, K must have rank n.   QED

Example 1.   Suppose that

$$\dot{x}_1(t) = x_1(t) + x_2(t) + u_1(t) - 2u_2(t)$$

and

$$\dot{x}_2(t) = -x_1(t) - 2x_2(t) - u_1(t) + u_2(t)$$

Then

$$A = \begin{bmatrix} 1 & 1 \\ -1 & -2 \end{bmatrix} \qquad B = \begin{bmatrix} 1 & -2 \\ -1 & 1 \end{bmatrix} \qquad AB = \begin{bmatrix} 0 & -1 \\ 1 & 0 \end{bmatrix} \qquad n = 2$$

[22] Theorem 4.5–1.

In this case, for K to have a rank n it is sufficient that either B or AB have rank n. Since both B and AB have rank n, the system is controllable.

The following special cases of linear differential systems are immediate consequences of Theorem 14.3–2.

Corollary 1 to Theorem 14.3–2   If B is an $n \times 1$ vector, b, then the linear system in Theorem 14.3–2 is controllable if and only if

$$K = (b\ Ab \cdots A^{n-1}b)$$

is nonsingular.

This corollary applies to the special case where there is only one control. For example, if

$$A = \begin{bmatrix} 2 & 1 \\ -1 & -2 \end{bmatrix} \quad \text{and} \quad b = \begin{bmatrix} 1 \\ -1 \end{bmatrix}$$

then

$$K = \begin{bmatrix} 1 & 1 \\ -1 & 1 \end{bmatrix}$$

Since $|K| = 2$, K^{-1} exists and thus the system described by A and b is controllable.

Corollary 2 to Theorem 14.3–2   If A is a diagonal matrix with distinct elements on the diagonal, then the linear system in Theorem 14.3–2 is controllable if and only if B has no rows with all zeros.

An even more special case of Corollary 2 to Theorem 14.3–2 would be where B was a vector b. This would mean that each variable was subject to control only by direct influence of its control variable. Thus, to be controllable, b could have no zeros.

The question of observability for an autonomous linear differential system is answered by an analogous theorem and corollaries.

If a linear autonomous system is observable at time t, where $t_0 = 0$, then

$$f^* = C\left[e^{At}x(0) + \int_0^t e^{A(t_0-\tau)}Bu(\tau)\ d\tau \right] + Du(t)$$

Hence the system will be observable at t if and only if it is observable at $t_0 = 0$, because information sufficient to determine the state $x(0)$ will also be sufficient to determine all future states.

Theorem 14.3–3   The linear system

$$\dot{x}(t) = Ax(t) + Bu(t)$$
$$f^* = Cx(t) + Du(t)$$

is observable if and only if the matrix $G = [C' \; A'C' \cdots (A')^{n-1}C']$ has rank n.

Corollary 1 to Theorem 14.3–3 If C is an n-dimensional vector, c, then the system is observable if and only if

$$G = [c' \; A'c' \cdots (A')^{n-1}c']$$

is nonsingular.

Corollary 2 to Theorem 14.3–3 If the matrix A is a diagonal matrix, then the system is observable if and only if C has no columns with all zeros.

The practicality of Theorems 14.3–2 and 14.3–3 and their corollaries is obvious for simple linear systems. This will also be demonstrated in later examples.[23]

Problems

14.3–1 By using Theorem 14.3–2 and its corollaries, determine which of the following systems are controllable:

(a) $\dot{x}_1(t) = 3x_1(t) - 4x_2(t) - u_1(t) + \frac{1}{2}u_2(t)$
$\dot{x}_2(t) = -x_1(t) + x_2(t) + u_2(t)$

(b) $\dot{x}_1(t) = 2x_1(t) + 2x_3(t) - u(t)$
$\dot{x}_2(t) = x_2(t) - x_1(t) + 5u(t)$
$\dot{x}_3(t) = x_1(t) + x_2(t) - 3x_3(t) - 5u(t)$

(c) $\dot{x}_1(t) = x_1(t) + u_1(t) - 3u_2(t) + 2u_3(t)$
$\dot{x}_2(t) = x_2(t) - u_1(t) + 10u_2(t) - 20u_3(t)$
$\dot{x}_3(t) = x_3(t) + u_1(t) + 4u_2(t) - 8u_3(t)$

(d) $\dot{x}_1(t) = -3x_1(t) - 4x_2(t) + u_1(t) - u_2(t)$
$\dot{x}_2(t) = 4x_2(t) - 5x_3(t) + u_2(t) - u_3(t)$
$\dot{x}_3(t) = 2x_1(t)$

14.3–2 Determine which of the systems in Problem 14.3–1 are observable for:

(a) $f^* = 3x_1(t) + 4x_2(t) - 5u_1(t) - 45u_2(t)$

(b) $f_1^* = 2x_1(t) + 3x_2(t) - 6u(t)$
$f_2^* = x_1(t) + 4x_2(t) + 7u(t)$

(c) $f_1^* = -6x_1(t) - 7x_2(t) + 4x_3(t)$
$f_2^* = 2x_1(t) - 3x_2(t) + 8u_1(t) - 9u_2(t)$
$f_3^* = -x_1(t) - 5x_2(t) - 4x_3(t) + u_3(t)$

(d) $f_1^* = x_1(t) - 3x_2(t) + x_3(t)$
$f_2^* = x_2(t) - x_3(t)$

---

[23] For nonautonomous linear or nonlinear systems, controllability and observability is much more difficult. See Kalman (1961) and Lee and Markus (1967).

14.4   THE MAXIMUM PRINCIPLE OF PONTRYAGIN

In this section we review some of Pontryagin's (Pontryagin et al., 1962) basic theorems for solving a control problem. The problem is to select an optimal control for a differential dynamical system. That is, for the state variables $x = (x_1, \ldots, x_n)$, where $x = f(x, u, t)$ is continuous and has continuous first partial derivatives, and control variables $u = (u_1, \ldots, u_m)$, where u is piecewise continuous and differentiable, find the control, u^*, that transfers the system from $x(t_0) = x^0$ to $x(t_1) = x^1$ in such a way that $J = \int_{t_0}^{t_1} f(x, u, t) \, dt$ is minimized.

By initially considering a special case of general control problems, we shall arrive at conclusions that can be generalized later. First let us consider an autonomous system with a fixed initial point, x^0; a fixed end point, x^1; and t_1 unspecified. This is illustrated in Figure 14.4–1 for two functions u^+ and u^* that constitute a solution to the differential equations $\dot{x} = f(x, u^+)$ and $\dot{x} = f(x, u^*)$; that is,

$$x^1 - x^0 = \int_{t_0}^{t_1^+} f(x, u^+) \, dt = \int_{t_0}^{t_1^*} f(x, u^*) \, dt$$

The problem is to select from a general class of functions one function that minimizes the performance criterion J and satisfies the initial and terminal conditions.

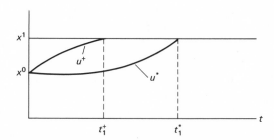

Figure 14.4–1   *Fixed end point, free time control problem.*

Suppose we have an optimal control, u^*. Then any variation in u^* cannot decrease the value of the performance criterion J. At the same time the control must transfer the system from x^0 to x^1. Therefore, what is needed is a system of "weights" to compare the different trajectories of alternative controls. These weights are developed by defining a Hamiltonian or (canonical) for the control problem, as is shown in Definition 14.4–1 and Theorem 14.4–1.

DEFINITION 14.4–1   The **Hamiltonian system** for the control problem of finding a function $u \in U$, the set of admissible piecewise-continuous controls, so as to

$$\min_{u} J = \min_{u} \int_{t_0}^{t_1} f^0(x, u) \, dt$$

where

$$\dot{x} = f(x, u), \; x(t_0) = x^0, \quad \text{and} \quad x(t_1) = x^1$$

is a system of $2n$ differential equations,

$$\dot{x} = \frac{\partial H(x, \lambda, u)}{\partial \lambda} = f(x, u)$$

$$\dot{\lambda} = \frac{-\partial H(x, \lambda, u)}{\partial x} = -\lambda_0 \frac{\partial f^0}{\partial x} - \lambda \frac{\partial f(x, u)}{\partial x}$$

where $H(x, \lambda, u) = \lambda_0 f^0(x, u) + \lambda f(x, u)$ is the **Hamiltonian function** (or simply **Hamiltonian**) and $\lambda = (\lambda_1, \ldots, \lambda_n)$ is a vector of variables termed **adjoint** or **costate** variables.

In other words, the Hamiltonian function is a solution to $2n$ partial differential equations and its form is the dynamic analogue of the Lagrangean function in static constraint maximization. The costate variables play a similar role to the usual Lagrangean multipliers. The objective to be minimized is the integral of $f^0(x, u)$ and the rate of change of the variables is determined (constrained) by the differential functions $f(x, u)$.

Theorem 14.4–1   If $u^*(t)$ is an optimal control for an autonomous, fixed end point, free time control problem for a differential system, then there must exist a nonzero n-dimensional vector function, $\lambda(t)$, corresponding to $x(t)$ and $u^*(t_0)$, such that

(1) $\lambda(t)$ and $x(t)$ are a solution of the Hamiltonian system for the differential system;
(2) the Hamiltonian function is maximum for $u^*(t_0)$ for all t, $t_0 \leq t \leq t_1$, for all $u(t_0) \in U$,[24] that is, $H[x(t), \lambda(t), u^*(t_0)] \geq H[x(t), \lambda(t), u(t_0)]$;
(3) $H[x(t), \lambda(t), u^*(t_0)] = 0$, for $t_0 \leq t \leq t_1$; and
(4) $\lambda_0 \leq 0$ and λ_0 is constant for $t_0 \leq t \leq t$.

---

[24] $u(t_0)$ denotes a piecewise-continuous function that is defined beginning at t_0. U is the class of all such admissable functions. The notational form $u(t_0)|_{t'}$ is the *value* of the function $u(t_0)$ at time t'.

The proof of this theorem is the essential content of Pontryagin's book *Mathematical Theory of Optimal Processes*. Even a sketch of the proof would require several pages and would not do justice to the proof itself. Therefore the interested reader should consult Pontryagin et al. (1962) for details.

One generalization of Theorem 14.4–1 is a consideration of a control problem with fixed initial (or left) and end (or right) target sets[25] rather than fixed end points. This is illustrated in Figure 14.4–2, where $x = (x_1, x_2)$, $x^0 \in S_0$, and $x^1 \in S_1$. The paths marked u^+ and u^* are two possible paths from S_0 to S_1.

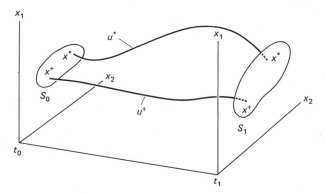

Figure 14.4–2 *Control problem for fixed initial and end target sets, S_0 and S_1.*

With a choice now of both initial and end points, we need a way of comparing the advantages and disadvantages of the various initial and end points within the sets S_0 and S_1. This method of comparison is known as the method of transversality conditions.

DEFINITION 14.4–2 For $x^0 \in S_0$, and $x^1 \in S_1$ and tangent hyperplanes T_0 to S_0 at x^0 and T_1 to S_1 at x^1, where the planes T_0 and T_1 are of dimensions $r_0 < n$ and $r_1 < n$, respectively, the vector $\lambda(t_0)$ satisfies the **transversality condition** at x^0 if $\lambda(t_0)$ is orthogonal to T_0. Similarly, $\lambda(t_1)$ satisfies the transversality condition at x^1 if $\lambda(t_1)$ is orthogonal to T_1.[26]

---

[25] Specifically, the target sets will be assumed to be **smooth manifolds** or **k-folds** in R^n, $0 < k < n$. S is a smooth k-fold in R^n if S is the intersection of $n - k$ smooth hypersurfaces, $f_1, \ldots, f_{n-k}$, whose gradients do not vanish, and if for every point $x \in S$ the vectors $(\partial f_1/\partial x)x, \ldots, (\partial f_{n-k}/\partial x)x$ are linearly independent. That is, a smooth k-fold is the intersection of $n - k$ tangent planes at every point and the vectors normal to each tangent plane are linearly independent. Furthermore, a smooth k-fold itself has a tangent plane at every point. (Are the sets S_0 and S_1 in Figure 14.4–1 smooth k-folds? Why?)

[26] Cf. Definition 10.6–2.

In other words, in Figure 14.4–3, $\lambda(t_1)$ satisfies the transversality condition at x^1 if for all $\theta \in T_1$, $\lambda\theta = 0$. At x^0, if $\lambda(t_0)$ is orthogonal to T_0, then for all $\eta \in T_0$, $\lambda\eta = 0$.

Theorem 14.4–2   If $u^*(t)$ is an optimal control that transfers some $x^0 \in S_0$ to some $x^1 \in S_1$, where S_0 and S_1 are r_0- and r_1-dimensional manifolds in R^n, with r_0 and $r_1 < n$, in the sense that

$$J^* = \int_{t_0}^{t_1} f^0(x, u^*)\, dt = \min_{u \in U} J$$

then

(1) there exists a vector function $\lambda(t)$ such that the Hamiltonian function $H(x, \lambda, u^*)$ is maximized;

(2) $H(x, \lambda, u^*) = 0$ for all t, $t_0 \leq t \leq t_1$ where $\lambda_0(t) \leq 0$ and $\lambda_0(t)$ is constant; and

(3) the transversality conditions for both end points of the trajectory are satisfied.

The effect on the necessary conditions for an optimal control of allowing target sets rather than points is that the costate (or adjoint) variables of the Hamiltonian must satisfy the transversality conditions of Definition 14.4–2. Intuitively, the transversality conditions pick out the best point from the given target sets.

Next let us consider the maximum principle for nonautonomous systems with fixed initial and end points and free terminal time. The technique of generalizing into nonautonomous systems is to define an additional variable, x_{n+1}, and convert the n-dimensional nonautonomous system into an $n + 1$-dimensional "autonomous" system.

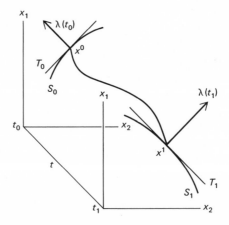

Figure 14.4–3   *Target sets S_0 and S_1 with tangent hyperplanes T_0 and T_1.*

For a nonautonomous system we have

$$\frac{dx_i}{dt} = \dot{x}_i = f^i(\hat{x}, u, t) \qquad \text{for } i = 1, \ldots, n \text{ and } \hat{x} = (x_1, \ldots, x_n)$$

$$J = \int_{t_0}^{t_1} f^0(\hat{x}, u, t) \, dt$$

If we let

$$x_0 = \int_{t_0}^{t} f^0(\hat{x}, u, t') \, dt'$$

and also define

$$\frac{dx_{n+1}}{dt} = \dot{x}_{n+1} = 1 \qquad x_{n+1}(t_0) = t_0 \qquad x_{n+1}(t_1) = t_1 \qquad x = (\hat{x}, x_{n+1})$$

we shall have

$$\dot{x}_i = f^i(x, u) \qquad \text{for } i = 0, \ldots, n \qquad x = (x_1, \ldots, x_{n+1})$$

$$u = (u_1, \ldots, u_m) \qquad \dot{x}_{n+1} = 1$$

or, in vector notation,

$$\dot{x} = f(x, u)$$

The corresponding augmented Hamiltonian system becomes

$$H^*(x, \lambda, u, t) = \lambda_0 f^0(x, u) + \lambda f(x, u) \qquad \text{where } \lambda = (\lambda_1, \ldots, \lambda_{n+1})$$

or

$$H^*(x, \lambda, u, t) = \lambda_0 f^0(x, u) + \sum_{i=1}^{n} \lambda_i f^i(x, u) + \lambda_{n+1}$$

Further,

$$\frac{d\lambda_i}{dt} = -\sum_{j=0}^{n} \frac{\partial f^i}{\partial x_i} \lambda_j \qquad i = 0, \ldots, n$$

(1)
$$\frac{d\lambda_{n+1}}{dt} = -\sum_{i=0}^{n} \frac{\partial f^i}{\partial t} \lambda_i$$

As in the previous theorems, for u^* to be the optimal control, it is necessary that $H^* = 0$ and also be a maximum. Thus, for $H^* = H + \lambda_{n+1}$ we have

(2)
$$H(x, \lambda, u^*, t) = -\lambda_{n+1}(t)$$

From the transversality conditions,

(3)
$$\lambda_{n+1}(t_1) = 0$$

since $\theta \in S$, and with a fixed end point, S is parallel to the x_{n+1} (or t) axis. Combining (1), (2), and (3), it follows that

$$H(x, \lambda, u^*, t) = \int_{t_1}^{t} \sum_{i=0}^{n} \frac{\partial f^i}{\partial t} \lambda_i(t') \, dt' = 0$$

Applying Theorem 14.4–1 establishes the validity of Theorem 14.4–3.

Theorem 14.4–3   If $u^*(t_0)$ is an optimal control for $x(t_0) = x^0$ and $x(t_1) = x^1$, then there exists a continuous nonzero function $\lambda(t) = (\lambda_0(t), \ldots, \lambda_n(t))$ such that

(1) $H(x, \lambda, u^*, t) = \displaystyle\int_{t_1}^{t} \sum_{i=0}^{n} \frac{\partial f^i}{\partial t} \lambda_i(t') \, dt'$ is a maximum for all t, and

further,

(2) $H(x, \lambda, u^*, t) = 0$ for all t.

In other words, when a nonautonomous system replaces the autonomous system in the premises of Theorem 14.4–1, the corresponding change occurs in the form of the Hamiltonian. Now the Hamiltonian must be an integral over the period t_0 to t_1.

Suppose we have a nonautonomous system where the right end point varies over time; that is, $x^1 = x^1(t)$. This will obviously affect the transversality conditions of Theorem 14.4–3. However, the effect is easily handled. For some admissable control $u(t_0)$, let

$$\frac{dx^1}{dt}\bigg|_{t_1} = (q_1, \ldots, q_n)$$

Then the target set containing the end point can be written as $S_1 = (x_1^1(\theta), \ldots, x_n^1(\theta), \theta)$, where the tangent to S_1 at $\theta = t_1$ is $(q_1, \ldots, q_n, 1)$. This, in turn, implies that the transversality condition for a moving end point becomes

$$\sum_{i=1}^{n} \lambda_i(t_1) q_i + \lambda_{n+1}(t_1) = 0$$

As in Theorem 14.4–3 for a nonautonomous system, we have at t_1,

$$H(x, \lambda, u^*, t_1) = -\lambda_{n+1}(t_1) = \sum_{i=1}^{n} \lambda_i q_i$$

where u^* is an optimal control. However, there is a difference in that before the system reaches the moving right end point, the Hamiltonian will not be zero but must account for the moving end point; that is,

$$H(x, \lambda, u^*, t) = \sum_{i=1}^{n} \lambda(t_1)q_i + \int_{t_1}^{t} \sum_{j=0}^{n} \frac{\partial f^j}{\partial t} \lambda_j(t') \, dt'$$

We can now state this formally as Theorem 14.4–4.

Theorem 14.4–4 If $u^*(t_0)$ is an optimal control for a nonautonomous system with a variable right end point, then there exists a nonzero function $\lambda(t) = (1, \lambda_1(t), \ldots, \lambda_n(t))$ such that

(1) $H(x, \lambda, u^*, t) = \sum_{i=1}^{n} \lambda_i(t_1)q_i + \int_{t_1}^{t} \sum_{j=0}^{n} \frac{\partial f^j}{\partial t} \lambda_j(t') \, dt'$ for $t_0 \leq t \leq t_1$;

(2) $H(x, \lambda, u^*, t) \geq H(x, \lambda, u, t)$ for $u \in U$;

(3) $H(x, \lambda, u^*, t) = \sum_{i=1}^{n} \lambda_i(t_1)q_i$; and

(4) $\sum_{i=1}^{n} \lambda_i(t_1)q_i + \lambda_{n+1}(t_1) = 0$.

In other words, by allowing a variable right end point, the necessary conditions that must be fulfilled are correspondingly expanded to include the requisite transversality conditions. This means that $\sum_{i=1}^{n} \lambda_i(t_1)q_i$, which is zero for a fixed end point problem, must be added to the Hamiltonian in (1). Thus, in (3) instead of the Hamiltonian being equal to zero at t_1, it must equal $\sum_{i=1}^{n} \lambda_i(t_1)q_i$, which reflects the penalty of having a different ending time.

Another generalization is the case where the terminal time is fixed. In such a case we gain some information, namely, t_1, and as a consequence, we lose one of the necessary conditions in the above free end-point theorems. Two special theorems for a fixed time problem will be considered:

(1) fixed time, fixed initial and end points, and
(2) fixed time, variable end points.

Theorem 14.4–5 If $u^*(t_0)$ is an optimal control for a fixed time, fixed end-point problem, then there exists a continuous nonzero function λ for the corresponding Hamiltonian such that

(1) $\max_u H(x, \lambda, u, t) = H(x, \lambda, u^*, t)$ and

(2) $H(x, \lambda, u^*, t) = H(x, \lambda, u^*, t_1) + \int_{t_1}^{t} \frac{\partial H}{\partial t} \, dt'$

[Note that $H(x, \lambda, u^*, t)$ is not equal to zero as in Theorem 14.4–1.]

Theorem 14.4–6 For a given t_0 and t_1 and given S_0 and S_1, which are, respectively, r_0- and r_1-dimensional manifolds such that $x^0 \in S_0$ and $x^1 \in S_1$, if $u^*(t_0)$ is an optimal control, then there exists a nonzero continuous function $\lambda = (\lambda_0, \ldots, \lambda_n)$ such that

(1) $\max\limits_u H(x, \lambda, u, t) = H(x, \lambda, u^*, t)$;

(2) $H(x, \lambda, u^*, t) = H(x, \lambda, u^*, t_1) + \int_{t_1}^{t} \dfrac{\partial H}{\partial t} \, dt'$;

(3) $\lambda(t_1)$ is transversal to S_1 at $x(t_1)$, which implies that $\lambda(t_1) = 0$; and

(4) $\lambda(t_0)$ is transversal to S_0 at $x(t_0)$, that is, $\lambda(t_0) = 0$.

(Again note the difference of conditions on the Hamiltonian along the path for t between t_0 and t_1; compare with Theorem 14.4–4, for example.)

Example 1. An Investment Problem and Control Theory[27] Suppose that Gigantic Steel Works Corp. wishes to attain an optimal stock of capital, based on demand considerations, in the shortest period of time. If we let

$$x_1 = \text{current capital stock} - \text{optimal capital stock}$$

$$x_2 = \frac{dx_1}{dt} = \text{investment rate} - \text{depreciation rate}$$

and assume that the rate of change in x_2 is a control variable for the firm bounded by upper and lower limits, that is,

$$\frac{dx_2}{dt} = u \quad \text{and} \quad |u| \leq 1$$

we have a time-optimal problem in control theory. The problem is to attain $x^1 = (0, 0)$ in the shortest possible time. That is, the objective is to have $x_1 = 0$ and the rate of change in x_1 also equal to zero as quickly as possible.

The Hamiltonian function is

$$H = \lambda_0 f^0 + \lambda_1 x_2 + \lambda_2 u$$

Since

$$\frac{d\lambda_1}{dt} = -\frac{\partial H}{\partial x_1} = 0$$

and

$$\frac{d\lambda_2}{dt} = -\frac{\partial H}{\partial x_2} = -\lambda_1$$

---

[27] Cf. the first example in Section 10.10 and the second example in Section 12.3, which deal with investment problems solved by the calculus of variations and dynamic programming techniques.

it follows that $\lambda_1 = C_1$, a constant, and $\lambda_2 = C_2 - C_1 t$, where C_2 is a constant. Since $f^0 \equiv 1$ for a time-optimal problem,

$$H = \lambda_0 + C_1 x_2 + (C_2 - C_1 t)u$$

By Theorem 14.4–1, H will be maximized along the optimal trajectory. Since $|u| \leq 1$, $u^* = -$ the sign of $(C_2 - C_1 t)$.

Suppose $u = 1$. By Theorem 14.4–1, $H = 0$ and we have

(1) $$x_2 = t - k_1, \; k_1 = \frac{C_2 + \lambda_0}{C_1}$$

and

(2) $$x_1 = \frac{t^2}{2} - k_1 t + k_2$$

where k_2 is a constant. Combining (1) and (2) gives

(3) $$x_1 = \frac{x_2^2}{2} + k$$

where $k = k_2 - k_1^2/2$. Similarly, for $u = -1$ we have

(4) $$x_1 = -\frac{x_2^2}{2} + k'$$

along the optimal trajectory.

The family of equations for Equation (3) is shown in Figure 14.4–4. If $u = 1$, the relation between x_1 and x_2 must lie on one of the parabolas to minimize the time to origin. Likewise, if $u = -1$, the optimal trajectory is one curve from the family of curves in Figure 14.4–5. By juxtaposing the two figures, the optimal path for the initial starting point a in Figure 14.4–6 is the curve abc. At a the optimal stock is greater than the initial amount of capital.

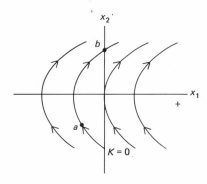

Figure 14.4–4 *Family of equations for $x_1 = x_2^2/2 + k$, and $u = 1$.*

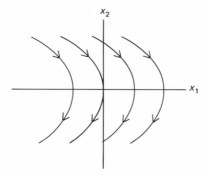

Figure 14.4–5   *Family of equations for $x_1 = -x_2^2/2 + k'$ and $u = -1$.*

Thus $x_1 < 0$, while $x_2 = 0$. The optimal investment procedure is to increase the rate of investment as rapidly as possible; that is, set $u = 1$, following the path bc in Figure 14.4–6 to the origin.

Line dd' in Figure 14.4–6 is the "switching" line of the combinations of x_1 and x_2 where the control switches from -1 to $+1$. Thus for any initial starting point lower than and to the left of dd', the optimal path begins with $u = 1$ until dd' is reached and then $u = -1$. For points above and to the right of dd', u is set at -1 until dd' is reached, then $u = 1$. The path efc is a time-optimal trajectory for the initial point e in Figure 14.4–6.

Example 2.   Infinite Utility Streams and Control Theory[28]   Suppose that we have an individual who wishes to maximize his utility over time, which is a function of consumption, C; leisure, L; and time, t. Let A be the assets of the individual, r be the rate of interest, T be the amount of time per period

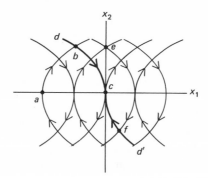

Figure 14.4–6   *Optimal relation between x_1 and x_2. dd' is the "switching" line.*

[28] A somewhat similar example and further details can be found in Arrow and Kurz (1969).

(i.e., $T = 24$ hours per day), and W be the wage rate in terms of consumption. Then the problem is to find the paths of $C(t)$ and $L(t)$ so as to

$$\max \int_0^\infty U(C, L, t)\, dt$$

where $\dot{A} = rA + (T - L)W - C$ is the individual's budget constraint. The Hamiltonian is

$$H = -\lambda_0 U(C, L, t) + \lambda_1(rA + TW - LW - C)$$

If H is to be a maximum for the optimal controls C^* and L^*, then

(1) $$\left.\frac{\partial H}{\partial C}\right|_{C^*} = -\lambda_0 \left.\frac{\partial U}{\partial C}\right|_{C^*} - \lambda_1 = 0$$

(2) $$\left.\frac{\partial H}{\partial L}\right|_{L^*} = -\lambda_0 \left.\frac{\partial U}{\partial L}\right|_{L^*} - \lambda_1 W = 0$$

and

(3) $$\frac{d\lambda_1}{dt} = -\frac{\partial H}{\partial A} = -\lambda_1 r$$

From (3), we find the solution for $\lambda_1(t)$ as

(4) $$\lambda_1(t) = \lambda_1(0)e^{-rt}$$

Conditions (1) and (2) state that at any point in time the individual should equate the marginal rate of substitution between consumption and leisure to their relative prices; that is,

$$\frac{\partial U/\partial L}{\partial U/\partial C} = W$$

The marginal utility of consumption is declining over time. If the utility function does not also vary with time, that is, if

$$\left.\frac{\partial U}{\partial C}\right|_{t_i} \equiv \left.\frac{\partial U}{\partial C}\right|_{t_j} \qquad \text{for all } i \text{ and } j$$

then Figure 14.4–7 illustrates the optimal relation between the marginal utility of consumption and time. The usual assumptions about the utility function are made, that is, $\partial U/\partial C > 0$ and $\partial^2 U/\partial C^2 < 0$. As a result, if r, the rate of interest, is greater than $(dW/dt)/W$ the individual should save, while if r is less than $(dW/dt)/W$ the individual should dissave.

Thus, if in early years the wage rate does not increase because of attending college, say, then increases rapidly for a time, and then levels off, the optimal consumption–savings path would be a Harrod humped savings diagram as shown in Figure 14.4–8.

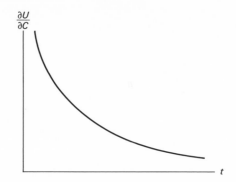

Figure 14.4–7 *Relation between marginal utility of consumption and time.*

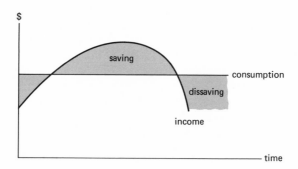

Figure 14.4–8 *Harrod humped savings diagram.*

Problems

14.4–1 State the Hamiltonian for the following control problems:

(a) $\min\limits_{u} \int_{t_0}^{t_1} (x_1 u_1 - x_2 u_2)\, dt$

$\dot{x}_1 = u_1 - x_1$
$\dot{x}_2 = u_2$
$x^0 = (0, 0)$
$x^1 = (1, 1)$

(b) $\min\limits_{u} \int_{0}^{t_1} (x_1^2 + u_2^2 - x_1 - x_2)\, dt$

$\dot{x}_1 = x_1 + x_2 - u_1$
$\dot{x}_2 = x_2 + u_1$
$x^0 = (0, 0)$
$x^1 = (1, 1)$

(c) $\min\limits_{u} \displaystyle\int_{0}^{20} -\frac{1}{x_1 x_2}\, dt$

$\dot{x}_1 = -x_1 - u_1 - u_2$
$\dot{x}_2 = -x_2^2 + x_1^2 - u_1 + u_2$
$x^0 = (0, 0)$
$x^1 = (10, 10)$

14.4-2 Suppose that we have a control problem of the following form:

$$\min\limits_{u} \int_{0}^{t_1} (3x_1^2 + 2x_2^2 - x_1 - 3x_2)\, dt$$

$(x_1^0, x_2^0) = (0, 0)$
$(x_1^1, x_2^1) \in S_1 = \{x|\ |4x_1^2 - x_2^2| = 0\}$
$\dot{x}_1 = u_1$
$\dot{x}_2 = x_1 + x_2 + u_1$
(a) Find the tangent hyperplane, T_1 for the target set S_1.
(b) State the transversality conditions for $\lambda(t_1)$.
(c) State the Hamiltonian.
(d) State the conditions necessary for the optimal control $u^*(t)$.

14.4-3 Use the maximum principle to find the control $u(t)$ that minimizes

$$J = \int_{t_0}^{t_1} (x_1^2 + 2x_2^2 + 3u^2)\, dt$$

where

$$\dot{x}_1 = x_2$$
$$\dot{x}_2 = u$$
$$(x_1^0, x_2^0) = (5, 0)$$
$$-1 \le u \le 1$$

under the following set of conditions:

(a) $(x_1^1, x_2^1) = (0, 0)$ (b) $2x_1(t_1) + 3x_2(t_1) = 5$

14.4-4 Find the control $u^*(t)$ that transforms $x_1^0 = 10$ into $x_1^1 = 0$ in the minimum possible time, where

$$\dot{x}_1 = -x_1 + u$$

and

$$|u| \le 1$$

14.4-5 Find the optimal control $u^*(t)$ that minimizes

$$J = \int_{t_0}^{t_1} e^{\sigma(t-t_0)}(x_1^2 + 2u^2)\, dt$$

where

$$\dot{x}_1 = u$$
$$\dot{x}_1 = 5$$
$$x_1^1 \text{ is free}$$

14.5 GENERAL RESULTS OF THE PONTRYAGIN MAXIMUM PRINCIPLE FOR TIME-OPTIMAL LINEAR SYSTEMS

In this section we present some general analytical results of the maximum principle of Pontryagin for time-optimal, linear, time-invariant systems. These systems are a generalization of Example 1 in Section 14.4 and can be descriptively termed "bang–bang" systems, since the optimal control switches from upper to lower bounds with no other intermediate values.

Consider the following linear differential system:

$$\dot{x}(t) = Ax(t) + Bu(t)$$

where $x = (x_1, \ldots, x_n)$, $u = (u_1, \ldots, u_m)$, and A and B are constant $n \times n$ and $n \times m$ matrices.

For simplification assume that for each control,

$$|u_i| \leq 1$$

The problem is to transform the initial state $x^0 = x(t_0)$ to the origin, $x(t_1) = 0$, in the shortest possible time.

For this system to be controllable it is necessary that the matrix

$$K = (B \ AB \ A^2B \cdots A^{n-1} \ B)$$

have rank n, [29]which we assume is true. The following theorem is an application of the Pontryagin maximum principle to the special characteristics of the foregoing linear system. It follows immediately from Theorem 14.4–1.

Theorem 14.5–1 If $u^*(t_0)$ is a time-optimal control for a given initial point, x^0, and a final point $x^1 = 0$, then it is necessary that there exist a nonzero $n \times 1$ vector function $\lambda(t)$ such that for the Hamiltonian function[30]

$$H = -1 + \lambda(t)'Ax(t) + \lambda(t)'Bu(t)$$

(1) $$\max_{u \in U} H = -1 + \lambda(t)'Ax(t) + \lambda(t)'Bu^*(t) = 0$$

(2) $$\frac{d\lambda}{dt} = -\frac{\partial H}{\partial x} = -\lambda(t)'A$$

(3) $$\frac{dx}{dt} = \frac{\partial H}{\partial \lambda} = Ax(t) + Bu(t)$$

---

[29] This was proved in Theorem 14.3–2.

[30] Note since λ_0 is a negative constant we can replace λ_0 with -1 in the Hamiltonian.

and, further, if $|u_i| \leq 1$ for all i, then

(4) $$u^*(t) = -\text{sign of } \{\lambda(t)'B\}$$

or

$$u_i^*(t) = -\text{sign of } \{\lambda(t)'b_i\}$$

for $i = 1, \ldots, m$ and where b_i is the ith column of B.

Part (4) of Theorem 14.5–1 reflects the "bang–bang" nature of the system. The optimal control switches from $+1$ to -1, in general, as the system moves from x^0 to the origin. However, part (4) does not specify the value of $u^*(t)$ if $\lambda(t)'B = 0$. If $\lambda(t)'b_i$ is zero for some interval between t_0 and t_1, then we have a period of **singularity** for the ith control over that interval. Thus the interval is a period where the control is ineffective and hence undefined. **Normal** problems have no intervals of singularity for any of the controls.

Theorem 14.5–2 The time-optimal linear differential system in Theorem 14.5–1 is normal [i.e., $\lambda(t)'b_i \neq 0$] except at a finite number of points (or it is sometimes stated as: $\lambda(t)'b_i$ is *almost always never zero*, between t_0 and t_1) if and only if the matrices $K_1, \ldots, K_m$ are nonsingular, where

$$K_1 = (b_1 \ Ab_1 \ \cdots \ A^{n-1}b_1)$$
$$\vdots$$
$$K_m = (b_m \ Ab_m \ \cdots \ A^{n-1}b_m)$$

PROOF *If*: Suppose that $K_i = (b_i \ Ab_i \ \cdots \ A^{n-1} \ b_i)$ is nonsingular. Since $u_i(t) = -\text{sign of } \lambda(t)'b_i$, then for normality either $b_i = 0$ or $\lambda(t)'b_i = 0$ for all $t \in (t_i, t_j)$, where $t_0 \leq t_i < t_j \leq t_1$. Since K_i^{-1} exists, $b_i \neq 0$. Since $d\lambda/dt = -\lambda(t)'A$, $\lambda(t) = \lambda(0)e^{-At}$.

A square matrix, A, satisfies its own characteristic equation, which in turn means that the first $n - 1$ powers of an $n \times n$ matrix are linearly independent. Therefore

$$e^{-At} = (1 \ A \ A^2 \cdots A^{n-1}) \begin{bmatrix} g_0(t) \\ \vdots \\ g_{n-1}(t) \end{bmatrix}$$

where $g_i(t)$, $i = 0, \ldots, n - 1$ are scalar functions. Thus

$$\lambda(t) = \lambda(0)(1 \ A \ A^2 \cdots A^{n-1}) \begin{bmatrix} g_0(t) \\ \vdots \\ g_{n-1}(t) \end{bmatrix}$$

$$\lambda(t)' = [g_0(t), \ldots, g_{n-1}(t)]\lambda_0 \begin{bmatrix} 1 \\ A \\ A^2 \\ \vdots \\ A^{n-1} \end{bmatrix}$$

and

$$\lambda(t)'b_i = [g_0(t), \ldots, g_{n-1}(t)]\lambda(0) \begin{bmatrix} 1 \\ A \\ A^2 \\ \vdots \\ A^{n-1} \end{bmatrix} b_i$$

or

$$\lambda(t)'b_i = [g_0(t), \ldots, g_{n-1}(t)]\lambda(0)K_i$$

Since K_i^{-1} exists and $\lambda(0) \neq 0$, $\lambda'(t)$ will be zero only when $e^{-At} = 0$, which can only occur at a finite number of points. The *only if* argument follows similar lines and is left as an exercise.

In Example 1 of Section 14.4, regardless of the initial point, the most that the optimal control could switch was once. In Figure 14.4–6, if the initial point were along the line dd', the optimal control would be constant, otherwise it would begin at one extreme ($+1$ or -1) and switch once. In a similar vein, Pontryagin et al. (1962) prove the following theorem for the number of switchings that can occur when the A matrix has both real and distinct characteristic roots.

Theorem 14.5–3   The greatest number of times that a piecewise-constant control $u_i^*(t)$ can switch from one extreme to another is $n - 1$ for the normal linear time-optimal system

$$\dot{x}(t) = Ax(t) + Bu(t)$$

$$|u_i(t)| \leq 1 \qquad \text{for } i = 1, \ldots, m$$

when the characteristic roots, $\zeta_1, \ldots, \zeta_n$ of A are real.

If the characteristic roots of A are complex, then the number of switchings will be finite but not necessarily less than $n - 1$. When A has complex roots, the number of switchings will depend upon the distance of x_0 from the origin, since $\lambda'(t)b_i$ will be a sinusoidal function.

Problems

14.5–1   Given the following time-optimal control problem for a linear differential system:

$$\begin{aligned} \dot{x}_1 &= x_2 \\ \dot{x}_2 &= u \\ (x_1^0, x_2^0) &= (5, 10) \\ |u| &\leq 1 \end{aligned}$$

(a) Find the matrices A and B.
(b) Is the system controllable?
(c) State the Hamiltonian and necessary conditions for u^*.

(d) What is u^*? Does it switch?

(e) Graphically sketch the optimal time-minimizing path of $x(t)$.

(f) Is this a normal problem?

(g) In terms of your graphical sketch, give the regions where initial values of x^0 result in no switching of u^*, u^* switches once, and u^* switches more than once.

14.5–2   Given the following time-optimal problem:

$$\dot{x}_1 = -2x_2 + u_1 + u_2$$
$$\dot{x}_2 = -3x_2 + x_1 + u_1$$
$$|u_i| \leq 1, \qquad i = 1, 2$$

(a) Is the system controllable?

(b) Is the problem normal?

(c) State the Hamiltonian and solve for u^*.

(d) Explain your results graphically.

14.5–3   If

$$\dot{x}_1 = x_2$$
$$\dot{x}_2 = -(a_1 a_2)x_1 + (a_1 + a_2)x_2 + bu$$

(a) Show that this system is equivalent to

$$\dot{z}_1 = a_1 z_1 - \frac{b}{a_2 - a_1} u$$

$$\dot{z}_2 = a_2 z_2 + \frac{a_2 b}{a_2 - a_1} u$$

(b) Are the systems controllable?

(c) If they are, find the optimal control. If not, add additional controls so that they are controllable.

(d) Find the optimal control u^* if $-1 \leq u \leq 1$.

(e) Is this a normal problem?

(f) Interpret all results in (a)–(e).

14.6   CONTROL THEORY AND MATHEMATICAL PROGRAMMING

Control theory is a specialized case of general mathematical programming and a generalization of the calculus of variations. In this section we shall illustrate the relation between control theory and mathematical programming and especially the relation of dynamic programming to control theory. In Section 14.7 we shall discuss how control theory is a generalization of the calculus of variations.

In Definition 14.1–2 we stated the control problem as finding control variables u that minimize the integral J, where u is contained in the space of admissable functions U. By defining the boundaries of U as $g(u) \geq 0$ (since U

is a subset of m-dimensional real vector space) and, if necessary, transforming the origin, we can convert the control problem to

$$
\begin{aligned}
\text{max:} &\quad -J \\
\text{subject to:} &\quad g(u) \geq 0 \\
&\quad u \geq 0
\end{aligned}
$$

which is a mathematical programming problem.

Richard Bellman's development of the dynamic programming technique[31] is a method of solving a particular class of nonlinear mathematical programming problems that includes those of control theory. The method of dynamic programming is more general than the theorems developed by Pontryagin for the control problem. However, the assumptions of dynamic programming are not in general applicable to a control problem.

To illustrate the difference we shall develop the dynamic programming solution for a time-optimal control problem, that is, where $J = \int_{t_0}^{t_1} dt$ and the end points x^0 and x^1 are given.

Let

$x(t)$ be the optimal trajectory;

$T(x_0) = t_1 - t_0$ be the optimal transition time; and

$T(x)$ be a function defined on $\Omega \subset X$, where Ω is the space of all possible optimal trajectories from x^0 to x^1.

Assume that Ω is open in X and $T(x)$ is continuous and possesses continuous partial derivatives in Ω.

Define $w(x) = -T(x)$. Then

$$
w(x) = -T(x_0) + t - t_0 = t - t_1
$$

Since $dx/dt = f(x, u)$,

$$
\sum_{i=1}^{n} \frac{\partial w}{\partial x_i} f^i(x, u) = \sum_{i=1}^{n} \frac{\partial w}{\partial x_i} \frac{dx_i}{dt} = \frac{dw(x)}{dt} = \frac{d(t - t_1)}{dt} = 1
$$

Similarly, the optimal time from $x(t) + dx$ to x^1 will be $T[x(t) + dx]$. Since $x(t)$ is optimal,

$$
T[x(t) + dx] + dt \geq T[x(t)]
$$

or

$$
w[x(t) + dx] - w[x(t)] \leq dt
$$

Since $dw = w(x + dx) - w(x)$, we have

$$
dw = \sum_{i=1}^{n} \frac{\partial w}{\partial x_i} f^i \, dt \leq dt
$$

---

[31] Bellman (1957).

or

$$(1) \qquad \sum_{i=1}^{n} \frac{\partial w}{\partial x_i} f^i \leq 1 \qquad \text{for } u \in U$$

Therefore the supremum[32] of the above inequality is equal to 1; that is,

$$(2) \qquad \sup_{u \in U} \sum_{i=1}^{n} \frac{\partial w}{\partial x_i} f^i = 1$$

This is Bellman's basic equation for solving the problem.
Now, letting

$$g(x, u) = \sum_{i=1}^{n} \frac{\partial w}{\partial x_i} f^i$$

and assuming that $g(x, u)$ has continuous partial derivatives, we obtain

$$\frac{\partial g}{\partial x_i} = 0 \qquad \text{for } t_0 \leq t \leq t_1$$

or

$$(3) \qquad \sum_{j=1}^{n} \frac{\partial^2 w}{\partial x_j \, \partial x_i} f^j + \sum_{j=1}^{n} \frac{\partial w}{\partial x_j} \frac{\partial f^j}{\partial x_i} = 0 \qquad i = 1, \ldots, n$$

Since

$$\sum \frac{\partial^2 w}{\partial x_j \, \partial x_i} f^j = \sum \frac{\partial}{\partial x_j} \left(\frac{\partial w}{\partial x_i} \right) \frac{dx_j}{dt} = \frac{d(\partial w / \partial x_i)}{dt}$$

(3) becomes

$$\frac{d}{dt} \left(\frac{\partial w}{\partial x_i} \right) = - \sum_{j=1}^{n} \frac{\partial w}{\partial x_j} \frac{\partial f^j}{\partial x_i}$$

Defining $\lambda_i(t) = \partial w / \partial x_i$ for $i = 1, \ldots, n$, then, we have

$$(4) \qquad \frac{d\lambda_i(t)}{dt} = - \sum_{j=1}^{n} \frac{\partial f^j}{\partial x_i} \lambda_j \qquad i = 1, \ldots, n$$

In addition, by Equation (2),

$$\sum_{i=1}^{n} \lambda_i(t) f^i = \sup_{u \in U} \sum_{i=1}^{n} \frac{\partial w}{\partial x_i} f^i = 1$$

or the Hamiltonian $H(x, \lambda, u) \equiv 1$ along the optimal trajectory.

---

[32] The supremum of $f(x)$ on an interval I is the maximum value of $f(x)$ on I if it exists and if a maximum does not exist, $\sup_{x \in I} f(x)$ is the greatest lower bound of a set of numbers, M, such that $f(x) \leq M$.

Thus, under the foregoing assumptions dynamic programming and control theory are equivalent. However, the assumptions employed in order to derive Bellman's equation (2) are not sufficiently general to be applicable to many control problems. Specifically, the assumption that $w(x)$ is twice differentiable, that is,

$$g(x, u) = \sum_{i=1}^{n} \frac{\partial w}{\partial x_i} f^i$$

has continuous partial derivatives, will not hold at points where "switching" occurs (i.e., where some control changes from an upper bound to a lower bound). Thus Bellman's equation would not apply to Example 1 in Section 14.4 or to other "bang–bang" systems in general.

14.7 CONTROL THEORY AND THE CALCULUS OF VARIATIONS

In this section we wish to demonstrate the relation between the calculus of variations and control theory. Specifically, we shall review Pontryagin et al.'s (1962) demonstration that the necessary conditions developed for the calculus of variations, as in Chapter 10, can be derived from the maximum principle of Pontryagin under special conditions. Namely, if the control region is an open set in R^n, then the Weierstrass necessary condition can be deduced from the maximum principle. However, if U is a closed set in R^n, then the Weierstrass condition is not necessary for an extremal to a functional.

The problem in the calculus of variations is to find all functions $x(t)$ that are extremals for the functional

$$J = \int_{t_0}^{t_1} f^0 \left(x(t), \frac{dx}{dt}, t \right) dt$$

where $x(t) \subset S \subset R^{n+1}$, S is open in R^{n+1}, and f^0 is continuous with continuous partial derivatives and defined for every point in S.

Now consider the following control problem for an nth-order differential system:

$$\frac{dx_i}{dt} = \dot{x}_i = u_i \qquad \text{for } i = 1, \ldots, n$$

$$\min_{u \in U} J = \int_{t_0}^{t_1} f^0(x, u, t) \, dt$$

where t_0, t_1, x^0, and x^1 are given, and

$$u = (u_1, \ldots, u_n) \in U$$

where U is equal to R^n.

This is a problem with fixed initial and end points and a fixed time period. The maximum principle, being a necessary condition for the control problem, must also, therefore, be a necessary condition for the same problem in the calculus of variations.

The Hamiltonian is

$$H = \lambda_0 f^0(x, u, t) + \lambda_1 u_1 + \cdots + \lambda_n u_n$$

or

$$H = \lambda_0 f^0(x, u, t) + \lambda_1 \dot{x}_1 + \cdots + \lambda_n \dot{x}_n$$

where

$$(1) \qquad \frac{d\lambda_i}{dt} = -\frac{\partial H}{\partial x_i} = -\lambda_0 \frac{\partial f^0}{\partial x_i}$$

Since the Hamiltonian is a maximum with respect to n along the optimal trajectory,

$$(2) \qquad \frac{\partial H}{\partial u_i} = \frac{\partial H}{\partial \dot{x}_i} = \lambda_0 \frac{\partial f^0}{\partial \dot{x}_i} + \lambda_i = 0 \qquad i = 1, \ldots, n$$

or

$$(3) \qquad \lambda_i = -\lambda_0 \frac{\partial f^0}{\partial \dot{x}_i}$$

Integrating (1), we have

$$(4) \qquad \lambda_i(t) = \lambda_i(t_0) - \lambda_0 \int_{t_0}^{t} \frac{\partial f^0}{\partial x_i} \, dt'$$

Combining (3) and (4), we have the Euler–Lagrange equations in integral form[33]:

$$(5) \qquad \frac{\partial f^0}{\partial \dot{x}_i} = \int_{t_0}^{t} \frac{\partial f^0}{\partial x_i} \, dt' - \frac{\lambda_i(t_0)}{\lambda_0}$$

Differentiating (5) with respect to t, we have

$$\frac{\partial f^0}{\partial x_i} - \frac{d(\partial f^0 / \partial \dot{x}_i)}{dt} = 0 \qquad \text{for } i = 1, \ldots, n$$

which is the Euler–Lagrange equation as derived in Chapter 10 (Definition 10.5–2).

[33] Definition 10.5–1.

Similarly, if $f^0(x, \dot{x}, t)$ has continuous second partial derivatives with respect to $\dot{x}_i$, $i = 1, \ldots, n$, then we can derive Legendre's necessary condition.[34] Specifically, the quadratic form of H must be ≥ 0, or

$$\sum_{i=1}^{n} \sum_{j=1}^{n} \frac{\partial^2 H}{\partial x_i \, \partial x_j} = \sum_{i=1}^{n} \sum_{j=1}^{n} \frac{\partial^2 f^0}{\partial x_i \, \partial x_j} \geq 0$$

The Weierstrass condition[35] states that if the trajectory $x(t)$ is an extremal for the functional J, then one can find bounded and measurable functions $\lambda_i(t)$, $i = 1, \ldots, k$, such that

$$E = \frac{1}{2} \sum_{i=1}^{n} \sum_{j=1}^{n} \frac{\partial H}{\partial u_i \, \partial u_j} \, du_i \, du_j \geq 0$$

where H is the Hamiltonian function. However, this condition is derived under the assumption that U is an open set. In other words, $E \geq 0$ must hold on the interior of U but at the boundary it need not be valid. The Hamiltonian need not obey classical "regularity" conditions for a maximum unless the control is in the interior of the control region U.

References

1. ARROW, K. J., and M. KURZ (1969), "Optimal Consumer Allocation over an Infinite Horizon," *Journal of Economic Theory*, **1**:68–91.
2. ATHANS, M., and P. L. FALB (1966), *Optimal Control*, New York: McGraw-Hill.
3. BELLMAN, RICHARD (1957), *Dynamic Programming*, Princeton, N.J.: Princeton University Press.
4. DORFMAN, R. (1969), "An Economic Interpretation of Optimal Control Theory," *American Economic Review*, **59**:871–881.
5. HAHN, W. (1966), *Stability of Motion*, Berlin: Springer-Verlag.
6. KALMAN, R. E. (1961), "On the General Theory of Control Systems," *Proceedings of the First IFAC Congress*, **1**:481–492, London: Butterworth.
7. KALMAN, R. E., and J. E. BERTRAM (1960), "Control System Analysis via the Second Method of Lyapunov," *Trans. ASME, Ser. D. J. Basic Eng.*, **82**:371–399.
8. KALMAN, R. E., Y. C. HO, and K. S. NARANDRA (1963), "Controllability of Linear Dynamical Systems," *Contributions to Differential Equations*, **1**:189–213.
9. KOPPEL, L. B. (1968), *Introduction to Control Theory*, Englewood Cliffs, N.J.: Prentice-Hall.

[34] Definition 10.7–1.

[35] See Sagan (1969).

10. LEE, E. B., and L. MARKUS (1967), *Foundations of Optimal Control*, New York: Wiley.

11. PONTRYAGIN, L. S., V. G. BOLTYANSKII, R. V. GAMKRELIDRE, and E. F. MISHCHENKO (1962), *The Mathematical Theory of Optimal Processes* (tr. by K. Trirogoff), New York: Wiley.

12. SAGAN, H. (1969), *Introduction to the Calculus of Variations*, New York: McGraw-Hill.

13. STRUBLE, R. A. (1962), *Nonlinear Differential Equations*, New York: McGraw-Hill.

14. WISHART, D. M. G. (1970), "A Survey of Control Theory," *Journal of the Royal Statistical Society*, **32**:293–317.

Index